PRAISE FOR PAUL M KEROUA

"At last, a nonfiction biography on Jack Kerouac."
—JOHN SAMPAS, Literary Executor for the Estate of Jack and
Stella Kerouac

"Kerouac research was for decades limited because his personal journals
were unavailable to scholars. That has all changed now that the New
York Public Library holds the Kerouac archive, which forms the basis
of MAHER'S work. . . . A useful piece in a difficult puzzle [that] sheds
new light on a writer of considerable interest."—*Library Journal*

"Representing a decade's research, *KEROUAC: The Definitive Biography*
uses the author's letters, journals, and lesser-known writings to separate
the private man from the public myth. . . . A thorough, readable, and
balanced portrait, this book represents an important and impressive addition to a growing body of Kerouac scholarship. . . . MAHER is at his
best examining Kerouac's poignant friendship with soulmate Neal Cassady whom he fictionalized as Dean Moriarty whose frenetic cross-
country travels fueled *ON THE ROAD*. . . . [and he] documents in ex-
cruciating detail the ruinous consequences alcohol had on his writing.
. . . Mixing sheer detail with a sympathetic eye to Kerouac's foibles,
MAHER gives his subject's final years a tragic humanity." —*Boston
Herald* and *New York Daily News*

"In the late 1950s and '60s, you could divide young people pretty well
by whether they liked *ON THE ROAD*. For some, it was a lot like the
new rock 'n' roll, a denial of traditional values. For those, MAHER'S
biography will be a surprise. Kerouac was born of a French-Canadian
family in Massachusetts. A high school athlete, he read literary classics
and studied at Columbia University under Mark Van Doren. . . . His
was a hand-to-mouth existence of sexual voraciousness, heavy drug use,

and a self-destructive lifestyle. But Kerouac's dream of writing the great American novel never dimmed."—*Dallas Morning News*

"Millions of readers all over the world can be overjoyed that a biography has been published that dispels the myths of the King of the beat generation and instead brings us the history of Kerouac himself, written in a heartfelt way that surely would have made Jack feel honored. PAUL MAHER has done the seemingly impossible. . . . He has written a truly definitive portrait, done with a purity of intent that shines through each page. . . . The dazzling amounts of new information, the priceless interviews with childhood friends, and quotes from many others who knew Kerouac during various phases of his later life make this book as hard to put down as the works of Kerouac himself."—composer DAVID AMRAM, author of *OFFBEAT: Collaborating with Kerouac* and *VIBRATIONS: Adventures & Musical Times*

"In this methodical extensive biography the gory details of Kerouac's life stack up. . . . The western world does not make writers like Kerouac any more, only pale pretenders."—GERALD DAWE, *Irish Times*, poet and author of *Heart of Hearts*, *The Morning Train*, and *Lake Geneva*

"This book should attract all who love Kerouac and all who wish to know more about his life. What makes Paul Maher's story of Jack Kerouac . . . stand out from other Kerouac biographies is his factual tone and his reliance on formal evidence in recounting Kerouac's life and making a case for his place in American letters."—*Smoky Mountain News*

"Just finished reading *KEROUAC* and thoroughly enjoyed it. Indeed, it does clear up the distorted accounts of a life 'particularly susceptible to agendas and animosity.'"—DONALD MOTIER, author of *GERARD: The Influence of Jack Kerouac's Brother on His Life & Writing*

"The artistic urges and carefree, reckless lifestyle of the 1950s Beat Generation is still most starkly and famously personified by the movement's enigmatic, controversial patron saint, Jack Kerouac. Kerouac was a walking contradiction: hopeless alcoholic and brilliant poet; blasé womanizer

and devoted Catholic. In this in-depth examination, MAHER takes a riveting look at the forces that shaped Kerouac's development into the original hipster artist, based wholly on a wealth of contemporary materials including letters, postcards, journals, and media accounts of the day."
—*Smoke Magazine*

"MAHER'S biography has brought back [Kerouac's] enormous importance to our literary history in the last half of the twentieth century."
—LAUREL SPEER, poet and author

"An outstanding Kerouac biography! MAHER has accomplished a truly great piece of work."—STEPHEN D. EDINGTON, author of *Kerouac's Nashua Connection*

"The virtues of *KEROUAC* are its concise prose style, inclusion of unpublished work by Kerouac, and refutation of anecdotal material uncritically accepted and printed as fact by previous biographers."—*Burlington Free Press*

Jack Kerouac's drawing of a crucified Christ sketched on a napkin at his
brother-in-law Nick's bar in Lowell, Massachusetts, circa early 1960s.
*(Photo courtesy of the late John Pendergast; permission for publication granted by John
Sampas, literary executor for the Estate of Jack and Stella Kerouac)*

Kerouac

His Life and Work

PAUL MAHER JR.

Foreword by David Amram

Taylor Trade Publishing
Lanham   New York   Toronto   Oxford

For Tina with all my love . . .

Published by Taylor Trade Publishing
An imprint of The Rowman & Littlefield Publishing Group, Inc.
4501 Forbes Boulevard, Suite 200
Lanham, Maryland 20706

Distributed by National Book Network

The hardback edition of this book was previously cataloged by the Library of Congress as follows:

Maher, Paul, 1963–
  Kerouac : the definitive biography / Paul Maher, Jr. ; foreword by David Amram.— 1st Taylor Trade Pub. ed.
     p. cm.
Includes bibliographical references and index.
  1. Kerouac, Jack, 1922–1969. 2. Authors, American—20th century—Biography.
  3. Beat generation—Biography. I. Title.

  PS3521.E735 Z77 2004
  813'.54—dc21
                                                      2003011738

  ISBN-13 978-1-58979-366-8
  ISBN-10 1-58979-366-8

∞ The paper used in this publication meets the minimum requirements of American National Standard for Information Sciences—Permanence of Paper for Printed Library Materials, ANSI/NISO Z39.48–1992.

Manufactured in the United States of America.

Contents

Preface

Between 1965 and 1976, I lived in Centralville Lowell and frequented many of the places that had been familiar to Jack Kerouac. But it wasn't until I took a class on the history of Lowell at Dracut High School in 1980 that I first heard his name. Even then, at that late date, the mention was brief—with no in-depth discussion of his myriad accomplishments—and only in the context of listing other famous folk born in Lowell. (Such illustrious persons included Bette Davis and Ed McMahon.)

It was then I realized that, during much of my boyhood, my footsteps had followed Kerouac's shadow. I had played along the same banks of the Merrimack River, had fished in its filthy waters, had thrown rocks at numerous fat river rats creeping around the same dump featured in *Doctor Sax*. I had roamed the streets on which Jack had loitered and raced. I had attended several wakes at the funeral home that sits diagonally from one of Kerouac's Hildreth Street houses, the one that seemed haunted by the ghost of Ti Jean's brother, Gerard. The pungent scent of burning incense and melting candle wax in the cool basement of St. Louis de France, where I had learned my catechism and where my first communion was held, was also the same church that Kerouac had experienced so indelibly (and later re-created in *Visions of Gerard*).

And like Jack, I, too, felt the same awesome and oppressive mortality bearing down on me whenever Saturday evening discussions, tinted with French Canadian accents, would turn to that day's obituaries: "Who's this in the paper today, the one who died suddenly? You knew her?" It was not difficult to believe that *someone* in the vast network of my family knew her and would be mourning; nor was it impossible to imagine that someday (always sooner than expected or desired) someone would be asking a similar question about myself.

I was in my twenties when I discovered that members of my own family (on the paternal side) had known Kerouac from their youths in Centralville Lowell, where they had been raised and where (by choice or circumstances) they had remained. My grandfather, Victor Maher, had shared a fourth-grade class with Gerard at St. Louis de France (my own elementary school for three years). Two great-uncles had trained in the boxing gym that Jack's father Leo had managed. My grandmother, Gertrude Maher, had often sat at the Kearney Square soda fountain with Caroline Kerouac, who confided to Gertrude details of her first marriage and its painful dissolution. One uncle, when he ever mentioned Jack at all, stated that Kerouac could have made something of himself. "He could have been a professional man working at the mills."

It was not until 1983 that, while serving in the U.S. Navy and stationed in San Diego, I first encountered Kerouac the writer. In a downtown used bookstore I came across an array of Kerouac paperbacks and selected two: *Visions of Cody* and *Doctor Sax*. The latter lured me with its backjacket squib about a "French Canadian growing up among the shadowy doorways and brown tenements of Lowell, Massachusetts." (I still own both volumes.) I read *Doctor Sax* along the trolley tracks outside the base of the Pacific Fleet and *Visions of Cody* during a trip to Tijuana. Kerouac's living descriptions, his alternating enthusiasm and melancholy, his precise powder-keg prose, floored me. To a twenty-year-old sailor exploring America as country and myth, Kerouac's work struck me to the core. Here was the once ghostly hometown acquaintance, known earlier by name mostly, whom I was now discovering as a distinct individual, as a writer who sought to forge a literary saga of his life from the scraps of a daunting existence. Such an encounter spurred me onward to learn more about Kerouac; this curiosity and desire has led, years later, to the biography now in your hands.

Regrettably, by the time I made that internal decision to devote myself to documenting, comprehending, and relating another's life, most of the valuable family witnesses to Kerouac's early life had died. Although their deaths precluded my obtaining perhaps new and illuminating anecdotes about Ti Jean, I still retain my lifelong connection to Lowell. My familiarity with its French Canadian culture and everyday life, with its physicality and psychological nuances, places me in a unique position *vis-à-vis* the plethora of previous Kerouac biographers. Many of my predecessors have produced inadequate and sometimes wildly distorted accounts of a life particularly susceptible to agendas and animosity. Kerouac was an extremely complex individual whose views evolved, fluctuated, and, yes, even regressed. And, like many of us, his contradictions were not always laudable, his actions not always admirable.

While writing the first Kerouac biography, Ann Charters was denied access to Jack's extensive archives. She was forced to construct her chronology and narrative from Kerouac's own admittedly fictionalized accounts in his novels and from the fallible or biased recollections of those whom she interviewed. Upon its publication in 1973–1974, it was a pioneering effort and valuable in many respects. However, it is unfortunate that subsequent biographers have chosen to rely heavily on Charters's book to confirm facts and to seek a balanced perspective on controversial aspects of Jack's life rather than make extensive use of recently opened archives.

Kerouac: His Life and Times stands apart from the rest in several key areas. First and foremost, I have meticulously and conscientiously based my work on primary sources contemporary to the events described: letters, postcards, diaries, journals, notebooks, newspaper and magazine articles, legal documents, and television transcripts. Whenever possible, I have chosen Jack's own views as this biography's brick and mortar.

Select portions of the archives currently available for research are replete with never-before-published information and new perspectives, but such treasures are easily overlooked. When one approaches the prodigious material with a preordained point of view, one tends to find only that which supports one's thesis. As a result, it is readers who suffer when spending their hard-earned money on an inferior or insidious portrait.

My hope in this biography is that readers will encounter a fresh and more accurate account of Kerouac, one that neither whisks away nor wallows in his flaws and frailties but seeks to do justice to the course and context of his sizable ambitions and singular achievement. When based on primary sources, familiar relationships, persons, and events appear in a new (and sometimes startling) light. The cornerstones of Kerouac's literary output, particularly *On the Road*, are reexamined, while many unheard-of and as-yet-unpublished works are discussed here for the first time.

Although a long list of well-deserved acknowledgments appears at the

Foreword

To the handful of us still here who knew Jack Kerouac, there remains among almost all of us a certain unspoken sadness. Most of us who loved the man for his spirit, generosity, and enormous gifts as an artist have been continually disheartened by the fear that the same myths and misinformation that plagued Keroauc himself, from the publication of *On the Road* in 1957 until his untimely death in 1969, would continue to besmirch the reputation of a true American original, distracting future readers and even objective scholars from a thorough appreciation of Kerouac and his work.

The term *Beat Generation* became another brand name that eclipsed the very person whom all consider to be the engine who pulled the train that this supposed generation was named after, Jack Kerouac himself. The term implied negativity, mediocrity, narcissism, and infantile behavior. In his letters and in many conversations Kerouac said, "I wish I had never used that term." It also became a thorn in the side of John Clellon Holmes, to whom the term was attributed as well. Poet Lawrence Ferlinghetti recently accepted an interview in the fall of 2002 for Canadian Broadcast System, in an hourlong special honoring his life's work, if it was understood that he would not be referred to as a "Beat" poet. "I'm a writer, Davey. I'm an author," Kerouac said to me on countless occasions, after our all-night poetry-music forays. "Don't they read my books?"

Nearly a half century later, little seemed to have changed. Those few of us still here felt that our only hope to clear up this clichéd way of discrediting and demeaning all of us with a label for a nonexistent movement (we never had badges, secret handshakes, a roll call, or a letterhead) would be for a real biography to emerge that would finally deal with Jack Kerouac the writer.

In the meantime, many of us would continue to have our spirits lifted when rereading Joyce (Glassman) Johnson's classic *Minor Characters*, her brilliant *Doors Wide Open*, and Carolyn Cassady's *Off the Road: My Years with Cassady, Kerouac, and Ginsberg*. These three works are universally acknowledged as being great books that bring the reader into the world about which Jack himself wrote so memorably. Both Joyce Johnson and Carolyn Cassady write in a loving, lyrical, and moving fashion about the true-life experiences they shared with Kerouac. This is why I wrote *Offbeat: Collaborating with Kerouac*. I wanted to share what it was really like, just as Joyce and Carolyn did. Many of us constantly returned to reread *Vanity of Dulouz*, Kerouac's own memorable account of his youth, most of which dealt with his life in Lowell.

Now in additon to Kerouac's close friends, millions of readers all over the world can be overjoyed that a biography has been published that dispels the myths of the King of the Beat Generation and instead brings us the history of Kerouac himself, written in a pure and heartfelt way that surely would have made Jack feel honored. Paul Maher has done the seemingly impossible. He has written a book that encompasses not only Kerouac's entire life and the history of the Kerouac family. This brilliantly researched new book also contains endless accounts of the town that Kerouac wrote about in so many of his most acclaimed works of fiction. That special place in Jack's life is the town of Lowell itself.

Paul Maher is a natural to tackle this enormous task. Like fellow Lowellian Paul Marion, editor of *Atop an Underwood*, which catalogues the early writings of Kerouac before *On the Road* was written, and Kerouac himself, Maher is of Franco-American heritage and a native of Lowell. Maher has an innate understanding and affection for the French Canadian roots of Kerouac and describes the stark beauty and multifaceted character of Lowell.

Maher has skillfully woven into this outstanding biography countless descriptions and historic events that make the reader feel at home. Maher obeys the principal rule of true reportage. He makes the subject of the story, rather than himself, the subject of the story.

Fortunately for all of us, instead of being a tell-all book of gossip and fictionalized non-events, *Kerouac: The Definitive Biography* is a truly definitive portrait of Kerouac the writer, done with a purity of intent that shines through each page. Maher leaves the fictional recounting of historical events to Kerouac himself, quoting from Jack during many parts of the biography. Maher himself has done years of painstaking research. The dazzling amounts of new information, the priceless interviews with childhood friends of Jack's, and quotes from many others who knew Kerouac during various phases of his later life make this book as hard to put down as the works of Kerouac himself.

This is the biography readers of Kerouac have waited so long to have published. It is the work of a true scholar, rather than another postmodern tabloid television–styled rehash of misinformation. It is a book that can further the appreciation of where Kerouac and his family came from and make the reader appreciate Kerouac's amazing journey in life.

Throughout this fascinating book, the soul of Lowell shines. This unique and ever-changing city has been as misunderstood as Kerouac himself. Today it remains a town where scores of languages are still spoken, and where the idealism and hopes of newly arrived immigrants remind us of what our shared American experience is all about. And that spirit is what Kerouac himself shares with us in his books.

This biography explores Kerouac's French Canadian heritage, his roots in the Catholic church, his devotion to his mother, and his love of his country and the entire American continent. Rather than dismissing, ignoring, or apologizing for these most crucial influences in Kerouac's life, Maher shows us how these experiences served as a rich source for Kerouac's work and his own personal development. Maher shares all of this information with us as a skilled tour guide, introducing us to the people and places that Kerouac cared about so much and wrote about in such a timeless way.

I have said hundreds of times when being interviewed and often in my own writings that to understand where Jack Kerouac was coming from, you had to go to where he came from. You had to come to Lowell. And I have said thousands of times when asked what Jack was like that you had to read his books, which were exactly what he was like. Now we have a biography that adds to our knowledge. *Kerouac: The Definitive Biography* gives all of us priceless information.

Paul Maher's biography is a much-needed addition for all students, fans, and readers of Jack's books. The true story of Kerouac is an inspiring and uplifting account of the struggles and ultimate triumph, albeit

PART I

The Seeds of Galloway

The Kerouacs of Nashua

January 1720-1925

And I begin to ask myself what it could have been, this unremembered state which brought with it no logical proof of its existence, but only the sense that it was a happy, that it was a real state in whose presence other states of consciousness melted and vanished.
MARCEL PROUST, *Swann's Way*

Urbain-François Le Bihan attended a wedding in the year of 1720, the first record of the earliest of Jack Kerouac's ancestors to come to the New World. That year he had attended a wedding in Huelgoat, a town in northwestern Brittany. After the wedding reception, Urbain-François went to the Auberge Fournel, a local tavern, with the bride's sister Constance, the groom, and several other members of the wedding party. They were sitting at a large table above the kitchen when Constance suddenly noticed that her money in a purse had vanished. For no other reason than that he was sitting there, she turned toward Urbain and accused him of theft. Urbain was brought down to the kitchen and physically searched. As the party continued its deliberations in the stables, suddenly someone shouted that the money had been located under the very table where they had been sitting only moments before. Despite Urbain-François's innocence, the Barthelemys, a local family of a distinctly lower social station, were outraged and were certain that Urbain had stolen three purses as he walked along the road to the village of Saint-Pol and had also taken forty sols from a man named Plassart. Since their shouting had attracted a

3

drunken crowd from the tavern, the motley group proceeded to undress Urbain, looking for stolen loot. Nothing was recovered.

Standing by the belief that his son was innocent, the wealthy notary François-Joachim Le Bihan de Kervoac brought the accusing crowd to court in the autumn of 1720. The accusers retracted their claim, claiming that too much drink had affected their memory. The family honor of Le Bihan de Kervoac was ultimately restored. Possibly the incident was nothing more than a social-class conflict. However, scholars will never know for certain since the legal documents of the Civil Tribunal for the Royal Court of Châteauneuf, Huelgoat, and Landeleau have vanished for the period between January 11, 1720, and March 2, 1723.

After the fifteen court sessions it took to deliberate the case, the troubled Urbain-François Le Bihan disappeared from all known records in Huelgoat. It is certain, however, that he had set off toward the English Channel to settle across the North Atlantic in New France. "The son of the notary of Huelgoat managed through his cleverness, audacity, and exceptional courage to make an impression at the highest level of government in his new country. Alexandre de Kervoach, '*coureur de bois,*' hunter, fur trader, and voyager, had ambition when he arrived in Canada and managed to rise to the top where he rightly belonged," writes Patricia Dagier.[1]

Among the mountains of Quebec, beside the flowing St. Lawrence River and its islands, a wedding ceremony took place on October 22, 1732. Monseignor de Samos, the coadjutor of Quebec, had granted a marriage license to Maurice-Louis Le Brice de Karouac and Louise Bernier in the presence of Nicolas Jean de Kerverzo. Maurice-Louis Le Brice had found some trade as a merchant in Kamouraska, Quebec, since his arrival in New France despite the formal training he received as a notary. Researchers of Kerouac genealogy had assumed that Maurice-Louis had one older brother, Alexandre de Kérouack, who also lived in Canada. It was also assumed that he had all but disappeared from history after signing a church document at the christening of his third "son," "Maurice-Louis." However, subsequent research by a Canadian genealogist has unearthed a different finding.

There was no older brother. Owing to inconsistencies with the very literate Maurice-Louis Le Bris de Karouac's usage of his name, various documents bear variants of the name. Maurice-Louis used the surname "Le Bris" only on three occasions over a period of five months during his nine-year stay. Simply put, tracking his whereabouts becomes difficult when one is unfamiliar with the casual adding and dropping of the articles of his full name. At some point during those nine years in Canada, the Christian name *Alexandre* was adopted and just as suddenly shed. Seemingly, Maurice-Louis had created a new identity, calling himself "Maurice-Louis *Le Bris de K/voac*" or the more Anglicized *Louis* and the alternate spelling of *Keroac*. On November 30, 1733, Maurice-Louis wrote a five-page letter from his home in Cap Saint-Ignace to Governor Beauharnois seeking assistance to denounce a church robber.[2] He got his wish, for Beauharnois passed the request along to a Superintendent Hocquart, who issued a command on December 3, 1733, that "order is given to all Captains and other army officers to give assistance to *Alexandre Le Breton* from Cap Saint-Ignace . . . to help capture the man."[3] By July 1735, Maurice-Louis had decidedly dropped his original Christian name and referred to himself simply as Alexandre, still using *Keroac* as his official surname.

Why was the youngest son of the family, Urbain-François, using the particle and surname *de Kervoac,* and not one of his two older brothers, Laurens and Charles-Marie-François, who were still living in Brittany? It was the custom that a son use the particle and surname only after the death of his father. In the case of François-Joachim Le Bihan de Kervoac, who had died in 1727, his two older sons found it necessary to attach to their family name another surname after the particle *de.* Out of this custom, the surname of *Le Bihan* was allocated to both. For each of them, it was an important choice, for they were notary-solicitors like their father. When the occasion arose to register with France's Royal Court of Justice, they would have to do so using their official title and signature at the same time. Out of these circumstances, the particle and surname *de Kervoac* was available to the third son. Urbain-François, now living in New France, was too far away from both his native land and his father. Feeling confident that the physical distance would give him this liberty, he decided to use the surname even though his father was still alive. After François-Joachim Le Bihan de Kervoac died in 1727, neither of the two eldest sons ever claimed the particle or the surname "de Kervoac." Quite obviously it proved that the family knew who was now using it.[4]

On March 5, 1736, thirty-year-old Maurice-Louis Alexandre Le Bris de Keroack died of an illness after a long, harsh winter, leaving two able-bodied and vigorous sons to perpetuate the Kerouac name (in all of its variants). Jack Kerouac unwittingly touched upon this piece of history in his novel *Satori in Paris* (1966):

Well, why do people change their names? Have they done anything bad, are they criminals, are they ashamed of their real names? Are they afraid of something? Is there any law in America against using your own real name?

I had come to France and Brittany just to look up this old name of mine which is just about three thousand years old and was never changed in all that time, as who would change a name that simply means House (Ker), In the Field (Ouac)?[5]

In North America, as in France, there are at least seven different ways to write the Kerouac surname: *Kérouac, Kéroack, Kirouac, Kyrouac, Keroach, Kérouack,* and *Kirouack*. Many of the later descendants were illiterate. Subsequently, in some of the older church records of Montreal, names inscribed into the ledgers were spelled wrong, including the more infrequent *Carouac, Carunoac,* and *Keloaque,* all of which shared Breton origins. The source of the prefix *Ker* is explained by Patricia Dagier of the Genealogical Centre of the Finistère (in the town of Quimper, Brittany):

> KER, the first syllable of our name, means house or village. In Brittany there are no less than 18,000 surnames and place names starting with KER. Interestingly enough, old Breton people often used to write a K followed by a stroke: K/ which stood for KER. So in our family too the signatures would vary and we found: K/voac, K/uoac, K/voach. The pronunciation of the surname is also of interest: K/voac would be pronounced: Kerouac, where v = u (in English it is pronounced OO) Even more tricky: the letters 'v' and 'u' in the Breton language could simply be left out when people wrote their name. In our case, that would give: Kéroac![6]

In 1941, nineteen-year-old Jack Kerouac wrote an imagined character sketch of his grandfather that he titled "The Father of My Father." He had to resort to his imagination, for young Jack never met the Kerouac patriarch.

Jean-Baptiste, or "Honest Jack," according to Jack's youthful account, stood five foot ten and was, by the accounts of his contemporaries, built like an oak tree. According to Kerouac, "Honest Jack" regarded his Catholic faith, like most of his countrymen, as an important part of his character and at times dared to shake his fist at thunderstorms as lightning jabbed fingers into the ground upon which he stood. This, of course, is highly charged with Kerouac's fecund imagination and is remarkably indicative of the young writer's tendency to mythologize a relatively mundane existence into a larger-than-life anecdote. The teenaged Jack also injected a not-so-flattering side of his grandfather's life in a seemingly transcribed recollection from his mother: "The old man! My Goodness, everyone in the town knew that your father's father was crazy! Absolutely crazy! A nut! And cruel! Oh my but how could such a man exist! He drank and drank and drank, killed his wife and himself with his drinking, leaving behind a snarling pack of cubs that were Kerouacs."

Jean-Baptiste Kirouac moved from Canada to the southern border of hilly New Hampshire, in Nashua, sometime in 1890. He left behind everything but his language, ethnic heritage, and devout Roman Catholicism to tie his identity into the complex social fabric of America. Kerouac imagines:

> A whole story in itself, the story of Emil [pseudonym for Leo Kerouac], his mad brothers and sisters, the whole troop coming down from the barren farm, to the factories of U.S.A.—Their early life in early Americana New Hampshire of pink suspenders, strawberry blondes, barbershop quartets, popcorn stands with melted butter in a teapot, and fistfights in the Sunday afternoon streets between bullies and heroes who read Frank Merriwell.[7]

Jean-Baptiste found his calling, at first working at odd jobs, and finally (after working as a carpenter's apprentice) mastering the carpentry trade that supported his wife and their surviving ten children for the rest of his short life.

On December 16, 1906, a Sunday afternoon, Jean-Baptiste Kirouac died an "instantaneous" death, just two days after his fifty-eighth birthday. His obituary was telling of his social standing: "The deceased was widely known and his straightforward, generous character made him dearly loved by a large circle of friends."[8]

Twelve of their fifteen children were born before Jean-Baptiste and Clementine's move south. The last three were born in Nashua. Between 1892 and 1896, the Kirouacs suffered heartrending tragedies, losing five of their children, ranging from four-month-old Marie Ann, a victim of cholera, to fourteen-year-old Bernadette, who died of dropsy.

Jack Kerouac's aunt Louise Kirouac Michaud worked as a dressmaker for most of her years and, according to her nephew, was particularly well read, reading everything from Arthur Rimbaud to Stendhal. At times Jack exclaimed that she was his favorite aunt.[9] Kerouac described Louise's sister, Caroline Kirouac, as the sister who turned out "sublime," as she joined the Sisters of Charity in Montreal. Her devotion took her across Sisters of Charity missions from the American Midwest to the Northwest, caring for the poor and infirm.[10]

Two years after Jean-Baptiste's death, on September 24, 1908, his widow succumbed to "heart failure" and not, contrary to her grandson's account, the cumulative effect of stress over her husband's drinking through the years. Jack's father, Joseph Alcide Leon Kirouac, the youngest son of the surviving ten children, Anglicized his name simply to "Leo" and chose to spell his last name with an "e" instead of an "i." Working amid cluttered tables of ink and paper and a wide array of printing presses at Nashua's leading newspaper, the *Nashua Telegraph*, Leo learned the primary trade that supported him for the rest of his life. An apprentice printer, he soon developed a mastery that exceeded that of his coworkers. (Until 1912, Leo worked as a writer and printer for the weekly *L'Impartial*, a French daily newspaper that reached "the French-American Population of New Hampshire and New England.") After Leo had worked devotedly for five or six years, Louis Biron, owner of the *Telegraph*, sent him south to Lowell, Massachusetts, to manage another newspaper that Biron had acquired. It was *L'Etoile* (The Star), a French Canadian daily newspaper that reported the political and social goings-on in Lowell; it was the leading, most enduring French newspaper up until the 1940s. Leo was twenty-three years old.

The Lowell office in which Leo worked was small, hot, and cluttered, *not* given to aesthetics and comfort but to economy of space, with printing presses taking priority over office space. An iron radiator at the bottom of the windows perpetually hissed steam and clanged as if being hammered by monkey wrenches. Mail and incoming articles were separated in long, boxed partitions along the wall; two little desks were outfitted with Underwood typewriters. Visored and cigar-smoking, Leo was a loyal and competent manager responsible for selling ads, editing text, and overseeing the physical layout of a weekly community newspaper. When Leo first arrived in Lowell, he lived with his married sister, Emma Vaillancourt, who was a mill operator. By 1915, he was confident enough in his ability to support himself that he boarded at a private residence on Ennell Street in the Centralville section of Lowell.[11] That year he also began making regular trips back to Nashua to court a French Canadian girl named Gabrielle Levesque.

Gabrielle Levesque was born in St. Pacome, Quebec, on February 4, 1895. Her mother, Josephine Jean Levesque, died a bit more than a year later, on March 6, 1896. Gabrielle's father, Louis Levesque, was remarried when Gabrielle was eight to a woman named Amanda Dube. They were a family, Gabrielle admitted, without "booklearning" or "culture."[12] On June 3, 1911, her father died of cardiac arrest and was buried two days later at the Saint Louis de Gonzague cemetery in Nashua. This left Gabrielle, the eldest daughter in the household, as sole supporter and housemaid not only to her siblings but also to her two half-sisters. For the next few years Gabrielle worked in the cramped, hot setting of the mills that peppered the New Hampshire valley. Despite this arduous and stifling life, she remained, as Kerouac recalls in *The Town and the City*, a "cheerful, rosy-cheeked, affectionate kind of woman in whom scarcely a trace of the effects of a tragic lonely girlhood were evident, save for an occasional air of grim quiet that orphans have in moments of reflection."[13] When she found a job at a Nashua shoe factory, Gabrielle moved out on her own to a nearby boardinghouse; "at the age of 14 there she was, at dawn, walking to the shoe factory to work till six that evening, till Saturday evening, 72-hour workweek, all gleeful in anticipation of that pitiful Saturday night."[14] It was while she was working at this factory that she met Leo Kerouac. In October 1915, approximately five years after the death of her father, Gabrielle had found a new father figure: five foot five, vigorous, blue-eyed, robust Leo, now twenty-six years old and working as an insurance salesman.[15] They were wed on October 25, 1915, at the Saint Louis de Gonzague Church, with Joseph Kerouac standing in as Leo's best man and Gabrielle's aunt Lydia Harpin serving as maid of honor.[16] Leo took the twenty-year-old Gabrielle back to Lowell after they married. Almost one year later Gabrielle gave birth to their first child.

At the beginning of the twentieth century, Lowell was a hodgepodge of textile mills, five-and-dimes, banks, printing presses, theaters, restaurants, shoe shops, and storefronts. Although it was far from a teeming metropolis, the city still had enough work to offer for those determined and ambitious enough to find it. According to city directories, Leo found work as an insurance agent at 8 Merrimack Street. Whether Leo worked two jobs or simply resigned management of *L'Etoile* cannot be determined, but his listing as an insurance agent continues for several years. He and Gabrielle lived near the agency at 476 Merrimack Street in a rented furnished apartment in what is now known as the Lowell Sun building in downtown Lowell's Kearney Square.

The Kerouacs' first child, François Gerard Keroack (as spelled on his birth certificate), was born on Wednesday, August 23, 1916, in Blanchard's Private Hospital in the neighboring town of Dracut. The next day he was baptized in Saint Jean de Baptiste Church, where younger brother Jack would have his funeral mass fifty-three years later. By fall 1917, the Kerouacs had moved once more, to 648 Merrimack Street, and after a year moved out of downtown Lowell altogether, settling in Centralville on Lupine Road. Two years after Gerard's birth, a little girl they named Caroline (and commonly referred to as "Nin") was born on October 25, 1918. On March 12, 1922, the Kerouac family would complete itself with the birth of Jean-Louis Lebris de Kerouac.

In 1843, the citizens of Centralville signed a petition for annexation. Lowell city hall quickly denied the request. Eventually, their persistence paid off, and in 1851 Centralville joined the rest of the city. Soon after the annexation, Centralville's population began to grow, the increase mainly due to French Canadian and Polish tenants who rented the scattered bungalows and cottages constructed by landowners (many of whom were also the owners of the factories in which their tenants worked). By 1890, approximately eight thousand people resided there. Some Kerouac biographers label Centralville a "slum." On the contrary, Centralville was regarded as one of the more affluent neighborhoods. If there was a Lowell slum, it was located across the river, on the outskirts of downtown. It was called, derogatorily, "Little Canada." But Kerouac may have been pleased to learn that twenty-nine years earlier, Centralville was overflowing with "hoboes" who begged door-to-door for cash and food. Many of them traveled on foot, hopped trains, or hitched rides on the farm wagons that came to Lowell from the north and from Boston. By the turn of the century, Centralville was cleansed of its vagrancy problems and was transformed into a section of the city for the moderately to superbly affluent.[17] Before long, the topography of Centralville began to reflect the stark contrast between its wealthier residents (factory owners and white-collar workers from the Locks and Canals Company) and those less fortunate inhabitants of a lower social status. Its higher elevations boasted larger, stylish homes that loomed above the tight rows of crowded tenements clustered near the river, which housed people who seemingly lived only to toil under the shadow of the Boott Mill Tower clock.

In the beginning Centralville was primarily residential. Late in the nineteenth century, Centralville already boasted three grocery stores, a women's clothing store, a butcher, a blacksmith, several carpentry shops, and a carriage maker. Churches and social clubs with exclusively French Canadian membership were soon erected. The Kerouacs immersed themselves in a city that for the most part had already reached its economic prime.

"Comes the cankerous rush of spring, when earth will fecundate and get soft and produce forms that are but to die, multiply. . . ."[18] It was March, and Lowell's long, cold winter was coming to an end. Gabrielle Kerouac was in the final stage of pregnancy with her third, and last, child.

On March 12, 1922, a fair, mild Sunday in Lowell, police made a liquor raid on a Bunting clubhouse. Twelve policemen restored order while Greek residents held their semiannual meeting at the Jefferson Street church. Such was the daily life, for better or for worse, that made Lowell much like its larger urban counterparts: illness and vice were rampant. It was a day hardly befitting the romantic mysticism attached to it by Jack Kerouac in his writing.

In the weeks before the birth of Jean-Louis de Kerouac, an unusually high mortality rate plagued the city: more than one hundred perished in the preceding three weeks, most from sporadic cases of diphtheria, scarlet fever, tuberculosis, and influenza. That Jack was spared nature's brutal process of elimination is miraculous. Dr. Victor Rochette, who tended to most of the Franco-American babies in Centralville, helped deliver Jean-Louis in the comfort of the family's Lupine Road home. The birth itself was unremarkable in that it attracted scant notice in the local papers; the village papers gave more mention to deaths than to births. One notice was printed in the Kerouacs' native French Canadian tongue, "Le 12 mars. à M. et Mme. Leo A. Keroack, 9 Lupine Rd, un fils.";[19] another in English, "March 12—[. . .] to Mr. and Mrs. Leo A. Keroach, 9 Lupine road, a son."[20] All too aware of the recent spate of infant deaths in the city, Gabrielle and Leo Kerouac watched warily for any hints of illness that might threaten their newborn son.[21]

The two-family tenement, numbered 7 and 9, on Lupine Road was the first of several residences for the Kerouacs. The house was equipped with a tiny yard just big enough to contain the three children and a wash line that they shared with the duplex's other tenant. At different times, the Kerouacs lived on both floors (Jean-Louis was born on the second floor).[22] Kerouac claimed that his mother could hear the sounds of the river as she gave birth to her last child, a dubious claim at best. Contradicting this claim, Lowell's chief newspaper, the *Lowell Sun*, reported on March 12, 1922, the conditions of the thawing river:

MERRIMACK RIVER ABOUT NORMAL — Several sheets of ice, not very thick and easily broken, drifted away from a point opposite the lower Gage icehouses on the river, at 10:20 this morning, moving quickly down the swift current and leaping over the Pawtucket dam to the rocks below. It wasn't a noisy plunge this time, the ice breaking into small pieces as it shot over the cap of the dam. The ice appeared to be very thin and the remainder of the river ice in the vicinity appears to be far from thick. The water was no higher this morning than yesterday. There is no evidence yet of any flood, and much of the river ice above the lower fields is said to be getting thin.[23]

As Gabrielle held the child in her arms, amid the erratic rhythm of dripping pine trees and ice melting from the tenement's eaves, a late winter sun set in a crimson smear over Lowell,[24] thus implanting into the recollections of both mother and son one of Jack's dearest recollections: "I was born. Bloody rooftop. Strange deed. All eyes I came hearing the river's red; I remember that afternoon, I perceived it through beads hanging in a door and through lace curtains and glass of a universal sad lost redness of mortal damnation . . . the snow was melting. The snake was coiled in the hill not my heart."[25]

In his writing, Kerouac's "snake," the underlying evil that plagues humanity in his novel *Doctor Sax*, is ever present in workaday Lowell. Traditionally, the serpent is connected with original sin, the accepted orthodoxy in the Catholic religion that everyone suffers the consequences of Eve's eating the forbidden fruit in the Garden of Eden. In the drama of his birth, Kerouac had set the stage for a "strange deed," the mysterious process of the emergence of life; he realized later, when reading various Buddhist texts, that to be born only means to suffer. This credo was already emblazoned on the family crest decades before the first Kerouacs reached the North Atlantic shore: "Aimer, Travailler, et Souffrir" (Love, Work, and Suffer). In a 1950 letter to Neal Cassady, Kerouac considers the remote possibility of recollecting his birth and its impact on his artistic and religious sensibilities. His birth occurs to him in a "peculiar eternity-dream vividness," prompting him to feel a connection to "late-red-afternoons." This memory made him think he had seen the afternoon of March 12, 1922, with "eyes a few hours old."

In the dark interior of Centralville's Saint Louis de France church, on March 19, 1922, Jean-Louis Kirouac was baptized according to the rite of the Roman Catholic Church by the Reverend D. W. Boisvert. His sponsors, or godparents, were Leo's brother Jean-Baptiste Kirouac, a shoemaker, and his first wife, Rosanna Dumais Kirouac.[26]

By the spring of 1923, Leo was successful enough as an insurance agent to acquire his own printing shop, which he opened at 26 Prince Street and called the Lowell Spotlite. The Lowell Spotlite, besides printing for downtown businesses, produced an eight-page weekly that covered the theatrical goings-on in downtown Lowell.[27] At this time, vaudeville and silent films were all the rage across the country, and Lowell was no exception. Numerous theaters were strategically placed around town, offering mostly vaudeville performances. ("High-brow" entertainment, such as opera, symphonic concerts, or Shakespeare, was more likely found in larger, more cultured metropolises like Boston.) The influence of early silent and talking films on Kerouac would later be seen in some of the more visual aspects of his writing.

Lowell's Northern Canal was bordered by Little Canada, where Franco-Americans lived in ghettolike conditions in crowded blocks of tenements. It is a cruel irony that industrial capitalism had given them the opportunity to raise large families but little else. Gabrielle thought it a matter of pride that her family had never resorted to living there, although they did live nearby at one point in Kerouac's youth (on Maiden Lane near Lowell City Hall).[28]

The social mores and language of Lowell's Franco-America endeared its people to Kerouac. In 1950, he wrote a letter to Yvonne Le Maitre (who had written favorably of his first novel, *The Town and the City*, in a Worcester, Massachusetts, newspaper) commenting upon using his native tongue as an approach to speaking English: "All my knowledge rests in my 'French Canadianness' and nowhere else. The English language is a tool lately found. The reason I handle English words so easily is because it is not my own language. I refashion it to fit French images."[29] Later he was comfortable enough to write some poems, an extended sequence of "Mary" (an early version of *Maggie Cassidy* drafted in four small notebooks), and an unpublished novella, *La nuit et ma femme,* in his native language.

Kerouac felt that, because they were Caucasian, his forebears successfully hid their "real sources," the fact that they were Canadians, in order to succeed in America: "Isn't it true that French Canadians everywhere tend to hide their real sources. They can do it because they look Anglo-Saxon, when the Jews, the Italians, they cannot."[30] But their white skin gained them no favoritism in Lowell. The hardships of day-to-day living were constant—especially when set against the backdrop of the country's constantly shifting demographics, economics, and politics. Beyond the provincial drama of Lowell, the world at large was taking on a more ominous hue. Kerouac's coming-of-age coincided with an important era for America, a period when it would be cast into the world's civil unrest and the darker forces of evil embodied by Adolf Hitler, Benito Mussolini, and Joseph Stalin. But Kerouac lived out his "childhood glee" unaware of the forces that would later shape him and his generation.

Sometime during the last few weeks of a very harsh winter in 1925, the Kerouacs moved from Lupine Road to a Victorian cottage several blocks away, at 35 Burnaby Street, keeping within the Centralville enclave. Leo also moved his business; the Lowell Spotlite was now renamed Spotlight Print and relocated to 463 Market Street.[31]

The Kerouacs stayed at the Burnaby Street residence for part of the year before moving to 34 Beaulieu Street, located one street away from the family's Catholic parish. This address was advantageous to the family for it placed the children closer to Saint Louis de France Church, where the children would attend grammar school. Perhaps the single address that had the greatest significance for Jack Kerouac, it was, as he recorded later in *Book of Dreams,* the imposing "house of dreams,"[32] site of the memory upon which all his others were built, that of Gerard slapping his face:

Just before he died he slapped me in the face. It is the last thing before he died. It was a gray morning, my sister was going to school, breakfast was being removed from the table. Gerard sat at his erector set before the magnificent structure of his brief career: it was huge, towering, a crane of some sort, arranged and hung in strange new ways and calculated to do a thousand strange feats. The contraption was on the edge of the breakfast table. Had he been older I'm sure he would have his second cup of coffee right then, he was so eager for his morning's work. But I had to come along and grab at his little arrangements: knock a subsidiary structure down, push the little wrench to the floor, whatever it was, disturbing him so suddenly that with understandable rage he impulsively tightened inside and his hand shot out and slapped me in the face. "Get away from here!" he cried. I mooned over that in the parlor. Gray vultures of gloomy day were feeding at the rooftops of time, I could see it outside the curtains. Gloom, grayness, faucet-ticking.[33]

Contrary to all the memories Kerouac claimed he had of his brother, he confided to his sister Caroline in 1945 that "all I remember about Gerard, for instance, is his slapping me on the face, despite all the stories Mom and Pop tell me of his kindness to me."[34]

Beaulieu Street, like much of Centralville at the turn of the century, was a motley collection of wooden cottages, most bordered by wooden picket fences and decorated with a bathtub-enshrined Virgin Mary stepping on the coiled snake representing Satan, dandelions sprouting between sporadic beds of grass, and trash cans bordered by gravel sidewalks. Nearby sat the Saint Louis de France rectory, school, and church, all constructed of brick and granite. The church was a gloomy edifice that barely topped the homes that squatted near it. Having little to no money when it was built in 1904, 696 families, primarily from West Centralville, settled for a basement-level church with unassuming stained-glass panels that, by chance and not by design, echoed the humility of its members. In 1907 it officially opened, staffed by ten Sisters of the Assumption, who taught 460 students.[35] Kerouac's memories of the church and school are unequaled in their clarity:

[F]irst you see the nun's home, redbrick and bright in the morning sun, then the gloomy edifice of the schoolhouse itself with its long-plank sorrow-halls and vast basement of urinals and echo calls and beyond the yard, with its special (I never forgot) little inner yard of cinder gravel separated from the big dirtyard (which becomes a field down at Farmer Kenny's meadow) by a small granite wall not a foot high that everyone sits on or throws cards against.[36]

Jack would later dream of the basement of the school turning into a cave, for to him it appeared "dungeon-like" and was pervaded by an aura of "damp gloom."[37] The nuns of Saint Louis de France were severe and strict in appearance, determinedly living up to their intimidating reputation if only to garner the respect and obedience of their young Catholic charges. The knuckles of many were rapped by wooden rulers in the main office. In the basement, the nuns combed the boys' hair, slicking it back with water dripping from the "pisspipes"; the smell of pails of sawdust used to clean up spills was pervasive. Despite the women's stern countenance, the institution supplied the cultural and social needs of Centralville, engaging eager volunteers to hold plays, recitals, parades, parties, fairs, club meetings, and dances. Leo and Gabrielle each volunteered their time to take part in such committees. Beneath the faith of the parishioners, however, there lurked an instilled hatred of Jews and Protestants. It was a simmering anti-Semitism and religious intolerance that escalated unchecked within the Catholic church. This was seeded deeply into Leo and Gabrielle's social sensibilities and, sadly, passed on to their children.

Kerouac was an impressionable child, easily swayed by the stories that his older brother and sister made up for him. Gerard told Jack, according to his various writings, that there was an abandoned cemetery beneath the Beaulieu Street house and suggested that the spirits interred there would shake and rattle the house. In an era when the mortality rate of a factory town remained unusually high, the dead of Lowell dotted the memories of its children. Most were accustomed to attending the wakes and funerals of relatives and children who succumbed to contagious diseases or tragic accidents (many drowned in the swift currents of the Merrimack River).

But there were good times aplenty to offset Gerard's dour disposition and persistent poor health. Visits to Leo's brother Joseph's corner store were weekly excursions for the Kerouacs; Jack remembered the barrels of pickles, the sawdust on the floor, and the smell of freshly sawed wood from a nearby lumberyard. There were also the drifting wisps of the Cu Babs his uncle smoked; the memory ultimately found its way into the novel *Doctor Sax* (1959): "[I]t was Godawful the scene of marijuana-sheeshkabob cigarettes he smoked for his asthma, Cu Babs." Kerouac remembered Uncle Joseph as an "extremely intelligent" man who could reel historical anecdotes off the top of his head. Jack also thought him the "saddest" of the family; he witnessed his uncle crying numerous times.[38] At other times, Uncle Joseph brought his family to Lowell, where they all sat on the house steps socializing together.

Neighborhood bazaars and Saint Louis's baked bean suppers anchored Gabrielle and Leo securely in the social bedrock of Centralville through the latter half of the 1920s. On weekend nights, they hosted relatives and neighbors at all-night parties in their parlor, singing French Canadian songs while Gabrielle played the piano in their parlor. The Kerouac children played with the other parish youngsters in the school's recess yard or in the cow pastures of upper Centralville (where Jack remembered lobbing green apples into steaming cowpies). In the summer months the Kerouacs picnicked at Salisbury Beach, on the northern coast of Massachusetts at the New Hampshire border. Salisbury Beach was an ocean resort of scattered beach cottages and an amusement park. Beachcombers walked along the boardwalk and watched their children splash in the cold Atlantic surf. Gabrielle and Leo stuffed themselves with cartons of fried clams and split hot fried dough among the three children. These were happy years, few as they were, that persisted until the untimely demise of Gerard.

2

The Ethereal Flower

1926–1933

I am moved by fancies that are curled
Around these images, and cling:
The notion of some infinitely gentle
Infinitely suffering thing
   T.S. ELIOT

The year 1926 was a promising one for Leo Kerouac. His business was growing successfully, and he was also working as an advertising manager for another company. But soon after Ti Jean, as the young Jack was known, turned four, his older brother, the sickly Gerard, received a visit from the "black suited bulk" of the family's attending physician, Dr. Nathan Pulsifer (Dr. Simpkins in Jack Kerouac's novel *Visions of Gerard*). He left the Beaulieu Street home "having given up hope a long time ago" about Gerard's rapidly declining health. Pulsifer had given the little boy less than a year to live. As the door closed, a shaken Gabrielle, consoled by the arms of her husband, watched the feeble invalid cry as he huddled in his bed, wracked with the violent pains that resulted from what would prove to be his lethal bout of rheumatic fever. Later, a procession of nuns from Saint Louis loomed over Gerard's bedside to pray. Gerard, to area children, was a "normal" child save for his pale, wan countenance. One contemporary, Roger Ouellette, remembers:

> I was about five or six. Gerard would take Jack and I around in my wagon. He was taller than Jack [at the same age], thinner and had

light brown hair and blue eyes. He was very friendly, cheerful and out-going [when well] and seemed bright. I visited him often the last few months he was sick. Jack, who was four at the time, got a little jealous and didn't want anyone else around Gerard. Neither of them were out [playing] very much even when Gerard was well. I remember seeing a picture of Gerard in his casket that somebody took.[1]

Others remember seeing Gerard wrapped in white blankets, sitting in the spring sun in the backyard with Gabrielle. "There was nothing excep-tional about him," neighbor Pauline Coffey recalls. "He was like any other kid—it was the mother—if you've ever lost a child, you would under-stand."[2] Gabrielle was patient and loving and devoted her life unselfishly to her children's needs. So faithfully did she abide by Catholic doctrine that she often clutched a string of rosary beads and hung prayer sheets around the house. But no amount of praying, no matter how prodigious and passionate, would alter the bleak outlook for her son. His waning days roused in Gabrielle a desperate hysteria, knowing that she was help-less to ease the boy's suffering or prevent his death. Father Jean-Baptiste Laboussiere came to the Kerouac home to give pastoral counsel to Gabrielle at her kitchen table.[3]

Rheumatic heart disease is a condition in which the heart valves are damaged by a process that begins with strep throat. If it's not treated, the streptococcal infection may develop into acute rheumatic fever, an inflam-matory disease that affects the body's connective tissues, especially those of the heart, joints, brain, or skin.[4] Kerouac wrote accurately of Gerard's suf-fering. In *Visions of Gerard* the enduring pain that "knifes into his jerking flesh" is a pain so savage that Kerouac naively imagines it inducing a spiri-tual hallucination causing an "ecstasy" that "unfolds inside [Gerard's] mind like a flower. . . . [A]nd he sees millions of white dots, like, and in another instant his legs are stabbing again and he's opened his eyes to con-centrate on the concentrating."[5] Gerard's last days were torturous as the illness reached its apex. On June 2, 1926, at 11:45 P.M., Gerard François Kerouac died in his bed. "Death," Kerouac writes in his touching elegy to his deceased brother, "is the other side of the same coin, we call now, Life."[6]

The Napoleon Bilodeau and Sons Funeral Home came to the house and took the body away in a "tidy basket" to be embalmed.[7] A day later, they brought the corpse back to lie in state at the Beaulieu Street home. Gerard lay for the next few days as a procession of friends, relatives, and nuns filed through the front parlor. Father Laboussiere presided over the funeral mass. Parishioner Edward Gregoire led the choir in singing a solemn "Pie Jesu" as Gerard's pallbearers, all friends of his from the Centralville neighborhood, filed down the church's front steps and placed the little casket into Bilodeau's horse-drawn hearse. On the day of the burial, Gabrielle and her children sat in the car as heavy rain drummed on the roof. When his sister and mother started to weep as the coffin was lowered into the little hole—an unmarked grave near that of his paternal grandfather, Jean-Baptiste—Jack did not know what was the cause of their crying. However, the loss would affect Jack all of his life; the memories of it, as vague as they were as he grew older, seeped into his sleep, coloring the worst and the best of his dreams. Artistically, such dreams would help fuel his creativity:

> ONE AWFUL CENTRAL SCENE, it's in the parlor brown and funeral and coffin-like, Gerard is dead in his coffin and all my writings are racked like candle flickers in a file box by the stuffed sofa in the suffocant gloom dark, literally writing in my brother's tomb—but it's the awful silence, the solemn ceremony of my papers all old some of them crinkled but all familiar and now—I see objects of a destined meaningful TOMB of meaning laid out and racked for use and observation and filing in the room of death—and so as if I was replacing life and sex by writing and death, I—antagonistic, dual, doom—Relatives don't even have to be there, I'm sorta alone with Gerard in the parlor playing with my papers.[8]

Jack's private universe of Jesus, Gerard, and Lowell, enmeshed into one, would be transmuted into his aesthetic sensibilities, ultimately forging the unique cast of his art.

As spring segued into summer 1926, the realization that something had gone awry in the Kerouac household slowly began to affect four-year-old Jack. The guilt associations he later developed over surviving his older brother nevertheless made Jack possessed of the conclusion that memories were inseparable from dreams: "When a man dreams he can't pluck his dream-image from the air that surrounds his bed; no, on the contrary, the image and the whole material in which it sits, is already in his mind; where did it come from; it comes from that part of his brain which has stored up a subconscious vision of an actual experience."[9]

Gerard is transmogrified into a "gaunt and ragged phantom" hovering over Ti Jean's crib: "After all I knew of his great goodness, what then was this vigil in the dark, and why had it frightened me, and why did I secretly believe he probably hated me after all? Because I cannot remember this enigma's first facts maybe I'll never know an enigma again and all's been lost. He who had been my great kind brother had also been my hater in the night."[10]

Jack retained the distinct recollection of being slapped by his older brother. Typically, a preschool child's perception of death is that it is reversible and that his thoughts and feelings have power over others. Jack's childish anger after Gerard slapped his face meant that he felt ultimately responsible for his death. He revealed to his sister Caroline in 1945:

I have this subconscious will to failure, a sort of death-wish, stems from something I did before I was five years old and which stamped upon me a neurotic and horrible feeling of *guilt*. . . . The psychoanalyst [the unqualified William S. Burroughs] figured that I hated Gerard and he hated me—as little brothers are very likely to do, since children that age are primitive and aggressive—and that I wished he were dead, *and he died*. So I felt that I had killed him.[11]

No doubt the lingering traces of their family tragedy continued to trigger profound bouts of sorrow for the family. Their comfortable family parlor was now seen as the site of Gerard's wake. It would come to be the one scene that pervaded the very doom and tragic circumstances of the family, "the coffin that's never been removed from the parlor of the Kerouacs—le mort dans salle des Kerouac—" as if the presence of the memory were a stigma. Also, their youngest child's physical resemblance to Gerard was eerie.[12] As Ti Jean grew that year, he slowly shed his infantile softness, and his blue eyes and pouted lower lip took on the "tranquil and compassionate" countenance of Gerard.[13] The inability to shake their sorrow prompted the family to move to nearby 320 Hildreth Street in August of 1927.[14] In a January 8, 1951, letter, Kerouac tells Neal Cassady: "My father was in the chips in 1926; he had gone all-out to take my mother away from the scene of her boy's death, possibly trying to please her with a fancy house too." In the fall of 1927, six-year-old Jack began his first classes at Saint Louis de France parochial school, walking the short distance through Centralville holding Nin's hand. It was a time, he wrote later, of an "utter lost-forever sadness of my unhappiness in one of the front desks of this room."[15]

If Ti Jean thought that he lived above a cemetery on Beaulieu Street, he knew for certain that he was not far from the real thing at their new address at 320 Hildreth Street. Life went on in the normal day-to-day fashion of labor and play. The rented home was a fourteen-room, cavernous manse with high plastered ceilings and spacious kitchen and dining room areas. The house, formerly a funeral home, was said to be haunted, and even present-day tenants testify to its walls shaking for no reason. Its hallways were dimly lit and cut diagonally through the house. An elderly couple lived upstairs. Gabrielle explored the nooks and crannies of every room as she moved her items in. As Kerouac recollected to Cassady: "My mother opened a closet door, something white flew at her, she screamed, and the thing whapped her on the head with terrible vehemence. I was stricken in my tracks." Gabrielle, doom and tragedy still heavy on her heart, jumped, shouting in French, "The Dead are in the house!" When she opened the door, a fold-in ironing board had fallen out of the closet and hit her on the head.[16] It was only in Kerouac's later fiction and personal letters that the house takes on the dimensions of a Gothic horror novel. The memory of Gerard and the remnants of his first few catechism classes were transmuted into a warped sensibility of life. Jack was greatly taken by the spectacle of Christ in agony in the garden of Gethsemane and each stage of torture on his path to the crucifixion faithfully rendered in the illustrated Bible used in catechism classes. The nuns stressed daily that life was nothing less than a struggle of sin and redemption. His six-year-old life had become entangled in the snare of familial dysfunction precisely at the time when it should have been imbued with healthy associations. They were also the years when Jack first sensed his independence from his family: "It was about that time I began discovering the fact that I was alive and could do things on my own. In the golden afternoon I stood on the sunporch among piles of unarranged furniture and made a complete speech, gestures and all, to a mattress leaning on the wall; I can never forget it."[17]

With an air of paranoia and French Canadian suspicion fostered by Gabrielle, Kerouac noted later that his "fears," as "insignificant" as they were, "were only just beginning." In *Doctor Sax,* the attentive reader can trace from Jack's elementary schooling the merging of life and death caught in the throes of religious mysticism. In class, the nuns fervently taught him the virtues of Catholic worship, of asking for penance in stuffy confessional booths, of praying not only to the Holy Trinity but also to the Virgin Mary, Sainte Thérèse, and numerous other saints. To hammer the point home to the impressionable children, the Sisters of the Assumption resorted to the cinematic trickery that was coming into vogue in the era of moving pictures. One such film, according to Kerouac, depicted Sainte Thérèse and incorporated a special effect that gave the illusion that the plastered statue's head was moving. This was branded into the memory of Ti Jean, for the importance of Sainte Thérèse was legendary in Franco-American Catholicism.

Pope Pius XI's canonization of Sainte Thérèse on May 17, 1925, lent her an air of special importance in Franco-American Catholic doctrine. This inspired the showing of the film on Sainte Thérèse. In Kerouac's letters, diary entries, and fiction, he often remarked upon Sainte Thérèse's "shower of roses," both figuratively and literally. As she lay dying in the convent infirmary, Thérèse could look out the window and see the rosebushes blossoming. As she reflected upon her impending death, Thérèse believed that her faith in God held great things in store for her. She explained: "After my death, I will let fall a shower of roses. I will spend my heaven doing good upon earth. I will raise up a mighty host of little saints. My mission is to make God loved." Shortly after her death, the rain of roses began (so explains the religious myth), sometimes appearing physically, other times as a distinctive fragrance in the air. Cures of painful and fatal diseases were attributed to her intercession. As a reward for their devout faith in Sainte Thérèse, her followers were imbued with inner peace and warmth of spirit.[18]

Thus, in Kerouac, passed down both from his parochial education and his mother's teachings, Sainte Thérèse was irrevocably entwined with the phantom of Gerard. A statue of the saint was prominently displayed inside the Kerouacs' home. On dark nights, the boy believed, this statue moved its head as in the film he had watched at school. Stemming from that experience, he also believed that Jesus Christ was pushing his bed at a later Centralville address in 1930:

We had a statue of Ste. Therese in my house on West Street I saw it turn its head at me in the dark. Earlier too, horrors of the Jesus Christ of passion plays in his shrouds and vestments of saddest doom mankind in the Cross Weep for Thieves and Poverty—he was at the foot of my bed pushing it one dark Saturday night (on Hildreth & Lilley secondfloor flat full of Eternity outside)—either he or the Virgin Mary stooped with phosphorescent profile and pushing my bed.[19]

In the home, Gabrielle's store-bought, priest-blessed crucifix hung from the parlor wall and glowed sickly green in the dark. Jack sat "motionlessly in the parlor, pale and thin." These events, gloomy and terrifying in their spiritual intensity, drove the frightened, sensitive boy deeper into self-absorption. He became frightened of the dark. Kerouac recalls in *Doctor Sax* the security of sleeping in his mother's bed. Such dependency formed the bedrock of the mother-son dependency that significantly marked Kerouac's life. His devotion and indebtedness to her for supporting him while he was writing are fundamental in understanding their sometimes unsettling relationship later in their lives. Gabrielle's work ethic, religious devotion, and encouragement were the pillars that upheld the Kerouac family before and after the death of Leo (in 1946). Jack felt justified in explaining this relationship in one of his novels, *Desolation Angels*, after numerous critics, writers, girlfriends, friends, and, later, biographers criticized his attention to her:

> I've noticed how most of my fellow writers all seem to "hate" their mothers and make big Freudian or sociological philosophies around that, in fact using it as the straight theme of their fantasies, or at least saying as much—I often wonder if they've ever slept till four in the afternoon and woke up to see their mother darning their socks in a sad window light, or come back from revolutionary horrors of weekends to see her mending the rips in a bloody shirt with quiet eternal bowed head over needle.[20]

It was to her he would remain indebted and committed, in youth as well as in adulthood.

The family moved again less than a year later, in 1928, relocating almost one block away, to 240 Hildreth Street.[21] Kerouac, sensing the disruption of his family's daily routine, began to invent ways to keep himself occupied. By virtue of his mother's memories, Jack knew that he played records like "Dardanella" on the old Victrola in the family parlor and acted out private movies he remembered from the serialized featurettes he watched in downtown Lowell's B. F. Keith Theatre. One of those was the Marx Brothers film *Animal Crackers,* which Kerouac claimed he saw six times when it was released that year.[22] Films and his relentless, restless imagination helped to blunt his sorrow and guilt and nurtured his imagination. Gabrielle, still active in the church, kept herself busy by participating in occasional church bazaars. On May 17, 1928, Ti Jean, clad in his best Sunday suit, took his first communion at Saint Louis de France.

In spring 1930, the family relocated to the last of their Centralville addresses, 66 West Street.[23] This time their stay lasted three years; memories of this time are Kerouac's earliest remembered (as opposed to *imagined*) recollections. In *Visions of Cody,* he recalls that the West Street address was a center for friendly gatherings: "I remember sitting in the parlor listening to the old pre–Basil Rathbone Sherlock Holmes on the radio with my father and Sis and suddenly in the kitchen I see a man creeping up like an Indian with twelve people creeping up behind him from the kitchen door and it's a surprise party which rocks house (small rose-covered cottage . . . on West Street Lowell)."[24]

In 1928 and 1929, the Kerouacs made trips on the Fourth of July to Montreal, "as all the New England French do,"[25] with Leo taking the wheel, Gabrielle singing French songs by his side, and Caroline and Jack huddled in the back with the luggage and food baskets. The idyllic lifestyle that they now enjoyed, seemingly on the upswing after the family tragedy four years earlier, would be short-lived. During these years (the last of Kerouac's Centralville childhood) the Roaring Twenties were coming to an end: a slackening economy, the first hints of civil unrest in Europe, and modernism were all on the rise. Herbert Hoover's 1928 presidential campaign slogan promised a "chicken for every pot," a vow that would linger in stark contrast later when the Great Depression descended upon America with the stock market crash of October 29, 1929. By late 1928, the portents were forbidding. Most major industries, chiefly steel mills, construction, and the prosperous automobile industry, began to slow production. In Lowell, textile and shoe factories began to lay off workers. Those of Franco-American extraction were among the first to be let go. The great mills were shutting their doors; some were razed to lower property taxes. Many Lowell families were compelled to pull their children from school to put them to work despite the relative scarcity of jobs. This trend fostered exploitation: many employers extended working hours and reduced pay. In the Merrimack Mills weave room, one woman remembered the working conditions that she faced on a daily basis: "When

I come out of there at night I was shaking. . . . [T]here we got thirteen dollars a week. . . . You really didn't need names, because everyone got thirteen dollars a week. Wouldn't do you any good to complain. . . . [T]hey were so petrified for their jobs in them days, it was pitiful."[26]

The Kerouacs were fortunate in never having to put their daughter or son to work. Leo's business still prospered at the Spotlite printing company, which catered almost exclusively to Lowell's theaters. The town had a glut of them; the Merrimack, the Crown, the Strand, the Royal, B. F. Keith's, the Tower, and the Rialto attracted the most recognized show business names. Despite economic hardship, many people attended the growing roster of films being produced in Hollywood. In downtown Lowell, Jack and his sister, Nin, sat in constant attendance in the balcony seats (pejoratively referred to as "nigger heaven" by the locals) of the B. F. Keith and Royal Theatres. They watched the movies for free, courtesy of Leo's business connections. In the balcony of the Royal Theatre, an ominous hook-handed usher (a "fine fellow" friend of Leo's) lurked in the shadows, intimidating unruly children, while on the brightly lit screen Tom Mix and Tim McCoy returned each week with cliff-hanger endings to entice audiences again and again. Often, backstage, Leo played blackjack with the vaudevillians who performed there. According to Kerouac's impassioned account of those years in *Visions of Gerard*, Leo was a "one-time ad man making up the B. F. Keiths Vaudeville ads" and was "well known by a lot of performers on the famous old circuit." One of the entertainers he socialized with was W. C. Fields, who billed himself then as "the Eccentric Juggler." Onstage Fields was customarily dressed as a baggy-trousered tramp, donning a fake beard and garish eye makeup, while his assistant, Hattie, wore a tuxedo with tight satin pants. Fields never spoke during his act but instead relied upon physical and character comedy. In one skit he would deliberately drop a ball and blame it on his assistant. Other times he faked behind-the-back throws by juggling two balls in one hand and waving a third ball behind his back with the other. In between shows he played cards backstage with Leo and other theater associates, as described in a bit of dialogue in *The Town and the City* (1950): "'Hell, I remember all of them. In those days they had the poker games, right here in B.F. Keith's and George [pseudonym for Leo Kerouac] never missed a one. They say he was the last man to go home and the first one to come back.'"[27]

Kerouac later described his father at this time as a "bustling jolly young businessman." If he was, he had every reason to be. With his own business and a growing family that he kept housed and fed ("lots of pork-chops and beans came to me via my old man's efforts in the world of business," Kerouac notes in *Visions of Gerard*), he had already achieved the Franco-American equivalent of the American Dream. In 1931, Leo moved his company again, bringing it next to an oily canal at 95 Bridge Street.[28] In his shop he employed local boys like Ralph Larrivee who helped him with small chores such as sweeping the floor and running the print jobs to different clients.[29] Aside from watching the occasional film, Leo seldom had time to spend frivolously. Gambling was his social mainstay: Rockingham Park, the horse-racing track in Salem, New Hampshire, was close enough for him to take a half-day trip, sometimes bringing his son.

Along with film, twentieth-century American literature had reached a creative zenith with the advent of modernist fiction. But this was of no interest in the Kerouac household, for Leo and Gabrielle seldom read much more than the Catholic Bible, some local French periodicals, and newspapers like *L'Etoile*, the *Lowell Telegram*, and the *Lowell Sun*. Young Jack read French children's books and slowly began to adapt to the task of learning a second language.

If we are to rely on the veracity of Kerouac's autobiographical fiction, his mother cried when Leo came in late from his late-night games of poker:

> She sometimes waited up late for him while he played poker with the boys backstage at B. F. Keith's, and when he got home she cried and he tried to soothe her tears, and then he would refrain from playing poker for two whole weeks and the honeymoon would resume. Each time he went back to poker her tears were less bitter and dumbfounded and, after each sad reconciliation, sweetly, meditatively, their marriage was that much sounder.[30]

As the 1930s began, there was no sign that the depression would abate. Gabrielle had a knack, as many French Canadian housewives did, for budget-minded resourcefulness. She was thrifty enough to make optimal use of her food leftovers, a lifelong skill Jack appreciated enough to capture in his later writing: "As for food, nothing went wasted: an odd potato half eaten ends up delightfully tidbit fried by a piece of later meat, or a quarter of an onion finds its way into a jar of homepickled onions, or old corners of roastbeef into a delicious homey burbling fricasee."[31] She fed

Jack and Nin mayonnaise sandwiches, ground pork scraps (cortons) for a meat spread, and on Saturday night served a generous pot of delicious baked beans. Some of her income she gained, like many families in Lowell, from the rag man, who plodded Lowell's cobblestone streets in a horse-drawn wagon. He paid a few pennies for old (but clean) washcloths, faded and torn clothes, and bedsheets.[32]

The constant uprooting of the two surviving Kerouac children from their friends implanted an early sense of the rootlessness that would plague them in later years. In 1934 the family moved yet again, this time to 16 Phebe Avenue in Pawtucketville, approximately one mile from Centralville. It was the address in which his remembrance centered on the family's brown desk, which was placed against the wall in the dining room, a room reserved for company. Beneath it were scrawled chalk marks made by Jack, Caroline, and Gerard.[33] Jack turned ten years old that March, and his move to economically depressed Pawtucketville he would later deem a time of "glee": "I had learned to stop crying in Centralville and I was determined not to start crying in Pawtucketville." Despite the loss and grief that marked his family's Centralville years, Kerouac looked upon them with profound fondness. In 1962 he told Pertinax (a pseudonym for his future sister-in-law Mary Sampas) in her *Lowell Sun* column, "The Rambler":

> I love Lowell for St. Louis de France in Centralville where I was baptized and where my brother was buried in a coffin as a hundred little boys sang on a rainy day and we carted him off in a procession to Nashua, N. H. and when he was lowered in the ground everybody cried except me. I was 4 years old and I thought he was in heaven and what was there to cry about?[34]

3

"Wits Abound in Lowell Too"

1933–1935

*O youth, still wounded, living, feeling with a woe unutterable, still
grieving with a grief untolerable, still thirsting with a thirst
unquenchable—where are we to seek?*

THOMAS WOLFE, "The Four Lost Men"

In 1930, Lowell's economic prosperity came to a sudden halt, sending the
town into a long, steady nosedive through the rest of the decade.

Leo, still gainfully employed in his own business, commuted around
Lowell in the family's 1929 Ford. The mill from which he rented space,
formerly Massachusetts Mills, had now gone into receivership (as had the
Suffolk, Tremont, and Middlesex Mills). It was subdivided into as many
as thirty-two different businesses, with Spotlite Print sharing space with
its competition, the Merrimack News Company.[1] The slackening of his
printing business over time, however, caused Leo to attempt to raise
money with family friend Armand Gauthier. Together they decided to in-
vest in and manage a boxing gym patronized by area teens. The venture
was short-lived.[2]

Jack had left Saint Louis de France school, for the upper grades were
exclusively for girls. He attended Saint Joseph's School, the last of his education in a Catholic institution, where he graduated in July 1933 as a
fifth-grader. During this time, under the tutelage of the Jesuits, Kerouac
served as an altar boy for Saint Jean de Baptiste Church. In September
1933, following an entrance examination in which it was determined that
he was advanced enough to skip a grade, "Jackie," as his Pawtucketville
friends now called him, entered public middle school. In the Bartlett

School he began to learn to read, speak, and write in English with the help of such educational books as *Mother Tongue* and the *Metcalf and Rafter Series*.[3] Kerouac quickly mastered the intricacies of English, so much so that it became his primary language for the rest of his life.

With the new language he took to with unnatural ease, Jack began to formulate fledgling ideas to use it with, most prominently writing. On the brown desk he rolled marbles imitating the horse races at Rockingham Park: "[I]t was when I got the idea for racing, they meandered a race under my eyes—it was a gray day—the whole idea of the *Turf* must have come to me like (as just now and not since 1948) that so-seldom experience of seeing my whole life's richness swimming in a palpable mothlike cloud, a cloud I can really see and which I think is elfin and due really to my Celtic blood."[4] According to Kerouac's own biographical résumé, written in the fall of 1957, he used ideas like the *Turf* as material created in one-page "newspapers" that were typeset and printed on his father's hand press. Jack titled one paper *Racetrack News*. Others he named *Turf Journal* and *Baseball Chatter*. The latter, a fantasy-baseball newsletter, saw four issues over his fifteenth and sixteenth years. At fifteen, Kerouac would write an ambitious, lengthy synopsis of all the racing action derived from his afternoon trips to Rockingham Park. He declared his first, fifteen-cent issue, dated April 1937, to be "America's Favorite Horse Racing Magazine," and beneath its dubious self-promotion, Jackie scrawled headlines like "Jericho Wins Futurity—Hunk Vincent's High Priced Babe Proved Worth!"[5] Another was titled "Stake Special—The Preakness." The specials were promised to be "published at every big stake classic." "Mighty Preakness run to-day before 90,000; Biggest Turf Classic Event yet; Eclipses spotlight attendance by 10,000; Immortal Turf Race worth highest ever—$500,000.00; Great Repulsion ranks favorite despite untimely defeats in hands of W. Watson's Romantic Head Play!"[6] The handwritten bulletin was a new way to express his interests, and he took to it with a skillful agility that eventually exceeded Leo and Gabrielle's capacity for communicating in English. However, it was also indicative of his self-absorbed tendencies, immersing himself in his imagination. It was, as Kerouac later said, a "sorry mess of scatological absorption."[7]

After Jack saw his first Boston Red Sox baseball game with his father at Fenway Park, he created a fantasy league of his own. It consisted of drawn cardboard sections from which he depicted the various actions of a baseball game. In his imaginary league (such as the "Summer League") he created teams like the Philadelphia Pontiacs, Pittsburgh Plymouths, Boston

Fords, New York Chevvies, Chicago Chryslers, St. Louis LaSalles, and Pawtucket Blues. Thus each (as eyewitness Stan Isaacs saw in 1961 after Jack offered to show it to him in his Northport, Long Island, home) represented a "single, double, strikeout, double play, stolen base, caught stealing and the like." Isaacs explains: "The fascination for me was the imaginative world of colorful characters Kerouac had created, and he mouthed a sort of play-by-play, sketching in their backgrounds as we played. He had wonderous players." Among Jack's many players was the leading home-run hitter "El Negro of the St. Louis Whites," described by Kerouac as a "big Negro from Latin America." There was the league's leading hitter, Wino Love of the Detroit Reds, who boasted a .344 average. Kerouac called him "Wino" because "he drinks, but he's still a great hitter." Then there was "everbody's favorite," a team player called Bill "Big" Louis. Kerouac explained to Isaacs, "I patterned him after Babe Ruth. One day I had him coming to bat chewing on a frankfurter." Another he created in the late 1940s was Pic Jackson, who was the "league's best hitting pitcher" and who, according to Kerouac, "likes to read the Sunday supplements; his name, 'Pic' is short for Pictorial Review." Isaacs recalls:

> I was taken with the name of Burlingame Japes, who Kerouac said "was 40 years old, a little left-hander who in his younger days was the league-base-stealing champ. I put him in for Joe Boston who broke his leg sliding and who wasn't helping the team anyway." Kerouac explained that the name Burlingame came from a town just south of San Francisco. I managed the Pittsburgh Browns, who beat Kerouac's Chicago Blues, 9-3. I was not accustomed to an afternoon of sipping wine, let alone the cheap stuff, and I was a bit woozy when I left the shaggy author late in the afternoon. But, as I wrote at the time, "It was a good game."[8]

Kerouac's fantasy baseball league was a continually evolving game that he continued to play with from 1933 through the 1960s. From this effort he spun out related writings depicting himself, in one published example, as the columnist for "Jack Lewis's Baseball Chatter" (1938).

At age eleven, Jackie attempted his first real literary effort that wasn't associated with sports: a pencil-written novel carefully scribed into his notebook and inspired by his recent reading of *Huckleberry Finn*.[9] The novel (since lost) was about an orphaned boy who runs away from home, a scene that would reappear in 1950 in the first part of his first published novel, *The Town and the City.* The effort was inspired when Jack ran away for a brief while in 1930 with his friend Michael Fournier. In *The Town and the City,* the Campbell brothers, along with little Mickey Martin, decide to run away in a boat that they had stolen from the boathouse on Galloway's northern border and row on the dark waters of the Merrimack. Kerouac's use of the river as a setting (most notably in the novel *Doctor Sax*) stems from his boyhood affinity for playing along its banks and the Merrimack's importance in the founding of Lowell as a textile town.

Jack also began to keep a journal, setting the groundwork for his lifetime tendency to observe the mundane and make it something special. For example, between January 23 and January 26, 1934, Jack records the progress of a Lowell snowstorm: "January 23—Started snowing in the afternoon. Snowed up to my waist at night. Still piling higher. Went to the club at night. Played pool with Harvey. Came back home all white. Snow" and "January 24—Still piling higher. No school! Snowbound. I'll make plenty of money shoveling snow. Plenty! Still piling up. What money I'll make. I'll bowl a lot with money for shoveling and 75 cents for watch." By the twenty-sixth, Leo, out of town in the family's new 1934 Plymouth, had telephoned Gabrielle twice to say he was stranded in the storm and had sought shelter at the same farm from which the family dog, Beauty, had been obtained. Kerouac finishes the journal entry by indicating that he slept with Beauty and watched the snow fall softly on the rooftops of Pawtucketville. Such scenes would later appear in his Lowell novels, tenderly reflecting the conscious mental workings of a boy bent on describing the events of the world as he encountered them.[10]

Kerouac's relative ease with English became increasingly evident in his personal writings and in his class work; they were, he claimed, linguistic feats attributed to the "higher aim of his parochial school education." At Bartlett Junior High School he joined the Scribblers Club and impressed his teachers with his urge to create characters and story lines, most lifted from his immediate world of everyday Lowell.

Then there was Kerouac's physical prowess. His interest in sports began to accelerate; his favorites were football, running sprints, and billiards. His adeptness at sports extended itself through his school years; he later joined the track and football team. Fond of creating lists (a habit that he kept for the rest of his life), Kerouac listed three "talents" in a 1934 journal entry: cartooning, writing, and billiards. Gerard had taught him how to draw: by the time he was eight, Jack was creating his own comic strips like "Kuku and Koko at the Earth's Core" and "The Eighth Sea." Sometime in his youth, Jack learned of a little boy in Nashua who lived near his relatives. Jack generously let him borrow some of his cartoons, but they were never returned. One comic book from his childhood now in the Kerouac archive (credited to "Jean-Louis Kerouac") addresses an imaginary audience. He drew a back view of himself drawing the opening scene, perhaps a nod to Vermeer, of whom he may have been aware from his visits to the Lowell City Library, which had many volumes of European art on its shelves. In the comic book's first panel, Kerouac states that it was "A New Story by Our Sensational Fabricator—The Gentleman from France" and titles it "The Whole World Is on Fire." In it are traces of the Kerouac trademarks. The comic strip, set in "Shakespeare, Iowa," features Luke Parent, a "railroad yardclerk." Especially intriguing is Kerouac's early grasp of his later writing style: "The house of life vibrating with early morning joy of human beings after sorrowful sleep of night." In the lower right corner of the first page, a young crippled boy named Little Tony Parent shouts, "Uncle Luke! Come see my new clay man!!" Kerouac, even at an early age, displays the keen empathy that he would retain throughout his life for those of a lower social station. This archival evidence illustrates the young writer's early awareness of suffering. He portrays men's vices in an equally compassionate light.[11]

Kerouac's pool-playing skills also grew, developed from taking advantage of his father's new job as proprietor of the Pawtucketville Social Club, which he took after his brief stint as a boxing club manager. The club was populated by French Canadian men from the Pawtucketville neighborhood and was typical of its kind in any town or city in New England. With its brass rails and rows of shining bottles, the bar had jars of eggs and kielbasa pickled in vinegar to feed the drinking men. The atmosphere of "hubbubs and echo-roars of the hall, click of pool games, laughter, and talk" was recalled by Kerouac and used in his novel *Doctor Sax*.

During the winters, preadolescent Jack took solitary excursions around the city and sometimes along the banks of the river or Beaver Brook (called Pine Brook in his writings), which flows out of neighboring Dracut. While his mother made roast beef (a rarity in depression-era Lowell) and simmered tapioca pudding on the stove in their little Phebe Avenue kitchen, Leo listened to sports and news on the radio and puffed his ever-present cigar. Outside, Nin was allotted the task of shoveling the walkways, allowing privileged Jack to wander after every beckoning notion. Even to his childhood friends it seemed that Jack was a favored child, fawned over by his mother as if her whole life revolved around him. Kerouac's explorations of his neighborhood were inspired by his newest author of the moment, Jack London. Donning his winter coat, rubber overshoes, and cap and mittens knitted by his mother, Kerouac would arm himself with a hockey stick to test the ice of Beaver Brook. He observed "the sweet rooftops of life" and, looking across the snow-blanketed river, he thought of the less privileged who labored within the red brick walls of the mills.

> I hear one dog, one farmerdoor slam a mile away — I hear a hoot of sledders, a keen shrill of littlegirl — I hear the tick of snowflake on snow, on limb — Ice is forming on my eyebrows — I come haunting, emerging from the forest, go down the hill to the brook, the stonewall has crystal icing in the heavy winter dim — Black bleak lines in the sky — my mouth is awed open, vapors puff out, it's stopped snowing and I've begun to sense a blue scene in the new night.

Reaching the top of a hill in Pawtucketville, he would gaze upon all of Lowell, to the peak of Lowell City Hall and the lower tenement roofs of Little Canada. After his walk, he would return to the "heat and warm joy" of his home.[12]

In the classroom Kerouac remained pensive, intense, and reticent, hardly ever uttering a word in class except when addressed. To one student he resembled "a tomb—all closed in."[13] Few sensed that a creative, fertile mind slumbered beneath his introverted persona. Kerouac's quick mastery of English helped him appreciate the poetry of Walt Whitman and John Greenleaf Whittier both inside and outside of class. He found increasing solace in the tall stacks of the Lowell City Library. But his education was not found solely in books, though books helped foster his artistic spirit. What he observed on a daily basis conditioned him to see beauty in every aspect of life. Even the walk over the Moody Street Bridge fascinated him. The white plumes of the cascading rapids below became a regular fixture in his Lowell writing.

Kerouac also passed a great looming crucifix constructed on a replica Golgotha when he crossed the bridge closest to the Pawtucket Falls. Beneath the hill a small, candlelit enclosure sheltered an altar that constantly flickered with dozens of prayer candles lit by Franco-American parishioners. Before reaching the altar, one first had to kneel and pray at the stations that were engraved into small black plaques: "II—Jésus est chargé de sa croix"; "III—Jésus tombe sous le poids de sa croix"; "IX—Jésus tombe pour la troisième fois." Gabrielle, like so many French Canadians in Lowell, made the Catholic grotto a standard pilgrimage. She wrote (in French) the object of her prayers in the little notebook that sat next to the burning candles. Often her children accompanied her.

In the hot and humid summer of July 1934 Gabrielle showed Jack how some parishioners kneeled at every step leading to the grotto's cross. The grotto was a popular place for local Catholics. There was an outdoor pulpit made of stone and cement where a priest would officiate at services beneath the enormous man-made hill on which the cross was erected. Weighted with his already overbrimming emotional baggage of impressions, Kerouac was taken through the dark, winding, narrow drive of the grotto as he remembers it in *Doctor Sax:* "So you kneeled there, at night, looking at faint representations of the Virgin, hood over head, her sad eyes, the action, the tortured wood and thorns of the Passion, and your reflections on the subject become mirrored from the funeral home where a dull light fixed in the ceiling of an overpass garage for hearses shines dully in the gravelly gloom."[14]

Near the grotto was a row of funeral homes that spread out from Pawtucketville's Saint Joseph's Hospital where Gabrielle had recently admitted Nin, who was stricken with appendicitis. Gabrielle's acute superstitions and paranoia, fostered by her abiding orthodox faith, her provincialism, and her ethnicity, which was fed by an undercurrent of Canadian folk beliefs, had the most influence over Jack. In *Doctor Sax,* Kerouac (writing as Jackie Duluoz) recalls a night in Pawtucketville when he and his mother walk a relative named Blanche home to Aunt Clementine's house after a trek through the grotto. They talk about family, lost loves, and dying and deceased relatives.

The Kerouacs of Leo's family began to splinter. His sister Emma had moved with her husband, Pierre, and their three children (Camille, Pierre Jr., and Leo, the latter two being children from Pierre's first marriage) north to Lewiston, Maine. By 1939, Pierre was dead; his wife followed him to the grave thirty years later (at ninety-seven years of age). Leo's brother, Joseph, who was by now gravely ill from asthma, still smoked the Cu Babs Jack remembered from his youth. He had lost his store at the beginning of the depression and, desperately needing income, sent his son Armand on errands around the neighborhoods of Nashua to collect money extended on credit. Shortly afterwards, he opened a store in Lowell, though it did not bring him the modicum of success that his

Nashua store had.[15] To compound his frustrations, his asthma began to take its toll. It seemed to Jack (as written in *Doctor Sax*) that he was "dying these past five, ten, fifteen years." A paragraph laments "the saddest Duluoz of them all" as "horrible, porcine, fat, sickfaced, bald, and green." Jack's perception of him was as a "slob with fear concerning nightmares."

Catholicism still ruled the Kerouac roost, and Jack was, more than ever, absorbed by the church interior when he attended Sunday services: the solemn flicker of altar candles, the smell of burning wax and incense, the magisterial sweep of the robed priest and his altar boys and the swell of the church's organ. A choir of children piped in high melodic tones from the balcony. From the pew when he sat at mass, the religious fixtures that were placed around the church transfixed him. For a young boy like Kerouac, the church's rituals and perceived magic were viewed with a palpable blend of dread and awe. However, Jackie soon gave up his stint as altar boy and started to focus his extracurricular activities on sports or on spending time with the gang of Pawtucketville boys that would become the creative fodder for the five Lowell books of his mature fiction.

Jack was also immersed in comic books like *Star Western* ("The Big Magazine of the West") and *The Shadow, A Detective Monthly.* He may have become familiar with the Shadow from the broadcasts that began on CBS radio on July 31, 1930. James La Curto was the voice of "the Shadow" when the program was heard on the *Detective Story Hour.* In September 1937, the voice of the Shadow took on a more distinctive dimension when it was performed by a new radio personality, Orson Welles (Agnes Moorehead played his love interest, Margot Lane), and the story had its own show. That year, Jack would have first heard the sinister laugh of the Shadow as he pronounced: "Mwee hee hee hee, the weed of crime bears bitter fruit. Crime does not pay, the Shadow knows. Mwee hoo hoo hooo."[16] The influence of *The Shadow* was significant in Jack Kerouac's novel *Doctor Sax.* In the 1959 novel a mysterious figure haunts the adolescent Kerouac (Jackie Duluoz) and stalks the shadows along the banks of the Merrimack River. His Sax was wrapped in a "wild and hincty cape," and his laugh was lifted directly from the radio speakers first heard in the Kerouac parlor. From the dark of the grotto the sound was heard, a "mwee hee hee ha ha" that "floats back sepulchral and glee-mad."[17] But *Doctor Sax* also recorded a time in Kerouac's life he recalled as being one of "glee." The worst was yet to come, however, not for Jack but for his family. Besides the country's economic collapse, the natural forces of the Merrimack River (coupled with the patriarch's gambling problems) would deal a severe blow in March 1936, the year Jack turned fourteen years old.

4

Now a Flood Will Bring the Rest

Spring 1936

Nowhere in this sinful world can a honest, hardworking man profit.
WILLIAM FAULKNER, *As I Lay Dying*

At the Bartlett School, Jack had met a boy who lived near him. The boy was Greek. His name was Sebastian Sampas; he was nicknamed "Sammy" and lived with his family on Martin Street on Rosemont Terrace in Paw-tucketville. Although they were the same age (born in May 1922, Sebastian was two months younger), Sampas was one grade behind. This chance meeting was paramount, for it was through Sebastian, Jack declared years later, in his introduction to *Lonesome Traveler,* that he was inspired to become a writer at seventeen years of age. Unlike Jack, Sammy was not physically strong. When a gang of local bullies set upon him, Jack defended Sammy. Though this meant nothing to Jack, Sammy remembered it for years afterward and looked up to Jack after he left Bartlett to continue his education at Lowell High School. Though they were closer friends in later years, they did realize that both loved the theater, poetry, and reading. The friendship became closer a year later because of their mutual interest and involvement in the Young Prometheans, a youth group that convened in the Sampas home to discuss the arts and philosophy. In Sammy's house there were books, plenty of them, on a bookshelf; the collection spanned world history, philosophy, and literature. Most of the books were from Charles Sampas; "Charlie" was born on August 23, 1911, and was educated in Lowell before moving on as an undergraduate studying journalism at Boston University and graduating in 1932. On the Sampas bookshelves sat works by Fyodor Dostoevsky, William Saroyan, and James Joyce (whose *Portrait of the Artist as a Young Man* was seminal for Kerouac; as a teenager he started to compose a work he titled "Portrait of an Artist"). Charlie Sampas had also subscribed to poetry magazines and the *New Yorker.* The Sampas family moved across the river to Stevens Street when they were forced to by the rising tides of the Merrimack River that early spring of 1936. It was a tragedy that hurt not only them but all of Lowell.

March 12, 1936, Jack's fourteenth birthday, was marred by news of an impending flood. The *Lowell Sun*'s headline warned, "Rampaging Merrimack to Hit Flood Stage Tomorrow Noon." On the thirteenth the headline was even bleaker, sending a chill to every Lowellian who owned a home or business near the river's banks: "River Threatens Widespread Destruction." The river was rising approximately four inches an hour. Not even the Locks and Canals Commission could give assurance to the frightened citizens, for it, too, feared that the flood would be the worst ever to hit the Merrimack valley. The residents of Lowell's Rosemont Terrace in Pawtucketville were warned that the river would probably flood them out of their homes by midnight. Days later, the *Sun* published a pair of photographs, two views of a landslide on First Street. Great surges of mud from the spring thaw cascaded down the river's flooded embankment and over the major roadway. Lowell was not alone in this devastation; virtually all of New England was faced with threats from various waterways. By March 14 the river had reached full flood stage as it crept up over the porch steps of the tenements and through the doors, damaging most homes with up to six feet of muddy, cold water. The Pawtucket Dam, which usually boasted beautiful falls and cataracts, was minimized to no less than seven feet over its capstone. At the brink of the falls, a sheet of ice still held on determinedly, cracking and bulging inward at the force of the overflowing river. Eventually, the ice succumbed before sending great jagged sheets into and down the river. Nearby, the Rosemont Terrace section of Pawtucketville fared still worse when Beaver Brook, rapidly flowing from Dracut, merged with the swollen river. Sebastian Sampas's home on Martin Street was destroyed, forcing the family to move up and across the river, to Stevens Street.[1]

Kerouac's later recollection of this ordeal would be vastly different from those of his contemporaries; he dramatized it with an infusion of childhood fantasy in *Doctor Sax,* making the formidable flood the result of the title character's prophecy. In real life, the teenaged boy watched the flotsam from the flood miles upstream flow by. Dead, bloated animals, trees, "brown foam, mud foam, dead rats, the roofs of hen houses, roofs of barns, houses" bobbed eerily in the ferocious grip of the water. School was canceled that week; Jack and his friends envisioned making a big raft from the floating debris. Amid the chaos of the flood, Kerouac also felt the adult concerns about the disaster: "We felt we'd grown up because these places and scenes were now more than child's play, they were now abutted in pure day by the white snow mist of tragedy." Although the flood did not reach the doorstep of the Kerouacs' house, it did reach Leo's water-level business, Spotlite Print. The flood damage was irreparable: "[R]ed-brick warehouses leading to the grimy door of my father's front floor hall-chamber . . . [were] all one vast and ghastly swimming pool made of mud, straw, cotton, machine, oil, ink, piss and rivers."[2]

A bounty was offered for killing the numerous rats evicted from their riverbank homes. Typhoid shots were recommended for the children in public schools. After receiving their shots, they were "sick and arm-swollen" for all of the following week.[3]

Throughout the remainder of March, while residents swamped the local Sears and Roebuck for tools to repair the damage, the river still "raged to her fury." Jack sought distraction from the flood's rampage by going to the Lowell City Library to read books. "A strange lull took place" in the flood's aftermath, as Kerouac writes in the opening pages of book 6 of *Doctor Sax.* This eerie lull enveloped Lowell. Kerouac's novelist friend John Clellon Holmes wrote in an essay about how he and Kerouac shared the same "rocks" in the "beds":

> Down river a few days later, beyond where the Pemigewasset flowed into the Merrimack, Kerouac watched those same trees under the Moody Street Bridge in Lowell on their way to that most austere of seas: The North Atlantic, and perhaps first heard the dire "mwee-hee-hee" of Dr. Sax echo in the roar beneath his shoes. We would discover this eerie correspondence in our lives only years later in New York, up way past midnight, the river of traffic in the clashing street below roaring as loud as the converging rivers of our boyhood, and bringing the memory back to both of us in the same instant.[4]

Particularly after the flood, the economic odds were stacked against the Kerouacs. Having little or no accident insurance and no savings, Leo could not repair the flood damage to Spotlite Print. Unemployed and searching for work, and therefore unable to pay his rent, Leo moved his family from Phebe Avenue to nearby 35 Sarah Avenue. (He eventually took a job carrying water buckets for the Works Progress Administration.) This home's yard had an apple tree that Kerouac jealously guarded. When apples (a sought-for treat during the depression) fell to the ground that late summer in 1936, Kerouac would not give one to his neighbor, little Jeanette Brown, who regularly watched him slug a punching bag he had made and hung from the apple tree. However, her mother's perception of Jack was that he was a precocious and strange boy from whom it was best to keep her daughter away.[5] Mrs. Brown also kept Jeanette away from the candy store where Jack bought his comic books; according to *Doctor Sax*, the proprietor was rumored to be a pedophile.

At Sarah Avenue, one of Kerouac's most vivid memories, he later revealed to Neal Cassady, was that his youthful habit of washing his own handkerchiefs met with an obstacle: his mother, who assumed he was doing so because he was masturbating. To combat this Catholic violation in her house, she would sneak up on Jack when he was lying in his bed: "my mother was real rough on me in that respect, she wouldn't allow any kind of sex in the house. They say that makes a man nutty. I guess I'm nutty then."[6] Despite this, Kerouac remembered the home on Sarah Avenue fondly. The unassuming house was furnished starkly yet comfortably. Kerouac recalled in *Doctor Sax*:

> I'm at the window in the parlor facing Sarah Avenue and its white sands dripping in the shower, from thick hot itchy stuffed furniture huge and bearlike for a reason they liked then but now call "over-stuffed"—looking at Sarah Avenue through the lace curtains and beaded windows, in the dank gloom by the vast blackness of the squareback piano and dark easy chairs and maw sofa and the brown painting on wall depicting angels playing around a brown Virgin Mary and Child in a Brown Eternity of the Brown Saints.[7]

Indoors, Jack played his phonograph records, choreographed the *Tarantella* for a stable of imaginary racehorses, and played the new fantasy-baseball game that he had invented by creating his own baseball leagues and keeping track of the statistics on the back of business cards kept in a wooden box. There were also mock horse races (with marbles), each "horse" with a different name and accounted for with detailed records and handicaps. Boyhood friend G. J. Apostolos remembered that each horse had a wealth of information attached to it. Leo had obtained for his children the next best thing to a marble horse, a real pony given to him by the mayor of neighboring city Lawrence, Massachusetts. The Kerouacs kept the pony for a short while in the backyard before it managed to escape; it was never recovered.

Jack also liked to draw pictures and curious symbols. One symbol he drew, when the steam hissing from the radiators or Gabrielle's "boilings" on the stove dripped beads of moisture on the kitchen windows, was a "crude swastika." Jack asserts that he knew of the swastika long before Nazi Germany appropriated it and put it to its evil use. For a while it was his favorite symbol. He may have first seen it at stores like the Walkover Boot Shop on Lowell's Merrimack Street, where it was plainly exhibited through the 1920s and 1930s, probably as a symbol of good luck.

Kerouac's reading continued unabated as he pored through an array of pulp magazines, French novels, Shakespeare, and, as always, Jack London. His dresser drawers were becoming crammed with more notebooks documenting faithfully each day of his existence. Deep in the core of the young boy was a sensitivity that surfaced often enough to become increasingly evident to his friends. G. J. Apostolos noted that "everything hurt the guy. Just a drizzly November day would zing him."[8] Another friend, Roland Salvas, recalled Jack's determination to make something of himself: "I think Jack wanted to be something out of life rather than just normal." It became apparent that the boy was beginning to envision himself as either an athlete or an artist.

Jack Kerouac was, even as a young teenager, deeply aware of the boundaries of his understanding. He was also able to act upon what he saw and understood. Also, his empathy exceeded that of most of his peers; he was able to intuit what others saw and felt. Jack also was unusually willing to seek out the alien, odd, and different when many of his peers and elders remained guardedly xenophobic. His openness toward others in a society bent on alienating other ethnic groups through a sheer need for survival was remarkable for a boy his age. Once, when Jack and his Pawtucketville gang encountered an old man staggering along the Textile Bridge, they took him home to a "big old house" (in G. J. Apostolos's recollection, the house was possibly the "castle" of *Doctor Sax*) where he fell off the bed and hit his head. They put him back in bed and left him there. For the next few days, they could not get over the thought that they had killed him and scoured the local papers looking for any mention of his death. When the *Lowell Sun* did not print his obituary after a time, they all sighed with relief. The boys in the gang became close friends with Kerouac despite his bookworm habits and classroom timidity. But it was the younger Kerouac's skill on the gridiron—he played tackle football with teams from other parts of Lowell—that began to earn him a favorable reputation around town. On one occasion, in October 1935, Kerouac submitted an ad to the *Lowell Sun* sports column: "The Dracut Tigers, ages 13-15, challenge any football team, ages 13-15, to a game at Dracut Tigers field (or any field) Saturday morning." Kerouac began to exude a charisma rooted in his natural ease and knowledge of sports. A raging urge to devour more and more books kept him up late at night reading in his bed. As he wrote in later years, he would never be as happy as he was in his "quiltish, innocent book-devouring boyhood night."

5

Order, Tenderness, and Piety

Fall 1936–Spring 1939

No bird soars too high, if he soars with his own wings.
WILLIAM BLAKE, *The Marriage of Heaven and Hell*

In the fall of 1936, Jack Kerouac enrolled in Lowell High School after graduating from Bartlett Junior High School. The high school was downtown near Kearney Square, bordered by the dark, placid canal. In the vicinity was Moody Street with its taverns and bars, its sidewalks walked prudently by market-bound women by day and prowled by shadow-drawn prostitutes at night. Bordering Little Canada, the street had a seedy enough reputation that most women feared walking it at any time of day. However, despite the stigma that it bore for most Lowell citizens, it was a magnet of vice for the town's male youth, who saw in it the appeal that would later plague their adulthood.

In his mid-adolescence, Jack's world began to broaden, further putting a stamp of impulse in the teenager who was developing an affinity for pool halls, athletics, and physical fitness. Leading a different life with his friends than what his parents suspected, Jack cruised the streets of downtown Lowell, ever the romanticist. This polarity would be a distinct aspect of his personality, one part of his world profoundly intellectual while the other, indoctrinated by the rabble-rousing rites of adolescence, embracing an appreciation for loose girls and exciting swing bands. On the riverbank the gang had a makeshift hangout that Jack called "Club de Paisan." It was located on the edge of the river dump where a row of ramshackle structures squatted. There Jack and his friends played pool and basked in "crude, raw escapism."[1] In keeping with his pronounced empathy, he noted (in a later piece of juvenilia) an old bow-legged Frenchman sitting near the stove "mumbling to himself"; the boys dubbed him "le Père."

Meanwhile, many girls flirted with Jack at Pete's, a popular soda fountain in downtown Lowell's Kearney Square. Sometimes, when the team got off the bus after an away game, the girls chanted the teammates' names. Their attention to Jack did not escape his notice, though his awkward shyness prevented him from courting them—his introversion ran counter to his athletic prowess and good looks. Over time, he would overcome his shyness when communicating one-on-one with a girl, but in groups he would become reticent, content to absorb what he heard rather than take part in conversation.

In class Kerouac sometimes displayed his intelligence with astute, articulate answers, but most times he kept to himself. He found self-expression chiefly through his writing. Classmates would sometimes see him reading a book and stopping intermittently to jot down a few thoughts. One classmate recalled that Kerouac's books were always dotted with marginalia that meant nothing to anybody but him.[2]

At home his sports fantasy world still prospered, as he continued to create handbills and reports like *Sports News* (one issue reported, "La Salles Win on Hiskey Homer in 6th!").[3]

By the summer of 1937, Kerouac was pitching junior league baseball for Pawtucketville on a team called the Pawtucket Blues. His strengths were most notable at the plate, where, in one game, he gained two of Pawtucketville's four hits in the team's sole victory. That summer the team placed last, with one win and nine losses. Kerouac was photographed for the *Lowell Sun* in a sleeveless T-shirt and jeans that he wore as a team uniform.

The next season he joined the junior varsity football roster as one of the team's two youngest players. Jack had grown to five feet, eight inches and a less-than-ideal weight of 155 pounds. His contribution to the team was still inconspicuous enough that the *Sun* didn't even get his first name right (confusing it with his father's) until late in the season: "Leo Kerouac turned in some real nice football yesterday afternoon and may see some action in the Lowell high backfield against Manchester [New Hampshire]." The sports reporter's observation was astute: Kerouac seemed to be well on the way to becoming an excellent ball carrier.[4] Kerouac disliked the high school pecking order that placed him on the bench while the seniors played first. In the locker room, the situation was the same. Kerouac nurtured a grudge against Hank Mazur, the "cornerstone of the 1936 Lowell team," for forcefully evicting him from the showers.[5]

In September 1938, Kerouac participated in the preliminary lineups of the Lowell High School football team after more than one hundred candidates reported to coach Tom Keady the last week of August. Among Keady's fourteen picks were his ten lettermen from the previous season, many of whom would figure prominently in *Vanity of Duluoz*. Keady had already named his definite starting backfield but retained Kerouac as "situation" ball carrier.[6]

Kerouac lacked the opportunity to prove himself to the local sports media, except for a few scant mentions by virtue of images from the newspaper's new speed camera. The *Lowell Sun* wrote: "Lowell High isn't a gifted nucleus of exceptional talent built around veteran 'stars' this year. It's merely the kind of club a 'coach's coach' likes to work on." By the next month, Kerouac would be noted for one thing: his amazing speed on the field. Yet he was always on the bench until late in the game and never made the grade to be in that "definite starting lineup."

On September 9, 1938, after a week and a half of daily workouts, Keady took his new, promising lineup to Medford High School for a scrimmage. On September 18, the "Red and Gray" team of Lowell High faced off with the "scrappy" sophomore-laden team of Greenfield High. Keady assembled his A team, including Kerouac, now number 35. He had been retained as one of Keady's halfbacks after boosting his weight to 160 pounds. During the last practice before the face-off, Keady changed his mind and replaced Kerouac with Warren Arsenault. Despite this decision, the game turned out to be quite eventful: Kerouac scored two touchdowns and made five out of the seven first downs, averaging a total of ten yards with each try. Despite his impressive efforts, he was only used for the last two minutes in the next game against Medford. Similar incidents occurred in the next several games, including a rival face-off against Manchester, New Hampshire, when Kerouac was benched (despite an impressive turn the previous game against Worcester Classical when he had "knocked off" two twenty-five-yard touchdowns). Coach Keady's seeming neglect of Kerouac infuriated Leo, who was convinced that favoritism influenced the coach's decisions.[7]

Through his high school social nucleus, Kerouac became friendly with many Greek boys from the Acre section of Lowell, an area that was largely foreign to him because of the prevailing isolation (by design) of different ethnic groups. Johnny Koumantzelis was a chum of Kerouac's but knew him solely from his track meets on the Lowell High team. Odysseus "Duke" Chiungos, a member of the football team, befriended the shy, reserved boy, whose name the girls chanted from the bleachers. His clearest remembrances of his friend Kerouac include Jack's physical prowess, good looks, and athletic abilities: "Kerouac was a really handsome, perfectly built kid. Though he wasn't very big, he was still as strong as anybody I knew at the time. His main thing was his obsession with physical conditioning."[8] Chiungos's description of Kerouac years later in a cocktail bar in Lowell was markedly different: "I didn't recognize the guy. His face was all beat-up, bloated and red. I couldn't help staring at him and wondering who he was and knowing somehow that I knew him from before. He was so intoxicated and banged out of shape that I couldn't put him together until later when he called my name. We had a few drinks but I couldn't relate, couldn't comprehend where he was coming from."[9] James Dowling, left guard in the 1938 lineup, did not know Jack well but observed his fellow teammate firsthand and admired Kerouac's football ability: "Jack played right and left end, no one could ever touch Jack in the field. I admire that he had the guts to play through sixty minutes of a whole game without getting tired. Jack played both defense and offense. In general, there were no substitutes for anybody on the team, but Jack was fast. He wasn't very strong in appearance. It was all in his legs."[10] Such are the testimonials of many Lowellians who remember Kerouac as he was in those glorious high school football days in the autumn of 1938 and who regard the accomplished writer as someone fallen from grace.

The Kerouacs now resided—for Leo's income had plummeted to a new low—at 736 Moody Street, the main drag of a low-rent tenement district populated mostly by French Canadians. For a short while, they lived in a tenement across the street from Saint Jean de Baptiste Church before moving across the Merrimack River to Moody Street, closer to their previous Pawtucketville residences.

The tenement was one of the taller structures on Moody Street, and in it the Kerouacs rented the top floor. In the furthest corner of the house, Jack had his bedroom, where he set up his toy pool table, a Victrola turntable, and a little green desk filled with his notebooks and other things gathered from "sorrows of pasts." On the tenement's bottom floor was a short-order diner. It was "across the street from the bowling alley, poolhall, at the bus stop, near the big meat market, with an empty lot on both sides of the street where kids played their gray games in brown weeds of winter dusk."[11]

In an adult dream, Kerouac visualized the tenement's back porches all collapsing one upon the other—a justified fear, for he remembered when Gabrielle habitually left one foot inside the tenement doorway in case the porch gave way beneath her. Many Franco-Americans besides the Kerouacs were housed in the same graying tenements where laundry flapped on clotheslines, where husbands and wives fought in a mix of patois and broken English, where irate men (their heads down, cursing the "hardass" world) returned home from their shifts of the textile and shoe mills. Jack Kerouac yearned to break free from this provincial world of struggle and despondency.

Although Caroline found some work to contribute to the family income, Jack was free of any such obligations, because it was expected that his academic achievement and performance on the gridiron would earn him a scholarship. On May 30, 1937, Caroline had married against her parents' express wishes, just after she turned eighteen. Her husband was Charles Morissette, a humorous older man who frequented the Pawtucketville Social Club and drunkenly bragged that his penis was bigger than the other men's. One-upping the others, he sometimes would "shove seven or eight or nine or ten quarters off a table with his piece."[12] This physical attribute, amusing as it was to his male friends, would plague his marriage to Caroline, as intercourse caused her physical pain and ultimately was a contributing factor to their irreconcilable differences.[13]

Gabrielle returned to work as a cutter in a shoe factory and Leo made do with whatever jobs were offered to him. Ultimately, he accepted a position at Sullivan Brothers Printing Company across the river. Using his expert skills as a linotypist, Leo worked the hot lead machine, setting type for the presses. Joseph Sullivan remembered Leo as heavyset and "classy." According to Sullivan, Leo was exceptional in his work, always on time and diligent (this runs counter to numerous charges leveled at Leo Kerouac by various biographers who have portrayed him as a gambling fanatic who irresponsibly contributed to the downfall of the Kerouac household). His pay at Sullivan Brothers was $89 per week—for the times, the best-paying job in town. With his new connections, Leo also obtained employment for Caroline in the ticket room, sorting out tickets and payment receipts. This regular income improved the Kerouacs' situation. Leo had one less mouth to feed. By late 1939 the three would move into a rented duplex on Gersham Avenue, one street away from the tenement.[14]

While some friends dropped out of school to pursue more immediate "worklife plans," Jack continued to set his sights on college, planning to earn a degree in journalism. Knowing that the lack of playing time could destroy any chance of winning a scholarship, he pleaded with Coach Keady to be used more often. In the game against Worcester Classical, Kerouac entered in the second quarter and completed the 43–0 victory with three touchdowns. The highlight of the game was Kerouac's jaw-dropping sixty-four-yard punt. In the following game, against New Hampshire's prestigious Manchester Central, Keady again kept Kerouac on the bench. The students in the stands repeatedly chanted, "We want Kerouac!" until Keady, at the game's final minute, yielded to their demands and put Jack in as quarterback. Some of Jack's teammates felt that Keady intentionally hid Kerouac from the eyes of the football scouts sitting in the bleachers.

The game against prestigious Keith Academy would turn the tide in Kerouac's favor. The *Lowell Sun* announced to the football-crazed townspeople who were eagerly anticipating a state championship for Lowell: "One of the fastest schoolboy backs in the state is expected to play a major part in Lowell's offense tomorrow." Eagerly the *Lowell Sun* staff photographer snapped his picture. Kerouac was the "speed merchant" the next day, scoring two touchdowns, breaking off a thirteen-yard tackle to score one of them. Lowell scored fifty-three points to Keith Academy's zero. However, the match that caught the attention of college scouts was a 19–13 loss to Nashua that still made Kerouac shine because of a hundred-yard rush, a sixty-yard scamper, and a returned forty-yard punt. Above all, Kerouac successfully garnered a twenty-eight-yard touchdown pass. To Kerouac, the Nashua match was the "most beautiful I ever played."[15]

Football came to a halt from September 17 to 20, 1938, when New England was buffeted by a large rainstorm that flooded many of the region's tributary rivers. This was followed on the twenty-first by a hurricane with wind gusts up to 138 miles per hour that swept across southern New England. The wind caused seven hundred deaths and six thousand injuries. The total damage loss rose to an estimate of $400 million (in 1938 dollars). Kerouac recollected the hurricane in *Visions of Cody* (mistakenly placing it in October but correctly remembering that it occurred close to the September 15, 1938, death of Thomas Wolfe):

> That afternoon began, in fact, the hurricane afternoon, clearly enough with the sudden riptide pace of thin, sniveled clouds across the glary pale above; to add to all that horror, of clouds racing so fast too that you didn't quite believe it and looked twice like at a comedian in a B-movie, a doubletake; so sinister an afternoon and introductory disaster that on the way home, in the grayness of Aiken Street [in Centralville] near the dump, a telephone pole had caught on fire and the engines were lined up putting out the fire with their hoses; engines and men that within an hour or two would suddenly be alerted as everybody and the authorities in a simultaneous amazement would realize that a fullscale hurricane was upon this northern manufacturing town in New England.[16]

On Thanksgiving Day—a severely cold morning that turned the Lawrence High School field hard and icy—Jack approached the field from the locker room and saw the seats filled to capacity with a crowd fourteen thousand strong. In some circles of Lowell High School, as well as among the most ardent devotees of high school football, Kerouac had attained temporary cult status. In the crowd were college recruitment scouts from Boston College and Columbia who came to watch Lowell High School in a clash of the "hallowed enemies" of the Greater Merrimack Valley.

Although Lawrence dominated the first half of the game, neither team scored. By the third quarter, with a 2–0 score, Keady took Kerouac off the bench. When a pass was thrown to Jack, he barely grasped it before barreling along the field's sideline, dogged by his Lawrence pursuers. Near the goal line Jack burst through two boys attempting to block him and scored the game's only touchdown. In the next day's *Sun*, a paragraph and photograph all but immortalized Kerouac: "With the ball on the Lawrence 14, Zoukis faded back to the 21 and tossed a neat pass to Jack Kerouac who grabbed off the leather on the Lawrence nine and outsmarted one Lawrence secondary man to score right at the corner."[17] In his fiction Kerouac would dramatize the event—suspending it, timeless and immortal, as epic as any Olympian moment. With each passing game, each glowing accomplishment, Kerouac kept his newspaper clippings safely guarded in his growing personal archive as a portion of the Kerouac legacy. He had become a small-town hero, perhaps gaining more fame for this feat than he ever would receive in Lowell during his lifetime for his literature.

At home, Thanksgiving dinner was especially joyous, with family, relatives, and friends showering the boy with appreciation for being the sole cause of a victorious match against the hometown rival. Leo had invited recruiter college scout Frank Leahy from Boston College to dinner before coach Lou Little's recruiters from Columbia could influence Jack's decision.

Leahy and Little knew each other all too well, with Leahy having left Georgetown University one year after Little did in 1931. Leo had high hopes that his son would redeem the family's tarnished name in Lowell and accept Leahy's invitation to come to Boston. His teammates, though, sensed that regardless of speed or prowess, there was something awry. Sam Samaras, who knew Kerouac from the mid-1930s ("when the Greek boys from the Acre would take on the boys from Pawtucketville"), expressed it most clearly: "He wasn't hungry enough. He wasn't the kind of guy who was real gung ho. He wouldn't hurt anybody." Kerouac's hunger for success was focused elsewhere. At season's end Kerouac placed second on the team with seven touchdowns. Lowell High School, in part through Kerouac's athletic contribution, finished 6–3–1 after starting 5–0–1.[18]

After the football season Kerouac spent the winter of 1938–1939 running indoor track at the Lowell High School annex. He fared well in the thirty-yard dash and the thirty-five-yard low hurdles for the rival challenge with Worcester. He frequently competed in the three-hundred-yard run, the standing broad jump, sprint relays, and low hurdles. Overall, he placed in several races and came in first in five of the meets. At the Boston Garden Kerouac was the lone scorer for the team, achieving third place in the forty-five-yard hurdles. By the spring of 1939, he was involved in outdoor track, varsity baseball, and (briefly) the American Legion baseball team. He was also in love.

It was the sixteen-year-old's first real love affair and began on January 1, 1939. Mary Carney, an Irish girl from South Lowell, lived with her parents on the banks of the slow-moving Concord River. Almost a year older than Jack, she attended high school with him and watched as he practiced his runs on the track, recording his times with a makeshift timer he had created. On nights after track practice during that winter of 1939, Kerouac would walk home, braving the gusts of Lowell's fierce winter winds.

Passing the places of his childhood pastimes, the Rialto and B. F. Keith Theatre, Chin Lee's restaurant, the unassuming streets of sprawling tenements, lazy smoke drifting from their chimneys, next to polluted canals, Kerouac listened to the cooing of roosting pigeons stirring in the dusk and the rattle of cars and horse carts bumping along the cobblestoned streets. He'd saunter past city hall and the great windows of the Lowell City Library, filled with what he imagined as its "scholars of the winter eve." This journey he walked habitually night after night, enamored of Mary, huddled in his arms for warmth. At 736 Moody Street, he was greeted by his mother, who would feed her love-struck son. As always, Leo sat in his chair puffing a cigar and scowling at the politics and racetrack results in the day's paper.

But Leo and Gabrielle had seen a change in the intensity of Jack's introversion. Sports provided a diversion, as did his interest in Mary. Because of her, his social world had broadened, so that his dependency on his family had lessened. Thanks to Mary Carney (as well as other girls), Kerouac began to realize that there was a world beyond fantasy baseball, football practice, and Jack London. Another relationship, with Lowell High School student Margaret Coffey, gave him his first introduction to sexual relations. (His own archives disprove his claim that he lost his virginity to a Manhattan prostitute in 1939; he kept a lifelong list of every woman he had sex with, along with the type and frequency of sex.) Between the two girls stood his mother, who reminded her son of the perils of premarital sex, illustrating her point with graphic pictures of "venereal sufferers." Although Kerouac thought Mary lazy and unresponsive, her dark hair and a body built like "fire" still attracted him. He was intrigued enough to take two buses and a cold walk to her house. Once there, though, his efforts, he felt, routinely paid off. She'd snuggle with Jack in the warm confines of her house where a steaming radiator fogged the windows. However, Jack and Mary never went further than passionate necking. The reasons for his hesitancy to go "all the way," whether through gallantry or awkwardness or both, are not clear. Yet a feeling of animosity undermined Jack's tenderness toward her. A later letter to Lowell friend John Macdonald reveals that Kerouac did love her but thought of her as a "wench" who "toyed" with his heart. However accurate this may be, it does make clear that he was once again a victim of his own indecision. In the same letter, he also writes that he is madly in love with Mary and considers himself a "lovelorn Marius," an allusion to the philosophical romance by Walter Pater, *Marius the Epicurean*, in which the noble Marius's death causes the Christian church to look upon him as a martyr. Mary had quipped to him that she wished he were older, to which he asked, "Why?" "You'd know more what to do with me." But he *did* know what to do with her. Despite the health hazards his escalating promiscuity may have posed (as his mother warned), it did not stop Jack and his friends from indulging in casual sex with the daughter of an usherette at the Rialto Theatre: "[S]he used to mop up the ladies' room after we gangbanged her daughter Filthy Mary in there all night, why you could go to the theatre any afternoon and get a handjob just by asking the usher at the door 'Where's Filthy Mary?' and he'd say 'Oh she's sitting in the backseat with Gartside there getting a blowjob up or something.'"[19]

Jack's sexual diversions lie in stark contrast to the idealistic relations befitting a morally grounded Catholic. It was another example of his dual personality. Jack was a gallant gentleman when he was around women he respected or was enamored of, and a shameless cad with needy women whom he deemed "easy." He was, as he described himself in *Visions of Cody,* "among the religious dirty old men of the world, chewing gum, like them, with a horrible beating heart—I can hardly think or control myself."[20] Mary's promise to Jack, should they marry, would be a comfortable and happy life together, an alternate path at a time when his brain was abuzz with thoughts of obtaining a scholarship and leaving Lowell. Throughout his life, when the pitfalls of his writing profession disgusted him, the thought of a cozy Lowell domesticity always intrigued Jack. But that allure was lessened by the predictable and provincial aspirations of many of his classmates, content to live out a blue-collar, working-class life—to find a job in a local mill, get married, buy a home, and have children. It was a prospect that Kerouac found bleak in every way. He was learning that life contained a plethora of choices, each in some way intriguing. He felt torn between his growing intellectualism and the Pawtucketville gang, a conflict that affected him tremendously. To boyhood chum G. J. Apostolos, Kerouac wrote that throughout his youth, he "stood holding two ends of rope, trying to bring both ends together in order to tie them." At one end of the rope, he said, was Lowell friend Sebastian Sampas, who symbolized Kerouac's intellectualism and "schizoid" self (an awareness of himself as a "bent and brooding figure" sneering at Lowell's provincialism). At the other end was Apostolos, a Pawtucketville friend who shared Kerouac's love of sports, raucous swing bands (appearing with increasing regularity at Lowell's Commodore Ballroom), and the flood of derelict humanity from the Moody Street bars. Kerouac's remedy to this in his early fiction would be to divide his personality into two or more different characters, as in the 1945 novella *Orpheus Emerged* and, on a broader scale, the numerous Martin siblings of *The Town and the City* (1950).

On those nights when he lingered too long with Mary, he had to walk because the buses had stopped running. He imagined himself a "far traveler looking for a place to sleep." This early yearning evolved into a tendency to imagine himself in another place and time. It was a constant desire to move onward to other experiences, for he quickly tired of the present. These yearnings contributed to his aspirations to be a serious writer, a goal that contradicted any long-range plans to marry Mary. By happenstance, Mary despised Jack's mother because she supported her son's desire to leave Lowell for New York City. When he decided to attend Columbia University, Mary was tremendously hurt and resented Gabrielle's support. Only later, in 1954, did Mary confess to Jack her naïveté, that she was, in fact, the "mixed-up kid" who did not understand his aspirations. Most of Kerouac's Lowell friends claim that they were not even aware of Jack's relationship with Mary; the extent of his relations with women, as far as they were concerned, was his ongoing affair with Margaret Coffey and his sex play in the dark shadows of the B. F. Keith Theatre.[21]

Kerouac continued to write. As usual, his feelings about girls, his adventures with the gang, and his thoughts about prewar Lowell all found their way into his journals. But now there was more: influenced by Jack London, Kerouac began his first serious writing attempts. His reading of Ernest Hemingway and, at Sebastian Sampas's suggestion, of William Saroyan inspired him to create "little terse short stories" echoing both their respective styles. Jack also read Thomas Wolfe and embraced that writer's "rolling" style of prose, since it suited his own fledgling endeavors, as did his reading of James Joyce. After Jack read portions of *Ulysses* (he was taken in particular by the Molly Bloom stream-of-consciousness style), he began working on an extended piece that was the earliest version of what became the 1968 novel *Vanity of Duluoz*. He also read Fyodor Dostoyevsky, Arthur Rimbaud, and William Blake, all of whom inspired an aesthetic awareness in his writing. This reading prepared Kerouac for college, where the demands of constant football practice and the actual games compelled him to cram his schoolwork late into the night. Kerouac had also accumulated a 110-page "sports diary" for 1938 documenting with tallies, play-by-plays, and newspaper clippings a year of his football and baseball games.

As Leo Kerouac labored over the hot Linotype, recruiters from Boston College visited his employers at Sullivan Brothers Printing. In one instance, coach Tom Keady went into the office of the chief editor of the *Lowell Sun* seeking a contribution toward a scholarship for one of his "star athletes" in 1939. "It so happened," the *Lowell Free Press* wrote in April 8, 1939, "that this boy had no financial support of his own in his quest for higher education." Keady was hoping that the chief editor would contribute the additional funds he earned as a city boxing promoter. The editor refused and apparently wasn't even willing to finance the carfare for the unnamed athlete to go "demonstrate to the football coaches that he had something they wanted."[22] Whatever the opportunity was, Jack had other means of proving himself. According to his account in *Vanity of Duluoz*, the recruiters' aggressive pursuit of Jack jeopardized his father's job. A surviving family member of the Sullivan brothers denies that a request for them to influence Leo Kerouac to change his son's mind was ever made.[23] In the spring of 1939, Kerouac weighed his options carefully as graduation drew near. Recruiter Frank Leahy made it clear that he intended to make Leo and his son choose Boston College over any other scholarship offer. Leahy mailed Sullivan Brothers Printing a postcard. On it was scrawled, "Get Jack to Boston College at all costs." Attending Boston College would leave Jack within the familiar perimeter of the Merrimack Valley. Above all, it would satisfy his sense of family obligations, not only pleasing Leo but also keeping him gainfully employed. However, regardless of her dependency on Leo's income, Gabrielle wanted Jack to leave Lowell to seek his fortunes elsewhere and not to remain in the depressing rut of Lowell's spirit-killing mill district. In midsummer 1939, Kerouac considered the Boston offer and visited Boston College to be interviewed by the Boston College Athletic Association. He stayed a few days in the city, where Leahy took him out to the theater district to see, at Kerouac's request, William Saroyan's *Love's Old Sweet Song*. The performance was marred, Kerouac reflected in 1943, by a "certain gentleman" who strategically seated himself behind Leahy and Kerouac as if he were tailing them. He turned out to be the freshman football coach for Columbia University.[24]

Although Kerouac's indecisiveness stemmed from his ambivalence over whether to honor familial loyalty and stay in Lowell or indulge his simmering restlessness and leave, sound advice from knowledgeable elders outside the family helped determine his decision. Charles Sampas, Sebastian's older brother, who had a degree in journalism, told Kerouac that if he had any aspirations to be a writer, then he had to leave his hometown. His "boyhood dreams" of being a writer beckoned to him beyond the limits of Lowell.[25] Meanwhile, Leo would be forced to resort to taking a train out of Lowell to find work, only returning home on weekends: "His only happiness in life now, in a way, considering the hissing old radiators in old cockroach hotel rooms in New England in the winter, was that I make good and justify him anyway."[26]

That March, Caroline and her husband, Charles Morissette, hosted a surprise birthday party for Jack. Photographers from the *Lowell Telegram* and the *Courier Citizen* took photos of Jack sitting with Mary Carney, his parents, sister and brother-in-law, and some friends. Outside, a blizzard started to develop. It would become what the *Lowell Evening Leader* characterized as the worst blizzard since the blizzard of 1888. Throughout New England, the storm ultimately claimed twelve lives. It "clogged highways, grounded planes, and paralyzed shipping"; more than sixty Massachusetts schools closed. The storm did not, however, prevent Ted Healey's "Famous 3 Stooges"[27] from appearing at Lowell's rat-infested[27] Tower Theatre all that week.[28] Whether or not he attended, Kerouac would incorporate the pratfalls of this vaudeville act into the pages of *Visions of Cody* during the early 1950s.

Kerouac graduated from Lowell High School on June 28, 1939. His report card reflected mediocre grades in language arts and math as a consequence of his lamentable attendance. Given these less-than-impressive academic achievements, Columbia's football coach, Lou Little, arranged for Kerouac to attend Horace Mann School for Boys, a prep school in the borough of the Bronx in New York City, to improve his grades.[29] He was required to take classes in physics, English, geometry, and algebra. Because the scholarship did not cover room and board, he planned to live with Gabrielle's stepmother in Brooklyn until he entered Columbia. If he passed all of his courses, Kerouac would earn a full academic scholarship.[30] As a last-ditch effort late that summer, Boston College's Leahy sent Kerouac a letter with an offer of matriculation and the promise to train the young athlete in the Notre Dame style of football play. Leahy thought Kerouac was best suited as a "climax runner type" who was "apt to break away for a long run anytime during a football game." Leahy assured him that a runner did not have to necessarily weigh the minimum of two hundred pounds to be used by a coach who employed the Notre Dame style of playing. Kerouac rejected the offer in favor of Columbia.[31] Gabrielle took Jack to McQuade's Department Store in downtown Lowell and bought him a sports jacket and some shirts and neckties. Her advice to him was sound and logical: to go on with his future and leave Mary Carney "at home."[32]

In late August, Kerouac boarded a bus in Lowell and rolled through the late summer woods, stopping first in Worcester, Massachusetts, and then dipping southwest over the hills of Connecticut toward the urban squalor of New York City. Behind him, as the bus sped onward, the Lowell that he had known for the last seventeen years slipped into the distance. Kerouac left—though not for the last time—the sad decaying tenements, the smoking mills, the sands and mysteries of the Merrimack, his doting mother, the grave of Gerard, and all of his friends (some of whom would soon perish in World War II). He left for New York City, ready to secure for himself an apprenticeship in the modern world—to become at last a paid writer. In his notebook he reminded himself of his motivations: "that I should not proceed in my literary ventures with such ease as would befit a typewriter. I feel that such a recurrence to the old method would sort of leave a silent tribute to those old gladiators, those immortal souls of journalism."[33] Despite his objective of earning a college degree in journalism, in his heart he felt capable of creating something completely different and new.

PART 2

The Dawn of Jazz in America

6

Aloof from Teeming Humanity

Fall 1939–1940

I will be able now to possess the truth within one body and one soul.
ARTHUR RIMBAUD

Jack Kerouac enrolled at the Horace Mann School for Boys in September 1939 against a backdrop of growing world turmoil of economic collapse, revolution, and social upheaval to which the United States responded by retreating into an entrenched isolationism. Although President Franklin D. Roosevelt paid close attention to the bellicose actions of Hitler, Mussolini, and Hirohito, he was adamant in preserving America's insular attitude. Two days after Hitler invaded Poland on September 1, France and Britain declared war on Germany. World War II had begun. On September 3, Roosevelt informed America over the radio that the country would remain neutral, and for the next two years and three months America maintained (at least outwardly) that stance.

Shortly after arriving at Horace Mann, Kerouac sat and wrote, as usual, in his journal. Still caught between opportunity and obligation, he firmly resolved to make his mark on the world. His journal, now more than ever, served as a "castle" that kept him "aloof" from the rest of humanity, even while that same humanity was spiraling into violent international conflict. In his journal Kerouac documented the continuous stream of ideas from his "turbulent" mind in carefully written pencil-and-ink notations. His writing, he reminded himself in an entry, would invoke the spirits of William Thackeray, Ben Jonson, and Charles Dickens. In another entry Jack vowed never to create his art with gratuitous ease. Rather he would write in the traditionalist mode, paying tribute to those of the literary canon who came before him.

But he could not concentrate solely on writing. To receive a full scholarship to Columbia, Kerouac first had to earn passing grades in his required courses at Horace Mann. He now found that his willful absence from Lowell High's classrooms had a price. Kerouac was determined to hone his intellect and devised a strategy of devoting himself exclusively to one subject per night. Indeed, he hoped to emerge from New York City not only as an artist but also with his scholarly integrity intact.[1] Walking the halls of Horace Mann, the provincial New Englander rubbed elbows with upper-class "incunabular Milton Berles." He enjoyed the raucous wit of some, especially an incessant wisecracker named Eddie Gilbert. According to Kerouac, Horace Mann's student-body hierarchy split three ways: the "wits," the "athletes," and those who actually studied. Clearly, Kerouac had a place among all three groups, yet he still stood out from his well-dressed and better-fed classmates, most of whom were Jewish, an ethnic group largely foreign to Kerouac. However, his sincerity, athleticism, and approachability made him a popular figure. Sensing Jack's indigence, Eddie Gilbert befriended his classmate and brought Kerouac home on weekends to his parents' house in Flushing, New York. As was his wont, Kerouac noted the details of Gilbert's bedroom with its pressed curtains and bedspread made for "little boys." Against a wall crisscrossed with tennis rackets sat a brass-handled bureau filled with clean, folded socks. In the closet a shoe-tree displayed tennis shoes alongside older leather ones. Each morning, the smell of bacon and eggs drifted upstairs and lured them to the kitchen as Eddie joked with the maid. Such casual wealth was alien to Kerouac. He was more familiar and comfortable with Gilbert's athleticism and musical talents. His friend was an active player on the varsity tennis and soccer teams as well as a skilled violin player. Most admirably, Gilbert was a jazz ballroom dancer, a talent that earned him recognition as "Best Dancer" in the Horace Mann yearbook. Together, Kerouac and Gilbert joined the school chess team and acquired enough skill to win an actual game. To earn spending money for his excursions to Gilbert's home, Kerouac wrote term papers for other students at "$2 a throw" and tutored French. It provided Jack with much-needed income. Eventually, he found work from sports editor Lou Miller by contributing to a sports news column in the *New York World-Telegram*.

By the time he had completed his required courses at Horace Mann, Kerouac seemed to have made a success of his most recent educational venture. His yearbook entry praised him as a promising asset for Columbia: "JOHN L. KEROUAC . . . Brain and brawn found a happy combination in Jack, a newcomer to school this year. A brilliant back in football, he also won his spurs as *Record* reporter and a leading *Quarterly* contributor. Was an outfielder on the Varsity nine."[2] Kerouac's yearbook photo presents a smartly dressed, polished young man with an intense, brooding stare. Alongside it is a snapshot of him in football uniform in midstride with the number 2 on his jersey. (The "prim, severe" dean stamped Jack with the pedestrian label "good citizen" in his year-end evaluation.)

Despite a heavy academic load and involvement in both baseball and football, Kerouac continued to pursue his personal writing. He labored over a football novella that he had started when he was sixteen. In it, Jack wrote of "Bill Clancy," a lonesome road traveler, football star, and American college boy. Sports was one of the few things he felt competent to write about at length for it made up the whole of his life experience thus far. Another extended piece of writing was a twenty-five-page baseball novella he titled "Raw Rookie Nerves." The story ends with the main character, a rookie second baseman named Freddy Burns, initiating a triple play that culminates in his team, the Blue Sox, winning the World Series.

Because he did not have a wealth of life experiences to draw upon, Kerouac's other choice was introspection. He resorted to mining the endless terrain of his musings and dreams. He described one such dream to G. J. Apostolos. After watching the film *Andy Hardy and Family,* in which Andy's mother was sick, Jack had a distressing dream that his own mother was ill. He awoke in a "big arm chair" staring at the waning coals in the fireplace until he fell into a meditative state.[3] (In future years, Kerouac would keep a dream diary alongside his other journals as if he knew that every scrap of detritus from the subconscious was fodder for his writing.)

To occupy his time, Kerouac played the fantasy-baseball game he had invented in 1933 in his Phebe Avenue home. Sometimes the game would carry over into his fiction (as it would later in prose pieces like "Ronnie on the Mound" [1958]). From his grade school through his college years, the galvanizing effect of playing, reading about, and writing about sports helped form his writing style.

Kerouac's year at Horace Mann initiated him into the frantic social milieu of Manhattan. Among his Horace Mann companions, Kerouac became friends with Donald Wolf, Henri Cru, and Seymour Wyse (the latter two staying lifelong friends). Wyse knew all the best jazz joints; together they made routine explorations throughout the city, from Greenwich Village to Harlem. There were plenty of seedy nightclubs and jazz haunts for Jack to check out in Manhattan. He and his Horace Mann comrades rubbed elbows with jazzmen, junkies, tourists, sailors, hookers, and pimps. In these clubs he heard the brassy brilliance of big band swing music. Measuring time with his fingertips on beer-splashed tabletops, Jack began almost intuitively to pick up the nuances of jazz. This appreciation of jazz found its way into print with some regularity when he volunteered to write for the *Horace Mann Record,* enthusiastically detailing local performances by the big band orchestras of Count Basie and Glenn Miller. Kerouac declared, "Count Basie's Band Best In Land: Group Famous For 'Solid' Swing" and astutely observed that "unlike the vacuous phraseology of pseudo-swing bands, Basie's stuff means something." And later, "He is a thrilling player with tremendous ideas." About Jo Jones, Count Basie's drummer, Kerouac stated bluntly that Jones was the "most finished drummer in existence." The intrepid jazz trio recognized the virtuosity of tenor saxophonist Lester Young, the Count's "outstanding soloist."[4] Kerouac acknowledged that his theories and opinions were not all his own creation, crediting Wyse and Wolf for their contributions.

Kerouac also tried his hand at detective fiction: a cliché-ridden short story for the *Horace Mann Quarterly.* In "The Brothers," the protagonist, Detective Browne, pursues the villain, Elmo, who attempts to murder Browne's brother. Another story, "Une Veille de Noel," set on a snowy Greenwich Village Christmas Eve, concerns a neighborhood bar where the appearance of an angel causes patrons to set aside their drinks and return home. Despite its temperance overtones, writing the story did not prevent Jack from imbibing.

Kerouac's off-campus drinking became reckless at times as the possibilities that the new city posed overwhelmed him. Through the haze of beer and cheap liquor, propelled by an insatiable impulse to explore and to record, Kerouac conquered his introversion and explored the massive metropolis on his own. The stale company of his rich classmates offered nothing that could not be remedied by a southbound subway to Times Square, where he roamed the neon-lit fantasyland. There, he haunted the balconies of the Apollo Theatre and took in such films as *The Lower Depths* with Jean Gabin. Kerouac's extra cash was enough for him to patronize the abundant Manhattan whores whom he relied upon to vent his overactive libido. The ensuing illicit experiences so sexually charged him that he boasted about them to his classmates and even callously suggested of some in letters to Mary Carney.[5]

The scholar-athlete could not succumb completely to his urge to roam; he had to confront nightly football practice. After all, he had to earn his full Columbia scholarship. Often Leo came to New York to cheer his son on, as he did when Horace Mann faced off against Garden City and Jack scored three touchdowns. His efforts culminated in a victory against Tome, during which he ran seventy-two yards for the game's sole touchdown. Kerouac's year at Horace Mann passed rather quickly. Although he had to repeat chemistry and French, he graduated with grades good enough to earn him the full scholarship. Not having enough money to rent suitable garb for the occasion, Jack did not attend his graduation ceremony. Always the outsider, he was content to spend the afternoon beneath a tree behind the school, listening to the proceedings and reading Saroyan and Whitman.

In Lowell during the summer of 1940 and back at his parents' rented Gersham Avenue house, he read Jack London and memorized new words by hanging them on signs around his bedroom. He also spent time with Sebastian Sampas, who had recently graduated from high school and was preparing to matriculate at Boston's Emerson College as a drama major.

Most of Kerouac's friends sensed only marginally the full depths of his aspirations to write, but one among them perceived more. Sebastian Sampas had grown into a tall, lanky young man with dark, curly hair. He had developed an intellect seasoned by Greek literature, William Saroyan, Thomas Wolfe, and Oswald Spengler. (He introduced Kerouac to all of these, equipping him with his first major writing influences.) Kerouac shared with Sebastian his love of Thomas Hardy, Emily Dickinson, Henry David Thoreau, and Walt Whitman. Sebastian and Jack also read *PM,* a New York daily newspaper (founded on June 18, 1940) that Charles subscribed to. *PM* accepted no advertising and relied solely upon income derived from its subscribers. It vowed to tell the "truth," was partial to no political party, remained uncensored, and was fundamentally antiestablishment. It attracted some of the best photojournalists, writers, and artists, including Ernest Hemingway, Erskine Caldwell, and cartoonist Dr. Seuss. *PM*'s principles cannot be ignored. Kerouac's sentiments for freedom of expression and his antiestablishment stance directly paralleled *PM*'s.

Sampas, like Kerouac, loved theater, and he often rehearsed his oratorical skills before astonished spectators in the street. Kerouac remained reserved, noting in his journals his appreciation for what he read and saw instead of resorting to extroverted measures. One enriched the other, so that by the summer of 1941, their acquaintanceship had metamorphosed into a deep friendship. This camaraderie fueled their ideas, writing, and aspirations. The amicable tenderness displayed so openly by these two young men echoed Walt Whitman's ideal of male friendship. Sampas would take his place as the first of many vital and inspiring personal contacts who helped influence the development of Kerouac's writing; Kerouac credited Sebastian in *Lonesome Traveler* for inspiring him to be a writer at seventeen.

During the summer Jack continued his voracious reading and writing. He was excited by the descriptive writing of novelist and poet Ivan Bunin (the first Russian to receive the Nobel Prize for literature, in 1933). He also eagerly read John Dos Passos's *Manhattan Transfer* (1925), a novel whose social criticism and interior monologue Kerouac found easier to imitate than several of the other writing styles he was trying to copy at the time. Sometimes he wrote little travel pieces in which he imagined journeying to far parts of the globe:

> If I were wealthy, here's what I'd do. Rather than to travel around the world having porters lug my enormous baggage, sit wearily in swaying rickshaws and look out with jaded senses at the Orient, drape myself tiredly in deck-chairs and gaze out somnolently at the surging surface of the sea . . . rather than that, I would work my way on tramp steamers, I would drink with the crew in every port, I would moil amid the reeking masses of the Orient, poking my nose into mysterious doorways and antique shops; I'd mush to the Arctic, I'd tramp through the jungles of Brazil and Africa, I'd have women in Capetown, in Singapore, in Port Said, in Istanbul, in St. Petersburg, in San Francisco, in Havana, in Liverpool, in Shanghai, in Morocco, in Sydney, in Sumatra.[6]

He sometimes chose more familiar settings. Some of his juvenilia centered on trains arriving and leaving the coal-sooted Lowell Depot, foreshadowing some of his best later prose centered on railroads, such as "October in the Railroad Earth." His other attempts at writing, apart from trying to imitate the exuberant prose of Wolfe or the cinematic techniques of Dos Passos, were patterned on the Modern Library edition of James Joyce's

Ulysses. But these led to frustrating results. Though Jack showed this work to friends like Connie Murphy and Jim O'Dea, they harbored little serious thought that Jack, as passionate as he was, had the makings of a real, credible writer. Among those who did appreciate his budding work was Billy Chandler, the president of the Lowell High School dramatic society, to whom Kerouac gave several samples of his writing. Writing to Chandler's mother in April 1950, Jack told her, "That you have some of my Billy's boyhood writings, and some of mine, moved me most; and I would sure like to see them, perhaps next time I visit Lowell."[7]

Kerouac and two friends attempted to stage a three-act play that summer when he returned to Lowell. Kerouac wanted to become a playwright and had written a piece of reflective writing, "A Play I Want to Write," which contained the first mention of Kerouac's later spontaneous prose: "This play of mine will have to be a spontaneous burst of passion which I will develop all of a sudden, then I shall rush to my typewriter and begin to extract pages from the book and begin writing my full-length three act play."[8] One of the friends, presumably Sebastian, agreed to perform while the other would produce Kerouac's fledgling creation. However, a shortage of income "made short shrift of [their] attempts." Instead, they condensed the work to fifteen minutes before it was finally performed over the local airwaves.[9] Kerouac also joined forces that June with friends G. J. Apostolos, Raymond E. Walsh, Frances R. Hayward, James F. Cuerden, Billy Chandler, and Sebastian to form the Variety Players Group. Especially for this group Kerouac wrote a radio script titled "Spirit of '14." The lead character, Jack, and his friend Jim join a "shell-shocked," handicapped World War I legionnaire who declares that he is an "intangible masterpiece" missing a hand. The legionnaire has become, to characters Jack and Jim, the embodiment of war. Hoping against hope that he would not be pulled out of Columbia, Jack is ambivalent: "I dunno. . . . I worked pretty hard to get to college. I'd hate to leave now to go to war and fight." The legionnaire's suicide by gunshot at the script's end declares loudly Jack's antiwar stance, one shared by a majority of Americans at that time. According to Kerouac, World War II was not being fought to prevent the spread of fascism but to "satiate the wild creative desires of society's foppish misfits." As the lead character Jack says to his friend Jim, it is "something you'll never understand." The thematic underpinnings of the script's idealism suggest an informed reading of H. G. Wells's *Modern Utopia.*[10]

In addition to writing for and with his friends, Kerouac maintained his frequent journal writing. Sitting on the Hildreth Street curbstone, he stared at his former home, envisioning past events good and bad: the "dream I used to have . . . and the nightmares too." Later, drawn to his past, he walked to Beaulieu Street. As "childish" and "vague" as these memories were, they were nonetheless deeply ingrained in his psyche. Shaking off disturbing reveries of Gerard's death and burial, Kerouac still could not easily discard recollections of his mother and sister crying those many years ago in the parlor: "Fools I think. Myself a fool. I must take it in slow now and look at the present and say to myself: Look, John, hold the present now because someday it will be very precious. Hug it, and hold it."[11]

Kerouac's profound sense of self would later infuse the "Duluoz Legend," an opus encapsulating the whole of his life. Kerouac's reading that summer—chiefly Walt Whitman, Henry David Thoreau, and Emily Dickinson—affected his writing style and philosophy tremendously. An essay titled "Nothing" pondered "nothingness," a prefiguring of his Buddhist preoccupations that marked the early 1950s: "I will be nothing someday because I will be part of the dust of the earth which will scatter to the winds of nothing . . . and I will scatter and fly about through nothing and be nothing."[12]

To boost his parents' skimpy income, Kerouac sold newspaper subscriptions. With his extra cash he scoured Moody Street dives looking for kicks and "quiff," those available women who flocked regularly to the servicemen on liberty from Fort Devens who patronized the bars. At other times, he staggered through the squalid bars of Boston's Scollay Square with Sebastian, as drunk from the experience of being among the throng as from the cheap draft ale poured out of brass taps. As summer ended, Kerouac was more than ready to begin his first semester at Columbia. This time he would live independently, housed on the Columbia campus in a less-than-stately room at decrepit Hartley Hall, overlooking Amsterdam Avenue. He packed his trunks, once more placing his journals and a few other manuscripts alongside the neatly folded clothes that his mother had placed there. Saying good-bye to his friends, Kerouac promised them he would write.

After driving through Massachusetts and Connecticut with some friends who were heading to the Flushing Meadows World's Fair, Jack and his father were dropped off at Columbia University. They lugged the trunks through the shadowy campus to Jack's room. For the next few days, Leo explored Manhattan with his son and watched the first football practices. Leo was interested not only in his son's physicality but also in coach Louis "Lou" Little's coaching style. Little had begun coaching for Columbia University in 1930 and would continue until 1956. In total, he coached 236 games for Columbia with 110 wins and 116 losses. The highlight of his career was bringing the Columbia Lions to the 1934 Rose Bowl and defeating Stanford by the score of 7–0. However, after 1936, Little's Columbia Lions fell on hard times because the school no longer gave full athletic scholarships and had a hard time attracting star athletes.

The first time on the field, Jack realized that the freshman section of the team was not of the same caliber as Horace Mann's team. The fullback and backfield were "slow" and "plodding." Despite the mediocrity of some players, Kerouac realized then that he might suffer the same fate he had endured at Lowell High School: he would not be part of the starting lineup. He began training four hours a day at Columbia's Baker Football Field. Running sprints and tackling dummies far into the cool autumn dusk, he saw the lights of Manhattan and knew that his destiny lay not in the rigors of academia but among the wilds of American society. He sensed, sourly, that whenever coach Lou Little walked by him among the freshmen, he never once "gave me the once-over."[13] Despite his feeling that he wasn't wanted by Coach Little, Kerouac was enlisted as the team's touchdown player. When Leo left to return to Lowell, after failing to secure a job from Little, he did so teary-eyed, telling Jack to "study, play good ball, pay attention to what the coach and the professors tell you, and see if you can't make your old man proud and maybe an All-American."[14] Not only would such advice go unheeded but it also seemed to be the catalyst for Kerouac's disenfranchisement from all that his family valued. It wasn't the aspiration for material well-being that concerned him, but instead the attainment of the "soul of man": "a component, a mixture, a swarming vat-like concoction of all the ideals of Man, embodied upon one portion of the Earth's crusty integument, and thrust upwards in a gesture of terrible finality and beauty that shall forever beckon." He realized that when he left Lowell he was "but a child" infused with "high dreams and mad dreams." But things had changed, his life had evolved. He was, at last, at the place "where the road begins."[15]

The "drear room" in Hartley Hall that Kerouac moved into in the fall of

1940 was infested with cockroaches and a bothersome roommate. Jack was used to having his own room, a retreat where he could play his fantasy-baseball game and read and write in solitude. Shortly afterward, Kerouac moved into a single room in another dormitory, Livingstone Hall. The window of that room overlooked Columbia's Butler Library and its resident hangout/eatery, the Lion's Den, where Kerouac gorged himself occasionally on sirloin steaks and ice-cream fudge sundaes. Most times, though, he ate at the training table in John Jay Hall; he reserved his knowledge of table manners (taught to him by Nin) for the one time that he was invited to dine at the on-campus residence of Columbia's dean. Impressed with Kerouac's manners, charm, and brightness, the dean sent Gabrielle a short, complimentary note (a source of never-ending pride for her).

After the first two weeks of school, despite the pride and thrill of being a young collegian in the big city, Jack found the responsibilities oppressive. To help defray his dining costs, he worked in the cafeteria as a dishwasher; after the first week, he quit to make room for his homework, late-afternoon practices, and inconsistent classroom attendance. Above all else, he had to earn grades decent enough to keep his scholarship. When he could relax at all, Kerouac did so in the seclusion of his dorm. The heavy load of courses did not stop Jack from his own intellectual pursuits. Butler Library sat to the right of John Jay Hall, and there Kerouac perused the tall stacks of world classics, philosophy, and history. On the corner of Forty-second Street and Fifth Avenue was the New York Public Library, where Kerouac spent a lot of his free time. Nearby, in Times Square, he went to the movies on Forty-second Street. Afterwards, he wrote reviews of what he saw for the *Columbia Spectator*. He continued to ghostwrite papers for his classmates, becoming a veritable "one-man typing agency" for the wealthier elements of Columbia's student body, as well as tutoring French. His resourcefulness, a family trait, gave him the much-needed income that a regular-paying hourly wage did not.

Jack's Lowell friends made occasional excursions to New York to visit. When they did, he guided them through both the upper echelons of Madison Avenue society and its downtown bohemian counterpart, Greenwich Village. Sometimes, they partied with whores in the New American Hotel. Lowell friend Scotty Beaulieu recalls:

Zagg [a nickname of Kerouac's] fixed me up with a girl named Lucille in the New American Hotel. This was the first time I'd ever been to a whorehouse. I was the last of the three to have her, all dressed up in my green suit and tie. Jack called me "Kid Faro" because of my green suit and hat, green tie, and green pipe—and gold tooth. Lucille was dressed only in a bathrobe. When we went into the room, she said, "Are you from Oklahoma too?" I wondered what the hell those crazy guys had told her, but then she took off her bathrobe and I forgot about the Oklahoma bit. You never saw anybody get out of their clothes so quick.[16]

Kerouac's casual attitude toward sex stemmed, in part, from his emerging existentialism, an indicator that he had shed his Catholic guilt for the time being in favor of fully embracing the possibilities of sexual union. Because "we are all animals," Kerouac postulates, then we are nothing more than an "ocean of sensateness" with "sickly gray entrails" only ceasing to make "noise" and erect "bridges" when we "rot and fall apart and absolve into dust." Sex was then nothing more than a by-product of that fleshly existence:

What is sex? Sex is rigid bone, covered in velvet skin, pounding and ripping into fleshy cavity with heart-pounding passion and blood-red lust. Sex is bang! Bang! That's sex, brother, and don't kid yourself. Bang! Pound! Bang! And then comes a rush of luscious fever, an ocean of pin-prick sensation, and a shuddering climax of gushing hot blood. Pow! And then to hell with sex. That's sex, kid.[17]

Kerouac's individualism did not lend itself to self-loathing. Less than one year later, he would realize that he was "august," a self-described trait derived from his reading of Walt Whitman's 1855 version of "Song of Myself" on June 4, 1941. Within this web of egocentrism there was no need to recoil from the stamp of shame imprinted upon such vices as prostitution and alcoholism. It was part and parcel of the legacy of the flesh:

What is this blurt about vice and about virtue?
Evil and reform of evil propels me. I stand indifferent.[18]

Kerouac was learning more and more that in becoming an artist, one must "steer" by the "pole-star" of "sincerity." Kerouac's logical extension of this was that the writing of a novel was the "story of man's development," which in turn was the story of "Fate." Kerouac, in essence, wanted to "kick in an original manner," a process that inevitably precluded collegiate football.

On October 12, 1940, Kerouac traveled to New Brunswick with the freshman football team to battle Rutgers University. He watched from the bench for the first half of the game, playing during the second. Columbia lost to Rutgers 18–7. Columbia's defeat only reinforced Jack's dismay at not being used to his fullest potential. Before long, friction developed between player and coach. Soon Kerouac's underutilization increased not only his frustration but also a lack of interest in the whole system of academics. Relief arrived, ironically, in the form of a painful leg injury suffered during Columbia's second game against St. Benedict as the result of a crunching football tackle. He complained of the pain to Lou Little, who, thinking it was only a sprain, made Jack continue the game. For the rest of that week, Kerouac attended practice diligently until X rays from Columbia Medical Center disproved the coach's notion: Jack had suffered a hairline fracture of his tibia. He was put in a cast, The fracture was severe enough to warrant injured-player status for the remainder of the season, thereby easing his schedule. Sitting by the fire in the Lion's Den during his convalescence, Kerouac spoiled himself with marathon sessions of reading and writing. He was, at last, far away from the rest of the bustling world, alone with "my thoughts, my self-confidences." Perhaps because he was living near the brownstone where Thomas Wolfe had written *Look Homeward, Angel* (1929), Kerouac immersed himself further in Wolfe's writing. The idea of America as one long, grand poem—and "not just a place to work and suffer in"—began to permeate his ideology. Thomas Wolfe had said on the novel's dustjacket that his fiction was

> loaded with invention: story, fantasy, vision. But it is a fiction that is, I believe, more true than fact—a fiction that grew out of a life completely digested in my spirit, a fiction which telescopes, condenses, and objectifies all the random or incompleted gestures of life.[19]

Those words could just as well have served as the emerging credo for Jack Kerouac. According to Kerouac, Wolfe was one of the greatest American writers thus far. Wolfe's rich use of language and distinctive literary style were exactly what Kerouac felt was missing in contemporary fiction.

While nursing his leg, Kerouac became giddy with artistic potential.

He began to yearn for something more substantial than the never-ending onslaught of stale academics. He was equally bored with football. As at Lowell High School, he was unwilling to conform to the disciplined lifestyle of collegiate academics. Increasingly, Kerouac felt himself an artist relegated to relating the bulk of his most passionate feelings into the pages of a journal. Wolfe's powerful prose left the young man reeling between indecision and an impulsive need to respond to the demands of his spirit. Wolfe's voice was entrancing, inviting, invoking perfectly that mind-set that captured the yearnings of Kerouac's romantic spirit. Wolfe's credo in *Of Time and the River* (1935) exactly matched Kerouac's:

> At that instant he saw, in one blaze of light, an image of unutterable conviction, the reason why the artist works and lives and has his be-ing—the reward he seeks—the only reward he really cares about, without which there is nothing. It is to snare the spirits of mankind in nets of magic, to make his life prevail through his creation, to wreak the vision of his life, the rude and painful substance of his own experience, into the congruence of blazing and enchanted images that are themselves the core of life, the essential pattern whence all other things proceed, the kernel of eternity.[20]

However, Kerouac insisted that his style, whenever he would achieve it, would be his own. Once, two hours after midnight, Kerouac, restless with creative energy, meditated upon his personal writing style and recorded his reflections, beckoning himself: "It is I, speaking to you." He recognized that following God's will (he had been reading the Bible every morning)[21] would compel him to be creatively driven. Although the page was "long, blank, and full of truth," it could just as well be "long, full, and empty with words" when he was done with it. He knew that he was not purposely trying to "copy" anyone but merely to be "truthful" to himself in order to become "endowed with words." That same night, he had ghostwritten a short story called "Black Gold" for a fellow student on his floor at Livingstone Hall. Knowing that he had cheapened his art for money (earning $1 for his hour-and-a-half effort), Jack also knew that what he did was done out of necessity. Squandering money was not a habit for frugal Jack. But since he had saved $10 in his desk and since he had squandered his talent to earn that temporary surplus of funds, Kerouac felt justified squandering the earnings from it. Earlier that day, he had been approached by a cruising homosexual, whom he had gently rebuffed; Kerouac later noted every nuance of the encounter in his diary. For $1.50 he ordered a meal of meatloaf and potatoes, doused in gravy, and devoured it. Feeling content, he bought a cigar and debated whether to smoke it before or after the film. During the movie, a comedy filled with pratfalls, "curves and curls," Kerouac sneered at the philistine audience and its eagerness to be so easily amused by Hollywood's heavy-handed box-office fare. Puffing his cigar afterwards, he walked through the night's cool fall air watching the lights glimmering along the New Jersey shore. Kerouac listened to the sound of the "all-engulfing roar of the earth and time" and recognized the futility of wandering Earth trapped in a prison of flesh. Being and nothingness were now the constant polarities of his consciousness. His introspection spiritually peaked as he reflected that "God is the thing" that made up his "consciousness." As God was a man, Kerouac reasoned, then man was God. Because God was the "thing," not much else seemed to matter. It is little wonder that Kerouac had no time to devote himself to the Columbia gridiron. By the second half of his sophomore year, the die had been cast. Art had bested the worldly demands of academia.

7

A Kernel of Eternity

February–Summer 1941

One minute before death, my iced foot touched
The lowest stair; and as it touched, life seemed
To pour in at the toes.
    JOHN KEATS, "Fall of Hyperion"

Sebastian Sampas was at Emerson College when he received Kerouac's postcards and letters from New York City. Evidently, Kerouac missed his literary rapport with Sebastian, and now that he was riding the crest of a burgeoning intellectualism, he was determined not to allow physical distance to destroy that rapport. In February 1941, he suggested to Sebastian that he write him daily and promised to reciprocate. Sebastian's sisters Claire and Stella (who was smitten with Kerouac) lived in the Sampases' Lowell home on Stevens Street. To prevent their reading his correspondence ("I'm being boyish," he explained to Sebastian), he mailed the postcards and letters directly to Emerson. For other friends and acquaintances like G. J. Apostolos, Kerouac did the same, thus keeping an active rapport with key Lowell friends, though the contents of his missives only hinted at the emerging artist within.[1]

During the second semester of his first year at Columbia, freed from football obligations, Kerouac used the time to read, write, and further explore Manhattan. He was still intensely taken with Thomas Wolfe as he delved into Wolfe's novels, most notably that winter, his short story collection *From Death to Morning*. In one story, "The Four Lost Men," Kerouac rightly felt that Wolfe used "too much language." Still, it was abundantly evident that Wolfe was not content to be a storyteller but wanted to evoke memorably an American experience from the commonality of the country's people. Although his copious use of adjectives to create atmosphere and mood bordered on descriptive overkill, it suited Wolfe's singular style and found a captive audience in Kerouac. (He would later emulate Wolfe's descriptive cadences in portions of his own first published novel, *The Town and the City*.) "The Four Lost Sons," a poetic reverie on Presidents Rutherford B. Hayes, James A. Garfield, Chester A. Arthur, and Benjamin Harrison, recounts the resurrection of an America existing vaguely in the mind of the narrator (presumably Eugene Gant, the pseudonymous stand-in for Wolfe) through his own father's past. The technique Wolfe employed is not merely to describe, but to evoke the period with sensory flashes:

> It was in the sweet and secret breasted heart of fragrant, all-engulfing night. It was in the sweet and secret rustling of the leaves in the summer streets, in footsteps coming quiet, slow and lonely along the darkness of a leafy street, in screen doors slammed, and silence, the distant barking of a dog, far voices, laughter, faint pulsing music at a dance, and in all the casual voices of the night, far, strangely near, most intimate and familiar, remote as time, as haunting as the briefness of our days.[2]

Despite his slight criticism of Wolfe's style, Kerouac thought such descriptive writing was what counted most in American fiction—that raw experience transposed into literary mythmaking was the essence of literature as art. In many ways Wolfe's life—mythologized through transmutation—eerily paralleled Kerouac's: the inauspicious upbringing in a working-class town; the obsessive aspiration to write; and the urge to eke out of the humdrum, day-to-day existence a life not merely endured but lived prodigiously.

Also on Kerouac's reading list that winter of 1941 was Jan Valtin's autobiographical novel, *Out of the Night* (1941), a sensational account of a man caught between two world wars. Valtin had been working as a merchant seaman and as an undercover agent for the Communist Party when he was captured and interrogated by the Gestapo. Kerouac credited this epic adventure novel with injecting wanderlust into his creative drive. Kerouac realized that to sail the seas and roam the world, he first needed to shed his current responsibilities.

On March 6, on weekend break from his classes, Kerouac thumbed a ride back to Lowell. There he met Sebastian and brought him a one-act play he had written while in New York. Of late, Kerouac had been attempting to delve into playwriting. Because his typewriter was broken, he wrote a draft of one play in his notebook. On March 23, at his parents' home, he wrote another small play, using his hometown as the setting. In the play, men lie nude in the sun at "Bareass Beach" sharing cigars and reclining indolently. Within this insignificant effort Kerouac's awareness of empathy as a working theme emerges. With cigar in mouth, the lead character, Zagg, has the courage to face the world and his fellow man without casting hasty judgment: "I'm Zagg and I've got a cigar and I don't give a damn for anything nor do I reject anything. I think that you've an ugly puss, but I like you because you inhabit this earth with me and we're both in the same boat."[3]

Trying to influence the steadfast and academically disciplined Sebastian with his own reckless wanderlust, Jack suggested that he also read Valtin. Kerouac's desire to reach beyond the limited means of the Columbia campus would cause Sebastian much chagrin. Jack proposed in a letter to Sebastian that they meet in later years in San Francisco and Moscow to fuel their prodigious appetites for literature, utopianism, and socialism. Kerouac theorized, in what he called "Kerouac's Socialism," that if the average American worker labored only for two- to three-hour shifts, there would be three working shifts per day, thus creating more jobs. Not only would this model broaden the American workforce, it would also overtly create a "new desire to live," so that people weren't merely "productive animal[s]" but could enjoy the "rights of man in the use of his divine intellect, a gift of God that is overlooked by our overloads of the present Industrial Era." Having come from Lowell, one of the centerpieces of the Industrial Revolution, Kerouac felt a profound connection to blue-collar workers. Their dismal plight determined his future and fueled his desire to leave Lowell and not be a part of the cyclical rise and fall of the family man bound by duty to place food on his table to the detriment of his mind, body, and spirit. The red brick exterior of the textile mills held just enough "smug tyranny" to make his "blood boil." As flawed as his idealism was, it worked for him because it accommodated his own interests but little else.[4]

Jack visited friend Howie Marton for two weeks when he returned to New York. They sat in the study of the opulent Marton residence smoking fifty-cent cigars and talking until five in the morning. Afterward, they walked in Central Park as the sun tinged the skyline a rosy pink. Kerouac also continued visiting the inner city, where he roamed its "vast and rich web" almost every night. When he had the funds, he would go to see films like *Philadelphia Story.* (Kerouac was finding it increasingly difficult to maintain his academic discipline and confessed to Sebastian that he rarely studied anymore.) For all the benefits of a crowded city, he still missed Sebastian. As he left the theater, Jack heard "I'll See You Again" playing from a nearby penny arcade, and tears welled up in his eyes. Another Lowell friend, G. J. Apostolos, visited him that spring: "we possessed the bodies of a few women; had a little discussion on Union Square with a few Reds; roamed Greenwich Village; and sat by the Hudson on Sunday, ending the afternoon by gazing rapturously at some original Greek sculpture from the Parthenon frieze and some oils in the Museum of Art and watching the famed Fifth Avenue Easter Parade! George also burped loud into the face of a genuine burper!"[5]

On May 22, 1941, Sebastian's birthday, Sebastian wrote Kerouac a letter in which he acknowledged his broadening intellect: "That definition of yours on Enthusiasm is so true—The more and more you write to me—the more you seem to be improving."[6] Sebastian was dating Doris Miller, a fellow drama student at Emerson. She had learned much about Kerouac through Sebastian and wrote him on October 17, 1941. She said she must meet him and asked if he was "real," "or is it just that Sebastian's idealism has made so much of you? May I know some day?" She did date Jack a few times, and often the two young men shared her between them.[7]

Kerouac was developing his keen ear for music of all genres: romantic crooners like Bing Crosby and Frank Sinatra, ebullient swing, and baroque and classical music like Bach, Mozart, Beethoven, and Sibelius. The sounds of all of them were prevalent in Manhattan, with several symphony orchestras, nightclubs, and jazz haunts. In April Kerouac saw Walt Disney's *Fantasia* and was impressed by Disney's fusion of classical music and color animation. Thus did Kerouac spend the spring semester of 1941 at Columbia, the last semester that he would be occupied solely with college.

That May Kerouac returned to Lowell, hitchhiking north in a series of several short rides. One was from a man "who loved books and music." He recited for Jack passages from William Cullen Bryant and praised the writings of Sir Walter Scott: "It was amazing, riding in a sleek car with a tender soul who loved the romance of Scott through streets strewn with realism—filling stations, stores, hydrants, straw hats, window fronts, no sign of Ivanhoe nor Rebecca."

In Lowell that summer, Kerouac spent most of his time with Sebastian. Together, they occupied their days living out the wanderlust that so plagued Kerouac's heart. Sometimes they hitchhiked to Boston to watch throngs of people on the Common. With other companions Kerouac ventured to the Boston docks and pondered the possibility of boarding a merchant vessel and seeing the world once and for all. There was also a trip north to Vermont with G. J., Scott Beaulieu, and Sebastian to visit some girls, a journey notable for its whiskey-soaked mishaps culminating in an automobile accident that left Kerouac so shaken that he had doubts about ever driving a car again in his life.

In June 1941, Kerouac noted in his journal his revisiting of Walt Whitman, remarking that the poet's "individualism cannot be beat." To Jack, Whitman's model was one to follow: to view himself as a poet who would celebrate his life lived on his own terms. In 1941 Kerouac wrote a free-verse credo echoing Whitman's definition of a poet:

> A poet is a fellow who
> spends his time thinking
> about what it is that's
> wrong, and although he
> knows he can never quite
> find out what this wrong
> is, he goes right on
> thinking it out and writing
> it down.[8]

A poet was someone who regarded life with "blind" optimism and who tried to be "timeless in a / society built on time." Most tellingly, he believed that he was "on the right track, / no matter what any of his / fellow men say."[9]

His views on the art of writing were becoming honed to the point where he no longer aspired to be a journalist with a degree from Columbia, not even as a trump card for the future should creative writing fail him. For Jack, the art of writing required more worldly considerations: the writer "wants to cut a slab out of the whole conglomerate mass-symphony of nature and life and present it to his readers." Kerouac knew now that art was a "readjustment of perception, from physical actuality to a perception expressed by the artist." But that consciousness in itself was not enough; it needed to be intensified. To write, one needed simply to document "reality" from one's sensitized perspective. Kerouac sought and, on occasion, found that reality, even when it was distilled in its harshest form.[10]

By the end of the summer, their prospects in Lowell having dried up, Gabrielle and Leo decided to leave the city, as recounted in *Vanity of Duluoz:* "My father, who'd been working out of town as a linotypist, sometimes at Andover Mass., and sometimes Boston, sometimes Meriden Conn., now had a steady job lined up at New Haven Conn. and it was decided we move there."[11] The thin strands of Caroline's marriage had frayed one by one. In 1940 and 1941, Caroline was still working as a bindery worker for Sullivan Brothers Printing and was living with Leo and Gabrielle and not with Charles.[12] The elder Kerouacs decided to move to New Haven and hoped for the best, but Caroline decided to stay in Lowell.

Idealistically, Jack viewed the move as fodder for his fledgling creative writing. In his journal he jotted down notes about leaving Lowell that would form the basis for another manuscript, "Farewell Song, Sweet from My Trees." In it Kerouac described his distinct Americanism and "American temperament." In the early morning hours before their departure, Jack sat on the steps of the house and listened to the wind blow through the boughs of the towering elm and pine trees. He remembered when his family first moved to Pawtucketville ten years earlier, the acquisition of new friends, the six-year-old mare that their father had gotten for them, the swims in Beaver Brook, every familiar nook and cranny of Pawtucketville's creaking tenements and tree-lined sidewalks. He recalled the familiar sight of his father on his recliner listening to music from the radio while his mother cooked caramel pudding. Kerouac would carry these associations with him for the rest of his life. Saddened, he said his farewells to the trees: "I look up at the trees, staring into their sorrowful profusion of night-green: 'So long trees. I've got to move along,' I whisper to them. 'So long . . . . . . so long . . . . oh so long.'"[13] Jack Kerouac was now nineteen years old, and his self-described role as poet was about to assert itself as his country slid inexorably toward war.

8

The Furious Poet

Fall 1941

Strange is the feeling that then presses in upon you—a feeling of enigmatic fear in the presence of this blind dreamlike earth-bound existence.
OSWALD SPENGLER, *The Decline of the West*

President Roosevelt's public reluctance to involve his country in World War II began to change in June 1941, when he gave American warships permission to retaliate should they be fired upon by German U-boats. In August 1941 the military draft, opposed by isolationist members of Congress, was extended for another eighteen months. It passed by an exceedingly slim margin, 203 to 202, in the House of Representatives. As that vote was being decided, Roosevelt met Winston Churchill secretly off the coast of Newfoundland. Churchill hoped to solicit a military commitment from the United States. The outcome of this rendezvous was the Atlantic Charter, in which Great Britain and the United States pledged not to seek territorial expansion or changes, to respect the rights of people to choose their own form of government, to promote free trade among nations, to encourage international cooperation to improve the livelihood of people worldwide, to build a secure peace based on freedom from fear and want, to disarm any aggressors, and to create a system that would make general security for all permanent. From this document arose the United Nations, which would promote the common purpose of its Allies in their struggle against the Axis powers. Twenty-six nations, including the Soviet Union and China, signed the declaration. Yet the question remained: How close to war was the United States? In the first week of September, a

U-boat fired two torpedoes at the USS *Greer*. Roosevelt, comparing the Germans to rattlesnakes poised to strike, ordered the U.S. Navy to pre-emptively fire upon German ships on sight. Later that month, another German U-boat attacked and sank the destroyer USS *Kearny*, killing at least one hundred sailors. Roosevelt's unwavering voice responded over the airwaves: "America has been attacked. . . . The shooting has started. And history has recorded who fired the first shot." However, Congress, despite the mounting toll of maritime fatalities, would not yet declare war.

A gale of August rain whipped the coastline along the broad expanse of Long Island Sound. Having secured a job in West Haven, Connecticut, Leo had gone ahead of his wife and son some weeks earlier. He had been traveling to Connecticut, working odd jobs he was able to find through his connections in the printing industry. With limited funds, he had taken an apartment, without first seeing it, in the ghetto district of New Haven. The moving van, minus their dog Tippy, who had jumped out of the van at Stafford Springs, Connecticut, was unloaded and left.

Their new living quarters were so deplorable that they sickened Gabrielle. She refused to live there once she had arrived with Jack by train, likening it to the worst she had seen in Lowell's Little Canada. Gabrielle, Jack, and his Horace Mann friend Burt Stollmack searched in vain for suitable housing. For the interim, their furniture was placed in storage, and they slept in a hotel room for the night. The next day Leo called a French Canadian realtor who arranged for them to move into his $40-a-month cottage on West Haven's Bradley Point on the coast of Long Island Sound.[1]

The amusement centers and clam shacks in West Haven reminded the Kerouacs of Salisbury Beach in Massachusetts. Gabrielle was content with the roominess of the cottage and was equally delighted that her bedroom faced the sea. Most of all, she was mightily relieved that they did not have to resort to desperate measures for shelter. Jack hung around West Haven with the idea of getting a job sooner or later to assist his parents. In the interim he swam in the sound, labored over his writings, and prepared for his sophomore year of college while his mother worked hard to make her new house a home.

Before he left West Haven, Kerouac sensed his mother's loneliness. He implored his sister to resign her job at Sullivan Brothers and move to Connecticut. Her divorce petition was filed, and her husband left the city.

Unwilling to leave her job and begin anew once more, she resisted Jack's exhortations. Kerouac had been wary of leaving his mother alone in the new home with his father away most of the time. Built for balmy summers, the cottage was not fit to inhabit during the harsh winter squalls that blew in from the sound. As he was packing for school in the cottage's attic, his feet fell through the "phony ceiling," and he slammed his testicles into the wooden beams. Writhing in pain, Kerouac cried for a half-hour.[2]

In September, Kerouac traveled the seventy-seven miles back to New York City from West Haven. Classmates picked him up in West Haven and drove him to Manhattan in a sports car. Upon arriving at Columbia, he went to Baker Field, where the rest of his team was exercising in uniform. According to Kerouac, Lou Little slighted him and the rest of the team cold-shouldered him for his tardiness. Practice and study resumed; before too long, Kerouac tired of the "hot September sun tacklings of silly dummies held by assistant coaches and idiots with cameras taking our pictures." He quarreled with Little over the coach's refusal to place him in the starting lineup and took to the field halfheartedly. With visions of hitchhiking, writing, and being free from Columbia's strenuous course load, Kerouac left campus abruptly by mid-September. It was one night after dinner that he resolved to pack his things and leave. Tired from the scrimmage, he limped by the table where Lou Little and his assistants sat. When the coach asked where he was heading, Kerouac said that he was going to do laundry at his stepgrandmother's house in Brooklyn. Kerouac left Harlem and took the subway to Grand Central Station. Eventually, he found his way to the idling buses of a Greyhound station. Indecisively, Kerouac bought a ticket south and boarded. He was filled with excitement and dread, for this was the most important decision he had made in his life. According to his juvenilia, this rebellion was sparked in part by his reading of William Saroyan: "Indolent, arrogant Saroyan. It ruined my first College year. But after the first drunken stage, I shortly gathered up my reins and began to direct those daring white steeds of rebellion into a more constructive direction—into a direction that was bound to be the beginning of ultimate, complete development & integration."[3]

Saroyan's message to budding writers was potent. He advised them that the "writer is a spiritual anarchist, as in the depth of his soul every man is. He is discontented with everything and everybody. The writer is everybody's best friend and only true enemy—the good and great enemy. He neither walks with the multitude nor cheers with them. The writer who is a writer is a rebel who never stops." So taken with Saroyan was Kerouac that Sebastian Sampas (declared by the U.S. government in early 1942 to be 1-A [available for military service] for the American draft) wrote Saroyan imploring him to write to Kerouac to boost his confidence as a writer: "God! if only you could read his manuscripts to see the stuff he has got."[4] It is not known if Saroyan ever did so.

The American eastern seaboard glided past the bus as it sped swiftly along the highway. Kerouac was, at last, rejuvenated despite a recurring undercurrent of dread. Movement of any kind refreshed him like shedding an old skin to progress toward something fresh and vivid. On the bus, he sat beside a black man from Newark, New Jersey, who was heading to "Virginny" to see his dying father. He told Kerouac that he had just won a game of pool but had also lost a hand at poker. Beneath the cresting wave of freedom and exultation there lurked an undertow of guilt and regret about disappointing his parents. To delay the dreaded moment of returning home to his parents, Kerouac transferred to a bus heading south toward Virginia. In Washington, D.C., he stepped off the bus and got a hotel room to stay for a while.

Inside the hotel in a low-end, treeless district of Washington, sweltering and sleepless, Kerouac sat and wrote letters to his friends. To Sebastian he confessed that he was "driven and weary": "I don't know what I've done—afraid to go home, too proud and sick to go back to the football team, driven and weary with no place to go, I know not a soul."[5] He wept. He brooded on the brick-walled exterior outside his window and felt it to be "one of the worst moments of my life." He thought that he had just "thrown up my cards completely." Restless with worry, he could not even escape the reality by sleeping because bedbugs had infested his sheets. He paced the room feeling overwhelmed by "the horrifying death of it all." Still, with irony, he viewed his sudden senseless excursion as "sadly humorous," telling himself: "I am a writer, and thus it will prove valuable for me to study this place. However, before I start writing in dead seriousness, I want to add one thing. One of the remedies for American sickness is humour—there isn't enough of it to go around—and I think it ought to be fed to the people."

America, Kerouac summed up, was a polarity of "pity and irony."[6] Although he was indeed surprised at his own impulsiveness, he felt content that his recent actions were for his own artistic integrity. To bolster his attempts at self-justification, Jack penciled a letter to Sebastian: "I speak to you from the hearts of all the lonely young writers that have ever lived on the earth. I speak to you from their hearts because now I am one of them."[7] Consumed with regret, Kerouac slowly began to doubt his convictions. The leap from college student and athlete to absolutely "nothing" no longer made sense to him because he knew it to be self-destructive. The next morning, surprised to have survived that first night in the hotel, Kerouac went to a bookstore and bought a used copy of Ralph Waldo Emerson's *Essays*. He spent the next few days in Washington brooding about the turmoil of his own indecision and the enlightenment provided by Emerson's essay on self-reliance: "There is a time in every man's education when he arrives at the conviction that envy is ignorance; that imitation is suicide; that though the wide universe is full of good, no kernel of nourishing corn can come to him but through his toil bestowed on that plot of ground which is given to him to till."[8]

However, Kerouac's "plot of ground" was littered with the stubborn stones of familial duty and academic obligation. As he later told Sebastian, he was a young man on a desperate flight, a "Hegira." (*Hegira*, an Arabic word for "the departure," included in its meaning the exodus of Muhammad from Mecca to Medina when he was expelled by the magistrates on July 16, 622. By extension, it has come to mean, as it most clearly was in Kerouac's usage, a journey undertaken by someone to avoid persecution.) Influenced by the cool autumn air and expansive blue sky, he decided to return home. Before doing so, Kerouac toured the nation's capital considering its "implications in the light of international complications." Although Jack hoped to catch a glimpse of Roosevelt, he was not terribly disappointed when he didn't because he did not "care for any politicians." He roamed through the immense National Gallery of Art, studying paintings by Rembrandt "simply because there before me was the original work of one of the world's really great artists." Visiting the National Archives, he nearly froze in its frigid corridors and was not impressed with the chaotic arrangement of its collection.[9]

Kerouac went to the bus terminal and bought his ticket home. At the hotel, for the last time, he picked up his bag and looked again at the infested bedsheets—he was still recovering from insect bites—and the thin tree that had sprouted "between fences and barrels," and left the hotel. Upon leaving Washington, Kerouac noted that the streets were like all others in the world. By the time the bus reached New England, he found life appreciably better and his bleak outlook lifted somewhat. Wolfe's credo of America as a poem now made more sense to Kerouac, who witnessed life now with his own eyes and not merely from the "meaty pages" of a book. Of all the moments he remembered about Washington, the most lasting image was the sight of three black men standing across the street from his hotel.

The relative enlightenment of his small journey faded quickly when he returned home. Enraged, Leo did not see any sense in rejecting a paid education, an opportunity that he never had, to try to be a writer. To avoid Leo's anger, Jack stayed in his room listening to Richard Wagner. From the window he watched an oyster steamer that had been anchored in the harbor for the past four days. He wondered about the men within: "I can picture the men on board, working all day, and playing cards in the musty hold at night, and perhaps one of them, young, is writing." As he sat watching the vessel, Kerouac read from *Leaves of Grass.* Kerouac quoted in a letter to Sebastian a passage from the twenty-fifth section of "Song of Myself": "My final merit I refuse you, I refuse putting from me what I really am, Encompass worlds, but never try to encompass me."[10]

On a train to Boston, Sebastian penned an enthusiastic letter praising Kerouac's "Farewell Song, Sweet from My Trees," which had been mailed to him. Before he left, he had written another letter from the Hotel Merrimack (across from the Lowell train depot). In the letter he composed a poem amid the "raucous laughter" of a "whore" who was smoking a cigarette and drinking a beer near him. Sampas had recently found a job with Woolf Fording Company working with trunks of ancient costumes. During his working hours, he tried on the different costumes "on the sly of course," favoring the Louis XVI hat that served as a prop.[11] Kerouac answered Sebastian's charge that he was neglecting to correspond with him. Kerouac, in fact, had written from Washington, assuring Sebastian that he had written him the more heartfelt missives (the letter written to G. J. Apostolos was merely "buoyant" and trivial). In those written to Sebastian he had laid his heart bare. Kerouac felt that Sebastian should be less egotistical and demanding, and more concerned and earnest in any present and future endeavors.

To appease his father, Kerouac promised that he would get a job. He went to a local rubber plant and filled out an application for employment. Soon thereafter he was hired as a laborer and worked through until the following morning, sweating it out within the noisy confines of the factory walls. Kerouac felt faceless, lost, and worthless laboring in the vast, arduous production line. Tired of the smell of rubber, of punching a time clock, and the demands suddenly placed on his time, Kerouac promptly left the job site without collecting any pay. It was not the first job that he would quit around this time. His experience in a cracker factory met with predictable results. He resented "wallowing in the mire of other people": "It is not right for me to give eight hours of my precious life to anyone at such a gory task every day. I should rather keep those eight hours to myself, meditating in the grass."[12]

In West Haven, not wanting to stay in his parents' house any longer than necessary, Kerouac escaped to the movie theater. One day he watched Orson Welles's *Citizen Kane*. On another day he took a train to Manhattan, where he loitered in front of a whorehouse. Lacking any money to eat, Jack accepted dinner from a homosexual pimp, who tried to work the young man who would not "break a deuce on anything but venus." Without a place to sleep, he found shelter inside a church.[13] By the time he left the city, he felt wearied, empty, cold, and feverish. At home Leo's quarreling and the guilt of watching his mother getting up to work each morning finally bested him, and again he fled. With the help of a friend, Kerouac went forty-eight miles north for a job as a "grease monkey" at an Atlantic Whiteflash station in Manchester, Connecticut. In his knapsack he brought along some works in progress, including "Farewell Song, Sweet from My Trees" (later sent to *Harper's Magazine*) and a collection of smaller, impressionistic poems and jottings. He boarded the Hartford train and wrote to Sebastian as he watched his fellow passengers staring out the windows at the "faint suggestion of mysterious and melancholy Oktober." Of late, Kerouac had written a number of small pieces reflecting his love for this month, including "Old Love-Light" and "I Tell You It Is October!" The former evoked Kerouac's train ride, the "railroad buildings, dingied / by scores of soot-years, / thrusting their ugly rears / at your train windows" that were a "sign of man's decay."[14] The latter, a free-verse poem imitative of Whitman, reveals one example of the wordplay that would be a hallmark of Kerouac's best writing: the "melancholy frowse of harvest stacks / The tender char of morning skies.[15] "Frowse," possibly a blend of "frown" and "drowse," was invented by Kerouac to evoke the image of a pile of harvested hay drying beneath gray, brooding skies. Kerouac, still impressed by *Citizen Kane,* brought along a piece of writing he called "Oktober," which he intended to send to the acclaimed director.

Kerouac's move to 106 Webster Street in Hartford marked the first time that he would live independently—a "little cheap room" for $4.50 a week, complete with a grease-splattered stove, steaming-hot radiators, the pungent smell of stale urine, and his own miserable furnishings. Despite the meager furnishings, it virtually guaranteed that he could act upon the advice of his spirit without the distraction of his "disconsolate and reprimanding parents."[16] At the automotive station he inspected car engines and checked oil as he watched October burn the New England trees crimson and gold. Around him, the leaves crisped and weakened before spiraling to his beloved "Indian earth," adding color to a world that he had formerly described as thoroughly "gray." The men with whom he worked were older and jokingly called him "college boy." Feeling somewhat accepted, he amused them with vivid stories of his travels. Bob (one of the younger men) gave Kerouac rides from Manchester back to Hartford. Kerouac's description of Bob in an early work could be aptly characterized as a prototype of Dean Moriarty in *On the Road*. Bob played "jive" music on the car radio, and as the music grew faster and sweetly urgent, he began to talk and drive with added enthusiasm and energy:

> until after a while he is tearing along at the rate of sixty miles per hour, dodging people, swinging around corners with a rhythmic flourish of his arms, hurtling over little lumps on the street floors with a beautiful and hot knee action, whisking and whipping along to the hot music, beating his hands on the wheel with the rhythm, tearing around the city in his car with the music blaring, tooting rhythmically at all the nice looking chicks that walk along the sidewalks with slender stockinged legs.[17]

It was among such people that Kerouac found he could most be himself without the pretenses of adapting to Manhattan city life among the wealthy poseurs he so detested. It was also in such company that he began to pioneer the most compelling and genuine portions of his early writing. Among such people, the kind his parents urged him to avoid, he did not feel the sting of his low social station. It was also in their presence, and under their influence, that he was better able to achieve a writing style that he could call his own.

Kerouac found time to pursue his love interests as well. One pretty seventeen-year-old girl named Kitty walked past the station every day while he worked up the courage to ask her out on a date. He made small talk with her at a lunch counter before asking. She accepted. He took the young girl to a "clump of bushes" outside a Pratt & Whitney Aircraft plant, read poetry to her, and spoke of Saroyan's books. When they emerged from the bushes, men leaving the plant saw them and cheered—one of them a friend from Kerouac's Lowell High School football days. It was Kerouac's objective to "make her" to win the approval of his coworkers, all of whom lusted after her. On the next date Kerouac and Kitty sat in her house playing records. She spoke of one day being married and having a "cottage with [a] white fence." Finally, she consented to sex, and Jack took her "hard and fast." Afterward, he walked the two miles to the bus stop to return to Hartford. When he passed by the service station, he tossed a used condom onto the Atlantic Whiteflash walkway for the men to see when they opened the next morning. Despairingly, Kerouac sensed they did not see the spent evidence of his "lastnight sorrow." He continued to date girls who were known among the locals as "loose." His libido, in most cases, strong-armed his gallantry.

Once back inside his "lonely dusty room," complete with a chorus of skittering cockroaches, Kerouac continued to churn out his stories, still striving to perfect his voice as a writer. His conviction to create was solid as he reminded himself:

> [W]hen you feel as if you cannot write, as if it is no use, as if life is no good, read this over and realize that you can do a lot of good in this world by turning out truths like these, by spreading warmth, by trying to preach living for life's sake, not the intellectual way, but the warm way, the way of love, the way which says: Brothers, I greet you with open arms, I accept your frailties, I offer you my frailties, let us gather and run the gamut of rich human existence.[18]

However, his attempts failed as he remained bogged down by the powerful influences of Saroyan, Wolfe, and Hemingway. He named this new collection of short stories (mainly prose sketches) *Atop an Underwood* and promptly sent one of them to *Harper's Magazine*, which had recently rejected "Farewell Song, Sweet from My Trees." *Harper's* promptly rejected the new story as well.

Having acquired at last a rented Underwood typewriter on October 13, along with a bonus ream of yellow paper, Kerouac composed the first few stories of *Atop an Underwood* so rapidly that eventually, as he claimed later, his new collection exceeded sixty pieces. His method of composition—more economically focused than fueled by a conscious aesthetic—was to fill each sheet of paper (from margin to margin, top to bottom) wrapping up his thought by the last line before finally typing "JK." His intention was to "augment their dignity" by not making the stories over-long, to instill importance into each, and to promote a "drive toward slower and more religious reading." This flurry of writing produced vivid, rich, sharp impressions of Hartford and Lowell, his family, recent jobs, and, when hunger began to set in, a sumptuous feast that he imagined eating—when all he had was bread, cheese, and bitter, black coffee:

> I begin to eat. The steak is huge, about two feet long and one foot wide, with a thickness of two inches. Through it runs a great bone, protruding at one end like the mighty hock of a beast. I grasp this bone and snarl into the steak, thrusting my mouth into the warm brown side of the meat, gnashing bestially with my savageful teeth and tearing off huge brown folds of meat, great flaccid flabs of bloody meat in massive mouthfuls.[19]

As autumn grew colder, Kerouac cut a conspicuous figure walking the empty streets of after-dinner Hartford in his red football jersey, green gabardine pants, and brown crepe-soled shoes. In his back pocket bulged his empty wallet. In his single bed he read, punctuated by short blasts of typewriting. Although living in penury (down to half a loaf of bread and some slices of cheese), he used the details in his stories, almost delighting in his self-imposed misery. Jack observed himself in the mirror, his self-absorption embracing the wild tangle of his "horrifying and crazy" hair, his "bright shining eyes," and the etched "lines down the side of the face." On November 12, Kerouac typed the last of his work and returned the Underwood to the rental agency.[20]

Kerouac's despondence embraced broader dimensions: the owner of Atlantic Whiteflash discovered that Jack was bluffing about his mechanical aptitude and demoted him to pumping gas. Walking the streets of South Hartford with a mere four cents in his pocket, Kerouac went into a drugstore. He was one cent shy of the price of a cup of coffee and wondered if he could finagle a cup. Instead, he blankly browsed the magazine rack, not having the nerve to ask. Later that day a friend came to his room and offered Jack a much-needed cigarette. Casually, he sifted through Kerouac's piles of fresh writing, with the author hovering anxiously over his shoulders. Inspired, they made tentative plans to drive to California to reap fresh experiences for Kerouac, but such plans were premature: Kerouac, without money, was stuck in Hartford: "I don't have a heart unless there's a typewriter somewhere nearby, with a chair in front of it and some blank sheets of paper."[21]

Under duress, and lonely for family at the onset of the holidays, Kerouac planned to quit the station shortly after Thanksgiving, to vacate his room, and to return to his family, who by then were making their own plans to leave West Haven and return to Lowell. Sebastian surprised Kerouac, stuck working a five-hour shift pumping gas for holiday drivers, with a Thanksgiving Day visit. He questioned Jack's motives for leaving Columbia. Kerouac replied that it was "allright to be an athlete if you think you're going to get something out of college. I wanta be a writer." They shared Thanksgiving dinner at a greasy diner: the "blue plate turkey special." That night, after attending two movies, they went to a bar with another Lowell friend. Kerouac almost got into a fight. Two weeks after Thanksgiving, Kerouac received a postcard from his family telling him to return to Lowell: Leo had been offered a job there. Gabrielle and Leo had tired of the summer cottage, and Caroline was still living alone. Jack realized that he could return with his head held a little higher, proud that he had written something of substance at the very least.

Leo, Gabrielle, and Jack were back under one roof in Lowell by December 1941. In what Kerouac describes as "the most delicious truck ride I ever had in my life," the movers had placed his father's easy chair at the tail end of the moving truck and Jack had sat in it, watching the road dissolve into the distance. They all stopped in Hartford for lunch at a diner. Kerouac describes his blue-plate dinner of roast pork in the first section of *Visions of Cody*: "The wonderful taste of what I guess was roast pork steamed and kept warm, going on a blueplate dinner with mashed potatoes, hundreds of great truckdrivers and even some of the boys from my station devouring it."[22]

As the truck pulled away from the diner and continued on its journey north, Kerouac watched the road unwind behind him until the environs became more familiar, "bearing me sadly back to the scenes of my boyhood."[23] Only a few days later, Japan's unprovoked attack on Pearl Harbor would finally push the United States into World War II.

9

The Wound of Living

December 1941–Spring 1942

Maybe all men got one big soul ever'body's a part of.
JOHN STEINBECK, *The Grapes of Wrath*

The Kerouacs joined Caroline and resided on the first floor of a two-family house on Crawford Street in Pawtucketville, less than a mile from the home in which they had lived the previous summer. Kerouac took to his books, reading Dostoyevsky's *Notes from the Underground,* Joyce's *Ulysses,* Thoreau, and Wolfe while he smoked his taped-up pipe: "After hours were spent in the Library studying, where I learned more in three months than I could have learned in three years at college. I delved into everything: history, sociology, psychology, the classics, philosophy, evolution, and even psychoanalysis."[1] Sebastian, knowing that Jack must get a job as soon as possible to keep his father off his back, suggested that Jack apply for a job at the *Lowell Sun,* where Sebastian's brother Charles was a writer.

On December 7, Kerouac went to the Royal Theater to see *Citizen Kane* once again. While exiting the dark theater, his head filled with the lushness of Welles's cinematic triumph, Kerouac heard a paperboy yell out the headline for the afternoon *Lowell Sun,* "U.S.-Jap War On! Bomb Pearl Harbor! Heavy Loss of Life as Bombers Raid Pearl Harbor and Manila!"[2] Walking home from the cinema, Kerouac was transfixed by the "wash stiffly waving in the cold moonlight snow wash lines of Moody and Cheever." He passed a mill worker returning from his night shift, and the two "exchanged quick suspicious glances" with a "nocturnal frown and scowl." Seeking the warmth of a late-night diner, Kerouac entered and sat among the blue-collar workers talking among themselves of the latest turn of world events. Kerouac placed a coin into a nickelodeon and sat, transfixed, by his own melancholy and felt "a grand vision of America swept in triumph before me."[3] His "grand vision" began to manifest itself in a transfusion of Joyce's "involuntary unconscious visions of the truth elicited through style" and Dostoyevsky's saintly orthodox compassion. Aesthetically, Kerouac's taste for literature expanded as he slowly left behind his "natural interest" for William Saroyan.

Impulsively, Kerouac signed up for the navy's V-12 program in the Naval Air Force and waited to be called to take his exams. Seeing the *Lowell Sun* being loaded into idling trucks, Jack took Sebastian's advice and inquired about a job as a driver delivering papers. When the hiring managers found out that he was a local football star and a player at Columbia as well as a journalism student, they hired him as a sportswriter. Three days later, according to Kerouac, he found himself writing 90 percent of the sports reports while his superiors retired to the local bar. For once, Leo could hold his head up high: no longer would Jack be at the beck and call of coach Lou Little, and his son was gainfully employed with what he deemed to be an influential position. Each morning at nine o'clock Kerouac left the house, crossed the bridge toward downtown, and fulfilled his obligations as a *Lowell Sun* staff writer. However, it was a bluff of a sort: he used the job to gain access to a typewriter and continue his personal writing. His superiors by turns angered and amused him: "I began to write a novel right in the City Room about Lowell and the three attendant ills of most middlesized cities: provincialism, bigotry, and materialism."[4]

One day while typing up the previous day's sports news, Kerouac began to envision a new work, *Vanity of Duluoz,* a novel about his hometown and the "three attendant ills" he had considered in depth the past several days. The lead character was Robert Duluoz. The name Duluoz, as he later explained, is a variant of the Breton surname Daoulas, which was also that of a prevalent Greek family then living in Dracut, Massachusetts:

> DULUOZ
> Name derived from early
> morning sources
> In a newspaper office
> Long Ago in Lowell Mass.[5]

The conception of the character Robert Duluoz had deep emotional roots for Kerouac. Robert Duluoz (and ultimately his offshoot, Jack Duluoz) embodies the youthful renegade and insurgent artist that divided Kerouac. Inspired by Joyce's *Ulysses,* he began to outline a fictional narrative using a stream-of-consciousness style, letting the words reel before him as he typed. In writing the first few pages, Kerouac was aware of how closely he was imitating Joyce, yet he realized that it was not enough to ape style. To achieve sincerity in art, one had to ultimately "suffer" for it.

Kerouac's ties to James Joyce were more than his innate understanding of the musical ear that he perceived in the Irish writer's raw, earthy language and in his incorporation of the Dublin vernacular. Kerouac related strongly to Joyce's *Portrait of the Artist as a Young Man* and *Ulysses.* As Joyce loved Dublin in his own unsentimental way, so Kerouac loved provincial Lowell. Like Joyce, Kerouac attended for a short while a Jesuit school and, like the Irish modernist, was every bit the individualist loner in the recess yard. They also had in common gambling, alcoholic fathers who were partially responsible for sending their respective families into spiraling economic decline. Both the Joyces and the Kerouacs constantly moved from home to home—as many as a dozen different houses in twelve years. Kerouac's attitude toward his writing mirrored Joyce's: they shared an unwavering dedication to their craft. Kerouac intended to invent his Duluoz character as Joyce had invented Stephen Dedalus.

Lowell's economy inclined Leo to remain. With the excitement of war, newspaper sales were high. By the middle of December, the *Lowell Sun* had published a report from the city's Chamber of Commerce that the pay envelopes of the city's workers were "much fatter" than the previous month. World War II had pulled the city up from its long, steady, and seemingly irreversible decline.[6]

Lowell still housed numerous ethnic groups in buildings that, for the most part, were old and on the verge of collapse. The less-than-affluent tenants who occupied them were paid an average annual salary of $1,000; ethnicity, and not skills and experience, determined their salaries. It is largely unsurprising (and perhaps this is the origin of Kerouac's interest in socialism) that Lowell had been a nonunion city ever since the nineteenth century. The city's mill owners and not its politicians controlled city hall. According to one historian, the "irony of victory" breathed new life into the dead city, for Lowell's prosperity depended on the mounting toll of war casualties.

While his father slept, Kerouac remained awake in his cold room sipping tea and rocking in his chair. After napping for a few hours, Jack reported diligently for duty at the *Lowell Sun,* completed his work obligations, and typed his own work. Afterward, he exercised at the Lowell YMCA and, with notebook in hand, returned to the library intent on learning everything that "ever happened on earth in detail." At winter dusk he went home, ate his cold dinner, and argued with his father. This was the cyclical nature of his last days as a young man in Lowell. Sometimes after the library closed, Kerouac stayed out late with Sebastian. These were the last few times Jack was with him during Sebastian's life. They caroused throughout the night, casting long, cold shadows over the cobblestoned streets of Lowell's downtown as they crawled the taverns and bars that opened their doors on virtually every corner.

To Kerouac's dismay, the *Lowell Sun*'s editors, when they typeset his sports column, almost never gave him a byline. When they did on February 19, 1942, they did so incorrectly as "Koruac." Disenchanted with the political machinery of the city's most influential newspaper, and bored by the local sports scene, Kerouac became restless. One afternoon, scheduled to interview a baseball coach from Lowell Textile Institute, Kerouac instead stared at the walls of his bedroom ignoring the strident telephone. Incensed, Leo later approached and asked, "Did you go to Textile Institute and interview the baseball coach?" Another fight erupted. With disbelief he asked Jack if he truly thought he could "do what you feel like all your life." Jack bluntly replied, "Yes." To make matters worse, Gabrielle defended her son's aspirations at all costs even if she was not clear exactly what they were.

Kerouac had put aside his nearly completed work in progress. He now planned to make the writing of the past few weeks the first part of a trilogy of novels: part 1, *The Vanity of Duluoz;* part 2, *The Vexation of Duluoz;* and part 3, *The Joy of Duluoz.* By the second book, his character would adjust his life to art's exigencies by leaving Galloway (the pseudonym for Lowell). The process of turning his life into fiction exactly as he was living it encouraged Kerouac to become detached from the very real consequences of doing so. This creative process, in part, sanctioned Jack's angering his father to provide him with material. Inadvertently, his art became a weapon, and with it came a price: Leo later read from Kerouac's manuscript and saw the less-than-flattering portrait of him. The broadening rift between father and son threatened to become irreparable.[7] Gabrielle continued to defend Jack whenever Leo was irked enough to begin yelling at him. Abruptly, Kerouac wrote a letter of resignation to the *Sun* and made plans to hitchhike south to visit G. J. Apostolos, who had left Lowell to seek employment. He packed a duffel bag and purchased a bus ticket. Having pocketed only a small portion of earnings from the *Lowell Sun* and armed with a letter of recommendation from a newspaper columnist he knew in Boston, Kerouac decided, at last, to leave. When Jack and an unnamed "comrade" made plans for a similar trip when Jack was living in Hartford, their planned approach was straightforward:

> He and I are going to sit in a car and drive straight out to California, in about three weeks. We mapped out the journey, figuring on going through the south where it is warm and where there are weeping willow trees with moss and old level porches. I told him I wanted to spend a whole hot sunny afternoon lying beside the Mississippi River, in New Orleans, sunning, yawning, slapping off the flies, dozing, yawning some more.[8]

Kerouac met G. J. in Washington, D.C. Once there, he made it his objective to make a "casual study" of the region. As noted before, Kerouac saw that there were more blacks than in Lowell. On one awful occasion, G. J.'s construction-worker roommate turned to Jack, asking, "Hey boy, want a Nigger?" He swerved his car, pretending to hit a black man riding a bike, much to Jack's horrified objections. Kerouac empathized with the black man, knowing what it was like to be despised by other races (as did many "Canucks" of Lowell).[9]

Plunking down $10 to join the local union, Kerouac worked for one and a half months as an apprentice sheet-metal worker for the New War Department in Arlington, Virginia, on its Pentagon construction project. However, as in most past attempts at conforming to time clocks and lunch breaks, Kerouac was distracted by the world around him. He heard a "Negro laborer" walking by, with a shovel on his shoulder, "singing the loveliest blues I ever heard" and followed to listen to him sing. Before long, his idle nature seized control and Jack simply slept off the brunt of the shift until it was time to punch the clock. At other times, Kerouac walked alone far into the Virginia woods and sat among the trees. Once he ventured to cross a bridge over the Potomac River while sipping from a pint of gin. He arose one morning and hitchhiked into Virginia to spend the afternoon wandering through open fields and villages before, once again, returning in time to punch out his time card. Eventually, the foremen became aware of his extended absences and fired him. Jack took a temporary job working at a lunch cart as a soda jerk and short-order cook before planning to leave Washington. One woman at the lunch counter offered to take Kerouac in. He spent a few nights with her before moving on. In Washington he whored around with G. J. Kerouac took his $60 paycheck and finally left Washington to travel further south. He was goaded on by the "cry of a train whistle" and the vision of "drowsing" on a wharf in New Orleans. He did not stay there long before taking a bus to Massachusetts.

When twenty-year-old Kerouac returned to Lowell, he wrote Columbia coach Lou Little asking to be reinstated on the team so he could matriculate as a sophomore for the fall semester of 1942. However, he needed $400 to pay his tuition, as his scholarship status was lost temporarily because he failed chemistry. Jack also felt obligated to help his family in the way of "economic security." To compound his dilemma, the war raged on, and he felt drawn to it by duty. With the war in full throttle, Kerouac knew that he wanted to be with his "American brothers."

> I wish to take part in the war, not because I want to kill anyone, but for a reason directly opposed to killing—the Brotherhood. To be with my American brothers, for that matter, my Russian brothers; for their danger to be my danger; to speak to them quietly, perhaps at dawn, in Arctic mists; to know them, and for them to know myself . . . an elusive thing, I speak of now, but I know it is there. I want to return to college with a feeling that I am a brother of the earth, to know that I am not snug and smug in my little universe.[10]

Impulsively he walked into the recruiting office of the U.S. Marine Corps, was examined, and passed. He was sworn in and hitchhiked back to Lowell. However, he thought twice, evidently, about his patriotic fervor and chose not to honor that duty in favor of another. Some days earlier, Kerouac met a Merchant Mariner, George Murray, from Lowell and talked with him until well past daybreak. He gave Kerouac full insight into the pay and benefits that the Merchant Marine offered. When Murray returned to sea, he gave Kerouac his leather-bound copy of *The Rime of the Ancient Mariner* for good measure. Inspired by this chance meeting, Ker-

ouac once again considered the option of going to sea. Entering the headquarters of the National Maritime Union in Boston, Kerouac applied
for—and received—his overseas passport. Soon thereafter, Kerouac for-
mally enlisted in the Merchant Marines as a laborer even though he had
been sworn in as a U.S. Marine. In the Seaman's Hall in Boston waiting
for assignment, Kerouac heard over the intercom a call for a scullion on
the SS *Dorchester,* a merchant vessel making dangerous runs across the Atlantic to assist the Allied war effort. That night he lay in bed "burn[ing]"
with feeling stirred by the blood of "my ancients." He thought that
maybe, because he was "tired of dull, prosaic living," all he really was, was
just a "fool." Besides the financial benefits the Merchant Marines could
offer him, there was the fresh material he could use to give added dimension to his writing. Clearly the material gleaned from his experiences at
Columbia University and in New York City and Lowell had run its
course; he had expended most of it on *Vanity of Duluoz.* If he escaped his
"little universe" and became a "brother of the earth," he would be able to
"write and write and write about the Merchant Marine." If he never came
back from sea, then he was never destined to become a "great writer. . . .
That is why I think I shall come back."[11]

Kerouac had plans for the money he would earn. Besides being able to
pay for college, he wanted to buy his mother a fur coat, expand his personal library with the eleventh edition of the *Encyclopedia Britannica,* and
buy some classical records. He signed on with the ship yeoman as a scullion, a low-level kitchen drudge, as John Keroach (the spelling that appears on his birth certificate); his scheduled departure date was July 18,
1942.

Shortly before Kerouac's enlistment, between July 4 and July 14, 1942,
Nazi torpedo-bombers and U-boats had launched repeated, devastating
attacks on merchant ships crossing the North Atlantic. The Germans' objective was to stop Allied aid to the Soviet Union by annihilating convoys.
On July 21 the SS *Dorchester* sailed from Boston Harbor with its military
escort of U.S. Navy destroyers. It was assigned to support bases established in Bluey West in Greenland. Upon arrival, it would disembark a
large construction crew needed for wartime labor.[12]

During World War II, the role of merchant shipping was critical: it determined what the Allies could or could not do militarily. If sinkings of
Allied merchant vessels exceeded production, or if slow turnarounds and
convoy delays severely taxed the transports, the war could conceivably be
prolonged for many months. Enlistment in such vessels took courage for,

like their military counterparts, they suffered tremendous casualties. Merchant ships faced a plethora of dangers, from submarines and mines to kamikaze aircraft. By war's end nearly 7,300 mariners were killed at sea, 12,000 were wounded (of whom at least 1,100 died), and 663 men and women were taken prisoner. Thirty-one ships vanished, presumably sunk. Kerouac was either brave or naïve when he crossed the *Dorchester's* gangplank to begin his first overseas journey.[13]

The night before sailing, Kerouac was drunk in Boston's Scollay Square. In a men's room at a bar he passed out and claimed to have been "pissed and puked on all night long" by several men. The next morning he awoke, dazed and hungover, and jumped into Boston Harbor to clean himself up. To Kerouac the more than 550 crew and troops could not have been better chosen. Here was the real raw material that he needed for his art: a motley collection of races from every walk of life representing all parts of the globe. There were "drunks, Indians, Polocks, Guineas, Kikes, Micks, Puddlejumpers (Frogs, me), Svedes, Norvegians, Krauts and all the knuckleheads including Mongolian idiots and Moro sabermen and Filipinos and anything you want in a most fantastic crew." However, Kerouac intuitively sensed the "flowers of death" in their eyes; he saw that all of them, like him, faced the possibility of perishing beneath the icy waves of the North Atlantic. Another more realistic fear was that there were not enough lifejackets for the whole crew.

The SS *Dorchester* steamed north into frigid waters, heading toward the fog banks of Newfoundland. Most times, the ship was swallowed in vast banks of fog. Lookouts were stationed in the drawbridge, forecastle, and stern to watch for periscopes peering amid the swells of the Atlantic. The *Dorchester* was a rusty tub, although it did have a small version of the stairs seen in the film *Titanic*. They led from the staterooms to the dining area, merging from both port and starboard sides.[14] Inside the ship's cramped galley (thought to be too small for the many crewmen it had to feed), Jack scrubbed mountains of pots and pans. When he wasn't working, he lay in his bunk idly writing in his journal. He took note of the vast array of crew members, better than any fiction he ever read, and wrote of them in his journal. Kerouac's bunk was filled with books stacked neatly beside his clothes and toiletries. He noted that as a sailor he was too introspective; the rest of the crew seemed to prefer "embittered cursing and bawdry foolishness."

By the end of July, the *Dorchester* was steaming off the coast of Nova Scotia toward the "shrouded Arctic." Soon the ship was in the more dangerous phase of its journey; Kerouac felt a pall descend upon the crew. Though some of the men developed "torpedo fever," many played cards and craps, seemingly unmindful of the peril of the invisible U-boats, only waiting for the cry of "Here comes Jo-Jo!," the maritime term for an incoming torpedo, before they reacted at all. "How do I feel?" Kerouac wrote. "I feel nothing but dim acceptance." Outside in the cold air, he enjoyed standing bare-chested while listening to the "pulse-beats" of the *Dorchester's* screws as they turned relentlessly, pushing the vessel onward to the northeast. There was one layover in Newfoundland before the ship completed the last leg of its voyage. The seas in the straits leading to Greenland were extremely rough (making many of the crew seasick) and were filled with ice and occasional looming icebergs. In the sky the crew saw the colorful shimmer of the Northern Lights.[15]

As the journey went on, Kerouac's self-esteem began to plummet. He felt he was of relatively little worth, observing that his hands weren't "sea-netted and chapped" from being a deckhand. Rather, they were prune-fingered from "pearl-diving" in the deep stainless-steel sinks with the end-less and thankless task of scrubbing and rinsing. Around his waist he donned "greasy aprons" and felt like an "idiot" with his hair hanging in wet, sweaty strands over his dishwater-splashed face.

To ease his despair, Kerouac corresponded with friends and family. Jack wrote to Norma Blickfelt on August 25 using stationery from a Puerto Rican cook with whom he worked during the dinner shift. Although Norma, who had attended Barnard College, was only a casual romance from New York City, a woman he had dated the previous April (he had met her in 1940), Kerouac thought it best to maintain ties since he anticipated returning to New York City soon. He wrote: "If anybody tells me I am disillusioning myself, or harboring 'pretenses to a high mentality,' or even 'trying to rise from the people,' as my father claims, I'll tell them they're damned fools and will go on writing, studying, travelling, singing, loving, seeing, smelling, hearing, and feeling."[16]

Kerouac continued his intensive studies of H. G. Wells's *Outline of History*, Thomas Mann, and ancient texts by Roman writers. Kerouac felt that his "true knowledge" was coming to fruition and, more than ever, he was bursting with ambition to write new material, having abandoned *Vanity of Duluoz* for the time being. "I've left aimlessness and paradoxical chaos behind me," he wrote. Seemingly, he indulged in these studies knowing he would lose the free time to do so once he recommenced his classes and football training.[17]

After the *Dorchester* docked in Bluey West, some crew members fished with bits of tinfoil taken from the inside of their cigarette packs. Using hooks fashioned from large pins (or whatever they could find) and some string, they threw their lines into the water and almost immediately got bites from within the cold, deep water that was brimming with cod. Near where the ship docked were dozens of Danish mining engineers working a silver mine. The land adjacent to the port area was relatively flat until it steadily rose to a sizable mountain with jagged glaciers. One morning Kerouac and crew member Joe Salzano left the ship to eat dinner on the base. They saw the mountain and decided, with no experience, no gear, and even less in the way of warm clothing, to scale it. At first it was easy, although they only gained a few inches of footing at a time as they scaled the mountain. Once they reached the peak, they looked down at a floating iceberg and marveled at the bluish hue that shone through. The ship, from where they stood, looked to be only about half an inch long. Descending the mountain took them hours. They had to carefully feel for the ledges as they clung to pieces of rock. Soon it started to get dark. By the time they reached the bottom, they were severely bruised and their clothing was in shreds. As he embarked on the *Dorchester*, Kerouac was arrested. He was fined two days' pay, $5.50, for "being AWOL in a foreign port."[18]

By the side of the ship Eskimos floated in tiny kayaks trying to sell their wares to the crew members. Kerouac, having no money to buy from their collection of carved walrus tusks and ivory jewelry, traded his Horace Mann sweater for a harpoon.

On the trip back, a German submarine attacked the *Dorchester* in the Davies Strait off the Newfoundland coast. The Canadian Corvettes and U.S. Coast Guard escorts dropped depth charges and eventually drove off the German submarine. In the galley, Jack felt the booming of the charges rock the frame of the vessel.[19]

Discharged from his scullion duties in New York City on October 5, 1942, Kerouac was revitalized and eager to begin life anew on land. In his wallet he tucked a payoff of $800. He gave $300 to his mother and she kept the remaining $500 to send to Jack in installments as he needed it. He returned to Lowell with Sebastian, who had been waiting for him at the docks, and upon arrival at his parents' Crawford Street home, Jack found a telegram from Coach Lou Little waiting for him. Little invited Kerouac to return to Columbia (the advent of war and lack of full athletic scholarships had made good men for his team hard to come by). Kerouac accepted and, passing up the opportunity to board the *Dorchester* for another crossing, returned to New York. He recalled his premonition about the crew with "flowers of death" in their eyes when news of the ship's fate reached him. On its next voyage the SS *Dorchester* was torpedoed by German submarine U-223 *(Wachter)* on February 3, 1943, 150 miles west of Cape Farewell, Greenland. En route from St. John's, Newfoundland, to Narsarssuak, Greenland, and holding 751 passengers, general cargo, lumber, and sixty bags of mail, the ship went down. Only 229 survived. Several of the dead had befriended Kerouac at sea.

Intending to salvage some of the remaining weeks of the first semester, Kerouac matriculated two days after receiving Little's telegram. At Columbia, Little toyed with Kerouac once again, deciding not to use him in the starting lineup since he had lost too much weight at sea. Needing the money to survive, Kerouac again took to washing dishes, this time in the school cafeteria. To foster some sense of nobility, he enlisted in the Officers' Training Program for the Naval Reserve but quit after he was made to wear a uniform. However, his study habits did improve, possibly because he knew this might well be his last chance to complete his degree.

There were also complications with his desperate father and a promise made by Little to secure Leo a job should he get Jack to come back. Kerouac had reminded Little of his promise but did not receive a response that satisfied his father. One October Sunday Leo appeared at the college and visited Little in his office. Sitting outside the shuttered office window, Jack could hear them yelling. When his father stormed back out, he said that the "wops" were cheating them both. Leo—unable to make gains on his own without using his son as a bartering tool—let his bigotry override events, a tendency that would also plague Jack throughout his life when he was at odds with his publishers.

Kerouac reconsidered his decision to stay at school and concluded that he felt more useful when he was at sea. After all, he was "more interested in the pith of our great times" than in textually dissecting *Romeo and Juliet*. With his family in dire financial straits, and with Leo still unable to find stable employment, Jack decided to rejoin the Merchant Marine, since he shunned military uniforms.

Leo left New York City and returned to Lowell, where he finally found work with the Works Progress Administration. This job required him to travel for extended periods, leaving Gabrielle alone with Caroline, who was still working for Sullivan Printers. Employment with the WPA, though welcome, did not pay Leo well; the relatively meager earnings of $23 per week he sent home to his wife. Because of his unavoidable extended absences and his clashes with Jack, which estranged him from Gabrielle, Leo had grown apart from his family. Gabrielle "guessed" that Leo resented his distance from the family and that he was being "left out." This, Gabrielle inferred, was the root of Leo's bitterness. There was also the consideration of his "dingy" living conditions. Gabrielle advised that Jack and Caroline be "lenient" toward Leo and let him have his say "or else."

Because he had opened one of his son's manuscripts to find a less-than-flattering portrait of himself, Leo was understandably upset with Jack. Leo sent Gabrielle a news clipping he cut out of a New York newspaper that shocked her. She wrote Jack that she was "sick all day" thinking about it. She asked Jack if he was having any conflicts with his coach and, perplexed, she could not "understand the change." The cause for her perplexity was that she truly believed that Lou Little wanted Jack on the team. She suggested that Jack immediately write to his father and sent him the clipping for verification. Gabrielle didn't mention in the letter what exactly the clipping said, but she correctly inferred from it that her son had left Columbia again after having an altercation with Lou Little.[20]

Two of Gabrielle's friends, Mr. and Mrs. Nel LeGrand, had gone to New York to attend one of Columbia's games and watch Jack. They did not see him. Gabrielle was relieved when Jack wired back to her that he was fine, refusing to acknowledge to her his boiling indecision. It was Gabrielle's wish to bring her family back to Lowell for Thanksgiving; she begged Jack to make amends with Leo by writing to him. Besides, Gabrielle faced her own hardships: she had broken her two upper teeth (it would cost $115 to repair them). She also hardly had enough stamps left over from her $198-a-year war ration book and resorted to closing off part of the house to keep warm (keeping only the kitchen heated). With Jack's consent she withdrew money from his savings from his *Dorchester* voyage, bought herself two blankets, and prepared for another Massachusetts winter, which had already dropped eight inches of snow. Of utmost concern was Leo's absence, which began to affect her both financially and emotionally. Her letters to Jack were constant; she told Jack that she was only "happy" when she heard back from him via letter. Her worries became frantic when "Pop" left the house stating "whats the use of sending money here if they wont ever get up and say goodbye!"

On the road, he stopped writing her one week and finally stopped sending her money at all. She wrote Jack that the "old budget was down." She contrived to "shake" Leo "out of his grouch" by writing him that she was ill. But her concerns were grave when winter began to creep slowly in.[21]

From New York, Jack begged Sebastian to obtain seaman's papers to join the Merchant Marine. Jack was unaware that Sebastian had recently enlisted in the U.S. Army Corps and would begin his training in February 1943 at Camp Lee, Virginia, as an Army medic, a position he chose in order to avoid having to kill. To ward off being drafted himself (and being sent where he didn't want to go), Kerouac relented and applied for the Naval Air Force V-12 program.

Kerouac's disenchantment with Columbia persisted. More and more, he skipped football scrimmages because he wasn't being used at all. During the Columbia-Army game, left on the bench again, Kerouac decided to drop the sport "for good." In his dorm room as he was preparing to go to a scrimmage, Beethoven's Fifth Symphony in C minor began to play on the radio. Jack decided, "I'm gonna sit here in this room and dig Beethoven, I'm gonna write noble words." His summary was blunt, that there was "nothing more logical or less . . . logical."[22] When sports journalist Stan Isaacs saw Little at a football game in the fall of 1957, he asked the coach if he remembered Jack: "'Kerouac . . . oh, yes, a good boy. He would have been a fine football player if he hadn't got hurt. Say, what is he doing now?'" He apparently harbored little resentment over Kerouac's hasty departure.

Although Kerouac was faring well, his perpetual ambivalence wearied him with self-doubt. Writing to himself as Howard Malcolm Marton III, Kerouac derided himself as an inferior, saying that he lacked culture and was burdened with poorly chosen friends. Jack had, however, recently become acquainted with Professor Mark Van Doren. Impressed with Kerouac's interpretations of Shakespeare, Van Doren encouraged Jack to pursue his writing independent of Columbia. Another instructor gave Kerouac an A in advanced composition, making his recent studies at Columbia an academic success. Although he had tutored French and written for the *Columbia Spectator* and *Jester*, two on-campus publications, Kerouac failed to raise the funds to return for the spring semester. His only obvious recourse was to rejoin the Merchant Marine. He wrote Sebastian in the middle of November: "I personally have seen enough of the Naval Regimentation here at Columbia. . . . I don't believe I shall join the Naval Reserve. My money is running low, and my family is once more in financial straits."[23]

In January 1943, Kerouac returned to Lowell by train with his disgruntled father. While sitting in the house with his mother, who had doted on him during his recent attack of German measles, Jack waited patiently for a call from the Naval Air Force V-12 program. When the navy did call, his illness caused him to postpone for two weeks to convalesce. In the interim, he committed himself to finishing a work in progress he titled *The Sea Is My Brother,* which he had started during his *Dorchester* voyage. The work had grown from a "little novel" to a "gigantic saga," as he told his friend Bill Ryan. As he had expected, overseas travel had provided plenty of fodder. During the voyage, his attention had turned to studying the "subconscious mind and dreams" in order to incorporate them into the novel.[24] The final work would total 158 pages.

In Lowell, Kerouac wrote to Sebastian that writing now encompassed a gargantuan fourteen hours a day for the whole length of the week of his return. At 35,000 words his health collapsed. Though he felt that to continue working would threaten his health, he also realized that he had to complete the work "before the Navy gets me." To pass the time and to earn a few dollars to help his family, Kerouac got a job at a car garage on Middlesex Street. He wrote more of "The Sea Is My Brother." He also made plans to adapt a short story, "A Time for Roses," written by Lowell friend Ian McCullough, into a three-act play.

Sebastian left for boot camp shortly after the New Year and was placed in the first platoon of Company C as a private. Kerouac corresponded with him, his letters lengthier than ever because he had a typewriter at his parents' home. One early Monday morning in February, after his work shift, Kerouac wrote again to Sebastian. The letter was little more than an itemization of Jack's thoughts coupled with a grand summation of their mutual theories on socialism, class struggle, and his artistry. Kerouac intended to defy the "exploiting group in society," those cigar-smoking superiors who comprised the "collective movement." Kerouac was bolstered in his belief by his recent reading of Thorstein Veblen's *Theory of the Leisure Class* (1899). Veblen's basic thesis was "conspicuous consumption," essentially the tendency of the wealthy to maintain their position in society by "wasteful expenditures," and of the less wealthy to purchase items they don't need on the "installment plan."[25] Kerouac advised Sebastian to avoid this "weary unstopping march of the common man."[26] When he failed the altitude tests and was disqualified as a candidate for officer training, Kerouac was declared 1-A in the draft. His number was up.

Among the Philistines

March 1943–November 1944

*I know of no more encouraging fact than the unquestionable ability of
man to elevate his life by conscious endeavor.*
HENRY DAVID THOREAU

Inflamed by alcohol and his vacillating temperament, Kerouac wrote Sebastian Sampas at boot camp. His pronounced sentimentalism was com-
pounded now by his awareness of the fragility of life. Reports of the casualties of war arrived with increasing regularity via paper, radio, and film
shorts. Kerouac assured Sebastian that he would arrive at Camp Lee to see
him off before he was sent overseas should he not hear from the navy. Jack
never got that chance.

Earlier that month, Sampas had written, annoyed with Kerouac's recent letters denouncing him for not looking at things "logically" and his
slighting remarks on "Prometheanism." Kerouac felt that he and Sampas
had "accomplished more" than their other friends in Lowell who were
part of the group that discussed literature and philosophy. It was a notion
that Sebastian thought pretentious since the core of the Young
Prometheans had been sent to all corners of the world to fight the war. He
also felt that Kerouac did not understand the essence of what the
Prometheans were trying to achieve: "Maybe the picture of being misunderstood and lonely, defying all mankind, appeals to you—it doesn't to
me."[1] With that precept, Sebastian was determined not to lead a "blind
life." One evening Kerouac awoke to the sounds of his mother playing an
acetate recording mailed to Jack from Sebastian. Sampas was reading pas-

sages from Thomas Wolfe. Afterward she told Jack that it was as if Sebastian had just sounded his own "death-knell."[2] On March 15, Kerouac wrote Sebastian from Lowell: "I failed to pass the Air Corps test, as you know. I'm glad now I'm going to be a gob after reading about officers in your camp." The following Sunday, Jack was alone in his parents' Crawford Street home. Leo was working in Connecticut, and Gabrielle was visiting her stepmother in Brooklyn. Caroline had quit Sullivan Printers and joined the Women's Army Corps, leaving Jack isolated from his immediate family. At four o'clock in the morning of March 23, he wrote to Sebastian after Margaret Coffey had just left. After he kissed her goodbye and shut the door, he lit a cigarette and paced the house until he sat down to write: "Sunday morning. I shall go to church at 8 A.M. and kneel with the faithful, not for the church's sake, but for the sake of humanity. I am all alone in this silent house, tonight. The ghosts of those I love haunt me in the sorrowful stillness, not leering, capricious ghosts, but loving ghosts who touch my lonely brow with tender care." He recalled the times in Lowell when those now empty rooms had been filled with gaiety, when his friends crowded at his doorstep, when the future still glimmered with opportunity. Now that he was drafted, the outlook seemed grimmer than ever, and he wept.

> I was alone. I don't know why, Sam, but tell me: Why did I begin to weep? I tell you I wept. . . . [M]y throat constricted, I sobbed, and tears went down my cheeks. I think it was the loneliness and the thought of humanity. I tell you, I had such a vision of humanity tonight, such a clear, powerful vision (tied up with me, my loved ones, and the human race), such a vision, I tell you, as I'd never expected to see, that it broke my heart and I cried.[3]

Closer to the truth may be that Jack realized he now was helpless to change the course of his life. Less than a week later, Kerouac entered basic training as a seaman's apprentice in the U.S. Navy.

At Newport, Kerouac had little in the way of an intellectual peer; luckily, he did have his handprinted notebook of the third draft of "The Sea Is My Brother," which he worked on during off-hours.

Not long after his arrival, Kerouac was straining against the incessant demands of military discipline. The violations of his "freedoms" initially were minor. He wanted to smoke when he chose to do so, not when an officer allowed it. There were other factors as well: the numerous work details like keeping barracks watch with a gun and holster around his waist and scrubbing latrines were demeaning. Kerouac maintained a convincing front for his mother when he wrote home, leading her to believe that he was without conflict. She replied that she was "glad to know where you are and know that you are O.K. I'm also glad you like it, I was worried."[4] Even toward Sebastian he kept his reserve and stuck to their discussions about philosophy, literature, and their shared Lowell past.

In the barracks Kerouac continued to assert his disdain for the military. Sometimes he went to sick bay seeking aspirin for his headaches (which he told his mother in a letter were caused by his car accident in Vermont). On his nightly watch in the barracks—equipped with a peacoat, trousers, leggings, bowcap, and a club slung from his white belt—Kerouac would watch the rest of the men sleep. "I mind my own business," he told Sebastian, "they can have their peckers hanging out for all I care."[5] After a while, the basic training, with the navy's entrenched practice of dehumanization, disgusted him. He saw no sense in washing garbage cans and enduring the endless repetition of marching drills. One day, as the rest of the company went through its routines, Kerouac declined to handle any weapon designed to kill his fellow man. He put his gun down on the ground and walked away "from everybody forever more." He strolled to the base library to read, where military police accosted him. Kerouac surrendered, telling the guards that he simply was not equipped to complete basic training. They prodded him with questions, which Kerouac answered matter-of-factly. "You're off to the nuthouse, kid," one of the guards taunted as Jack was carted away in an ambulance.

Kerouac fired off a letter to his parents telling them of his "condition," which he surmised might have stemmed from his frantic writing of "The Sea Is My Brother." While in the hospital, he was placed under psychiatric observation, given a neurological test, and administered a written IQ exam. (He passed both, and Kerouac claimed he had the highest intelligence quotient in the history of the Newport base.) Afterward, Kerouac suspected that they had thought him a Communist. But he knew that his behavior amounted to merely a "maladjustment with military life," a fact upon which both he and interviewing psychiatrist Dr. Conrad Tully seemed to agree. Tully noted in his report:

As one somewhat defiant in accordance with his beliefs as to the rights, duties, and behavior of human beings in an organized group, and as one who follows the promptings of his conscience, one might conceivably guide his conduct, in such cases, in accordance with principles unsafe to follow under military conditions. A member of the armed forces, whether enlisted or drafted, is not considered to have the right to act differently than the military unit; individuality is subordinated to obedience and discipline. Anyone not conforming to this regimen is of no use to the organization.[6]

Kerouac saw no shame in his passive resistance and, ironically, took pride in Dr. Tully's description of him as being afflicted with "extreme preoccupation." Trying to establish a prognosis by first inquiring into Kerouac's emotional attachments, the psychiatrist questioned him further. Kerouac revealed that he "wasn't in love with any girl," contradicting his emotional letters to Norma Blickfelt in New York City and a new girl named Edie Parker, whom he had first met briefly in the fall of 1942 when she was dating Henri Cru, Kerouac's Horace Mann classmate. Jack had no plans for marriage; callously he reduced his liaisons to either "mistresses" or "various promiscuous wenches." He said that his relationships with his male friends made him feel more "closely attached," both spiritually and emotionally. In Kerouac's opinion, he was "pouring it on thick" to test the young doctor's reaction. However, Tully's reaction to his patient's statements remained neutral.[7]

With both children gone, Leo (fifty-four) and Gabrielle (fifty-eight) left Lowell for the last time as a couple and moved to New York City. However, their feuding and Leo's extended absences gave Gabrielle ideas of separating from him until he found a steady job—by no means a certain prospect, given her husband's age. Eventually, when Leo was securely employed, she moved into an apartment in Ozone Park, Queens, at 133-01 Crossbay Boulevard, near her stepmother. After a while, Leo joined her and lived out the last three years of his life in fitful insolence and fractured pride.

Initially, Jack's being drafted encouraged Gabrielle to buy into the navy's patriotic, prowar propaganda; she sent even more letters to boost his morale. But the underlying reality of Jack's personality could not be denied. Ultimately, she realized that Jack had not just temporarily run afoul of the military but that his "maladjustment" placed him firmly and entirely outside the conventions of military discipline. On May 3

Gabrielle wrote to her son inquiring, "What seems to be all the fuss out there?" In a letter Jack had asked her to attest to his "symptoms" (she had noted his hands shaking as he was drinking a cup of coffee) to the doctors.[8] It was Leo who relayed to her the news that Jack had refused to proceed with his training—or "in other words refuse to serve your country," as she stated bluntly in a letter to Jack.[9]

Leo, however, sympathized with Jack's subversive defiance of authority and lauded his courage and convictions, while Caroline expressed concern for her brother's welfare. She felt that his enlistment would be a "lot safer" for him, rather than pursuing the reckless path that he had been following for the past two years. Tired of his sister's incessant badgering, Jack did not bother replying.

Kerouac was transferred to Bethesda Naval Hospital in Maryland. Identifying himself with Dostoyevsky's Raskolnikov, a guilt-ridden Kerouac worked in his hospital room on "The Sea Is My Brother," which the naval doctors had already perused. However, Sebastian Sampas responded to Kerouac that he had "misunderstood" the novel *Crime and Punishment* and the foundation of its protagonist: "At the beginning of the book, Raskolnikov is the over-refined, polished, finished product of the Western World. It is only through great suffering that he forgets himself—his own, Razumikhin's (who was a product of the Russian earth, a friend, a brother, and who never knew the Western World) and Sonya's. In this great suffering he forgets himself."[10]

Influenced by literary and philosophical ideas that he had already encountered, Kerouac remained stoic in his decision to withdraw from the war effort. He said that it wasn't that he "[would] not accept discipline; I cannot." Ideas ranging from Thoreau's philosophy of passive resistance to Whitman's "Song of Myself" led him to delve into the core of his "extreme preoccupation." At Bethesda, Kerouac was surrounded by wounded vets and shell-shocked soldiers, and he sympathized greatly with those fallen comrades in black body bags unloaded onto the tarmac. Later in *Vanity of Duluoz*, he wrote that he "could have gained a lot out of loyal membership to that outfit." By war's end, when several close friends and casual acquaintances had perished, he would be haunted by the pall of death that seemed to plague him. (His later support for the military as embodied by the American soldier in both the Korean and Vietnam conflicts would find him once again out of step with his times.) Ultimately Kerouac realized he was in possession of "creative powers" and just needed, as he told Lowell friend John "Ian" Macdonald, "faith" in himself to fully realize his potential: "I must change my life, now, I have reached 21 and I am in dead earnest about all things. This does not mean I shall cease my debauching; you see, Ian, debauchery is the release of man from whatever stringencies he's applied to himself. In a sense, each debauchery is a private though short-lived insurgence from the static conditions of his society."[11]

Kerouac, in his introspection, began to align himself with various writers of merit. In a letter to a Lowell friend (after giving himself a "searing self-analysis" from which he determined that "Fate closes portals to us and opens others; until all are closed at Death, Fate's master-stroke") he listed books he had read and his assessment of each: Joyce's *Portrait of the Artist as a Young Man* was "the Artist as an independent soul bending to nothing"; John Steinbeck's characters from his recent book *The Moon Is Down* were "Conquerors conquered by the people"; Dostoyevsky's *Crime and Punishment* contained a "violent d.p. [dementia praecox] Raskolnikov—part schizoid—a Hamlet too destructively intelligent to live"; Hemingway's *Farewell to Arms* portrayed "War as it is—the price of love—the lost gene'rion" and *The Sun Also Rises* revealed a "sex-drive in life gone" with "bullfights for release." Kerouac's assessment of Hemingway was that he was a "supreme craftsman, investigation of American ideals on native grounds." His own novel "The Sea Is My Brother" Kerouac described as "Fate, the scheme of things, as a directing force in life."[12]

In May 1943, Sebastian Sampas still engaged Kerouac in discussions of "Western Man" and Spengler's Faustian Culture. In addition he corrected Kerouac's perception of Dostoyevsky that the Russian author was "one of ourselves." For Kerouac, this comparison was apt, for he was attuned to the philosophical profundities that Dostoyevsky's novels offered. Kerouac detected rich veins of ideas and literary techniques that he could use in his own work. There was also Dostoyevsky's insurgent fermentation of utopian socialism, nihilism, and radicalism (Dostoyevsky, like many Russian radical comrades, scorned czarist Russian society). Sebastian responded that Kerouac "misjudged the man and his goal." Sebastian's understanding derived from Oswald Spengler's *Decline of the West*:

Russians are children of another earth, not of this old earth, but seeds in a new soil. Earth-children of an unborn culture, great young souls—unfound and formless—their music, their literature, the profound melancholia of an unfulfilled Destiny and not Western man's infinite longing through individual endeavor for fame, intellect and riches for a soul that has already died; their unbelievable dynamism, the birth-pangs of a whole new world, not the death-throes of your overlived meaning.[13]

The Decline of the West would prove seminal to Kerouac's aesthetic as well as being one of the key intellectual cornerstones of the beat generation. Thus, Sebastian may be credited with alerting Kerouac to the *fellaheen*, a term derived from Spengler's concept of the "fellah-peoples," those primitive peoples that "assemble the human material of a population into groups" with "little or no alteration . . . occurring in the stamp of man."[14] Kerouac also credited Spengler with contributing to his prose style. Spengler's "blind dreamlike earth-bound existence"[15] could be argued to be a direct forebear of Kerouac's adjective-driven "wild echoing misty March night" and "invisible brooding landscape" found in *The Town and the City*.

Five days before his discharge, Kerouac wrote a short essay titled "The Wound of Living." In it he reveals perhaps part of the reason he did not pass chemistry at Columbia:

> Here I will say the foundation of my knowledge of truth rests on science; but I am forced, and willing to add that my house of knowledge, its very foundation (which is science), is set in the soil of Art, or Belief, or Beauty (or religion of the spirit), and that furthermore, Art is also my roof and shields me from neurasthenic and impossible fears that assail the scientific and unhealthy psyched minds of some men.[16]

Kerouac's aim was to write not to achieve fame but to share his "rich" and "ripe" vision of the world (as egotistical and self-driven as he knew it to be): "I may sum up and cast off confusion, by saying I see something that the world doesn't, that suggested itself to me; and was nourished by the Gants [of Wolfe's *Look Homeward, Angel*] and Dedaluses [of Joyce's *Portrait of the Artist as a Young Man*] of world culture when I realized I wasn't alone in my vision."[17] His dual personality that he wrote of on April 7, 1943, the schizophrenic "Raskolnikov–Dedalus–George Webber–Duluoz" side, countered his "normal" side; his friendship with Sebastian Sampas characterized the former side, his friendship with G. J. Apostolos the latter. Each of these comprised a "world." He knew that to succeed in realizing his unique world vision, he would have to synthesize these two and create a composite from which he could draw. Excited by this realization,

Kerouac changed the title of "The Sea Is My Brother" to "Two Worlds for a New One."

Kerouac received a medical discharge for an "indifferent character" from the navy on June 30, 1943 (making it possible for him to receive some benefits made available to World War II veterans under the brand-new G.I. Bill). He was given $50.67 upon his discharge and five-cents-a-mile travel expenses to his parents' new home in Ozone Park. He was, however, denied a veteran's pension. Kerouac reasoned to Connie Murphy that he was not "ashamed" of his "maladjustment," because he was eager to return to the Merchant Marine.[18]

Upon arrival Kerouac sent some of the smaller works he had written over the last several months to magazines; all of his submissions were rejected. Occasionally, he ventured beyond the security of Ozone Park to be with Edie Parker. In apartment 15 at 421 West 118th Street, Kerouac wasted no time in renewing his social skills, this time in the company of two women who, in part, would be responsible for introducing him to those people who would prove seminal to his artistry. Perhaps recognizing that the majority of his writings were chaff, he stopped submitting his writing (approximately half a million words' worth) to magazines and redoubled his efforts to produce quality writing that reflected his current inner state and not the fodder of his youth.

One cold day during the first month of 1944, Kerouac took to his journal, driven by the despair of his introspection:

> We are all too sensitive to go on: it is too cold, and our bodies are too exhausted. There is too much life around. The multitude is feverish and ill. There is war where men sleep on the snow, and when we waken from sleep we do not desire to go on. I hiccup very violently, twice. This is an age that has created sick men, all weaklings like me. What we need is a journey to new lands. I shall embark soon on one of these. I shall sleep on the grass and eat fruit for breakfast. Perhaps when I return, I shall be well again.[19]

In January 1944, Sebastian Sampas was one of thousands who stormed the shores of Anzio, an Italian seaside town close to Rome. At Anzio the fighting lasted for five months, until May 1944. During the relentless combat, Sebastian stuck to his poetry; two poems were published (posthumously) in *Stars and Stripes*, "Cote D'or" and "Taste the Nightbane," the latter of which is printed below in full:

> In the tortured hours like these when all looms black,
> (Unless it be the weird flame of our flak.)
> I do not weave strange scenes I'll never live to see;
> For Madame Fate with white cross spun my destiny;
> I have forgotten stardust and the sapphire gleam.
> I have remembered but your wet-eyed face
> When you did kiss me in our last embrace.[20]

The editor of the Puptent Poets section of *Stars and Stripes,* Lieutenant Ed Hill, wrote Sampas soliciting more poetry to publish. However, the request would never be answered. Shrapnel from an explosion at Anzio wounded Sebastian, who was evacuated to an offshore medical ship. On March 2, 1944, he died. In the middle of March, Kerouac mailed a farewell letter to him: "Sebastian, really, your death has never ceased making of me a damned sentimentalist like yourself. . . . You bastard, you, I shan't ever forgive you!"[21]

Kerouac had lost another important comrade and once again fell into despair. As with Gerard, the memory of Sampas would be sheltered in Kerouac's mental storehouse of grief and dispensed in his literature. By war's end, other friends of Kerouac's, like Johnny Koumentzelis and Billy Chandler, would also perish. In 1950, Stella Sampas mailed Sebastian's "old Goethean card" to Kerouac, who found it full of "valuable memories." In his thank-you letter he bleakly assured her that "we'll all be dead sometime." Sebastian was laid to rest in Lowell in the Sampas family plot of Edson Cemetery.[22]

Between 113th and 114th Streets, at 2911 Broadway, sat an unassuming building emblazoned with the words "The West End" across its exterior. It was a Columbia University replica of a Greenwich Village dive. It was divided in two with a lunchroom on one side and a long, narrow bar on the other. Diana Trilling, author and wife of Columbia's Lionel Trilling, described the place in an article for the *Partisan Review* as a "dim waystation of undergraduate debauchery on Morningside Heights." There many of the earliest participants in what would later be labeled the beat generation gathered for socializing and intellectualizing as well as for indulging in more sordid behavior.

Frankie Edith Parker, the daughter of a physician and a Grosse Pointe, Michigan, socialite, was only six months younger than Kerouac. She regularly cruised Columbia University's social circles and frequented the college bars and undergraduate hangouts. She was wired with a prodigious thirst for men, good times, and any path that promised the most radical detour from her Grosse Pointe upbringing. She studied art with George Grosz and dabbled in the curriculum until she found a major that seemed to suit her. After meeting Henri Cru at the West End Bar, she maintained a relationship with him before meeting Jack. Cru had introduced Edie to Kerouac, who began an affair unbeknownst to Cru.

Unimpressed with her antibourgeois, pseudo-bohemian ways, Kerouac instead was consumed by Edie's down-home friendliness and sexuality. It would not be long before they were having sex, sometimes doing so under the deaf ears of Edie's grandmother, with whom she lived for a while in Asbury Park. Soon Kerouac's social itinerary was established—much to the chagrin of his parents. Weekdays were spent with Edie, weekends with his parents.

Kerouac's guilt regarding his restlessness and failure to follow through weighed intensely on his mind. Despite his military discharge, he still felt a moral obligation to stand beside his fellow Americans in a time of war: "My generation . . . is making the sacrifice. It is suffering. Only through suffering does one learn love and fulfillment. I believe I am correct in saying so. My generation, my world is not lost."[23] Although he was seldom alone, Kerouac continued to feel isolated psychologically. Edie sated Kerouac's burgeoning lust, but she was no artist; despite her companionship, he was anxious to pursue his art with others. In this phase of his life, Kerouac found a new social niche that would more than fulfill this desire. In one regard, it surfaced with an intellectual incarnation of Sampas. However, he would not be Greek and not from Lowell. He was Jewish and from Paterson, New Jersey, a point of contention for Jack's anti-Semitic and xenophobic parents.

Seventeen-year-old Irwin Allen Ginsberg was born on June 3, 1926, in Newark, New Jersey. He was a Columbia University student attending on a Congress of Industrial Organizations scholarship, was knowledgeable, well read, and had already won the recognition of the prestigious trio of English professors and literary scholars Mark Van Doren, Lionel Trilling, and Raymond Weaver. Although Ginsberg had originally aspired to be a labor lawyer, the influence of these professors convinced him to switch his major to English. In a short time he was writing poetry and began to send some to the *Columbia Jester Review*. In short, he was a model student who absorbed the windy rhetoric of lectures unharmed and conversed at length with his superiors on literature, philosophy, and the arts. Ginsberg also frequented the outskirts of the campus with a select few who straddled the fine line between unbridled village bohemia and the stale polish of academia. He spent time at Edie Parker's apartment conversing with two other men who completed the friendly circle, Lucien Carr and David Kammerer. Also there was Céline Young, an admirer of Lucien's who competed for his affections with rival Kammerer (a homosexual who for several years had made unrequited advances toward Lucien). Edie's apartment was a refuge for Lucien and Céline whenever they wanted to avoid Kammerer's aggressive and intrusive behavior. Kerouac spent enough time with Edie for them to be considered lovers. Kerouac and Lucien became avid conversationalists; Lucien's all-encompassing intellect impressed him. In turn, Lucien told Allen about his new friend, stoking Ginsberg's curiosity.

In their fevered discussions in the weeks after his discharge, Lucien and Jack formulated a "New Vision" for themselves. The New Vision asserted that self-expression was both the route and summit of artistic endeavor. Using Emerson's philosophy of self-reliance, the New Vision sought to discard the limitations of traditional writing in favor of a credo of personal experience uninhibited by technique and structure.

During this time Henri Cru helped Kerouac enlist as an ordinary seaman on the Merchant Marine steam vessel SS *George Weems*, bound for Liverpool, England. While he waited to go to sea, he continued his nightlife; at the Three Deuces on Fifty-second Street, Kerouac watched Ben Webster, Duke Ellington's tenor saxophonist. He later told Edie that "no one can beat his tone."[24] A few nights after the show, on August 18, the *George Weems* left New York City.

Against the dreary rigors of shipboard life, Kerouac penned long letters to Edie; he also spent his free time reading, now concentrating on English authors Hugh Walpole and Radclyffe Hall, as well as *Heirs Apparent* by Sir Philip Gibbs (which he felt was "stupid"). He also read *The Forsyte Saga* by John Galsworthy, an English novelist and playwright whose long epic about three generations of the affluent Forsyte family comprised six novels. Kerouac took Galsworthy's idea and formulated his own version of it using his life as a backdrop. He still preferred American novelists, who he felt were superior to the British. Writing to Edie, he praised Thomas Hardy as one of the "very greatest English novelists" but not as "supremely powerful" as Herman Melville. Contrasting Hugh Walpole and John Galsworthy against Hemingway and Wolfe, Kerouac felt that there was no comparison stylistically.

In Liverpool and London, Kerouac caroused in several pubs and in London attended a concert of Tchaikovsky's music at the Royal Albert Hall. In the port of Liverpool (on September 21, 1943) Kerouac wrote a note titled "The Romanticist" on a sheet of American Republic Lines stationery. At the conclusion of a lengthy list of his accomplishments, he stated, "I have walked the streets, a lonely U.S. Navy gob, and sought women. . . . I have languished in hospitals and shuffled cards in melancholy abstraction. . . . I have written reams and reams of writings." He ended on a note of uncertainty: "And through it all, I have always been restless, unhappy, and seeking new horizons. What shall I do?"[25]

Back in port in October, Jack sought out Seymour Wyse, a friend from Horace Mann he had met through classmate Donald Wolf and a fellow jazz enthusiast, hoping that he could "get leave" and hang out with him, Edie, and Henri Cru. Wyse had introduced Kerouac to jazz. He had since joined the Canadian Air Force and, after eighteen months, returned to New York City in the early months of 1943. Upon Jack's return from sea, they went back to the jazz clubs. After the clubs closed, Jack, Edie, and Wyse loudly swapped jazz riffs in the silent city streets. Kerouac and Wyse also went to the theater to see Laurel and Hardy and Humphrey Bogart films. However, Peter Lorre's portrayal of Raskolnikov in *Crime and Punishment* (1935) had the biggest impact on them. Kerouac shared his passion for literature with Wyse, turning his friend on to Thomas Mann, Thomas Wolfe, Louis-Ferdinand Céline, and John Dos Passos.[26]

Jack had written Edie passionately from sea, telling her that he loved her and calling her a "Dostoevskian creature." Sensing the potential for hazards in Manhattan, he pleaded with her to stay out of trouble. Jack was eager to have her meet his parents (Edie met Gabrielle and Leo Kerouac when she went to their Ozone Park apartment for Jack's radio). Acting upon his conviction that Edie was the girl for him, Kerouac planned a trip to Lowell to meet his old Lowell friends Ian Macdonald and Cornelius "Connie" Murphy, a move he later regretted. His friends laughed at him after they met Edie, and Kerouac felt slighted. He was affronted by their blatant sarcasm and found it an "ordeal" to go through with his best intentions. Besides, Lowell held painful memories for him. Sebastian had died only a few weeks earlier, and he still reeled from the loss. Walking the streets of Pawtucketville he revised his "theories on human nature." Kerouac decided to turn away from Lowell and to look toward the future embodied in New York City. After leaving his hometown, he wrote to Ian Macdonald informing him that he had never trusted Connie, a stark expression of the betrayal that Jack felt. Weeks later, he assured Ian that Edie was a woman with heart and had an "admirable lack of hypocrisy." Yet, Jack told him that his plans for the next six months, despite her "anger," did not include Edie.[27]

On February 21, 1944, asthma had finally claimed Jack's favorite uncle, Leo's brother, Joseph, who died at sixty-three. He was buried in Nashua, fifty yards away from his nephew Gerard.[28]

During the winter months of 1943–1944, Kerouac found work in Warren Hall Residence Club as a switchboard operator, a job that only lasted a few weeks, for the writing of "Galloway," an early version of *The Town and the City,* consumed much of his time. By March 1944, he had written 30,000 words. Concurrently, he was composing a four-part poem titled "Supreme Reality" as well as an elegy to Gerard, "Dear Brother," which he planned to be a 150,000-word ode to "my brother, whom I have created in the image of my spirit." (It was the earliest configuration of his later published novel *Visions of Gerard.*)[29] He also attempted to rewrite the 80,000-word novel "The Sea Is My Brother" with its new working title, "Two Worlds for a New One." Another short story, "The Boy from Philadelphia," Jack loaned to Lucien Carr to submit as a term paper for a composition course at Columbia. Simmering beneath it all was his obsession with the New Vision, which Allen Ginsberg conjectured was Kerouac reacting "verbally and intuitively out of longing, but also out of a funny kind of tolerance of this universe."[30]

Ginsberg, still attending Columbia, wrote poems, modeled largely after Poe, and took part in a debating club. He also maintained an intellectually stimulating rapport with Columbia's professors. By the late spring of 1944, after Lucien's constant effusive praise of Jack's prolific writing and genuine convictions as a writer, Allen Ginsberg set out to meet Kerouac. Jack was at Edie's 118th Street apartment writing in his journal as Edie cooked him breakfast. Allen climbed the steps to the sixth-floor apartment, knocked on the door, and entered a four-room apartment. Kerouac's arms were burly, his shoulders thick. He offered Allen a beer; Allen declined with the quip, "Discretion is the better part of valor." Instead, he settled for breakfast.

Kerouac's reputation awed Ginsberg: Jack's literary output had already exceeded, by his count, one million words. Allen's rhymed and metered poetry paled in comparison, and he felt that he was brushing up against the inherited spirit of Melville or London.

After their first meeting Ginsberg and Kerouac walked through the Upper West Side. Ginsberg, moving from his room at a theological seminary, had to return one last time to retrieve some dishes. During the walk he discussed with Kerouac the infiniteness of space and their smallness within it; they spoke "about the phantomlike, ghostly nature of moving place to place and saying farewell to old apartments and rooms." They climbed the seven flights to the seminary room and got the dishes; as they descended, Allen "bowed and saluted" each door and step. Kerouac responded, "Ah, I do that, too, when I say goodbye to a place."[31] Ginsberg and Kerouac became both friends and valued literary comrades. It was a relationship that fused—by chance, not design—Emerson's principles of friendship and Walt Whitman's concept of camaraderie. When Ginsberg mentioned his intentions of becoming a labor lawyer, Kerouac countered, "You never worked in a factory. What do you know about labor or law? They're all Mafia in New Jersey anyway."[32]

A few months after meeting Kerouac, Ginsberg admitted his attraction to men and expressed his love for Kerouac (an emotion that he felt toward almost anybody at the time who appealed to him intellectually and physically). Ginsberg remembered:

At that time Kerouac was very handsome, very beautiful, and mellow—mellow in the sense of infinitely tolerant, like Shakespeare or Tolstoy or Dostoevsky, infinitely understanding. . . . [A]s a slightly older person and someone who I felt had more authority, his tolerance gave me permission to open up and talk, you know 'cause I felt there was space for me to talk, where he was. He wasn't going to hit me. He wasn't going to reject me, really, he was going to accept my soul with all its throbbings and sweetness and worries and dark woes and sorrows and heartaches and joys and glees and mad understandings of mortality, 'cause that was the same thing he had.[33]

Edie Parker understandably grew anxious, wishing Kerouac would propose. Though he continued to spend most of his time with her, his attention was occupied by his reading and writing. At Ozone Park, Gabrielle wrote Caroline to intercede, as she was alarmed at her son's nonchalant attitude toward cohabiting with Edie, as Gabrielle suspected. On July 12, 1944, Caroline wrote her brother a letter from St. Louis, where she was working as a recruiter for the Women's Army Corps. She was boarding in an apartment with L. Belle Pollard, a board of education home economics supervisor, as well as seeing a man named Paul Blake (who was a private in the army). In the letter she chastised Jack for messing around with the "wrong woman" and urged him not to make the same mistake she had made when she married Charles Morissette:

> I don't quite understand this business of you living away from home! What's the story Moe! Are you living with Edie? If so I'm terribly disappointed in you. In behaving thus, you're not being my own sweet brother who was fine, dignified and on his way-up to a bright future. That kind of living is for other people Jack dear, but not for us. We may be poor and havent always had the best but we must always have family values for Gabe and Leo. They brought us up to have high moral standards and its our duty to see that we keep them through life. For the best fortunes come to those who lead a good clean life. Believe me.[34]

To soften her harsh criticism of Jack's relations, she urged her brother to contact an acquaintance of hers from Hollywood, the film actor Lon McCallister, who was at the time working on the motion picture *Winged Victory.* Caroline told Jack that McCallister's film contacts might be of use to him, since he was interested in screenwriting, and she gave him the actor's Malibu home address. Jack never wrote, even when he was in Hollywood in September 1947, feeling that he lacked the skills to write for the screen—his strengths, he realized, lay in the descriptive novel.[35]

The summer of 1944 waned as Kerouac's fascination with his new friends who hung around Greenwich Village waxed. Edie began to realize that he was deeply preoccupied and often had no use for her or her views. His new friendships were what he needed; in February 1944, a meeting with William Seward Burroughs would be seminal.

Kerouac later described the day David Kammerer brought the wizened, gaunt Burroughs to meet Kerouac in Edie's apartment:

> [S]ee Elly [Edie Parker] was sleeping, it was the middle of the afternoon, I had just fucked her and—and I had got up, took a shower and they rang the doorbell as I was coming out of the shower, with a towel

around me. So I opened the door, and I put on my wino pants, chino pants, and they came in, and I sat on the hassock and they sat on the couch. The sun was always shining, it was always hot, into this room, the top floor of a pad, see. One hundred and eighteenth Street, and I said "Well, shipping's pretty good, Bull [Burroughs] you can go out there and you can get papers."[36]

Kerouac had heard of Burroughs from Lucien and others and had pictured him as stocky and dark-haired; he was the exact opposite. Burroughs was "tall and bespectacled and thin in a seersucker suit as tho he's just returned from a compound in Equatorial Africa where he'd sat at dusk with a martini." Kerouac sensed that his visitor was gifted with a "terrible intelligence." Later, Kerouac visited Burroughs (some nine years his senior) with Ginsberg. The seeming nobility of Burroughs and his natural grasp of literature, science, philosophy, and anthropology impressed him; he was a man who had no use for mysticism, which he said was just a "word." Rather, he was "concerned with facts on all levels of experience." Burroughs turned to his bookshelf, grabbed two books, and made a gift of each: to Ginsberg, Yeats's *A Vision,* and to Kerouac, Spengler's *Decline of the West.* "Eddify yer mind, me boy," Burroughs drawled. The triumvirate of what would become the charter members of the beat movement was now complete.

On August 14, 1944, Kerouac's life took on dimensions of a movie drama, and Gabrielle and Leo's worst fears about their son's city acquaintances were confirmed. Lucien Carr had been drinking with Kerouac and Ginsberg at the West End Café. After leaving Lucien, Kerouac saw David Kammerer on the Columbia campus. David asked where Lucien was. Kerouac pointed toward the West End and left. At the café Lucien argued with Kammerer. They left together and walked toward Riverside Park along the Hudson River. Once there, Kammerer became aggressive and made an "indecent proposal," as described by Lucien's Wall Street attorney, Kenneth M. Spence. Lucien wielded his Boy Scout knife and stabbed Kammerer twelve times. David, fourteen years older than Carr, died in his arms. Lucien removed his white shirt, tore strips from it, and with them tied stones to the corpse. After stripping completely, Lucien waded chin deep into the warm waters of the Hudson to dispose of the body. Despite being weighted with slick river stones, Kammerer's corpse did not sink. Instead, it floated face down just below the surface.

Confused, Carr first went to see Burroughs, then living in Greenwich

Village. Lucien offered him a smoke from Kammerer's bloody pack of Luckies. Flushing the cigarettes down the toilet, Burroughs implored Lucien to get himself a good lawyer, turn himself in, and plead self-defense. Carr left Burroughs and went to see Kerouac. Edie slept as Lucien told Jack what happened. Lucien asked Kerouac to go to Harlem with him so he could dispose of the evidence in his possession: Kammerer's eyeglasses and the bloody knife. In Morningside Park, Kerouac pretended to urinate into a bush while Lucien buried the glasses. They proceeded to 125th Street, where Lucien threw the knife down a sewer grate. From there, they went to Park Avenue, where Lucien confessed his crime to his psychiatrist as Kerouac sat in the waiting room. They then left, saw a war film called *The Four Feathers,* wandered the Museum of Modern Art, and finally lingered in Times Square in desperate procrastination. Planning to have his aunt call her Wall Street attorney, Lucien left Kerouac to see her. That evening, as Kerouac sat in the apartment with Edie, who did not know yet what had occurred, two plainclothes detectives knocked on the door. As soon as she let them in, they began making inquiries about Kammerer's murder. Kerouac was arrested as a material witness, being an accessory after the fact, and spent the remainder of his evening in a jail cell.

The next morning, detectives questioned Kerouac at length. Although aware of his involvement, they seemed more interested in his sexual preference. After asking if Burroughs, the other person held as a material witness, was a "homo" (Kerouac told them Burroughs wasn't), they let Jack know that Burroughs's father had bailed his son out of jail for $5,000. However, there was an air of understanding among the authorities, for the crime was considered an "honor slaying," since Lucien had been defending himself from a much older homosexual, a circumstance that would ultimately reduce the charge to first-degree manslaughter. Should Lucien prove to be homosexual, the detectives assured Kerouac, the first-degree murder charge would change the outcome of his sentence. In the waiting room of the Bronx jail, Edie was brought in for questioning along with Lucien's girlfriend, Céline Young, and Allen Ginsberg.

In the magistrate's court, Lucien and Kerouac sat side by side awaiting arraignment as rain fell furiously outside. Clutching two volumes of literature, Rimbaud's *A Season in Hell* and *A Vision* by Yeats, Lucien was anxious and scared. It was of major importance that their sexual identities be established firmly, and he stressed to Kerouac that it must be "heterosexuality all the way down the line." When Kerouac was brought before the bench, a throng of people approached and asked his name. Until now,

Kerouac had managed to keep the sordid events secret from his parents. Kerouac's naïveté and trusting nature led him to assume his questioners were legal professionals, when actually they were members of the press. By the following day, his name would find its way into the papers.

Shivering in a flimsy blanket, Kerouac slept restlessly in his cell. He was told he would not be charged as an accessory after the fact. The police gave him permission to call his father, who was then working at a Fourteenth Street printing plant. Jack told him, after describing what he was involved in, that all he needed was a $105 cash bond, set against an enormous bail, and he could go home. Leo, however, was livid and told Jack to "go to hell" before hanging up the phone. The police took Kerouac to the bottom floor of the Bellevue Morgue to identify Kammerer's body. Jack later recalled that the corpse had been blue with the color of his "spiritual torment." With morbid curiosity he also noted that Kammerer's penis was "still preserved."[37]

Back in his Bronx cell, Kerouac spent the next few days reading Aldous Huxley's *Brave New World* and W. Somerset Maugham's *Cakes and Ale*. On August 23, he wrote a poem, "The Prisoner's Song."

> Platinum blonds go shopping, their men
> are busy stealing,
> In their apartments the radio is on and
> the maid is busy sweeping
> Here, men who have killed, kill time.[38]

He also composed some brooding "Jail Notes": "The intellectually honest man is today still faced with the same problem, but to him there cannot be conceded fervour of originality, since his is the battle, lost long ago, which he must renew in the knowledge that he cannot triumph, and the [sic] which is old enough now to assume a decadent aspect."[39]

Eventually he obtained the number of a bail bondsman, yet was still unable to secure the funds from his angry father. In distress, Kerouac called Edie and asked her to borrow the money from her family. Before going to her family, she attempted to solicit the money from Lucien Carr's mother (among others). They either could not or would not help. She was careful to avoid Jack's parents, for they lumped her in with the wrong crowd that had "corrupted" their son. Before getting the money from her parents, Edie wanted to make sure Jack loved her. She made him agree to marry her. Jack promised her that they would move to Grosse Pointe to work and repay her mother. (However, he actually planned to board a merchant vessel and send her the rest of the money while at sea.) Edie consented and wired her mother, who promptly sent back $105 to set against his $5,000 bail. In the company of a plainclothes detective, Jack was taken downtown to meet Edie, who brought along Céline, who was her maid of honor (the detective was best man). Kerouac married Edie Parker on August 25, thus releasing him from one confinement into another no less binding.

The bride and groom went to Ozone Park and slept under his parents' roof as husband and wife, much to the approval of Gabrielle. The next day, Jack argued fiercely with Leo. In the next room, Edie sat at Jack's desk writing a letter to Lucien Carr complaining about the "bourgeois" mentality of her in-laws and decrying their destitution. When Leo found the letter, he scrawled his own note disparaging Edie's discontent with the social status of her in-laws.[40]

On September 1, at Edie's urging, Kerouac wrote her mother in Grosse Pointe. He stressed his willingness to resolve his debt and made it clear that he and Edie had never cohabited before their marriage: "I was aboard a merchant ship, in drydock, when the tragedy occurred. The ship was not paying, since it was in drydock, and consequently I found myself, when all this happened, broke as usual. I had counted upon my pay as a material witness, but that doesn't come until the case is disposed of— probably September 15."[41]

Edie and Jack struggled to come up with the fare to make the trip to Grosse Point; eventually Jack got the money from friends. After Labor Day they boarded a crowded train to Detroit. In a rocking carriage Jack sat opposite Edie on the coffin of an American soldier.[42]

In "the best job I ever had," a job obtained by Edie's father, Kerouac worked the midnight shift at a ball-bearing factory. He was thrilled to be working in some way toward the war effort. However, he managed his duties to his benefit and not always the job's demands. At the foreman's desk he jotted down notes and read American literary criticism. He stayed at the job through the month of September, paying back Mrs. Parker each week in $20 installments. At home Edie and her mother, anxious to see Jack as a competent husband, were alarmed that he spent most of his free time in the bathroom reading Shakespeare and the Bible.[43]

Gabrielle wrote to Kerouac on September 15, after a hurricane had slammed Long Island Sound and had drenched Manhattan in pouring squalls of rain. She enclosed a clipping about Lucien Carr's case from the *New York Post:* "Lucien Carr, 19-year-old Columbia University student, today pleaded guilty to first degree manslaughter in the fatal stabbing of David Kammerer, 33, a former teacher, of 48 Morton St., last Aug. 14."[44] On October 6, 1944, Lucien was sentenced for an indeterminate amount of time to Elmira Reformatory in upstate New York.

Kerouac had made amends with his parents, who were content to believe that his incarceration was the result of his association with Times Square miscreants: "They looked on me as an errant but innocent son victimized by decadent friendships in the evil city."[45]

They were also well aware that Jack had married into money, a fact that went a long way with Leo (who was more than eager to initiate a social acquaintance with Mrs. Parker).[46] However, Gabrielle continued to stand behind Jack. She assured Edie that with the support of a "good wife," he would become a "great" writer.[47] However, Leo had long since given up challenging his son's unrealistic aspirations. Gabrielle still believed that Jack should be pitied and loved for his errant ways and his writing ability. His irresponsibility was that of turbulent genius. She missed her boy sorely; each time she looked out her window, she expected to see him walking down the street. "I know that you don't belong to me anymore but that's life and sooner or later I'll get used to the idea."[48]

Grosse Pointe did not sit well with Kerouac, and his marriage to Edie had run its course in less than two months. There was not enough "tragedy" in Grosse Pointe, Kerouac claimed. Kerouac needed headier fodder than china plates and silk cushions. Shortly afterwards, Edie's father arranged a free truck ride back to New York. Kerouac was eager to go, for he wanted to resume work on his Galloway novel. He made tentative plans, at war's end, to go to Paris with Edie, Lucien, and Céline Young. It was his new goal, he told Ginsberg, to work hard and establish his "fortune swiftly" and buy a "decent flat" in Montparnasse. He encouraged Allen to discontinue his studies at Columbia and join him in Paris, where the "New Vision would blossom." This time, his attention shifted away from Lucien, and he alerted Allen to the differences between them:

Lucien is different, or at least, his egocentricity is different; he hates himself intensely, whereas we do not. Hating himself, as he does, hating his "humankindness," he seeks new vision, a post-human post-intelligence. He wishes more than Nietzsche prescribed, . . . I prefer the new vision in terms of art—I believe, I smugly cling to the belief, that art is the potential ultimate. Out of the humankind materials of art, I tell myself, the new vision springs.[49]

In October 1944, Kerouac boarded a merchant vessel, the SS *Robert Treat Paine*, in New York after a frantic evening of partying. For a series of nights, he made forays into the city as he waited for the day of departure. In the West End Café, two nights before leaving, he watched Céline flirt with two naval officers who thought him and Ginsberg "queer." After practicing his punches in the men's room, Kerouac asked the sailors to step outside. The ensuing fight caused him to weep on Céline's belly in Ginsberg's room later that night, ashamed of his actions. When the ship sailed, he was relieved to be at sea with the "wind, the cleanness, the dark, the quiet blue light in the bridge where hand holds wheel and course is set. The sleeping seamen below."

The chief boatswain's mate, enamored of Kerouac, pursued him aggressively. When the ship docked in Norfolk, Virginia, to load its cargo and fuel for Italy, Kerouac disembarked. He returned to New York by bus and stayed with Ginsberg at Warren Hall on the Columbia campus. He also contacted Céline and embraced her before ending their huddle with an argument. He did manage to bed her once. However, he was personally discomfited by the fact that he had discovered warts on his penis one day while he was sitting on the toilet.

Content to be left alone, he kept his whereabouts unknown to Edie and his parents. Before he left, Jack had told Gabrielle that he was sailing to the South Pacific and would not be back until the following spring. It would be his first Christmas away from the family, Gabrielle sadly noted to Edie. The hemorrhoid-stricken Gabrielle, in physical pain and despondent, wrote Edie on November 24 urging her to give Jack a "chance." She was expecting a visit from Caroline for New Year's Eve and was preparing the house for her arrival. With good intentions, she informed Edie:

I don't mind telling you dear Jack is quite irresponsible he never worked before I mean at a real job and Im afraid that will take time, he's still a young man and his career requires a lot of time before he will be able to profit by it. That's why and I guess that's where you come in, he'll need your help and more ways than one if he's to be a success. Writing is a long grind before it gets profitable. At any rate I know everything will be all-right for you two.[50]

Edie was still unaware that not only had he jumped ship in Virginia but that he had also done the same with their marriage.[51]

Kerouac was uneasy because Céline had been Lucien's girlfriend and he discerned her as a "tease."[52] During Lucien's incarceration, she flirted with Kerouac mercilessly. More often than not, she had little use for him otherwise. On October 26, 1944, she stood him up as he waited for her in a wooden booth at Flynn's Bar in the Village. Jack wrote in his notebook that he found reality, especially now, hard because he was such a sensitive person, because he was so "soft." He felt guilty because of his "ignorance" and "incapacity" to forge his life into something meaningful. Neurotically, he even found the lessons of Ecclesiastes, which he habitually read, to be too difficult to follow anymore: "Remove sorrow from thy heart, and put away evil from thy flesh: for childhood and youth are vanity." Kerouac was twenty-one now, and he felt his youth slipping rapidly behind him. With adulthood came responsibilities, and with sinning there were consequences. There was a penalty to be paid, he felt, for his narcissistic self-absorption. Although he sensed that Céline would not come that night, he still felt that her "beauty" was worth the "loss of pride." He realized that part of his problem was the harsh indigence that he endured to carve a niche for his art. He reasoned that if he had the money that he so desperately needed, perhaps he could be "saved" from his own shortcomings. Writing was easy enough, he supposed. It was making a living at it that was the problem. How could one survive in this materialistic world, yet preserve one's poetic integrity? He dreaded the bleak prospects of paying taxes at age thirty and pondered ruefully the life of a criminal and being reduced to stealing money to survive. He was in love with Céline but also knew that without work, and subsequently money, she would never want him. Once again he faced a crossroads: to lead a conventional path through life with his marriage to Edie or to pursue his art. "I have no more money, I do not want to give myself up to my family. I do not want to be lonely or to work, I cannot be practical and I cannot die and I am an apprentice nihilist."[53]

Kerouac, free from the grip of marital strife and again wandering the cool autumn streets of New York, would attempt life at the fringes of hard-core bohemia. He would pass his days jobless and broke so he could focus solely on reading and writing. In the following weeks, what he did write of substance, he burned. He cut his finger and scrawled onto a card "The Blood of a Poet" and included a quote from Nietzsche, "Art is the highest task and the proper metaphysical activity of this life," before bandaging his finger and hanging the card on the wall to remind him of his "calling."[54] "The new vision can be achieved in art. Art, commonly assumed to employ the six senses, may in itself be a sense, or system of senses, potentially capable of transmitting universal forces as yet blind and numb for the six senses."[55]

After reading Kerouac's handwritten novel "The Sea Is My Brother," Columbia professor Raymond Weaver introduced Jack to many Eastern texts. He also suggested that Jack read Emerson, Thoreau, *The Egyptian Book of the Dead,* Plotinus, Herman Melville's *Pierre,* and some samplings of Gnostic scripture. For Kerouac and Ginsberg, it was their first taste, besides the two Transcendentalists, of theological and Far Eastern writings. Kerouac also borrowed Ginsberg's library card and checked out works by Nietzsche, the Comte de Lautreamont's *Maldoror,* Aldous Huxley, Yeats, and Rimbaud. He embarked upon a series of readings drawing from many sources: sexual neo-Platonism, political liberalism, the decline of religion in the Western church, the psychological theories of Freud, H. G. Wells's humanism, and the "conflict between modern bourgeois culture and artistic culture in Thomas Mann, in Rolland, in Wolfe, in Yeats, Joyce."[56]

On November 16, Kerouac estimated his written output: "I wrote close to half a million words since 1939, when I first began to write—Poems, stories, essays, aphorisms, journals, and nine unfinished novels. That is the record—600,000 words, all in the service of art—in five years. . . . Tonight I stored away my writings of the past month, plus an unfinished novel, a total of 75,000 words, in my drawer." Again, via "Self-Ultimacy," he saw a "new vision" in which he "cravenly turned it to a use in a novel designed to gain me, the man of the world, respect, idolatry, sexual success, and every other thing that goes with it."[57]

Throughout November 1944, Kerouac was reduced to sharing potato soup out of the same bowl with Ginsberg. At night they slept in separate beds in Ginsberg's room. Their living arrangement led to problems when a local bartender reported to the dean that Ginsberg was drinking alcohol every night with Kerouac after the two stayed at the West End until well after 3 A.M.

Kerouac returned to 360 Riverside Drive, near the scene of Lucien Carr's murder, and stayed with William Burroughs, who had just returned from St. Louis after being implicated in Kammerer's murder. Burroughs found Kerouac's quest for Self-Ultimacy absurd, seeing no use for self-destruction as a means of achieving high art. Burroughs recommended instead a "bang of morphine." Under the influence of his first morphine shot, approximately ½ grain, he wrote two poems, one of which began, "Straighten your limbs or you will not become an arrow for a flight along a parallel." Kerouac sat at Burroughs's feet listening to the man pontificate his strange worldviews. He would take another "voyage to morphine" on January 19, 1945; from this experience he gathered notes dwelling on the use and misuse of Aristotle's "Logos." On Christmas 1944, Edie returned to Kerouac in New York and lived briefly in Dalton. Afterward, they moved in with Joan Vollmer, who soon thereafter took in William Burroughs as a boarder. It was an apt introduction to 1945, a year Kerouac later characterized in *Vanity of Duluoz* as one of "LOW, EVIL DECADENCE."

True Thoughts Abound

1945–Spring 1948

My debauchery I undertook solitarily, by night, covertly, fearfully,
filthily, with a shame that would not abandon me. . . . I was then
already bearing the underground in my soul.
FYODOR DOSTOYEVSKY, *Notes from the Underground*

A flood of writing by Kerouac and Ginsberg marked the new year, with
Ginsberg feeling he had written enough quality poems that he dared to
call them his "first poems of genius." Kerouac was busy collaborating with
Burroughs on a novel. Burroughs, until then, had only dabbled occasionally in writing. For this effort, they decided to alternate chapters of a dramatic rendering of the Carr-Kammerer murder, with Burroughs using the
pseudonym Will Dennison and Kerouac writing as Mike Ryko. They cast
about ideas for titles, such as "The Ryko Tourian Novel," "The Philip
Tourian Story," and "I Wish I Were You," before settling on one taken
from a radio broadcast about a fire in a London zoo: the absurdist "And
the Hippos Were Boiled in Their Tanks." It was not, as Burroughs recalled
later, a distinguished effort despite its sensational subject matter. On a
page of the novella-length manuscript, Kerouac wrote, "And the Hippos
Were Boiled in Their Tanks by Jack Kerouac & William Lee."[1] An added
benefit of Kerouac's affiliation with Burroughs was Jack's introduction to
the New York underworld of drugs, thieves, pimps, and whores:

> One of our "friends" who came in to stash a gun one day turned out,
> after he hanged himself in the Tombs some months later, to have been

the "Mad Killer of Times Square", tho I didn't know about that: he'd walk right into a liquor store and shoot the proprietor dead: it was afterward confessed to me by another thief who couldn't hold the secret he said because he hurted from holding it.[2]

Burroughs was eager to share his fascination with the underworld with his younger friend. In the seedy nest of Times Square, it was not long before Kerouac was experimenting with a wide array of drugs. He smoked some pot (first introduced to him by Lester Young in a cab, according to Edie Parker),[3] ate the soaked paper from Benzedrine inhalers, and ingested the ever-present morphine (Burroughs's drug of choice). The profuse sweating and loss of appetite from the speed caused Kerouac's weight to plummet by thirty pounds. The Benzedrine made him hallucinate and fall into depression. At one point, a redheaded woman who had contributed to his overdosing applied pancake makeup to his face. It didn't help. Kerouac's Ozone Park visits gave new reasons for Leo and Gabrielle to indict Burroughs and Ginsberg.

In January 1945, Jack declared simply in his journal: "Edie all right." Though Edie had first attempted to bond with her in-laws, she found the Kerouacs to be too provincial and Leo's fawning attempts to ingratiate himself into her privileged Grosse Pointe world (from which she was so eager to escape) pathetic. However, there was ample reason for compassion.

Leo had been diagnosed with Banti's disease, a disorder characterized by congestion and enlargement of the spleen and, for him, a harbinger of the cancer that would kill him. One symptom was progressive anemia aggravated by a bleeding esophagus, which caused recurring vomiting of dark blood. Before long, Leo was unavoidably unemployed, the relentless disappointments of his life having come full circle. Resigned and nearly vanquished, he sat at home playing the radio "full blast,"[4] waiting for death's coup de grâce. Jack lamented his father's misfortunes in *Vanity of Duluoz:* "My poor father had to see me, while dying of cancer, come down to all of this from that beginning on the sandlot football field of Dracut Tigers Lowell when the ambition was to make good in football and school, go to college, and become a 'success.'"[5]

Leo, blanched countenance and detached manner remarkably pronounced, watched his son come and go between home and Ozone Park. In tow, at times, was Allen Ginsberg or William Burroughs, both of whom Leo distrusted. Gabrielle, often ruled by her bigotry and anti-Semitism, did not like them either; she thought Ginsberg was the "devil himself." Sometimes, Leo would reluctantly discuss politics and religion with Ginsberg, whose poetic worldviews sparked Leo's disdain. Similarly, he refused to accept the legitimacy of his son's ambitions and clung to the belief that one day Jack would recognize his naïve ways and pursue more respectable work. In his father's estimate Jack appeared wanting when contrasted with his sister, who had married again (to Paul Blake). She had followed the conventional path in life, while Jack sought more exotic byways. Kerouac had his reasons, deeply rooted as they were. He reminded his sister that his life operated in "cycles, " that he tended to "flit from, say, Edie to the merchant marine, home and writing and then back again to Edie in a continuous blind circle." He reasoned to Caroline that

> my aimlessness and laziness are not just ingrained in my personality—
> they were put there by the hard nature of life when I was just four or
> five, and can be extracted again, like a bad appendix. The only thing I
> don't like about all this is that I lose self-respect, I feel as though I
> don't have a mind or will of my own. But then I realize that, well anyway, get operated on for the hell of it—because if I start to exercise my
> so-called will on my own again, it will blindly lead me back along the
> rounded rut of that circle I'm in. Gadzooks, I'm sick of that circle.[6]

In Burroughs's lay psychoanalysis of Kerouac, conducted in early 1945, he revealed that Jack simply did not want to be successful and that something destructive in his subconscious willed him to failure. Burroughs's conclusion was that Jack had hated his brother, Gerard, and had wished him dead, "and ever since, mortified beyond repair, warped in my personality and will, I have been subconsciously punishing myself and failing at everything." The failure became most pronounced, Kerouac reflected, when he first left Lowell for Columbia, and he began to exercise a "malicious and destructive will against myself."[7] The "psychoanalytical probing," Kerouac wrote in his journal, "has upset me prodigiously."[8]

Despite Jack's defiant "aimlessness and laziness" in the face of his father's disapproval, his writing continued unabated. The month that Edie returned, he wrote a poem, a story, and an essay—all from "new ideas." In February 1945, he completed his collaboration with Burroughs; an essay centering on Yeats, Nietzsche, and Blake; a short story titled "God's

Daughter"; as well as the novella *Orpheus Emerged.*[9] He and Burroughs submitted "And the Hippos Were Boiled in Their Tanks" to Simon & Schuster, which duly rejected it.

Orpheus Emerged, or The Half Jest, began as a series of notes in his January 1944 journal. Kerouac's jottings included an outline of the novella's thirteen characters, the last one being Marcel Orpheus, who is "never seen." He divided the story into ten parts. The work is critical in the Kerouac oeuvre for his first extended attempt to use his friends as pseudonymous characters as well as for incorporating elements of himself into various personas (prefiguring *The Town and the City*'s characterizations of the Martin family's brothers). Kerouac used his journal entries as fodder for criticism between the characters "Leo" and "Paul":

> "Here's the way it goes," Leo says, beginning to read. "Contemplate the universe—close your eyes—and, like God, begin to sense, without words or image, sound or shape, the impulse of all creation. This is the pure moment of God's imagination before the epileptic fit of fault and history begins."
>
> "That," interrupted Paul, "that is rather strange and I don't understand it."[10]

Orpheus Emerged is an allegorical story peppered with references to Kerouac's readings and the music he was listening to at the time; it also portrays Kerouac as both twenty-two-year-old Paul, the "genius of life and love," and twenty-two-year-old Michael, "the genius of imagination and art." According to Kerouac's notes, Michael has "suffered the wound of his calling and deliberately sold out Paul. The story concerns Paul's return and the ultimate rejoining, and the struggle with appropriate principles involved."[11] The underlying symbolism of Michael and Paul was Kerouac's attempt to portray the former as transcending "human emotions to those of God—emotions of creation, or of Eternity, etc." To do so, Michael had to discard his "human self" and strike off for the "High Regions," as Orpheus had tried to do when he ventured to the underworld in an attempt to lead his wife, Eurydice, back from the dead. In the High Regions Michael becomes "lost, lonely, and out of his element." His humanity holds him back, and he "finds that his life exists unquestionably on human terms." His "wholeness" of being is only achieved in being the "Lyre of God." Michael, in essence, embodies the "new vision" that had obsessed Kerouac for the past year. Scattered throughout are allusions to

Goethe's *Faust,* Lucretius's *On the Nature of Things,* Nietzsche's *Also Sprach Zarathustra,* Kenneth Patchen's *Journal of Albion Moonlight,* and the works of T. S. Eliot, Brahms, and Stravinsky, among numerous others. In short, this bold attempt by Kerouac is his "artist as a young man" portrayal of himself.[12]

Before beginning the typescript, he typed his name on the title page as "John Kerouac." Upon completion, he took a pencil and crossed out his first name. Above it he wrote the less formal "Jack." The novella was completed and stored with his expanding collection of manuscripts, letters, journals, and notebooks for future consideration. But Jack would find that his emerging style outstripped any real possibility of mining his juvenilia for publishable material. In a journal entry he named "Book of Symbols," Kerouac assessed his written output, categorizing it in stages. His written output was representative of his belief that he did not live by a "calendar of personal events" but by the "almanac of artistic directions." Beginning with his "Sunset at Six" short story written in Hartford, Connecticut, in October 1941, which he categorized as his "Saroyan" period, he escalated each year afterward with another stage of artistic development based upon his literary forebears: "Galloway" (an alternate, fragmentary version of the 1944 *Vanity of Duluoz*) was his Joycean period; "The Haunted Life," his Wolfean period; "I Bid You Lose Me," his Nietzschean period (neo-Rimbaudian); *Orpheus Emerged,* his post-Nietzschean Yeats period. The 40,000-word novella "Philip Tourian" belonged to the Spenglerian period of 1945; "The Sea Is My Brother," the American period (Dos Passos); "Supreme Reality," his Self-Ultimacy and "post-neurotic" periods. Kerouac felt that he had "severely misused" the "new form" of his Dos Passos period, for he opined that Dos Passos was a "truly creative artist hampered by excessive naturalism."[13]

Joan Vollmer Adams's serviceman husband, Paul Adams, had returned home to find her and her new friends strung out on drugs. Disgusted, he left, leaving her the sole guardian of the baby daughter who wasn't even his. Joan's $80-a-month, five-room apartment was huge and costly. Because she wanted to complete her degree at Columbia, she took on boarders like Edie and Jack to ease her rent woes. William Burroughs dropped his suitcases at her door, as did Allen Ginsberg and the Times Square junkie and thief Herbert Huncke. Huncke, seven years his senior, was to Kerouac the apotheosis of *beat,* the Manhattan drug-world slang for being reduced to one's essentials. Huncke's high, guttered, ecstatic, bleak existence impressed Jack. Another tenant, Haldon "Hal" Chase, a Columbia student of anthropology and a wooer of women, received Kerouac's respect for his outgoing ease and sexual prowess. The culmination of this chance gathering was the "Night of the Wolfeans," a literary discussion that split the tenants into "non-Wolfeans" (Ginsberg and Burroughs) and "Wolfeans" (Kerouac and Chase). The non-Wolfeans associated themselves with the French Symbolists, while the Wolfeans were fundamentally traditionalists. In a broader sense, the split also reflected their sexual identities, with the former pair being predominantly homosexual and the latter, heterosexual. Such literary discourses were vital for Kerouac's developing artistry. Exceptional too was his openness toward new ideas.

In March, Kerouac spent more and more time with Burroughs, sensing the "Gidean" overtones that the strange gentleman emitted. In his journal, Kerouac quoted a line by French writer André Gide that he felt epitomized the Burroughs mystique: "The bastard alone has the right to be natural." Such a line, Kerouac reasoned, "elicits a picture of the Burroughs thought." During this time, Burroughs's frequent psychoanalysis continued to upset Kerouac. In part, the intuitive Burroughs told him that his close relationship with his mother would affect him later in life.

On March 16, a perturbed Kerouac visited Ginsberg to discuss Burroughs's prediction. Kerouac had been spending more time with his mother, especially during the final stages of his father's fatal illness. In their mutual grief, Gabrielle and Jack took solace in each other's company and watched despairingly as Leo, huddled in pain in bed, waited for his stomach to be drained, his only paltry relief. Still, so unnerving was Burroughs's comment that Kerouac began to wonder whether his writing reflected his mother's ideas rather than his own. Kerouac and Ginsberg both had maternal issues, and Allen felt that Jack should at least consider Burroughs's remark. For both, maternal influences (negative or otherwise) were seminal in key portions of their writings. At seven years old Ginsberg saw his father break the glass of the bathroom door to get to his wife, who had locked herself in. In December 1941, at fifteen, Allen was forced by his mother to follow her around Paterson by bus searching for a rest home for her. The next day, Allen's father retrieved them. It was these related series of distressing events that proved seminal in Allen's artistry. His turbulent bond with his mother culminated when he signed the papers authorizing a prefrontal lobotomy the doctors ultimately prescribed to treat her severe schizophrenia. The result of this tragedy was one of Ginsberg's poetic masterworks, "Kaddish," initiated a little over one year after Naomi's death on June 9, 1956.

Kerouac had made a habit of sleeping in Ginsberg's dorm; a convenience for Kerouac despite his persona non grata status on the Columbia campus. Ginsberg had already raised Associate Dean Nicholas McKnight's ire when he had begun work on a novel centering on the Carr-Kammerer episode, with numerous references to homosexuality. The high-profile murder—centered around the Columbia campus—was an embarrassment to the university and, undoubtedly, they preferred it to be swept under the rug as soon as possible. After Ginsberg had turned in the first chapter, McKnight cited "college policy" and ordered Allen to cease writing on the subject, which he considered "smutty." McKnight also told him that his good friend Jack Kerouac was a "lout." Allen's hesitant steps toward asserting his artistic integrity would never be as daring as Kerouac's; good behavior was required to maintain his scholarship because his father, the poet Louis Ginsberg, could not afford to pay his tuition. One of Jack's former assistant coaches, Dean Ralph Furey, had recognized him one day when he had burst into Ginsberg's room and saw him leaping out of Ginsberg's bed and into his roommate's, where he pulled the blankets over his head. The crude violation of privacy was prompted when a cleaning woman had registered a complaint to the university after Ginsberg had written in the dust on his dorm windows, "Butler [president of Columbia, Nicholas Murray Butler] has no balls" and "Fuck the Jews." The latter comment was intended to antagonize the cleaning woman, whom Ginsberg perceived to be anti-Semitic (as well as neglectful of her duties). Ginsberg was ordered to leave the campus and advised to stay with his father for the weekend. He was also billed $2.63 for having an unauthorized guest. However, Ginsberg was relieved that nothing suggesting his homosexuality was ever reported to his father.

Allen eventually resided in Joan Vollmer Adams's West 115th Street apartment in late March. Burroughs was romantically entangled with Joan. Joan was attracted to Burroughs's expansive knowledge and streetwise sensibilities. Being cultured and literate (preferring James Joyce, Immanuel Kant, and Marcel Proust), she also had a visceral obsession with New York City's underworld. Her upbringing placed her squarely in the upper class, a social status against which she revolted when she married law-school student Paul Adams. He was eventually drafted, and his long absences ignited her infidelity, which resulted in the birth of a daughter. But casual sex also made her a learned lover; she once taught Edie Parker how to properly fellate a man, a lesson that no doubt pleased Kerouac.

Burroughs impressed Joan not only with his "cocksmanship" (she was aware of his homosexuality, but still thought him good enough in bed to be a "pimp") but also with his intellectual prowess. She offered him the best room in the apartment: furnished with bookcases, a desk, and a bed. Likewise impressed, Burroughs thought her the smartest of the bunch and the only one capable of inspiring him in new directions. Adams's addiction to Benzedrine caused her to experience auditory hallucinations: she imagined that she heard discussions between an older married couple in the apartment beneath them. Burroughs's descent into heroin addiction made them an ill-suited pair, united only in their despair and declining health.

Frequently, Burroughs took Joan, along with Kerouac and Ginsberg, for a tour through the gay bars in the Village, as well as through the city's dangerous and depraved underbelly, which not only excited her enthusiasm but also gave Kerouac fodder for his current works in progress. When Burroughs led Kerouac along Eighth Street, they often ended up in Kieran's and Dineen's, a bookie bar.[14]

By July 1945, Edie Parker had firmly decided to leave Jack and move to Asbury Park, New Jersey, with her grandmother, abandoning any further attempts at keeping their marriage intact. Later, Kerouac went to look for Edie. When he found her, they went to the beach with Joan. The two women festooned Jack with seashells and earrings. Subsequently Jack and Edie became painfully sunburned. Regardless of her discomfort, Jack still had plans to bed her. They took a stroll along the boardwalk; Jack assured Edie that he still loved her. He went into a drugstore to buy a condom and Noxzema. When Edie asked what he went in there for, he lied and told her he was buying aspirin. They went to Jack's motel room (across the street from Edie's grandmother) where he sensually rubbed her body down with the lotion. Once Jack was undressed, she said to him, "I knew this would happen." Afterward, Kerouac passed out and Edie returned to her grandmother's home. When Jack went to the house to pay his respects to her family the following morning, Edie came down the stairs with a painfully swollen face.[15] In his journal, Kerouac reflected on his increasing tendency to selfishly exploit women to suit his needs, physical or otherwise. It was a loathsome trait, he realized; however, it was necessary to fulfill his libido.[16]

Burroughs moved to St. Louis, where his parents lived, leaving Joan to suffer the disintegration of her addiction alone. Joan's addiction to Benzedrine became evident when her pale skin erupted in sores and hallucinatory voices began calling her a "whore" and "dope fiend." The rent on the apartment went unpaid, stolen merchandise (courtesy of Herbert Huncke) cluttered the rooms, dope paraphernalia littered the tables. Jack's altercations with her unsettled him. One day he went to the apartment to see her and Huncke:

[S]he was out of—out of her fucking mind on Benzedrine, and she came in, and she immediately stripped. I said "June [pseudonym for Joan] what are you doing?" She said "Who are you strange man, get out of this house." Standing there . . . she didn't strip . . . she, ah—Yes! [. . .] Man she *stripped!* I was sayin "I'm not a strange man June, I'm Jack." Huck [Herbert Huncke] was sleeping in what used to be Val Hayes' [Hal Chase's] bedroom, she went in there, knocked on the door, he said "Uuuh," and she goes, she says "Jack is trying to rape me, Jack is . . . bothering me, Jack is annoying me"—Huck says "Well ba-by, I don't know what to do." She said, "Well you've got to do something about him." Finally she closed the door behind her and went in to talk to Huck about it.[17]

With all her tenants gone now, Vollmer took in an array of shady characters chosen by Huncke because he deemed them responsible enough to pay the rent on time. By November, strung out and gaunt, she was picked up by the police in Times Square and brought to Bellevue for a ten-day stay. Burroughs drove back to New York in early December and retrieved her from the hospital. That night they made love, and she conceived a child, the ill-fated William Burroughs III.

With Leo Kerouac unemployed and Gabrielle struggling to keep the family solvent, Jack was finally pressured to contribute some income. In the summer of 1945 he tried valiantly to work at a summer camp, where he was hired to scrub toilets, but failed. At the urging of his parents, he came closer to home; downstairs from them was a drugstore where he worked as a soda jerk.[18]

From August through September 1945, having joined the U.S. Maritime Service, Ginsberg sent Kerouac a series of letters, with words of encouragement, critical suggestions, poetic meditations, and philosophical musings, all of which stoked the intellectual fire that Kerouac so sorely needed to create his art. During this time, Ginsberg had caught a cold that escalated into pneumonia, leading him to the Maritime Union's sick bay. The recovery left him free time to read a good portion of *War and Peace*. Completing his obligation in November after two brief stints on ships, Ginsberg was discharged and rejoined his friends.[19]

Kerouac sat at the typewriter and wrote with minimal effort, yet created nothing of any sustained quality, as he began to realize when magazines routinely rejected his frequent submissions. He was wrapped up in his own world, engrossed in his preoccupations, which he justified blazingly on September 5: "I know now, as I write this, that I shall never be allowed the favor, admiration, and love of my fellow beings—and that is because I am partly mad from my art, my god, and my princes." The path was clear, and he would take to it with no reservation about the sacrifices he would have to make to realize his art: "I dedicate myself to myself, to my art, my sleep, my dreams, my labours, my sufferances, my loneliness, my unique madness, my endless absorption and hunger—because I cannot dedicate myself to any fellow being."[20]

He still dropped Benzedrine into his coffee and, by his own account, became so addicted that the consequences, he thought, finally snared him in December 1945. While crossing the Brooklyn Bridge with Ginsberg, Kerouac collapsed. He was hospitalized in Queens. Deep within his leg blood clots had developed, and he was diagnosed with thrombophlebitis. Although Kerouac claims in *Vanity of Duluoz* that excessive Benzedrine consumption caused his phlebitis, the symptoms of such an addiction, according to current medical science, do not include phlebitis, which results from hereditary tendencies, inactivity (such as prolonged bed rest and long periods of travel in a confined space), or a traumatic injury to the legs, such as Kerouac's Columbia football injury on October 12, 1940.

In his hospital bed he brooded:

I began to understand that the city intellectuals of the world were divorced from the folkbody blood of the land and were just rootless fools, the permissible fools, who really didn't know how to go on living. I began to get a new vision of my own of a truer darkness which just overshadowed all this overlaid mental garbage of "existentialism" and "hipsterism" and "bourgeois decadence" and whatever names you want to give it.[21]

To him life was a "brute creation." The very rain that dewed the morning flower served only to hasten its death when the moisture "encouraged the bud to flower out just so's it can fall off sere dead dry."[22] Such a philosophical underpinning would color most of his fiction in the years to come.

With the help of some anticoagulant medication and a few weeks of bed rest, Kerouac was back in his parents' apartment to recuperate, more determined than ever to write something of significance. As Jack recovered, Leo reached the final stages of his illness. Because of their financial problems, Gabrielle continued working at a Manhattan shoe factory, leaving Jack to care for his moribund father in the depressing Ozone Park apartment. While keeping an eye on Leo slumped in his favorite chair, Jack sketched out an outline for his next work, a considerably longer novel in which he would explain "everything to everybody." Jack watched as doctors and nurses visited every other week and lanced Leo's belly to drain his abdomen of fluids. As Kerouac put it, his father "withered" before his eyes. On the afternoon of May 17, 1946, a Friday, after such a visit, Jack was arguing with Leo over how to brew coffee when his father asked him to "take care of your mother whatever you do. Promise me." Without another word, and before Jack could respond, Leo slumped forward in his chair. Jack assumed he was asleep; however, he never woke up. Jack, with "awful understanding," reached for his father's wrist, placed his hand on his forehead, and was surprised that it was still warm. Leo had died in his sleep at the same age as his father, Jean-Baptiste, at fifty-seven. In *The Town and the City* Kerouac would dramatize the moment:

> "You poor old man, you poor old man!" he cried, kneeling in front of his father. "My father!" he cried in a loud voice that rang with lonely madness in the empty house. He still refused to believe it, with a sense of terrible wonder he reached out and stroked his father's cheek, like a child, and the notion that now he could stroke his father's face at will because he was dead and did not know it was awful, it strangled in Peter's throat. That he could cry out and talk like that, mad and foolish, even though his father was sitting there, too flooded his brain with uncomprehending horror. Without thinking he wiped the mouth of spittle, brushed back the poor ragged hair a little, held his hand on his father's head unbelievingly, and kissed him on the forehead with a feeling of gentle crumbling relief, and madness, and fear.[23]

In 1965 Kerouac would reflect on the day when the "man who gave you hopeful birth cops out & leaves you flat with the burden (yourself) of his own folly. He sits in death almost satisfied."[24] Jack would also note that all Leo had to show for his struggles was the ink indelibly stained into his dead fingertips.

Leo Kerouac's body was brought to the city of his forebears. His wake was held on May 19; the funeral was the next day at the same church in which he had been married. Among the pallbearers were Jack, thin and out of place, and his new brother-in-law, Paul Blake. They mournfully carried the casket with some of Leo's brothers to the Saint Louis de Gonzague Cemetery to be buried in the unmarked grave where his firstborn son lay.

After Leo's funeral, Kerouac set out to transform his notes into the first truly mammoth undertaking of his career. Drawing from a number of Lowell sources, he began to create a sprawling, patchwork novel out of his chaotic past. His trips into the city, for now, became less frequent as he chose to focus his energy on the chapter layouts and plotting of his new novel. When he did venture out, he chose to stay, despite his unwanted status at Columbia, with Hal Chase at Livingstone Hall. Chase had, for a time, stayed in Joan Vollmer's apartment. Another student Kerouac met was a friend of Hal's, Ed White, who was taking classes under the G.I. Bill. (White would eventually become an architect.) White's habit of carrying notebooks around with him encouraged Kerouac to follow suit, a simple act that would be a significant factor in the evolution of Kerouac's later spontaneous prose style. After graduating from Columbia, White returned to Denver and sustained a prolific correspondence with Jack. The move also motivated Kerouac to make Denver a vital stopover during later cross-country trips as well as in his mythic account of these travels, *On the Road.*

Hal Chase also hailed from Denver. He regaled Kerouac with tales about a young man named Neal Cassady, whom Hal considered something of a mad genius. Cassady, according to Chase, had a propensity for car thefts and relentless womanizing. Son of a Larimer Street flophouse alcoholic, Neal sought his destiny and pleasures on Larimer Street and its environs. Chase had a collection of Cassady's letters from reform school, which he let Ginsberg and Kerouac read. Almost five years younger than Kerouac, Neal was brought up in a $4-a-month cubicle that he and his father shared with a double amputee. At age nine Cassady lost his virginity, and, after that, his libido knew no bounds. He had sex with everybody he could, from prepubescent girls to the elderly. Before long, his sexual identity was a blur; he would move with schizoidal ease from boy to girl and back, purely on the caprice of the moment. His car thefts matched his sexual conquests in their frequency: he stole an estimated five hundred cars (by Cassady's count) between ages fourteen and twenty-one. Cassady was a sociopath who refused to resign himself to society's conventions, preferring to ride the razor's edge of experience strictly for thrills.[25] Intrigued, Jack and Allen were eager to meet Cassady. Kerouac, though, was hot on his new project and was determined to see his manuscript through to completion.

On September 18, 1946, in Michigan, Edie Kerouac filed a decree requesting an annulment of her marriage to Jack. In the decree, Edie asked that her maiden name be restored and that Jack pay her $1:

> this provision made for the said Frankie Edith Parker herein shall be in lieu of her dower in the lands of her husband John L. de Kerouac, and he shall hereafter hold his remaining lands free, clear and discharged from any such dower rights and said provision shall also be in full satisfaction of all claims that she may have in any property which the said John L. Kerouac owns or may hereafter own, or in which he may have now or hereafter any interest.[26]

Her request was granted. (This document would later come to light when, after Kerouac's death, she again voluntarily took his last name. Edie threatened a lawsuit in an attempt to claim a portion of his estate but retracted this threat, aimed at Stella Kerouac, when this public document surfaced from Kerouac's archive.)[27]

Kerouac worked on his novel at his mother's kitchen table. It was as if Leo's death and the ensuing grief fueled Jack as he strove to realize the sweeping narrative that had been growing in his mind for several years. Impressed by his friend's determination, Ginsberg dubbed him the "Wizard of Ozone Park." Kerouac's chronicling of a mill-town family (in the thinly veiled Lowell setting he called Galloway) was full of insightful, vibrant characterizations. Some scholars theorize that the Martin family is based on Sebastian Sampas's family, who lived on Martin Street before the flood in March 1936. Each member of the Martin family evoked both a solid underlying familial bond and an individual fragility capable of splintering into conflict. Kerouac resorted to his own life for the structure of the novel as well as its characters. It would end with the death of the family's patriarch and a subsequent reunion of the Martin family. Besides the traditionalist "town" setting of Galloway there existed its polar opposite, the "city" of New York. This real-life duality, regularly encountered by Kerouac, gave him material to manipulate the English language like origami and create long bursts of colorful prose. Benzedrine and the constant bebop that he played on the radio in his mother's kitchen also helped. *Orpheus Emerged* had given him some practice in using Village friends to lend a hipster edge to the conventional narrative; such characterizations included incorporating Ginsberg into the novel as the pseudonymous Leon Levinsky. Kerouac had become equally adept at using the vernacular of Manhattan: the hipster slang, the barroom banter, the bebopper streetwise jive talk—he tuned in to it all and sought to re-create those idiosyncratic phrases and rhythms into the pages of *The Town and the City.* For Kerouac, it was a bold new direction to take in his writing, and each day he plunged into the process with renewed vigor and excitement.

In his journal, Kerouac pleaded for divine inspiration in helping him complete the novel—evidence of how deeply Catholicism had sown its seeds in him. One such entry reads:

> And what do I owe You, God, for my gifts:
> I owe you perspiration and suffering and
> all the dark night of my life:
> God I owe you godliness and diligence,
> God I owe you this blackest loneliness,
> and terrified dreams—
> but humbleness, God, I have none and
> I owe it to You: for I would have You
> reach down a hand to me, to help me
> up to You—oh I am not humble.
> Give me this last gift, God, and I will
> be humble, I will owe You humbleness,
> but only give me the gift.[28]

Before he would commit himself to a spell of writing, Kerouac prayed to Jesus Christ and read from the Holy Bible that he kept on his writing desk.[29] For further inspiration, he read Leo Tolstoy's moral essays before turning to Dostoyevsky, whose literature was (in Jack's view) more humanistic than Tolstoy's, for Dostoyevsky's writings evoked Christ while portraying man's "lust" and "glees." It was Kerouac's hope that should he successfully reconcile "true Christianity" with everyday life in America, he would do so by remembering his father, who exemplified both of these things to him.

In December 1946, Jack met Neal Cassady.

Neal Cassady Jr. was born in Salt Lake City, Utah, on February 8, 1926, to Neal and Maude (Scheuer) Cassady. A daughter, Shirley Jean, was born on May 22, 1930. In addition, Neal Jr. had five stepsiblings from his mother's previous marriage. Both his parents were in their early thirties when he was born. His father was a barber, his mother a home-maker. Shortly after Neal Jr.'s birth, the family moved to Denver, where the marriage promptly dissolved. Afterward, any stability there had been in Neal Jr.'s life all but vanished. Skid-row flophouses became the daily setting for the young boy as his father descended into alcoholism. Cassady remembered in his autobiography, *The First Third and Other Writings* (1971):

> For a time I held a unique position: among the hundreds of isolated creatures who haunted the streets of lower downtown Denver there was not one so young as myself. Of these dreary men who had com-mitted themselves, each for his own good reason, to the task of finish-ing their days as pennyless drunkards, I alone, as the sharer of their way of life, presented a replica of childhood to which their vision could daily turn, and in being thus grafted onto them, I became the unnatural son of a few score beaten men.[30]

The Denver winos, perpetually stewed on canned heat (denatured alco-hol), called the duo "the barber" and "the barber's boy." Meanwhile, the barber's former wife died in Denver in May 1936. After Neal's mother died, Neal went to live with his half-brother, Jack Daly. Neal, now twelve, was returned to his father in October 1939. Daly had married, and his wife did not like or want the boy around the house. Meanwhile, Neal Cassady Sr. was constantly being arrested for public drunkenness. On July 19, 1940, the Denver Catholic Charities filed an application on behalf of young Neal to the J. J. Mullen Home for Boys, remarking on the form that he was a "Catholic child in a non-Catholic environment." His intelligence level was listed as "high": "The school reports and adjustment of Neal in Cole Jr. High since grade 7B through 9B show a significant correlation with home conditions. On entry to Cole Jr. High, Neal was found to have an IQ of 120. He was placed in what was termed a 'core' class, that is, a group of advanced pupils."[31]

Despite his evident intelligence, Neal's grades turned dismal by the ninth grade; he had a B average in science and C's and D's for the rest of his courses. Neal was "anxious" to enter the home to improve his domestic environment but, despite the Catholic Charities' best efforts, the boy's life became increasingly peppered with criminal acts. At fourteen he stole his first car. He became a constant tenant of reform schools. In 1945, Neal met Hal Chase, who had been attending Columbia University and was already acquainted with Jack Kerouac and Allen Ginsberg. Enthusiastically, Chase shared with Neal his correspondence with Kerouac and Ginsberg, fueling the young criminal's desire to travel to New York. Neal, by this time, was married to a sixteen-year-old girl named Luanne Henderson whom he had met in a Walgreen's drugstore booth. In December 1946, driving through snow and wind, they set out for New York City in a stolen car.

In late 1946 twenty-year-old Neal and his young wife arrived in New York. Their first objective, besides a slapdash honeymoon, was to find Hal Chase and a place to live. With $35 in their pocket (left over from $300 they had already stolen), they moved into a cold-water flat in Spanish Harlem. At a Village bar with Hal Chase, they met Allen Ginsberg who was sitting with a companion. Because Allen was with someone with whom Hal was not familiar, they sat in separate booths. Neal did not see Allen again, by his own estimation, until January 10, 1947.[32]

Ed White and Hal Chase brought Kerouac with them to meet Neal. Neal answered the door nude; Jack could see Neal's teenaged bride lying on the couch trying to compose and cover herself. Kerouac's impression of Cassady was that he looked like a young Gene Autry; lean, with a raw-boned visage seemingly etched by hard living. Blue-eyed and ruggedly handsome, Cassady possessed the swagger of confidence that Kerouac knew he himself lacked. Neal's conversation sometimes bordered on gibberish and was laced with occasional pseudo-intellectual smatterings. Kerouac knew Cassady was a con, yet he felt that there was some worth to befriending him. During Kerouac's last few months of writing *The Town and the City,* he gathered notes and made journal entries about days spent with Cassady.

One night, as Gabrielle cooked for Jack, they were surprised by a knock on the door. It was Neal who had come to ask Jack to help him write. Over the course of that night they talked, and Neal revealed his scattershot chronology of his life and ambitions. It was plain to Kerouac that here was a man worth writing of. In Neal lurked various and partially formed personalities: the intellectual powerhouse, the sexual dynamo, the charismatic showman. These aspects of Cassady embodied the rush that Kerouac felt was lacking in his prose. One night, Neal's request to learn to write devolved into impatient pleas for Jack to finish his writing so that they could go out and find women. On another occasion they went out to obtain some pot; Cassady had never smoked it and was curious. They went to a woman whom Kerouac knew of on West Eighty-ninth Street, Vicki Russell, to buy some. There, they found Allen Ginsberg. Ginsberg was, by now, taken by Neal who had been raised to legendary status by Hal Chase. Neal and Allen paired off and left Kerouac "shambling" after them. Although Cassady had turned off many people in Kerouac's Village circle, clearly Jack saw something genuine and resonant that others did not.

Cassady boarded a Greyhound bus and left for the west to Denver on March 4, 1947. His short stay did not allow much time for Kerouac to get to know him. However, Jack and Neal made tentative plans to meet in the West. At home, Kerouac took a map and drew a red line from New York to Colorado, planning to follow Route 6. The most opportune time, he estimated, was in July. For now he went south to North Carolina with his mother to visit Caroline and Paul. As usual, he carried some books with him: *The Oregon Trail* by Francis Parkman, a U.S. history textbook, a biography of George Washington, and a historical account of the Revolutionary War. This expanded knowledge of America would anchor his saga, but he also deemed it necessary to experience the country, to know it like the "palm of his hand," every river, mountain, highway, and city.[33]

On June 16, 1947, Jack "made one of those great grim decisions of one's life": to hold back his manuscript from the eyes of editors and publishers until it was completed, "all 380,000-odd words of it." The work physically and mentally exhausted him, but Kerouac realized that there was honor in hard labor and sacrifice, that his "Niagara of a novel" would not simply materialize by daydreaming and windy discussions regarding writing and literature. From late afternoon to early morning, he would write and then sleep, waking by noon to continue the cycle. Generally, he completed twenty pages per sitting or, as he liked to express it, "batting .330 again." Through mid-July 1947 his writing faltered as the summer heat sapped his stamina. He socialized with Ginsberg, went to Fire Island for a break, and, when he returned, wrote a long journal entry incited by the sight of a black man shuffling along the subway. After rereading Dostoyevsky's *Notes from the Underground*, Kerouac realized that "true thoughts abound" throughout the pages of *The Town and the City*.

On July 17, 1947, Kerouac left New York to follow Route 6 as he had planned, but he found that the actual physical trek required more complicated planning than the map's simplicity intimated.

Kerouac first boarded a northbound train and, realizing his error too late, vented his frustration in his road journal. He returned to New York and bought a bus ticket to Chicago. Once he reached Chicago, he checked into a cheap room at the YMCA and spent most of the night listening to jazz in the Loop. The next day, he bummed a ride from a truck driver, who took off through the summer heat. Kerouac rode with him until they reached the Illinois state line. After several more rides, the peaks of the Rockies appeared in the west. In Shelton, Nebraska, he sent a postcard to his mother telling her that he was well fed (having eaten apple pie and ice cream for virtually all of his journey).[34] It was important to give a positive shine to his trip lest she worry unnecessarily about him. In Cheyenne, Wyoming, on July 24, he witnessed Wild West Week and was dismayed at the crass commercialism of the festivities. On July 28, Kerouac reached "clear and cool" Denver.[35] He was penniless and, by the next day, already anxious to travel to the West Coast. San Francisco was his eventual destination; there he planned to score a Merchant Marine job with his friend Henri Cru. Because he did not expect to hitchhike across the high mountains and hot deserts, he telegraphed Gabrielle, asking her to wire him $25 through Western Union.[36]

While in Denver, he visited Columbia friends such as Alan Temko, Ed White, and Hal Chase. He failed to find Neal at first, and Jack's other Denver friends, who did not like Cassady, had no idea where to find him. A new acquaintance, Bob Burford, eventually took Kerouac to them. However, Burford was less than impressed with Cassady: "I think that Jack just picked up the wrong hero in Neal. There was a character treatment, and then he exaggerated it, and he blew it out of proportion to anything that was real."[37] Through Burford, Jack was not without female companionship. He dated and bedded Burford's sister, Beverly, who remained enamored of Jack. They spent many of his Denver nights together.

Neal Cassady also had a new girl in his life. He had separated weeks earlier from Luanne, though he continued seeing her. Carolyn Robinson was blonde and comely and, according to her, it was an affair tolerated with Luanne's consent since she was doubtful her marriage to Neal would last.[38] Unlike Luanne, Carolyn was educated, having a degree from Bennington, and was pursuing a graduate degree in fine arts at the University of Denver. To woo her, Cassady used Ginsberg's love poems to him as his own. Kerouac found Cassady with Carolyn at the Colburn Hotel. Again, the girl was on the couch, and Ginsberg was hovering nearby. It was a trying week for Allen, for he was in love with Cassady and had to listen to Carolyn's panting as Neal made love to her at night. Worse, she was not the only one. Cassady confessed to Ginsberg a "fatherly concern" for Luanne, feeling that the teenager had fallen into a "complete apathy toward life" since they separated. On the other hand, Neal was disgusted with her chronic "lying," though it was a character trait he shared.[39] Eventually Ginsberg found some graveyard shift work vacuuming floors at the May Company and rented a basement-level apartment on Grant Street.

Neal introduced Carolyn to Kerouac. They shared dances with her. Kerouac's warmth, sensitivity, and simmering masculinity impressed her. His romantic, brooding nature was more to her liking than Cassady's brash ebullience, but as she and Kerouac slow-danced, he whispered in her ear, "It's too bad, but that's how it is—Neal saw you first."[40] Equally impressed with her sweetness, beauty, and talent, Kerouac went to see her perform in a play at the University of Denver. As if encouraging the relationship, Neal left the two together much of the time. He harbored a desire for a threesome, a situation that Kerouac, being modest and shy about undressing in front of others, could not carry through. While Carolyn admired Kerouac, she was shocked and disgusted by Ginsberg when she caught him nude in bed with Neal and Luanne later that summer. Horrified, Carolyn slammed the door and vowed never to see Neal again. It is a testament to Neal's charm that he not only won her favor again but also convinced her to marry him (on April 1, 1948).

To let the situation cool, Ginsberg and Cassady left Denver and went south to New Waverly, Texas, to visit Burroughs, who had moved there with Joan Vollmer Adams and her daughter, Julie. She was pregnant and now declared herself Burroughs's common-law wife. On July 21, 1947, she gave birth to William Burroughs III.

Preferring his more reliable friends like Ed White and Hal Chase, Kerouac went to Central City, Colorado, for a theater festival that summer. Kerouac saw Beethoven's opera *Fidelio,* which so moved him that it would figure prominently in *On the Road.* That night, having fully satisfied himself with the possibilities of Neal Cassady's Denver, Kerouac left for the West Coast.

Getting off the Greyhound at Market Street, Kerouac arrived in the fog of San Francisco on August 10, 1947. Before he left Denver, Neal had made plans to join him in San Francisco, but he ultimately failed to do so. Shortly after arriving, Jack became restless. He found Henri Cru, only to discover that no vessels were ready to ship out. To compensate, Cru got him a job as a security officer at a construction company. It paid $45 a week, most of which Kerouac sent back to New York for his mother. As with previous jobs, there was one benefit: the office had a typewriter that Jack could use. On it he wrote Cassady, relaying his experiences of the day, giving every minute detail, in emulation of a letter Cassady had written on his bus ride to Denver while he was stoned and drunk. Kerouac was wording his correspondence to suit Cassady's hyperactive attention span or, as Kerouac phrased it, to "maintain your neat standards of reportage."[41] For now, he lived with Cru and his girlfriend. In his room, Kerouac kept three cats and a box of kittens, sheltered in a hole in the floor. They had little money to spare, since Kerouac dutifully mailed 75 percent of his income to his mother and often had to pilfer food to make ends meet. At one point during his stay Kerouac realized his fantasy of plunging his forearm into a bucket of ice cream to eat from it after they raided a closed cafeteria.

The job soon grew tedious, and before long Kerouac enacted outrageous antics to amuse himself. Pretending to be a New York City mafioso, he waved his gun at women and later intimidated a "fag." In this disgraceful act, Jack dubbed himself "Nanny-Beater Kelly" from Chicago.[42] Over the ensuing weeks, Kerouac grew increasingly lonely and missed the company of his Denver and New York City companions. Most desperately, he missed Cassady. Writing to him, Kerouac made suggestions to help Neal hone his quick intellect into that of a writer. Jack urged him to continue reading and recommended Balzac. He also boasted to Neal of two women anxious to "fuck" him, saying he had declined. Another woman, Odessa, after whom Kerouac clamored, was more of an attraction since she was "hard to get." Manipulatively, he told her he was going to Hollywood because he knew many of the producers down there. But eventually he settled for "bang[ing]" her roommate at their apartment shortly before Odessa returned home. At San Francisco Bay, Kerouac watched Henri Cru and his girlfriend, Dianne, row around the harbor waters. Relaxed and uninhibited, she stripped naked and lay in the boat as Cru continued to row. Kerouac had always wondered if her pubic hair matched the blondness of her head. Gazing lustfully, he saw that it did and proudly wrote of his discovery to Cassady. Later Henri, Dianne, and Jack examined the ghostly remnants of an abandoned freighter, left to rust placidly at anchor in the harbor. Looking for copper to strip and sell for extra cash, Kerouac and Cru boarded the vessel. It was, Kerouac imagined, an ideal place to sleep for a few nights—if only to be amid the lonely blasts of the foghorns, to be shrouded within the dense, drifting banks of fog that blanketed the city's waters.[43]

While in San Francisco, Kerouac tried his hand at scriptwriting. Over the course of a week, he completed a draft of one script; it came to forty thousand words, which meant his efforts would hold little value for Hollywood executives with no time to wade through his voluminous descriptive prose (as William Faulkner discovered to his dismay, though he did make a small career out of screenwriting).

In early October, Kerouac left San Francisco. On the bus ride to Los Angeles, Kerouac fell in love, as he was wont to do, this time with a Mexican girl named Bea Franco. This romantic connection had its consequences, for it meant that he would miss meeting up with Neal Cassady, who was driving east from Texas with William Burroughs and Herbert Huncke to deliver some pot. (After quarreling with Cassady, Ginsberg had shipped out from Houston on a merchant ship sailing for Africa.) For over two weeks, Kerouac drifted through the sunny San Joachim Valley with Bea and her son. Later, they met up with her family, and he joined them to pick cotton for $1.50 a day before anxiously returning to his work in progress. It was October, the season that beckoned Kerouac home, because "everybody goes home in October." He left Bea, taking with him a portrait of her (which is now in the possession of the Kerouac archive). For some time afterward they maintained correspondence, but he never saw her again.

Upon arriving in New York and finding himself in the heart of Times Square, he was struck momentarily by the sharp contrast between the teeming metropolis and the lonesome, rolling, open space of America's heartland. In Ozone Park, Gabrielle remarked on Jack's gauntness but had no clue that the journey he had endured had its merits, his privations notwithstanding. In his rucksack rested the journals containing the heart of his next novel, *On the Road*.

In December 1947, turbulent and unhappy, Neal Cassady wrote to Kerouac that "something in me . . . wants to come out," something that needed to be articulated without resorting to writing, for

> words are not the way for me. . . . I have found myself looking to others for the answer to my soul, whereas I know this is slowly gained (if at all) by delving into my self only. I am not too sure that the roots of the impulse to write go deep enough, are necessary enough for me to create on paper. If, however, I find writing a must (as you've seemed to) then I know I must build my life around this necessity; even my most indifferent and trivial hours must become an expression of this impulse and a testimony to it.[44]

Cassady's ebullient extroversion was everything Kerouac yearned for. Kerouac longed to snap free of his shyness and the introversion that kept him locked out of his own instincts, to dive deeply into the crashing waves of a raw, furious life. Neal was, in a sense, Gerard, the lost brother whom Kerouac sought in vain in his friendships with Sebastian Sampas and Allen Ginsberg; one died prematurely, the other could never embody the machismo that Cassady emitted so effortlessly. He also handed Kerouac the blueprint to his emerging writing style: "I have always held that when one writes, one should forget all rules, literary styles, and other such pretensions as large words, lordly clauses and other phrases as such. . . . Rather, I think one should write, as nearly as possible, as if he were the first person on earth and was humbly and sincerely putting on paper that which he saw and experienced and loved and lost."[45] One cannot help but wonder what written work Cassady could have produced if he had dedicated himself to writing with the same unwavering focus as Kerouac, or at the very least with the same unbridled devotion with which he pursued his sexual encounters.

On January 1, 1948, Kerouac had written almost the whole of *The Town and the City*. Its length was Wolfean, a staggering 280,000 words at that point. He retyped a page of the manuscript and sent it to Neal, who responded with scant reference to it, much to Kerouac's chagrin. Allen Ginsberg visited and listened as Kerouac read the manuscript. Ginsberg told him that it was "greater than Melville," that what he had achieved was the "great American novel." Kerouac was hesitant to accept Ginsberg's grandiose assessment of his work. He regarded Allen as "just like any other human being" and that, in Kerouac's view, was what "drives him to wit's end." Reflecting on Ginsberg, Kerouac asked himself, "How can I help a man who wants to be a monster one minute and a god the next?" Ginsberg's amorous obsession with Neal annoyed Jack, yet he needed Allen to foster his artistic growth. Ginsberg was a convenient sounding board for Kerouac's ideas. He could write feverishly and send the results to Ginsberg, whose effusive encouragement buoyed the sometimes skeptical Kerouac during these important months.[46] Despite Ginsberg's concern for his friend's work, Kerouac still debated the worthiness of such associations in his journal:

> These Ginsbergs assume that no one else has seen their visions of cataclysmic emotion, and try to foist them on others. I have been a liar and a shifty weakling by pretending that I was a friend of these people—Ginsberg, Joan, Carr, Burroughs, Kammerer even—when all the time I must have known that we disliked each other and were just grimacing incessantly in a comedy of malice. A man must recognize his limits or never be true.[47]

Throughout the spring of 1948, Kerouac continued polishing *The Town and the City*. In early May, he finished the first draft and immediately began work on the earliest draft of *On the Road*, this version of which was imitative of Theodore Dreiser's naturalism. Later, Kerouac would realize that "naturalism fails to express life," that it was too studied a technique for what he had to express. Around the same time, he was inspired, oddly enough, by Lionel Trilling's refusal to recognize him on the street "in the most farcical way, as if I'd suddenly acquired leprosy and it was his rational duty to himself as a Liberal Enlightener of Intellectuals to repair at a safe distance from the area of my septic running sores." Kerouac was determined that his work would compel such people to recognize him. But even more work and self-sacrifice were required before this happened. Trilling's earlier critique of a 20-page typescript titled "God's Daughter" elicited a curt handwritten response that Kerouac was "trying to blend realism with symbolism." Van Doren's response was that the "traveler" needed a "destination."

12

Toward a New Vision

Summer–Fall 1948

I await God, hungrily.
ARTHUR RIMBAUD

Neal Cassady was much on Kerouac's mind. In principle, Neal embodied everything that Kerouac instinctively felt lacking, not only in himself but also in his characters thus far, including those found in *The Town and the City*. Although Hal Chase resembled Cassady in some ways, he was too self-destructive (according to Kerouac) and self-absorbed, too vain, to be of much use to Kerouac's artistic retrospection. However, Cassady was different; he represented a genuine, unexpurgated catalog of primal man. Although Cassady seemed a bit of a con artist, his aims were not, at least superficially, selfish. Rather, they reflected a free soul acting purely on instinct and inspiration, as unhinged as those advisers could be.

Kerouac spent most of the summer of 1948 editing and retyping sections from the first draft of *The Town and the City*. During the last week of June, he accompanied Gabrielle to Caroline's home in Rocky Mount, North Carolina, so that she could help Caroline after the caesarean birth of her son, Paul Blake Jr. The difficult birth and extended stay in the hospital racked up the medical bills, putting the Blakes deeply in debt. To Paul, Kerouac said that there were worse things than debt (something Jack knew nothing about, having had no debt in his life so far). While in North Carolina, Kerouac carried on a casual acquaintanceship with a nurse named Ann. But she was a far cry from Manhattan girls, who were more licentious, and not much ever happened between them. After a short stay in North Carolina, he returned to Ozone Park without his mother. In Gabrielle's absence, he managed the bills and cooked for himself. Selling his manuscript took precedence over all things—domestic, romantic, or otherwise. He had a contact, through his friend Ed Stringham, with the chief editor of Random House and arranged a meeting. He also renewed his Columbia contacts despite his persona non grata status with Columbia officials. Kerouac gave the manuscript to literary scholar and *New York Times* book critic Alfred Kazin. Kerouac intended Kazin to use his *own* contacts to arrange a book deal and was even resigned to accepting an advance as small as $2,000, so that he could move to California. But his plan stalled as publishers balked over the book's unwieldy length, a quality no longer in vogue with American book buyers.

Neal Cassady, who had married Carolyn after having his marriage to Luanne Henderson annulled, wrote Kerouac that he and Carolyn were expecting their first child. Cassady supported wholeheartedly Jack's idea of purchasing a ranch where Gabrielle, Jack, and the Cassadys would live. Cassady reasoned that, since Carolyn and Gabrielle were "exactly alike," they would "get on together famously." In a way, they were alike: both were domestic servants to their wayward men.[1]

Burroughs wrote to Kerouac and Ginsberg on June 5, 1948, informing them that he had been arrested in Texas for drunk driving and public indecency. Since his arrest had placed him under reasonable suspicion, he feared a raid on his farm, where a crop of marijuana grew under the hot sun. Staying in Texas would be "very uncool," he said, and for that reason alone, he prohibited Ginsberg and Kerouac from any future visits until he had established permanent residence elsewhere. He also congratulated Kerouac on the completion of his novel.[2]

Kerouac felt that Neal's affirmation of the ranch plan "solidified" their friendship. Kerouac needed that external stimulus to prod him toward achieving his goal of earning a living as a writer. Furthermore, he simply did not like to be alone. The empty apartment in Ozone Park oppressed him, as he wrote to Cassady: "Alone in the house . . . cooking, sweeping floors, washing dishes, working, sweating, sleeping, terrified dreaming, and the most yearning lonesomeness." Expressing obliquely his need for companionship, Kerouac strove to orchestrate the ranch idea to fit every aspect of his life. By living on a sprawling ranch, he would fulfill Leo's express wish that he provide for Gabrielle, he would have Neal by his side for inspiration, and he would be free to write. In Kerouac's view, "To be alone in a *house of home* is the last unhappiness. I think of it. The house is empty. It broods, it's haunted . . . all those things."[3]

Kerouac's employment prospects in California, as he informed Cassady, ran the gamut from high-paying Hollywood jobs to working as a railroad brakeman to once again shipping out to sea with Henri Cru. Never settled on any single preference, Kerouac still did not deviate from his intention to move with his mother across the country. He expected to obtain the necessary funds by selling his novel (from which he hoped to reap an income sufficient to support them both). What he feared was that Cassady would back out eventually or, worse, never commit at all. Jack hoped that they would metamorphose their first frantic letters into a body of literature that would revolutionize American culture and thought. Their partnership, Kerouac told Cassady, meant that they were destined to become the "two most important American writers someday."

Cassady did not share Jack's enthusiasm. His own writing, he told Ginsberg in a letter in May 1948, was "terrible, awful, stupid, stupid trash. . . . I see no greatness in myself." This letter's contents contrasted starkly with the bold, confident, and eager Cassady who had taken Ginsberg to his bed in Denver. Despite the praise Kerouac and Ginsberg had showered upon him, Cassady felt "simple-minded" and "child-like." He scoffed at Ginsberg's poetics. When Ginsberg wrote that he had an "image" in his mind of the "vast realistic visions you spoke of," Cassady blasted back, "bullshit." Venting his frustration at being unable to write even a single sentence after a month of steady effort, Cassady was convinced that his interests had "degenerated" so much that he was unable to understand any conversations about artists like Cézanne and Shakespeare. Included in this list was Jack Kerouac, whose writing, Neal admitted, was "beyond me."[4] Embittered, Cassady insisted that Allen was "wasting" his "time and love." Cassady's estrangement was so severe that even Carolyn and his baby were "removed from my consciousness and are on a somehow, secondary plane." Women in general were reduced to "whores." His only way out was his love of hard bebop, an affinity that he shared with Kerouac: "I become truly unaware of all bullshit in life only when I dig it." Cassady's final admonition to Ginsberg was cold and clear: "Let us stop corresponding."[5] Ginsberg felt that Cassady's letter was a "great mortal blow to all of my tenderest hopes." He had been aware that Neal's recent marriage to Carolyn and her subsequent pregnancy would ultimately exclude him. But he was accustomed to Cassady's vacillating temperament and still resolved to be a part of his life one way or another.

Ginsberg replied that the "light broke for me several times in the past week, partly owing to your letter." Of late, Ginsberg had been living a relatively calm, ascetic life, adhering to a vegetarian diet and reading Saint John of the Cross, the Bible, Plato, Saint Teresa of Avila, and William Blake. Shaken by Cassady's rebuff, Ginsberg's response was to take no offense, focus instead on his poetry, and wait for the light of inspiration to shine.[6] The inspiration first came via an auditory hallucination one evening while he lay in bed in his East Harlem apartment reading Blake and idly masturbating. From the bed, he could see the "cornices of Harlem and the sky above." After he came, he lay there pensively:

> I wasn't even reading, my eye was idling over the page of "Ah, Sunflower," and it suddenly appeared—the poem I'd read a lot of times before . . . and I suddenly realized that the poem was talking about me. . . . [S]uddenly, simultaneously with understanding it, I heard a very deep earthen grave voice in the room, which I immediately assumed, I didn't think twice, was Blake's voice.[7]

Like Kerouac, whose loneliness was mostly self-imposed, Ginsberg felt isolated. He felt the absence of Kerouac, busy retyping his novel in Ozone Park. Other friends were also distant. Herbert Huncke, though due to be released soon, was still jailed in Rikers Island. Burroughs had moved to New Orleans. Ginsberg's only other social outlet was Cassady, who resumed his correspondence with Ginsberg by August 1948.

Cassady wrote to Kerouac regularly throughout the spring of 1948 continuing to express his enthusiasm for the idea of a communal ranch or, as he phrased it, their "Shakespearean house." Though Carolyn Cassady portended her apprehension, Kerouac assured her (in his letters to Neal) not to worry. The lack of privacy mattered little to him, nor did the "unavoidable, true, and Biblical matter of female incompatibility" trouble him.

Ginsberg had taken Kerouac's finished novel to read; he returned with it on June 2, 1948, as Kerouac was finishing his dinner. Ginsberg declared that the novel's ending was "big and profound" and said he thought it would finally earn Jack his much-deserved financial success, though he thought that Kerouac wouldn't know what to do with that success. For that matter, as Kerouac noted in his journal, neither did he. Despite Kerouac's earlier suspicions of Ginsberg's assessment of his work, his attitude toward Ginsberg shifted when his assessment of the novel was positive: "The madness has left Allen now and I like him as much as ever."[8]

Kerouac's retyping of the manuscript had been hard work, but he stuck to it with fierce perseverance. By July 22, he had retyped nine hundred pages and had an estimated two hundred to go; he completely rewrote ten pages of conversation between the brothers Francis and Peter Martin. He bought a five-inch-high packing box to store the new draft in and saw, with awe, that it was not deep enough.[9]

Throughout the first half of 1948, Kerouac was "painfully lonely" for female companionship. As he typed, girls constantly passed by his apartment window and it drove him "crazy" that they remained oblivious to him. He wondered why, if a man was doing important "big work," such as his devotion to his novel, did it mean that he had to be "alone and poor" most of the time. Why couldn't he find a woman who would devote her "time and love" to him exclusively? Evaluating himself in his journal, he considered himself healthy and sexual, "riven" by an unsated desire to possess the body of every girl who crossed his path. Throughout that summer, Ginsberg hosted parties regularly in his East Harlem apartment. On July 3, Kerouac attended one (and subsequently spent over three days on a drinking binge, "squinting and sweating"). He met a "vivacious" girl, who looked, to Jack, as if she had stepped out of the lost generation; regrettably he learned later that she was sexually frigid. Awash in desire and desperation, Kerouac walked during a heat wave three and a half miles to her place, only to lie on her floor and "look out of a dream." Inner turmoil and discontent plagued him; his drinking and his weariness of the "beautiful ugliness of people" undermined his spurts of optimism. To add to Jack's misery, Herbert Huncke, recently released from prison, told him that he had declared to Edie Parker in Detroit that Kerouac still loved her. Kerouac wondered in his journal if he indeed did and concluded that maybe, regrettably, it was true.[10]

Near the end of July Kerouac went to Ginsberg's apartment for another party and met a "rose": a sixteen-year-old girl named Jinny Baker, who he felt was "weighted down by the horror of her kingdoms." She was there among the hardened Village types like Vicki Russell and Herbert Huncke. But before she left the party to go home, she made a date with

Kerouac for the next day. He stayed until late with Ginsberg, Huncke, and Vicki discussing voyages to Dakar and Panama.[11]

Jinny and Jack went to the beach, where they swam in the surf of Long Island Sound and lay in the July sun. Later, they ate dinner in his apartment and went for a walk in the "odorous darkness." After she left, he returned to the city and wandered through the Bowery, drinking beer and "thinking love-thoughts." He met Lucien Carr, drank even more, and found Ginsberg crying "because he thought nobody wanted to hear his new 'silence and transcendence' visions." Kerouac thought Allen might be going crazy.[12]

Despite the prior night's excessive drinking and the hangover that followed, Kerouac didn't mind: "I think I got drunk for the first time simply because I was happy, no other big reason, and because I was in love."[13] However, his feelings of "love" were not sufficient to dispel the summer heat that sapped him until he was "wearied by ragged literary work." Questioning his own self-worth, Jack pondered in his journal whether he was any good for anybody. His one spark of redemption, at least for now, flickered in Jinny.

> My eager gleeful girl is not a grand passion, it's a wife I shall love and live with, a girl who will allow me my soul somehow, yet love me. I was jealous of the world for awhile there and really started to hate everybody because I could not take the attention of my spirit off little Jinny Baker. I was locked up in madness of blind greedy desire and jealousy . . . "passion" in short. For me it should be something else, I fear. I fear all limitations. Allow me that fear. It is a fear of the "artist."[14]

In his journal he taped a photo of the young actress Shirley MacLaine and wrote next to it, "Jinny's exact likeness." He contemplated marriage to Jinny but feared the limitations that it would inevitably place on his writing. He continued to toil over *The Town and the City* manuscript. Otherwise, he remained young, horny, moody, and as impulsive as ever. Once when he was alone, to alleviate his randiness, Jack flicked out a hole in the ground. He dropped his pants and "fucked the earth."[15]

By the end of July 1948, Kerouac had read Dostoyevsky's *Notes from the Underground,* Conrad's *Heart of Darkness,* and Twain's *Tom Sawyer Abroad.* The sparseness of Conrad's writing style and his superb usage of personification forced Kerouac to reconsider his own work. Taking *The Town and the City*'s last chapter, he rewrote it in a more relaxed style to see how it would work. He realized that while he had used "too many words," by doing so he had let "true thoughts abound," which "nullifies the slight harm of wordiness." Nonetheless, Kerouac was prepared now to downplay his novel's message and retain the exhilarating expansiveness of his prose style. This realization was the true turning point in Jack's evolution as a writer. In his journal he disclosed that he was formulating a "new principle" in his writing. During the retyping of *The Town and the City*—after the white heat of its initial composition when the spirit of Thomas Wolfe had held him entranced—the transparency of his initial imitative technique, the structured, "wordy" style of it, struck him as a first step in the right direction rather than a final destination.

Babe Ruth's death on August 16, 1948, may mark the genesis of Kerouac's shift of ideas for his road novel. In an August 17, 1948, journal entry, Jack wonders who Babe Ruth's father was and asks who "spawned this Bunyan? What man, where, what thoughts did he have? Nobody knows. This is an American mystery."[16] This American mystery is the wellspring of all subsequent versions of *On the Road* and, to some extent, *Doctor Sax*.

The rain-swept night and America's seemingly endless stretch of new highways reaching west continued to intrigue him. For his next work Kerouac had in mind a novel about two men who hitchhike to California in search of "something they don't really find." Instead, they return to their respective hometowns hoping to find "something else." Kerouac was unclear on what that "something" was. His concept, however, was obvious. It was the gradual loss of the country he knew and his intuition that the post–World War II nation was rapidly sliding into consumerism:

> In Russia they slave for the State, here they slave for Expenses. People rush off to meaningless jobs day after day, you see them coughing in subways at dawn. They squander their souls on things like "rent," "decent clothes," "gas and electricity," "insurance," behaving like peasants who have just come out of the fields and are so dreadful tickled because they can buy baubles and doodads in stores.[17]

On August 23, Kerouac developed these ideas, as he perceived them at the time, into a story line. Stumped for a working title, he called it *On the Road*.[18]

In the first week of September 1948, Kerouac started editing selected chapters from *The Town and the City* (at one point titling it "The Soul of a Family"). This task included extracting from his 1,100-page family saga a lengthy excerpt for the perusal of publishers. He revised portions and wrote "explanatory interims." It was especially difficult for Kerouac because he felt the novel had the "sort of structure that cannot be represented in piecemeal chapters" and that those chapters chosen would have to show "the substantial elements of the theme and its main preoccupations." Although he realized that tomes of Wolfean grandeur were no longer popular, he still hoped the bulk of the novel would be preserved in its published form. That month he also began the arduous, tedious job of sending it out to publishers. He planned to shop the manuscript to the larger publishing firms in New York City: reputable houses such as Scribners (his first choice because they published Wolfe's novels); Random House; Houghton Mifflin; Knopf; Little, Brown; and Macmillan (the first to reject it).

After two and a half years of labor, Kerouac knew that he had to emerge from the "warm sweet shell of creation" into the "dusty marketsquare" to prove himself to the "world of men."[19] To help Kerouac in this endeavor, his friend Allan Temko, an architectural critic and professor, gave him a list of publishing contacts. Temko recognized Jack's talent as a writer but had no use for his friend's coterie of writers, poets, and con men. Temko could not understand why they fascinated Jack and how they served as source material for his characters. Temko recalls that Jack "thought they were America" and that Neal was Huckleberry Finn and another friend, Bob Burford, was Tom Sawyer. (Temko would appear as Roland Major in *On the Road.*)

With no word from Cassady, Kerouac began to feel distanced from him. Jack wondered if he had offended Cassady in some way, or if his friend thought he had been excluded from Jack's plans for the future. Perhaps, Kerouac noted to him in a letter, Cassady created certain "levels" into which he sorted his friends. If so, Kerouac wondered, was he "plopped . . . into one of those levels, and therefore excluded"? While this modus operandi was true for Kerouac, who categorized his own family and friends in this manner, it was not apt for Cassady, a lifelong opportunist. He had simply not needed Kerouac and company lately. During this period Ginsberg occupied himself with an ongoing study of French impressionist painter Paul Cézanne. He also attempted to write original poetry but quickly became impatient and frustrated with his efforts. His poetic sensibilities confined him (for now) to rhymed verse emulative of John Donne, William Blake, and Andrew Marvell, even while seeing potential in the free verse of T. S. Eliot and Walt Whitman. Ginsberg's frustrations went beyond the literary; without an outlet, his sexual tension built to a point where he made a pass at Kerouac in a subway station and began frequenting gay bars in Times Square, a habit that he loathed. Furious with his inability to resist, Ginsberg begged Kerouac to beat him up. Awkwardly, Kerouac declined, and they continued their relationship, tense and tenuous as it could be.

Gabrielle left again to visit Caroline, Paul, and their new baby. Her absence allowed Ginsberg to visit Kerouac in Ozone Park, an infrequent occurrence lately. Rarely tolerant of any of her son's visitors, Gabrielle singled out Ginsberg for disdain because of his Jewish ethnicity and, more than likely, his homosexuality. One friend, John Clellon Holmes (whom Kerouac met in July 1948), passed muster with Gabrielle. Holmes once remarked upon Gabrielle's extreme orderliness: "I went out there to Ozone Park. It was a very, very formalized situation. Memère was the other side of Jack wrought to its uttermost. She was very precise and very fastidious and hated disorder but was herself very irrational."[20]

Kerouac told Ginsberg that he felt "lost" in the Ozone Park apartment, as he had in July when Gabrielle had gone to Rocky Mount. Once again the parlor struck Kerouac as stark: "It broods, it's haunted." John Clellon Holmes once theorized: "Jack had no center to begin with. His center had begun to disintegrate with the death of his father and the move from Lowell, and he was looking for some kind of new center. Neal seemed to offer, not a center, but a trajectory out."[21] Attempting to fill this hollow core, this centerless center, Kerouac persisted in his daydreams about building a ranch with Cassady. But without money this was impractical. Kerouac's utopia depended upon the publication and financial success of *The Town and the City*. He wrote Cassady and told him that he was entitled to $5,000 from the G.I. loan program if he could prove that he could reap a profit from the ranch. While conspiring with Neal to parlay this possible opportunity into a guaranteed gimmick, Kerouac soon realized that he lacked the audacity required for success.[22]

Reluctant to leave the city in case a publisher should accept his novel, Kerouac gave himself till the new year for it to happen. On September 9 he received a form rejection card from Macmillan. Although it angered him, it also increased his confidence in *The Town and the City*.

I'm getting more confident and angrier each time something like this happens, because I know "The Town and the City" is a great book in its own awkward way. And I'm going to sell it. I'm ready for any battle there is. Even if I have to go off and starve on the road I won't give up the notion that I should make a living from this book: I'm convinced that people themselves will like it whenever the wall of publishers and critics and editors is torn down. It is they who are my enemies, not "obscurity" or "poverty."[23]

By October, he was impatient as his indigence became a reality: he needed money to pay rent. Kerouac wrote to his brother-in-law, Paul Blake, that he'd be visiting Rocky Mount sooner than expected. Blake offered Kerouac a job helping to run a parking lot adjacent to the annual county fair—a great opportunity to earn fast, easy money, and to see his newborn nephew. Near the end of September, Kerouac left Ozone Park and hitchhiked south for another false start, one of many to come. Leaving the city, he also left behind his romance with Jinny Baker:

The girl was sixteen, and beautiful; she wanted me to treat her rough and I couldn't do it. It seems that her mother was a martinet and she had no father, and she had the tragic sense of being left out in the cold by her two sisters who went to Paris. It's a girl looking for someone to stick pitiful needles in (her little needles are so sad). Well it hurt me to part from her—I'm still devising schemes to see her again. We had a wonderful day last summer, and nights. Looking at the thing objectively, may I suggest that our prophecy concerning 16-year-olds was in no way inaccurate. How I felt like old Karamazov himself!—(no piddling Dmitri). Shortly after that I hooked up with a woman more than twice her age, and was disgusted. Little Jinny (16) had slanted green eyes, little bangs on her brow (which perspired), a little slight body (in slacks), and a way to clinging to my bared wrists on subways and busses that was like desperation. I still don't understand it.[24]

When not helping Paul, Kerouac wrote in the Blakes' shack, which he had helped build on an earlier trip, in May 1948, as he listened to the radio. The rain never stopped (so it seemed) and the gospel singing of Mahalia Jackson from the radio depressed him. The race relations of the South also bothered him. He told Cassady in a letter that he "didn't come down here to mourn the Negro's lot, but I do."[25]

The Kerouac-Blake moneymaking enterprise was a literal washout; the rain turned the parking lot into a muddy quagmire. "Now it's all mud," he wrote to Cassady, "and I'm broke."[26] He was so "broke" that he didn't have enough money for a bus ticket home. Rocky Mount offered little to do for a twenty-six-year-old man accustomed to the debauchery of New York City and away from his archive of writings. There were the old-timers in the country store to chat with, but not much else. He tried dating (once more) the Blakes' neighbor and friend, Ann, whom he had first met in May. Although engaged to a medic, Ann had continued to correspond with Kerouac that summer. Kerouac desired her to the point of distraction, yet he hesitated to make the first move, feeling that he was unworthy of her. The sight of Ann rocking his nephew on her lap made him feel "trampish." However, he envied stability, especially the domestic kind:

> Next door, a young couple:—young wife looks like Luanne, husband like us [Kerouac and Neal Cassady] . . . he's barefooted in new hardwood house, casual, khaki pants, drinks like fish, goes to work in morning. "Luanne" listens to radio, writes letters. Great marriage. I want a girl who'll be all things. Ann may have to learn these things, see? These are my doubts. As to love, who have I ever loved? I am too insane to love anybody else but me, but I have decided to change. Therefore, I think I will chase Ann (I'm mad about her anyway) and marry her. Real, sensible, practical girl. I feel like a fool beside her, she feels "why would I want her?" Son. What a life![27]

However, Ann could not tolerate such an erratic and unstable personality, though she became another in a long line of women that Kerouac considered as potential life partners. Needing to return to his novel, Kerouac cut his trip short and left North Carolina. To appease Gabrielle, he planned to move his sister's family north to Ozone Park.

Once in Ozone Park, Kerouac enrolled in classes at the New School for Social Research with his G.I. Bill benefits—not for his edification but "only to pay the rent," he told Ed White.[28] This $75- to $90-per-month stipend gave Kerouac the time needed to hone *The Town and the City*. Writing to Cassady on October 18, he implored him to correspond more often, even though Jack knew that Neal's "sufferings" were rooted in "pure unreasonable demand arising from loneliness." Though he and Cassady were physically separated, Jack felt closer to him than ever. Kerouac praised Cassady's literary aesthetics and called him the "great Walt Whitman of this century." That afternoon Kerouac read *Leaves of Grass* (the

"Calamus" and "Children of Adam" sections) in Union Square, from the little volume that he had kept all his life. These two sections affected Jack, particularly because they represented a departure from a transcendentalist celebration of the unity of all things to a recognition of the "self" in a world of ruthless change and unfulfillment. Unwittingly, this "world" would foster the rise of the beats. Whitman's intonations coupled with Kerouac's new perspective on his life, art, and America allowed him to discover the poet's work anew. Particularly taken with passages from "Spontaneous Me," Kerouac quoted lines from it in his letter to Neal:

> Love-thoughts, love-juice, love-odor, love-yielding, love-
>   climbers, and the climbing sap,
> Arms and hands of love, lips of love, phallic thumb of love,
>   breasts of love, bellies press'd and glued together with
>   love,
> Earth of chaste love, life that is only life after love,
> The body of my love, the body of the woman I love, the
>   body of the man, the body of the earth,
> Soft forenoon airs that blow from the south-west,
> The hairy wild-bee that murmurs and hankers up and down,
>   that gripes the full-grown lady-flower, curves upon her
>   with amorous firm legs, takes his will of her, and holds
>   himself tremulous and tight till he is satisfied.

By bringing these poems to Cassady's attention, Kerouac insinuated that Cassady was Whitman's Adamic man, the sexual revolutionary who would become On the Road's star attraction. Recently released passages from the On the Road journals reveal the erratic path of the novel's development and strongly imply that Kerouac was awash in romantic ideas about art and artists; that he owed his vision to no one philosophy, person, or event in particular, but rather to a broad confluence of ideas and events, though certainly the Whitman-Cassady idealism and enthusiasm stimulated Kerouac's new shift in characterization. Whitman was, to Kerouac, a literary figure "greater than Melville." He was Shakespeare's equal as a "bard of the humans," a poet of the intellect, a prophet who wrote in "waves of verse" and celebrated the "holiness of the body." Kerouac quoted with evident relish to Cassady: "Oh furious! O confine me not!"[29]

Kerouac was relieved to be back in the city, at least in Manhattan where he was never at a loss for things to do. In mid-October, Kerouac attended a Lennie Tristano concert with David Diamond. As usual, Jack roamed a never-ending circuit of parties hosted by friends. Feeling "utterly sad and lost," he spent part of his time searching for Hal Chase. Chase had kept his new address from Kerouac, but Jack was determined to find him. He was eager to invite Chase and Jack Fitzgerald to join him on his planned trip.

In October and November 1948, Kerouac sketched out three novel-length works. One, "The Imbecile's Christmas," which never came to fruition, concerns an "Imbecile," based loosely on himself, who invests faith in "everybody" and "everything." The Imbecile passes no judgment on his fellow man and has no means of transportation other than relying on others for rides. Like Kerouac, the Imbecile cannot drive a car.

The other two works, pure Americana, were developed in part from his recent academic course on the American novel, in which he studied the techniques of novelists like John Dos Passos, Thomas Wolfe, Theodore Dreiser, and Sinclair Lewis. In October 1948 he outlined what was to become *Doctor Sax* in his journal with its alternate title, "Myth of the Rainy Night." *Doctor Sax* explores the "American myth" and its relationship to children. Kerouac's obsession with this myth embraced the recurring rains that descended to earth and ascended as fog and vapor into the atmo-sphere, baptismal associations, the flowing of the river. Based on his Lowell adolescence, the nonlinear plot concerns childhood, "concentrations of evil," "glee," "townspeople," and "mysterious occurrences"—all placed against a metaphysical backdrop. Kerouac would later shed its naturalistic elements in favor of a postmodernistic flavor. *Doctor Sax*'s plot would ultimately climax with the 1936 flooding of the Merrimack River. However, after an earnest start, Kerouac shelved *Doctor Sax,* eager to begin *On the Road.*

In November 1948, Kerouac outlined his road novel idea, which had been percolating in his mind for months. To Kerouac, this "American-scene picaresque" would detail the arduous realities of road travel, of hitchhiking the American dark highways, of the "sorrows," "hardships," "adventures," "sweats and labors" of being an American writer searching for identity. This theme consumed him so much that he felt unable to conceal it from strangers whom he accosted drunkenly in bars.

Kerouac's attempts to write these three works coincided with his courses at the New School for Social Research, an institution founded in 1919 that stressed a radical alternative to higher education. Located near

Greenwich Village on 66 West Twelfth Street, the New School was known as a refuge for European intelligentsia fleeing the Second World War. Kerouac observed bitterly that "ugly Jewesses and generally ugly intellectuals" made him "sick." He resented the "baldfaced" educators who incorporated "Marxian overtones and under-rumblings" into their lectures on the literary canon. The influx of soldiers seeking education from institutions such as the New School aggravated the existing tensions between the privileged upper class and those underprivileged who attended by the grace of the G.I. Bill. This fostered snobbery. Kerouac—the seemingly provincial Lowellian hayseed—was only the most obvious embodiment of this new breed of intellectual outcast, a fact that perhaps explains in part his intense disgust with the New School's administration and its curriculum: "The New School is a battleground for European ideas-of-disintegration, as you already know, but direct constant experience of it gives me a fresh feeling of mistrust and loathing."[30] As bitter as his diatribe toward the school was, Kerouac made a friend at the college: professor and lecturer Elbert Lenrow.

Kerouac registered for credits on October 8, 1948. The course he enrolled in was Lenrow's "The Twentieth Century Novel in America," which covered F. Scott Fitzgerald, Ernest Hemingway, Willa Cather, Theodore Dreiser, Stephen Crane, Sinclair Lewis, and Thomas Wolfe, among others. Lenrow had perused his roster and saw the name Kerouac and immediately remembered it from an acquaintance who had mentioned the young man to him when he had considered placing Jack in his literary magazine. When the time came for Lenrow to meet with each student individually to discuss a possible research topic, Kerouac told Lenrow that he was at work writing a novel.

Kerouac was an eager and intent student who avidly listened to Lenrow's lectures. Regularly, Ginsberg would accompany Kerouac and on one occasion they invited their professor to join them at a Sixth Avenue bar. They were joined by Lucien Carr, who helped spark a high-spirited, ebullient conversation that "refreshed" Lenrow for its "carefree zest."[31]

Later that autumn Kerouac brought to class his *The Town and the City* manuscript. Lenrow read it and was impressed with Kerouac's observational powers and imaginative language. By November, Jack revealed to Lenrow that he was starting a new novel called *On the Road*. Near December's end he submitted his first term paper for "partial fulfillment of credit requirements." It was a subject of Kerouac's own choosing: "Dreiser and Lewis: Two Visions of American Life." Kerouac asserted at length (and by virtue of doing so, displaying his keen critical powers of literature at age twenty-five) that of the two writers, he favored Lewis:

> They are different orders of men. Sinclair Lewis was a prophetic type and Dreiser was not; Lewis supported many theories and movements in his hectic career, Dreiser has supported not many, if any, with a degree of fervor. One of the most un-Lewislike things in Dreiser's writing is the simple and even profound conclusion young Frank Cowperwood arrives at in "The Financier" when he observes the famous lobster slowly diminishing the famous squid in the tank: Dreiser does not seem to be moved at all. "Who feeds on men? Men." It is not that he fails to be aroused by this awful thought, as Lewis certainly is with all his haggard fury, but Dreiser accepts the truth of the thought and considers it a fact and does not deign to controvert the sentence handed down by his deities.

On January 27, 1949, Kerouac took his final exam for the course. Filling out the identification panel on the face of the blue book, Kerouac wrote inside on the first page, "I do not feel capable at this time of taking an examination and I beg to be excused, at least temporarily, from the responsibility." Lenrow did excuse Kerouac based on the advanced writing of his Dreiser-Lewis paper. Lenrow also knew that Jack was better read than many of his classmates.

Although Kerouac borrowed Dreiser's naturalistic style of writing for the initial stages of *On the Road,* he criticized Dreiser in a five-page double-spaced essay for fitting so snugly into literary critic William Troy's theory of the pattern of "old great literature." Using *Sister Carrie* as a basis for comparison, the essay contrasted Dreiser and Sinclair Lewis. Kerouac saw Lewis as a fevered writer tormented by a keen sensibility and social consciousness. Kerouac's essay included the notion that Thomas Wolfe had based the character of Lloyd McHarg in *You Can't Go Home Again* on Lewis. Kerouac perceived Lewis's "torments" as "comparable to fury assigned by gods." Kerouac felt that Lewis's characters were more "spiritual" than Dreiser's, for they sought the calamities that Dreiser's characters dreaded. Dreiser's characters were unable to step beyond the boundaries of their own moribund conventions. They were not "capable of wildness, irresponsibility or naivete." After reading the essay, Lenrow noted that Kerouac had an "easy command of conventional academic analysis."

When Kerouac asked to defer his final exam, Lenrow asked Kerouac to write a second paper. This Jack did after reregistering for the course on February 11, 1949. This time he focused on the little-understood writer Thomas Wolfe. Typing the paper over sixteen hours of concentrated study, Kerouac turned in a nine-page essay, "The Minimization of Thomas Wolfe in His Own Time." Beginning his paper with a statement that he rejected Marxist criticism because he felt it too dominating and stifling, Kerouac instead explored Wolfe's "mysticism," minimized by critics and academics (who condemned, falsely it appears, Wolfe's works as being constructed piecemeal from one large manuscript). Kerouac argued that modern criticism was "near-sighted" and that classical criticism overemphasized style. Exploring Wolfe's concept of time, Kerouac contended that Wolfe towered over his contemporaries by virtue of his wonder and that profound sorrow and loneliness infused his work:

> Wolfe's thesis of "dark time" expands and expands until it becomes no longer a matter of time, but a real description of timelessness and preordainment in our spaces. Although his imagery which is employed to these things is never specifically necessary within its medium, and sets itself no rich limits, and is really not an imagery that can be bitten into, there is a structure of architectural solidness that supports it and sometimes throws it off towards interesting "variety of types of combination." (In this connection it may or it may not matter that he aims at his 'America' theme.) Wolfe falls by his repetitive imagery even though it might have been intended to suggest the rhythm of litany; the same combined words in different pictures seem to grow watery; but he stands again by the poetry of his whole, real structure, all stylewise tricks aside; since, again, his Americana always succumbs to the great varied treatments of 'dark time' in the burning moments.[32]

It was a loosely structured paper peppered with random imagery, but Lenrow valued the passion that Jack invested in it. To accommodate his student's interest in Wolfe, Lenrow allowed Jack to visit his home on West 55th Street to peruse his collection of Wolfe manuscript memorabilia and photographs. Sometimes Kerouac was accompanied by Ginsberg, Cassady, or John Clellon Holmes. On one occasion Lenrow recalled:

[I] explained to Jack how I had once joined Wolfe, seeing a mutual friend off to Europe from the Cunard Line piers, and how we had walked together across Manhattan from the Hudson river to midtown, at a midnight hour, while I listened to an unbroken, unrestrained monologue from him; of how I had visited Wolfe's apartment at 865 First Avenue to gaze at those legendary packing-cases stuffed with his manuscripts.[33]

Jack was especially interested in Lenrow's inscribed copies of *Look Homeward, Angel* and *Of Time and the River* that he had acquired in 1935.

In retrospect, Lenrow sensed Kerouac's "self-doubt" and that he was greatly saddened by the fact that Wolfe had died only three years after his last published novel and that he would not live to see another. On March 11, 1949, Kerouac wrote eight lines of verse in Lenrow's apartment:

> Of what pearls are made of, poor pearl,
> Of laving weave of changed silk
> In waving water boughs enamoured,
> where seahorses' nimble thimbles sailor-eyes
> entangle, in dust of coral balconies,—
> or of mere mystery, thine own beauty,—
> O immemorial pearl, so art wove,
> and wove so sure, thou must endure.[34]

Subsequently, Kerouac frequently remarked on the scope and usefulness of Lenrow's library and remained, for the duration of his life, an infrequent "friend & admirer" of Lenrow.[35]

Writing to Ed White on October 29, Kerouac made plans with him to accompany Bob Burford and Frank Jeffries to France, since he (erroneously) assumed Caroline and Paul would be living with Gabrielle in Ozone Park. They planned to visit the Parisian bistros and "Haute-Savoies." However, Kerouac's plans, like those for a family ranch with the Cassadys, still hinged solely upon his advance from *The Town and the City*. Since the parking lot debacle he had been essentially unemployed.[36]

A string of New York parties continued to occupy Kerouac's nights and weekends. Rousing Louis Ginsberg from his sleep, a drunken but ebullient Kerouac called Allen Ginsberg one November midnight to make plans to attend a party given by John Clellon Holmes. Holmes worked odd jobs as a ghostwriter for $50 a month to support himself while he wrote fiction and poetry. Kerouac wrote Ed White: "The thing that distinguishes these people from my Carr-Burroughs-Adams-Ginsberg crowd is that they try their best to be humanly good, while still 'knowing as much,' in a way, as the others. I don't feel cold and lost among them." Such an assessment reveals why Holmes's friendship, lasting from 1948 until Kerouac's death, remained consistent.[37]

To Holmes, Kerouac and Ginsberg were the "most interesting people" he had met after the war. He was eager to host them in his Manhattan apartment more often. Kerouac's junior by five years, Holmes was old enough to sense intuitively Kerouac's integrity as a serious artist and thought him a "tremendously gifted and unique human being." Kerouac accepted Holmes as a close friend almost immediately. (He later described Holmes, called Tom Saybrook in On the Road, as a "sad, handsome fellow, sweet, gentle, amenable.") According to Holmes, Kerouac showed him all of his journals and The Town and the City manuscript, but not The Sea Is My Brother. Holmes was exceptionally excited about Kerouac's journal: "It impressed me, generally first, with the infinite variety of the human being, the fathomless fluctuation that is in everyone, and specifically, with the intensity of your quest accompanied as it was with self-searchings, condemnations, postulations of premises, self-lacerations and psychological pick-me-ups."[38] Holmes also witnessed the development of On the Road:

During that period he was trying to write it. First he tried to write it the way he'd written The Town and the City. He had phalanxes of families and characters. I remember it vividly, because it was so good. On the Road started in New York with a rich family, a poor family, all kinds of crazy things. The opening scene was in a penthouse. The mother was based on my mother, whom Jack knew quite well by then. Then there was a whole phalanx of younger children. And then there was the character who was to be the major character—he then called him Ray Smith. This was to be the moment when he decided to reject all this and go out on the road. And the scene itself—it couldn't have been more than 5,000 words long—was enormously funny and real and good, but in the style of The Town and the City. He rejected it. He didn't feel right about it.[39]

What Kerouac rejected was the static naturalism that, in his view, had undermined the efficacy of Dreiser's prose. He was eager to fuel his road tale with a new lyrical dynamism. His resolution to develop a more innovative prose style for *On the Road* was sparked by a letter in November 1948. Neal Cassady had finally made contact.

Writing to Kerouac, Neal Cassady inquired about the availability of work on an oil freighter (he had lost his railroad job). Anxious to kick-start his stalled road novel, Kerouac dashed off a response that they should ship out on the Standard Oil freightliners and each earn $200 a month. Willing to leave as soon as January 1949, Kerouac felt that he no longer had reason to stay in New York to wait for news about *The Town and the City.* Those responses from publishers that Jack had received were grim. Little, Brown, the latest of the lot, rejected the manuscript, not on grounds of quality but because of its hefty page count. Disgusted by the huge pile of manuscript pages to which he had devoted nearly four years of his life, he told Cassady that he refused to go on "banking on the fantasy that I will make a living writing." He wasn't going to waste time waiting on those "cocksucking bastards with their sheep's brains" who he felt would grovel for his work once he had become an established author, which he was certain would happen in five years. For now, shipping out together would enable Cassady and Kerouac to start saving money for the ranch. If that opportunity fell through, Kerouac suggested working overseas on a construction unit, where together they would net a potential $10,000. (Neither plan would come to pass.)

William Burroughs wrote to Kerouac from New Orleans, where he had bought a farm and was having some success growing cotton, peas, and lettuce. His property bordered some swampland, where he would fire his guns into the swaying boughs of dense Spanish moss: "I've got enough guns here to stand off a siege," he wrote Kerouac.[40] Desperately trying to keep his mind occupied as he battled heroin addiction, Burroughs also hunted small game. As Kerouac mapped out his January travel itinerary, he planned to swing down and visit his mentor.

Waiting for Cassady's letter was tiresome, and the frustration of doing so boiled within him. He was eager to leave the East Coast. He felt betrayed by publishers and friends. Of the elusive Hal Chase, for whom Kerouac continued to search, Jack raged to Cassady: "Fuck him seventy eight times. . . . Fuck the whole lot."[41] He also aimed his hostility toward Ginsberg:

> I hate you. Because years ago you and Burrows [*sic*] used to laugh at me because I saw people as godlike, and even, as a husky football man walked around godlike, and Hal did that too, and still does. We long ago realized our flesh happily, while you and Bill used to sit under white lamps talking and leering at each other. I think you are full of shit, Allen, and at last I am going to tell you.[42]

Kerouac's only outlet was casual romances. One was with a model for artist Alan Wood-Thomas (whom Kerouac had met in the fall of 1948) named Pauline, who was married to a New York City mechanic who did not like to "get his fingers wet" and whom she derided as a "Minute Man." Kerouac eagerly embraced the opportunity to compensate for her husband's sexual shortcomings: "A very beauteous thing: Lombardian, tall, sloe-eyed, Edie-naïve but not bitter, a girl with a background perhaps like Neal's (no breaks). This girl moves me in every possible way but I don't like to interfere in marriages so much and I'm just glad I know her." The other woman he was seeing, an "eyepopper" Jack found to be too sad, told him she just needed a friend. He wrote Ed White that he was also "gunning innumerable women so much that I sometimes confuse them in my sensual thoughts—an orgy of arms and legs: all kinds of mad creatures, most of them from the Middle West strangely."[43]

On December 15, Cassady placed a long-distance call to the pharmacy below Kerouac's Ozone Park apartment and said that he had borrowed some cash from Al Hinkle, had confiscated Carolyn's savings, and with the combined funds financed a 1949 Hudson Hornet straight from the assembly line. As elated as he was that Cassady now had a way to visit him, Kerouac was also suspicious of Neal's circumstances. He suspected that Cassady had stolen the car or was running from creditors. What did not occur to Jack was that Cassady had used the money that he and Carolyn had saved—the money for the much-discussed ranch. It was an impulsive purchase that Carolyn felt to be foolhardy when they had no other savings account, no reliable source of income, a newborn baby to care for, and were living in a "cardboard dump" furnished with orange crates. Despite his reservations, Kerouac agreed to join Cassady if he came to Rocky Mount. Jack's one stipulation was that he and Neal drive Gabrielle and her belongings from Ozone Park to North Carolina. Having his aging mother safe with his sister eased his ambivalence about leaving her alone while he pursued "joys, kicks, darkness."

On November 20, 1948, Kerouac wrote a draft of an essay for a literature course with Alfred Kazin. In "Whitman: A Prophet of the Sexual Revolution," Kerouac lists the several "revolutions" that man experiences—religious, political, economic, and social—and asserts that they all cause man to stray from the "point of real unspeakable human desire." The ultimate "breakthrough" Kerouac called the "Forest of Arden," his term for an Edenic state of mind and body. In Kerouac's view, the only revolution worth fighting was the physiological or sexual revolution: "a world where it is finally admitted that we want to mate and love, and eat and sleep, and bask in the days and nights of our true, fundamental life." In essence, Kerouac tapped unknowingly into the future credo of the beats: the pursuit of a primitive state of consciousness no longer inundated by consumerism, a social revolution no longer tied to the larger conventional society, but to the grand vessel of life itself.[44]

New School still bored Jack: "it's like signing for checks, that's all it is for me." After his classes ended, Kerouac left New York City and went to Caroline's home in Rocky Mount to spend Christmas with his mother. His nephew, Paul Jr., who had begun to talk, was taught to call Gabrielle "Mémère," the French Canadian version of Grandmother. Kerouac's presence was, at best, tolerated by his brother-in-law, who was disturbed by Jack's typewriter clacking through the late hours of the night. Jack was viewed as an oddity by the Rocky Mount locals, but Gabrielle defended her boy and assured whoever would listen that he would be famous one day.

On Christmas Day, a dirt-splattered Hudson pulled into the Blakes' driveway. Kerouac had been playing Dexter Gordon's "The Hunt" on his phonograph when Neal Cassady, his ex-wife, Luanne Henderson, and Al Hinkle arrived in the "Slow Boat to China" (as they called the Hudson). To Kerouac, the trio looked like "dead people," "victims" of Cassady's "frantic tragic destiny."[45] Obnoxiously, a tee-shirted Cassady played the Gordon record again loudly in the Blakes' small parlor. When Jack said that his sister could not understand the concept of bop, Cassady boosted the volume. While he grooved to the record, sweating and full of kinetic motion, Gabrielle, the Blakes, and their relatives watched, unblinking and "somber," beyond fathoming this apparition from the west, a "stranger for all intents and purposes from California." For a few days, Cassady, Henderson, and Hinkle hung around the Blake residence eating and resting before making two round-trips to New York City with Kerouac to move Gabrielle's belongings to her daughter's place.

In the car, on the final trip north, Kerouac observed that Cassady had been "completely in charge" of the situation when making the seating arrangements. They all sat in the front, with Luanne (Cassady's "honey-cunt") sitting beside his knee, Jack next to her, and "big warm" Al Hinkle near the passenger door. The "Slow Boat" fishtailed through the slushy winter night, passing through Washington, D.C., Baltimore, and Philadelphia before arriving in New York City. Allen Ginsberg had been waiting patiently for them to celebrate the New Year together. Their New Year's Eve was festive, frantic, and high, an atmosphere that contrasted sharply with Gabrielle's quiet night at home watching the Guy Lombardo special. Jack, Neal, Luanne, Ginsberg, and Pauline (Jack's girl of the moment) were also celebrating Lucien Carr's release from Elmira State Reformatory. Although Kerouac was somewhat interested in Pauline, he was also aware that, to her, he was nothing more than a fling. He became more entranced by Luanne, who assured him that Neal would desert them both once they reached the West Coast. They made plans to be together once they were free of Neal. All night they partied frantically, trying to keep up with each other in their jazz-drenched, stoned-out, drunken, sprawling revelry.

From the party in Ginsberg's apartment they planned to circulate among a network of friends' places. On February 2, 1949, their escalating arguments would prompt Cassady to try to strike Luanne across the head. His hand deflected off her brow, hurting his left thumb. This caused an incomplete fracture of four bones around the base of the thumb.[46] The turmoil added an air of hostility to the group staying at Ginsberg's apartment over the next few weeks. When they were ready to depart, they left Ginsberg behind. Jack, Al Hinkle, and Luanne all piled into the Hudson Hornet, with Neal Cassady at the wheel, purely in his element, oblivious to everything, even to the plight of the wife and children who were waiting for him.

While the group was in New York City, Burroughs was mailing letters north from Louisiana to Allen Ginsberg wondering where they were: "I would like to know what gives with the Hinckle[sic]-Kerouac-Cassady expedition. Does this Hinckle [sic] character expect to billet his wife on me indefinitely? His performance is an all time record for sheer gall and irresponsibility."[47] Although Hinkle's wife paid her own way, Burroughs was still amazed that Hinkle could be so callous. But Hinkle had only known

Helen for a short time, having decided to marry her a few days after they met. Cassady used Hinkle's rash union to his advantage. Combining the newlyweds' need of a car for a makeshift honeymoon with Jack's need for transportation west, Neal told Carolyn that he was the one, "ol' Cass," coming to "everybody's rescue." To ease Carolyn's anxiety, Cassady kept the best part for last, as if it would vindicate his selfishness: Helen Hinkle was "loaded," thus making it a "free ride."[48] According to Burroughs, Al Hinkle had married Helen at the Cassadys' instigation to lay siege upon her money.[49]

The road seemed by turns formidable and inspiring. Anchoring his self-doubt from turning to sheer panic, Kerouac resorted to spirituality to guide him: "God is what I love," he closed his journal entry with that first day on the road.

It was around this time, in 1948, that Jack Kerouac coined the term "beat generation" with novelist John Clellon Holmes, who went on to write an essay, "This Is the Beat Generation" for the *New York Times*. "Beat" originally meant "spent": "bad or ruined." It suggested to be "beaten down" or exhausted, both physically and materialistically, and referred to the generation who had come of age during the Second World War but could not polarize themselves as either clean-cut white-collars nor dutiful militants. "Beat" metamorphosed into a conscious objection to straight but spirit-killing jobs, with its adherents preferring to eke out their existence on that dividing line between material comfort and bohemian squalor, at best, or in outright indigence, at worst. This struggle to survive often encompassed selling or using narcotics, promiscuity, a kind of restlessness, and sometimes a sense of spiritual bankruptcy.

To this original meaning Kerouac added a second: "beatific." In this sense, beat captured a sort of holiness that came with being among the downtrodden masses—comparable to what Prince Myshkin experienced in Dostoevsky's *The Idiot*. In Kerouac's world, these masses included lost sailors, dusty hoboes, drunk and despondent husbands, disillusioned soldiers, and truck stop diner customers. Just the type he was about to meet on the road.

PART 3

Essence of Mind

13

*He was on the road again, traveling the continent westward, going off
to further and further years, alone by the waters of life, alone, looking
towards the lights of the river's cape, towards the taper burning warmly
in the towns, looking down along the shore in remembrance of the
dearness of his father and of all life.*

JACK KEROUAC, *The Town and the City*

On January 19, 1949, the Hornet crossed the tunnel to New Jersey, emerging into the raw drizzle of a winter night. New York City's chaotic despondence was fading behind them, both literally and figuratively, and their single objective, the "one noble function of time," was to move. Luanne recognized that Cassady was feeling "panicky." He was eager to push her and Jack together, perhaps sensing that she felt a "definite attraction" toward Kerouac, which she felt was, in part, Neal's doing. As she recalled, "There was really no need for pushing on Neal's part, but Al [Hinkle] said that if Neal was aware of that, he would have been very unhappy. He was later, when he found out I was really attracted to Jack, and it wasn't Neal's idea but Jack's and mine also. He was very unhappy about the situation, and he tried to reverse it which wasn't easy to do."[1]

Beating the dashboard in time to the erratic bebop rhythms, the four of them plotted their trip on a road map as the Hornet swept through the frozen roads of winter. Although Kerouac was thrilled to be on the road finally, he also felt "haunted" by something, though familiar, "yet to remember." Leaving behind the predictable timetable of his Ozone Park days and freed of the guilt caused by his disapproving father, Kerouac confidently embraced the spontaneous risks of traveling penniless.

Regarding Cassady, Kerouac had every right to harbor reservations about what the trip had in store for him. John Clellon Holmes, who hosted Neal and Luanne at his home during December 1948, immediately intuited what Jack saw in Neal:

> I believe Neal was a psychopath in the traditional and most rigorous sense of the term. That is, he acted out everything that occurred to him. He wasn't an ugly person, and he wasn't really a very violent person, but when he saw a chick, he poured it on and everybody melted. . . . The reason why "Dean Moriarty" became the sort of image or metaphor that he did become was because people were feeling that way. Why Jack fastened on this is peculiar to him, but it's peculiar to genius to pick out instinctively—he didn't do it cognitively—something that was going to be the next move.[2]

In Cassady's presence, Jack felt "inauthentic," as many people did; for example, when Neal stole a car or scammed a gas station attendant, this put a scare in Jack, who still for the most part retained his middle-class, Catholic, small-town values. Kerouac's desire to split life open, to seize the belly of the beast, outside of his writing, could be experienced vicariously through Neal. The dislocated Kerouac, Holmes explains, was thrown off-kilter by the death of his father and his departure from Lowell. Neal offered Kerouac not a center but a "trajectory, out." For this reason, Kerouac's urge to dare dwarfed any internal ambivalence or foreboding.[3]

In the front seat of the car, Kerouac, Cassady, and Luanne talked excitedly: "Haunted by something I have yet to remember. Neal and I and Luanne talking of the value of life as we speed along: 'Whither goest thou America in thy shiny car at night?' Seldom had I been so glad."[4]

As the Hornet bucked along over the course of the next few days, Kerouac felt "glad" as his legs rubbed the lean thighs of Luanne, enjoying the bebop playing on the radio and listening to Neal fill in the spaces with his seemingly nonstop talk. For the most part, their trip remained uncomplicated. In Maryland, Cassady drove around blindly searching for a shortcut to Route 1. After losing his way, he wound up on a narrow forest road on the outskirts of Baltimore. Cassady quipped, "Doesn't look like Route

One," which amused Kerouac (later he entered the comment into his journal). Near Elmira, Virginia, the Hornet's seats proved snug when a "mad hitchhiker" joined the group for a stretch. The stranger apparently made his living by knocking on doors across the country proclaiming his Judaism: "I am a Jew!—give me money." To this, Cassady cried out jubilantly, "What kicks!" In Virginia the speeding Hornet, this time driven by Hinkle, was stopped by a police car. Frantically, Luanne shoved all their pot down her pants. Nervously, Neal explained to the cop: "I'm on my way to my wife and this is my ex-wife." This alerted the suspicious cop, who did not believe the nubile blonde, sitting between two grown men, was eighteen. Thankfully, they were able to get off with a warning.[5]

In South Carolina, Kerouac hesitantly took the wheel and drove through the night. By the time they reached Mobile, Alabama, the car's ball bearings were shot from long distance and high speeds. But, according to Kerouac, they began to hear "rumors of New Orleans," heard back-alley bebop, and smelled odorous drifts of "chicken, jazz 'n' gumbo." A week into their trip the car finally crossed the "humpbacked" Mississippi.

Nearing Algiers, Louisiana, as he filled the tank of the Hornet, Cassady yelled, "Smell the people!" New Orleans's "rickety streets," the movement of the boughs of palm trees, and the great masses of late-afternoon clouds drifting over them contrasted sharply with the snows of the North that they had left behind. The "smell of people and rivers," Twain's raw, muddy Mississippi, the shine of the hair of southern girls, and children shouting through "soft bandannas of air" all enriched Kerouac's journal entries.[6]

When the wheels squeaked onto Burroughs's rented property in Algiers, they saw that his house was a decrepit structure. From the front door emerged the gaunt figure of Burroughs, who received Cassady coldly. Burroughs had met Cassady when he and Ginsberg visited Burroughs in Texas; Burroughs suspected Cassady of being a con man. According to Burroughs, Cassady asked him for money to continue their journey. Burroughs refused, partially out of principle (remarking to Ginsberg in a January 30, 1949, letter, "As a matter of principle I would not have contributed one cent, if I were wallowing in $") but also because he was broke from trying to pay the basic expenses of his home. However, Kerouac's gentility and disposition "favorably impressed" Burroughs, who was perceptive enough to see that Cassady would abandon both Kerouac and Luanne once they reached San Francisco. Burroughs felt that they deserved such a fate for having the "weakness" to let Cassady continuously "con" them. Writing to Ginsberg on January 30, Burroughs explained at length his thoughts on Cassady:

> Neal is, of course, the very soul of the voyage into pure, abstract, meaningless motion. He is The Mover, compulsive, dedicated, ready to sacrifice family, friends, even his very car itself to the necessity of moving from one place to another. Wife and child may starve, friends exist only to exploit for gas money . . . Neal must move. To shift into less figurative gear: He takes $1000 (which could have been a down payment on a house to take care of his family), makes a down payment on a car, leaves his wife and child without $ one, cons other people (Luanne, Kerouac) into sending a few $ for their support while he refuses to do a lick of work, or even send his wife a single letter. Then he arrives here and has the unmitigated gall to expect me to advance $ for the continuation of this wretched trip.[7]

When Burroughs wrote Kerouac in February—after Cassady had indeed dumped them—he castigated Neal for assuming that "others are under some mysterious obligation to support him." Unlike Ginsberg and Kerouac, to whom Cassady endeared himself, others, including Lucien Carr, had no use for Neal or his antics.

Cassady introduced Luanne as his wife to Helen Hinkle, who had, in fact, been introduced in late 1948 to his *other* wife, Carolyn, in San Francisco. Helen, who had made phone calls to Jack's mother's house repeatedly, was furious with Al for abandoning her. She recalls in *Jack's Book*: "Al and I immediately repaired to the bedroom to do some arguing. Al didn't argue. I argued. And Jack busied himself, started immediately to fill the vacuum. It was a weird scene. Burroughs was enraged, and I had known Burroughs for all of a month. So everybody's kind of embarrassed when these people walk in."[8] Jack immediately offered to heal the rift by cooking crêpes suzette from his mother's recipe. Helen (brought up by a family that forbade the use of lipstick and going to movies) was taken aback when Luanne casually asked amidst their arguing, "Aren't you going to screw? I'd like to watch."[9]

Helen and Luanne each noticed immediately Joan's copious use of amphetamines. According to Luanne, "Joan was really involved in speed, that inhaler trip. We cleaned Algiers out and then had to start going over into New Orleans, making trips to every drugstore in town, because I think at that time—I'm not positive—she was taking about eight tubes a day."

Once, when a druggist offered Helen twelve tubes (under the pretense that she wouldn't abuse them), she accepted only one, assuming that the labeled six months it was expected to last would suffice. Helen had no idea what they were for until the unkempt Joan, who never wore a bra or shoes, broke the cap off the dispenser, extracted the soaked cotton, and swallowed it. The leftover capsules Bill used as targets for the gun he kept in a shoulder holster. Joan's exhausting the supply of Benzedrine inhalers out of every drugstore in the area echoed her habit in Texas, where she recruited people, such as Neal Cassady and Herbert Huncke, to go into Houston to score more. Luanne never saw Joan sleep. She was always engaged in some form of obsessive activity, whether it was washing the kitchen walls, scrubbing the floors, or scraping chameleons off of trees at four in the morning.[10]

Burroughs, though less bizarre, was still an eccentric. According to Cassady, who witnessed the thirty-five-year-old Burroughs's schedule in Texas, he would go to bed by 8:30 in the evening and emerge from his bedroom "dressed complete in a tie and everything" by 10:30 the following morning. Sitting on his porch, Burroughs would take potshots with his air pistol, read, or unwind one of his morbid narratives. Many evenings the group sat around Burroughs, who was almost always in a rocking chair talking to the group. It seemed to Luanne that he aimed his conversation mostly toward Jack when mentioning New York or Kerouac's writing. Neal's response was to draw attention toward himself by irritating Burroughs with his agitation, which emerged whenever he felt inadequate around people. Being alienated by someone like Burroughs would "speed him up even more, and then he would get into things that normally wouldn't be a part of him."[11]

Although he remained civil toward Jack, Burroughs could not wait for the group to depart (though he suggested that Kerouac remain behind). Al Hinkle and his wife decided to stay in New Orleans to look for work. On January 28, Kerouac, Cassady, and Luanne left, this time aiming the nose of the Hornet toward California.

The first leg of the trip, from New York to Louisiana, appears in chapter 6 of part 2 of *On the Road*. From the beginning of the chapter, underscored by allusions to Cassady's and Hinkle's spousal abandonment, the narrative reverberates with the ruthless desertion of familial obligation for the sake of self-fulfillment at best or mere self-gratification at worst.

Physical reality is interchangeable with metaphysical possibilities till both become untenable. For Dean Moriarty (Cassady), there is "no need in the world to worry, and in fact we should realize what it would mean to us to UNDERSTAND that we're not REALLY worried about ANYTHING."

Traveling through the Louisiana bayous, Neal drove as Jack, in a voice Luanne compared to the Shadow's, told the story of David Kammerer's death:

> It was really wild. He had me just with shivers up and down, and he was talking in that kind of voice deliberately. We'd been listening on the radio, 'cause at that time, all our spook stories were on, like *The Shadow* and some other old-time radio shows, and that's just how Jack related it. Speaking in a low, mysterious voice, and picturing the whole thing of the river, the darkened streets. He really went into vivid detail, and I felt like I was there, and I got the shivers.[12]

In Texas, Luanne undressed and cavorted in the nude with Neal and Jack among the sagebrush and cacti. When a car approached with some elderly tourists, Neal climbed to a column among some desert ruins and posed like a statue. Jack and Luanne watched from the safety of the car, ducking down to gauge the response of the shocked observers. Needing gasoline, the trio pulled into an El Paso bus station hoping to hustle a few bucks. Neal suggested that they should mug somebody for money and wandered off, only to return later with the required funds. By dawn, they had left Texas.

On February 1, the Hornet headed north through the rainy night to San Francisco, with Kerouac miserably sulking in the backseat. High on hashish, he was hypersensitive to Cassady steering the Hornet's wheel, a simple act that became a veritable wild machine of "kicks and sniffs." Cassady's "maniacal laughter" made him feel like a "kind of human dog." Cassady was beginning to wear on Jack; instead he missed his midnight conversations with Ginsberg. Kerouac stuck his head out the car window and looked upon the "whole world" with "Billie Holliday eyes." He thought that his eyes looked as contemplative and sad as those of "whores" in the "mud-shack" saloons of Richmond, Virginia. Yet, his altered, blissful state also made him paranoid. In such times he sensed Luanne's "sullen, blank" hatred for him and was swallowed into insignificance.[13]

When they reached San Francisco, Kerouac saw how perceptive Luanne's New Year's Eve comments, Burroughs's harsh estimate, and his own stoned paranoia had been. Not five minutes after the car stopped at the corner of O'Farrell and Grant, Cassady dumped Luanne and Jack, both stone-broke except for the loose change in Kerouac's pocket. Kerouac had spent his money on food and gas when Hinkle's ploy to marry for travel funds failed, and what money Hinkle did get from his family he kept to himself.[14]

In a seedy hotel room the following night (they had stalled the owner by promising payment in one week), they lay clothed on the bed as a red neon light outside their window flashed incessantly. Kerouac whiled away the night telling Luanne about the "Great Snake of the World," a concept he was developing for his next novel (*Doctor Sax*). Unimpressed, she suggested that instead they go out and find money for food. They walked the streets looking for handouts. From there, according to Kerouac, who recounted the events of that night to Cassady in 1951, Luanne descended to the desperation of prostitution with a "sugar daddy."[15] What Jack and Neal did not know was that he was Luanne's "secret" fiancé, Ray Murphy, whom she would marry in the summer of 1949.

With his last sixty cents, Kerouac bought a dozen oysters at a bar; after eating them, he retreated into the dark doorway of an apartment building and waited for Luanne. When he saw her emerge with an older man and another girl, Jack flicked the ash from his cigarette to attract her attention, but she stepped into the older man's car and was gone. Because Kerouac did not want to be around when she returned, he took to the cold streets huddled in a leather coat. He stopped "dead in his tracks," with the "tremendous sensation" that he had no "consciousness whatever." This abrupt and visceral epiphany sent him into an "unbelievable and heavenly rapture." Bruised and betrayed by Cassady's callousness, stranded on the opposite side of the continent by his supposed friend, Kerouac tried to transform a near calamity into an "experience" through the sheer force of his optimism. However, Neal later showed up and brought Kerouac back to his home minus Luanne.

Cassady's injured thumb became infected; the pain forced him to the hospital for treatment. Nauseous from the medication and miserably depressed, Cassady seemed helpless to prevent the collapse of his relationships. Luanne no longer wanted him (she had confided to Carolyn that she was secretly engaged). Carolyn had no intention of forgiving Neal for his infidelity and for endangering the security of their family. The battered Hudson Hornet, on which the payments were two months in arrears, was now discarded on a side street and waited for the repo man's inevitable arrival.

With a check from Gabrielle, Kerouac bought a bus ticket back to New York City. At the bus station he said goodbye to Cassady but refused to give him one of the fifteen bologna sandwiches that he had made to eat en route (all but five would spoil by trip's end). Although he felt somewhat remorseful, the stinginess was perhaps justified. Kerouac did not feel right toward Cassady for several months afterwards.

More than likely, when Jack was confronted with self-doubt and disappointment, he turned to his psalms, written throughout numerous journals:

Oh god how I rejoice in sorrows now, as though I had asked You for them, and You had handed them to me, how I rejoice in these sorrows. Like steel I will be, God, growing harder in the forge-fires, grimmer, harder, better: as you direct, O lost Lord, as you direct: let me find You now, like new joy on the earth at morning, like a horse in his meadows in the morning seeing the master a-coming across the grass—like steel, I am now, God, like steel, you have made me strong and hopeful.

Strike me and I will ring like a bell!

The bus departed the first week of February and headed northward before veering east, where, unknown to Jack, *The Town and the City* was only weeks away from being accepted by Harcourt, Brace.

14

Back East

February–April 1949

So long as man remains free he strives for nothing so incessantly and so painfully as to find some one to worship.

FYODOR DOSTOYEVSKY, "Dream of a Ridiculous Man"

On February 6, 1949, Kerouac's bus left Portland, Oregon, and drove east toward Butte, Montana. Aboard the bus with Kerouac were two drunk hoboes "bound for The Dalles [Oregon]" and busily scheming to con the bus driver out of a couple of bucks on the fare. Kerouac napped as the bus slid into a blizzard blanketing the Columbia River valley. When he woke, he chatted with the two hoboes for a bit. One said that he would be an "outlaw" if J. Edgar Hoover hadn't made it against the law to "steal." Kerouac responded by fabricating the criminal scope of his trip west: he claimed that he had driven a stolen car from New York to San Francisco. He went back to sleep, and when he woke, he felt "hairy horrors" when he saw columns of ice hanging "hundreds of feet high." Crossing the Columbia River valley and passing cities like Connell, Sprague, and Cheney, the bus rocked and swayed through the gusts of intermittent storms.[1]

On February 7, the bus reached the western part of Montana. In Miles City, Jack wandered through desolate streets empty because of the snowstorm: "In a drugstore window I saw a book on sale—so beautiful!" The book was *Yellowstone Red* (1948) by Tom Ray, a dustjacketed hardcover chronicling the exploits of a pioneer of the western valley. "Is this not better reading in Miles City than *The Iliad*? Their own epic?" Historian Douglas Brinkley determined that "Kerouac was intent on creating his own Yellowstone Red story, only in the modern context, where existential jazz players and lost highway speedsters would be celebrated as vagabond saints."[2] Traveling through mountain passes and valleys, Kerouac watched the isolated shafts of light from desolate shacks nestled in the dark pockets of gulches. Two young men driving by in a car almost swerved off the road, narrowly avoiding a collision with the bus. When he reached Butte, Kerouac stored his bag in a bus depot locker and walked through the town. He refused an invitation from a "drunken Indian" to go drinking with him. As the sun dropped below the horizon, the temperature in Butte plunged below zero. To ward off the cold, Jack stopped in a saloon to warm himself with a "giant" beer. In another bar, clusters of drunken Blackfeet Indians drank whiskey in the bathroom, while others openly played cards for money at the tables. One gambler "tore" Kerouac's "heart out" because he reminded Jack of his father. In Big Timber, Montana, in an "old ramshackle inn," Kerouac watched a huddle of "old-timers" playing cards as snow blanketed the prairie:

> A boy of twenty, with one arm missing, sat in the middle of them. How sad!—and how beautiful he was because he was unable to work, and must sit forever with old-timers, and worry about his buddies punching cows and roistering outside. But how protected is he by Montana. Nowhere else in the world would I say it were at all beautiful for a young man to have but one arm. I shall never forget that boy, who seemed to realize that he was home.[3]

In Billings, Montana, near the Crow Indian Reservation three girls were dining in a cafeteria "with their grave boyfriends." The idealisms were glaring to Kerouac: "You can have your Utopian orgies: I should prefer an orgy with the Montanans." Journal entries such as these show that Kerouac was being carried along willingly by the full sway of his self-cultivation; he was learning to individualize his cultural conscience to suit his artistry. With these fresh experiences, Kerouac was deepening, shaping, and perfecting his own aesthetic. Therefore, such relatively common and mundane details as the "asthmatic, laborious sadness" of old men playing cards changed his whole concept of *On the Road*. Intuitively, he sensed that he was tapping the lifeblood of the real America found tucked into pockets of isolated obscurity, such as men down on their luck or pretty girls sitting with their boyfriends at drugstore soda fountains.[4]

The next day, the bus navigated its way through North Dakota snow-drifts and almost skidded off the road. The unfazed driver persisted until he encountered impassable snowdrifts one mile beyond Dickinson. By midnight the snow grew too intense for safe driving. On the Saskatchewan Plain, the bus was caught in a traffic jam where a truck carrying slot machines to Montana was rutted in the deep drifts and men with snow shovels toiled in the "bitterest cold." Despite the inclemency, Kerouac "wished" that he was "born and raised in Dickinson, North Dakota."[5] Minnesota was "uneventful," and Kerouac was bored by the flat landscape. Upon reentering the eastern half of the United States, Kerouac declared that there were "no more raw hopes; all was satisfied here."[6] Starving in Pennsylvania, for the remainder of his sandwiches had spoiled, Kerouac stole apples from a grocery store to eat during the last few hours of his bus ride. By the end of February 1949, Kerouac was back in New York City. It had been a harrowing yet rewarding trip, for Kerouac reaped an abundance of material for his writing. He wrote in his journal the "sad fact" that modern American cities had "none of the strength of the metropolis and all the ugly pettiness" of the great open lands of the Midwest. Already he was weary of people who spent their lives as "drunkards in bars" and who roamed the "dismal streets" leading "dismal lives."[7] Enviously, he watched Ed White and Bob Burford board the *Queen Mary* en route to France. Nothing had changed in Jack's absence; the city appeared nothing more than a bleak, gray, metropolis-sized prison. Nevertheless, he was happy to be home once again in Ozone Park by his mother's side, and he prepared to submit his manuscript to more publishing houses. Several rejection slips for *The Town and the City* had arrived in his absence.

At his writing desk, Kerouac eagerly took out his works in progress and recommenced work on them. In his notebook he had envisioned *On the Road* as a picaresque "quest" novel echoing *Don Quixote*. He intended to blend the scenes and people encountered on the road with his renewed perception of experience and spirituality, both lacking (he felt) in his earlier draft. His hero would emulate the gentle but impoverished "Knight of the Sorrowful Countenance." At the end of March, Kerouac developed more "definitive" ideas. Ray Smith, the novel's principal protagonist, became also its sole narrator, who "tells the story with ravenous absorption, & with great beauty (*naturellement*)." He likened his narrator to Melville's "Confidence Man," who dupes his fellow passengers on board the *Fidele*. Kerouac's mid-twenties "hero" of "many talents & personalities" would wind up in jail. After "lingering" in New York City with his cohorts (characters like "Junky" [Herbert Huncke] who peopled the city of *The Town and the City*), Ray Smith would take to the road with Pip, an "idiotic" boy of gentle nature, "too saintly for this world." Pip was recycled from an earlier work, "The Imbecile's Christmas," and in time would be discarded from *On the Road*. The quest of Red Moultrie (an early manifestation of *On the Road*'s Dean Moriarty) was to find his father. On March 25, 1949, Kerouac characterized Red Moultrie extensively; he was to be a veteran of minor league baseball, an ex–seaman/truckdriver/jazz drummer/college student from London University now imprisoned in a jail cell after being incarcerated for robbery. There was also to be a lost inheritance. As he awaits his imminent release, Red studies from his Bible and prays. The night before his release, Red was to have been lying in his bunk and listening to his fellow inmates falling asleep, a moment, Kerouac writes, when they were closest in spirit to that of a child. As Red broods upon the sounds, attuning his ear to the conversations near him, gradually his consciousness would drift further and further from the jail block to the outside world until it becomes an indistinct roar of sound; it would be nothing more than the "sounds of the universe as we sleep." This parallel would compare the jail cell to a ship at sea, a notion Kerouac was very familiar with. Tim Hunt explains:

> Once Kerouac introduces the metaphor of the jail as a ship, everything else all but disappears. The passage from that point on largely ignores the initial setting of the jail and proceeds to survey the New York neighborhoods visible, presumably, from Red's cell window. This voyage of New York moves on a swell of long vowel sounds and by means of an associative logic controlled by the sound and by the emotional resonances of words more than by their explicit meanings.[8]

In the passage, Kerouac inserts some wordplay imitative of Whitman's "Out of the Cradle Endlessly Rocking." His aim, it seems, was to suggest a lyrical, imaginative universe that ultimately usurps Moultrie's external world. Upon his release, Red ventures into New York City and meets with some Times Square characters from *The Town and the City*. He also meets with Smitty and Pip and together they all head west to rendezvous with Moultrie's acquaintance Vern Pomeroy (an early prototype for Neal Cassady). It was Kerouac's intention to transmute his 1947 road trip into Moultrie's characterization and merge it ultimately with that of his early impressions of Cassady. Red locates his lost father in Montana; Vern finds his in Denver.

Kerouac's attention eventually steered away from the immediate action of the novel (though it was hardly plot-driven) and focused instead on the richer character development of Red. To accomplish this, he planned a dynamic journey of Moultrie's character in five steps: The first was to be his incarceration where we would see Red in his purest embodiment of mind and spirit. In the second, during his road journey west, the "pure" Moultrie would sink into apathy as a result of his copious drug usage. Third, the derangement of Red would result from a chaotic gambling expedition in Butte, Montana. The fourth phase would be Red's attempt to reconnect with his initial purity. The conclusion would have Moultrie repenting and recovering the lost joy of his innocence at the novel's outset. Kerouac planned to end the novel in California. The work would be fashioned in the spirit of those pioneers who headed west in covered wagons seeking land for themselves and their families. The work's tragic characters would be those men who "unhitched" their horses from the wagon train for a sole materialistic purpose—the pursuit of gold. "All the gravity and glee and wonder of their lives and their loves was forgotten, for mere gold." Kerouac felt that this unbridled pursuit of wealth and power was precisely what was wrong with his contemporaries; they had "unhitched the horses from the wagons—from their souls and gone off like whores for a little gold." They had unhitched for the surrender of "simple truth" and "gone off sweating after the golden, glittering, false solution." Overall, though, the wagon train of America, Kerouac felt, was "still rolling!"[9] Despite the extensive work he put into both the chapter treatments and character developments, Kerouac would ultimately discard a great portion of the work and keep only his concept of the open road and the search for *something* intact.

Frustrated with editors and publishing houses, Kerouac heeded Allen Ginsberg's advice and let Mark Van Doren read his completed manuscript and two chapters of the fledgling work *Doctor Sax*. With little mention of *Doctor Sax*, Van Doren responded that he was impressed with Kerouac's perseverance to be a writer and the quality of his writing in *The Town and the City*. Van Doren telephoned his friend Robert Giroux at Harcourt, Brace and suggested that the company publish *The Town and the City*. By the close of March, Giroux sent a letter of acceptance offering Kerouac a $1,000 advance against royalties for his work. Kerouac tinkered with the narrative structure for *On the Road* as he impatiently awaited word from Giroux about the editing of his manuscript. Soon, Giroux made contact, and they agreed to work together on the manuscript. They spent several early evenings making extensive cuts and revisions. The work that they did satisfied Kerouac, although he later criticized the results in an unmailed letter in which he complained that Giroux had edited *The Town and the City* "rather badly but not from any mean motive."[10]

Kerouac's first impulse, in mid-April 1949, was to flee the city, for it no longer held any "mystery" for him. He felt isolated lurking in Times Square while his fellow "geniuses" brooded in prison: "In the past week, Bill, Allen, and Huncke were all arrested and put in jail—Bill for narcotics, in New Orleans, the others for robbery and etc. in N.Y."[11] However, the acceptance of his novel had changed his outlook. He no longer felt "beat," but eager to start anew. Refreshed by his recent trip west, Kerouac yearned to cross the Great Divide once more and decided to realize his communal ranch idea with Cassady—unaware that he had spent his money on the repossessed Hudson Hornet and did not plan to relocate his family. Cassady had been unable to find employment on the railroad; to compensate, Carolyn took a job as an assistant in a doctor's office. Two weeks later, despite her conscientious efforts to practice birth control, she was pregnant again. Regardless of Neal's travails, Kerouac was determined to move himself, Gabrielle, and his sister's family to Colorado once the bulk of his editing work for Harcourt was completed in June. He also planned to marry within two years. It was, he declared in the pages of his journal, the "turning point, the end of my 'youth' and the beginning of manhood. How sad."[12]

In the middle of April, Kerouac worked earnestly on another draft of *On the Road*. One way of doing this was to structure the novel with three concepts of unification: American places, seasons, and Red Moultrie's inheritance. The inheritance had important implications for *On the Road*: not only was it lost to Red, it was meant to impart the loss of America's innocence. To harness the stylistic shifts of his erratic prose, he read Dostoyevsky's tale "An Unfortunate Predicament," noting the usefulness of developing an "idea" before arriving fully at "what *actually* happens in the story."[13] Excited by his progress, he included passages in a letter to Ed White, who was still in France with Frank Jeffries (Sam Shepard in *On the Road*), another friend of Kerouac's from Denver. During the first two weeks of May, Kerouac wrote eight thousand more words of the *On the Road* draft; he created an itinerary of travels on April 27 and a sixteen-page outline of the novel. He then put it aside and made preparations to leave for Colorado.

Kerouac had planned to continue his studies of the modern novel. The 1949 spring semester syllabus at the New School would cover early American modernists like Ernest Hemingway and William Faulkner (Kerouac had a serious interest in the latter). He also delved into Tolstoy once more, exploring the "moral dilemma" the Russian author faced in his later years. Kerouac regarded Tolstoy's novels *War and Peace* and *Anna Karenina* as representing this dilemma through his manipulation of his characters: "Modern thinking has put its stamp of disapproval upon Tolstoy's dilemma, which was perhaps less a dilemma to him than to most of us, and after all was said and done perhaps served him in his great turbulence in a way which we cannot imagine in a singularly shallow century."[14] As intriguing as a career in literary criticism would have been for Kerouac, he only toyed with such ideas before moving on to his own work. Immersed in editing *The Town and the City* and in writing his ongoing road novel, Kerouac did not complete the semester. He dropped out to go on the road once again.

During the first week of May 1949, Kerouac went to Poughkeepsie with Jack Fitzgerald, his wife, and some friends of theirs. The weekend turned into a drinking bout as they spent the long afternoons guzzling beer till their thirty-quart supply was reduced to a few bottles. They went for a bar crawl and returned afterward to begin drinking anew. The intoxicated musings included Fitzgerald's declaration that he knew a "lot of dumb sonofabitches who're going to be fucked when they find out there's no heaven after this one to finagle for. . . . I like people who are conscious of the gigantic sadness of the whole mad thing." Kerouac sympathized. As usual, Fitzgerald's pessimism affected Kerouac, who wrote to Ed White soon afterwards: "Every time I go see Jack Fitzgerald I come home feeling different—as though the world was full of sad, dumb bastards who are at bottom amazingly funny to behold." Fitzgerald's outlook complemented Jack's innate "morbid nature," which sent him sweating at the midnight hour with his own "perspiring vision." Of late, Kerouac's ideas had been springing from nightmares and dreams that seemed to define his peculiar personality and frenetic interactions with others:

It took place in the late afternoon somewhere . . . among many excited people, friends, lovers, relatives. Dozens trooped into front parlors and argued and harangued about something. God knows what it was but I was the center of it all. I was trying not only to pacify everybody but actually to make a separate peace with each individual. This involved many difficulties—since some relationships were more intense than others. But that seemed to make no impression on my dull, beating brain. All I wanted to do was win the mad approbation of everyone.[15]

Kerouac could not reconstruct the dream verbatim for his *Rain and Rivers* journal, only recalling that the "feeling" gave him the notion of his own "falseness": "The sum of it was: how could all these people be so blind to my monstrousness, how could they be fooled, why couldn't they see?" In the late morning of April 12, the day of a lunar eclipse, Kerouac discussed with Allen Ginsberg the "shrouded stranger," a concept gleaned from Jack's rapidly filling dream journal. In his dream a stave-carrying "Hooded Wayfarer Without a Name" pursued him through the expansive plains of the Midwest kicking up slow plumes of billowing dust. To be saved, Kerouac had to reach the "Protective City." Prompted by Ginsberg for the identity of the stranger, Kerouac "proposed that it was one's own self merely wearing a shroud." Even at birth, Kerouac reasoned, the baby is able to "get what he wants" and the "maturity" of the child's soul is intact even before the brain starts to metamorphose its thought processes. Was not Beethoven, Kerouac reasoned, simply a "soul peeking from the mighty darkness of his own creation"? Kerouac's dream of the Shrouded Stranger made him realize that there was "another world" that ultimately emerged in glimpses from our "shrouded existence which was given in darkness, before the light of life arrived," a light that Kerouac felt would only be discernible to us at the hour of death.[16]

On April 16, William Burroughs wrote Allen Ginsberg: "Just took a fall. Possession. The bastards are trying to send me to the State joint at Angola which is one of the worst of the South." The local police had initiated an antidrug crusade. On the streets they interrogated known street addicts and examined their arms for recent tracks. On April 6, Burroughs and known drug addict Pat Cole cruised slowly along Lee Circle looking to score a fix of heroin. A policeman in his prowl car passed them and recognized Cole. They were pulled over. As he searched the car, the policeman opened the glove compartment and found an unregistered handgun Burroughs had brought along to pawn. Also, a recent letter from Ginsberg discussing the sale and purchase of marijuana led them to the conclusion that Burroughs was a big-time dealer. They next searched his house and found a jar of marijuana, some heroin, and a collection of firearms. Burroughs was brought in for questioning and then locked up with three other addicts. Painfully addicted, Burroughs was suffering withdrawal in jail and was brought to a private sanitarium for a shot of morphine and a one-week Demerol treatment. Writing to Ginsberg on April 13, Joan Burroughs informed him that the cops had found his letter. She advised him, since they might notify the New York police, to clean up his apartment.[17]

Things weren't much better on Ginsberg's end. After Kerouac and Cassady's departure in January 1949, he remained at his job as a copy boy at the Associated Press. Herbert Huncke, just released from Rikers Island prison (this time for marijuana possession), needed a place to stay. During February 1949, Huncke had been homeless upon being released from Rikers, subsisting mainly on doughnuts, coffee, and, to his detriment, Benzedrine over a period of ten days. Against Burroughs's, Kerouac's, and Lucien Carr's sober advice, Ginsberg's kindly and sympathetic nature got the best of him and he took Huncke in. Ginsberg biographer Michael Schumacher assesses Ginsberg's act of charity astutely: "In many respects, Huncke was an apparition of Ginsberg's vision of a tragic Dostoyevskian figure."[18] He took Huncke in after first turning him away (Huncke had stolen $200 worth of personal effects from a friend of Allen's a year before). Ginsberg nursed the ailing man for the first two weeks. He peeled the shoes off Huncke's feet, against the sick man's advice, and saw that his toes and heels were scabbed and blistered. Ginsberg washed them with a solution of boric acid and water. Huncke slowly took over the apartment, moving furniture and wearing Ginsberg's clothing. Huncke's Times Square underworld friends soon were bringing their stolen merchandise to the apartment to stash. Heroin junkie Vicki Russell and her safe-robber boyfriend, "Little Jack" Melody, began storing their wares all over the apartment. On April 22, 1949, Ginsberg had the misfortune of needing a ride. He took up Little Jack's offer and stepped into a stolen car filled with pilfered loot. In Queens, Melody drove the wrong way down a one-way street and was immediately flagged by a police officer. A squad car chased them at speeds of up to sixty miles per hour in the cluttered streets. Six blocks later the car jumped a curb, bounced off a telephone pole, and rolled over twice. Ginsberg was basically unharmed, but his eyeglasses were shattered and the papers he had brought along mixed with the stolen material littering the street. In the distance, the faint wail of a police siren could be heard. Ginsberg grabbed his 1943–1945 journal and fled the scene. He bummed enough money for a subway token and a phone call and telephoned Huncke at the apartment. He warned Huncke to clear the rooms of stolen loot. Despite these efforts, Ginsberg, Huncke, Russell, and Melody were all arrested. Ginsberg's Columbia professors, Mark Van Doren and Lionel Trilling, advised him to plead insanity. In court the twenty-three-year-old Ginsberg followed their advice and was sentenced to the Columbia Presbyterian Psychiatric Institute for psychoanalytic therapy.[19]

Neal Cassady had begun writing, after much support from Jack and Allen, an autobiography he titled *The First Third.* The actual writing was difficult, for his thumb was in a cast. It had become infected with osteomyelitis from changing dirty diapers. Writing to Kerouac, he itemized his misery stemming from the incident when he had tried to punch Luanne in New York the previous January:

> Jazz-hound C. has a sore butt. His wife gives daily injections of penicillin for his thumb, which produces hives, for he's allergic. He must take 60,000 units of Fleming's juice within a month. He must take one tablet every four hours for this month to combat allergy produced from this juice. He must take codeine-aspirin to relieve the pain in the thumb. He must have surgery on his leg for an inflamed cyst. He must rise next Monday at six a.m. to get his teeth cleaned. He must see foot doctor twice a week for treatment. He must take cough syrup each night. He must blow and snort constantly to clear his nose, which has collapsed just under the bridge where an operation some years ago weakened it. He must lose his thumb on his throwing arm next month.[20]

Though Cassady was elated that Kerouac had found a publisher for *The Town and the City,* he was also swift to respond that Jack had never been as poor and miserable as he and others (like Huncke) had been for practically their whole lives: "To be blunt, you were never in jail so many goddam times you had nightmares of future arrests. You were never actually obsessed with the year-by-year, more-and-more apparent fact that you couldn't escape the law's stranglehold. You, in short, were never where Huncke is now."[21]

The recent spate of misfortunes affected Kerouac, putting him into a "particularly stupid state of mind." Writing to Alan Harrington, he assessed his situation:

> I am no longer "beat," I have money, a career. I am more *alone* than when I "lurked" on Times Square at 4 A.M., or hitch-hiked penniless down the highways of the night. It's strange. And yet I was never a "rebel," only a happy, sheepish imbecile, open-hearted & silly with joys. And so I *remain*. It is all ominously what you said about my "innocence"—even though that Lucien business years ago, when everybody went unscathed except me (that is, me, & the actual pale criminal). But now (as I promised myself) I want to go on to *further considerations*.[22]

Placing himself squarely apart from his beat associates, Kerouac envisioned a "new" life on a more idealistic and broader plane. He had aspirations to pursue a career in Hollywood, where he would realize motion picture adaptations of *Look Homeward, Angel; Heart of Darkness;* and *Passage to India*.[23] In addition, he labored on *On the Road* "in earnest," and felt he could finally have a house and, ultimately, his own family: "Within two years I'm going to marry a young lady. My aim is to write, make money, and buy a big wheat farm."[24]

After Jack had Nin take publicity photos of him for Harcourt, Brace, he pondered in his journal the "leisurely, playful, casual" days with his family. Part of his tension was relieved because his talent was "recognized." The future held positive prospects: "Do we need a Jesus? — is the time coming? And will this Lamb reveal? Shall he reveal the secrets of joy in the land, and shrouds? For all this is too much of a scramble for me and already I foresee, I foresee . . . I foresee Waste in my own house, and Dull Lust, and Laziness, and Snarling Sin. I am thinking." Jack stressed his seriousness of the matter soberly, insisting on not "learning" his riches like Solomon. "I am he, John L. Kerouac, the Serious, the Severe, the Stubborn, the Unappeased; he who is pursued by the Hooded Wayfarer."

In the middle of May, Kerouac set out again.

15

Denver Doldrums

May–June 1949

There is that in me—I do not know what it is—but I know it is in me.
WALT WHITMAN, "Song of Myself"

Acting on a "swift decision" (a disingenuous phrase since he had brooded over the decision for more than a year) to "establish some kind of 'homestead' for myself and family," Kerouac arrived in Denver on May 15. On the day he left New York, Kerouac had been invited by Elbert Lenrow to attend a screening of Carl Dreyer's *Passion of Joan of Arc* at the Museum of Modern Art in Manhattan. However, he was too eager to begin his westward journey after finally convincing his family in April to move to Denver with him. He planned to leave ahead of them and arrange living quarters. There was also to be a contingent of Columbia University associates who would greet the budding novelist in Denver. His mother helped pack his things and he boarded a bus.

He planned on Hal Chase assisting him in finding a place to rent until he had earned enough from royalties to buy a house outright. He was committed to spending the bulk of his funds on "making my home out here come hell or high water." To that end, he had spent only 90 cents during the entire bus trip. His thriftiness had been easy because of the free distractions of the journey west. Near Deer Trail, Colorado, next to the East Bijou River, he watched the sun "blushing" on the lonesome plains, where one farmhouse stood bathed by sunset, the very "blush of God Himself."[1]

In Denver at last, Kerouac tried to call Ed White's father but couldn't find his name in the phone book. Instead, Jack "casually" called Justin Brierly, a friend of Hal Chase, who picked him up at the bus depot and brought him to a YMCA. Kerouac rented a room and in these lonely confines wrote on a rented typewriter (which cost him 10 cents) while drinking from a bottle of Scotch that Brierly had given him.[2]

Later Kerouac moved his rented typewriter and rucksack to a rented house on 61 West Center Street in Westwood, Colorado. To hasten the growth of his savings, Kerouac applied for a construction job. During his off-hours, he read French poetry by François de Malherbe and Jean Racine (dubbing the latter the "French Shakespeare"). He also read Western dime novels while he lay in bed and admired the rich geographical descriptions of the American West. To form his own impressions, he took long solitary walks over empty roads and through abandoned fields. Likening himself one Sunday afternoon to the Flemish painter Rubens, he carried his notebooks with him and jotted spontaneous impressions.[3] Soon enough, Kerouac felt on the verge of becoming a "Thoreau of the Mountains."[4] His plan was simple: at Larimer Street he would buy a saddle for a $30 saddle horse, an army surplus sleeping bag, cooking utensils, some food, matches, and a rifle; he would "go away in the mountains forever" and turn "[his] back on society." Preoccupations with solitude and his being "like Thoreau" recurred throughout Kerouac's life, most strongly after his abrupt fame. Despite his eagerness to have a wife, his optimal state, it seemed, was solitude and self-sufficiency:

> I want to be left alone. I want to sit in the grass. I want to ride my horse. I want to lay a woman naked in the grass on the mountainside. I want to think. I want to pray. I want to sleep. I want to look at the stars. I want what I want. I want to get and prepare my own food, with my own hands, and live that way. I want to roll my own. I want to smoke my deermeat and pack it in my saddlebag, and go away over the bluff. I want to read books. I want to write books. I'll write books in the woods. Thoreau was right; Jesus was right. It's all wrong and I denounce it and it can all go to hell. I don't believe in this society; but I believe in man, like [Thomas] Mann. So roll your own bones I say.[5]

In June his family arrived with their furniture and tried to absorb the vast mountainous land that Kerouac found so fascinating. Making no effort to accommodate his pessimistic family, Kerouac preferred to keep his distance. Trying to adapt was awkward for Jack's family, who were accustomed to the East Coast, and soon their confidence in Jack and the rightness of his assumptions began to crumble.

Most nights through May and into June 1949, Kerouac made further notes for *On the Road*. Generally he slept until noon, ate breakfast, and began his writing. Stopping infrequently, sometimes he kept at it until almost midnight. He wondered in his journal whether the final product would be "any good." Accurately, he predicted that it would be "popular," knowing that it would differ greatly from the conventional narrative of *The Town and the City*.[6] He hoped to be able to solicit an advance for *On the Road* from Robert Giroux, who was scheduled to travel to Denver to meet with him on July 15. Kerouac was eager to spend some days with Giroux, knowing the editor was far too busy to socialize when he was in New York City. However, Kerouac was mistaken when he assumed the editing of *The Town and the City* was going to be "light."[7]

By the Fourth of July, not more than a couple of weeks after her move, Gabrielle had had enough of Kerouac's Golden West. It was, according to Jack, "one of the saddest days I've ever seen," as he and his sister watched Gabrielle board a train at the Denver depot. There had been no "send-off stroll to the bar." Instead, they sat in chairs while little Paul's wailing resonated within the vast walls of the station and Paul Sr. idly flipped the pages of his *Popular Mechanics* magazine. Kerouac watched with "pale eyes" as the train rolled away and the idea of his aging mother traveling alone through the dark badlands of Nebraska, heading back to her penurious life punching the clock at the Brooklyn shoe factory, consumed him. Caroline and her two Pauls followed soon thereafter. Despondent, Jack wrote to John Clellon Holmes that his "big ideal Homestead idea" was "collapsing." He was desperate, having already spent his advance money, and now he needed more funds. (He planned a half-baked scheme to sublet the house and "take it on the lam" by joining Cassady in San Francisco. There, he could continue living as he saw fit—listening to bop and supporting himself as a fry cook.) In other ways, though, he was relieved; freed of "familial burdens," Kerouac experienced an "opening" of his "eyes" inscrutably leading to the "real import of the prayers" he said each day. However, he was torn by indecision. Standing in the yard, he watched the plains flicker with heat lightning. Looking west, he sensed that the lightning seemed "strangely wild" while that in the "mystic" east was more "intense": "I had a desire to go in both directions at the same time."[8]

Several weeks later, still in Denver, Kerouac greeted another train bearing his editor, Robert Giroux. During Giroux's visit he suggested to Kerouac that there was no need to write metaphysical sagas, such as "Myth of the Rainy Night," but that he should write solely of people and guard his writing from the "mush" of "oversymbolization." Excited, Kerouac wrote Cassady:

> My editor of Harcourt, Brace—Robert Giroux, a big literary cat, the Golden Boy of Publishing right now (only 35)—came to Denver to work on the manuscript with me. B [Bob Burford, a friend of Kerouac's in Denver] kindly took us all over (other expenses on the publisher), but the main thing is that we became close friends. I must admit that he has influenced me, to wit, he pointed out that I had no need to write about wizards like Doctor Sax, but only about people. He knew how Allen had influenced me with mad image-makings and crazy "oops!" writing. (He is however interested in Allen, I talked it up plenty, and Allen may now take his volume of works to him.) I agreed with him; I saw the *mush* in oversymbolizations . . . I even now see the reality of people as phantasy—*of course!*
>
> Who are Allen and I to invent poetic myths in a real, serious world? (A world like yours and your poor infected thumb.)[9]

Over time, his Denver experience helped him develop an appreciation for the western "myth," for the "great classless mass of Americans" who abided by the dictates of their own American mythology. Kerouac admired their allusions to Roy Rogers and Dale Evans just as he admired his Columbia classmates' comments about "Dostoevsky and Whittaker Chambers." He watched family softball games played under the bright arc lights of gas tanks and felt silly for being too "longfaced" to join them: "I said to myself, 'What's the use of being sad because your boyhood is over and you can never play softball like this; you can still take another mighty voyage and go see what Cody [pseudonym for Neal Cassady in *Visions of Cody*] is finally doing.' Oh the sadness of the lights that night! . . . the great knife piercing me from the darkness."[10]

Yet, as much as he admired the honest and bold "classless Americans" of the Midwest, Kerouac missed the frequent discussions of literature, jazz, philosophy, and art over cups of coffee, or being high on speed or *tea* (hipster slang for marijuana; Kerouac described Proust as "an old teahead of time"). In his correspondence with friends, references to literature and writing predominated. In his June 24 letter to John Clellon Holmes, Jack encouraged the budding novelist to keep writing about New York City's social milieu and the characters who frequented the San Remo, a hipster hangout in Greenwich Village on the corner of Bleeker and MacDougal Streets that served beer, hard liquor, and coffee. The descriptions in Holmes's writing, Kerouac suggested, should depict "the bars, the mad parties, big swirling vortexes" as in Dostoyevsky's novel *The Possessed;* he shouldn't concentrate on any one person but instead paint a "large impassioned portrait" as Charles Dickens had done. Already attempting a novel about 1940s New York, Holmes had asked Kerouac for an objective portrait of Ginsberg. Jack replied: "Burroughs is his father. Neal is his God-Bone. Lucien is his Angel."[11]

To counter the Western dime novels that he read avidly, Kerouac devoured Alain-Fournier's *Le Grand Meaulnes,* Cicero's *Offices,* Matthew Arnold's *Study of Celtic Literature,* Keats's *Letters,* and Spenser's complete poems (purchased for fifty cents in a Denver bookstore). Spenser helped "sharpen" Kerouac's appetite for appreciating singular words for their poetic power and potential wordplay. In a letter to Elbert Lenrow, Kerouac described his method: "I conduct private philologies of my own in a notebook, concentrating mostly on tremendous words like 'bone' and 'door' and 'gold' and 'rose' and 'rain' and 'water.'" Through Spenser, Kerouac "kicked off" the conception of his own poetry. Celtic literature, from which Kerouac gleaned "perfect bones of images," also contributed to his development. Kerouac's eclectic grasp of poetry would help revolutionize the postmodernism of American poetry and would propel the reexamination of many of its essential aspects. That revolution would begin with Allen Ginsberg, who would describe himself in 1992 as an "imitator of Kerouac."[12]

After spending the middle of June typing and organizing 10,000 words for *On the Road,* Jack considered it to be its "true beginning." He realized two weeks later in his "road-log" journal that one does not actually begin "writing a book till you begin to *take liberties* with it." One section of *The Town and the City* that he needed was in the hands of Vicki Russell. She had been indicted on some drug charges and Jack feared that his "Levinsky and the Angels on Times Square" was probably in the hands of the New York Police Department by now. Even so, he wanted it back.

16

Go Moan for Man

July 1949–Summer 1950

The sign and credentials of the poet are, that he announces that which
no man foretold.

RALPH WALDO EMERSON, "The Poet"

At the Columbia Presbyterian Hospital, Ginsberg "questioned" his "own sense of reality." He could not decide whether his "illuminative experience" back in 1948 was, as he recalled in 1989,

> a kind of traditional religious experience that you might find within (William) James's book *The Varieties of Religious Experience,* where there is a sudden sense of vastness and ancientness and respect and devotional awareness or sacredness to the whole universe, or whether this was a byproduct of some lack-love longing and a projection of the world of my own feelings, or some nutty breakthrough.[1]

Ginsberg hoped that the Columbia psychologists would give him the answer. Instead, they helped him "relate to my own desires"—sexual, intellectual, or otherwise. Ginsberg's hospitalization did make possible his encounter in the hospital corridor with fellow patient Carl Solomon, who had shuffled toward him after receiving a series of insulin treatments. Trying to engage him in conversation, Ginsberg confessed to Solomon his own earlier visionary experiences. Unimpressed, Solomon responded that Ginsberg was "new here" and that he would "meet some of the other re-

pentant mystics." Stunned, Ginsberg resorted to his arsenal of literary allusions and responded that he was Prince Myshkin. Solomon surpassed
him by responding, "I'm Kirilov." Ginsberg's Myshkin—the noble who at
first displays an odd, unconventional frame of mind and eventually suc-
cumbs to mental deterioration—had encountered Solomon's Kirilov, the
character from Dostoyevsky's novel *The Possessed*, who cannot accept the
divinity of God or endure the human condition and responds with the ultimate self-negation, suicide, which permits him to play God and exercise
power over life and death.

Kerouac empathized with Ginsberg's predicament: "Your stories of the
madhouse are so actual that I feel again as I did in the Navy nuthouse—
scared and seeing through heads. I used to sit with the worst ones to learn.
Be kind and allow that I sought to see. Oh for krissakes, I know everything . . . don't you know that? We all do. We even all know that we're all
crazy. All of us are sick of our sad majesties." Jack advised Ginsberg not to
be so "pedantic." To cheer his friend, Kerouac told Ginsberg that he had
shown Robert Giroux some of Allen's *Book of Doldrums* poetry. Giroux
had suggested mild revision, such as excising some words to better evoke
images and insights instead of burying them with excessive wordiness. He
suggested, Kerouac told Allen, a meeting in New York. All Ginsberg had
to do, in Jack's view, was be "smart" and not "shit" in his pants, for the
world was only waiting for its poets to "pitch sad silent love in the place of
excrement."[2]

On July 3, Cassady wrote Kerouac from San Francisco. The letter served as
a "case history" that Cassady, echoing Proust, called his "remembering of
things past." In the letter, Cassady details his past incarcerations (portions
would later appear in part 3 of *On the Road),* an inventory of criminality
useful for Kerouac's writing:

> My first job was on a bike delivery around Denver. I meet a lad named
> Ben with whom I used to steal anything we saw as we cruised in the
> early A.M. in his 27 Buick. One of the things we did was smash the
> high school principal's car, another was steal chickens from a man he
> disliked, another was strip cars and sell the parts. I bought the Buick
> from him for $20. My first car; it couldn't pass the brake and light in-

spection, so I decided I needed an out of state license to operate the car without arrest. I went to Wichita, Kansas to get the plates.

Cassady told Kerouac that he had been arrested ten times and had served fifteen months of his life on six convictions.[3]

Despite the imminent publication of *The Town and the City*, Kerouac felt that being a published writer was merely a "sad affair." The "laurel wreath," as Giroux told Jack in Denver, was donned at the moment of writing. Kerouac felt, after he had seen Giroux off at the airport and hitchhiked back through the "mammoth plains dusk," shallow and insignificant. Certain that his writing achievements were not enough, "I saw how sad he [Giroux] was, and therefore how the best and the highest that the 'world' has to offer was in fact empty, spiritless; because after all he is a great New Yorker, a man of affairs, a success at thirty-five, a famous young editor."[4] Kerouac was also saddened by the fact that he had failed to extract money from Giroux to live on. In desperation he found work loading and unloading fruit crates in Denver's food market.

To work at the Denargo Markets fruit wholesalers, Kerouac woke up at two in the morning and walked four miles to work. He punched in at 4 A.M. and worked until 6 P.M. loading and unloading crates of cantaloupes from boxcars. It was, as he writes in *On the Road,* "the hardest job of my life." However, when he was asked not to return after a shift, Kerouac assumed it was because he "was not as fast as the Japs."[5]

It was not difficult for Jack to decide which direction to take once he left Denver. His family had already disappointed him by leaving to pursue their predictable lives back east; his $1,000 advance had been thrown away. His family's shallow pursuit of materialism had sabotaged Jack's ideal of a peaceful, communal life where he did not have to worry about his mother's welfare. Instead, consumerism was rampant: "My sister and brother-in-law were sitting worrying about money and work and insurance and security and all that, in the *white-tiled* kitchen."[6] Kerouac wrote to Cassady: "You remember how you and I dug the old railroad men we saw all over the country last winter?—we saw them with their lunchpails in the night in Baltimore and Carolina and Texas & Bakersfield. We dug them as old workmen, we understood something about them."[7] Kerouac had no use for the materialism of the East exemplified by his family. Instead he invested his faith in the downtrodden; the fertile ground of his emerging literature was the woes and laments of workingmen, the homeless, and the minority races that increasingly dotted the landscape. In *Visions of Cody* he wrote of his disillusion during his last days in Denver:

> I came to feel that the alleys, the fences, the streets were the "holy Denver streets" I called them, and just because of this particular softness—I walked along that, feeling low, seeing how the successful young executive, mysterious Boisvert, was just a bored old Tiresias completely beat and sighing; with nothing to do in his soul but flounce around and yawn and wait, always wait, wait; the dullness of the heart gone dead, the heart never got anything. The highest glamor he had, and was as sad as an old dishrag; in fact we stood on top of a mountain together at Central City and overlooked a hump of mountains with their special snowing iceclouds flying along a heavenly golden cloud ridge, the roaring day of the Colorados, high up, and didn't think much of it together; by myself I might have marveled or by himself he might have . . . but it meant nothing, to see, own, and possess the world from a height physical and social, to either of us. He talked some other nonsense, anecdotes of boredom maybe. You've got to get that World of mind. So I walked the streets of Denver in the night, and passed the dark shapes of women with soft voices, and children with soft voices, and the fragrant smoke from the pipes of workingmen resting on the porch in the evening; at one point in fact a young colored girl peered at me on the sidewalk and said "Eddy?"[8]

Kerouac focused on the immediate future, on Cassady, on the promises of the West, for "there was nothing behind me any more, all my bridges were gone and I didn't give a damn about anything at all."

Cassady beckoned to Kerouac by mail. Because his thumb had failed to respond to medical treatment, the doctors decided to amputate it at the first joint. He was now available for the next two weeks for the length of his convalescence: "Carolyn will be working all day including Saturday, and we will have the house to ourselves." He was excited and told Jack they could while away the hours playing music, talking, and, at night, visit the "nigger joints" and listen to bop.[9]

In August, Kerouac prepared to go to San Francisco to meet him. He had made tentative plans to hitchhike to Detroit to meet Edie Parker but changed his mind when his mother warned him not to go. However, Cassady *had* written and urged Jack to go to California. Kerouac insisted that

Cassady was wasting his time recapping tires and should be writing instead: "I'm convinced you should attempt to make yourself a writer—and an existence in it—a living. Also, there's nothing you have to learn. You know enough. All you need is the habit of work. Now that I can push your work with authority, there's no reason for you to be childish about having to work." It was time, Kerouac advised Cassady, to "play the game."[10]

Having saved some money from his last job, Kerouac journeyed west to San Francisco in a "travel bureau" car—a paying job requiring the driver to bring the car to a destination assigned by the bureau. At the Colorado state line, Kerouac witnessed a cloud formation "huge and massed above the fiery golden desert of eveningfall" and envisioned the "great image of God with forefinger pointed straight at me." The admonition was clear enough, and to Kerouac it seemed prophetic; "go moan for man . . . and of Cody [pseudonym for Neal Cassady in *Visions of Cody*] report you well and truly."[11] This he did, stockpiling anecdotes about Cassady in his notebooks that would eventually find their way into the ever-evolving *On the Road* and the notebooks for *Visions of Cody*.

He reached San Francisco after midnight; by two o'clock in the morning, he was knocking on Cassady's door. Neal answered the door stark naked. Although Kerouac felt that his arrival made him feel like a "strange most evil angel," both Carolyn and Neal welcomed their dear friend. Carolyn recalled, "My supersensitivity made our few encounters strained, and the more I behaved like the disapproving parent, the more they treated me as such—the mother, to be lied to and evaded."[12]

One morning, not long after Jack's arrival, he needed to urinate. To reach the bathroom, he had to cross through the Cassadys' bedroom. That night he saw Carolyn crying in bed. To avoid involvement in their domestic matters, Kerouac hit the sidewalks of Russian Hill looking for an open bar and an empty bathroom, but finding neither, urinated outside in the street. Returning to the Cassadys', he slinked past Carolyn into the bathroom. Uncomfortably he overheard Carolyn and Neal shouting outside the locked door.

One night they took Carolyn with them, having found a babysitter for Cathy. However, Carolyn felt like a "fifth wheel" when Neal and Jack discussed people, places, and things she knew nothing about. The first half of the night Neal spent racing through the Fillmore section of San Francisco searching for marijuana. An hour later he scored some and parked in a dark residential area to inspect his purchase. He had been "duped" when he hadn't received what he expected. Angry, he abandoned the search and took Carolyn and Neal to a hotel where a friend of Luanne's was staying. Carolyn and Jack attempted to make conversation, but Carolyn realized it was not the same as the last time he had visited. Afterward, they went to a seedy strip club where Carolyn was mortified watching Neal flirt with the female vocalist on the stage above them. She demanded to be taken home, and Neal, happily, obliged her. At their house he let her out as he impatiently gunned the motor. Jack and Neal did not return until the next morning. William Burroughs, it seemed, had been right when he remarked to Kerouac that Cassady had finally reached the "ideal state of absolute impulsiveness."[13] Rashly, Neal left Carolyn only a few dollars and a curt note: "Carolyn: Am leaving today. Won't ever bother you again. I won't come back in a month to make you start it all over again." He informed her that he was driving to Denver, Detroit, and New York City and that he was not seeing Luanne Henderson.[14]

Kerouac and Cassady drove back to Chicago. From there they continued east, stopping off to see Edie Parker in Grosse Pointe, a trip described in the April 1951 "scroll" version of *On the Road* but later excised from the published version. By late August, Jack and Neal were back in New York, where Kerouac answered correspondence and completed the final revisions of *The Town and the City* with Robert Giroux at the Harcourt office. In September, Kerouac and Giroux attended the Ballets Russes at the Metropolitan Opera House. Kerouac felt the ballet the "most exquisite of the arts" as he saw for the first time a "strange little death" with its girls dancing en masse bathed in blue light, looking at once "Oriental" and "Russian." Afterwards the two visited Leon Danielian, "the Old Death's Head Impresario of the Ballet," in his dressing room. In the city, Kerouac found that his forthcoming novel was slowly garnering him a bit of celebrity: "I learned that I have to change now—being so much in 'demand' it is impossible to accept all invitations to lunch, and equally impossible to try to communicate with everybody, as I've always done out of mere joy. Now I'll have to start selecting. Isn't that awful?"[15]

Burroughs had written to Kerouac from Pharr, Texas, on September 26. He invited Jack for a stay on his farm and, afterward, to take a sojourn into sunny Mexico, where "a single man could live good for $2 per day," with the abundance of seedy whorehouses, cheap restaurants, and even cheaper liquor. Burroughs was still under the impression that Kerouac was well off financially from his book advance. (Nothing could have been further from the truth. Kerouac's indigence was so extreme that in May 1950 he wrote a letter to the Internal Revenue Service explaining that his income for 1949, a total of $1,250, had been also his primary source of revenue since 1946. Not able to afford the $89 that he owed to the government, Kerouac asked for permission to pay the tax in 1951, when he felt he would be in the position to pay both the tax and interest.) For now, Burroughs, fearing the wrath of post office censors, warned Kerouac against mentioning anything about drugs in his letters, "[n]o references to junk or weed." Signing off "As Ever," he awaited Kerouac's response.[16]

Rather than reply to Burroughs right away, Kerouac wrote to Charles Sampas, Sebastian's older brother, who was living in Lowell and writing a regular column for the *Lowell Sun*. As in his high school football glory years, Kerouac wanted to make his hometown proud. To Sampas, Kerouac described the genesis of *The Town and the City* and reminded him that one of the "heroes" of the novel, Alexander Panos, "the melancholy young Greek," was fashioned after Sebastian.[17] Incorporating into his letter long excerpts from the novel's opening chapter, Kerouac assured Sampas that he would receive a review copy and reminded him of his earlier advice to "stay out" of "[s]trange, dark" Lowell if Jack wanted to make it as a writer. To Kerouac, Lowell was the same as any other city, whether it be Anderson's Winesburg, Ohio; Hawthorne's Salem, Massachusetts; or Wolfe's Asheville, North Carolina. It was the

> place where the darkness of the trees by the river, on a starry night, gives hint of the inscrutable future Americans are always longing for. And when they find that future, not till then they begin looking back with sorrows, and an understanding of how man haunts the earth, pacing, prowling, circling in the shades, and the intelligence of the compass pointing to nothing in sight save the starry passion . . . strange, is strange, how we be-dot infinity with our thoughts and poor rooftops, and hometown, then go away forever.[18]

On January 23, 1950, Kerouac received advance copies of *The Town and the City* and promptly sent books to friends like Beverly and Bob Burford, William Burroughs, Ed Smith, and Allen Ginsberg. To accompany Ginsberg's copy, Kerouac composed a poem in his friend's honor, "Lines Dedicated to Allen Ginsberg on the Occasion of the Presentation of My Book to Him," writing that he was "tied to dark-trod earth" with a "trembling veil."

Anticipating *The Town and the City*'s imminent release, he pondered in his journal, "Will I be rich or poor? Will I be famous or forgotten? Am ready for this with my 'philosophy of simplicity' (something which ties in a philosophy of poverty with inward joy, as I was in 1947 and 1948)."[19] By the middle of February, Kerouac was still waiting for the first book reviews. While he waited, Kerouac wrote an early version of an opening to *On the Road* stopping after four handwritten pages. He dated it February 1, 1950.

The Town and the City was published in March 1950. On March 5, the *New York Times* reviewed the novel. The reviewer, John Brooks, was exceptionally aware of the technical and spiritual scope of Kerouac's writing. He compared Kerouac's Massachusetts settings to Wolfe and the descriptions of the New York City underworld to Dostoyevsky: "One gets the feeling that the author grew spiritually and improved technically while writing 'The Town and the City.' The early scenes in Massachusetts tend to be overly idyllic in content and wordy, even ungrammatical, in presentation. On the other hand, Mr. Kerouac's somewhat Dostoevskian view of New York City life is certainly exaggerated in another direction, but it is powerful and disturbing."[20]

Another prominent review appeared in the *Saturday Review of Literature* by a Harvard professor, Howard Mumford Jones, on March 11:

> In the present amorphous state of book reviewing this will likely be hailed as a novel displaying great life, energy, and realism. Life, energy, and realism of a kind it certainly has. It belongs to the category of the "big" novel—the lengthy book, in which a prodigious splashing about, general emotional appeals in the "lost, lost, lost" cadence of Thomas Wolfe, and a rather simple notion of what constitutes fictional characters are supposed to compensate for radical deficiencies in structure and style.[21]

Despite the early reviews, Kerouac remained optimistic that his road novel would be his breakthrough book. He planned to exercise every day at the local YMCA and to curtail his drinking, for he wanted to create a "new" and "real" life for himself. In his writing Kerouac vowed to "express more and record less in *On the Road*. You have to believe in life before you can accomplish anything."

Charles Sampas wrote in the *Lowell Sun* for the novel's first excerpted serialization on March 12, 1950:

> Writing is the loneliest job in the world and I don't doubt that Jack had many moments while writing this novel when he must have felt lonely. He must have felt mighty lonely for so many of his youthtime friends who went Over There and never came back. He felt lonely for the young spring days when life was an adventure and every forest a jungle of surprises. He felt lonely for the days of football at Lowell High School and the big game with Lawrence.
>
> To spend day after day, night after night, away from Lowell, evoking the scenes of yesteryear in Lowell, with no promise of having your novel ever published, that is the great test of any writer; and Jack passed that test.[22]

Alongside the excerpt, photographs of the "broad and placid" Merrimack River and downtown Lowell illustrated the novel's fictional counterparts. The Martin family was identified as the Kerouacs, and Alex Panos as Sebastian Sampas. Later that month, as part of his promotional tour, Kerouac returned to his hometown. Standing in the Bon Marché Book Shop and wearing a suit and tie (the only time he would ever do so in connection with a novel's promotion), Kerouac signed copies of his book at a sparsely attended signing. One attendee, Mrs. Elmer P. Rynne, who was the wife of the owner of Lowell's sports apparel shop, Lull & Hartford, went out of compassion for the hometown author who failed to draw even a respectable crowd from his hometown. Standing in the shop with three women (including Rynne), Kerouac was photographed by a *Lowell Telegram* photographer as part of its regular feature: "Camera News of Greater Lowell." The *Lowell Sunday Sun* noted the novel in its column, "What Lowell Is Reading," which was bylined by the city's librarian. Beyond that, Kerouac failed, as he did with the rest of the country, to make a splash with his novel.

In Lowell, he did find time to visit with close friends, including the Sampases. He later wrote to Stella Sampas that he wished his visit to Lowell had been spent anonymously and jesting that next time he would grow a beard and don a slouch hat.[23]

Despite Kerouac's efforts at publicity, *The Town and the City* was selling poorly; expected advance sales of twenty thousand copies, a $7,500 advertising plan, and the novel's acceptance by a British publisher (Eyre and Spottiswoode) had negligible effects on increasing sales (though he was pleased with the handsomely bound British edition). The novel, however, received positive reviews in Ireland and England. He wrote his London editor, Frank Morley, expressing gratitude that his novel was being published in England. He revealed to Morley that Giroux had rejected *On the Road* and that for now, he would be his "own editor." The London critics had wisely suggested that Kerouac move on and find a different style that did not emulate Wolfe so closely. But such sound criticism had an adverse effect. His spirits plunged, and Kerouac (once again) turned his eyes to the road.[24] He toyed with the idea of creating a sequel to *The Town and the City*. For the duration of seventeen pages he typed and corrected his prose. On page five, he headed the section "On the Road" before abandoning it altogether.

When Burroughs wrote to thank Jack for the book, he nonchalantly asked when he could expect Kerouac to visit. Burroughs was no longer a citizen of the United States (having taken citizenship in Mexico) and had begun writing his first novel "about junk."[25] Desperate to revive the lagging sales of his book, Kerouac convinced Harcourt, Brace to pay the majority of his expenses for a book signing in Denver. In early May 1950, Kerouac went to that city to publicize his book and did not arrive in Mexico until June, accompanied by Cassady. Neal had decided to meet Jack in Denver and drive him down—this time in a 1937 Ford that had definitely seen better days. It was, Kerouac remembered in *On the Road,* "the most pleasant and graceful billowy trip in the world."

While in Denver, Kerouac appeared at the Denver Dry Goods Company. Justin Brierly, Bob and Beverly Burford, and Ed White visited the store to see him; afterward, they went to the city's Elitch Gardens to smoke marijuana in the darkness of the waving tree shadows. Ed White, his sister, and her upper-class friends, anxious to host a New York City author, threw a congratulatory party for Jack. To Ed's sister's dismay (and probably to Kerouac's relief), Cassady and some Larimer Street blue-collar friends crashed the gathering. Bob Burford did not think highly of Cassady and could not understand Kerouac's fascination with him. Burford believed that Ginsberg kept the fire of Cassady's persona alive in Kerouac's mind: "I think there were many characters that he could have written about, and really would have developed his talent more than playing around with Cassady. Cassady just wasn't that interesting." The rowdy group kept Kerouac suitably high for the duration of his visit. On the day before he left, they all gathered in the dingy bar of an even dingier hotel where young Neal and his derelict father had once lived.[26]

Upon his arrival, Kerouac viewed Mexico City as similar in many ways to Lowell. As with his hometown, the noon sunlight fell on the close-knit communities that sprawled outward from the hub of Mexico City, and those who lived and died by the guiding light of Catholicism populated these quarters predominantly. There were the downtrodden trekking to and from the hot fields and shops at sunset. New York and his failed novel were far behind Jack, who spent the summer of 1950 in Mexico City in pot-clouded bliss. As he described in a letter to John Clellon Holmes from Cerrada Medellín that hot July, he was smoking enough large bombers to see, echoing Louis-Ferdinand Céline's novel of the same name, the "end of the night."[27] To Ed White, Kerouac described Mexico as "much fun," a place where he tanned darkly in the sun, dined on steaks, and indulged in numerous young Mexican prostitutes. On one Sunday afternoon Kerouac crossed the baking-hot plains from an ancient Indian village of stone huts to a newer housing development. Hallucinating, he sat at the base of a shimmering pile of orange bricks (in his view a makeshift altar) envisioning God. Jack's state of mind was distorted not only by drugs, but also by the violence of a bullfight he had watched at the Cuatro Caminos earlier that morning. He had witnessed the matador's sword plunged to the hilt into the bull's shining, sweaty body until the blade tip pierced the creature's heart; until the bull vomited "spewing rivers of blood" and consequently gagged on its "choking mass." A team of horses dragged away the carcass while men shoveled the coagulating blood into buckets. Disgusted, Kerouac thought that Ernest Hemingway, the "fat ass," was nothing more than a "fool" for writing of such gory spectacles with such unabashed zeal: "a bull dies too big a death for the cowards in their seats." "Everybody wants death. Young boys rush off to get killed in great wars before they've had their first tender fuck with a woman, who prefers them to die, it would seem. Everything is oriented toward death. I don't know what to do. I feel almost like the Jew in the tank scrawling his name, his statement and the date on the wall with blood."[28]

Such exploited violence evoked a number of other scenarios, such as the "young Negro cat" tenor saxophonist playing "I'll Remember April" in a "sawdust saloon" of whom Kerouac wondered why the cops would "smash his head with clubs." The bullfight, his pot-addled brain, the violence of Mexico City, and Burroughs's own sinister countenance caused Kerouac to reflect that he lived in an "evil world" with nothing to look forward to except the "transient bliss of such moments" as getting high. Tired, wearied, and doomed, Kerouac decided to "resign my optimism in this odious and oppressive place we call the earth." At the brick altar, swirling images arose, and among them was the penitent "Great Walking Saint" he had incorporated into a working draft of *On the Road*:

> Out of it emerged—much like Tony the Imbecile rising from my desk in Richmond Hill—the Image of the Great Walking Saint of On the Road . . . who, as a penance, walks around America till the day of his death, no Nature Boy, but a man digging all women, men and children, dogs, cats, squirrels, birds, trees, rivers, and flowers that fall in his path as he trudges. He stops and speaks with the children. He sits on a rock in front of a Coca Cola sign and listens to the hum of time. He stands on the side of Highway 66 looking at all the cars that pass, saying "Whither Goest Thou?" and when a car stops he repeats the question to the driver, and stares at him. He sits in the middle of Mexican shacktowns in the afternoon and chatters with the people in his own strange tongue they can all understand. He walks on. He will do so till he's a hundred years old. I decided to do this from seventy on . . . or sixty on . . . or anytime. Meanwhile it goes in my book. Someday like old Gogol and old Tolstoy, why not, I will do that . . . if it comes to pass that the light is not of this world. I have seen the light. That's what is at the end of the night. The Light. That Which God Hath Wrought. The Light.[29]

His sole literary balm while in Mexico was a review of *The Town and the City* by Yvonne Le Maitre, a columnist for a newspaper in Worcester, Massachusetts, who praised the book. Her review "touched" him more than the others because he felt that she "understood" him best. He informed her in his response on September 8, 1950, that his reason for naming his family in *The Town and the City* Martin was that it could "also be a French name. . . . Norman. It was one of the few personal clues I wanted to establish. Because I wanted a universal American story, I could not make the whole family Catholic. It was an American story. As I say, the French-Canadian story I've yet to attempt." This review made Jack antsy to return to the United States, where he still aspired to the status of literary lion. By August, he was home again.[30]

Kerouac had stayed in contact with Ginsberg throughout the summer of 1950. Ginsberg—living now in Paterson, New Jersey, with his father and Louis's new wife, Edith—was depressed and moody. Although no longer under close psychiatric scrutiny, Ginsberg still wondered if he was indeed "doomed to incompletion." He continued his intensive studies of Cézanne and Dante, but—despite his diploma from Columbia—found it difficult to find a "career." In a letter to Kerouac, Ginsberg complained that he knew how "strange and actually sordid the atmosphere here among those who run the city officially" was. Indeed, it was an environment where "friendship is actually political." Believing the answer to this problem existed solely in art, Ginsberg worked on his "Book of Doldrums," while Kerouac wrote in his journal that one had to believe in life before one could "accomplish anything. That is why dour, regular-houred, rational-souled State Department Diplomats have done nothing for mankind." Life, in its every aspect, was too sacred to while away its precious hours frivolously. "Why live if not for excellence?"[31]

One of Kerouac's staunchest supporters, Ginsberg was proud of his friend's achievement and was equally incensed by Harcourt, Brace's lack of commitment. (Because the sale of the novel hardly brought in enough to pay back Kerouac's advance, he would earn no royalties from it.) To Kerouac, he wrote: "This may sound like old wives gossip but my original optimistic prognosis, reinforced in my mind by reviews, is being rapidly undermined in my own mind by fears about some commercial slip up unforeseen brought on by Harcourt. Do something. Man the lifeboats . . . You have a duty to protect your investments. . . . Time is crucial."[32] By June 1950, however, it was too late to man the lifeboats. After four months of floundering, the book sank without a trace. John Clellon Holmes remarked:

> I think Jack had to have *The Town and the City* published and had to
> go through the bad times of the editing of the book—the book was
> cut by a third—and get sick of it. Get sick of the scene, but also take a

look at what he really wanted to do. I think if it hadn't been published, he would've been cranky and hung up on it. This way he was freed from it and he could look at it and say, as he used to say, "It's alive."[33]

On the Road continued as a work in progress (among Kerouac's several other active writing projects). In the mid- to late summer of 1950, he typed up seven chapters and gave it a setting in Iowa. He titled it "Gone on the Road" and penciled extensive corrections over the type before scrapping this version. Kerouac submitted what he felt were the best portions of *On the Road* to Robert Giroux, who rejected them. Upset with Giroux's reaction, Kerouac gave up on Harcourt, Brace as an option and instead sent the manuscript to Farrar, Straus & Young. Although the company did not reject the manuscript, it advised Kerouac that the work required extensive revisions before it would be publishable. Taking the company at its word, Kerouac attempted to revise the work but then decided to start over. He sent portions of the manuscript to John Clellon Holmes, who helped Kerouac acquire an agent, Rae Everitt from MCA. This development left him with one responsibility: to write. Reaching back to 1947 and his first trip cross-country with Neal Cassady, Kerouac started writing again.

Meanwhile, Neal Cassady did all he could to encourage Jack's propensity to drop what he was doing and head west. His September 25, 1950, letter detailed his commiseration with a hallucinating hobo sunning atop an S&P boxcar. Neal's vigorously charged letters would accelerate over the coming months to pierce and crack Kerouac's stylistic breakthrough. He was almost there.

17

Shadow Changes into Bone

Fall 1950–Spring 1951

In the knowledge of truth, what matters is having it, not what made
one seek it, or how one found it.
FRIEDRICH NIETZSCHE, *Human, All Too Human*

Listening to the fall 1950 World Series on the radio at his mother's
house in Richmond Hill, Kerouac noted the frantic banter of the sports
announcer, Gene Kelly, and found worth in what he heard. Having mastered the lingo of capturing this speed rap on paper, Jack was no stranger
to sports talk. As a boy he wrote (or typed) play-by-play imaginary baseball games. It wasn't necessarily the World Series itself that fascinated
Jack, but the sound of it, a banter uniquely American in its frantic yet
focused delivery. He made a tentative plan to create an "American Times
Series" narrated by various American voices: the chatter of a ten-year-old
Negro boy; the drone of English "sagas"; the utterances of Native Americans; the working-class vernaculars of myriad ethnicities; the monologues and the peculiar rants of America's Italians, hoboes, hipsters, west-
erners, and dilettantes. Kerouac told Neal that it was the "voice" that
determined a book's pacing and how the narrative sounded in the
reader's ear, that ultimately the "voice was all." Straight traditional narrative was insufficient for what Kerouac had to say. He tested various
voices in a letter to Neal. There was the "effeminate" drawl of a Manhattan socialite; the New York cry of Herbert Huncke the "jailbird"; the

217

western vernacular of hoboes and Cassady sidling down Larimer Street drunk "as he ever was." It was the voice that mattered, and Kerouac would test it for all it was worth.[1] He continued tampering with his palette of American voices and, in the beginning of October, Jack began a new work titled "Pic." A later inventory of his work, which Kerouac made at age thirty-two, describes "Pic" as merely a "fragment" of fifty thousand words[2] containing a "nigger dialect": "AIN'T NEVER NOBODY LOVED ME like I love myself, cept my mother and she's dead."[3] It was a minor work, similar to others that Kerouac attempted to write at this time when he was striving for his stylistic breakthrough.[4]

Needing money, Kerouac synopsized scripts for Twentieth-Century Fox. However, his constant intake of marijuana and experimentation with morphine, alarming to even his closest friends, thwarted this venture. Similarly reckless was Bill Cannastra, an Ivy League graduate, renowned switch-hitter, and "collaborator" with Kerouac. (Kerouac claimed that he did a couple of "collaborations" in bed with Cannastra in "lofts" with "blonds.")[5] Cannastra had been a fixture in the Village. One chilly autumn night, Ginsberg read his poem "In Judgement" (a work based on Cannastra and Huncke) and discussed "death" for five hours with Cannastra till they closed the San Remo bar:

> Who talks of Death and Angel now, Great Angel fallen
> out of Grace?
> O Lord why has Thou taken him
> There was such beauty in his face.[6]

A few nights later, after leaving a party with a friend and boarding a subway, Cannastra discussed returning to the Bleeker Street Tavern and, on impulse, made as if to go there through the train window. He stuck his head out into the acrid air of the subway's labyrinthine depths and, pushing himself out even further, spied the supporting pillar of the tunnel racing toward him, and began screaming. The pillar wrenched his neck and bashed his skull. He was dragged along filthy unyielding tracks, his face of "beauty" destroyed.[7] Cannastra left behind girlfriend and roommate Joan Haverty. Joan was another San Remo patron able to match wits with Cannastra and Ginsberg with relative ease (contrary to Allen's description of her to Neal as a "tall dumb darkhaired girl").[8]

Feeling the "Presence of fate" near him after Cannastra's death, Ginsberg knew that every tragedy had its prophetic warnings, and he heeded them by willing "pleasure" instead of death. He lost his job working for a labor newspaper and, realizing his inefficiency, knew that he hadn't the knack for being even a "pissyassed" reporter. He applied to work at a ribbon factory and was provisionally hired but was fired soon thereafter. From his perspective it wasn't his fault, but that of a "couple of nasty cunts."

Kerouac maintained a prolific correspondence with Cassady, who was planning to come to New York City in January 1951. Neal had been staying in San Luis Obispo for a few weeks alternating his manic life with spurts of caring for his daughter, Cathy. Railroading was laborious; despite that, he loved the work and it was perfect for his temperament. However, his employment at the railroad was problematic: Cassady was a risk for the railroad to have around. During his employ, there were over seven railroad mishaps at the Southern Pacific and Cassady was almost fired for two of them (on one occasion, the station was tied up for sixteen hours). As usual, it was life on the edge for Neal, but it was beginning to affect those who relied on him. Carolyn had had enough, but Neal thought that she just did not understand him. For Allen, he deconstructed his frantic everyday life: he was unable to do "ordinary things" because of his infected thumb; the car needed fixing; his health problems were mounting; he needed to acquire railroad passes for his trip back east; and, as always, the financial burden of supporting his family weighed heavily. Cassady hardly had time to write anymore. To increase the pressure further, a woman he had been seeing in New York, Diana Hansen, had become pregnant and given birth to a boy, whom she wanted to name Neal III (much to Carolyn's chagrin). Despite Neal's problems, the newly divorced Carolyn became economically independent and lived on her own. Shortly after his marriage to Diana, Neal asked Carolyn if he could move back in. Hesitant at first, Neal appeared at the house more and more to see his children. It was, in Carolyn's words, a "strictly business arrangement." By October 1950, Neal persuaded Carolyn to let him move back to their Russell Street home permanently "for the children's sake." Neal devised a plan to give each of the women a "test period"—Carolyn would be granted July through December, Diana the other half of the year. This, by Neal's logic, would show him who would be the "better wife." As alarmed as Carolyn was at Neal's twisted logic, she found it easy "to slip back into a married feeling with him."[9]

When the spirit seized him, Cassady worked on *The First Third*. He attempted to use an Ekotape tape recorder, but it was more frustrating than facilitating. Cassady felt that a tape recorder would benefit Kerouac more than it did him and urged his friend to try it.[10] Once when Cassady was high, he picked up copies of Wolfe's *Of Time and the River* and Proust's *Remembrance of Things Past* and read portions of each into the machine and sent the reel to a delighted and receptive Kerouac.

Neal Cassady continued to manipulate the people around him: "Never, in recent years, had I so consciously drawn out and controlled a piece of talk," he told Allen in November 1950. Neal told Kerouac that to write, he should portray himself as the first person on earth and "sincerely" place all of his thoughts on paper: everything seen, everything experienced, "loved and lost." Such encouragement and declarations endeared him even more to Kerouac, regardless of his ambivalence about Cassady's lack of acknowledgement of *The Town and the City*. For months, Cassady said nothing, and Jack felt slighted because of it. Kerouac's fragile ego could be wounded easily. Still, for now, Cassady remained his friend.

Kerouac's second marriage occurred precisely at the same time that he was achieving a crucial peak in artistic growth. Neal's letters were coming fast and furious, and *On the Road* (in various configurations) was continuing to gestate. Allen noted Kerouac's absence from the city; he began to sense that Jack seemed sober and more "settled in reality." It was, Neal contended, that Kerouac was actually stoned to distraction—having reached a "final and most disheartening realization of himself."[11]

In his journal Kerouac recorded his meeting with Joan Haverty on November 7 in her loft. To the best of Joan's recollection, he first appeared on the street below her window looking for Lucien Carr's party. In her sixty-by-thirty-foot undivided loft with her sometime boyfriend, Herb, Haverty appeared at the window and threw her keys down to Kerouac. Minutes later, he appeared at her door holding an attaché case. Herb asked him what he did for a living. "I wrote a book," Kerouac replied. He withdrew from his case a fresh copy of *The Town and the City* and gave it to Joan. She insisted on an autograph, which he signed "For Joan," telling her, "When I know you better, I'll add something to that." Joan retreated into the kitchen, leaving him alone with Herb. She overheard Kerouac asking him if Joan was Herb's girl. "Nope," he said, "she's fair game." Kerouac insisted that they both come with him to Lucien's party. They talked enthusiastically and, during the party, prompted by John Clellon Holmes, a discussion arose about Louis-Ferdinand Céline. An older partygoer remarked on Céline's nihilism and cynicism and on the French writer's comment that "women are all housemaids at heart." Joan Haverty remembered that Kerouac agreed with the sentiment but restated it by proclaiming that women were just "big beautiful children, that's all." The way that Kerouac got himself "off the hook" charmed Joan. The older partygoer challenged him by asking if he meant women were "inferior." Jack retorted, "Nah! Not inferior! Are children inferior? They're beautiful. I love 'em."

Jack endeared himself to Joan from the start. Her relationship with Herb, or what was left of it, ended essentially that evening. Merely a few days passed before Kerouac was beneath her window calling up from the street. She let him in. During the course of that Sunday evening he proposed to her. For Joan, "Jack's appeal lay more in what he was not than in what he was. He was not sexually aggressive, not intellectually curious concerning me, not anxious for me to achieve goals or improve myself, and he was neither critical nor demanding except in regard to domestic matters."[12]

Joan recognized that she was being wooed because suddenly Jack was anxious to have a family, another in a long list of reckless behaviors and impulsive decisions. She also felt that, having already garnered Gabrielle's semiapproval, she was especially desirable to Jack. Joan was a threat neither to Jack nor to his mother, and she knew how to cook, sew, and keep house. Joan and Kerouac also "shared a dream of children." He was bright, young, handsome, and seemingly sensible; she figured he could serve as a "means to an end." To her, marrying Jack was the "least of a number of evils."[13]

In mid-November, Joan and Jack went for blood tests and a marriage license. For a while, their wait for Jack's annulment papers from his marriage to Frankie Edith Parker delayed matters. A phone call to Jack's attorney confirmed that the annulment had actually occurred. On the following Friday, November 17, they were waiting at City Hall for the justice of the peace to officiate when news that they were thirty-four minutes shy of the required seventy-two-hour waiting period thwarted them. Incensed, Jack pleaded with the authorities at city hall to stay open a half-hour longer so that the brief ceremony could take place. (The reception had been planned for that night.) His pleas went unheeded. Joan suggested that they simply tell their guests they *were* married, an option that Jack declined. He did not carry off deception well. They took a subway to Greenwich Village and found a friend of Jack's with the authority under New York law to marry them. Judge Vincent Lupiano, in his Horatio Street residence, presided; Lupiano's wife and secretary were witnesses. Joan wore Gabrielle's wedding ring, blessed by the pope. After the ceremony Lupiano poured them both a shot of booze and reminded Jack that he never kissed the bride. "Oh yeah. That's right," Kerouac said.[14]

The party was under way by the time they arrived. Allen Ginsberg, Lucien Carr, and Potchki Lehmann all served as "bestpeople" at the rooftop ceremony, although Allen was skeptical about what good a second wife could do for Jack (or what good Jack could do for Joan). John Clellon Holmes and his wife, Marian, stood by the beer keg in the kitchen. Holmes told the newlyweds that he believed in their union. Joan felt that maybe Holmes thought they needed the support because they lacked any real comprehension about what they had just done. Joan noticed that Jack, halfway into the party, seemed to not be really drunk but simply acted that way out of a "conditioned response." The party consisted mostly of Jack's friends; Joan remembered bitterly in her memoir that it was "his party" because it was "his wedding" and that "none of it seemed to have anything to do with the rest of my life." During the party Jack and Allen went to the roof and had a "loving symbolical conversation." The partygoers dispersed early Saturday morning, leaving the bride with her drunken groom (despite her earlier suspicions that he was faking intoxication). By the time she turned off the light and slipped her nightgown over her head, Jack had passed out cold. Joan remembered thinking that, so far, the marriage had lived up to her "expectations."[15]

Carolyn Cassady received a letter from Jack a few days after his wedding. The news of the marriage shocked her and Neal, who wrote to Allen that it was a willful "blindness" stemming from a "perverted sense of wanting to help the girl and just plain what the hell." Cassady concluded that if Jack had not been high all the time on Mexican weed, he would not be married.[16] (Kerouac himself confessed that for much of the fall of 1950 he was smoking regularly "three bombs a day" because he was so unhappy.) On a positive note, his prodigious pot use sometimes took him inside the music that he listened to, as with George Handy's "The Bloos." Handy's music was "sacrificing" the "joy" that Jack felt existed "naturally in his heart for the glooms and despairs and great disappointed deaths, the deadly loss of ego, the last acknowledgement of self": "The music seemed to say 'There are still a few things that you can cling to and this I supposed you should be soothed about — ha ha — but you won't even regret that — though there's joy in our souls (bop interlude) we are nothing but shits and we'll all die and eat shit in graves and are dying now.' Pretty powerful talk!"[17]

Neal, who had planned to travel alone with Kerouac in the coming months, felt hurt by the abrupt marriage (though his own commitment as a friend would fail Jack in the coming months). Carolyn felt that Jack's "Catholic dogma" and "convictions regarding women" made such a union particularly fragile.[18] After receiving Allen's letter describing the ceremony, Neal summoned the spirit to write to Jack on December 7:

> I'm sure happy to hear you got married, naturally, I was as surprised as all git out but I knew you had to do it sometime. When a man approaches 30 (ugh) without being well on the way to have little kiddilies, it begins to become a teensy bit too late and soon all he can do is write books. It'd be fine, then, if your "impregnated on the 18th" is right and there is a building in the mixer a miniature K. with big ears and a bigger thingajigger.

Kidding aside, Neal tapped intuitively into the core of his friend's nature: "Jack, with all your fooleries, you can never escape your serious and overconcerned nature nor the destiny of your blood and your inclination to the Home . . . and all the times you've spoken about, and otherwise revealed, to me the hankering for a family."[19]

On December 14, Carolyn received an anxious letter from Jack, who had not yet received Neal's reply and was "waiting on pins and needles" for his reaction to Jack's nuptials. Overall, Kerouac's attitude was positive: he had a wife to ward off his loneliness and a new book he felt was "hogtied and thrown." How much of the optimism toward wife and work was genuine and how much feigned are difficult to determine.[20]

Echoing Allen's feeling that Joan was making a "shrine" of the Cannastra loft, Kerouac felt uncomfortable with her insistence on leaving the bed where it was and also with where she wanted to place his writing desk (one of the first things he and his friends had moved). Jack reasoned that since Bill Cannastra was dead, he no longer needed the loft and its possessions; but Joan felt that it was best to maintain his things as they were when he died. Jack, however, persuaded Joan, and soon the apartment was arranged to Jack's preference. In the process, Kerouac found several twelve-foot-long rolls of paper in one of Cannastra's cabinets. Asking Joan for coffee, he fed one end of the roll into his typewriter and began typing. "It just about guarantees spontaneity," he assured Joan, and proceeded to fill four feet of the new paper before putting it aside.

They traveled upstate to just outside Poughkeepsie to visit Joan's mother. Lucien Carr and Allen Ginsberg gave them a ride. The newlyweds returned in dire need of money to pay December's rent. Because Jack slept by day and entertained friends at night (he claimed such socializing was necessary for his books), his financial contributions were negligible. It wasn't long before Jack took Joan to live with Gabrielle. Standing in her floral-print housedress and slippers, Gabrielle wept with joy that her boy had returned to Richmond Hill with his new bride. Jack moved his writing desk back to its original spot, and Gabrielle placed his slippers under it. She also relinquished her much larger bedroom to the couple. The den was refashioned into a sewing room for Joan, who was mindful of both her domestic duties and her planned career as a dressmaker. The room, though tiny and unheated, quelled Joan's worst fears that there would not be one place for her to be "herself" in. Although Kerouac promised the room to her, it was Joan alone who had to remove the accumulated clutter, clean the space, and move her things in while Gabrielle worked at the shoe mill and Jack slept soundly in bed.[21]

For now, Jack was happy. Under one roof he had both mother and wife—both caretakers to his domestic needs and the latter a regular source of sexual fulfillment. To help ward off total poverty, Joan took a temporary job in a department store during the Christmas rush. No longer counting on *The Town and the City* for his fortunes, Jack needed to complete *On the Road,* his "REAL BOOK," to earn an advance. To accomplish this, he had to circumvent his mental roadblocks. Jack wrote into his journal more potential titles: "Souls on the Road," "Home and the Road," "In the Night on the Road," "Love on the Road," and "Along the Wild Road." Perhaps needing more hands-on experience to kick-start his imagination, Jack anxiously awaited Neal's arrival in February. Should that fail, Jack would resort to "plan 2": moving to San Francisco with Joan so that he could get a job at a newspaper and she could continue her career as a clothing designer.

In the fall and winter of 1950, Kerouac remained resentful that *The Town and the City* wasn't being publicized in Harcourt, Brace's promotional Christmas lists. It was the "worst shitluck" he ever had—the "curse of Melville," as he called it. Books that he deemed mediocre were rated above his own. He assumed that critics couldn't think for themselves, that they waited to see what other critics said, and that, when they said nothing at all, their silence sank the book into oblivion. Calling the publishing world "cocksuckers," Kerouac swore off ever again writing such a carefully crafted work. He told Cassady:

> Now you see why my thoughts turn to Mexico; if I can land a little job with some American company I can stay there the rest of my life . . . some American money turned to pesos . . . and have five kids moreover . . . and my wife is the gal for such a life. Same dream I had in 1947 when I wrote you those wild imprctible [*sic*] letters and Allen said my T & C manuscripts might very well be "the production of a cracked brain." Why am I telling you this, my dear friend. Well so you'll know. And anything I write from now on is my own business and my own personal possession and have no fear that it will be useless.[22]

High on pot, he sat at the typewriter while Joan showered and his mother watched the news on television. Communist troops from North Korea were routing the South Korean army, but more than ever, Kerouac remained outside of world crises and politics.

In December 1950, Jack retrieved Neal's latest letter from the front steps and opened it. Leaving the house shortly thereafter, he took the letter with him on the subway to read and later went to a cafeteria for two hours to peruse it again before finally returning home in the early evening. Joan read the letter and was enthralled by Neal's autobiographical comical misadventure. Jack showed it to Alan Harrington and John Clellon Holmes; neither was impressed. Neal's rambling prose style did not suit everyone. Yet Cassady's correspondence was a crucial catalyst in the transformation of John Kerouac, the author of *The Town and the City,* into Jack Kerouac, America's Poet of the Open Road.

Jack had found his writing breakthrough. The thirteen-thousand-word letter was a rambling scattershot narrative assaulting the reader with its reckless verbosity. It was no less a letter than autobiographical fiction. However, to Kerouac, it all made sense—the door to Cassady's demons was cracking open little by little. Kerouac placed the tale of Cassady's Christmas in 1946 Denver in the same league as Dostoyevsky, Joyce,

Wolfe, and Céline, feeling that its honesty would spark a new "American Renaissance." Excited, he showed the letter to Ginsberg, who also saw promising literary merit.[23]

Neal's imagery unraveled for Jack the answer to *On the Road*. That night, Jack wrote to Neal: "Just a word, now, about your wonderful 13,000 word letter about Joan Anderson and Cherry Mary." Cassady's technique, Kerouac explained,

> will be published. It was a moment in lit. history when I received that thing & only sweetwife & I read it & knew. Ah man it's great. Don't undervalue your poolhall musings, your excruciating details about streets, appointment times, hotel rooms, bar locations, window measurements, smells, heights of trees. I wait for you to send me the entire thing in disorderly chronological order anytime you say and anytime it comes, because I've just got to read every word you've got to say and take it all in. If that ain't life nothing ain't.[24]

Kerouac told Neal his work had elements of the best of the Western canon: Joyce's experimentation, Céline's frankness, Proust's minute recall, and Dostoyevsky's confessional mode—all combined with Cassady's "muscular rush." He told Neal that not even Melville, Wolfe, or Fitzgerald (all of whom, in Kerouac's view, failed to cast off static literary conventions) had touched upon Cassady's approach. Cassady so impressed Kerouac that he saw "no harm" in devoting his future oeuvre, a proposed ten books, to Neal. To further affirm the creative worth of Neal's writing, Jack made plans to show the letter to Robert Giroux in the hope that the letter could be published. In Carolyn's estimate, Jack went "overboard" and failed to see the flaws in Cassady's writing style.

Kerouac was leery of lending the letter to Allen for fear he would lose it. By chance finding himself in the apartment in Gabrielle's absence, Ginsberg took the letter from Jack's writing desk. After reading it, Allen wrote Neal and called it an "almost pure masterpiece" (though Neal responded that he could write the same kind of letter "anytime"). At the very least, it was an impressive display. Cassady's reply to Ginsberg in November was, as always, candid and vulnerable. Neal began by describing the tormenting "vacuum" within and by claiming that he was at a loss to communicate with anybody (especially Diana Hansen, who had given birth to their child). "I can't overemphasize," he told Ginsberg, "how ugly my life has become, simply because of this 'do nothingness,' and how low

I've gotten by realizing emotionally every damn moment what a really disgusting fish I am." Neal listed his more miserable aspects in a blatant display of self-loathing, before leaping into a new paragraph describing the "soul."

The letter's references to soul can be traced to Spengler's *Decline of the West*, which both he and Carolyn were reading at the time. It was one of the more influential works of the beat generation. Less than ten years earlier, Kerouac had discussed Spengler with Sebastian Sampas. Now Spengler was on Neal's mind. Cassady stressed the futility of getting an "exact fix" on the "ever-mysterious soul." The essence of soul is not found in its "abstract thinking," Cassady explained, but is most feasibly encountered in its more physical manifestations, much as the "likenesses" found in Rembrandt's self-portraits manifest the painter. Of relevance to Neal and Jack's literary camaraderie, Cassady states that "certain ineffable stirrings of soul can be imparted by one man to the sensibility of another man through a look, two bars of melody; an almost imperceptible movement."

Two days after receiving Neal's epic letter, Kerouac sat down to pen a series of letters that would become his own "confession" to his new high priest of modern prose, though never mailed. To do so, Kerouac had to reach far back, to the day of his birth in Lowell, and dig further into himself, beyond his sense of "falseness." To be truthful in his writing, Jack felt that he had to "renounce" any prospects of writing fiction for profit. The first by-product of this new belief was a "full confession" to Cassady mirroring—if not in style, at least in spirit and conviction—his letter. Jack hoped that this series of letters, which would occupy most of his time for the next two weeks, would "become more interesting and less literary" and would finally arrive at the "actual truth of my life." The glowing beacon that lit the dim hallways of his uncertain days and quelled the nagging feeling that he was "false" was his acknowledgment that "God is light and truth."[25]

Kerouac's realization that writing was his only means of redemption became glaringly apparent in his December 28 letter, written in an inspired fury as snow fell outside his apartment in the "pit of night." He began by eradicating any preconceived notions of himself:

My sin—the fact that I am a subtly dishonest man generally recognized and probably by all means rightly referred [to] as a "swell guy," you see which has nothing to do with it—began, brother Neal, on the day of my birth. Before I'm finished you'll know everything about me.

Value given is value received. What God hath wrought. All that. When a man is born dust takes a flyer. Dust of dust, you may as well know of my dust. My report to you in the pit of night, and to God in the pit of night, will carry me through.[26]

The description of his birth resembles closely the version published later in *Doctor Sax:* the March thaw on the day of his birth, when the snow melted from pine trees and "snowy banksides" crumbled under their own weight as little streams ran under them. Other references to *Doctor Sax* include the "world snake" and his conviction that Christ is "the son of God" who "died for our sakes truly." Interestingly, Kerouac asks Cassady not to destroy their correspondence but to save it for posterity.

Kerouac took a break from his writing during the waning days of December and walked through Manhattan. Seeking shelter from the freezing cold (after he left Grand Central Station "looking around in futile sorrow for a place to sit and think"), he sat in St. Patrick's Cathedral and watched the dusk glow blue through the immense stained-glass windows. As he sat in the pew listening to novenas, his mind turned to Lowell and he thought of his childhood home on Hildreth Street that his family had moved into after Gerard's death. He saw again the midnight memories of Jesus Christ pushing his bed, heard once more his mother's grief-stricken shrieks and crying, and recalled the ominous green glow of the family's black-lacquered crucifix. A newfound misery set in as Jack began to reason that he was now the biblical Judas figure and Gerard, the ethereal "do-no-wrong" older brother, was Jesus. This survivor guilt fragmented his already fragile sensibilities. He overheard two priests nearby speaking with winter-hoarse voices and began to weep.[27] Kerouac reflected on his new marriage and home life, already spinning out of control after only three months. In the cathedral he tried to divert his thoughts from the fact that he was subtly "torturing" Joan. Lately she had been uncomfortable with their sex life and told him that she felt like a "frog" during intercourse. She also did not want to be touched during menstruation. In the pews of St. Patrick's Cathedral he brooded on a shawled woman kneeling in prayer in front of him:

I saw how all earthly life, with its gutty sufferings, really passes like a river through the body of a woman while the man, unknowing of these things and "clean," just cuts along arrogant. I saw how it is the woman who gives birth, and suffers, and has afterbirths dragged out of her, and navel cords snipped and knotted and bleeds—while the man boasts of his bloody prowesses. I saw how it is the woman who suffers for the sins of man. Suffers especially more so, because the earth is so much in her, temptation drives her mad. I had even been annoyed at the poor girl lately because she conducted long secret meditations of her own in the bedroom while I "wrote." What are you thinking about?" I'd ask slyly. What's going on in her great soul now? I'd ask myself sarcastically. Bah, bah, bah, and all that; as if, and certainly BE-CAUSE I was a "writer" she, a mere girl, could not possibly have a soul like mine worthy of hours of deep contemplation.[28]

Although he empathized with women in general, he grew irksome with his wife's accelerating complaints.

In early 1951, Kerouac continued his series of confessional letters to Cassady. As Jack wrote, he displayed a new confidence in his narrative method, previously restricted to his personal notebooks. Within Jack's reveries simmered long-harbored fears of God and the searing iron of Catholic superstition—all spiked with a liberal dose of Gerard's "ragged phantom" spirit forever clambering through his younger brother's labyrinth. Kerouac flatly stated, "It's to YOU I have to tell everything." Although Kerouac aspired to be a "life-changing prophetic artist," he also realized that such an ambition was a by-product of vanity. For the next few years, his writing would be difficult even for close friends like John Clellon Holmes and Allen Ginsberg to read. Neither could understand why Jack refused to bend a little to write more conventional and salable prose under the duress of his crushing poverty. Kerouac's latest writing had evolved into a narrative fractured by personal asides and flashbacks that defied linearity. Ginsberg viewed Kerouac's letters to Cassady as a "long confessional of two buddies telling each other everything that happened, every detail." Such an undertaking "required sentences that did not necessarily follow exact classic-type syntactical order, but which allowed for interruption with dashes, allowed for the sentences to break in half, take another direction (with parentheses that might go on for paragraphs). It allowed for individual sentences that might not come to their period except after several pages of self-reminiscence, of interruption and piling on of detail, so that what you arrived at was a sort of stream of consciousness visioned around a specific subject . . . and a specific viewpoint."

Sitting in their bedroom alone, Joan Haverty Kerouac felt like a child under Gabrielle's oppressive authority, conducting her "long secret meditations." Joan saw that her husband did as his mother asked because he was indebted to Gabrielle, who provided physical and emotional comfort to such a degree that he would never be comfortable anywhere (or with anyone) else. Joan thought of herself as playing a minor part in the daily drama of Gabrielle's and Jack's lives. Gabrielle's firm resolve was that his work as a writer was more important than being a husband, a notion not too far removed from Jack's own convictions. He was, as Joan belatedly discovered after their rash decision to marry, a man brimming with inner contradictions. Though he was, most times, generous and kindhearted, Jack could also be irascible and unapproachable. His nature was introspective. The high-spirited extrovert her husband became when he was drinking easily metamorphosed into a deeply melancholic and introspective man when sober. Jack was a mass of conflicting feelings and aspirations and, though essentially a unified personality, was not to be judged by the contrasting characteristics that he had inherited from his very dissimilar parents. Nor was he to be judged by isolated actions of his own (most of which sprang from his inner impulses rather than from mature deliberation) but by the moral purpose that remained constant throughout his life. These traits held all the contrasting elements together.

One night, after a long day spent working in the department store, Joan came home to find Jack eager to have a spice cake. Gabrielle, attending a union meeting at the shoe factory, was not there to bake it for him. Joan refused, and Kerouac replied that a "woman's comfort" depended on her husband's. When she changed out of her business clothes, Jack told her not to undress in front of him if she had no intention of "doing anything about it." "I didn't ask you to follow me in here," she countered. Soon afterward, Gabrielle returned, and Joan smelled the aroma of spice cake drifting through the bedroom vents.[29]

Jack was also jealous of Joan's male friends and acquaintances. One afternoon he went to a local bar, leaving Joan alone on a barstool while he played pool; when he looked back, he saw that she was talking to a Richmond Hill neighbor. Jack went over, took her arm, and exited hastily from the bar. "You've got to learn to tell guys like that to fuck off," he reproached. Joan felt as if she were Jack's "possession," but that he was not worthy of possessing her. Such incidents piled one atop the other.[30]

On January 9, 1951, Kerouac finished the last of his five confessional letters (approximately 22,500 words over twenty-nine pages) and signed off, "Goodnight Sweet Prince." Cassady was due in New York in February. Kerouac had enmeshed Neal fully into his past and present. Meanwhile, Burroughs (preparing to leave Mexico for South America) mailed a manuscript that he was working on to Ginsberg and Kerouac. The work, simply titled "Junk," was an account of his experiences with heroin. Enthusiastically, Kerouac wrote to Burroughs asking how the novel would conclude. Burroughs's straightforward writing style was suitable enough for Kerouac to borrow, and he revealed that he was "imitating" from Burroughs a "kind of Dashiell Hammett of Wm. Lee [pseudonym for Burroughs in *Junky*]," which may have contributed to his breakthrough on *On the Road* that forthcoming April.[31] John Clellon Holmes was also working on his manuscript titled *Go.* In March he brought Kerouac the manuscript on which he had been laboring since August 1949. His influences were similar to Kerouac's (chiefly Dostoyevsky), but, unlike his friend, Holmes found that "truth wasn't half enough." It needed to be sparked into a fictional treatment: "I was dealing in extremes of spirit, excesses of behavior, violent emotions or *lack* of them." Much to Kerouac's chagrin—he later thought he had been plagiarized—*Go*, published in the fall of 1952, would be the first beat novel to emerge.[32]

Before Cassady arrived in February, Kerouac intended to save money (for Cassady's impending visit) from his at-home script-synopsizing job, but it only earned him roughly $35 a week. With their combined funds and Neal's help, they would acquire either railroad passes or a panel truck; load the truck with furniture, a mattress, and cushions; and leave for a nonstop trip to San Francisco. But Cassady's visit had a sober purpose: he had a child less than one year old there—his son with Diana Hansen—and Neal's paternal negligence had begun to wear on him.

Cassady, shuffling from foot to foot, arrived on the doorstep of the Richmond Hill apartment house. Kerouac was out somewhere, so Joan offered Neal a beer, a warm pan of water to wash and soak his sore feet, and a pair of Jack's socks. She enjoyed Neal's presence and admired his ability to process an event "on several different levels" without losing the "thread" of any. In his rap, she caught elements of geography, philosophy, poetry, natural history, and social commentary. Next to Neal, she felt herself a "well-mannered, numbed excuse for a living being" cast into the world by what Cassady deemed a "divine design."[33]

One thing that Joan did not feel toward Cassady was physical attraction. She refused his request to engage in a ménage à trois with him and Jack. According to Joan, Kerouac reasoned that Cassady could show her "what it's all about," while showing Jack what he was doing "wrong." Not wanting to "know what it's all about," she gave her consent—half humoring them and half serious—for them to look for girls. Joan detected a change in Jack once his friend arrived; Kerouac's dualism became all the more evident to her. Years later, she could compare accurately and objectively *The Town and the City*'s Ti Jean with *On the Road*'s Jack: the shy, brooding man who required from his wife an air of unworldliness versus the spirited, boundless Jack intent on unleashing her libido.

During the week of Cassady's stay, Jack and Joan, along with Henri Cru, attended a Duke Ellington concert. Cru, not fond of Cassady, denied Neal a ride to Forty-second Street despite the night's freezing temperature. Joan asked Henri why Neal could not attend the concert with them. Fearing Neal would embarrass him, Cru said that Cassady's presence was out of the question. To her, Neal embodied the spontaneity of music. It was an excitement that, in some ways, she felt Jack lacked. Having secured neither panel truck nor railroad passes for the Kerouacs, Neal left the city. Jack's last glimpse of Cassady was of him walking away in his "moth-eaten overcoat" in the winter harshness of the city. Although Kerouac did not know it yet, it was his ending for *On the Road*. Jack would soon be bidding farewell to his marriage, too. For Joan, there would be no life apart from the French-speaking Cerberus so zealously guarding Jack, who refused to tear himself away. Kerouac wrote to Alfred Kazin that he was "trapped" in an "American Tragedy roominghouse newlywed marriage all soaked in dolors."[34]

Miserable but determined, Joan worked as a waitress to save money for a studio apartment. She intended to live there by herself and eventually did. She hired a moving company and drew a floor plan of the Richmond Hill apartment for the movers to take out all of her belongings. During a break at her job, she hurried down to her new studio to see what progress was being made. There, on the sidewalk, were Jack and his writing desk. He could not get the key to the door from the movers. If she was leaving, he decided, then so was he. The movers relented, telling him to wait until they got permission from Joan to give him the key. When she refused, they told her that husbands had "rights," too. She admitted that Jack was her husband and, to add insult to injury, she had to fork over an extra $10 to have his desk moved up to the studio. Once in, he set to work on his writing. Desperate for more cash to fund a projected trip to Mexico, he accepted more scripts. Working at Joan's apartment, however, was too distracting; his own writing constantly beckoned him away from his script work. He set his sights on Mexico to focus his efforts on his writing without the need to earn money. Burroughs, detached now from the optimism with which he once regarded the country, scoffed at Kerouac's idealism and flatly stated that Mexico was not Lowell, but a nation that reflected "2000 years of disease and poverty and degradation and stupidity and slavery and brutality and psychic and physical terrorism." This did not dampen Kerouac's enthusiasm, and Mexico remained in the forefront of his mind.[35]

Jack had written Sebastian Sampas's sister, Stella, shortly after his marriage to Joan that he hadn't been able to come to Lowell because he was "penniless" and in debt to publishers. He told her of his new marriage and his plans to move to San Francisco with Joan. However, he remained uncertain of his self-identity and his stance toward the Korean War, though he loved America: "Where am I going? I'm going to try to go the way of the soul and not the way of the jet-plane, as long as I can. I believe in the people of America but I can't get patriotic about fighting in Korea because I don't see why we went there in the first place." In short, Kerouac yearned to "try to live a simple life of love." "Suffering as Sammy well knew, is for the salvation of the soul." Though he could not visit them anytime soon, he reminded Stella that she and her family remained close to his heart: "I think you are all wonderful and of the same noble cloth as your noble brother, my friend."[36]

On April 2, 1951, Kerouac took Cannastra's rolls of paper and taped them together, end to end, to create one continuous roll. He fed the end of it into the typewriter (atop the rolltop desk his sister and brother-in-law had gotten him in 1950) and had Joan brew the many cups of coffee he would drink to fuel his prodigious writing output. On April 2 he started a marathon session that resulted in the breakthrough novel that would make his name as a writer. Holmes was the first person to read the scroll once it was completed. Kerouac handed it to him on April 27. The single-spaced manuscript was virtually one long paragraph and was sparsely punctuated. The characters bore the names of actual persons, perhaps to expedite the writing process. Holmes also observed Kerouac's lack of conventional structure to "capture the onrushing flow of his thoughts and impressions."[37]

Kerouac's estimate of his output merits notice, if only to demonstrate his desire to re-create the same channeled energy evident in his December 27, 1950–January 11, 1951, letters to Cassady. Ten days into his typing, Jack wrote to Ed White that an estimated 86,000 words had been written thus far. Kerouac was exhilarated that it was going so smoothly: "I don't know the date nor care and life is a bowl of pretty juicy cherries that I want one by one biting first with my cherry stained teeth."[38] By April 22, Kerouac had completed a 125,000-word novel. Rejuvenated and thrilled, he explained to Cassady that the work was about "you and me and the road." Ginsberg, who had read from the work in progress and had seen that Kerouac had used real names in lieu of pseudonyms, told Cassady that the "hero is you."[39] Because Kerouac had been struggling over an appropriate ending, Ginsberg suggested that Cassady recommend one. Cassady asked Ginsberg to tell Kerouac to end the novel with him as an "ulcerated old color-blind RR conductor who never writes anything good and dies a painful lingering death from postate [sic] gland trouble (cancer from excessive masturbation) at 45." Cassady went on to fabricate a future for himself: being sent to San Quentin for raping a teenaged girl and ultimately drowning in a "slimy cesspool."[40] The design he set for his own demise illustrates Cassady's self-loathing as well as his less-than-overwhelming regard for Kerouac's newer work. *On the Road* was no exception; Cassady suggested to Ginsberg that Jack

> must either forget it or enlarge it into a mighty thing that merely uses what he's written as a Book 1, since what he's done doesn't lend itself to stuffing he should create another and another work (like Proust) and then we'll have the great American Novel. I think he would profit by starting a book 2 with the recollections of his early life as they were sent to me and then blend that into his prophetic DR. SAX. Of course, I'm sure I don't know what I'm talking about, but I do worry for him and want him happy.[41]

But he did know what he was talking about; unwittingly he had touched upon the literary concept Kerouac would ultimately expand upon for the remainder of his life, the Duluoz legend. (Inspired by Galsworthy's Forsyte saga, the Duluoz legend was Kerouac's attempt to chronicle the saga of his life from birth to what he hoped would be old age. It eventually comprised the published novels *The Town and the City, Maggie Cassidy, Vanity of Duluoz,* and many others.) Kerouac learned of Ginsberg's intercession and wrote immediately to Cassady. Concerned about Neal's possible negative reaction to his impassioned work and its portrait of his friend and idol, Kerouac stressed that his portrayal of Cassady—unlike those of Lucien Carr and Allen Ginsberg (Jack's comparison)—was one of "life," "energy," "love," and "greatness."[42] Neal's response was positive, because he had "trust" in Kerouac, but he felt the novel's theme was too "trivial." On April 27, 1951, John Clellon Holmes took the manuscript back to Kerouac's apartment and related his impressions of the novel. He was all too aware that they would not be objective, because he was so close to the subject matter and had read all the earlier incarnations of *On the Road*. Together, they walked to a waterfront bar; afterwards, for fifteen minutes they stood on the pilings of the pier in the cool spring night. With a few minor revisions, the novel would "make exciting and stimulating reading," Holmes said. Jack replied, "You know, kid, your book and mine constitute a new trend in American literature!" To which Holmes could only say, "Amen."[43]

Joan claims in her memoir that during *On the Road*'s composition Kerouac took breaks to be with her. One night, he was typing in his bathrobe. As the screen surrounding his desk separated him from the bed, Jack appeared from behind it and jumped into bed with Joan. "Quick!" he exclaimed. The next morning, she looked at what he was typing. According to Joan, it was a passage about Terry, the Mexican girl (pseudonym for Kerouac's short-term girlfriend Bea Franco in *On the Road*) whom he had met at a Bakersfield, California, bus station in September 1947. In one section of the passage, Terry is angry with Sal Paradise (Kerouac's pseudonym in the published version of *On the Road*) when she suspects he is a pimp (after Sal suspects, in turn, that she is a whore):

> In reverent and sweet little silence she took all her clothes off and slipped her tiny body into the sheets with me. It was brown as grapes. I saw her poor belly where there was a Caesarian scar; her hips were so narrow she couldn't bear a child without getting gashed open. Her legs were like little sticks. She was only four foot ten. I made love to her in the sweetness of the weary morning. Then two tired angels of some kind, hung-up forlornly in an L.A. shelf, having found the closest and most delicious thing in life together, we fell asleep and slept till late afternoon.[44]

By Joan's count, a child was conceived on May 10, 1951 (*On the Road* was completed almost three weeks earlier). By June, she concluded that she was indeed pregnant. Expressing doubts, Kerouac sent her to Nin's obstetrician. Joan felt that it wasn't that he didn't want a child, but that they couldn't have one *yet*.[45] Kerouac denied paternity and believed that Joan was involved with a Puerto Rican coworker at the restaurant where she was working whom he had caught in their apartment. Though she insisted he was just a friend who visited her, Jack firmly believed that it was he who had fathered the child (as he also believed that he was sterile when he and Edie were unable to conceive a baby). Insulted, Joan kicked him out of the apartment. The split was final. They went their own ways, their future child their only link for the remainder of Kerouac's life.

Kerouac moved his scant belongings into Lucien Carr's loft. But before he did, Kerouac took the scroll manuscript to Giroux's office at Harcourt, Brace and dramatically unrolled a portion of the scroll onto the floor at the feet of his horrified editor. Instead of offering approval and an immediate advance, Giroux asked, "How the hell can the printer work from this?" Furious, Kerouac rolled the scroll up and left. Giroux had stood by Jack from his first novel's acceptance and publication and introduced him to New York City's literary circles. But the editor never read a word of his author's masterwork in its rawest form. Kerouac retyped the scroll into a more conventional format with numerous alterations before sending it to Harcourt, Brace, which ultimately rejected the work.[46] On June 10 he wrote Cassady from Lucien Carr's loft (Lucien thought the *On the Road* scroll was "shit")[47] where he was staying: "Now I sit here, with sore phlebitis foot, my book finished, handed in, waiting for word from Giroux, a book about you and me, I sit here, my wife's not here, she's at her mother's, presumably tomorrow I move out and we part, I don't know what to do, where to go, on June 20 I may have a thousand dollars or more, meanwhile I stay with Lucien and Allen in loft."[48]

John Clellon Holmes suggested that Kerouac bring the manuscript to Rae Everitt, his agent, who declined to accept it in its current form. Jack ignored her suggestions for revision, for he knew that his writing another *The Town and the City* was impossible. Kerouac viewed everything that he had written before as "lies," and he was not about to start creating new ones.[49] What Kerouac needed to do was forget his audience and rely purely on his instinct to capture his conception of Neal. He first began by sketching storefront windows, people walking in the street and sipping coffee in diners, seeking to convey them exactly as he saw them. The idea was to isolate each event or moment, thereby making it sacred. Kerouac described his new technique (adapting Ed White's idea of sketching) as "SKETCH—a sketch is a prose description of a scene before the eyes. Ideally, for a BOOK OF SKETCHES, one small page (of notebook size) about 100 words, so as not to ramble too much, and give an arbitrary form."[50] It was an experimental writing technique that lent itself easily to his emerging spontaneous prose style. The immediacy was comparable to that of an artist roaming the countryside with a sketchbook and pencil, except that there was no pastoral setting from which to draw his inspiration. Instead, his keen eye took in the mundane and that which remained beneath most people's notice: bums eating boiled potatoes and meat: "I saw the flash of their mouths, like the mouths of minstrels, as they ate"; "piss in urinal sloshes"; men's room walls; and the New York City streets.[51] It was a culmination of over ten years of artistic struggle that finally stamped itself so remarkably on the notebook page. The notebook sketching would be used to its greatest extent when Kerouac applied it to Cassady in *Visions of Cody*, his emerging new work. Unlike *On the Road*, *Visions of Cody* would be merely a character study. It would evolve into an "enormous paean which would unite my vision of America with words spilled out in the modern spontaneous method." It would be a "metaphysical study" of Cassady's character and his relation to America.[52]

To alleviate Kerouac's anguish over *On the Road*'s initial rejection, Neal Cassady invited Jack to stay with him in San Francisco. Cassady had reconciled with Carolyn (now pregnant with their third child). He wrote Jack:

> I have absolutely the greatest bed in the world on the floor of my extraordinary attic; I got books and shelves, great huge desk that's bigger than any desk could possibly be, since Carolyn made it out of 6 ft. by 6 ft. piece of plywood, with immense dictionary of 30 lbs, and foot thick proportions, and fine lamps and good radio (one downstairs too) and wondrous tape recorder made for not only endless kicks on sound but for dictaphone type writing and recording of thoughts, hi and otherwise.[53]

It was an option that would give him the time he needed to work on *On the Road* freed from financial duress. He didn't have the money to travel to Mexico, as he wanted; the Guggenheim Foundation denied his grant request. Kerouac also knew that, before long, Joan would be after him for child support. In Jack's words, he was "completely fucked" by *On the*

Road's first rejection. Jack responded to Neal that he lacked money to travel west to live in San Francisco. It dawned on Kerouac that he always depended on others. He felt himself a burden not only to his family but also to Neal, who had his plate full with two children and a pregnant wife. He was sure that his presence there would promise "fuckups." To confound his frustrations, he was still dismayed by the lackluster response to his new novel by his editor and publisher. Kerouac wrote to Neal on June 24:

> Giroux didn't take my book. Harcourt won't publish it, tomorrow I have to get agent like beat young first novelists do only worse. Giroux says HE likes book but is sure President of the company and the Sales Manager won't—even tho it's "like Dostoevsky" (he says) they don't even ready Dosty and don't care about all that shit and bums etc. Giroux says Harcourt expected me to write AGAIN like *Town & City* and this thing so new and unusual and controversial and censorable (with hipsters, weed, fags, etc.) they won't accept.
>
> Because of this, Allen re-reads my book and decides it's really beat after all. Lucien thinks it's shit. John Holmes still stands by it. I know you would like it. Anyway here I go. Don't know what to do. Have no money to even GO to your attic; and once there, would have to work; and have necessity of writing further book in peace & silence.[54]

To escape the city in August 1951, Kerouac went to his sister's home in North Carolina, planning to read, walk, and write; he thought that there he couldn't possibly "fuck up" anything except his own life. But he was not at peace even there. Once again stricken with phlebitis, his fifth attack since 1945, Kerouac became bedridden for a month. For a time Nin and Gabrielle cared for him, but he needed more qualified medical help. Since Kerouac couldn't afford treatment from a personal physician (though he did spend some time in the Rocky Mount sanitarium), it was more practical for him to return to New York, where he was able to use his Veterans Administration benefits. Once he entered the Kingsbridge VA Hospital in the Bronx on August 11, his physical misery and anxiety at being so close to Joan sent him deeper into despair. It was also the day he was supposed to leave with Lucien Carr and Allen Ginsberg to go to Mexico. He wrote Cassady, "My wife, having sent the law after me to support, has never given me the affection I still need from somebody, anybody."[55]

18

Beat Fellaheen

Summer 1951–Fall 1952

I would rather be a superb meteor, every atom of me in magnificent
glow, than a sleepy and permanent planet. The proper function of man
is to live, not to exist. I shall not waste my days in trying to prolong
them. I shall use my time.

JACK LONDON

Planning on going to Mexico to visit Burroughs, Kerouac had no idea that his friend would be catapulted into the most tragic of circumstances. Playing "William Tell" with his wife, Joan, Burroughs aimed his Star .380 automatic at a shot glass balanced on his wife's head and fired. Whether she flinched at the last second or whether Burroughs simply had a shaky aim, the result was the same: she lay in a bloody heap on the floor. The foolish game and its hideous outcome plagued Burroughs for the rest of his life.

While Burroughs's tragedy unfolded, Kerouac lay for two months convalescing in the Kingsbridge Veteran's Hospital. The doctors insisted that Kerouac stop smoking and take blood-thinning pills to minimize clotting. Penicillin also helped. To pass the time he read Proust and socialized with the parade of friends who visited his bedside. When by himself, he wrote in a diary, attempting to create a recollection of his own life in the Proustian manner. He also outlined a series of novels that would ultimately compose the "legend" of his own life. Near the end of his recovery, a bored Jack roamed the corridors in his wheelchair; snapped a picture of himself in hospital garb; and made forays outside, where the reek of New York City in August contrasted with the acrid disinfectant of the hospital's corridors. Outside, he watched a funeral procession from the funeral parlor next door and the children playing at the Four Chaplains Memorial Swimming Pool (dedicated to four chaplains who perished aboard the SS *Dorchester*). Brooding on the sad fate of his brother mariners he had once known and the pool built in their memory, Kerouac wrote Cassady that "the pool of life, which would never have existed if the S.S. Dorchester, that yr. blood brother sailed in 1942 just before it sank with the chaplains, had died. Woe and saddest death on all sides, he, yr. faithful brother, sat a long time there in the dark steeped in the joyous melancholy of the organ, the funeral remembrances of the ship, how dirty the old tub was."[1]

When Kerouac left the hospital, he went home to Richmond Hill. Once he got there, two police cars pulled up to the apartment and took him to the precinct station. He was arrested for spousal nonsupport and jailed for thirty minutes. Kerouac had promised Joan to pay $5 a week for her medical bills. To avoid his reneging on his obligation, Joan went through the court system to ensure payment.[2]

Kerouac felt compelled to leave the city for good and even got new seaman's papers to ship out on a merchant vessel. He also briefly considered returning to Lowell. He wrote to Stella Sampas that he wanted to "revisit the tenements of Centralville where I jabbered on the porch with little kids long before I even knew how to say 'door' in English—I want to re-visit the mysteries of my past, which is my job; the mysteries of my source, my soul, the things that now teach me the meaning of universal love." Jack told her that his marriage had "fizzled" ("it'll teach me not to ask a girl to marry me the first night I met her—and be wary of any quick acceptance of such a crazy proposition") and inquired whether her brother Nick (who had just purchased the Old 66 bar, a future drinking haunt of Jack's), who was stationed in the army in New York, was still making trips between Lowell and New York City. However, despite his romantic desire to return there, Lowell, he knew, was too provincial for a man who aspired to be an artist.[3]

Confused, with a "reeling" mind and desperate for cash, he asked Neal about a brakeman's position on the Southern Pacific Railroad. His current $25-a-week earnings from script synopsizing were insufficient, for he had to pay $5 a week to Joan and $10 a week to his mother. Gabrielle wanted to leave New York and live with Caroline. This, should it happen, would be a burden lifted from Jack, for then he could travel more.

On the Road was now typed onto separate pages in an attempt to make its appearance more conventional and thus more appealing to publishers (he would retype the manuscript at least twice in 1951 and 1952). Jack scribbled annotations on some pages, added typesetting suggestions, crossed out passages, and proposed textual insertions. Jack realized that the vast pendulum swing of his trips crisscrossing across the country had to be brought into a tighter focus. His cuts to *On the Road* precede Malcolm Cowley's suggestion that he shorten the manuscript, contrary to previous biographers' assertions that Jack had insisted on maintaining the text as he originally wrote it in April 1951. Jack realized, aesthetically and practically, that such revisions would create a necessary sense of linear order in the narrative. In the hospital Jack wrote to Ed White that he was "completely re-writing" his "Neal-Epic." Actually, Jack was creating "inserts" originally conceived to place between selected chapters of *On the Road* (much as Hemingway inserted short vignettes throughout *In Our Time*). However, Kerouac decided that these inserts would make an interesting novel on their own and saved them for a future work.

In October, the concept of sketching hit Kerouac "full force." Writing this way took personal courage, for to be successful there had to be total "personal honesty." The technique, as he described it to Ginsberg, should not take more than fifteen minutes' worth of effort since it exhausted the mind. Jack wrote these sketches into his nickel notebooks and found that following his criteria created neat little chapters. At first the sketches seemed like the "confessions of an insane person," but by the next day, Kerouac read the results as "great prose." In October 1951, he sent Neal three pages of this text. He was on to something new and wanted Cassady and Ginsberg to be the first to read it. He advised Allen to select some sketches to show publishers and felt that what he sent was "publishable." Little did he know that patient, open-minded Allen thought Jack's writing was anything but publishable.[4] It was challenging reading, even for Kerouac's most liberal-minded, adventurous thinkers. No longer restricted to the "horizontal" method of writing about Cassady and the road, Jack felt that he now could simultaneously create a more "vertical" and metaphysical study. This approach allowed Kerouac to convey several facets of Neal's character for which Jack felt *On the Road* was not suitable. The syntax grew more complicated and the writing style freer as Kerouac gradually dispensed with punctuation. His spontaneous method echoed the wild improvisatory jazz playing of Lee Konitz, Lester Young, and Charlie "Yardbird" Parker. Passages reflecting this influence included those about Cassady's boyhood. John Clellon Holmes claimed that Jack's writing was influenced by his marijuana use.

Have you ever seen anyone like Cody Pomeray?—say on a streetcorner on a winter night in Chicago, or better, Fargo, any mighty cold town, a young guy with a bony face that looks like it's been pressed against iron bars to get that dogged rocky look of suffering, perseverance, finally when you look closest, happy prim self-belief, with Western sideburns and big blue flirtatious eyes of an old maid and fluttering lashes; and if it's a suit it's with a vest so he can prop his thick busy thumbs in place and smile the smile of his grandfathers; who walks as fast as he can go on the balls of his feet, talking excitedly and gesticulating; poor pitiful kid actually just out of reform school with no money, no mother, and if you saw him dead on the sidewalk with a cop standing over him you'd walk on in a hurry, in silence. Oh life, who is that?[5]

Experimenting with a tape recorder at friend Jerry Newman's record shop, Kerouac attempted what he termed "jazz writing" by creating on-the-spot impressions directly into the microphone. He was eager to record that way with Neal. Jack was so excited by this innovation that he envisioned taking on merchant seaman gigs to raise money to devote all of his time to what he felt was a genuine artistic endeavor. He looked forward to recording the street sounds of San Francisco's "Little Harlem" and the lusty "fucking-sounds in beds," if only to transcribe as closely as possible the heart of the human condition. Kerouac recommended to Cassady that he should try reading the typed portions of the manuscript sent to him into the recorder, in much the same fashion as Jack had in the record store.[6] Cassady's enthusiasm for writing, however, had dimmed since he no longer had either weed to write on or time to write because of the demanding nature of his railroad job. (He complained to Ginsberg that he was seldom in San Francisco for more than eight hours at a time.)[7]

Kerouac stayed at his mother's house in Richmond Hill until October 25. While there, he contacted Carl Solomon at the publishing house A. A. Wyn. Out of the visit, and through the adept dealings of his agent, Rae Everitt, Jack was able to obtain an advance of $1,000 for *On the Road*, with $250 due upon signing (a signing that never took place, as Wyn eventually withdrew it's offer). With money finally in his pocket, he had the means to leave the city. First, Jack went to see his mother in North Carolina. To further elude pursuit by Joan, her lawyer, and the domestic relations court, he accepted Cassady's offer to stay with him on the West Coast.

Kerouac had earlier contacted Henri Cru, who wanted Jack to berth with him on a merchant marine vessel. Though Cru assured him that a job was available, one did not open up. To fund Kerouac's trip, Cru lent him $60 for the cross-country bus trip, which seemed to proceed at a crawl. Kerouac made notes in his journal, as alternating patterns of shadow and light swept the ever-changing landscape, and drank booze generously given to him by a fellow passenger. Over a week later, Jack was in southern California. In San Pedro he tried to board another vessel that Cru had supposedly lined up for him, but again the job fell through. (Reliability was not one of Cru's strongest traits, in Kerouac's view.) Jack headed north, following the coast till he reached San Francisco. He went to Russell Street and knocked on the door, which opened to reveal Neal Cassady. Kerouac was shown his room in the small attic, which he relished for its dimness and the antiquated charm of its woodwork. The drawback was that he had to cross through Neal and Carolyn's bedroom to enter and leave the space.

Neal was thrilled by his friend's arrival; he pictured himself and Jack as the "Van Gogh" and "Gauguin" of American literature. Cassady promised his guest a vast array of material items and pleasures: typewriter, automobile, tape recorder, drugs, women, and ultimately the opportunity to bed Carolyn. He would also assist Neal on his stalled autobiography with hands-on editorial advice. Most important, Jack had the means to support himself for one of the few times in his life. Kerouac worked at a job that Cassady found for him on the Southern Pacific, hauling mailbags into boxcars. From San Francisco, Kerouac wrote to Carl Solomon looking for news about A. A. Wyn's decision on the publication of *On the Road* as a paperback. Jack also proposed to Solomon the chance to publish Neal's work in progress, *The First Third*.

Kerouac's prospects seemed promising, and he relayed his optimism in his letter to Carl, who was still perusing Kerouac's submissions and also becoming inundated with Neal's writing (through the overzealous efforts of Ginsberg, who had appointed himself both Cassady's and Burroughs's agent). To Solomon, Jack described his new writing technique: talking into the tape recorder and then typing the results directly in their unexpurgated, unedited, spontaneous glory.

While Jack read excerpts from *Doctor Sax* into Neal's tape recorder, the cold rain spattered the windows of the house. At other times, Jack taped himself reading his latest prose or his stoned conversations with Cassady. One such example reads:

> CODY. Goddamn it . . . this evening . . . and it's fat, man, and best of
> all it's loaded with a lot of great shit. This isn't any old stick of

tea, man, when you get this down your gullet gonna have to give me a match (hee hee hee hee *as J. goofs*). Forty-six eighty-three Seventeenth Street, where the god's hell we ever gonna get out there. We're gonna have to do that, immediately! Ha! Humph! If this doesn't get you high man, nothing will. Here take this (*as J. seeks a roach*). Hmm (*exhale*)

JACK. But did you dig this? (*indicating typewritten sheet*)

CODY. Yah, that's what I've been in this process of doing here.

JACK. Boy that's really something. . . . You don't want to dig it now, do you?

CODY. Do whatever you say (*disposable*). Get high, get h-i-g-h. . . . See . . . I know you got the recorder on, if I . . . ah, even if I . . . (*laughing*) damn him.[8]

However, even *Visions of Cody* (as the work was ultimately published; during writing it was titled "Visions of Neal") had its share of problems; other works were constantly crowding Jack's active imagination. His work on *Visions of Cody* came to a halt when he concluded that what he was actually writing was not about Neal but instead about himself and . . . Lowell.

Once again, Lowell was pervading his spontaneous writing, and he filled the notebooks with prose that would be published as the novel *Doctor Sax. Doctor Sax* describes Kerouac's adolescence in Lowell through the pseudonym of Jack Duluoz, but also blends dream sketches and memory with scattershot fantasy—an amalgam of transmutation of Kerouac's artistic sensibilities. To focus solely on these visions of his past, Kerouac turned his attention to his hometown and its "downtown red brick neon." The words came swiftly until, once again, he felt cursed by his fecund creativity: two separate works were emerging and competing for his energy and time. Jack began to realize that if he confessed the whole of his life, not only would he be freed from the relentless urge to write it, but he would also get everyone off his back. He suffered from the weight of what he termed his "Canuck" dualism, a duality that reached as far back as his forebears, who arrived in the United States still craving the traditions, culture, and social mores of Canada, yet immersed themselves and their children in their new country's technology, prosperity, and freedom.

Although Kerouac was honing his own literary style, many writers continued to influence him. He imagined various literary figures duking it out to reign over his artistic sensibilities—Wolfe versus Proust, Whitman versus Dostoyevsky, Melville versus Céline, and Faulkner versus Genet. Jack felt that parts of him touched upon all of their stylistic and thematic concerns. In his own words, he became a "Keroussadian Ginsbergian Shakespeare."[9] In November 1951 he wrote in his journal that he hoped that his increasing grasp of his destiny, wrung from grief and galling hardship, would signal a new reality for himself. Kerouac sensed that this changing perspective would mean very little for his immediate future but hoped that fifty to a hundred years from then the work completed in his lifetime would prove meaningful. (Jack was being modest; it would take less than thirty years for this to occur.)[10]

Kerouac continued living with the Cassadys through the winter and into the spring of 1952. On February 16, Joan gave birth to Janet Michelle Kerouac. He still firmly denied paternity, and Gabrielle, too, believed that the child was a result of Joan's alleged relationship with a coworker. The money that Jack sent east (from his $35-a-week paycheck working as a baggage handler and yard clerk for the Southern Pacific) went into his mother's pocketbook. In the Cassadys' attic, Kerouac spent hours typing epic visions of Neal from his notebook. At times, Carolyn peeked over his shoulder. Jack integrated the sketching that he had done in New York City into the work. The words came as swiftly as he could type them. John Clellon Holmes once remarked that Jack was a superb typist both in speed and accuracy; he could transcribe his thoughts directly onto paper with his eyes closed. Focusing on a "jewel-point" of detail, he would let other details flower until the whole picture swirled with sensations of sight, smell, and sound. His objective was to create imagery as multifaceted as possible. He sent an excerpt to John Clellon Holmes.

Holmes, author of the newly published *Go* (1952), most appreciated what Kerouac was attempting, and Jack knew this. He assured John that rather than "putting off" writing to him, he in fact "practiced" his letters to Holmes to perfect the prose. The letters were filled with creative tangents; to illustrate this quality, Jack enclosed a few unmailed letters in the March 12 mailing. In that latest letter he admitted feeling that he had reached his "peak maturity" with respect to writing and that he was "blowing such mad poetry and literature that I'll look back years later with amazement and chagrin that I can't do it any more." Evident throughout was an emerging ability for wordplay, much as a jazz musician would improvise from a snatch of melody:

You pissy ass Seattle, you dullpoke old Minneapolis St Paul, you lakey crakey flakey Minneeapolakey, you wild up Duluths of the blue moose and doggerel of the snow, you hoar river, you beginning wildlands, you never did piss on me enough you damn river.[11]

While writing the letter, he incorporated the sounds that he heard from a new Oscar Peterson record playing in the background. Kerouac compared himself to a tenor/alto saxophone player blowing notes like Stan Getz, a musician whom he admired. The letter recounted a wild night with Neal, the events of which were preserved for posterity not only in Kerouac's letter to Holmes but also in the posthumously published *Visions of Cody* (1972). This dual use of material proves that Jack's letters were not merely documents of communication but also launching pads from which to explore and demonstrate his prose style. However, the actions of Neal and Jack—no matter how compellingly portrayed in the three recollections (the letter to Holmes, *Visions of Cody*, and Carolyn Cassady's own *Off the Road*)—were such that they began to topple the precariously balanced Cassady household.

In Kerouac's version, on a "tragic" Saturday, after punching out from his night job on the railroad, Jack went out on the town without Neal. Courtesy of his free rail pass, he caught the local train into the city and stopped at a bar on the corner of Third and Howard Streets that (like many in that area) catered to the working class. High and drunk and playing jukebox jazz, a stumbling Kerouac dropped his money on the floor and consorted with street hookers who frequented the Little Harlem bar. He met a prostitute (who, he tells Holmes, was the only woman he had been with since arriving in San Francisco), and inspired by the possibilities she presented, Jack phoned Neal at home. He interrupted, yet again, a lovemaking session. He persuaded Neal to leave Carolyn and join him. After all, it was Neal's birthday. In Cassady's station wagon they all left the bar to find a drug dealer named Charley to purchase some marijuana. In Charley's apartment they watched the girls play strip poker. Horny and high, Neal and Jack brought the whores home, where Carolyn was rocking the crib of their crying newborn baby. Infuriated, Carolyn threw them all out of the house. They piled into the car and drove around until Jack's hooker, Lulu, passed out (before he could even make it with her). "Crestfallen," Neal and Jack returned to the Cassady household, and Jack, wearied and regretful, retired to his attic.

Carolyn's memoir, *Off the Road: My Years with Cassady, Kerouac, and*

Ginsberg, reveals several aspects of this event that Kerouac neglected to note. Neal's birthday had been a special occasion for Carolyn and the children; after all, it was one of the few events eligible to be called a "family moment." It was also an attempt to bond. Cassady was thrilled that Carolyn had baked a cake and cooked a steak dinner and that there were presents. All were puzzled by Jack's absence. After the celebration the children went to bed, as did Neal and Carolyn. Later, the phone rang only eight feet away from the bed. Cassady sprang from the bed to answer it, as he often did when he received late-night calls from the railroad, so as not to wake the children. But it was Jack, not the Southern Pacific, on the other end. Neal told Carolyn that Jack was drunk and in jail and needed to be bailed out. Carolyn spent the rest of the night restless and in pain from an attack of Bell's palsy that had erupted that day. Her husband did not return that night.

The next morning, after the children had awakened and after Carolyn had taken care of their personal needs, she washed her hair. While rolling her blond hair up under a towel, Carolyn noticed Neal coming down the stairs and Jack escorting a "young black woman" to his attic room. Appalled, Carolyn followed her husband into the kitchen and asked where he had been. Neal admitted that Jack had not been jailed. The lie had been Jack's drunken way of getting Cassady out of the house. Carolyn insisted that Neal go upstairs and evict the young woman. After a few minutes Neal, Jack, and the woman came down and passed through the Cassadys' bedroom on their way out. The hooker "lunged" toward Carolyn like a feral cat, hissing violent words that she could not understand. The woman walked toward the bureau, picked up Neal's keys, and insisted on being driven home. All three left the house, leaving Carolyn to wonder why she was trying to raise a family with a man like Cassady.

On their return, Jack went back to the attic and did not come down for over a day. Carolyn's concern for him overrode her anger; she had Neal check on him. He reported that Jack was just "sulking" and busy "reading and writing." On Monday, the first day after the "infamous" weekend, Neal stayed home from work and brought Carolyn to the hospital. When they returned, she saw a book on the dressing table that hadn't been there earlier: their copy of *The Town and the City,* which Jack had autographed before presenting it to them. Jack had now taken the liberty of adding to his inscription a heartfelt apology to Carolyn. His remorse touched her, and she brought it downstairs to show Neal. Relieved and happy that Kerouac had broken the ice, he went upstairs and brought Jack down. They opened beer and wine and "eagerly gave up any thoughts of sorrow or condemnation in our efforts to restore a state of mutual comradeship." They even went out in the street and photographed each other.

True to Kerouac's prediction back in Richmond Hill, his zeal for kicks with Neal resulted in a "fuckup." The only gain was one of hundreds of minute sketches that Jack noted in his notebooks. His time with the Cassadys had exceeded its bounds. During the last few months, and almost at Neal's urging, Carolyn and Jack's platonic relationship became a sexual one. Before long, Neal turned uncommunicative toward Jack. Although Carolyn was delighted with Jack's attention, the open affair also made Kerouac one part of an increasingly awkward triangle. It was time to leave. He wrote to Burroughs in the spring of 1952 asking if he could visit. Lonely for companionship, Burroughs agreed.

Neal dropped Jack off in Sonora, Arizona, where he hopped the wire fence into Mexico. Once across the border, he noted a key difference between Mexico and the United States. It was—as he remarked in a story created from his Mexican sojourns—like being sent home from school sick at two o'clock or donning overalls after wearing Sunday clothes to church. It was the taste of freedom, the shedding of an America now stale with laws, rules, and modernism. It was the "fellaheen feeling about life," where joy abounded everywhere, where the sounds of cantina music lifted like smoke into the air, where marimba bands played and smiling dark faces flashed white teeth. He felt it to be a positive environment, unlike that portrayed by Hollywood. It was as though the influence of a "civilized" society diminished the farther south one went.

Frugally, Jack purchased second-class bus tickets for the journey south. The bus was high and narrow. Passengers sat on wooden benches that ran on either side down the length of the bus's interior. Some of the passengers boarded with their animals, and some of the children sat on the roof. They transferred often to other buses during the thousand-mile trek to Mexico City. The bumpy passage included starlit deserts and dense jungles; at one point the bus crossed a shallow river and water surged to the tops of its wheels. In Jack's enthusiastic assessment, it was a "tremendous journey."

In Guaymas, Kerouac met a Mexican named Enrique, who tried to teach him some Spanish. He also showed Jack how to partake of the peyote cactus for a hallucinogenic high. Jack ate tortillas as pigs brushed against his legs and drank the "greatest milk in the world," an unfermented pulque extracted from the agave plant and then made into a thick alcoholic drink. It triggered in him a laughing fit. Leaving Guaymas to continue his journey, he stocked up on mangoes to eat en route. In the back of the bus Kerouac drank mescal and sang "Scrapple from the Apple" and "Israel" to entertain some Mexican singers. They, in turn, sang for him in their native tongue.

At a midnight stopover in the western city of Culiacán, Jack, Enrique, and his tall footman named Girardo left the bus and walked through a group of silent huts to the outskirts of the little village. Enrique knocked on a door, and a white-garbed Spanish Indian, wearing a wide sombrero that reminded Jack of Herbert Huncke, opened it. Inside, the Indian's wife sat on a bed, while another man—goateed, barefoot, and sitting on the edge of the bed—lit some opium. Nearby, a soldier snored loudly in an opium-induced slumber. Enrique conversed in Spanish as Jack listened. After a few minutes the goateed Indian handed Jack a pellet of opium, which they sprinkled into a "cigar" of weed and lit. Kerouac was stoned by the second drag. In his high he felt comfortable enough to attempt to talk with them in Spanish. He showed them his notes about Mexican culture. After a while, they all went to sleep, but not before offering Jack either the soft ground or a straw pallet on which to sleep. Using his seabag as a pillow, he chose the ground. He stayed awake for a while listening to the sounds of the night.

The next morning, Enrique scored for Jack: two ounces of weed for the equivalent of $3. However, Kerouac got the shakes from the opium-laced pot. The men who had gotten him stoned the previous night gave him some hot pepper soup and a bottled soda to alleviate his misery. The opium hangover made him feel as if he were being hung upside-down on a cross, "skewered," and "burned at the stake." Although the soup burned his throat, sipping it helped. Later, he was startled when some soldiers and policemen surrounded him. They wanted to score some weed, which somehow they knew he had. Although relieved that they weren't arresting him for possession, he was also disheartened that he had to give up the majority of his marijuana. Enrique took out his own stash, cut it in half, and gave it to the authorities. They took their extorted weed and squatted on the ground to roll cigar-sized joints. Enrique and Jack stored what remained inside a wooden radio and left the village. To escape momentarily the seething heat, they stopped at a church before continuing their trek.

They boarded the bus in Culiacán and headed for the next city,

Mazatlán, on the coast. Enrique found a place for them to sleep, and they swam in the Acapulco surf. On the beach, stoned and beatific, they sat watching three young Mexican women approaching them from miles away. As the trio strolled closer, Kerouac felt them to be the "center of the world." Afterwards, the men swam in their underwear in the surf. Jack experienced one of the "great mystic rippling moments of my life." He saw the sun set over the three sister islands floating in the warm Pacific waters. Jack and Enrique decided not to stay the night and instead moved on to Guadalajara, northwest of Mexico City. In the heart of the city Jack strolled through the marketplace stalls eating fresh fruit. He boarded yet another bus for the final leg of his journey to Mexico City. By dawn, the bus arrived. Not wishing to wake Burroughs just yet, Kerouac chose to sleep for five pesos in a "criminal's hovel," where he was told to be on the lookout for a "gun-wielding" man (Burroughs, now infamous for his wife's death) said to be lurking in the neighborhood.[12]

From Jack's journey through Mexico, he was able to eke out a short travel piece, "Mexico Fellaheen," that would be published as part of the novel *Lonesome Traveler* in 1960. In that story he expounds at length on the subtle virtues of a fellaheen (or peasant of the earth) society: the accepted casual drug use, the pervasive Catholicism, and the underlying primitivism that made him feel as if he had been exiled to paradise. Jack visited a church in Mexico City, an experience he felt was similar to visiting St. Patrick's Cathedral in New York City or St. Jeanne d'Arc's Church in Lowell. While there, he experienced an epiphany:

> I pray on my knees so long, looking up sideways at my Christ, I suddenly wake up in a trance in the church with my knees aching and a sudden realization that I've been listening to a profound buzz in my ears that permeates throughout the church and throughout my ears and head and throughout the universe, the intrinsic silence of Purity (which is Divine). I sit in the pew quietly, rubbing my knees, the silence is roaring.

After Joan's death and his release on bail, Burroughs had remained under suspicion and close scrutiny by the Mexican authorities. If the ballistics experts found evidence of foul play, Burroughs would face considerable prison time. One alternative was to flee the country. In the event of his expulsion, he had as few as five days to leave the country. The other possibility was being forcibly deported to the United States. In his homeland there were no spectacles as "brutal, bloody and degrading" as those he enjoyed in Mexico. Burroughs frequented cock- and bullfights. He took Kerouac to a bullfight that wasn't as "real" as those held during Mexico's winter season. After the fanfare, the bull entered the ring and charged the matador. Lances pierced the animal's hide between its shoulder blades, and soon the bull was streaming blood. The orchestra punctuated its torturous death with bass-drum rattles. Jack compared its lance-riddled body to that of St. Sebastian. After the matador plunged the final sword into the bull, the animal buckled to the dusty ground and began vomiting copious amounts of blood. Because the creature wasn't quite dead yet, an "extra idiot" came out to end its misery with a dagger. Jack's reaction was far removed from Hemingway's adoration of bullfighting as a skilled and epic battle between man and beast. Kerouac wrote: "And I saw how everybody dies and nobody's going to care, I felt how awful it is to live just so you can die like a bull trapped in a screaming human ring."[13]

Burroughs spent the majority of his time typing what would eventually become his second novel, *Queer*. He may have thought—as Neal did when writing his autobiography—that Kerouac's experience as a novelist could help him forge his manuscript into a publishable work. Burroughs noticed a dispirited air about Jack and rightfully assumed that it stemmed, in part, from A. A. Wyn's rejection of *On the Road*. Jack's writing was considered too experimental; such uncompromising prose was certainly not geared toward the general readers to whom Wyn catered. The publishing company specialized in mysteries, comic books, and science fiction. Ginsberg had written to Kerouac in San Francisco in early 1952 that his *On the Road* manuscript had been forgotten at the bottom of MCA's closet. Allen knew that Jack's writing eclipsed in quality and innovation those that filled A. A. Wyn's immense catalog. But he also knew that his friend's brilliant writing alone would not be enough to compel a mass audience to buy the book. Kerouac had urged Ginsberg to read *On the Road* in its entirety and judge it for himself. Allen did, but his opinion remained less than favorable. He wondered why Kerouac, certainly able to write prose that could meet the needs of publishers, flirted intentionally with "rejection" and "fate." He could not comprehend the method to Kerouac's madness. In July 1952 Ginsberg wrote, "He was not experimenting and exploring in new deep form, he was purposely just screwing around as if anything he did no matter what he did, was O.K."[14] Jack replied to Allen that the prose was comparable to Joyce's *Ulysses* "and should be treated with the same gravity." He decided that he would not allow an editor to cut the story up. "Intelligibility" didn't enter into Jack's designs, for he knew that his prose (a derivative of his *sketching* method) would define him as a serious artist. To further secure his reputation, he also planned an American Civil War epic in the tradition of Tolstoy's *War and Peace,* but the project never progressed beyond the note-taking stage. The little he had read from *On the Road* pleased Burroughs. Like Neal, he had neither the time nor the inclination to peruse the whole work till much later. He did think that Jack's skill as a writer had improved measurably since *The Town and the City.*

After a while, Jack's spirits lifted. Although his woes were many, the distance between himself and New York helped. *Doctor Sax* was taking shape, as he scrawled page after page into his notebook. By May 27, Jack wrote to the Cassadys, he had completed twenty thousand words. Much to Burroughs's displeasure, for he could ill afford to run afoul of the Mexican authorities, Jack continued to smoke cheap Mexican weed in cigar-sized blunts. To ward off Burroughs's nagging, Jack stayed in the toilet. In there, *Doctor Sax* came to life, replete with scatological references and pot-induced visions of Lowell.

When night fell, Kerouac would hike five miles around Mexico City, venturing as far as the slum outskirts, where he encountered only restless dogs and rats. On one such journey he walked to the whore district and paid a peso for a seventeen-year-old prostitute named Luz. Accompanying her into a low-ceilinged hovel, they waited while another whore played with the "pecker" of a Chinese man. Afterwards, Kerouac and Luz reclined on a curtained-off cot, where he guiltily enjoyed his purchase.[15]

Jack also accompanied Burroughs into the mountains of Tenencingo with "Old Dave" Tercero and a "Catholic Indian" named Esperanza Villanueva. They all attended a Mexican fiesta; Burroughs, with his .38 Colt revolver, shot at targets. Skeptical Kerouac was leery of entering the mountains with Burroughs, who frightened Jack (intentionally) with tales of tree-dwelling vipers and the bellicose "Auca" tribe, which thrived on killing men. They parted for approximately one hour before planning to meet back in Tenencingo. Other excursions included the Ballet Mexicana and the Turkish baths. Burroughs was everything a host should be: gracious and willing to spend his time and knowledge on Jack. In return, Jack helped Burroughs assemble many pages into one solid work. Kerouac's distance from friends, family, and his hometown gave him the necessary objectivity to write. The blended subject matter of Mexico City fellaheens and provincial Lowell Canucks invigorated *Doctor Sax*'s composition. Kerouac viewed the fellaheens of Mexico as similar to those who toiled in the mills and factories of Lowell; both groups worked with their hands to subsist. Describing his new work to John Clellon Holmes in June, Jack termed *Doctor Sax* "invisible," a work in progress to be pursued solely as a "hobby." Burroughs urged Kerouac to focus entirely on his road chronicles and not to be distracted by a novel that he considered less publishable than "Visions of Neal."[16]

Kerouac opens *Doctor Sax* with his dream of being a boy once again sitting on Moody Street in Lowell. With pencil and paper in hand the boy suggests to himself that he "describe" the sidewalk and iron picket fence surrounding the Lowell Textile School in the town's Pawtucketville section. But to bring that picture, blurred by some twenty years, into sharper focus, Kerouac wills himself not to think of that past in words, but rather to "think of the picture better." His conjuring would merge memory with dream. It was pure Proust, as Kerouac's recent reading of *Remembrance of Things Past* permeated his composition of *Doctor Sax:*

> I am the pudding, winter is the gray mist, a shudder of joy ran through me—when I read of Proust's teacup—all those saucers in a crumb—all of History by thumb—all of a city in a tasty crumb—I got all my boyhood in vanilla winter waves around the kitchen stove. It's exactly like cold milk on hot bread pudding, the meeting of hot and cold is a hollow hole between memories of boyhood.[17]

From the "wrinkly tar" of the "sidewalk" on Gorham Street, his thoughts travel to Gersham Avenue, one of his family's rented duplex homes in his youth. There he sees his father standing with fellow Canadians after Sunday church and bemoaning the sermon's length. A boy, Joe Plouffe, shuffles past, heading home for breakfast. Joe has no father, because he abandoned the family. This is Jack's way of underscoring the social and familial dysfunctions of depression-era Lowell, a society that thrives despite emotional and physical deprivation. Childhood glee (as Kerouac once described the theme) is linked arm-in-arm with the societal maladies of urban life: teenaged sex on the weedy banks of the Merrimack, a village idiot tending a smoldering riverside dump, and an ailing proprietor who beckons little boys to the back of his candy store to play with their "ding-dangs." A strong preoccupation with sex, in both deviant and innocent incarnations, haunts the novel.

Gerard's death and Catholicism suggest sources for Kerouac's lifelong anguish over the inevitability of suffering. This concept would justify his upcoming Buddhist studies; "All existence is suffering" was all too obvious to Jack as he strolled through Mexico City's slums, the embodiment of Mexico's suffering. On the notebook containing his Lowell saga Jack wrote "A Novella of Children and Evil" and "The Myth of the Rainy Night." By June 3, he had written forty-five thousand words of *Doctor Sax;* should *On the Road* sell like "wildfire," he would instantly have another work (one that he deemed a masterpiece) ready for the presses.

Kerouac felt at the height of his creative mastery, and excitedly he wrote to John Clellon Holmes on June 5 while riding the crest of a tremendous peyote high. Jack's "discovery," which began in December 1951, was an explosion of "wild form" that took him beyond superficial description into "revealed prose." His sketching technique had freed him from the constraints of linear form and imbued him with the accuracy of a photographer. However, this euphoria evaporated once Burroughs grew annoyed by Kerouac's selfish consumption of his food and his pot smoking. Before long, Jack had no doubt that he had overstayed his welcome. The negative aspects of his life became magnified once he realized that he would soon be cast into a hostile and relentless world. As much as he resisted the idea of living in the United States, his family felt otherwise. Nin and Gabrielle were certain that Jack would meet an untimely end in Mexico and were leery of Burroughs's inimical influence. Jack wrote:

> I am starving to death. I have no more money, not one red cent. I weigh 158 lbs. Instead of 170. Bill thinks I am mad at him because I was writing when he got up and retired to the bathroom with my tea and pencil pads, so he's gone, has only money, nothing to eat in his house, it's cold. . . . I sit here yearning to get back to food and drink and regular people.[18]

Miserably, Jack assessed his life's progress thus far and again wrote to John Clellon Holmes, this time evaluating his situation more gravely. For the first time he reconsidered his responsibility for fathering Jan: "What have I got? I'm 30 years old, broke, my wife hates me and is trying to have me jailed, I have a daughter I'll never see, my mother after all this time and work and worry and hopes is *still* working her ass off in a shoe shop; I have not a cent in my pocket for a decent whore."[19]

As Kerouac confronted the realities of his life—his indigence, no newly published works for sustenance, the failure of *The Town and the*

City to earn him any meaningful income—one would predict that he would suffer, if not a physical and mental breakdown, then at the very least an erosion of purpose. Instead, Kerouac summoned his spirit to create even more experimental works in the coming months. From where did such missionary zeal stem? No doubt Gabrielle's faith in him as a writer instilled enough confidence in him to persevere. His inner resolve was a brutal taskmaster, yet he would complete the bulk of his literary oeuvre between 1951 and 1956. Kerouac was able to put aside the darker aspects of his life and write.

Broke and dependent on Burroughs, Jack wrote to Carolyn in June complaining of his extreme poverty: his seabag had a hole in it; his raincoat had been stolen; he had 60 cents to his name; and again, as usual, he felt that he was getting "fucked" by his publisher. He was convinced that they were conspiring to keep his most important works from being published. Jack hoped that the Cassady clan would pack their bags and move to Mexico to be with him in his squalor. This setup, in his view, could bring only positive results; for one, this would allow him and Neal to work side by side on their own projects. Even more important, Jack assumed that he and Carolyn could carry on their sexual relationship unabated. He questioned Neal's reactions; he felt that Cassady was not actually "jealous" but instead "just didn't know what we expected him to do, and we didn't either." For Jack, there were no consequences except "life and death" and all that mattered was "eternity."[20]

Meanwhile, Kerouac and Burroughs continued to get on each other's nerves. Burroughs's chief complaint was Jack's voracious appetite (no doubt from the pot that he smoked). Desperate to leave Mexico and relieve his penury, Kerouac wrote to Carolyn Cassady pleading for some money for bus fare. However, despite losing bail money to shady Mexican lawyers, Burroughs came through first and gave him $20 on condition that it be paid back.

On his last day in Mexico City, during the late afternoon, Jack went to a little church in the nearby town of Redondas. After slugging down two beers, he entered the church and sat on its floor. He looked up in wonder at a huge statue of the crucified Christ. "Mon Jésu," Jack said to the statue, equating Christ's tortured grimace with both Robert Mitchum's scowl and the squinty-eyed, stoned gaze of Enrique peering at Kerouac through opium smoke. He implored the statue to pray for him.

Here Holy Spain has sent the bloodheart sacrifice of Aztecs of Mexico a picture of tenderness and pity, saying, "This you would do to Man? I am the Son of Man, I am of Man, I am Man and this you would do to Me, Who Am Man and God—I am God, and you would pierce me my feet bound together with long nails with big stayfast points on the end slightly blunted by the hammerer's might—this you did to Me, and I preached Love?[21]

Jack left Mexico on July 1 and trekked northeast to North Carolina with only $5 in his pocket from Texas on. He hitchhiked to Houston where he met up with a "drunken construction worker" who invited Jack to shower in his hotel room. When Jack emerged wet from the bathroom, he found the man nude on his stomach, "begging me to screw him." He resisted and then left the man, who was crying. Shortly thereafter he arrived at North Carolina, where his mother and sister nagged him for not having a stable job and for his reckless forays into a country light-years away from the ordered Franco-American domiciles of Lowell.

The stinging criticism in Ginsberg's June 11 letter infuriated Jack, as did the lackluster reception by publishers of his newest writing, his so-called "spontaneous prose pieces." Kerouac answered months later:

> My heart bleeds every time I look at *On the Road* . . . I see it now, why it is so great and why you hate it and what the world is . . . specifically what you are . . . and what you, Allen Ginsberg, are . . . a disbeliever, a hater, your giggles don't fool me, I see the snarl under it. . . . Go ahead and do what you like, I want peace with myself. . . . I shall certainly never find peace till I wash my hands completely of the dirty brush and stain of New York and everything that you and the city stand for . . . and everybody knows it.[22]

Denigrating everything New York City stood for in shaping him as an artist, Kerouac reduced his situation to a spectacle—that of being nothing but an "almost humorous chronicle of a real dumb lil abner getting taken in by fat pigjaws." He lashed out at Giroux and even Cassady, who he claimed had stolen a book from Giroux's office back in 1949. Such was the depth of his despair that he wrote to Stella Sampas in December that he had been experiencing "long, dark depression with thoughts of suicide sometimes." Again, he remained hostile to New York City's literati: "The rich homosexual literati of New York at first offered me alluring scholarships and then withheld them when it became apparent that I wouldn't be famous—This includes my own editor, Robert Giroux." Kerouac felt that they were unsympathetic to his medical condition, which made it hard to work on his feet:

> Because I'm not famous they don't care—and I don't exist anymore. But what they don't know is that I am going to be famous, and the greatest writer of my generation, like Dostoevsky, and someday they'll see this and the emptiness of their lives spent chasing after fashions & glittering Italian islands—when the soul of man is weeping in the wilderness, and little children hold out their hands for the love of Christ.

His distress turned toward his hometown and Sebastian, who was killed in World War II, and he made clear to Stella his attitude toward warfare and, perhaps, his real reason for bowing out of the navy under a feigned psychological condition:

> Ah I wish Sammy had lived—what a great man he would have been—Wars don't advance mankind except materially—The loss of people like Sammy, and even Johnny Koumentzelis, and even Jimmy Scondras, makes the earth bleed, & kills something—Billy Chandler, Chuck Lozeau—so many were killed—from Lowell—for nothing. The survivors build new apartment houses and think they've gained an "era"—They've got an "error"—Jimmy O'Dea, machine politician, and Bobby Rondeau, union leader are the survivors of what in Sammy's day was a Spirituality & thoughts of the ideal of God.[23]

In Stella, Kerouac felt he had found a more grounded and objective correspondent to whom he could open completely his pained and compassionate heart. In return, she suffered his stormy angers and rejoiced in his accomplishments. It was to Stella that Kerouac returned again and again. She was strong, having suffered many familial hardships, and intelligent. To Kerouac she epitomized the idealism of his charmed Lowell youth.

Kerouac wrote to Carl Solomon in August 1952 comparing his present situation with *On the Road* to the experiences of Dreiser, Hemingway, and Joyce, all of whom had works deemed "unprintable." He derided Solomon's rash readings and remarked that he approached such difficult books as Joyce's *Finnegan's Wake*, Malcolm Lowry's *Under the Volcano*, and Marcus Goodrich's *Delilah* by seeking to understand the writers' "intellect," "passion" and "mystery." Prophetically, Jack assured Solomon that *On the Road* would be published eventually and would gain the recognition that it deserved. He also insisted that, in the end, the publisher of *The Town and the City, Doctor Sax,* and *On the Road* would be "proud" to have them in its catalog. The book could not be appreciated in the present, but it would affect future generations. Jack was uncannily prescient about the impact of his road novels.

Furious still with Ginsberg's judgment, he was also angered by John Clellon Holmes's recent success with the publication of his novel *Go.*

> And now even John Clellon Holmes, who as everybody knows lives in complete illusion about everything, writes about things he doesn't know about, and with hostility at that (it comes out in hairy skinny legs of Stofsky and "awkward" grace of Pasternak, the sonofabitch jealous of his own flirtatious wife, I didn't ask for Marian's attentions . . . awkwardness indeed, I imagine anybody who walks on ordinary legs would look awkward around effeminate flip-hips & swish like him)— And the smell of his work is the smell of death . . . Everybody knows he has no talent . . . and so what right has he, who knows nothing, to pass any kind of judgement on my book—He doesn't even have the right to surl in silence about it—His book stinks, and your book is only mediocre, and you all know it, and my book is great and will never be published. Beware of meeting me on the street in New York.[24]

Traditional to his nature, Kerouac's irascible turn of character was just as easily forgotten days later when he would write another letter forgetting completely his disparaging attack on their character and work. One reason for this was his copious drug use. In his own estimation, marijuana made him paranoid toward Ginsberg, Joan Haverty, Lucien Carr, Neal and Carolyn Cassady, Philip Whalen, and Gary Snyder (those whom he trusted while high were his mother and sister, Norman Mailer, Ed White, Gregory Corso, William Burroughs, and, in Mexico City, Esperanza Villanueva).

Despite the sound criticism his friends gave him, Jack was so convinced of the rightness of his method that he began a new series of notebooks (fifteen breast-pocket notebooks in total) that would be complete in 1957. He called this collection of prose "Book of Sketches."

Anxiously writing Allen Ginsberg, Burroughs inquired into Kerouac's whereabouts, concerned that Jack pay back the $20 loan sooner rather than later. Cassady also sought Kerouac, having mustered the thoughtfulness to write a letter of recommendation for Jack. For unknown reasons, the letter was addressed to J. C. Clements, the captain of police in Rocky Mount, when he applied for a job with the railroad as a trainman. Cassady wrote that "no man has all the superlative virtues I seem to be attributing to Mr. Kerouac, nonetheless, he is the only man I know into whose hands I could entrust the use of my saxophone, fountain pen or wife and would rest assured that they were honorably and properly taken care of."[25] However, despite Cassady's raves, Kerouac did not get the job. Financially strapped, Jack seemed to owe money everywhere. He put the finishing touches on *Doctor Sax,* placed it in his seabag, and left North Carolina. He headed west for San Jose, where Neal had arranged a job for him as a brakeman on the Southern Pacific. The Cassadys had moved from Russian Hill to a rented one-story house in San Jose with nut and fruit trees on the front lawn, and Neal wanted Jack to live there.

When Jack took his seabag, with all of his worldly belongings inside, and left through the back door of Caroline and Paul Sr.'s home, he just missed Neal's letter with its instructions on how to circumvent a new Southern Pacific ruling that prohibited hiring new men over thirty. Without this vital news, Jack left with a renewed air of optimism, hoping again for financial and social stability.

19

The Shrouded Traveler

Fall 1952–Fall 1953

My bones are carried out on the train
Westward where the sun has gone;
Night has darkened in the rain,
And the rainbow day is done;
Cities age upon the plain
And smoke rolls upward out of stone.
      ALLEN GINSBERG, "Ode to the Setting Sun"

Kerouac stopped in Denver en route to California. From Denver, he sent a postcard to Neal. After receiving it, Neal posted an extremely urgent telegram and wired $25 from his own pocket so that Jack could arrive ahead of Southern Pacific's imminent deadline. Thrilled to have Jack back in their home, Carolyn prepared a room for him.

When, days later, he reached the West Coast, Kerouac called Cassady from San Francisco. Neal arranged passage for his friend on the Zephyr (nicknamed the "Zipper" for its barreling, straight-through passage to Los Angeles and back).

Neal and Carolyn drove a Model-A Ford to the train yard to pick up Kerouac. Leaving his wife to sit alone, Neal left the car to meet Jack. After waiting a few minutes, she could see the two familiar outlines illuminated by the glare of the train's light. Jack got into the car and Carolyn sensed the warm sensuality. Because Cassady had to work in Watsonville that evening, Kerouac, on his first night back, would be alone with Carolyn. After he took a hot bath, he met Carolyn in her bed. When they finished, she returned to her bed as was her wont. It was her rule that, should one of her children waken during the night, she should be found in her own bed.

The next day, Kerouac spent time with the Cassady children at the nearby ball field. Carolyn noticed how relaxed he was, how at ease he was with children. Around adults of either gender he was self-conscious and often relied on alcohol to make possible the gregariousness that some contemporaries associated with him. With the new job, his status as trainee continued for two weeks. Each night Neal and Carolyn had to encourage him to return the next day, for he soon tired of the rigors of brakeman's school. When he completed the training, Jack continued working as a brakeman. He was thrilled to be dressed like Neal, to be one of those men he saw sauntering up and down the tracks and riding the cars. However, Jack soon discovered that writing about railroads was more appealing than the job's actual arduous labor. His stout frame, more suited for the gridiron than for chasing railroad cars, was not an advantage when he had to rely on swiftness to execute the job properly. Also, the men called him "Carraway Seed," to which Kerouac took offense. Before long, the prospect of returning to Mexico began to beguile him once more.

While Neal worked, Carolyn and Jack continued to spend time together, often reading to each other or discussing literature. They recorded some of what they read, and when Neal was home, he also read with Jack. Kerouac read from his *Doctor Sax* notebooks, Cassady from Proust, and all of them from Shakespeare's plays.

Carolyn remarks in her memoir:

All this pleasure and my partial descriptions of it to Neal pleased him less and less. Jack was now more interested in Neal's family than in Neal, whose lonely brooding on long runs stoked his jealousy and resentment. Where was his old partner in crime? Where his excuse and sidekick for his own private desires? Then the chill of winter arrived and with it, the cold rains and the colds in our noses. When the railroad work slowed, the men were home together more often, and the feeling of confinement increased the restlessness and irritation in them both as they waited for the calls that never came. There was nothing interesting to do in San Jose, and San Francisco was too far to go without a good excuse. It was evident that wanderlust was tugging at Neal again and the Mexican sun at Jack, and in me the seed of dread began to sprout.[1]

Neal's receptiveness to his old friend and their shared discussions of art, philosophy, and literature were diminishing rapidly. Neal now talked only of work, home expenses, and the lack of money (Cassady's daughter Cathy was suffering from osteomyelitis of her left leg, an ailment that was covered by the S.P. insurance. Cassady was dismayed that Kerouac wasn't even smoking as much weed as he liked, for his crop of pot had been growing into long, "medusa-like," six-foot lengths. His assessment of Kerouac was harsh with jealousy in an October 4 letter to Ginsberg: "Jack's the lonely fucker of Carolyn, who blows him; he was almost capable of going 3 ways, but hope for that is about given up since he's so morose all he talks of now is moving from up here to way down there on skid row 3rd street, to be near work (he brakie now too) and write."[2]

Kerouac told Holmes that he did not like Neal anymore (calling him an "asshole") and was done being conned by him.[3] It was as if an older brother were shunning the younger. Jack's platonic love for Neal may also have clashed with his physical love for Carolyn; Neal's desire to create a threesome undermined both relationships. Jack was too modest for a ménage à trois.

These multiple complications prompted Kerouac to leave. Relieved and guilty, Neal drove Jack to San Francisco, where he lived in a seedy flophouse on the corner of Third Street and Howard near his much beloved Little Harlem. He likened himself to the winos and hoboes who leaned in doorways and skulked in corners. To Holmes, he declared himself a "true hobo" who lived like an "indian." He was more able to live up to the image of one when he was laid off that December. His brakeman job, which he worked seven days a week, had earned him $600 per month. His frugality made the income last; a hotel room cost $4.20 a night. The flophouse's shabby hallways and thin walls did not bother him, for they all were fodder for the prose sketches that he regularly jotted into his notebooks. Jack also slept on the cabooses of the trains, thereby getting more sleep when he needed it. In his notebook he documented his expenditures: 35 cents for a fifth of wine, 20 cents for coffee, and 25 cents for breakfast (two eggs with toast, coffee, and oatmeal). Despite his careful budgeting, sometimes he went hungry. The harshness of it wasn't wasted, for he found it occasionally made for good poetry, evoking Mallarmé's dictum that poetry was a product of a state of crisis:

The rat of hunger
Eats at your belly,
then dies &'s left
to rot & bloat there.[4]

Kerouac continued making entries in his book of sketches and wrote little "pomes." He also wrote regularly in his journal. His drug of choice these days was alcohol. He often joined the Third Street winos to drink from a grimy fifth of Tokay. On that rough high Jack pulled out his sketchbook and began writing a spontaneous prose piece titled "October in the Rail-road Earth," a meditation on the railroad, the streets of Little Harlem, and the denizens of Southern Pacific train yards.

The sweet flesh intermingling, the flowing blood wine dry husk leaf bepiled earth with the hard iron passages going oer, the engine's saying K RRRROOO AAAWWOOOO and the crossing it's ye famous Krrot Krroot Krroo ooooaaaawwww Kroot—2 short one long, one short, 'sa thing I got to learn as one time the hoghead was busy telling a joke in the fire-man's ear and we were coming to a crossing and he yelled at me "Go ahead go ahead" and made a pull sign with his hand and I looked up and grabbed the string and looked out, big engineer, saw the crossing racing up and girls in sandals and tight ass dresses waiting at the flashby RR crossing boards of Carnadero and I let it to, two short pulls, one long, one short, Krroo Krroo Krrrooooa Krut.[5]

This sweet prose freedom gave him license to record every impression and sensation exactly as it struck him. His sensitive ear caught the conversations of all, young and old, rich and poor, black, Indian, white, Mexican, Chinese. He placed hobo conversations alongside the abrasive expressions of the blue-collar men with whom he worked. "Neverthefuckingless" merged the words exactly as they sounded to him; "your" was changed to "yr"; "nothing" to "nathing"; "Mom" to "Mam"; "the" to "de." Kerouac captured the western lexicon as accurately as Faulkner did the southern with his Snopes trilogy and Steinbeck the Okie depression-era saga. Even train sounds, the push-pull of boxcars, the scream of loud steam-fueled horns were written out in the spirit of *Finnegan's Wake*. Most tellingly,

"October in the Railroad Earth" was Jack's first complete mature work written in his spontaneous prose style that did not involve Cassady or Lowell.

One evening when Kerouac was sleeping on his ratty couch, he woke to see Neal standing over him and urging him to come back to San Jose. Jack obliged since he was short on cash after the railroad laid him off. He soon found himself back in his makeshift bed and within Carolyn's warm embrace. He became so enamored of her that he implored her to come with him to Mexico. She considered the offer, justifying it as a much-needed vacation, but Neal insisted on taking Jack to the Mexican border alone.

Cassady rushed Kerouac to Mexico and, scoring some marijuana, left the country just as swiftly. In Mexico City, Burroughs tried to sort out the utter shambles that his life had become. After the arrest of his lawyer for shooting a boy in the leg, Burroughs's bond was increased beyond his financial means. Not wishing to be imprisoned, Burroughs jumped bail and fled, by way of Panama, to Rio de Janeiro shortly before Kerouac's arrival. When Kerouac arrived in Mexico City, he found himself alone and assumed residence on Burroughs's rooftop at 210 Orizaba. He adjusted himself once more to the simple, uncluttered lifestyle that he preferred. From this vantage point he could observe the fellaheen, the Mexican Indians. With his knowledge of Spengler, he perceived them to be genuine denizens of the earth.

High on Benzedrine, Kerouac lay on his bed and plotted out the components of his Duluoz saga. But sometimes he departed from the comparatively tame goings-on of Duluoz. In one notebook, titled "Benzedrine Vision—Mexico Thieves Market—Memoirs of a Bebopper" (which would culminate in an eighty-four-page manuscript), he created a meditation filled with mental anguish and a yearning to be released from suffering. Ben Giamo explains, in his study of Kerouac's spirituality, that in the sketch Kerouac, while walking along Mexico City's streets, "begins to lose his sense of reality, soon becoming a pitiable homeless figure in the Mexican night":

> In this state, he has a vision of his mother, offering consolation and help. The bebopper, overcome with weariness and exhaustion, eventually finds his lair and, with a flimsy roof over his head, the rain of disturbing thoughts turns into two visions. The first vision is of heaven,

in which "everyone was simply a level higher than they are on earth," and the second is one of madness, which he witnesses when looking at his reflection in the mirror. The bebopper then considers three options: (a) "give myself up to a madhouse, to the VA hospital for mental treatment"; (b) "go on as before"; or (c) gain immediate relief from "the burden of time—just a good big overdose of morphine." The sketch concludes with the bebopper taking the final option: "Get a needle and works in a drugstore, a supply of M. from D., get in bed, heat spoon over alcohol flame, melt tablet or powders. Therein, suck up in dropper, put on needle, then aim for big blue Ti Jean athletic muscle, and puncture, til blood comes up in dropper, then slowly push down to ecstacy of death—no more possible worries of any kind."[6]

Another notebook from this period would later be reworked extensively into a larger work titled first "Mary Carney" and then *Maggie Cassidy.* In the same notebook Kerouac worked on pieces he titled "The Blessedness Surely to Be Believed," "The Ecstacy of Life and Death," and "The Happy Truth." The last was translated from a piece written originally in French. This translation, completed over a six-day span from December 16 to December 21, concerned the relationships among a wino named Dean Pomeroy, his son Dean Pomeroy Jr., and a stepson named Rolfe Glendiver. Like much of his work, it was set in the month of October. As with his road novel, the characters were heading east from Denver to New York in a Model-T Ford. The stepson, Rolfe, was a cowboy from Gunnison, Colorado, who worked at the Robeson Bar Ranch breaking broncos and castrating bulls. Like Jack, Rolfe had blue eyes and a movie-star-handsome face and was preoccupied with his own thoughts. Rolfe's kin back home did not understand him. Dean Pomeroy Sr., modeled after Neal Cassady's father, was an old wino carrying a bottle of port and stumbling around Larimer Street in Denver. Together, all three meet "Old Bull Balloon," a character about whom Jack wrote at greater length in a French novel of forty thousand words. Unlike his current writing, "The Happy Truth" was written linearly. The French novella, "Old Bull Balloon," was completed in five days. As he described it in a letter to Cassady, it featured Neal and Jack as children in 1935 and was much like "The Happy Truth" in both setting and narrative.[7] Against the noisy backdrop of Chinatown, they would meet Old Bull Balloon, a composite character based on W. C.

Fields and William S. Burroughs. The two boys, together with their fathers and some lithesome blondes for company, would take off in a Model-T for an adventure that would ultimately tie up the plots of both *On the Road* and *Visions of Cody.* Jack left the novel untranslated and untyped in his notebook.

Life was easygoing in Mexico, though Jack grew lonely. He wrote to Carolyn with plans for her to visit. To pass the time, he visited Burroughs's junkie acquaintance, Bill Garver. But even Garver did not plan to stay in Mexico City for long. Kerouac's $12-a-month, two-room apartment was small and unassuming. He decorated it with pottery handmade by Indians, who sold it in street stalls. A Mexican Indian woman did his laundry, and he dined on oysters (three dozen fried in butter for 35 cents) and chased them down with imported Chianti. In the morning he ate steak and eggs for 30 cents. It was just what Jack wanted, living in faux opulence for next to nothing, to avoid compromising his writing time with any real-world obligations that would have bogged down his efforts in the United States. Also, Kerouac had stocked up on drugs: goofballs, laudanum, opium, speed, and pot. Kerouac's drug use continued despite the threat of the Mexican government and the depressing spectacle of gaunt junkies with festering sores along their bony, dark arms.[8] He wrote to John Clellon Holmes:

> Burroughs is gone at last—3 years in Mexico—lost everything, his wife, his children, his patrimony—I saw him pack in his moldy room where he'd shot M all this time—Sad moldy leather cases—old holsters, old daggers—a snapshot of Huncke—a Derringer pistol, which he gave to old dying Garver—medicine, drugs—the last of Joan's spices, marjoram, new mold since she died & stopped cooking—little Willie's shoe—& Julie's moldy school case—all lost, dust, & thin tragic Bill hurries off into the night solitaire—ah Soul—throwing in his bag, at last, picture of Lucien & Allen—Smiled, & left.[9]

Recipients of Kerouac's letters during this time read them under his new name, Señor Jean Levesque, a combination of his French first name and his mother's maiden name. Writing to Holmes (now handling Jack's literary affairs), he inquired into the possibility of reprinting *The Town and the City* and the prospects of publishing *Doctor Sax.* To cajole Holmes, Jack inquired on the "progress" of Holmes's novel, *Go.* He forgot (or chose to forget) his jealous assessment of Holmes's writing skills less than two months earlier.

Finally, before leaving Mexico City as suddenly as he had appeared there, he wrote back to Stella Sampas, perhaps hinting that he wished to be with her:

> My dearest hope is to come back to Lowell, with my mother, and make a home—eventually get married again—to some girl that loves me, not hates me—hate is madness, my wife I believe is insane—But it's too late—But nothing can prevent me from returning to Lowell, and revisiting the house where I was born, Lupine Road, Centralville; and the house where my brother died; in the night I can return to Lowell and walk all I please those hallowed streets of life.[10]

After Jack wrote to Stella, he went to the union hall and signed up for a four-month voyage on a merchant vessel destined for Korea, a journey that would reach all of the countries in Southeast Asia. This luck, he informed Stella in a postscript, was because of her, his "lucky leadingstar." He would make a gift of his paycheck to his mother "for all the years she supported me while I wrote & now the years she goes on slaving at shoe shop skiving machine while I roam." However, his plans to ship out were aborted; instead, he returned to New York and risked being caught by Joan's lawyer so that he could spend Christmas with his mother, who had returned to Richmond Hill.[11]

During the holiday Kerouac attended a party at Lucien Carr's and passed the time in Ginsberg's apartment on the Lower East Side by reading the complete works of Jean Genet while listening to WHOM's radio broadcasts of Lester Young. He left the apartment with Genet's oeuvre under his arm, leaving a note asking Allen to show *Doctor Sax* to Mark Van Doren. He was excited, in spite of his earlier disgust with Manhattan. All his friends were there, and he jumped around the city visiting Ed White and John Clellon Holmes. On New Year's Eve, Jack was stoned and went to Jerry Newman's record store. By night's end, he returned home in a cab alone and weeping. Allen did not know why he was crying, other than perhaps his realization that, though older, he was no wiser. Although he was excited to see his friends, Jack was becoming more seclusive. Ginsberg felt ignored by him; those conversations of the past, the New Vision and Spengler, were behind them.[12] Kerouac was extremely preoccupied with his favorite subject—himself—and used that preoccupation as fodder for his work. His next effort, drawing from working notes written in Mexico, centered on his adolescence and romance with seventeen-year-old Mary Carney. On the opening page of his notebook, he wrote, "[I]n the great forgetful night a hollow-eyed lost mother's son in a flapping blue suit hung from the rear-end of a train" before crossing it and the rest of the passage on that page out with a diagonal line. In text he retained, Jack depicted pure boyhood: carousing with friends, wandering the streets of Lowell after dusk, listening to Count Basie, dancing to "Stella by Starlight" at the Commodore Ballroom, teen romances as pristine as the snow that falls in the opening of *Maggie Cassidy*. Kerouac's Lowell novels served a distinct purpose for him. They were testaments to his youth. In his Richmond Hill apartment, with Gabrielle in the next room for company as needed, Jack began his labors anew. Sometimes he would discuss with her their lives in Lowell and would add her memories to his own.

In *Maggie Cassidy*, Kerouac's Duluoz chronology continued where *Doctor Sax* left off in Pawtucketville, where his character lived near the top of a four-story tenement:

> He lived with his mother, father and sister; had a room of his own, with the fourth-floor windows staring on seas of rooftops and the glitter of winter nights when home lights brownly wave beneath the nearer white blaze of stars—those stars that in the North, in the clear nights, all hang frozen tears by the billions, with January Milky Ways like silver taffy, veils of frost in the stillness, huge blinked, throbbing to the slow beat of time and universal blood.[13]

Whereas *Doctor Sax* was narrated in seemingly spontaneous flourishes of language between reverie and dream, *Maggie Cassidy* is recollected in crystal-clear imagery that creates, despite its depression-era backdrop, some heady romanticism. Kerouac dispenses with his sketching style in favor of a straightforward narrative structure. His unorthodox phrasing often results in passages of startling originality:

> The rutted mud of hardrock Time . . . was it wetted, springified, greened, blossomied for me to grow in nameless bloodied lutey naming for her? Wood on cold trees would her coffin bare? Keys of stone rippled by icy streaks would ope my needy warm interiors and make

her eat the soft sin of me? No iron bend or melt to make my rocky travail ease—I was all alone, my fate was banged behind an iron door, I'd come like butter looking for Hot Metals to love, I'd raise my feeble orgone bones and let them be rove and split the half and goop the sad eyes to see it and say nothing. The laurel wreath is made of iron, and thorns of nails; acid spit, impossible mountains, and incomprehensible satires of blank humanity—congeal, cark, sink and seal my blood.[14]

Immediately after this reverie, Maggie appears unable to see, hear, or read what poetic feats honor her absence (he thinks that she has stood him up). "What are you so quiet about, Jacky Boy?" she asks.

As Kerouac settled down in New York to create his next mature fiction, he did so unbothered by the demands of contemporary society and his own friends (who, he thought, always seemed to want something from him). His reasons for shunning his New York friends still puzzled Ginsberg, who noted to Cassady that Jack avoided large crowds and noise. But Allen had not traveled with Jack and shared his experiences on the road. To Kerouac, despite momentary bouts of euphoria, New York City still contained all he resented: Joan, the literati of Fifth Avenue, the poseurs and players, and, most of all, his contemporaries who seemed to find success easier to obtain than he did. To Neal Cassady, in January 1953, he unleashed a bitter diatribe and railed against several friends behind their backs. He thought that Ginsberg was "fat-faced and ugly," Al Ansen looked like a "pig," and Holmes's expensive overcoat flapped as he chased Manhattan cabs with his wallet full of cash from *Go* (a $20,000 reprint advance for the never-published paperback edition of *Go* planned by Bantam Press). Kerouac remained bitter about Holmes's success. Jack found all his acquaintances "tiresome" and "dull" and remarked that only Cassady was "fascinating." Jack could not accept that the world was moving on, that his friends were growing older, that some had found a modicum of success. He had returned to New York to find many friends had changed. Some, including Lucien Carr, attained a level of maturity that escaped Jack. Mustached and sporting horn-rimmed glasses, Lucien was removed from the beat scene of the late 1940s. Their being overfed and comfortably well-off irked Jack to no end. He preferred to live by Thoreau's credo, opting to sit on a pumpkin rather than a crowded velvet cushion.

In addition to forging a domestic exile for himself, Jack needed to detoxify himself to recollect with clarity. Although he still got high once each month, the serenity of Gabrielle's parlor was therapeutic, giving him the calmness needed to surrender himself to thoughts of Lowell.

In February 1953, Kerouac joined famed editor Malcolm Cowley for lunch to discuss his manuscripts. Cowley felt that all Jack's work required revision and that *Doctor Sax* could potentially earn him $50,000 if he excised the entire fantasia portions, leaving intact only the passages concerning his boyhood. Jack resisted and disregarded Cowley's advice. He felt that if William Faulkner had written *Doctor Sax,* it would be published. Cowley said that if Viking did publish it, the company would do so at a loss. Cowley had edited *The Portable Faulkner* in 1946 and was responsible for enlarging America's awareness of its greatest living writer.

Carl Solomon's association with Ace Books allowed him to option Kerouac's manuscripts by offering him a $250 advance. By virtue of his contract, Kerouac presumed he could offer the pulp-paperback publisher short books, such as selections from *Visions of Cody* that he had gathered and bound together into one typescript. However, Jack ignored similar requests to revise other manuscripts that he had submitted, after the company rejected the earliest incarnation of the sixty-thousand-word "Springtime Mary." Despite refusing to do so for Ace, he revised the novel directly on the manuscript pages. Archival evidence indicates the addition, deletion, and translation of passages originally written in French. After rejecting "Springtime Mary," Ace's three-book option expired with none of Kerouac's work being published.

Ginsberg sent Jack a draft of a press release concerning Ace Books' imminent publication of the pseudonymously authored *Junky* (written by "William Lee"). It was ill timed. Now using the address of his agent, Phyllis Jackson at MCA, Kerouac denied permission to use his name in the book. He also prohibited the use of his name for publicity purposes: "I do not want my real name used in conjunction with habit forming drugs while a pseudonym conceals the real name of the author thus protecting him from prosecution but not myself and moreover whose work at the expense of my name is being bruited for book trade reasons."[15]

Kerouac also disassociated himself from his beat associates. As he grew into his own style, he had less need for his New York City acquaintances. Kerouac also resented that his publishing prospects were tainted by the

Lupine Road, birthplace of Jack Kerouac.
(Photo by Paul Maher Jr.)

Beaulieu Street, where Gerard Kerouac
died and was waked.
(Photo by Paul Maher Jr.)

The Kerouacs and family friend Armand Gauthier, circa early 1930s.
(Courtesy John Sampas)

Jack Kerouac at his sister's home at 45 Crawford Street for his surprise seventeenth birthday party, March 12, 1939. Mary Carney is seated at left. Jack is seated at right.
(Courtesy John Sampas)

Jack and Caroline Kerouac on the back porch, 726 Moody Street, Lowell, Massachusetts, circa 1939.
(Courtesy John Sampas)

Kerouac with his fellow members of the Lowell High School
football team, 1939.

Kerouac in the Merchant
Marines, 1942.
(© *Estate of Jack and Stella Sampas)*

Kerouac in Central Park.
(Photo by Wilbur Pippin)

Jack Kerouac (seated left) and Hal Chase,
New York City, circa 1944.
(Courtesy John Sampas)

Kerouac at a signing for *The Town and the City* at the Bon Marche bookshop
in Lowell. *(Courtesy Gil Topjian)*

Neal Cassady in 1955. *(Corbis)*

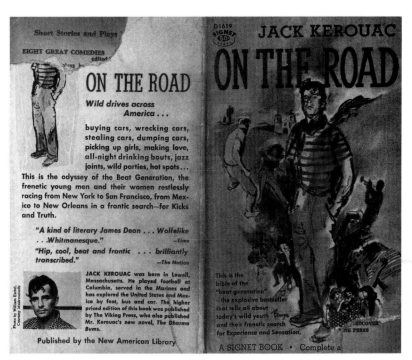

First paperback edition of *On the Road.*

Collaborators taking a break from the 1959 filming of *Pull My Daisy*. From left to right: poet Gregory Corso (back to camera), artist Larry Rivers, Jack Kerouac, composer David Amram, and Allen Ginsberg. *(© John Cohen)*

Kerouac, Northport, Long Island, 1962.
(© Antonio A. Rubino)

Northport, 1962. *(© Antonio A. Rubino)*

Lowell, Massachusetts:
Jack Kerouac at the Sac
Club, late 1960s.
(Courtesy George Poirier)

Jack and Stella, Lowell, 1968.
(Courtesy John Sampas)

John Sampas and Jack Kerouac, Lowell, 1968.
(Photo by Stella Sampas; courtesy John Sampas)

Grave of Jack and Stella Kerouac: "He Honored Life." *(Photo by Paul Maher Jr.)*

belief that he was heavily into drugs and that his agent thought him a "dope addict." Writing to John Clellon Holmes, echoing his mother's suggestion to discard his friends and start off "clean and alone in literary reputation," Kerouac vehemently protested any linkage of his name with Burroughs and the emerging beats in general: "I have ask'd that my name be withdrawn from all yr. councils—I have my own new ideas about the generation, this isn't 1948, there's nothing beat about these sleek beasts & middleclass subterraneans, it's just another pose & all of it was accurately & politically prophesied & then blue penciled by Giroux out of T&C [*The Town and the City*]."[16]

Several reasons buttressed Kerouac's reluctance to involve him with this work, which he had praised to Burroughs mere months earlier. He wished to avoid any attention that cast him in a negative light. Besides protecting his good name and literary reputation (nascent as it was), he was trying to avoid the possibility that Joan Haverty or, worse, her lawyer, would knock on his Richmond Hill door. His decision was "strictly business"; he did not want to be connected to the "beat generation" as depicted in Holmes's *Go,* and rejected Holmes's offer to credit him in print for cocreating the term "beat." Wishing to retire from the New York literary scene for now, Kerouac wrote to Carolyn (expecting her to speak on his behalf to Neal) and asked about open positions at Southern Pacific. His one concern was further gibes from the brakemen, which caused her to wonder why Jack cared at all what people thought of him. Cassady answered his letter. Neal had received a call from the railroad and could have a job for his friend. Once again, Jack was invited to stay at the Cassady residence. Carolyn was uncertain whether his presence would help lessen her husband's growing estrangement or only broaden the rift between them. Cassady had been injured on the job in Millbrae on April 10. While he was setting the brake of a car, it had collided with a bumper, causing him to tumble from the roof of the car and land on the toe of his boot. His foot bent backward, breaking the bones of his ankle and foot. Neal faced a lengthy convalescence. After a month, he was discharged from the hospital and returned home, where he had to sit with his leg raised to ease the pressure on the healing bones. True to his con man nature, he had already made plans for the money that he would receive from the railroad.

When he arrived, Kerouac decided against staying with the Cassadys. Neal was still in the hospital, and Jack may have felt awkward staying with Carolyn. Instead he rented a $6-a-week hotel room in San Luis Obispo.

His stay in California was for practical reasons: to earn money to take him to the next phase of his artistic journey and to move his mother away from his sister, who wished to raise her family without the added burden of Gabrielle. Jack wrote to his mother shortly after arriving in California. He told her that by Christmas he hoped to have saved $2,000. He also wrote her about advertisements that he had read in a San Luis Obispo newspaper for economy-priced trailers for them to live in.

In his room Jack cooked his own food and ate it while gazing at the mountains of California. Work was only a short walk away. At night he slept soundly to the pulsing chorus of crickets. He felt good, revitalized. As he told Gabrielle, his move west brought him back to life. However, Jack was eager to free himself from San Luis Obispo, which he likened to a "sanitarium," and to reenter the "feverish intensities" of San Francisco. Kerouac was pondering the next steps of his life, and that always threw him into vacillation. His immediate plans were to retreat into the mountains, where he envisioned his life as an exile similar to that of John the Baptist. Afterward, he would return to Mexico and take up residence with a "cunt" (as he callously put it to Cassady).[17]

With extreme difficulty Jack started writing again. His lack of weed left him uninspired and disinterested in his work; soon, despite what he told his mother, life in San Luis Obispo took its toll. Jack began to regret declining Neal's offer to live with them. The tedium of working full-time began slowly to drive him "insane." Life had set an "economic trap" for him. He grew so disenchanted that he even began to resent Catholicism; he no longer set his hopes on God. Jesus Christ was a "liar," "jealous of the Pharisees," "afraid of the black cunt." Instead of saving himself, he chose crucifixion. Literature also held little interest as depression descended on him. The literary merits of Wolfe and Melville, of Proust and Joyce, no longer intrigued him with the same intensity. So obvious was Jack's disillusionment that even Neal could see that his friend was threatening to topple headfirst into the "deep end."

Ginsberg remarked to Neal that Jack should "lay down his wrath," so that his own true self could shine through "untroubled and tender."[18] Lately, Kerouac's behavior affronted Allen, who was certain that, somewhere in the American west, he was spreading slander about Ginsberg and his poetry. He even felt that Jack had "infected" Neal with the "anti-semitic paranoia he inherited from his mother." Still, Ginsberg strove to remain patient and understanding. He pursued Jack through the U.S. mail system, needing power of attorney forms signed before peddling his two manuscripts (*Doctor Sax* and "Springtime Sixteen"—previously called "Springtime Mary"). Kerouac's own agent, according to Ginsberg, was not even sure if Jack wanted to publish *Doctor Sax* at all and demanded a note from Kerouac confirming his intentions. In Allen's estimate, Kerouac could publish all of his works if he only tried.[19]

Kerouac began a new notebook on May 11 and titled it "Book of Daydreams—San Luis Obispo." In his "Editorial Explanation of Various Techniques of the Duluoz Legend," Kerouac described "Daydreams" as a "prose description of daydreams, wish-dreams during waking hours, example: 'Wearing top hat with black cloak with red lining, with T. S. Eliot, walking into premiere of DOCTOR SAX, through crowd of queers, handsome.'"[20] Throughout the work, Kerouac interspersed passages about his friends with wordplay. He tucked the notebook into his backpack and later filed it in his archive.[21] The following month, on June 28, he began a new notebook of short prose pieces he called "Tics"; a tic was a "vision suddenly of memory. The ideal, formal *Tic*, as for a *Book of Tics* is one short and one longer sentence, generally about fifty words in all, the intro sentence and the explaining sentence."[22] On one page he dashed out several: "Cold Fall mornings with the sun shining in the yard of the St. Louis school, the pebbles—the pure vision of world beginning in my childhood brain then, so that even the black nuns with their fleshwhite faces and rimless glasses & weepy redrimmed eyes looked fresh and ever delightful."[23] He also had aspirations to assemble a Book of Prayers:

> O Lord Avalokitesvara
> Emptiness Without End
> Bless all living & dying
> > things
> In the endless past
> In the endless present
> In the endless future
> > amen.[24]

Neal no longer had much confidence in Jack or his reliability. Scornfully calling him a "Wandering Minstrel" in a letter to Ginsberg, Cassady admitted he did not know where Kerouac was. Allen had originally mailed the letter and power of attorney forms to Neal, who left them in a "nigger hepcat's" pad after Jack did not arrive at his home. Eventually, Neal had the letter rerouted to Jack's ship, which was heading through the Panama Canal. In the letter was Allen's poem "The Green Automobile," which contained lines created by using Jack's "original rhythms" writing.

Kerouac had quit the railroad in late May 1953 and signed on to the SS *William Carruthers*. Al Hinkle, who had visited the Cassady home with Jack, went there alone one afternoon to tell Carolyn that Kerouac had gone to sea. Al Sublette, a mutual friend of Jack's and the Cassadys', had been with Kerouac on his last day ashore, and they had celebrated with an ill-advised, all-night bar crawl. The next morning, Jack woke with a start at five o'clock with barely time to make the ship. Throwing his seabag over his shoulder, he hurried through the gray mist of the San Francisco morning to catch the "A" train across the bridge to the army base, where the ship was already turning its screws. Up the gangplank he sprinted, twelve minutes late, which annoyed a German man of some authority. He immediately assigned Jack to duty in the officers' pantry.

The vessel passed the Golden Gate Bridge, remaining close enough to shore that the thin crust of the western coast shrouded by fog was always in view. Donning a white jacket, Jack gulped down some Benzedrine and sped through his duties, not even unpacking his seabag until later that evening. Before long, he again found out that, though the sea contained boundless joy and freedom for him, the vessel floating upon it did not. Rather, it had become "one vast new iron nightmare."[25]

As the *Carruthers* steamed south, Jack watched the western coast of his beloved Mexico (as *Heart of Darkness*'s Marlow scanned shrouded Africa's western coastline)—where he had ogled *muchachas* and smoked opium with Enrique only months earlier—pass by. Just beneath the surface of the serene Pacific, sharks cruised for prey. Seabirds swooped and dipped after little schools of flashing fish. The warm air of the sea and Mexico's Three Sisters Isle reawakened Jack's passion for Melville. He calculated the ship's progress at 350 miles a day as it voyaged south to Panama before heading northeast past Yucatán and the island of Cuba. Each day his routine was structured. He began his morning with a grapefruit, which he ate at the ship's rail. There he watched the porpoises swim among the cresting swells that split and rose from each side of the ship's bow. At other times, he watched the waves crash over and spray the deck as driving rain fell. From these encounters Kerouac composed a haiku:

Useless, useless!
Heavy rain driving
Into the sea!

If there was a place to lose himself from the woes and worries of the world, then this was it. However, according to Carolyn Cassady, a thirst for alcohol, a dependency that gradually began to trouble him more and more, gripped him, and he jumped ship in Panama. Neal, as Allen noted, had Jack "pegged," for Cassady had accurately predicted that Kerouac would not stay onboard long enough for the vessel to leave coastal waters. However, Kerouac's discharge papers tell a different story from that of Carolyn Cassady. His discharge date, June 23, 1953, left him a free man on dry land in New Orleans, Louisiana. If he "jumped ship," he did so officially, witnessed by a yeoman who signed him offboard, releasing him from his duties. He wrote Carolyn in August 1953 that he did not want to be imprisoned within the iron holds of a ship that contained him not only physically but also spiritually. Again he was able to redeem his memories of this travel experience by writing about the largely uneventful voyage in a memoir magazine piece, "Slobs of the Kitchen Sea" (later collected with other prose pieces in *Lonesome Traveler*).

Life began anew in New York as Jack again moved in with his mother in Richmond Hill. He avoided her nagging by sitting in his room writing in his journal and composing letters, sometimes by the light of his brakeman's lantern. In a "cock"- and "cunt"-filled letter to Ed White, he casually referred to a new woman in his life, a half-black, half–Native American named Alene Lee, who had made Jack declare that there was no difference between black and white "pussy." She was a warm addition to the "subterraneans" Jack was becoming acquainted with. Kerouac spent time in the Village with Burroughs, who had returned to the United States with a clutch of "dried telepathic vines." During his exile Burroughs maintained a voluminous correspondence with Ginsberg, who kept the letters for a later book. While Burroughs was in New York, he and Allen worked on these letters, which were ultimately published in 1961 as *The Yage Letters*. Kerouac dubbed Burroughs and his crowd from the Village "subterraneans" and considered them poseurs and parasites of the New York avant-garde.

Although "cunt" had "ruled his thoughts" by the end of that summer in New York, Kerouac had worked through the smog and heat typing his railroad prose sketches, which he titled "Wine in the Railroad Earth." He also attempted to maintain a correspondence with Cassady, but Neal did not reply. Perhaps Jack's feelings for Carolyn had worn Neal's tolerance raw. Kerouac was convinced that Neal was intercepting his letters to Carolyn. In August, Carolyn wrote to Jack concerned that she hadn't heard from him in some time. He wrote her back immediately. Apparently, this letter got through, for she discussed it at length in her memoir. In the letter Jack assumed optimistically that his last "long letter" to her had been lost in the mail. He assured her that he had shipped out on the *Carruthers* not to avoid her but to appease the whims of his restless nature.

Visiting the San Remo bar one evening in the company of Ginsberg and Burroughs, Jack met Gore Vidal. Accounts differ as to what happened that night. According to Gore Vidal's *Palimpsest,* a sodomous bacchanal ensued. In Ginsberg's version, Jack, drunk, fell in Vidal's bathtub, unable to maintain an erection hard enough to please his suitor. In *The Subterraneans,* though Kerouac adopts an apologetic tone toward Vidal "for leading him on," there is no mention of this event in Kerouac's journals.

During the early fall, Kerouac prepared his next work, one more link in the chain of his Duluoz legend. His fling with Alene Lee had fizzled. She remembers Kerouac as "insecure and paranoid to the point where if I went into the hall, he imagined I was sleeping with someone in the hall. If he was outside the door, I was in bed with someone." His paranoia may have been somewhat justified in the case of Gregory Corso, who had bedded Alene. To Kerouac, it was a crisis, even though Alene did not take her relationship with Jack seriously. Years later, in 1958, a remorseful Corso wrote to Kerouac:

> You see after reading *The Subterraneans* again, this time with an awareness, I realized the hurt I had caused you, and I wanted to tell you it wasn't my fault. Oh it was my fault all right, but not *my* fault, *me,* what is really me. It was the fault of a boy who was only two years out of a past that rightly calls "institutional." [Corso had been institutionalized in various orphanages, a psychiatric ward, reform schools, and prison after the disappearance of his mother when he was only a year old.][26]

Kerouac garnered enough from their brief fling to write a piece of autobiographical fiction. He also worked her telling of one of her dreams into his dream notebook:

IRENE'S [a pseudonym for Alene Lee] DREAM AUG. 9, 1953

"Francesca—a piece of clay—I mold it, it wants to come to life—it struggles under my manipulation—I try to tell others that it is breathing and wants to live—Then it is Francesca dying, as they come over—My sister Bessie looks at her, she is worried about other things—I take the figure inside the hall—it stops struggling to live—it is icy cold and rigid—I lay it down—The nurse comes to take over—As I lay there I smooth the figure—I begin to mold it again and she struggles—I tell the nurse and she tells me to go away—She believes in her death, as I am going to the door I see the figure rise, and as I go down the hall I look back expecting to see it walking but the people in front are behaving as normally."

That Kerouac bothered to record her dream reveals his respect for her emotional and intellectual fiber. So much did he revere her that *The Subterraneans* centers around their relationship, a tribute he paid to only two other women (Lowell's Mary Carney and Mexico City's Esperanza Villanueva). It was a neat multiethnic triumvirate revealing Kerouac's disregard for race and color. This did not bode well to Gabrielle, who enclosed in one of her letters to him a newspaper clipping about a rape in a subway, scrawling on it, "There's your damned niggers!" Her patience with Jack and his wanderings began to waver as well: "So you want to roam & leave—well don't you dare do anything that will dishonor your father's name!"[27]

From October 21 to 24 Kerouac typed the whole of his account of the Village subterraneans. He immediately showed it to Burroughs, Ginsberg, and Alene Lee. Burroughs admired the younger writer's stamina and determination. Allen was impressed with the work, although he felt that once again Jack was deliberately thwarting his chance for success. Alene Lee also read it: "Jack showed me *The Subterraneans* probably four or five days after he wrote it. He sent me a telegram: 'Have soul surprise! Wait for me. See you Friday.' Like a child who was going to receive a magical gift, I waited." When Jack met Lee on a Friday night, he walked in, sat down at the fireplace and handed her the manuscript. She started to read it and immediately was shocked by Jack's version of their times together: "I could look at it one way and feel it was like a little boy bringing a decapitated rat to me and saying, 'Look, here's my present for you.' These were not the times as I knew them and the people, with the exception of his friends, were not as I knew them."[28] Kerouac offered to throw the complete manuscript into the flames, but of course he did not.

The Subterraneans centers on a circle of Village bohemians: writer William Gaddis; saxophonist Alan Eager; record producer and store owner Jerry Newman; Burroughs and poets David Burnett, Alan Ansen, Allen Ginsberg, and Gregory Corso. Throughout the narrative, related in a spontaneous first-person stream, Jack (Leo Percepied) is a weary soul romantically involved with Mardou Fox (Alene Lee). They quarrel a lot, as she is an independent woman. She displays an air of nonchalance toward him, but she strikes him as a "thief of some sort and therefore was out to steal my heart, my white man heart, a Negress sneaking in the world sneaking the holy white men for sacrificial rituals later when they'll be roasted and roiled."[29] Leo applies the theories of radical German psychoanalyst Wilhelm Reich (whose *The Function of the Orgasm* [1940] Kerouac had just read) to Mardou: "A million doubts of Mardou, now dispelled, now (and even without the help of Reich who shows life is simply the man entering the woman and the rubbing of the two in soft—that essence, that dingdong essence—something making me now almost so mad as to shout, I GOT MY OWN LITTLE BANGTAIL ESSENCE AND THAT ESSENCE IS MIND RECOGNITION—) now no more doubts."[30]

Reich's theory contends that "normal" and "abnormal" sexuality are both treated as "dirty," punishable, and undesirable. In *The Function of the Orgasm* Reich posits that healthy sexual needs must be fulfilled, or else dissatisfaction and repression would be destructive. Of most relevance to Kerouac (perhaps leading the way toward his studies in Buddhism) was Reich's belief that the waste of intellectual potential by those who spend a major portion of their energy fighting with their sexual desires drains the energy that otherwise could be available for further growth and work. Kerouac's pursuit of sexual kicks with either sex points more toward an egocentric personality than a sincere evolved sexual attraction to men and *some* women.

In a dream on October 14, 1953, Kerouac returned to Lowell. In the dream, it was sleeting all over Pawtucketville:

> The fine sleet white strengthens my belief in the unreality of the older "snow dream" of Moody but the thinner (more believable therefore) realities of this one-Kid Gringas in the sad dusk has that same sharp and humangrieving reality I saw in the 'moonlight bum caps of Amsterdam' and many other dreams where figures stalk cleanly and sharp in soft gloom clouds of poor nap (H horror) brain."[31]

Kerouac experienced rejection not only in waking life but also in his dreams, in which he was intensely reluctant to relinquish the past or to acknowledge that new generations must arise. Another Lowell dream that Kerouac had at this time occurred at his family's former West Street residence in Centralville. In the dream he returned to live with his father, back from the dead. Jack, thirty now, felt "closer than ever" to his father, and they shared "profound absorptions." In another dream, Leo was jobless and homeless in Lowell and was assisted only by the spirits of his own past acquaintances. Like his son, he "doesn't care any more." Leo ignored his son in this dream while haunting the Pawtucketville pool hall of the 1930s: "So different than he was in real life—in haunted life I think I see now his true soul—which is like mine—life means nothing to him—or I'm my father myself and this is me."[32]

Through Ginsberg, Kerouac once more asked Cassady about railroad work in Yum and El Paso. He also wanted to know if Cassady still "loved" him, and if he did, was it still that same brotherly affection that helped fuel *On the Road* and *Visions of Cody?* Ginsberg suggested to Cassady that maybe Kerouac could be persuaded to join him on his trip west planned for early 1954. Ginsberg had resigned himself to experimenting with his own poem, "The Green Automobile," much like Cassady's (by chance) and Kerouac's (by design) experimental writing. Ginsberg wrote to Cassady on June 22, 1953:

> In new poem I am beginning to explore some of the uncharted verbal rhetorical invented seas that Jack (& yrself) sail in. More I think of it the more interesting Jack's blowing is. After Empty Mirror, which for me strips yakking down to modern bones, I would like to build up a modern contemporary metaphorical yak-poem, using the kind of weaving original rhythms that Jack does in his prose, and the lush imagery. I been dry too long.[33]

Kerouac and Ginsberg hatched an idea (never realized) to create a company that would publish books in quantities of a thousand or fewer, and at a loss, if only to see their works in print. Enthusiastically, Ginsberg collected his poems in preparation for the venture. Burroughs had other plans. He intended to visit Tangier, where he would continue to compose some of the many satirical "routines" for which he had become known and where, perhaps, he would stand out less as a "pernicious foreigner." Soon he left, as did Ginsberg, who left the East Coast just behind a trunk of manuscripts sent in advance to the Cassadys.

Once again, Kerouac was saddled with another rejected novel. Ginsberg wrote Cassady: "Jack's novel [*On the Road*] is rejected, I think for good."[34] In May 1953, Kerouac's MCA agent, Phyllis Jackson, responded to Malcolm Cowley's request to publish excerpts from the rejected *On the Road*. Despite his eagerness to have his work published, Kerouac did not want *On the Road* published in excerpted form.[35]

In November 1953, Kerouac met again with Malcolm Cowley, who had received a letter from Viking editor Helen K. Taylor (who would later edit *On the Road* for publication) late in October 1953. She told Cowley that the novel "stirred" her for two reasons. First, she felt that Kerouac possessed "bold writing talent" that was by turns "lavish" and "reckless." Despite its recklessness, the seeming carelessness was effective because it built up energy on its own "that is all-pervasive by the end of the book." She also observed that "it is almost as if the author did not seem to exist as an outside agency of creation." Second, Taylor felt that the novel depicted a "raw sociology" of the "hipster generation." It was "a life slice so raw and bleeding that it makes me terribly sad." Though her perception of the characters was harsh ("There is no redemption for these psychopaths and hopeless neurotics, for they don't want any"), the portrayal of Dean, the antihero, was "gargantuan but believably pitiful." Taylor's suggestion to Cowley, should Viking accept it, was "large-chunk cutting" to reduce the length and the "lightly touching pencil, for refinement has no place in this prose." In essence, though she wasn't alarmed by the "obscenity," she felt it to be "very challenging" and recommended publishing it quietly "with no touting, pre-viewing, or advance quotes from run-of-the-mill names."[36] At the meeting, Cowley offered to show Kerouac's work to Arabelle Porter, editor of the journal *New World Writing*. Jack considered the option and replied in mid-November, assuring Cowley that if she wanted his work, he would send her excerpts for consideration. In an attempt to flatter Cowley, Kerouac called Gore Vidal a "pretentious little fag" for berating Cowley's critical methodology in an issue of *New World Writing*:

> What's troubled me is . . . certain dull individuals who happen to be homosexual who have grabbed off the limelight and therefore the temporary influence, second rate anecdote repeaters like [Paul] Bowles,

pretentious silly females with flairs for titles . . . clever dramaturgists, grave self-revellers too naïve to see the shame of their position like [Gore] Vidal, really it's too much, I think I'll come out soon and make a statement—every single original musical genius in America, for instance, has been to jail or prison; I assure you the same holds true for literature.[37]

Whenever there was a need for discretion, Kerouac instead revealed whatever came to his mind. It is small wonder that he later found himself at such unmerciful odds with New York critics and other substrata of the city's literati. Apart from any conflicts arising from his prejudices toward those he viewed as obstacles to his success as a writer, Jack changed agents to one more willing to temper his stubborn prose stylings: Sterling Lord of the Lord and Colbert agency (who would serve as Kerouac's literary agent during his life and after).

Cowley's parting advice to Kerouac, whose immediate prospects of getting published were bleak, was to "take a job for a while." Soon after, Cassady offered him a job as a parking lot attendant so that he could again escape New York, that "overcrowded frosty fag town." Labor, no matter how menial, was never beneath Jack when under duress. He told Carolyn that such a job was "made to order." He was prepared to board a bus to California after Christmas, but he only had $30 to his name. Cassady answered Kerouac, assuring him that the attendant's job was still available. Kerouac planned to keep the job until spring, when he would hand it over to Ginsberg.[38]

Waiting for more money before leaving, Kerouac was dismayed when he learned that it would not arrive by Christmas. With haste, Jack wrote the Cassadys telling them that he expected to leave by the first week of January. Neal, having promised his employer a warm body for the job, was now in the lurch. Jack attempted to resolve the problem by asking Cassady for railroad passes that he could use to reach Nogales, Arizona, from where he could dip into Mexico to obtain some pot. Neal spat to Carolyn that he couldn't get the "jerk" any more train passes.[39] By the end of January, Jack was still a no-show. Finally, on January 29 he left New York after assuring Neal that he need not worry. Kerouac would learn all he needed to know in the parking lot in "one day."

Kerouac's trip west included a miserable two-hundred-mile journey on an open flatcar, where he endured the night's cold huddled in a thin blanket. Starving, he ate grass when he reached Watsonville, California. When he arrived in San Jose, he started at once at the parking lot. Although he was somewhat experienced from working as a young man at the Middlesex Garage, he proved inept with clutches and brakes.

Neal had immersed himself in the writings of Edgar Cayce, which he urged Jack to read. Cassady felt Cayce integrated the reincarnation found in Hindu and Buddhist beliefs into those of Judaism and Christianity. Instead, Jack was becoming enlightened by his readings at the San Jose Public Library. On his thirty-second birthday he attained "transcendental understanding" as he watched the sun through a purple stone until he blinded himself temporarily.

Kerouac put the Cassadys on edge again. Despite having invited Jack, Neal intimated to Carolyn that his friend was a "freeloader." One night, as they sat eating a dinner of pork chops around the kitchen table, Neal remarked that the food they were eating was there because he had earned it. Jack vowed to go out the next day, buy a hot plate and some food, and cook in his room. The breaking point occurred when Neal and Jack were dividing a pile of marijuana and got into a fierce argument. Neal told Jack that he was supposed pay the $20 for the pot, while Jack assumed the cost would be shared evenly by both. Although Jack protested, Neal insisted it was so. That night Jack went drinking with Al Sublette and did not return. Kerouac went to San Francisco and stayed for a week in a $3 room in the Cameo Hotel before returning to New York.

While in San Francisco he wrote a poem, composed in a spontaneous burst, "San Francisco Blues." Gazing out his window at Third Street while sitting in a rocking chair, he watched the whores and bums and noted random elements in his notebook: hunch-backed old men, mustached blacks, firemen, Mexican laborers, young girls, thick-lipped kids, an old man chasing a young woman, a whore with her pimp, cops, topcoated gangster-types—all of them, among others, living against the backdrop of San Francisco.

The poem is divided into eighty "choruses" fashioned after the musical choruses of bebop. In the preface, Kerouac explains that his "system" was to confine each chorus to one small page of the breast-pocket notebook that he carried habitually in his shirt pocket. "It's all gotta be non stop ad libbing within each chorus, or the gig is shot."[40]

> This pretty white city
> On the other side of the country
> Will no longer be
> Available to me

I saw heaven move
Said "This is the End"
Because I was tired
Of all this portend.

And any time you need
    me
Call
    I'll be at the other
    End
Waiting
    At the final hall[41]

Kerouac did not stay at the Cameo for long. He put the notebook containing "San Francisco Blues" into his knapsack along with a copy of Dwight Goddard's *Buddhist Bible* lifted from the San Jose Public Library. When Kerouac reached home, after an arduous bus trip during which he went without food for lack of money, he wrote to Carolyn. He recognized the tensions between them, especially the conflict between the Cassadys' immersion in Cayce and his Buddhist studies:

> I don't believe in karma; and just found out I'd made a dreadful mistake, thinking Emptiness had preceded the Now World; a big mistake; it's not that the world is "empty," but, that you say about it, neither IS, or IS NOT, but merely a manifestation of mind, the reflection of the moon on a lake; so the next porkchop you eat, remember, it's merely a porkchop reflected off water, and your hunger, and you the hungerer, Narcissus you. . . . but for purposes of this world, I say let wine and porkchops flow, anything to put us asleep, or put ME asleep leastways. Who me? Who you? Who you ever be who ever I be send what ever is. Someone was trying to tell me something, maybe, and I want to see.[42]

Neal read and dismissed the letter, tossing it back to Carolyn.

20

Lake of Light

December 1953—April 1955

And I discovered that profound truth, so difficult to perceive, difficult to
understand, tranquillising and sublime, which is not to be gained by
mere reasoning, and is only visible to the wise.
THE WORD OF THE BUDDHA (Paticca-Samuppada)

Kerouac's introduction to Buddhism in December 1953 would help open
the door to a later generation's acceptance and practice of it in the Western world. At the San Jose Public Library he had picked up and perused
Dwight Goddard's *Buddhist Bible*. He began to amass reading notes and
added his own Catholic insights. Eager to share this amalgamation with
someone, he typed a hundred pages of it for Ginsberg. Kerouac did not
mail him these right away. They would form part of *Some of the Dharma*,
posthumously published by Viking in 1997.

The Buddhist Bible (1932) was intended by Goddard to import the
essence of Buddhist scripture without bogging the reader down with
"matter not bearing on the theme of the particular Scripture," interpreting
only what was "necessary" and "advisable." He intended to create an
anatta (no soul) doctrine, thus illuminating the "unreality of all concep-
tions of a personal ego." The anthology contains selections from Pali, Sanskrit, Chinese, Tibetan, and modern sources and concludes with a summary of the dharma of the Buddha. The book sought to awaken a new
faith from the bedrock of self-doubt. Kerouac came across *The Buddhist
Bible* at precisely the right moment.

Buddhism, he hoped, would be the key to correcting all of the negative character traits that he felt skewed his behavior. Lust for women and for alcohol, for example, clouded his thinking. Concerning women, Kerouac had neither the time nor inclination to establish any new or meaningful relationships during this period. He did keep casual company with a suicidal, heroin-addicted woman recently hospitalized from an attempted overdose (thus continuing his tendency to attract the addicted, the married, or the helpless). During his drinking sprees he felt mired in unhappiness and found it difficult even to sleep. When he did manage to doze at all, he had nightmares, many of which he recorded in his dream journal.

By the time his *Book of Dreams* was completed in 1960, it spanned eleven handwritten notebooks totaling a staggering 1,955 pages. *Book of Dreams* stands as a testament to Kerouac's spontaneous prose method. Kerouac preserved these dreams, not for any Freudian analysis (he disdained Freud's theories), but rather, as poet Robert Creeley so aptly explains, to explore the "dream contents." In his foreword to the published version (1961) Kerouac states the aptness of such a publication when viewed in conjunction with his other published works: "The heroes of *On the Road, The Subterraneans*, etc. reappear here doing further strange things for no other particular reason than that the mind goes on, the brain ripples, the moon sinks, and everybody hides their heads under pillows with sleepingcaps."[1]

Dreaming is the one common denominator that ties all humankind together, Kerouac reasons in his foreword. Thus, it proves that "the world is really transcendental." In his dreams he was in Lowell or San Jose or Denver or back in San Francisco and was visited by the living and the dead. Leo Kerouac appears again and again, sometimes accusatory, sometimes fatherly. Gabrielle is also a constant fixture, as are Ginsberg, Burroughs, Huncke, and Corso, among others.

There was also, in addition to *Book of Dreams*, his poetry from San Francisco that he would add later to his collection of "blues" poems. In his Richmond Hill apartment he began "Richmond Hill Blues" (not as inspired as its West Coast counterpart). Kerouac also wrote twenty-thousand words for a novel which he later abandoned. On the cover he wrote in blue magic marker the title *Cody Deaver*.

Kerouac told Ginsberg that, despite his battles with alcohol and depression, he had found the "path" at last. His recent immersion in Buddhism had taught Kerouac that his miseries and his sufferings were not meaningless. He memorized the Four Noble Truths (or, in Pali, *Ariya Satta*): all life is sorrowful; the cause of suffering is ignorant craving; the suppression of suffering can be achieved; the way is the Noble Eightfold Path. Through knowledge of these four truths came the Noble Eightfold Path, which guided the way toward "Holy Ecstasy" but was difficult to attain when saddled with a lust for women and booze. Kerouac gave Ginsberg a reading list: *The Buddhist Bible; Texts from the Buddhist Canon Known as Dhamapada; Life of Buddha* by Asvaghosha the Patriarch; *The Gospel of the Buddha* by Paul Carus; *Buddhism in Translations* by Henry Clarke Warren; *Buddhist Legends* by E. W. Burlingame; *The Dialogues of the Buddha* by Digha-Nikaya; *Visuddhi Magga* by Buddhaghosha; and *The Sacred Books and Early Literature of the East*, volume 18, *India and Buddhism*. Allen thought Jack was wasting his time. Writing to his father, stepmother, and brother, Ginsberg observed: "Everybody appears to be either off their rockers or getting religion. Cassady has some mediumistic cult that has changed him so that he kneels and prays with his children; the doctrine is screwy and absurd, almost on a *Reader's Digest* level, but the seriousness of the search for uplift is real enough and respectable; Kerouac seems all hung up on Buddha doctrine of life as a dream." He told his family that he would "eventually" read from the list of books recommended to him, as there was "nothing like a wide range of information."[2]

Because he was officially laid off from the railroad, Kerouac continued to receive unemployment checks, which he used to support himself and his mother. He also worked two days on the New York Dock Railway as a yard brakeman, earning $18.35 a day. His phlebitis threatened to flare up again, and he needed medicine for it. He started a garden in the backyard and tended it faithfully, meditated, and read from his Catholic Bible as he pursued the Thoreauvian ideal. Gabrielle continued to work in the shoe factory, and Jack prepared dinner, often joining her in a cocktail. At other times, any notions of abstaining were lost when he went into the Village. One night, he was so intoxicated that he thought a "tangle-haired," "mad-looking" man standing on the street corner was Ginsberg and called to him.[3]

Like Cassady across the continent, who finally received his settlement from the railroad, Kerouac was for once financially stable. However, the unemployment agency did not feel that he was trying hard enough to find a job and informed him that the agency would cease issuing him checks. "When they do, I will tell them to go to hell." But he decided against that option, and against collecting unemployment, because he felt that life was not "worth living." He was making a concerted effort to avoid relationships with women, reporting to Carolyn that women were offering to "fuck and suck" him, but he refused. Instead, he continued reading his Buddhist texts, writing, and meditating, perhaps heeding the text of the Surangama Sutra:

> When anyone becomes inflamed by sexual passion, his mind becomes disturbed and confused, he loses self-control and becomes reckless and crude. Besides, in sexual intercourse, the blood becomes inflamed and impure and adulterated with impure secretions. Naturally from such a source, there can never originate an aureole of such transcendently pure and golden brightness as I have seen emanating from the person of my Lord.[4]

It was, in theory, the exact opposite of Reich's *Function of the Orgasm*, which Kerouac had read earlier. His meditation brought into focus all of the mistakes that he had made thus far. For now, he made no plans to return to California. The only way he would ever go back, he wrote Carolyn, was if he were personally driven in a car or if he earned sufficient money from the manuscript now titled "Beat Generation" (*On the Road*). In other words, if the opportunity was right, he would suspend his self-imposed exile to pursue further kicks.

Kerouac dismissed the Cassadys' Cayce readings, telling them that they were being "duped." Instead, he recommended to Carolyn that she read *Jataka* (or *Stories of the Buddha*). In one story, a devout monk surrenders his beliefs because he is "tired of trying" to reach supreme enlightenment. The Buddha visits the monk and tells him that in another lifetime he was a young traveler in the desert ready to give up until the leader of the caravan told him to split a rock in half. When he did so, water shot straight upward like a geyser. In that lifetime, Buddha says, he was the traveling boy and Buddha was the caravan leader. Tales like these mirror the parables of Christ, and it was perhaps this quality that attracted Kerouac. From his window, Jack was able to make casual observations and to apply his Buddhist readings to them. The tree in the front yard existed because it *is*. It was merely a "dream," like much of what Kerouac ascertained life to be. While Neal's reading of Cayce taught him that life was perpetual until perfection was attained, the Surangama Sutra states:

The reason why sentient beings by their previous lives since begin-ningless time have formed a succession of deaths and rebirths, life after life, is because they have never realized the true Essence of Mind and its self-purifying brightness. On the contrary they have been absorbed all the time busying themselves with their deluding and transient thoughts which are nothing but falsity and vanity. Hence they have prepared for themselves the conditions for this ever returning cycle of deaths and rebirths.[5]

The Sutra also states that "the lives of human beings who are always being troubled by worldly attachments and contaminations" cause "their percep-tion of sight to become inverted and unreliable," thus "seducing their thoughts and causing them to wander about ignorantly and uncon-trolled."[6] At a time when "control" of any sort was beyond Kerouac's grasp (except in his own writing), this insight must have hit him hard. Small wonder that he dismissed the cessation of his unemployment checks as unimportant.

Kerouac's Buddhist learning did not erode the complex beliefs of his Catholic upbringing but caused him to ponder creating an amalgam that would clarify and enrich each orthodoxy. If Christ had reached India, Kerouac reasoned to Carolyn Cassady, "one dab of Buddhism would have wiped clean from his mind that egomaniacal Messiah complex that got him crucified and made Christianity the dualistic greed-and-sorrow Monster that he is." The difference between Christ and Buddha, accord-ing to Kerouac, was that Buddha never claimed to be God or the Son of God but merely a man who had attained enlightenment. Clearly, echoes of Leo Kerouac's anticlerical attitude were subtly affecting his son's be-liefs.[7]

Another summer arrived, and Kerouac, who detested the heat of New York, started itching for action of any kind. Despite the simplicity of liv-ing that Buddhism preached, Kerouac had money in his pocket once more from his sporadic employment and wrote to Cassady with plans to travel. One possibility was meeting Burroughs in New York and together traveling to San Francisco, where they could work and save enough money to return to Mexico. Kerouac was keen on seeing the "grapey dusk" of the California landscape and imagined himself cooking hot dogs over a fire. He was again free, but this time in the broader sense of the word: beyond the restraints of the physical body. He told Carolyn that the Kerouac whom she knew was "false and phantasmal." It is small wonder that when he visited Mary Carney in Lowell in October 1954, in what he called the "Great Lowell Trip," she sensed that he was a changed man, one worlds apart from the shy college boy she had known ten years earlier.[8]

He walked the streets of Lowell immersed in its autumn colors. Kicking through the fallen leaves on Wannalancit Street, he walked toward the Bartlett School to reconnect with his past (jotting his impressions into his journal). For some reason he avoided Stella Sampas and instead walked along the Boston and Maine train tracks until he reached South Lowell. There, he came to the home of Mary Carney. When she knew him as a Columbia student, Mary had sensed that he no longer wanted to be associated with Lowell or her world. Even though she had resented Gabrielle for supporting Jack's decision, she now realized that his mother had stood by him for the right reasons: to reach beyond the provincial limitations a small town places on you, it is necessary to leave.[9] The visit was nostalgic but awkward for her. Kerouac asked one of Mary's daughters if her mother was "still married." After the visit, Mary wondered if the past would repeat itself and if they would become lovers again. They had had little privacy during the short while he was there. After he left she imagined running after him and creating the ideal union that they both sought.[10]

Kerouac went to a Boston and Maine railroad bridge that crossed the Concord River and started to write in his notebook:

> But I'm too sad to care that I understand everything.
> Lowell is a happy dream but just a dream.
> All's left, I must go now into my own monastery
> wherever it's convenient.
> My life went from culture of Town, to civilization of
> City, to neither of Fellaheen.[11]

He crossed the bridge over the Merrimack into Pawtucketville and continued walking through Lowell's downtown section. As was his habit, Jack sat in the dim recesses of the empty basement of St. Jeanne d'Arc church near his boyhood home on Crawford Street. The next day, he got drunk with some friends and, hung over, took another walk. This time he walked past Stella's house "afraid to go in." He stopped before his birthplace where he stared at the porch light's fluted globe and remembered his picture taken there as a baby in a wicker basket.[12]

Revitalized with fresh impressions, Kerouac polished the Lowell sections of his novels. Mary, Lowell itself, all that had preceded, and all that would follow were currents in a dream river coursing through the "Universe Canyon of mystery."[13] Mary Carney urged Jack in a letter to keep pursuing his life goals. She wrote him soon after he left Lowell that it was "pleasant" to see him after so many years. It was, she said, an occasion she found "hard to believe." Between her and Jack there existed a huge gulf: her satisfaction extended to a simple day at the beach watching her children play in the surf; his was cerebral, buried beneath literary and religious detritus. Love, being pleasant, was a very easy thing to consider (though heartbreaking), but it was not enough to compel one to surrender one's own ambitions.[14] Jack's visit with Mary left her with several questions, among them whether his two marriages were "real" or whether he was "lying." Her situation wasn't much better, she said, for her alcoholic husband had met and bigamously married a seventeen-year-old girl in Monson, Massachusetts. Unsure of where she stood in Jack's life, she wrote him one last letter in 1954 telling him that if he did not answer, she would "understand." He apparently never did according to archival sources.

At home with his mother on Easter Sunday, Jack was brooding over his notebook. That evening he wrote a small meditation about his mother and his growing awareness of the "Void":

It broke my heart in the rainy night to see the glazed Easter Egg cakes in the bakery . . . the kindness of poor people trapped in this world so unreal that tonight, napping fitfully, I heard my mother talking to me about the same thing on both sides of Eternity during which I was unconscious, asleep, and thought all infinity had pass't, but in "reality" it must have been 15 seconds or so . . . that therefore she thought she was talking to "me" breaks my heart, for I love the world and the people in it because they are really so sweet, helpless and lost—and I wish I could do something to ease their fears, for now I'm convinced that there's absolutely nothing to fear—sadness yes, and no name to it— What I wish I could do, that would be of use, or good, beneficial, does not exist in this mortal sea—My mother talking "to me" to and into the Void—O—[15]

In the summer of 1954, before Kerouac left for Lowell, his agent, Sterling Lord, convinced Malcolm Cowley to reconsider a short prose piece, "Jazz of the Beat Generation," which documented Jack's year with Neal in 1949. To Cowley, the essay was impressive, perhaps the best he had read recently and the one that best documented the post–World War II generation. Its content was novel and sincere: "Out we jumped into the warm mad night hearing a wild tenorman's bawling horn across the way going 'EE-YAH! EE-YAH!' and hands clapping to the beat and folks yelling 'Go, go, go!'"[16] Cowley brought the manuscript to Arabelle Porter, who was impressed by the work (and trusted Cowley's judgment). She scheduled it for the April 1955 edition of *New World Writing;* for his efforts, Kerouac received $108 (after agent's fees).

Nervous that Joan Haverty might see this second piece of published writing since *The Town and the City* and demand a lien on his meager earnings, Kerouac used the pseudonym Jean-Louis. He told Ginsberg that he used the pseudonym to preserve anonymity, so that he could observe the world unnoticed as he wrote. His biography, when the piece was published, read: "This selection is from a novel-in-progress, *The Beat Generation.* Jean-Louis is the pseudonym of a young American writer of French-Canadian parentage. He is the author of one published novel." Malcolm Cowley, however, was not happy with the name change, as he had been plugging Kerouac's real name in association with *On the Road.* Kerouac immediately wrote to Cowley when he heard of his unhappiness with his decision:

> I want you to know, and I'm positive you could never be bugged after knowing, that I changed my name for no eccentric beret-and-cravat reason but because I have an ex-wife who is continually trying to get me in the workhouse for non-support and was recently (after the name-change) stymied by a judge's verdict that, because of my chronic thrombo-phlebitis which I have all the time (all over my body at different times, the brain not yet or I wouldn't be writing this letter), I am not liable to prosecution but "disabled." . . . For instance, were I to start smoking butts like everybody else I'd die in 3 months. The girl tried everything to get me banged behind bars. . . . as soon as she finds out I am Jean-Louis, for instance, there'll be more trouble . . . but by that time I'll be in Africa or someplace I hope. . . . You understand, Malcolm, the reason,—altho now I really feel like using my full name, which is John (Jack) (Jean-Louis) Kerouac.[17]

It would not have taken a tremendous mental leap for Joan to figure out the pseudonymous writer was her former husband. Even more incriminating than the conspicuous bio was the prose style that was uniquely Kerouac's at the time. He did give some of the money he earned to Gabrielle to help pay her bills. As for work, he felt "too old" to railroad in Brooklyn (as suggested by Carolyn Cassady). He felt that the arduous labor exacerbated his phlebitis.[18]

On July 28, Kerouac attempted to begin a new work, "Book of Samadhi." He had taken to meditating in his Richmond Hill yard (on one occasion even fainting), and on that day he saw that "I cant write my visions of the Dharma except as I write my dreams, swiftly, surely, undiscriminated, purely from my mind—So I hereby end this book SOME OF THE DHARMA." Kerouac appended "Book of Samadhi" as a postscript. It was Kerouac's first extended exploration of writing (foreshadowing seminal works like *Mexico City Blues* and *The Scripture of the Golden Eternity*) that incorporated Buddhist texts:

> Only if at death my body vanished into thin air—for its destruction among worms or in fire is only a vague rearrangement of atomic worlds infinitely empty in all directions moving about in imaginary hassle inside vast universes of worm cell or in universes of empty fire gas—in no sense vanishment of the primal mistake of false-existence—Is it all in the mind, the escape? the breakthrough? As I lay unconscious it wasn't "I am dead," it was "mind essence is mind essence." (This is why, when walking at night on my favorite sidewalk going under low trees I say "Bend the head, your low branches wont hurt")—Nobody dies; there is nothing to die except aggregates of imagination that is not real in the first place but we cling and call it "ego-personality"—Where is the escape?[19]

Unable to sleep on the night of July 29, Kerouac began book 3 of *Some of the Dharma*, apparently unsatisfied that he had exhausted all that he wanted to say in his notebooks. It was easier for him to project his "Bliss Screen of Movies" onto blank pages than to try to discuss it with his mother, who was intolerant of all religions other than Roman Catholicism.[20]

On August 24, he had plunged to the "lowest point in my Buddhist Faith" since he had commenced his practice the previous December.

> Here I am in America sitting alone with legs crossed as world rages to burn itself up—What to do? Buddhism has killed all my feelings, I have no feelings, no inclinations to go anywhere, yet I stay here in this

house a sitting duck for the police who want me for penury & non-support, listless, bored, world-weary at 32, no longer interested in love, tired, unutterably sad as the Chinese autumn-man. It's the silence of unspoken despair, the sound of drying, that gets me down. . . . I MUST GO AWAY ALONE.²¹

By the fall of 1954, Kerouac had completed five major works, written purely on his terms. After seeing Alfred Kazin in a televised roundtable discussion on Melville, Jack offered to send him *Doctor Sax* and *The Subterraneans*. He wanted to impress upon Kazin the development of his prose style since *The Town and the City*, saying that the words themselves stemmed not from logic but from their aural magic. Kerouac explained his writing method to Kazin: "The main thing, I feel, is that the urgency of explaining something has its own words and rhythm, and time is of the essence—Modern Prose."²² A response from one of New York City's leading literary critics would bolster the validity of his spontaneous prose method. Also, Kazin had connections with Harcourt, Brace, a fact not lost on Kerouac.

As 1954 drew to a close, Kerouac was no closer to having any of his mature fiction published. All that December he typed deep into the night a manuscript of "The Beat Generation" for Knopf, which rejected it in January 1955. Kerouac wrote to Ginsberg in mid-December, shortly before Allen arrived in New York, assuring him that they were "fellow disciples before the Awesome Law," for he hesitated to embrace the role of master teacher. However, the law of another sort arrived to arrest him. Joan Haverty had prepared to sue him for child support. This crisis caused his spirit to spiral downward into the "lowest beatest ebb of my life." He felt trapped by the law. His friends, he felt, only plagiarized his work. He felt "scorned" and "cheated." His family did not understand him, perhaps impatient with his Zen attitude toward life: "Everybody is getting mad at me for knowing the truth now."²³ His physical health was in jeopardy by his own doing; his mind was frazzled from Benzedrine and goofballs, his smoking scorched his throat and lungs, and the booze drowned him in a gasping pool of "alcoholic sorrow." His obligations to others only "dragged" him down. Bitterly, he knew that he was "considered a criminal and insane and a sinner and an imbecile, myself self-disappointed & endlessly sad because I'm not doing what I knew should be done a whole year ago when the Buddha's printed words showed me the path . . . a year's delay, a deepening of the sea of troubles, sickness, old age creeping around my tired eyes, decrepitude and dismay, loss of solitude & purity."[24]

His brooding carried him to the heights of spiritual understanding and the depths of self-loathing. Three nights before Christmas, he wrote "Night Dhyana," in which he reveals that he now realizes the death of his father's body and mind, and by virtue of it, the elimination of all human manifestations. That realization contained concepts of "Beginninglessness" and "Endlessness." The understanding of Mind Essence by human thought could be achieved by rationalism whereas an animal (Kerouac uses a frog in his example) knew it by "mere sensation." When he prayed on the floor with legs crossed, the throbbing ache that he felt in his ankles was different from that of the "pain of Western Praying in the knees." The morning after, he concluded with a "Morning Dhyana" and succumbed to a "useful realization of the triviality of the activities of people in civilizations." This continued throughout Christmas Day until midnight, when he finally attained "at last" a "measure of enlightenment."

Allen Ginsberg came to Kerouac's rescue once again. His brother, Eugene Brooks, was a lawyer. In January 1955 they went to court to contest Haverty's suit. Brooks's defense was that his client was too disabled from phlebitis to work full-time. Missing from Brooks's briefcase was a letter from Kerouac's personal physician prescribing bed rest "until his acute condition subsides." However, they had another plan. Kerouac demanded a paternity test. Should the strategy fail and he be incarcerated in the notorious Tombs, Kerouac had brought with him a manila envelope filled with his typed notes of *Prajna* and *The Buddhist Bible* (Joan disparaged his interest in Buddhism as his "little game").[25] Kerouac was sure that Joan had learned about the proposed test and that was why she did not bring her daughter to court. He was surprised when Joan asked Jack if she could sit with him. They talked pleasantly. He was pleased to hear that she had converted to Catholicism. Endlessly, she brought up Jesus Christ, the Virgin Mary, and her own attainment of inner peace. From her wallet she took out photos of Jan. Writing to Ginsberg, Kerouac admitted, "She looks like me, especially frowning square-browed photo, so may be mine." Despite his feelings, Joan did not want Jan to be in contact with the Kerouacs. In the judge's chambers they all met: Eugene Brooks, Kerouac's female probation officer, and Joan's lawyer. Somehow, the medical records turned up from the veterans' hospital in the Bronx, and the judge decided that the case had to be set aside if the defendant couldn't work. The case was suspended for a year, "unless Joan gets mad or I get rich and famous."[26]

Kerouac had many works floating around New York (four complete novels and several shorter pieces), and he wrote to Sterling Lord asking if perhaps there were too many eyes perusing his writings. Thus far *Doctor Sax* had been rejected by A. A. Wyn, Viking Press, and New Directions; "The Beat Generation" *(On the Road)* by Harcourt, Brace, Ballantine Books, Farrar, Straus, Viking, and Vanguard; and "Mary Cassidy" (*Maggie Cassidy*) by Wyn, Viking, and New Directions. "Visions of Neal" (*Visions of Cody*) was dismissed roundly as "unpublishable." Kerouac decided in February that he really hadn't given Lord the opportunity to circulate his works thoroughly. His agent planned to send *The Subterraneans* to France as well as circulate the prose piece "October in the Poolhall" (also called "October in the Railroad Earth"). On January 11, Kerouac learned that Knopf had passed on 'The Beat Generation."

By the spring of 1955, he was still studying Buddhist writings and recording dreams. Soon, Gabrielle tired of her job in the shoe factory and decided to move south to stay with her daughter and son-in-law. On February 13, Kerouac escorted his mother to Rocky Mount and stayed there because he did not have the money to maintain an apartment on his own in New York. Again he slept in the room with a desk and typewriter. Two days after arriving, he hiked into the woods with Bob, one of the Blakes' two dogs. There he sat at the base of a pine tree and meditated in the heat, while the dog rested at his feet. Another time he walked with his nephew, Paul Jr., to an old sharecropper's farm, empty save for a crying puppy chained to a porch. Kerouac asked himself, "What's the use of all this suffering? Why was he born?"[27] Despite going "bugs in the cotton-fields" of his sister's oppressive household, Kerouac remained productive. He completed a seventy-thousand-word, pencil-written biography of Buddha, "Your Essential Mind, The Story of Buddha," which he had started on February 18. Basing the piece on his Buddhist readings, he merged actual biography with his own perceptions to recount the rise of Buddha. It was to be, according to Kerouac, a "handbook for Western understanding." At different times, Kerouac gave it different titles: "Buddha Tells

Us," "Wake Up," and "Buddhahood: The Essence of Reality." Opening the work with an aphorism by ancient Sanskrit poet and scholar Ashvaghosh, Kerouac wrote:

> Buddha means the awakened one.
>
> Until recently most people thought of the Buddha as a big fat rococo sitting figure with his belly out, laughing, as represented in millions of tourist trinkets and dime-store statuettes here in the Western world. People didn't know that the actual Buddha was a handsome young prince who suddenly began brooding in his father's palace, staring through the dancing girls as though they weren't there, at the age of twenty-nine, till finally and emphatically he threw up his hands and rode out to the forest on his war horse and cut off his long golden hair with his sword and sat down with the holy men of the India of his day and died at the age of eighty a lean venerable wanderer of ancient roads and elephant woods. This man was no slob-like figure of mirth, but a serious and tragic prophet, the Jesus Christ of India and almost all Asia.[28]

Kerouac continues Prince Siddhartha's story with his marriage at sixteen to Yasodhara and the birth of his son, Rahula. At twenty-nine, Siddhartha encounters three stages of suffering: old age, sickness, and death.

> I fear birth, old age, disease, and death, and so I seek to find a sure mode of deliverance. And so I fear the five desires—the desires attached to seeing, hearing, tasting, smelling, and touching—the inconstant thieves, stealing from men their choicest treasures, making them unreal, false, and fickle—the great obstacles, forever disarranging the way of peace.[29]

Subsequently, he leaves behind his wife and child and departs on his horse in the middle of the night. Siddhartha also leaves behind the opulent palace to pursue a life of spirituality. One of the first things he does in preparation for his vow of homelessness is to shear off his hair and trade his clothes for those of a beggar. Siddhartha sits under a bodhi tree and vows not to rise from the spot "until, freed from clinging, my mind attains deliverance from all sorrow." Siddhartha becomes liberated as a consequence of discovering the Four Noble Truths and the Noble Eightfold Path and achieving full enlightenment. He becomes known as Shakyamuni Buddha. However, Buddha delays his entry into Nirvana until all "sentient beings are freed from suffering." He gives a sermon in Benares, forms his first sangha, and delivers his Fire Sermon in front of a thousand fire worshipers. His sermon addresses the nature of reality and the inconstancy of the self. By the close of Kerouac's story, Buddha is eighty years old and, to his assistant Ananda, proclaims his preparation to enter Nirvana: "Now I have given up my term of years: I live henceforth by power of faith; my body like a broken chariot stands, no further cause of 'coming' or of 'going,' completely freed from earth, heaven and hell, I go enfranchised, as a chicken from its egg."[30]

In April 1955, Kerouac typed from his handwritten manuscript. Naively, he thought he could sell the work to publishers when his lack of income put him against the wall. As passionate and knowledgeable Kerouac was about the Buddhist canon, the work was destined to remain unpublished during his lifetime.

His sister and mother were badgering him to contribute to the family income. Frantically he wrote to Lord about the status of his submitted work, saying he did not even have five cents to buy a Popsicle at the county store.

Kerouac returned to New York to retrieve more of his mother's belongings. In the city he went out with some friends, who ultimately "bored" him, so he did what he always did—he got drunk. Guiltily, he was all too aware of how he contradicted his Buddhist beliefs and how his drinking distanced him from his friends and family.

> Drinking heavily, you abandon people—and they abandon you—It's a form of partial self murder but too sad to go all the way—Make it a rule not to drink without eating outside your own home (degrisez . . . sobered up). Because, the kind of drinking that seeks to abandon people, is done in public. The kind of drinking that seeks to allay boredom, is done at home and is self controlled.
>
> DON'T DRINK TO GET DRUNK
> DRINK TO ENJOY LIFE[31]

His abstinence from alcohol was short-lived. The lack of news from his agent and what he perceived as desertion by his friends made him feel "crushed by almost everything." Hungover and distraught the next morning, he wrote Neal Cassady: "I want no more bullshit between us any more; and believe me and don't mistrust your senses, when I say, it was all my fault and you were not to blame, because you're always the same, and very constant in your own way that I understand now."³² Kerouac was willing to put aside the arguments over unpaid loans and splitting weed. He tried to create the illusion that things were now as they had always been. To cajole Cassady into writing back, Kerouac desperately flattered him as "the greatest writer in America." Kerouac was ready to board a truck and head west, but Neal had changed, at least for the present. He no longer needed kicks with Kerouac. Cassady simply did not write back.

In the city Kerouac wrote a poem while looking out the window of a friend's apartment, "Macdougal Street Blues in the Form of 3 Cantos." The poem incorporated several allusions to Buddhism and culminated in a prayer and plea to humankind:

> I shall pray for all
>   sentient human
> & otherwise sentient
> beings here & everywhere
> now—
>
> No names
>   Not even faces
>   One Pity
>   One Milk
>   One Lovelight
>   s   a   v   e ³³

In March he wrote "Bowery Blues," in which he stated that the "story of man / Makes me sick." Jazz no longer interested him either; he dismissed it as "simpleminded noise."³⁴ He felt at odds with society but prevented himself from completely going off the deep end through the "transcendental brilliance" of Buddhism. In a feverish frenzy, Kerouac transcribed The Diamond Vow of God's Wisdom on a typewritten forty-foot-long scroll.

Perhaps sensing Neal's lack of interest in him, Kerouac wrote two letters to Carolyn once he returned to Rocky Mount and saw no letters from Neal waiting for him. Again, he praised Neal's writing as as "great" as Joyce's but felt he was "too far gone" to ever want to write anymore. Penury, as usual, thwarted Jack's plans to go west. He was left to confront the constant scowls of his sister, her husband, and his mother. Immersed in Thoreau, Kerouac again contemplated a hermitage where he could meditate, compose prayers, and escape the pressure to "contribute."

WHY DO I WANT TO LEAVE SOCIETY? (in my case) Lou Little making me run a week on a broken leg in 1940—the way drivers sneak their cars up to your knees when you cross with the red light— the way the gang at the Pawtucketville Social Club punched me in the sandlot football pileups and called me "*L'ti Christ a Kerouac*"—Kerouac's Little Christ (Leo's Little Bastard) because of some grudge against my father and so against his innocent child—the time 1954 I called at a friend's house uninvited and I never was told that it signified "Don't call us we'll call you"—the slap in the face I got from my brother, whom I shadowed like Ananda his Lord—the slap on the top of the head I gave Lil Paul once for yanking at my slip of paper I was reading—all this contemptuousness, cold drollery, viciousness, hypocrisy, and derangement convinces me man must leave society and learn to live by himself purely in a solitary out-of-the-way hut, and feed himself by whatever means are kindly.[35]

To evade his family's harsh dismissal of his Buddhist interests and writing, he escaped into the woods with the Blakes' two dogs and meditated. In the forest his intentions were noble; if he planted seedlings of dharma, they would grow into full plants, from which he could harvest the "Crop of Enlightenment." When meditation didn't alleviate his misery, a potent cocktail of ginger ale, orange juice, rum, and white lightning did.[36]

To Kerouac, Manhattan did not seem the same. The bohemian circles where bebop had raged only years before had suffered a serious and premature loss: on March 12, 1955, Charlie "Bird" Parker died. Max Roach commented, "New York isn't New York any more without Bird." In Greenwich Village, Kerouac had lunched with Malcolm Cowley and Viking Press editor Keith Jennison. Kerouac asked for a monthly stipend from Viking to support him while writing in Mexico and showed them the twenty-seven pages of *On the Road* that Cowley had requested. They were impressed with his writing, but they still turned him down flat. Kerouac also mentioned a work by Burroughs, now called, at Jack's suggestion, *Naked Lunch*. Cowley recognized Burroughs's name from Kerouac's "Beat Generation" manuscript but was unimpressed by the erratic, nonlinear nightmare of Burroughs's prose. What Cowley did praise was poet Greg-ory Corso's book, *The Vestal Lady on Brattle and Other Poems*. With little accomplished, the meeting ended. Discouraged, Kerouac drank away what little money he had and was broke once again.

Lucien Carr invited Kerouac to stay in his Greenwich Village apartment till his wife, Cessa, returned from Vermont. Carr, now working at United Press International full-time, was a responsible workingman whose days of discussing the New Vision were long behind him. Carr was opinionated and blunt. He declared that he thought Kerouac and Ginsberg were living a literary illusion and that neither could write for "shit." Instead, Carr praised the work of Paul Bowles, arousing Kerouac's envy. While Carr was working, Kerouac used Carr's old typewriter ("fuck this typewriter it's a awful typewriter") to compose letters. He began circulating his work once more. He called Robert Giroux concerning "Buddha Tells Us" and prepared "cityCityCITY" for the science fiction magazine market (apparently with Cowley's blessing). He sent a note to poet William Carlos Williams asking him to pen a recommendation to Random House (he declined). Not giving up on "Beat Generation" (*On the Road*), he had it submitted to Dodd Mead. But all of these efforts led to nothing. Carr's wife, Cessa, returned and Kerouac had no place to stay, so he returned to Rocky Mount. Hoping to escape from Caroline and Gabrielle's domestic order, he planned to buy a sleeping bag and return to Mexico.

On Independence Day, in sweltering North Carolina, Kerouac lacked money to buy even a beer to enjoy the festivities. To remedy his circumstances, he had Cowley working on getting a grant, had earned money helping his brother-in-law load televisions for a paltry 75 cents an hour, and had received $25 from his lawyer, Eugene Brooks, and the same amount from Ginsberg's crowd from the West Coast to entice Kerouac west. Not that Kerouac needed enticing; all he needed was the money and the opportunity. That Fourth of July he noted in his journal that he would soon leave "home" and, forgoing its comforts, eke out a "homeless" existence in the riverbeds of California or in a Mexican hut to fashion a Thoreauvian lifestyle.

Making a last-ditch effort to take care of business before leaving the States, Kerouac sent a copy of the *Doctor Sax* manuscript to Sterling Lord to replace his missing copy. Now heading his own agency, Lord was busy with other clients but still attended to Kerouac's affairs with unwavering devotion. "Buddha Tells Us" was submitted to the Philosophical Library in New York for its consideration. While the company agreed that the work warranted publication, they offered to publish only if he would guarantee the sale of 600 copies for $3.50 each. To Ginsberg, Kerouac wrote in September that he did not know "600 people with $3.50."[37]

In July 1955, Kerouac reappraised his circumstances and decided to retrieve all of his circulating manuscripts and, instead, submit "Buddha Tells Us" to publishers.[38] Despite these plans, he dug out and reworked the manuscript of "cityCityCITY," which he had written during the Army-McCarthy hearings. He saw it as relevant now, as America struggled in the vise of the Cold War, and felt the theme would most appeal to Burroughs. Kerouac sent him the story and proposed a visit to Tangier. With some good hash to smoke they could transform the story into a novel, much as they did with "And the Hippos Were Boiled in Their Tanks." Also, he wanted to continue to work on a manuscript he called "Visions of Bill," for which he had written preliminary notes. He felt Burroughs's character, his strange humor and intelligence, was intriguing enough to warrant a novel. If he felt connected to Burroughs artistically, it may be because Burroughs had adopted a variation of Kerouac's sketching method. Recently, Burroughs had mailed copies to Kerouac and Ginsberg of his routine "The Finger." In it, Kerouac saw the qualities that would help shape "cityCityCITY" into a novel. Burroughs would read the manuscript while trying to kick his heroin habit in Tangier (in 1956). His criticism was astute, as he had more of a grip on the genre than Kerouac: "One thing about City; you must concentrate on specific characters and situations involving them. No doubt you intend to do so, and what you sent me was introductory. I found so many of my own kicks, control through broadcasts of feeling, etc. I want to see the rest of it as you get done."[39]

Burroughs, preoccupied with his "Interzone" world (his name for Tangier), was living near Place Amrah in Tangier's Native Quarter. He was so close to Paul Bowles's residence, Burroughs told Kerouac, that he could nearly spit on Bowles's roof if he wanted to. (Jack had no interest in Bowles's work and noted in his Dharma journal that the writer was "defiling" young boys "in the land of Pali Scriptures.")[40] Burroughs was at full throttle now with his writing and wanted Ginsberg or Kerouac to help bring order to the chaos of pages rapidly piling up around his writing table. Like Kerouac, Burroughs was broke; at one point, he went thirty-six hours without food or heroin. In desperation he sold his typewriter. Until the money that Ginsberg owed him arrived, he dined on fried apple peels and fatty pieces of bacon. To pass the time, he sat in the Café Central eyeing Arab boys as they walked by, comparing the action to a lizard turning its head as it followed the course of an ant. However, the man whom the Mexicans nicknamed "El Hombre Invisible" was stalking his own peculiar prey within his Harvard-educated brain; his imagination was churning out routines involving "talking assholes" and the sinister Doctor Benway.

When not writing or meditating in Rocky Mount, Kerouac read, including Dostoyevsky's short story "The Ridiculous Man" and the theological writings of Boethius. In Dostoyevsky's story, he felt the Russian writer's flaw was that he was too emotionally attached—a surprising contention considering that Kerouac's forthcoming works would embody numerous displays of pathos.

Perhaps wanting to help her discouraged brother, Caroline expressed interest in acting as his agent. However, she wasn't happy with her brother's apparent idleness and lashed out at him in anger:

> My sister got mad at me and said I thought I was God, I said, What are ya jealous?—O what a dreadful household this is, I'm in. . . . leavin again. . . . everybody is resenting my cool Sihibhuto sittings in the morning, cool trances, they work hard to show how busy they are, they putter around, restless, proud, indignant, call me this and that, O if I were not greased cool by the wisdom of the Indes (which is French for Nothingness) I would be madder yet and have more reason to be madder than even in 1952 when I was mad at everybody even you.[41]

Kerouac resented the authority of his sister, mother, and women in general. To Ginsberg he went on a misogynistic rant: "As for a woman, what kind of man sells his soul for a gash? A fucking veritable GASH—a great slit between the legs lookin more like murder than anything else."[42] Already discouraged by Lord's slow responses, Kerouac was further dismayed when—after spending two dollars on a long-distance call to Lord's office to inquire about his eighty-one-page manuscript "Buddha Tells Us"— Lord questioned whether it was "any good." It wasn't just Lord; Kerouac felt that his communications were being cut off on all fronts. He was convinced that the Cassadys were "crazy." Unaware that Burroughs had been hospitalized for two weeks trying to kick heroin, Jack fretted that he had not heard from Burroughs about "cityCityCITY," after having spent a precious sixty-six cents in stamps. When Burroughs replied in June, he suggested that "cityCityCITY" needed to spotlight specific characters and that Jack should develop the situations that involved them. Burroughs did congratulate him on the publication of "Jazz of the Beat Generation." But Burroughs was too far away to help ward off Jack's constant bouts with loneliness. The only one who seemed available now was Ginsberg. Although he was in San Francisco, he wrote Jack more often than his other friends did. Anxious to promote his friend's writing, Ginsberg offered to show selections to William Carlos Williams.

Despite his feelings of abandonment, Kerouac was slowly gaining recognition. "Jazz of the Beat Generation" had been published in *New Directions* in April, and its appearance did not escape notice. Many readers contacted *New Directions* editor Arabelle Porter praising the conversational writing technique. Critic and jazz scholar Stanford Whitmore requested an explanation by the author of his writing technique, as Whitmore intuitively saw a similarity between it and bebop. Kerouac responded with his own personal creed, "Belief and Technique for Modern Prose," composed of twenty-seven principles. He condoned artistic expression for personal fulfillment without regard for reader or critic. By being a "crazy dumbsaint of the mind," one could explore the "holy contour" of life with neither shame nor fear. One could then compose "wild" and "undisciplined" prose. The writer was a "genius all the time" who created "Earthly Movies produced in Heaven."[43] But when Malcolm Cowley wrote Kerouac in June 1955, he did not express any interest in "cityCityCITY" and "Buddha Tells Us." Cowley viewed Jack's deviations into Buddhism and "automatic writing" as unnecessary and indulgent; instead, he valued Kerouac's natural storytelling. Cowley asked for a brief passage from *On the Road* to show George Plimpton, editor of the literary journal *Paris Review*. This gave Kerouac the impetus to return to New York City, a trip made possible by the $10 that his mother gave him.

Kerouac alerted Carolyn that he now planned to travel west by train. Traveling was never the problem; the difficulty was what to do upon reaching the destination. Even if he hopped a freight train, he knew that on arrival he would be a burden to somebody. He did not want the Cassady children to see him in the same impoverished state as when he last left them. Yet, it wasn't for lack of trying that he was not more widely published. In part he blamed the booming sales of television sets and the popularity of drive-in theaters, which had eroded book sales. Even Neal Cassady had "changed." Kerouac had not written to Neal in almost a year, and now he made another impassioned appeal:

I want you and I to be big buddies again, not that we're not big buddies anyhow; in thinking about Reincarnation and Cayceism I'm not too sure that maybe you arent my brother Gerard reborn, because he died in the summer of 1926 and you were born . . . when? in 1927. Sometimes I explain it to myself that way, what is almost the holy feeling I have for holy Neal, maybe he's my brother at that; it was you first said we were Blood brothers, remember?[44]

Cassady did not bother to answer. He was consumed by his own demons that sought to destroy him with insatiable appetites; writing to Carolyn on May 10, 1955, he confessed, "I am in full fear of my feeling that once a man starts down he never comes back—never." Things were no different for Jack; no amount of "egolessness" and "emptiness" would alter things now. The world was a "torrent of suffering" from which there was no escape—except to keep tunneling through it like a blind mole in the cold, dark earth.[45]

> Release yourself sweet escapee,
> Death owns bones;
> But infinite Emptiness
> Of pure perfect Mind
> who how much owns?
> All, all of it

PART 4

The Consolidation of Fame

21

The Sage of Rocky Mount

July–December 1955

For nonconformity the world whips you with displeasure.
RALPH WALDO EMERSON, "Self-Reliance"

An attack of phlebitis during Kerouac's Rocky Mount stay was staved off with penicillin (stolen by a friend in the medical profession). Confident he would receive a $200 stipend for which Cowley had recommended him to the National Academy of Arts and Letters, he left his family and headed southwest toward Texas.

It was a bad trip for Kerouac. He hitchhiked from Rocky Mount to Victoria, Texas. During the journey he hardly slept after he had passed through Gainesville, Georgia. He had intended to hitchhike straight to San Francisco to meet Ginsberg, who had helped finance the trip, but his phlebitis was bothering him and he needed treatment. He decided to dip down into Mexico City to seek some penicillin before traveling northwest. By July 29, he found himself in Monterrey, Mexico. There he declined a skid-row bed to save 48 cents and chose to wander the streets after sleeping on a park bench. He visited modern churches, ancient cathedrals, and market stalls and sauntered barefoot in a park eyeing the Mexican women.[1] In his dharma notebook he wrote:

> Mexico—no organized viciousness as in America,
> no organized pessimism as in France—Did sweet
> Jesus indirectly sweeten this former Aztec land?[2]

Kerouac arrived at last in Mexico City. He stayed first in Bill Garver's apartment and then in the adobe rooftop hut at 212 Orizaba Street. Unlike Garver, cleaned up now and off the junk, Kerouac took on the first day some substance that instantly made him sick. It wearied him tremendously so that he felt even more aimless and sadder than usual. Mexico was different now: Burroughs had left, his friend Dave Tercero had died, and the creative overdrive that had dominated his last stay was at first hard to conjure. He also suffered from dysentery.

Kerouac fell in love with Tercero's widow, prostitute and junkie Esperanza Villanueva (nicknamed "Saragossa" on the streets), whom he had met during a previous visit to Mexico. She reminded him of jazz singer Billie Holiday: "gorgeous ripples of pear shape her skin to her cheekbones, and long sad eyelids, and Virgin Mary resignation, and peachy coffee complexion and eyes of astonishing mystery with nothing-but-earth-depth expressionless half disdain and half mournful lamentation of pain."[3] Their sexual trysts were frequent despite his Buddhist vow of celibacy.

Inspired, Kerouac began an extended prose piece centered around Esperanza that he called *Tristessa*. Kerouac's portrait focused on his perception of her as a holy (but morphine-addicted) Madonna cast against the squalid backdrop of Mexico City's slum district:

> Her eyes are radiant and shining and her cheek is wet from the mist and her Indian hair is black and cool and slick hangin in 2 pigtails behind with the roll—sod hairdo behind (the correct Cathedral hairdo)—Her shoes she keeps looking at are brand new not scrawny, but she lets her nylons keep falling and keeps pulling on them and convulsively twisting her feet—You picture what a beautiful girl in New York, wearing a flowery wide skirt a la New Look with Dior flat bossomed pink cashmere sweater, and her lips and eyes do the same and do the rest. Here she is reduced to impoverished Indian Lady gloomclothes—You see the Indian ladies in the inscrutable dark of doorways, looking like clothes holes in the wall not women—their clothes—and you look again and see the brave, the noble *mujer*, the mother, the woman, the Virgin Mary of Mexico.—Tristessa has a huge ikon in a corner of her bedroom.[4]

The relationship was doomed to failure. Esperanza was too far gone in her drug addiction, and Kerouac felt awkward embracing her skeletal frame: "I feel we are two empty phantoms of light or like ghosts in old

haunted-house stories diaphanous and precious and white and not-there."
By the end of August, she was covered in cysts and paralyzed for a short
while.[5]

In another burst of creativity, Kerouac created 150 spontaneous choruses, with each confined to the length of the notebook page. The poem,
Mexico City Blues, along with essays and reading notes, ultimately filled six
notebooks. Writing to Ginsberg, Kerouac made tentative plans to arrive in
San Francisco between September 15 and October 1. By August 7, Kerouac was despondent:

> I have no eyes for anything but occasional drinking, got sick first day
> on shit—Feel aimless, ephemeral, inconceivably sad, don't know where
> I am going, or why—Wish I was in Frisco now but such a long trip—
> Will make it to Nogales on SP Railroad in Mexico for $10—accompa-
> nied as far as Chihuahua by Bill—dig-in about a month. Meanwhile I
> been sleeping on Bill's floor. Tomorrow I get rooftop adobe. All I want
> as far as life-plans are concerned from here on out, is compassionate
> contented solitude.[6]

If Kerouac had known that Viking had received another enthusiastic report on *On the Road* from one of its staff editors, Evelyn Levine, he perhaps would have been less despondent. Levine was entranced by the male
characters, the "search of their identity," and their attempt to find themselves by driving all over the United States. Unlike the "Lost Generation,"
Kerouac's heroes "stay right here—and try to find themselves." She was
troubled by the female characters, who, in her opinion, were unconvinc-
ingly drawn; "almost none of them are real." Regardless, her contention
was that the "novel must be and will be published eventually." Kerouac
was a "fresh, new (and fascinating) talent" who she felt was more honest
than Saul Bellow. He was a "jived up Walt Whitman." Though the manuscript needed a lot of work, she thought that it should still be published
"even if it's a literary and financial failure."[7]

After Carolyn Cassady kicked Ginsberg out (for another sexual dalliance
with Neal), Ginsberg shaved off his beard, trimmed his hair, donned a
tweed suit, and found a job at the market-research firm Towne-Oller for
$250 a week. As part of his new image, Ginsberg cast away what he per-

ceived as his outward appearance of homosexuality and moved in with a twenty-year-old woman, Sheila Williams Boucher, in her elegant apartment on Nob Hill. At the same time, Burroughs was courting him through letters, and Cassady was anxious to pursue further sexual relations. However, Ginsberg was not sexually attracted to Burroughs and rejected him via letter. However, Ginsberg's "confessional" impulse possessed him and he revealed his proclivities (his sexual relations with Cassady) to Boucher. Thereafter, she refused to share a bed with him.

Before long, Ginsberg rebounded with a relationship that would endure till the end of his life. One day, at painter Robert LaVigne's place, Ginsberg noticed a nude study of a young blonde man. Ginsberg inquired and LaVigne replied that the very same model was in the apartment right at that moment. The model was named Peter Orlovsky, an eccentric twenty-one-year-old local discharged from the army for being mentally unfit. He had told an army staff psychiatrist that "an army is an army against love." Orlovsky's mother was deaf and three of his four siblings had been in and out of mental wards. No stranger to mental illness himself, Allen became enthralled by the pathologically shy but (at times) brilliant Orlovsky.

Ginsberg's job at Towne-Oller was going well until he unwisely suggested that an IBM computer could be more cost-effective than hacks like Ginsberg and he was replaced. Laid off, Ginsberg was once again on the skids. He was eligible for thirty dollars a week in unemployment benefits, which, though representing a significant drop in income, gave him the opportunity to work on his poetry for six months and to continue his psychotherapy. Ginsberg perused the poems that he had labored over for months now. San Francisco poet and small-press publisher Lawrence Ferlinghetti had already rejected them for publication, and soon even Ginsberg could see why. One night, after drinking and bringing home a "boy," he woke from a vivid dream about Burroughs's slain wife Joan, in which she came to him and inquired about the "living fate" of her and Ginsberg's mutual friends. Of Kerouac, Ginsberg told her that

> Jack still jumps
> with the same beat genius as before,
> notebooks filled with Buddha.
> I hope he makes it, she laughed.[8]

When Ginsberg asked about the knowledge of the dead, she faded away till all he saw was a rain-wet tombstone in a Mexican garden. It was, in Ginsberg's words later in life, a "sympathetic encounter with her spirit." After writing the poem, Ginsberg sent it to Burroughs who responded that, jaded as he was, he had experienced a "distinct shock at the end." By virtue of Ginsberg's words, he could now see her smiling and talking again. Ginsberg also showed the poem to poet Kenneth Rexroth, who thought it too academic to break any new ground in a city seething with aspiring poets.[9]

One week later, Ginsberg sat in his furnished 1010 Montgomery Street pad in North Beach that he now shared with Orlovsky (who was visiting his family that month). Ginsberg slipped in a fresh sheet of paper and began typing—only this time Kerouac's aesthetics guided him. He typed, "I saw the best minds of my generation destroyed by madness." The poem was inspired, in part, by the incarceration of Carl Solomon, who had been fired from his uncle's publishing company and held in the same hospital as Ginsberg's mother. Allen found that this experimental method of writing suited him. It represented the "manifestation of the mind's moving in time and the attempt to change and revise and restructure and reorient was, in a sense, a lie."[10] He made a clean copy and sent the first six pages to Kerouac. At the top of the first page, he wrote in pink pencil "Howl for Carl Solomon."

By August 30, Kerouac had forwarded the pages to John Clellon Holmes (who did not return them to Ginsberg until 1980). Even though numerous emendations and crossed-out passages made it difficult to read, Holmes knew that the poem possessed an unmatched verbal power. Kerouac was also very pleased with the poem, but when he saw the crossed-out words, he advised Ginsberg not to revise passages to suit "time's reconsidering backstep." Ginsberg responded that his strategy was simply to let the words "blow." He told Kerouac that the first few pages were sent to him "as is." Ginsberg already had an offer of publication from Lawrence Ferlinghetti.

As pleased as Ginsberg was with "Howl," Kerouac was equally pleased with the postmodern poetic masterpiece that he had just completed in Mexico. Kerouac wrote excitedly to Sterling Lord about the new work, which used a form of "lingual spontaneity" more liberally than had any of his previous poems.

I hitch hiked through the awful South and Texas to get here, and am relaxing very high. In fact so high I wrote a big volume of poetry (150 poems) in past week MEXICO CITY BLUES which will do for poetry what my prose has done, eventually change it into a medium for Lingual Spontaneity . . . a kind of challenge Jazz session for letters— (about time). These poems are of no gainfully commercial significance right now, so I'll just hold them, (sending a copy to Cowley).[11]

Sterling Lord sold an excerpt from *On the Road,* "The Mexican Girl," to the *Paris Review* for $50. The selection was one of the more superbly written sections and certainly helped gain renown for Kerouac, for it contained some of his most memorable writing:

> I had bought my ticket and was waiting for the L.A. bus when all of a sudden I saw the cutest little Mexican girl in slacks come cutting across my sight. She was in one of the buses that had just pulled in with a big sigh of airbrakes and was discharging passengers for a rest stop. Her breasts stuck out straight; her little thighs looked delicious; her hair was long and lustrous black; and her eyes were great blue windows with timidities inside. I wished I was on her bus.[12]

Kerouac corresponded with several people about his latest cycle of poems, *Mexico City Blues.* It was to him a literary landmark. In an author's note placed before the poems when they were published in 1959, Kerouac specified his objective and technique:

> I want to be considered a jazz poet
> blowing a long blues in an afternoon jam
> session on Sunday. I take 242 choruses
> my ideas vary and sometimes roll from
> chorus to chorus from halfway through
> a chorus to halfway into the next.[13]

Kerouac described to Malcolm Cowley how his writing avoided "crafty" revision by maintaining a spontaneity that tapped into the "very sound of the mind." The quality that Cowley saw in Kerouac—the storytelling ability plainly evident in *On the Road*—took a backseat to raw experience and sensory expression. In Kerouac's view, what a writer eliminates through revision, what he tries to "hide" through excision, was precisely what modern literature desperately needed.[14]

Cowley wrote to tell Kerouac that *On the Road* had stalled at Viking. Kerouac had preserved the real names of his characters because he felt that the people portrayed in the book would not object. Viking was unwilling to take that chance. Until this legal roadblock was removed, Viking was postponing publication. In September 1955, Kerouac consented to change both the names and some locales to distance fact from fiction.

When Kerouac's marijuana use rendered the penicillin treatment worthless, he decided to suffer the phlebitis and move on. Before leaving, Kerouac converted the first installment of his stipend to traveler's checks and flushed his remaining pot down the toilet. Then he boarded a bus and headed northwest to Ginsberg's newest place, a cottage in Berkeley. The bus rolled along the highway past "dry cracked ravelled arroyos at the base of vein bleeding mountains of sand, rock, and rustle." The landscape was stark and pale as he scanned the "sad brown twilight of it all" and jotted his fresh impressions into his *Some of the Dharma* notebook.[15]

Jubilant at seeing his old friend again, Ginsberg wanted Kerouac to appear at a poetry reading that he was organizing at the Six Gallery in October. Kerouac was reluctant to take the stage because of his shyness and preferred that Ginsberg invite local poets, including Michael McClure, Philip Lamantia, Philip Whalen, and Gary Snyder. Kerouac's visit coincided with a revival of the San Francisco arts scene initiated some nine years earlier by Kenneth Rexroth, who would preside as master of ceremonies for the Six Gallery reading. The reading was held on October 13, 1955, in a refurbished former car repair shop on Fillmore Street that now served as an artists' workshop. Ginsberg had one hundred postcards made to advertise the event.

Kerouac crammed into Ferlinghetti's car along with Ginsberg and Peter Orlovsky for the ride to Six Gallery. On arriving, they saw that Ginsberg's publicity had been successful; it was a standing-room-only crowd. Cassady was there in his brakeman's uniform (having come straight from his shift). Kerouac overcame his shyness enough to solicit loose change from the crowd to buy jugs of California burgundy, which he circulated through the audience. The event culminated with Ginsberg's streetwise, free-form poetry. Kerouac beat on a wine jug in time to Ginsberg's reading and scat-sang between Allen's measured phrasings. Kerouac's genuine enthusiasm visibly annoyed Rexroth. Sometime after the reading, he invited Kerouac, Ginsberg, Snyder, and Whalen to his home for dinner and conversation. At the dinner, according to Rexroth, Kerouac became aware that most of the guests were not only knowledgeable about Buddhism but also knew at least one Eastern language.

At Rexroth's, alcohol soon liberated Kerouac from his better senses; he was so boisterous that Rexroth was afraid Jack would wake his children. Rexroth began to criticize *Doctor Sax* and called Kerouac "unmannerly." Kerouac called Rexroth a "*bouche*" ("dirty German").[16] Insulted, Rexroth ordered them all to leave.[17] Kerouac's social drinking was metamorphosing to alcoholism. He wrote to Cassady in April 1955, "As I write to you I'm drinking brown beer and regular beer mixed together in little wineglasses and every now and then I get up and refill because without beer, with hangover, my whole system shakes, I'm just the biggest drunk in town."[18]

In September, Kerouac began preliminary work on two new novels. The first, about his impressions of the Southern Pacific Railroad, he planned to title "Brakemen on the Railroad." The other novel concerned his first six years; he would title this effort *Visions of Gerard*. In Kerouac's estimate, by the late summer of 1955, he had completed seven volumes of the Duluoz legend. Kerouac felt that it justified his hardscrabble years and that his "entire life-work" was beginning to "shape-up" at last. He told Malcolm Cowley that September that the Duluoz legend was purely conceived and reflected an artistic integrity unmatched by any of his contemporaries in American literature. Eventually, he hoped to abandon his writing as "just so much sad, human, and arbitrary poppycock" and to retire in a hut by the sea to practice "tranquil meditation unto the grave."[19]

In October, Kerouac hiked into the mountains of the Sawtooth Range with his new acquaintances Gary Snyder and John Montgomery. Snyder was a Buddhist scholar who, like Jack, possessed an intuitive knowledge of much of the Buddhist canon. Montgomery was a librarian. The climb along the Sawtooth Range was both athletic and spiritually stimulating. The silence of Matterhorn Peak was far different from the rabble of North Beach. Kerouac was grateful for the time spent with Snyder and later wrote about this period in *The Dharma Bums* (1958).

Visions of Gerard can be traced in part to a dream: "One awful central scene, it's in the parlor brown and funeral and coffin-like, Gerard is dead in his coffin and all my writings are racked like candle flickers in a file box by the stuffed sofa in the suffocant gloom dark, literally writing in my brother's tomb—but it's the awful silence, the solemn ceremony of my papers. . . ."[20]

In Kerouac's journal, this dream includes an incestuous episode involving Caroline. Kerouac remembered that the dream contained no actual act of incest but the "understanding all night long that there had been incest and we should be punished soon." Kerouac, much like Ginsberg, borrowed actively from the detritus of his dreams and used them in his fiction. Combined with conversations with his mother, these dreams allowed Kerouac to transport the reader back to 1920s Lowell, a decade filled with personal tragedy and Roman Catholic mysticism. In December, on a train to a racetrack in San Jose, Kerouac translated some notes from their original French. He knew the novel's centerpiece would reveal Gerard to the reader as Kerouac saw him: "pure, tranquil and sad."[21] To execute this project, Kerouac relied on his prose method and a steady intake of tea, wine, and Benzedrine. Starting each writing session "fast," he would "blow" the words out alternately in spontaneous bursts and long, "slow" sentences. To facilitate these momentary flashes of insight and memory, Kerouac planned to incorporate "pops, tics, flashes" and "blues" within each chapter to create an experimental novel equal to *Doctor Sax* in scope and ambition. (As defined by Kerouac, a "pop" is an American haiku consisting of short three-line poems, a "tic" is a "vision sudden of memory," a "blues" is one complete poem a notebook page in length, and "flashes" are "short sleepdreams or drowse daydreams of an enlightened nature describable in a few words." None of these methods were actually used to write the novel.)[22] After making these preliminary notes, he put the book aside until he reached the East Coast that Christmas.

Cowley responded to Kerouac's September 1955 letter later that month and suggested that he discard "Beat Generation" and instead use *On the Road* as the title for his road novel. Kerouac agreed, knowing that he could use "Beat Generation" for another, related work. Later that fall, Cowley wrote again to Kerouac, concerned with the libel issues of *On the Road*. "We are still thinking very seriously about publishing *On the Road*. The difficulties are still the ones I mentioned in my last letter, and the principal difficulty is the danger of libel. For the last two weeks the manuscript has been in the hands of the Viking lawyer, who will mark the dangerous passages and submit a brief to us."[23]

It wasn't just a matter of changing names and places. What mattered to Viking's legal department was Kerouac's depiction of some of the characters' actions and the repercussions it could create for the company if Kerouac's portrayal sparked "shame or ridicule." The best resolution, Viking's attorney told Cowley, was to have Kerouac obtain signed waivers from Cassady and Ginsberg, who figured prominently. Cowley remained optimistic that the problems could be ironed out and they could soon sign a contract. On November 8, Cowley wrote Kerouac once again, repeating attorney Nathaniel Whitehorn's advice:

> You must remember that in a book of this type every character starts out with two fixed points of reference and identification. Each one of them is a friend of the author or has had some contact with him in the manner reflected in the book, and each of them is also a friend or acquaintance of Dean. In addition, each of them is a friend of one or more of the other characters. As a result, it takes but a little more definite reference to identify any particular character.[24]

Whitehorn had used as an example a mention of the Windsor Hotel, which he said "can serve as an example of the difficulty of disguising a person or place. I am sure the author had changed the name of the hotel. Nevertheless, it is easily identifiable by the fact that Lucius Beebe [poet and columnist for the *New York Herald* in the mid-1930s] visits it once a year. Probably everybody in the area is well aware of Beebe's visit to a hotel. The fact that another name is used would not be sufficient disguise." The lawyer was especially troubled by the Denver section because it touched upon the lives of many "respectable" people. Kerouac obtained waivers from Ginsberg and Cassady and mailed them to Cowley.

The three months in California were arguably the best time in Kerouac's adult life thus far. The wine flowed freely, he had friends and acquaintances with similar passions, and another book was on its way to bookshelves across America. For once Kerouac could enjoy the prospects of potential commercial success from *On the Road*. If the novel was successful, the rest of his unpublished work would at last see the light of day. Kerouac also imagined selling film rights for $150,000 with Marlon Brando as Dean Moriarty and Montgomery Clift as Sal Paradise. (Eventually, this daydream would come true, after a fashion. Film director Francis Ford Coppola would option the film rights for *On the Road* on April 1,

1978. On March 4, 1980, the famed director of *The Godfather* and *Apocalypse Now* purchased the film rights for $95,000.)[25]

Kerouac's freedom allowed him to hitchhike and hop freights between cities whenever the whim moved him. He resorted more often to the railroad, particularly since the average American tourist had become increasingly paranoid about picking up dusty hitchhikers. Once, Kerouac lucked out and caught a ride to San Francisco from a 1955 Mercury Montclair–driving, lithesome young blonde wearing a strapless white bathing suit:

> I am bloody well afraid to look at her, the curl of her milk armpits, the flesh of her cream legs, the cream, legs, curls, love, milk, wow, did I love that, not looking, but giggling, hearing she has been driving all the way from Fort Worth Texas without sleep I say "O how would you like some Mexican Benzedrine?" (which I have in big battered pack that I just been sleepin on beach in cold night of sea fog coast with, sad, talking to old sad Greeks at noon, the old Greek taking his annual vacation wanders up and down the sands looking at driftwood)—"Crazy!" she yells, I whip out my Benzedrine, yanking out all my dirty underwear and unspeakable Mexican raggedy junks and give her, she takes two, very much, we stop at a coke station and she mumps out jumping, the sweetest little perfect everything you know.[26]

She dropped Kerouac off and they made a date to see each other again. Although he didn't see her again, he wrote about the encounter in a short piece of fiction later published in *Playboy* (January 1965).

With the final monthly stipend of $50, Kerouac purchased a new poncho and a down-insulated sleeping bag that came in handy when he hiked the Yosemite mountains. When Kerouac visited the Cassadys, he slept in his sleeping bag in their yard for several days, before leaving for the East Coast. Toward the end of his California stay Kerouac spent some time with Neal drinking wine and going to the racetrack. As usual, Cassady was reeling from bad fortune. He had coerced his latest girlfriend, Natalie Jackson, into forging Carolyn's signature on $10,000 worth of savings bonds (purchased with compensation from the railroad after his accident). Soon after, Natalie killed herself by leaping off a roof. Jack was shaken by the news, having been the last to speak with her. He wrote in his dharma journal: "About this time Natalie Jackson committed suicide—I tried to tell her everything was empty, including her paranoic idea that the cops were after her & all of us—she said O YOU DON'T KNOW! then the next day she was found dazed on the roof and when a cop tried to catch her she jumped, off Neal's tenement roof."[27]

Distressed and visibly shaken, Cassady returned to his family to restore some semblance of normalcy to his life. He intoned some prayers to save Natalie's soul from limbo. During the day the Cassady children took turns reading back to Kerouac the poems that he had written. On Kerouac's last day with the Cassadys, Neal wanted Kerouac to accompany him to the track with $300 in cash Kerouac had somehow come across. Thinking better of it, Kerouac told Carolyn that he had better leave before he was again penniless.

Jack traveled to San Jose, where his earlier frugality allowed him the luxury of buying some raisins, peanuts, carrots, and canned food. The moisture of carrots, he learned, made the peanuts softer. Still, he found it all a "nutritious mess" and nibbled from it while trekking eastward. He went to the trainyard, cautious of the guards patrolling for the vagrants who, of late, were breaking the seal of boxcars, shattering the windows, and littering the cars with empty bottles. By six o'clock, after the sun had set, Kerouac was chilled to the bone. Still, he waited till 8:40 P.M., when he learned that the train wasn't going to show. He sat in a weedy bed by the rails, lit a small fire, and heated a can of macaroni. He conversed with some on-duty switchmen, who advised him to move to the other side of the yard to elude detection by the night watchman. Later that evening, Jack boarded a flatbed, unrolled his sleeping bag, and slept the length of his twelve-hour journey through the Diablo Range. When the train stopped in Watsonville, north of Salinas, Kerouac saw flashlights playing along the sides of the cars. With his bundle on his back, he jumped off and hid in a nearby lettuce field. When the Zephyr blew its whistle before departing, he ran under cover of the darkness and boarded once more. He continued this strategy till eight o'clock the next morning when he reached Los Angeles.

Kerouac disliked Los Angeles tremendously. Its smog burned his eyes and hurt his sinuses. Huddling by the side of a highway, he watched the Zephyr as it was readied for its journey to its ultimate destination, Arizona. This time Kerouac was almost injured: the train picked up steam faster than he estimated and nearly threw him off balance. When he was onboard, he noticed that, among the fourteen cars, there was no flatbed to sit on. He decided to jump back off before the train picked up speed. He landed in a ditch and there he stayed, resigned to the reality that he would not be going anywhere anytime soon. After another dinner of beans and macaroni, he unrolled his bag and slept fitfully among the jarring sounds of slamming train cars.

The next day, December 14, Kerouac went to a Los Angeles bus terminal to catch a local bus to Riverside. While waiting, he went to a coffee shop on South Main Street. His restless imagination took over, and he scribbled some prose and composed a poem shortly before he left, "Little Main Street Blues":

> Farewell South Main Street,
> I go now,
> Till another time,
> Sour sorrow smashes
> down sweet parting
> ere my prap's been
> crowded outa bins
> and banks of green
> clay water grass
> and erst I saw
> the elf on high
> —tsa pall of billshit
> —Cram!
> I'm out.[28]

Once the bus arrived in Riverside on December 15, Kerouac headed straight to a dried-out river bottom. There he lit a small fire, drank tea, and ate a supper of beans. Sleeping there for the night, he took out his notebook, recorded the date, and wrote another poem, "Little Pureland Blues":

> The Lord Buddha
> and I got a headcold
> sinus and try to stand
> on my head 5 minutes
> to lubricate it, nothin
> avails, the tight asses
> pretty California girls,
> everywhere makes

me hard and juicy
and I say "Wouldn you
lak to be layin
me stead a lookin
at me?"—[29]

A local man warned Kerouac of the danger of being arrested for vagrancy. Despite this warning Kerouac stayed until the next day, when he hitchhiked to Beaumont. Amid a group of high school kids, Kerouac ate a hot dog, hamburger, and fries and drank a strawberry shake. In Calexico, a watchman on patrol nearly arrested Kerouac for trying to urinate at a construction site. He searched out another river bottom to sleep for the night, but a local deaf-mute Mexican gestured to Kerouac that he would be robbed or murdered if he stayed there. Gesturing to the mountains south, the Mexican indicated that the they were safer. Later that day, Kerouac finally reached the border between California and Mexico and crossed into Mexicali. He walked around, digging the girls, and wrote in his dharma journal, "Thank you O Lord for returning me my zest for life, for thy ever recurring forms in Thy Womb of Exuberant Fertility!" Later, Kerouac went to a drugstore and bought sixty *codienattas* and fifty Benzedrine inhalers for $3.50. When he returned to the border, an American border patrol guard stopped him and searched his bag but narrowly missed the flap pocket in which he had stashed his wares.[30]

In El Centro, California, at the southern border of Imperial Valley, Kerouac tried to catch the Zipper out of town, but learned from a conductor that he would have to jump a freight train through Mexico. Instead, Kerouac took to the road and flagged down a truck driver named Charley Burchette, who promised to give Kerouac a ride all the way to Springfield, Ohio, if shown a good time in Mexicali that night. They parked the truck in Calexico, crossed the border, got drunk together on tequila, and consorted with some "sultry" Mexican whores. On December 20, four nights later, Charley dropped him off in Springfield. Kerouac boarded a bus to North Carolina for $12.[31]

The day before Christmas Eve, Kerouac arrived outside the Big Easonburg woods. He walked three frozen miles along Route 64 under the winter moon to Caroline's house. When he reached the yard, he stood in the dark watching his mother, "piteous-faced," wash dishes. He thought, "I'll never hurt you again."[32] The family had been expecting him, and he apologized to Gabrielle for his tardiness. Caroline prepared the couch for her brother, but instead he chose the back porch, where he could sleep in his sleeping bag and watch the frost shining in the moonlit backyard. After the family retired, Kerouac stepped outside, poncho over his clothes, and, accompanied by the family dog, Bob, went to his favorite meditation spot in the woods: "I sighed because I didn't have to think any more and felt my whole body sink into a blessedness surely to be believed."[33]

On Christmas Eve, Kerouac sat drinking from a bottle of wine while watching the Christmas mass televised live from New York's St. Patrick's Cathedral. Afterward, he read from his Bible and wrote "Drinking Pomes"—

> You blest me
> Sweet cat
> With yr arrival
> On my lap[34]

—and scribbled notations (now more Catholic than Buddhist) in his almost-completed dharma journal.

After the excitement of the Christmas holiday, the Blake household was quiet. Gabrielle left for New York to attend the funeral of her stepmother, Amanda Dube. Caroline and Paul returned to their jobs, and Jack went to the kitchen table to write. He removed his notebooks and journals from the rucksack, ingested some Mexican Benzedrine, and wrote in his dharma journal: "O Lord, reveal to me My Buddhawork and give me the great intense eager ecstatic excitement of the Holy Words, amen."[35] Two days after Christmas, at a candlelit table, with Benzedrine coursing through his bloodstream, he began to write, "Gerard Duluoz was born in 1917 a sickly little kid with a rheumatic heart and many other complications that made him ill for the most part of his life which ended in July 1926. . . ."

22

Passing Through

January–December 1956

What am I to do? Stay Awake
JACK KEROUAC, *Some of the Dharma*

The temptation, it would seem, was for Kerouac to record immediately his latest West Coast forays. There was a fresh influx of friends who were not only artists but also practicing Buddhists. There was the San Francisco renaissance, which he recognized as a legitimate literary movement in his posthumously published poetry collection *Scattered Poems* (1971):

> The new American poetry as typified by the SF Renaissance (which means Ginsberg, me, Rexroth, Ferlinghetti, McClure, Corso, Gary Snyder, Philip Lamantia, Philip Whalen, I guess) is a kind of new-old Zen Lunacy poetry, writing whatever comes into your head as it comes, poetry returned to its origin, in the bardic child, truly ORAL as Ferling said, instead of gray faced Academic quibbling.[1]

Kerouac had impressions, journal entries, and poems from the time spent wandering among San Luis Obispo, San Francisco, Los Angeles, and Mexicali on foot and by rail, bus, and truck. Rather than write a novel to document this period for the Duluoz legend, he gazed further back into his early childhood and began writing *Visions of Gerard*. His Catholic sensibility reasserted itself, sometimes overwhelming his Buddhist jottings. References from St. Paul's letters to the Corinthians resided side by side with quotes from Visuddhi-Magga. He spent the first days of 1956 "drunk with Shakespeare's power" after reading *Henry IV.* By January 7, he had written six thousand words of confessional and schoolyard scenes. A fresh reading of parts of *Finnegans Wake* contributed to his own novel's verbal experimentation, as his speed-whacked mind grew nauseated from the Benzedrine. On January 10, Kerouac finished the "Christmas Eve" chapter after spending a "Long Night of Suffering" during its composition. Twelve pages completed on January 12 went to waste when Kerouac crossed out all of the work. He decided to take a three-day break. The scene that he planned to write next was the most daunting of all: Gerard's funeral. On January 16, Kerouac wrote the novel's last line shortly after midnight. He considered it a "modest" closing: a gravedigger poised above the open grave with a shovelful of freshly turned soil. In his journal he jotted: "O rainy bleary face of graves! Wont they get sick of me for this one?"[2] In Kerouac's assessment, the novel was significant. He wrote to Gary Snyder, now in Japan, that it was his "best most serious sad & true book yet." After finishing the novel, Kerouac prayed to "St. Gerard" to "protect" him from getting drunk again.[3]

Despite his apprehension over the strength of his sobriety, he left for New York two days later to retrieve Gabrielle. Once there, he saw "The Mexican Girl" in the *Paris Review.* He stayed two weeks before returning to North Carolina with his mother in tow. Kerouac was miserable in New York. Jack's sister rebuked him for Gabrielle's having to work to support him instead of the reverse. When he claimed that he had given his mother $50 of his stipend, Gabrielle denied it. He was still coming down from the bennies, which left him depressed. The "sudden" wine that he drank copiously (apparently without St. Gerard intervening) sickened him further. He felt "old" and "futile" mixing with the Village poets he perceived as "enthusiastic fools of the future." Miserably, Kerouac saw Alene Lee kissing other men as he watched her through a tavern window from the sidewalk. Unwilling to return to his stepgrandmother's house, Kerouac chose instead a frozen bench.[4]

He took time to compose poetry. On January 28, he wrote ten choruses of poetry, "Brooklyn Bridge Blues." The second and third choruses included his disbelief that his mother had denied receiving his $50. Increasingly, Kerouac suspected his family of turning on him. Despite those feelings, he returned to Rocky Mount with his mother. He had to endure Caroline and Paul's rancor over his perceived idleness. Anxiously, he awaited word from Viking; good news could free him from his familial dependency. Kerouac was also eager to hear about a fire-lookout job on Mount Baker in Washington State, which he hoped to have secured by June. In early February he received a letter saying that he would be assigned to Mount Baker for three months.

Kerouac wrote principally to Snyder and Whalen during this time. He hardly communicated with Ginsberg, who was busy with his own career as he read "Howl" (among other numerous new works) to audiences throughout California. With Whalen, Kerouac shared passages from *Visions of Gerard*. He advised Whalen to read "real" writers like Balzac, Dostoyevsky, and Shakespeare. Writers unworthy of even the slightest glance included Gertrude Stein, Ernest Hemingway, Henry Miller, Thomas Hardy, and Goethe. Whalen also received letters demonstrating Kerouac's growing enmity toward Kenneth Rexroth. Jack was still bitter that Rexroth had criticized *Doctor Sax* and that he had created a less-than-favorable portrait of San Francisco for Jack. His bitterness and frustration finally boiled over in a letter in January 1956:

> Fuck you all! I'll shower and bombard you with prose works and verse works and shit works that'll inundate Frisco and make you all go mad you bunch of mad motherfuckin no good bastards and cocksuckers divine . . . I'll make you sorry you ever fetched lip and grabbed to crawl outa your mother's hole. You bunch of shits![5]

His paranoia peaked in mid-February when he still had not heard from Malcolm Cowley. Kerouac wrote to Sterling Lord, fearing that Viking would forget completely about *On the Road* after the verbal agreement to accept the manuscript. He asked Lord to send Viking the recently typed manuscripts of *Visions of Gerard* and *Tristessa*. Wanting to be closer to the action, he planned to return to New York in the late spring.

Kerouac's run-ins with Caroline and Paul Blake multiplied. The dog, Jack's only companion in Rocky Mount to whom he could relate, was not allowed to run free anymore. Kerouac asked, "How would you like to be tied to a chain and cry all day like the dog?"

"It doesn't bother me," Paul replied with indifference.

"I don't care," Nin added.

Kerouac wrote in his *Some of the Dharma* journal: "If you don't heed the cries of a dog on a chain, how do you expect God to heed your cries?" In passive protest Kerouac "banished" himself to Big Easonburg woods.[6] Indifferent to his brother-in-law's protest, Paul remained reluctant to offer his cot and porch to Jack. The Blakes were sick of the tight quarters in which they were living, causing their son to have to sleep in the same bed as his grandmother. The agreement, Gabrielle reminded her daughter, was that her investment in Paul's television business would "cover" her and Jack's room and board. Soon, Gabrielle tired of Caroline's attitude and decided to leave with Jack when the opportunity presented itself. Tentatively, Kerouac planned to move to San Francisco and rent an apartment for them both before leaving for his fire-lookout job in June. Months later, Kerouac would write about the "cold eyed sister / that made a bum outa me."[7]

Kerouac labored through March on *Some of the Dharma* and completed it on March 15. He also planned a sequel to *The Town and the City* that he titled "The Martin Family"; it was never completed. The next day, he wrote to Carolyn Cassady telling her that he was leaving to go west the following day. Kerouac also needed to work on the *On the Road* manuscript with Cowley, who was in Palo Alto teaching writing courses at Stanford University. Kerouac alerted Carolyn that Gabrielle would be writing her for help finding a job in San Francisco.

Kerouac left Rocky Mount alone after borrowing $50 from Gabrielle to reach the West Coast. When he arrived, to his dismay he found that Cowley had left after completing the winter semester. Disappointed, he did not bother writing to his mother, who was waiting anxiously for word to move west. With only himself to worry about, he moved that spring into a Mill Valley cabin owned by Gary Snyder, who was waiting to depart once more for Japan. According to poet Michael McClure, who visited Kerouac there, the cabin was basically a shack. It sat on a slope near the Mill Valley home of Snyder's friend Locke McCorkle. Situated forty minutes outside of San Francisco, Mill Valley was a relatively small rural community. Snyder's unfinished cabin sat within some evergreens and patches of pungent eucalyptus.

Kerouac wrote, at Snyder's prompting, a Buddhist sutra called *The Scripture of the Golden Eternity*. He also planned to write, with Bill Garver, a historical novel that would encompass the culture and history of the Mesoamerican Zapotec Indians. Kerouac was eager to assist researchers who had recently found artifacts on Monte Alban. William O'Dwyer, a former ambassador to Mexico and now an attorney in Mexico City, had requested the book. However, Kerouac needed a publisher, and Cowley failed to respond. Attempting to paint a portrait of his indigence, Kerouac told Cowley that his jeans were torn and that he was living in a shack. He still hadn't heard from Cowley about *On the Road, Tristessa,* and *Visions of Gerard* by the time May had arrived. When at last Cowley responded, he indicated that *Visions of Gerard* was promising if Kerouac would discard all of the Buddhist references incorporated into the manuscript.[8] Cowley also wrote to Bill Garver on May 15 expressing interest in the novel about the Zapotec Indians. However, he also wrote Kerouac discouraging him from focusing on such a book at that time.[9] As if to slight Cowley of his damning advice, Kerouac resorted to an even more radical foray in his writing.

On April 1, Kerouac began the first of five notebooks containing a startling work of literary experimentation, "Old Lucien Midnight," named after Lucien Carr (who rejected Kerouac's nod to their friendship, causing Kerouac to publish it as *Old Angel Midnight*). He wrote John Clellon Holmes on May 21 that he was "doodling" an "endless automatic writing piece which raves on and on" directionless, without any narrative. It was modeled, in part, on Carr's speech pattern. Kerouac labored on this writing as turkey vultures circled the valley and the scent of eucalyptus wafted through his open window.

> The Mill Valley trees, the pines with green mint look and there's a tangled eucalyptus hulk stick fallen thru the late sunlight tangle of those needles, hanging from it like a live wire connecting it to the ground— just below, the notches where little Fred sought to fell sad pine—not bleeding much—just a lot of crystal sap the ants are mining in, motionless like cows on the grass & so they must be aphyds [*sic*] percolatin up a steam to store provender in their bottomless bellies that for all I know are bigger than bellies of the Universe beyond.[10]

Though many of Kerouac's contemporaries saw little to no worth in his newest work, Michael McClure remained an admirer, having read and recognized the poetic worth of *Mexico City Blues.* He realized that "Kerouacian prose allowed people to be the spirit lives that they were. Kerouac was prepared to be an athletic and visionary bop prosodist by the spring of 1956."[11]

In May 1956, Gary Snyder left for Japan. Kerouac was left alone in the Mill Valley cabin. He invited local poets Robert Creeley and Bob Donlin to the shack. Four years younger than Kerouac and born in Massachusetts, Creeley was a Harvard graduate who taught at Black Mountain College. Kerouac described Creeley to Holmes as "lonely, sad, restless, one eye, tragic Spanish dark." Creeley and Kerouac went out drinking, sometimes at the Cellar in San Francisco, where Jack protected his friend during bar fights. Another time, Creeley got drunk at a fellow Black Mountain poet's house and was embroiled in two confrontations. Kerouac regretted these drinking sprees, not only for Creeley's sake, but also because they made him spend money. To help "purify" himself, Kerouac hiked the Sierra Mountain trails alone. But this was not without consequences. Without Snyder's eye for the terrain, Jack ended up getting lost twice. At the end of his hiking expeditions, Kerouac made camp and slept under the stars. Footsteps of bounding deer stirred his slumber: "I cooked my supper naked then lit a huge nice bonfire to drive away the mosquitos and slept that night under a moon that was like a streetlamp in my face and continually awakened by the hoofbeats of deer and in the morning a bull grabbed my shirt off a stick and playfully swung it around and rejoined his cows."[12] The next morning, he breakfasted on "black-eyed-peas-and-port stew."

Sporadically, Kerouac saw Ginsberg, with his lover, Peter Orlovsky. Kerouac noted Ginsberg's increasing tendency to strip nude onstage to dramatize the nakedness required by poetry. Jack became acquainted with a Berkeley girl who, by his description, looked like Marilyn Monroe. He took her to Ginsberg's home, where the shocking sight of a nude Orlovsky massaging a naked Ginsberg offended her. They left and Kerouac brought her to Mill Valley and nearly made it with her, until she learned that he didn't own a car; "I ain't seen her since."[13]

In mid-June 1956, Kerouac hitchhiked to Skagit Valley in northwest Washington, to begin his stint as a fire lookout on Desolation Ridge. Because of the exceptionally dry weather of that spring, recently hired fire-watchers who had just completed fire school were told to report to duty earlier than expected. Jack made passage up the rushing Skagit River, swollen from its spring thaw. At some point, on the river's banks, he composed haiku:

Satisfied, the pine
Bough washing
In the waters[14]

Dismayed, he realized he would be without alcohol, and he was afraid that he could not endure abstinence. His sleep was fitful; a dream of his father dying in his bed and his mother sent to an insane asylum marked one long night he spent staring into the dark. In his fire tower, he spent hours in a canvas chair facing the north, where Mount Hozomeen loomed before him in its natural splendor. At the table Kerouac wrote upon, he could stare south toward Jack Mountain: "Jack Mountain as always receives his meed of little cloud at highbrow base, his thousand football fields of snow all raveled and pin, that one unimaginable abominable snowman still squatted petrified on the ridge." In his notebook he sketched in pencil a monster snowman holding a bow and arrow. Taking in the whole panorama of the Hozomeen terrain, the landscape was stark and spooky.

Inside the lookout tower, Jack had a stove on which to cook his canned food. At night, lying awake in his sleeping bag, Jack could hear the sounds of mice in the cabin and of deer foraging within the perimeter of the campsite. He passed some of his time listening to the "big event in the loneliness" which commenced promptly at eight o'clock. It was radio chatter crackling between fire towers scattered throughout Mount Baker National Forest. When he wasn't playing his fantasy-baseball game or doing his job, Kerouac wrote by the light of his kerosene lamp. Kerouac's accumulated ten spiral notebooks (numbering roughly 615 pages) contained an array of different works he attempted to write simultaneously. Some of the material would later be included in the first half of his novel *Desolation Angels* (1965). Another never-completed novel was about his Ozone Park years of the mid-1940s.

By the end of July, fire watching bordered on drudgery. There were, thus far, no fires, as he dourly noted; "O I looked forward to come up here, why don't I eat my own dreary enthusiasms."[15] There was nothing to stare at anymore but the great mountain vistas, which humbled him to insignificance. To Kerouac, Mount Hozomeen appeared as a "Chinese mountain" spiked with pointed firs and burdened by huge gray boulders of basalt: "[M]y God look at Hozomeen, is he worried or tearful? Does he bend before storms or snarl when the sun shines or sigh in the late day drowse? Does he smile? Was he not born out of madbrained turmoils and upheavals of raining fire . . . ?"[16] By night the distant lights of the other lookouts sparkled from the engulfing darkness of the mountain valleys. At night, after standing on his head, a self-prescribed exercise to ward off phlebitis, Kerouac wrote "thousands of words." The next morning, after making his breakfast and washing up, he returned to fire watching. Staring at the same views began to weary him.[17]

While at Desolation Peak, he recalled and recorded football board games with his father during winter blizzards; warm June evenings on Pawtucketville's Phebe Avenue; the "marshmallow lips" and "silk thighs" of Mary Carney; and Jack's final surrender to eternity: "when I'm old by my final stove, and the bird fritters on his branch of dust in O Lowell . . . it might have been better than what it may be, lonesome unkissed Duluoz lips surling in a tomb."[18] Kerouac also completed a blues poem, "Desolation Blues," in which he declared, "I don't know / I don't care / and it makes no difference." Kerouac descended from the mountain in September. Checking into a hotel, he contacted Ginsberg and moved his belongings into Allen and Orlovsky's apartment.

While Kerouac scanned for fires in August, *Howl and Other Poems* was published as part of the City Lights Pocket Poets series. Ginsberg's poetry was interesting enough to provoke *Mademoiselle* magazine to shoot pictures of the "Flaming Cool Youth of San Francisco Poetry." In the photo, a tired and drawn Kerouac, with a silver crucifix dangling from his neck, stands unassumingly among the group of San Francisco poets.

Kerouac suggested to Sterling Lord that they submit excerpts from *The Subterraneans.* Creeley took two of Kerouac's pieces for the *Black Mountain Review.* Not waiting to cement publishing deals in America, after two weeks of drunken carousing in San Francisco, Kerouac hopped a freight train to Mexico City.

By the late fall of 1956, Kerouac was still anxiously waiting to hear from Cowley. Jack felt that he had given Viking enough time. He considered asking for the manuscript back and publishing it as a cheap pulp paperback. However, not only was *On the Road* under consideration, but Cowley's interests also extended to Kerouac's two Lowell novels, *Maggie Cassidy* and *Doctor Sax,* which he wanted to "weld" into one work. Such a union would have produced jarring results, and Kerouac refused despite Cowley's estimate that Jack would earn at least $40,000 should the merged novel be accepted for publication. Kerouac felt that he was now capable of standing firm: "I've been through every conceivable disgrace now and no rejection or acceptance by publishers can alter that awful final feeling of death-of life-which-is-death."[19]

As he was hiking through Arizona on the way to Mexico City, Kerouac was stopped by the police for vagrancy. What puzzled the authorities was that he had the fire-lookout money, which he had converted into five-dollar traveler's checks which would have paid for a decent motel room:

> I'm 34, regular looking, but in my jeans and eerie outfits people are scared to look at me because I really look like an escaped mental patient with enough physical strength and innate dog-sense to manage outside of an institution to feed myself and go from place to place in a world growing gradually narrower in its views about eccentricity every day—Walking thru towns in the middle of America I got stared at weirdly—I was bound to live my own way.[20]

Kerouac caught a bus out of Nogales, Arizona, to Mexico City, where he rented his now-familiar Orizaba rooftop hut overlooking the "drear, even sad, darkness" of the city. Almost immediately, he emptied his rucksack. lit a candle, and began writing a new book about his fire-lookout experience and San Francisco forays.

Kerouac wrote five hundred pages of what would ultimately become *Desolation Angels*. He also completed another blues poem, "Orizaba 210 Blues," consisting of seventy-one choruses derived in part from his attempt to re-create from memory a series of poems, "Fellaheen Blues," the manuscript of which had been stolen on his last trip to Mexico City. Kerouac even considered titling this new attempt "Pickpocket Blues." "Orizaba 210 Blues" drifts from wordplay to free-associative imagery and reveals more than ever Kerouac's intuitive command of language. Kerouac incorporated within the work eleven verses about Bill Garver, who lived beneath Kerouac's rooftop domain. Garver was still junk-sick, seemingly helpless, and dependent upon Jack to run errands for him. The verses appear to be a word-for-word record of Garver's account of his New York City exploits as a thief stealing to satisfy his drug dependency. By the forty-second chorus, Kerouac turns abruptly once more to wordplay. In the forty-eighth and fifty-first choruses, Kerouac switches to French. The sixty-ninth chorus is an invocation: "God, protect me! / See that I don't defecate / On the Holy See." The poem closes, "I'll be dyin / down in Innisfree /Waiting for ye / Mary Carney."[21]

One morning, after a late night of "scribbling poems and blues" by candlelight, Kerouac was awakened by Allen Ginsberg, Peter and Lafcadio Orlovsky, and Gregory Corso. Together, they walked through the Thieves Market and the Tenochtitlán pyramids. Although the history and mythology of Mexico impressed Ginsberg, Corso could not understand why anybody would want to be among a people so depressed by poverty and sickness. Corso moved to a hotel with a semblance of hygiene shortly before flying to Washington, D.C., to meet with the esteemed poet and Library of Congress poetry consultant Randall Jarrell.

Not long after Corso left, Kerouac, Ginsberg, and the Orlovskys answered an ad for passengers to share a car to New York. Shortly after they started their journey, the heady smell of pot curled within the confines of the car. After three days, they arrived in the November chill of a Manhattan morning. The driver deposited Kerouac on the sidewalk. Once again, he stood homeless, penniless, and frozen. Gaunt from his travels and the day-to-day struggle for survival, Kerouac suspected (wrongly) that he had contracted tuberculosis. Once again, he was bailed out by finding a new girlfriend, Helen Weaver. She was an English literature major from Oberlin College and had divorced her husband after three years of marriage. Not having any idea what she wanted to do and newly liberated, she moved to Greenwich Village and took a job at Farrar, Straus. She found an apartment on West Eleventh Street at the top of an ancient brownstone, where she did her dishes in a bathtub, wore sunglasses at night, and learned to speak the bohemian lingo popular in the mid-1950s. Her roommate, Helen Elliott, had first met Kerouac and Ginsberg when they were at Columbia and she was attending Barnard. One morning, as snow dusted the November sidewalks of the Village, Kerouac, Ginsberg, and Orlovsky appeared below their window. After they argued over the merits of Thomas Wolfe and Henry James, she fell for him. For the remainder of his time in New York, Kerouac stayed in her apartment. She was also enamored of Ginsberg, but in a different way:

> I fell in love with Allen, too, the way you fall in love with friends, I loved the way he and Jack talked very gentle, often quiet, but fast, with such a rush of energy, noticing everything, excited about

everything, so loving of each other and their friends: "You've got to come to Frisco and meet Neal! Wait till you see Gregory! You would really dig Burroughs!," etc. They had this tremendous childlike faith in each other as writers and in the power of words themselves, as if being writers meant they had a sacred mission to wake up America.[22]

To Weaver this type of "love and belief" between men was a new experience. She perceived that Ginsberg and Kerouac would make a name for themselves in literature and that their passion and conviction were heartfelt. "Looking back, I think maybe it was this mutual belief, this spiritual vitality they shared, rushing headlong into the vacuum of the utter faithlessness and joylessness of that time, that account for the ease with which they captured the public imagination and ultimately changed the spirit of their age."[23]

Kerouac also bonded with Helen Elliott's German shepherd, Treff, and played with the dog on the wooden floor. He took Treff for walks through the city, although he had trouble controlling the animal. Kerouac planned to return to his family—Gabrielle and the Blakes were now living in Orlando, Florida—for the holiday, promising to see Weaver again in January.[24]

Before leaving New York, Kerouac contacted Sterling Lord and Viking, which finally had accepted *On the Road,* contingent on his editorial changes. The release was scheduled for the fall of 1957. However, fearing further libel suits, Viking asked Kerouac to obtain more release forms. With renewed optimism, Kerouac completed Viking's requirements and then left Manhattan with four dollars earned from helping Herbert Huncke move a gas stove up six flights of stairs.

Shortly before Jack left, Ginsberg appeared at Weaver's door with Orlovsky. Together they took Kerouac to the Russian Tea Room to meet surrealist painter Salvador Dalí, who was courting celebrities and journalists. Dalí was now painting immense gauche oil panels commissioned by wealthy patrons. In a private room he greeted Ginsberg and Kerouac. Next to Dalí sat his wife, Gala, notorious for her riveting stare that cut down those who dared to approach Dalí without "vast quantities of cheques." Dalí rested his chin on his cane; his curled moustache sprouted from the thin face, jowled with age. He informed Ginsberg and Kerouac that an artist was only as good as the money that he earned. Present nearby was Marlon Brando, and Ginsberg told Dalí in Spanish that they wanted to meet the actor. Wriggling three ring-clad fingers toward Kerouac, Dalí exclaimed, "He is more beautiful than Brando."[25]

23

Before the Fall

January–September 1957

As the world cracks by
thundering
like a lost lumber truck
on a steep grade
in Kerouac America

LAWRENCE FERLINGHETTI, "The Canticle of Jack Kerouac"

En route to Orlando, Kerouac stopped in Washington to visit Gregory Corso, who was staying with poet Randall Jarrell. Corso arranged for Kerouac to sleep in Jarrell's basement while he crashed on the couch. Jarrell showed Kerouac sheaves of poetry, which Kerouac appreciated, praising him as a "great poet." Kerouac spent an afternoon writing a new blues poem, "Washington, D.C. Blues." Between Jarrell and Corso, Kerouac found himself defending his theory of spontaneous prose. Whereas Jarrell and Corso polished their poems in the spirit of craftsmanship, Kerouac reasoned that prose/poetry should read spontaneously: "If it's gibberish, it's gibberish. There's a certain amount of control going on like a man telling a story in a bar without interruptions or even one pause."[1] Kerouac showed Jarrell the manuscript of *The Subterraneans*, which Jarrell predicted would be "popular."[2]

The night that he left, Kerouac sketched the older of Jarrell's teenaged daughters and drank half a bottle of Jack Daniels before catching a bus.[3] After a cop confronted him on suspicion of vagrancy, Kerouac slunk away to the station and boarded the bus, with his return ticket in his backpack. When the bus reached Roanoke, Virginia, Kerouac, who had passed out, woke up and found his backpack missing—stolen, he thought, somewhere back in Richmond. When he reached Orlando, the first thing that he saw on his sister's porch was his rolltop desk, holding all of his unpublished work, and the couch on which he slept.

In December, Kerouac had written to Ginsberg, thanking him for all of his help and telling him he was preparing to go to Tangier at the invitation of Burroughs, who was now living there.

> Far from sending you the $6 I owe you, I've already asked Lord to lend me $40 for my return trip with the mss. because of Merry Xmas I had down here buying turkeys and whiskey for everybody and presents. Also, I don't know where those passports photos went, so I'll have to apply for my passport around Jan. 8 and so, three weeks from then will be Jan. 29 which oughta be just a hairline under our sailing date so I guess we'll make it.[4]

The day after Christmas, Kerouac considered Viking editor Keith Jennison's inquiry whether Jack had any special "demands" regarding *On the Road*'s publication. Kerouac wanted to retain the title *On the Road* (the publisher was vacillating). Kerouac felt that the title conveyed the "picaresque" tone of the novel. Besides, as Kerouac explained, *On the Road* was the "definite road of beatness." He skimmed through the typescript, at the request of Jennison and Cowley, "trimming it of unpraiseworthy libellous touches." On March 22, 1957, Viking issued an interoffice memo determining that Kerouac's book had been checked for libel and could be "released for printing." A manuscript acceptance report was passed out on April 4 with a summary of the novel for the sales representatives and marketing team:[5]

> This is a narrative of life among the wild bohemians of what Kerouac was the first to call "the beat generation." It carries us from New York to Denver, from Denver to San Francisco, then back to New York (with a detour through the Mexican settlements of the Central Valley)—then New York, New Orleans, San Francisco, Denver again, Chicago in seventeen hours in a borrowed Cadillac, Detroit, New York, Denver once more, and a Mexican town—the characters are always on wheels. They

buy cars and wreck them, steal cars and leave them standing in fields, undertake to drive cars from one city to another, sharing the gas; then for variety they go hitch-hiking or sometimes ride a bus. In cities they go on wild parties or sit in joints listening to hot trumpets. They seem a little like machines themselves, machines gone haywire, always wound to the last pitch, always nervously moving, drinking, making love, with hardly any emotions except a determination to say "Yes" to any new experience. The writing at its best is deeply felt, and extremely moving. Again at its best this book is a celebration of the American scene in the manner of a latter-day Wolfe or Sandburg. The story itself has a steady, fast, unflagging movement that carries the reader along with it, always into new towns and madder adventures, and with only one tender interlude, that of the Mexican girl. It is real, honest, fascinating, everything for kicks, the voice of a new age.[6]

Proudly, Kerouac signed the contract making him an author under the auspices of Viking.[7]

Kerouac spent the first weeks of 1957 typing the first half of *Desolation Angels* (the second would be written in 1961). Through Sterling Lord, he attempted to create a flurry of publishing activity, having him submit a seven-thousand-word excerpt from *Visions of Cody* (at that time titled "Vision of Neal") to Michael Grieg of Paperback Editions Limited in San Francisco. Thinking that printing an excerpt from it (at no cost to the publisher) would stir interest in the rest of the manuscript, Kerouac endeavored to get part or all of *Visions of Cody* published. He also prepared a typescript of *The Subterraneans* and additional material to be incorporated into the *Tristessa* manuscript. Charging a penny per word, Kerouac anticipated earning $500 from *The Subterraneans*. Kerouac advised his agent to inform Barney Rossett, Grove Press's publisher, of the worth of the manuscript; Donald Allen, Grove's editor, had recommended that Rossett buy the novel back in July 1956. Allen felt that Kerouac's writing captured effectively the "moods, emotions, and stance of the hipster life." Jack planned to see Allen in early January and to bring a suitcase filled with work. Trusting Allen, Kerouac intended to leave with him not only *Desolation Angels* and *Visions of Cody* but also the newly typed manuscripts for *Book of Blues, Some of the Dharma,* and *Book of Dreams*. Kerouac stressed that he most wanted to see *Some of the Dharma* and *Visions of Cody* published.

In the first week of January, Kerouac boarded a Greyhound bus to New York. Arriving January 8, he dropped off his belongings at Helen Weaver's apartment and went straight to Viking with the manuscript for *On the Road* under his arm. He hoped to meet Cowley and present him with the final version of his opus. In the elevator he unscrewed the cap on a pint of bourbon and downed it minutes before entering Cowley's office. When Kerouac left, he joined Ginsberg, Corso, and Orlovsky to celebrate in the Village. By January 11, Kerouac had finalized and signed his contract with Viking. During those weeks, in the early morning hours, a jubilant Kerouac returned often to Weaver's apartment unmindful of her need to sleep after eight hours of work. She soon learned that his disregard was a constant characteristic. In her apartment he would play records at high volume, listening to music as diverse as Chet Baker and Bach's *St. Matthew's Passion.*

Though he remained friendly with Ginsberg, he began to feel that the poet was latching on to him parisitically. Kerouac explained to Edie Parker (Dietz): "Allen never loses track of me even when I try to hide. He does me many favors publicizing my name. Well, we're old friends anyway. But I cant keep up the hectic 'fame' life he wants and so I wont stay with them long in Tangiers, I'm going to get me a quiet hut by the sea on the Spanish coast, then join them in Paris in the Spring."[8] Although Edie had remarried, Kerouac expressed his love for her, telling her that he dreamed of her often. He was anxious to explain the Buddhist teachings he had studied over the past few years:

Hearing your voice at night over the phone, in a hotel where I'd gone to hide out to work, was like a strange & beautiful dream. You sounded warmer and more mature. You will always be a great woman. I have a lot of things to teach you now, in case we ever meet, concerning the message that was transmitted to me under a pine tree in North Carolina on a cold winter moonlit night. It said that Nothing Ever Happened, so don't worry. It's all like a dream. Everything is ecstasy, inside. We just don't know it because of our thinking-minds. But in our true blissful essence of mind is known that everything is alright forever and forever and forever. Close your eyes let your hands and nerve-ends drop, stop breathing for 3 seconds, listen to the silence inside the illusion of the world, and you will remember the lesson you forgot, which was taught in immense milky ways of cloudy innumerable worlds long ago and not even at all. It is all one vast awakened thing. I call it the golden eternity. It is perfect. We were never really born, we will never really die. It has nothing to do with the imaginary idea of a personal self, other selves, many selves everywhere, or one universal self. Self is only an idea, a mortal idea. That which passes through everything is one thing. It's a dream already ended. There's nothing to be afraid of and nothing to be glad about. I know this from staring at mountains months on end. They never show any expression, they are like empty space. Do you think the emptiness of space will ever crumble away? Mountains will crumble, but the emptiness of space, which is the one universal essence of mind, the one vast awakenerhood, empty and awake, will never crumble away because it was never born.

He signed the letter, "Your eternall old man, Jack."[9]

As Jack attempted to renew ties with Edie, his romantic bond with Helen began to unravel. She soon found out that Jack could be romantic as well as inconsiderate and moody. The same man who would fly into a rage over the ineffectiveness of her Olivetti typewriter could also entertain her with erotic drawings. One such gift was a self-portrait, created in Mexico. Attached to the drawing was a note: "Dear Helen / I love you and / I want you to know that / I love you."[10] The other, a portrait that a Mexican peasant drew of Kerouac, revealed a man who, despite the rigors of the road and the excessive drugs and alcohol, still appeared to be youthful and handsome. She came to know "the dark underside of all this enthusiasm." She found him "erratic" and "unpredictable." Soon, she feared for her own mental health and sought advice from a psychoanalyst. He advised her to break up with Kerouac, who had been living with her only two weeks. "The abyss in his eyes was familiar, but that didn't make me want to climb back into it with him. . . . I watched at a safe distance as, unable to live up to the heroic legend he had created for himself in his books, he continued his spiral descent into illness and death."[11]

Although Helen continued to see Kerouac on and off after 1957, she did so only as a friend and, on a few occasions, a last-minute lover. He moved from her apartment in the Village to an Eighth Street hotel. There, through Ginbserg's arrangement as matchmaker, Kerouac brought another woman into his life.

Ginsberg had known Joyce Glassman since she was sixteen years old and felt comfortable enough to consider pairing her with Kerouac. She had heard of Kerouac when she was a secretary at the MCA literary agency (the staff there remembered his unmarketable manuscripts and unmannered behavior). The author's photo on a copy of *The Town and the City*, pilfered from MCA's book shelf, appeared to her to contradict MCA's description of him; he looked brooding, handsome, necktied, and authorial. However, in *Mademoiselle* magazine, she saw a photo of the Kerouac whom the staff at MCA knew: dark featured, with unruly hair, wearing an open-necked lumberjack shirt, a crucifix dangling from his neck. Joyce would soon come to know both sides of Jack.

At a friend's apartment, she received a call from Ginsberg, who said there was someone who wanted to speak with her. From a phone booth near his hotel, Kerouac spoke to her for the first time. He asked her to come right then to a Howard Johnson's restaurant in the Village. She agreed. Among Howard Johnson's drab clientele, Kerouac stood out with his blue eyes, jet-black hair, and red-and-black flannel shirt. They talked for a while. Joyce bought him dinner, and then he asked meekly if he could go home with her. "If you wish," Joyce replied. She had a ground-floor apartment in a brownstone on 113th Street. That night and for several nights thereafter they were together. Kerouac often left her bed and slept in another room in his sleeping bag with the window open. (He told her that cold air helped his phlebitis.) Joyce remembered Kerouac's silent, sullen moods, "so deep you'd be afraid to break into them." He was edgy and deeply preoccupied with his internal world of Duluoz. An aspiring novelist in her own right, she found that Kerouac treated her as his equal, though their writing styles were worlds apart.[12]

Kerouac visited friends around the city; exhausting bar crawls through the Village would ultimately end in Glassman's apartment. After one such night, Kerouac and Glassman took the subway uptown. Before entering the Ninety-sixth Street station the train stopped abruptly; someone had leapt onto the tracks and killed himself. Sensing the doom of the situation, Kerouac was overcome. It was time to leave New York; he wished that he were back on Desolation Peak amid the mind-numbing wilderness.[13] On February 15, Joyce Glassman, along with Lucien Carr and his wife, saw Kerouac off as he set sail for Tangier aboard the Yugoslavian freighter, SS *Slovenija*.

Burroughs, now a Eukadol-dependent writer in exile in Tangier, Morocco, was writing his next novel. He had incorporated into his letters to Ginsberg the numerous "routines" he had written over the past few years. The routines, Swiftean dashes of social satire, revealed a "hideous new force loose in the world like a creeping sickness." Burroughs realized the work's power but knew that he needed what he termed "routine receivers": "Whenever I encounter the impasse of unrequited affection my only recourse is in routines. (Really meant for the loved one, to be sure, but in a pinch somebody else can be pressed into service.)" In April, Burroughs wrote to Kerouac that he was working on a new novel and enclosed some routines for his friend's perusal. One routine derived in part from Kerouac's dreams involved "overcrowded cities of the future" and "purple-assed baboons."[14]

Burroughs's new locale helped him focus on his writing after battling to overcome his drug dependency. With assistance from Kiki, an adolescent Arab boy, Burroughs made a valiant effort to kick his drug habit. Kiki locked Burroughs into his room and listened to the agonized groans of withdrawal. When that failed, Burroughs sought medical assistance. The doctors raised and lowered his morphine levels and even experimented with sleep therapy, none of which was successful. He tried other hospitals until Dr. John Dent prescribed an apomorphine treatment. In theory, it would regulate the physiology of the cell through metabolic manipulation. In four-hour intervals Burroughs received apomorphine injections, thereby reducing his morphine dependency from thirty grains to zero. The process was not easy: nightmarish insomnia gripped him for four days; his gaunt frame was wracked with cramps and bouts of vomiting. The treatment, however, appeared to work, and Burroughs seemed free of the narcotic grip that had clutched him. Trying earnestly to resume a routine and productive lifestyle, he rented a single room, equipped with a typewriter and an orgone box, at the Villa Muniria. He ate simply—balls of *majoun* and Moroccan tea. In this state of stability and good health, perhaps his healthiest in years, he typed. Burroughs systematically dropped each page to the floor after typing it till the chaos of manuscript pages needed objective eyes to approach his work. He created different titles for it: "Word Hoard," "Interzone," "Grand Tour (Hell Is Where Your Ass Is)," "Meet Me in Sargasso," and "On the Road to Sargasso." It wasn't until Kerouac arrived in March 1957 that, at Jack's suggestion, the title was changed to *Naked Lunch*.

Part of the trip east to Africa was rough for the crew of the SS *Slovenija*. Ensconced in his bunk (he and his crew members tied themselves securely in with straps), Kerouac read Kierkegaard's treatment of Abraham's near sacrifice of his son Isaac in the Old Testament. Of late, Kerouac's preoccupation with religion had shifted from Buddhism to Catholicism. His belief in God came to the fore and he exclaimed at one point, "Everything is God, nothing ever happened except God—and I believed and still do."[15] When the seas grew calm for a ten-day stretch, Kerouac walked the frigid decks for fresh air. He slept when he could and, when awake, continued reading books on world history. He was the healthiest he had been in years. Kerouac grew restless and was eager to reach port. By the end of February, he could see the yellow-and-green coastline of Africa.

Tangier was an internationalized city turned over to Morocco in 1956 after a long, bloody struggle for independence from France. The city was also an illicit crossroads for cocaine and hashish trafficking. For this reason alone did it draw Burroughs as expatriate. Upon Kerouac's arrival, Burroughs took him to the city's many sidewalk cafés where they smoked marijuana in the open terraces. Kerouac noted the mysterious veiled women walking through the Medina and wished that he had money to patronize one. He rented a $20-a-month room furnished with a patio facing the sea. In the local quarter, he dined for as little as 35 cents. Burroughs took him rowing in the sea. At night, Kerouac drank Malaga wine and brewed his own coffee. But Tangier's squalid living conditions also sickened him. When he wasn't writing, he read voraciously: the New Testament, Genet, and Van Wyck Brook's study of the American renaissance, *The Times of Melville and Whitman* (1947). He also corresponded with Don Allen, Malcolm Cowley, and Sterling Lord.

In December 1956 Don Allen had received a libel release from Alene Lee, the love interest in *The Subterraneans*. She had consented to her thinly veiled portrait and signed the waiver on the condition that changes to the manuscript would be made to distance her from her fictional counterpart, Mardou Fox. Kerouac turned the typescript over to Don Allen. No doubt with good intentions to increase sales, Allen heavily edited *The Subterraneans*. Perhaps assuming that Kerouc's numerous dashes and run-on sentences were unintentional, Allen thought no harm was done. However, Kerouac thought differently when he read photostats of the emendations; he said they violated the "impulses of my own heart" and "riddled" the manuscript with editorial "buckshot." Sentences separated by em dashes had been punctuated by commas and periods. Kerouac had already accommodated Allen by removing some overt sexual references, but he refused to change the writing style to make it more palatable for the general public. Because of Allen's "Big Castrating Scissor" the "swing, the heartbroke sound, the blues style, the rush of lowdown confession" had all but disappeared from the text.

From the Hotel Mouniria, Kerouac wrote to Sterling Lord asking him to retrieve from Don Allen *Some of the Dharma*, a 250-page typescript of *Book of Blues, Tristessa,* and *Visions of Cody*. Again Jack stressed that his prose, a "series of rhythmic expostulations of speech," used an unorthodox grammatical structure to sustain a "spontaneous word-flow." Kerouac compared himself to Hemingway, who, if he had succumbed to editorial pressures and publishing trends, would never have developed his "Hemingway Style." (Kerouac's determination not to alter any of his work would be less problematic for Lord after *On the Road* was published.) There were also financial issues; money was owed from *New Directions* and from editor Martha Foley, who had chosen "The Mexican Girl" for inclusion in *The Best American Short Stories of 1956*.[16]

The advance for *On the Road* was now available. Kerouac made provisions with Lord to divide it between Jack and his mother, with the first payment to go to Kerouac and the second to Gabrielle. However, his payment would not appear till sometime in April. Until then, he typed Burroughs's manuscript in exchange for meals.

Cowley stayed in contact with Kerouac but did not have a very high opinion of the other projects under consideration. *Desolation Angels*, Cowley thought, was uninteresting because of its "formlessness"; he urged Kerouac to develop its plot and characters. Cowley viewed the references to Buddhism as problematic because they cluttered the prose with words unfamiliar to average readers. He again suggested that Jack merge *Doctor Sax* and *Maggie Cassidy* to create one manuscript. However, all of Cowley's suggestions met with Kerouac's characteristic resistance.

Kerouac took Cowley's rejection of *Desolation Angels* detachedly and adamantly defended his writing style to James Laughlin of *New Directions*. Kerouac argued that his novels were written in "poetry sheeted in Narrative steel." He also insisted that his writing was as earnest and impulsive as a jazz saxophonist's solo. He told Laughlin that the novel form was "dead," that his work was akin to the outlaw writings of Genet, Céline, and Burroughs. Kerouac was seeking a publisher who catered to the writer, not the marketplace: "I will no more have my prose cut up than would Paul Bowles or Hemingway or any other conscientious artist." Laughlin did not respond.

After several weeks with Burroughs, Kerouac tired of Moroccan living. The publication of *On the Road* neared as Kerouac retyped the nightmarish manuscript pages retrieved from the floor of Burroughs's room. *Naked Lunch* was "so horrible that when I undertook to start typing it neatly doublespace for his publishers the following week I had horrible nightmares in my roof room—like of pulling endless bolognas from my mouth, from my very entrails, feet of it, pulling and pulling out all the horror of what Bull [Burroughs] saw, and wrote." Burroughs explained that he was "shitting out my educated Middlewest for once and for all. It's a matter of catharsis where I say the most horrible dirty slimy awful niggardliest posture possible—By the time I finish this book I'll be as pure as an angel, my dear."[17]

Kerouac began to miss his clean-sheeted bed, his morning bowl of Wheaties, and his mother's doting. World travel was starting to weary him. He suffered a "listless dispiritedness" from some arsenic-tainted hashish that he smoked. He sweated through hours of diarrhea and cramps from drinking local water. Kerouac planned to leave Morocco shortly after Ginsberg and Orlovsky arrived in Tangier to assist in the construction of Burroughs's novel. They worked dutifully on the manuscript, sometimes for as much as six hours a day, and were rewarded by Burroughs's cooking a feast for them. Afterwards, they would relax over cognac and Moroccan weed. The trio (sans Burroughs) visited local taverns and watched stoned men slide checkers across a board while smoking pot through long pipes. Arab whores tempted Kerouac by offering their services for three dollars, and he wished he had the money to accept. The gay scene of Tangier did not impress Kerouac in the way that it impressed Burroughs, who made ample use of boy prostitutes. Lonely for female companionship, Kerouac wrote Joyce in March:

Look forward to seeing you, lonely here, don't like whores anyway and no girls speak English . . . mostly fags abound in this sinister international hive of queens . . . have had everything in my books, smoked opium, ate hasheesh, don't want any of it, just musing in my room, lights out, face sea, moon, liquid lights of anchored ships in bay, good enuf . . . the blink of lonely headland lighthouse . . . Grove Press really pulled a fast one on me and cut the novel subterraneans by 60 per cent of all things and ruined swing of prose so I wrote and called it off . . . I will not stand any more of this castration of my careful large work by liverish pale fag editors.[18]

By April 5, Kerouac had prepared to leave Africa. Having developed a fixation on his genealogy, he decided to go to Europe to initiate what would become a lifelong obsession. The night before he left, there was a get-together at Burroughs's place. There, in the haze of marijuana smoke, Jack spent his last hours in Tangier with friends and hangers-on.[19] Already, with *On the Road* linotyped for press, he was tired of the scene that would later be distorted from his beatific philosophy into the "beatnik" phenomenon of the late 1950s. It was all mere posturing, an unsettling "sociological coolness," a desire to join the scene without contributing anything directly to it, intellectual or otherwise.[20] As Kerouac left, Burroughs held his hand and said, "Take care of yourself, Jack." Ginsberg and Orlovsky accompanied Kerouac to the dock and watched his ship sail for Europe where, within one week, Jack would pick up 68 pounds advanced to him by Andre Deutsch for the U.K. edition of *On the Road.*[21]

In 1957 American readers were captivated by Ian Fleming's *From Russia with Love,* Ayn Rand's *Atlas Shrugged,* William Faulkner's *The Town,* and Vladimir Nabokov's *Pnin.* With cultural icons Elvis Presley and James Dean hot in the American media, rock-and-roll music pouring out of jukeboxes, and television a burgeoning commodity, the time was ripe for Kerouac's breakthrough. Intuitively, Cowley knew that Kerouac's book, though not the greatest he had ever read, was as effective as those by Hemingway or Fitzgerald and would affect American culture.

Kerouac kept on writing. On the trip from Africa to London, he drafted an outline for a new novel, seeming to heed Cowley's advice to forge a work more palatable to the readers whom Viking wished to reach.

In a letter written before he left Tangier, he told Gary Snyder that the novel (now called *The Dharma Bums*) would center around the events of his life in the fall of 1955.[22]

In Europe, Kerouac was detained at the border; his vagabondish appearance made him suspect to authorities. It wasn't till he showed the officials his copy of the *Nation* that they recognized him. In Paris, he stayed with Seymour Wyse for a short time before Wyse sent Kerouac on his way. Still, Kerouac kept his appointment with Andre Deutsch and researched his surname at the Bibliothèque Nationale. In that institution Kerouac found his family crest, which bore the legend "*Aimer, Travailler et Souffrir*" ("Love, Work and Suffer"). This, he told Snyder, was incidentally the theme of *The Town and the City.* Kerouac needed a place to stay for several days in the city. Besides Wyse, he had no other connections in Paris who would offer him shelter. Even Jimmy Breslin refused to let Kerouac spend a night on his floor. Giving up his habitual frugality, he found a hotel room for one night. To make matters worse, he met Gregory Corso, who encouraged him to spend his money, so that most of it was expended his first night there. Corso found him gloomy. Kerouac felt that his depression was exacerbated by Corso seeing right through him, that he was indeed "gloomy and bugged." With no other recourse, Kerouac took to the streets. He attended Catholic masses and admired the architecture of the city's cathedrals. Not all of Paris, however, was pleasing to him.[23] He saw more of the poseurs who of late populated the Village cafés and the San Remo. Cool, lounging, smoking, and high, they were, in Kerouac's view, the worst part of bohemian culture. Before going to London, Kerouac explored France for five days. He took a bus through van Gogh's Arles, where he noted the yellow tulips in windowboxes and the wind-tossed cypresses. He hitchhiked twenty miles through the French countryside, finding the effort more difficult than it was in America. He covered twenty miles and explored the beautiful countryside he knew so well from the paintings of Cézanne. In Paris he walked the corridors of the Louvre. In London he sat in St. Paul's Cathedral absorbing the haunting intonations of *St. Matthew's Passion.*[24]

Before returning to the United States, Kerouac wrote to Sterling Lord suggesting a title change for *On the Road.* He thought it would be a marketing advantage for the title to reflect American youth's rising interest in rock-and-roll. Songs like Elvis Presley's "Jailhouse Rock" and Chuck Berry's "School Day" were expressing the energy of America's youth. "It occurred to me," he wrote to Lord, "maybe it would double the sales to change the title to Rock and Roll Road or at least to invent a similar subtitle."[25] Kerouac, it seemed, was not above capitalizing on American culture.

On April 20, Kerouac left Europe on the SS *New Amsterdam,* a $190 trip that he considered "one big drag." He prowled the decks, waiters glaring at his lumberjack shirt and blue jeans. At the end of April he was in New York at last and back in Joyce Glassman's apartment. In Kerouac's absence, Glassman had found a job as an editorial assistant at Farrar, Straus and Cudahy. There she became acquainted not only with Kerouac's old editor Robert Giroux but also with his old flame Helen Weaver. Glassman found her likable enough and befriended her (although she suspected that Weaver and Kerouac still had feelings for each other). Glassman had made the rounds of Manhattan's social scene, catching jazz acts at the Five Spot and Café Bohemia and drinking in the Cedar Tavern. Encouraged by Kerouac, she delved into Buddhism and found that its teachings gave her new insights into Jack's personality. She saw him as both a "believer" and a "seeker." Understandably, his belief in himself fueled her own ambition and she labored away, sometimes during working hours, on her novel.

What Joyce did not realize at the time was that Kerouac intended to stay in New York only until he could go to Florida to collect his mother and move west. Kerouac invited Joyce to join them, provided that she find her own place, and she made tentative plans to follow him.[26] Once he reached New York, Kerouac could expect another advance check to be waiting for him at Lord's office. With these funds he could afford another move to California—this time bringing his mother along and allowing her to quit her job. He wrote Neal:

> Unluckily am low in funds and just look mostly . . . Well neal, I have a proposition now to make to you. My mother and I wanta move lock stock & bullshit to California once for all and when I mentioned my plan to give you a week's railroad wages plus gas & oil plus expenses ($400) to come get us in Florida, you remove seats from Nash Rambler and we come back with me, you, my Ma and the TV set, clothes, my boxes of Manuscripts, a box of books, clothes, a box of dishes, no more, we zoom back to coast, all done in one fast week . . . would you like to do that?[27]

Cassady never replied.

Kerouac had reason to make himself scarce: Joan Haverty, "that bitch" (as he called her to Ginsberg and Burroughs), was looking for him again. He wrote to Ginsberg:

> . . . and I was feeling so good because no lushing and happy thoughts of concentrating on Duluoz Legend, damn her, she's like a snake snapping at my heels. . . . She got some doctor to prove that she couldn't work and support her child, because of TB. . . . She made sneaky calls to Sterling who dug her right away without my telling him and kept mum. . . . So what I'll do Allen, when I get their roundabout letters, is answer them, mail the letter to you to mail from Casablanca, as tho I was there.

All this scheming was for nothing. Haverty only wanted Kerouac to sign papers so that she could obtain a divorce and remarry.[28]

Kerouac left Manhattan for Orlando, filled with dread. He disliked the swampy humidity, relentless heat, and bloodsucking insects. His sister and her husband resented being burdened by Jack's visits. He didn't stay long this time, leaving Florida on May 6 with Gabrielle in tow. In their luggage they stowed Coca-Cola bottles and bourbon to toast America from a Greyhound bus window.[29] Two weeks later, they arrived in California. Kerouac found a small place for them in Berkeley. Philip Whalen was there to greet them, and Gabrielle took to him right away. With nothing else to do (neither his trunk of manuscripts nor his typewriter had arrived), Kerouac drank with his mother. On the first night in their cottage, they got drunk, and the next morning he awakened to the sounds of his mother groaning with a hangover. It occurred to Kerouac that they were already "cursed." Gabrielle's French Canadian superstitions began working overtime, and she soon predicted earthquakes. Every bit as impulsive as her son, she turned to him one day and announced that California was "sinister" and that she wanted to spend her Social Security checks in Florida. Besides, Jack wasn't exactly good company when preoccupied with reading and writing—or drinking. She missed her daughter and grandson and the security that her son's precarious lifestyle couldn't provide. Kerouac wrote to Sterling Lord near the end of June requesting that Viking combine its payments for July and August, so that he could send Gabrielle back east.[30]

Kerouac was not enjoying Berkeley that much either. He said the city fostered a "killjoy culture" that dampened his zeal. He wanted "ecstasy of the mind all the time," he told Snyder.[31] He was incensed particularly at being fined for jaywalking; he and Whalen were also stopped when they were drunk and singing in the streets. Even walking to work with shovel over shoulder (Kerouac helped John Montgomery with some labor for pay), he was hassled by the authorities. It was one of many complaints that Kerouac wrote to Joyce Glassman to ward off her impending visit. She detected Kerouac's unusual bitterness toward the elderly at that time (which may be because of his mother). He even felt alienated from Neal and Carolyn Cassady: "I saw Neal here, who is become mindless, borrowed $10 from me, made no explanation for not coming to get me, disappeared, and now his wife writes a vituperative letter saying I'm a bad influence on her poor innocent hubby . . . so you see it's sinister everywhere."[32]

The stifling atmosphere did not prevent Kerouac from working on "Lucien Midnight," "A Dharma Bum in Europe," and *Book of Dreams*. He said that "Lucien Midnight" had become "verily the writing of what I hear in Heaven." Moroccan speed aided its composition. The work, begun in the spring of 1956, came to a close as he shut the last notebook and added it to his projects in the hope that it would be published someday. He also removed fifteen notebooks of prose sketches, the "Book of Sketches," from the trunk once it arrived in Berkeley and began typing them into the form of a prose poem so that readers could "discriminate between written verse and written-prose."

Unbelievable levels of flawless blue bay water like in upper Chinese heavens shifting and moving in irradiant tumbling tides, with beyond that, the lil Cleopatra needle of Berkeley Tower like a distant view of a lighthouse—the perfect little No Clouds popped up there in the deepning afternoon blue like cold dogs horizoning in shame as ship bawls and traffic bothers me and boom the big wave from the big ship is Ignorating in. (*writ on Embarcadero*)[33]

He planned to rewrite *Vanity of Duluoz* in order to fill the gaps in his Duluoz legend. The first 1942 draft was now stylistically dated. Rewriting the novel was necessary to complete the "Lowell picture": his job as a sports reporter, his frequent run-ins with Lou Little, and his germinating artistry would compose the bulk of the novel. What remained unwritten was the portion about the 1940s, culminating in his father's death and the composition and subsequent publication of *The Town and the City*. No doubt

On the Road's imminent publication contributed to Kerouac's optimism. His creativity was greater than it had been in months. He wrote to Malcolm Cowley asking why he had not seen the final galleys of *On the Road,* closing with a quote from Mark 13:11: "Take no thought beforehand what ye shall speak, neither do ye premeditate: but whatsoever shall be given you in that hour, that speak ye: for it is not ye that speak, but the Holy Ghost."[34]

When Cowley responded, he ignored Kerouac's inquiry into the final galleys' whereabouts and advised him that, though the Holy Ghost might speak through Jack, he should also know how, as an artist, to employ the conscious and unconscious minds and to cut what needed cutting. This was advice aimed at the composition of the new work Kerouac mentioned in his letter:

> I'm thinking about writing the second half of DESOLATION AN-
> GELS and can all the sentiment and give those "angels" the works, the
> subsequent shoddy events all the way to Paris. . . . when it's all to-
> gether and we've removed some of the surplus chronological heaviness
> (which even I don't like) it will be another "Road" picaresque. This
> item will take care of 1956-1957 in the Duluoz Legend.[35]

Sterling Lord informed Kerouac that the review copies of *On the Road* were printed and ready for shipping. Jack had some reviewers in mind for advance copies: poets William Carlos Williams and Carl Sandburg. Viking publicist Patricia MacManus was, at this point, his sole contact with the company. He was not receiving steady correspondence from Keith Jennison or Malcolm Cowley, which distressed him. In the first week of July, Kerouac's advance copies of *On the Road* arrived. When the mailman delivered the box to the Berkeley cottage, Neal Cassady, Luanne Henderson, and Al Hinkle were present. After opening the box, Kerouac handed Cassady the first copy, since Neal was the "hero" of the novel. In the center of the shiny black dustjacket was an impressive red-and-blue abstract of a cityscape. What Kerouac held in his hands not only irrevocably changed his life but also, in due course, would alter American culture. He revealed in a letter addressed to Allen Ginsberg, Peter Orlovsky, and Alan Ansen that Luanne wanted to "fuck" him the next night after seeing his book. However, he declined that offer, because he had to get ready to leave Berkeley.

Before leaving, Kerouac gave his first interview concerning his second novel to the *San Francisco Examiner.* Preparing to go west to be with Jack, Joyce Glassman was stunned when she received a letter from him saying that he had changed his mind about staying there. Kerouac instead encouraged her to go to Europe, saying that California had fallen into the hands of a "Total Police Authority." If she insisted on coming to California, he wrote, she could leave from there to join him in Mexico. He ended the letter to her opaquely with "Do what you want."[36] Fortunately, Joyce still had her job if she wanted it, even though she had given notice, but she had also given up her apartment and had to rent a hotel room until she could find a place of her own. After much thought, Joyce realized that she could have her "own adventure with or without Jack." She had received news from Hiram Haydn that Random House had accepted her novel and offered her a contract and a $1,000 advance. Now that she had the money and the movitation, she only had to shake her indecision. But Kerouac mailed a postcard immediately after the letter, shortly before leaving California: "Dear Joyce, Disregard last letter, I think I exaggerated conditions here in gloomy mood. . . . Go ahead as planned, I'll be with you all the way . . . all the way to Mexico, eventually I have an idea . . . and you must write a novel about Mexico too!"[37] Following her intuition, she decided to go to San Francisco, if not for Jack, then for a female friend who was in need of her company. She worried, however, that he would change his mind once again. She remembered years later: "There was a certain bravado in this new plan, but when I got some good news about my novel at the end of the following week and a more optimistic sounding postcard from Jack, all my confidence returned."[38]

In mid-July, Kerouac stepped off the bus into the humid heat of Orlando. He found a place for his mother for $45 per month, only to realize that virtually all of the money from the last two-thirds of his advance (except $33) was now spent. The small home had a large yard with a grove of orange, grapefruit, and tangerine trees. Having settled his mother, he prepared to leave for Mexico City, where he planned to stay for six weeks. He intended to rent a "solitary room" and write by candlelight the further material that Cowley suggested for *Doctor Sax.* However, before leaving, Kerouac needed to take care of business with Viking. He sent a letter to Malcolm Cowley asking him to send more money.

> Now, Malcolm, I'm depending on you—in order to recreate the conditions under which Doctor Sax was written, that is, by candlelight in a solitary dobe hut in cool summer Mexico City, I am going there to-

morrow and will arrive just about the time you read this (Tuesday) with only $33 in my pocket, and will start right in on those extra childhood scenes for Doctor Sax, as well as an article "explaining the beat generation" for Patricia MacManus [his Viking publicist] for Harper's or Sat. Review.[39]

He wrote MacManus, for she conveyed enthusiasm for his work and eagerly promoted the novel by placing it in the hands of prospective readers and critics to garner it some attention. She suggested that Kerouac write an article defining the "beat generation," which he was willing to do once he reached Mexico City.[40]

Although now broke from "resettling" his mother, he left for Mexico regardless of his indigence. Relieved to escape the "heatwave horror" of Memère's "paradise," he boarded the bus with his knapsack (which he filled with raisin bread, meat, and cheese) over his back. Cowley replied that he could send Jack some money to his agent's office. His funds secured and his immediate future certain, Kerouac planned to complete *Doctor Sax* by a proposed deadline of October 1, 1957.

Upon arrival in Mexico City, Kerouac discovered that his old acquaintance, Bill Garver, was dead and that the locals did not know where Esperanza Villanueva was. He rented a room at the Hotel Luis Moya, a converted whorehouse with mirrored walls and marble floors. Kerouac went to work handwriting the article for Viking, which he titled "Explaining the Beat Generation." He derived part of his definition of "beat" from Oswald Spengler's *Decline of the West* and his term "Second Religiousness," which Spengler defined as falling between the balance of "primitive" culture and as starting with "Rationalism's fading out in helplessness, then the forms of the Springtime become visible, and finally the whole world of the primitive religion, which had receded before the grand forms of the early faith, returns to the foreground, powerful, in the guise of the popular syncretism that is to be found in every Culture at this phase."[41] Thus Spengler asserts that the Second Religiousness "appears in all Civilizations as soon as they have fully formed themselves as such and are beginning to pass, slowly and imperceptibly, into the non-historical state in which time-periods cease anything."[42] The relevance of this passage for Kerouac's definition of "beat" is particularly important. In keeping with Spengler, Kerouac wrote, "Strange talk we'd heard among the early hipsters of 'the end of the world' at the 'second coming,' of 'stoned-out visions' and even visitations, all believing, all inspired and fervent and free of Bourgeois-Bohemian Materialism."[43]

Thus, Spengler's Second Religiousness, according to Kerouac's philosophy of beat, was being fulfilled. Evidence could be found in the photos of American youth with their "slouchy look," "cool and beat." Kerouac asserts in the essay that "beat," with its Spenglerian associations, had disappeared after 1950 when the actual subjects of On the Road "vanished into jails and madhouse, or were shamed into silent conformity; the generation itself was short-lived and small in number." It was Spengler's "first, genuine, young religiousness" that On the Road's beat characters strove to secure.[44] Although Kerouac determined that the term "beat" was no longer relevant, it wouldn't be long before America redefined and distorted its meaning. If Kerouac's characters were no longer beat, the media would reinvent the term in a way that in time would stigmatize his life and art.

On July 26, at 3 A.M., an earthquake rocked Mexico City, killing thousands. Kerouac awoke suddenly in his bed in the hotel. Above him, the ceiling creaked violently, and the shaking floorboards tossed the bed. It was, Kerouac told Ginsberg, one "horror after another as usual in Doom Mexico."[45] Jack simply went back to sleep recognizing that "all this living & dying & wrath" originated from the "Diamond Silence of Paradise." He wrote to Joyce, inviting her to his "earthquake-proof room" and assuring her that her cash advance would go a lot further in Mexico than in the United States. He added that, though he originally wanted to be alone, he realized after the earthquake that "no one can be alone, even one's own body is not 'alone,' it is a vast aggregate of smaller living units, it is a phantom universe in itself." Drug-free and sober, he could only "stare healthily at the interesting world."[46] He tried to kill some time visiting the city's churches, going to the movies, and eating steaks and drinking Cokes, not trusting Mexico's water. Nonetheless, he contracted Asiatic flu and had to leave.

By mid-August, he was back in Florida. He was suffering immensely from the lingering illness made worse by his not drinking any water in Mexico to keep himself hydrated. He was barely able to walk, his testicles swelled, and he ran a high fever. When he arrived at his mother's Clouster Street residence, she wasn't home. Without a key and unable to walk, he curled up on the grass and slept till Gabrielle appeared.[47]

He managed to write Joyce, who was preparing to meet him in Mexico, to stay put and work on her writing. He promised to meet her in New York when Viking advanced him more money. Joyce found another apartment, on West Sixty-eighth Street, and sent Kerouac the $30 needed to bring him to her this time. With *On the Road* only weeks away from official publication, it was vital that Jack come to the city. He cashed the check at his sister's bank and bought a Greyhound bus ticket.

In mid-August, Kerouac wrote to Philip Whalen looking for some photos of himself that he could bring to Viking's publicity department. Kerouac mailed the first of the new insertions for *Doctor Sax* to Malcolm Cowley, those being the first of several new chapters derived from his mother's memories of Lowell. He was also concerned about the essay that he had written in Mexico City: "it's the only statement I ever made about the Beat Generation, and that is the only statement about it ever made by the originator of the idea (3 or 4 people have already written about it) and that tho my article may seem deceptively light-headed it really is the score."[48] From Orlando, Kerouac asked Joyce to inquire to Patricia Mac-Manus about the essay's status. His primary concern was the "impostors" who would distort the sacred symbology of the phrase in order to distract prospective readers from *beat*'s more "profound basis."[49]

Kerouac arrived in Manhattan on September 2, rang the doorbell of Joyce Glassman's brownstone, and went with her to find the midnight edition of the *New York Times*. Anxiously, they flipped through the pages in Columbus Avenue's Donnelly Bar to find the first review of dozens that would follow. His luck was good for a change: Charles Poore, the original intended reviewer of the book, was a book critic with a conservative bent. He was replaced for that day's issue by Gilbert Millstein. Millstein's assessment of the novel, combined with the influence that the *Times* wielded, would launch Kerouac into fame as a cultural icon and one of the twentieth century's most significant writers. Millstein started the lengthy review with, "'On the Road' is the second novel by Jack Kerouac, and its publication is a historic occasion in so far as the exposure of an authentic work of art is of any great moment in an age in which the attention is fragmented and the sensibilities are blunted by the superlatives of fashion (multiplied by a millionfold by the speed and pound of communication)."[50] Millstein predicted that some critics would misunderstand *On the Road*, that its theme and narrative would be "condescended to" and dealt with "superficially": "But the fact is that 'On the Road' is the most beautifully executed, the clearest, and the most important utterance yet made by the generation Kerouac himself named years ago as 'beat,' and whose princi-

24

Everything Exploded

September 1957–April 1958

And I am an unhappy stranger . . .

JACK KEROUAC, "Mexican Loneliness"

The day after publication, Kerouac had a dream: "I had a white bandage on my head from a wound, the police are after me around the dark stairs of wood near the Victory Theatre in Lowell, I sneak away—come to the boulevard where a parade of children chanting my name hide me from the searching police as I duck along their endless ranks keeping low."[1] The next morning, the phone began ringing in Joyce's apartment and did not stop. The obscurity that Kerouac by turn loved and loathed had vanished. He began drinking.

Millstein threw a party for Kerouac. John Clellon Holmes attended (Millstein had read Holmes's article, "This Is the Beat Generation," and reviewed his novel, *Go*). Millstein, who had never met Kerouac, hoped that Holmes could entice him to come to the party. Kerouac phoned Holmes at Millstein's party: "I can't come down," he said, "I'm hung over." Although he claimed to be suffering from delirium tremens, it was really the endless requests for interviews that exhausted him. He asked Holmes to leave the party and visit him at his apartment. Holmes took Millstein aside and explained that Kerouac would not be coming. It was ironic, Holmes felt, that this "new, young Marlon Brando of literature" could not attend the party held in his honor because he was holed up in his bedroom frightened by all the sudden attention. "This so discombobulated him that for the rest of his life he never, never got his needle back on true north."[2]

Those requests for interviews and appearances often bypassed Lord's office and reached Kerouac directly. He could never refuse, even when it was in his best interest to do so. At first in earnest, he sought to explain (or sometimes justify) the philosophy and wisdom of being beat. His good intentions often came to nothing when reporters would write what they wanted.

Not all of the reviews were positive. Herbert Gold, writing for the *Nation,* compared Kerouac to a "perennial perverse bar mitzvah boy." Phoebe Lou Adams's review in the *Village Voice,* though finding his writing style "distinctive" and "readable," criticized the novel for its "severe simplicity." Adams felt the novel disappointed: "It constantly promises a revelation or a conclusion of real importance and general applicability, and cannot deliver any such conclusion because Dean is more convincing as an eccentric than as a representative of any segment of humanity."[3] Kerouac never promised any such thing, but Adams, like many critics, failed to see that Dean Moriarty and Sal Paradise's quest was to pursue the whims of their spirit along America's highways hoping to discover "something." The novel wasn't about closure but about the open road in all its grandeur and grief.

On the Road's rapid success did give Kerouac money to spare, so he was able to repay Ginsberg for his passage to Tangier. The rest of Jack's funds went to Gabrielle. There were other sources of income as well: an advance for an Italian translation of *On the Road,* Grove Press's purchase of *The Subterraneans,* Esquire's $400 purchase of a baseball story, $300 for an article for *Pageant,* and payment for a foreword to Robert Frank's collection of photos. In addition, Hollywood was showing growing interest in purchasing the film rights to *On the Road.* A Village hipster named Leo Garen even offered to produce a play about Neal Cassady if Kerouac would write it; he declined.

Through mid-September, publicity-related appearances on talk shows and magazine interviews abounded. On John Wingate's television show, *Nightbeat,* a terse and uncommunicative Kerouac declared that he was waiting for "God to show His face." After the show, he and Wingate went out on the town for drinks. In Goody's Bar on Tenth Street, Jack was dressed in a "battered royal-blue polo shirt, his white T-shirt showing beneath," with a pack of cigarettes poking out of the rumpled shirt pocket. He periodically drank from a bottle of Schlitz. He told *Village Voice* writer Jerry Tallmer, "I can't make it. I'm cutting out." Tallmer asked Kerouac whether he was scared during his interview on *Nightbeat.* "Yeah man, plenty scared," Kerouac replied. "One of my friends told me don't say anything, nothing that'll get you in trouble. So I just kept saying no, like a kid dragged in by a cop. That's the way I thought of it—a kid dragged before the cops."[4] Kerouac preferred to shun the spotlight and have the attention focused only on his book. Often, before he sat down to be interviewed, he drank. Alcohol, it seemed, made it easier for him to play the extrovert. The fear even seeped into his dreams:

> My ass naked sitting on a stool in the field full of people I'm reading some book and the Jack Paar show is going on in the field but I don't care—Suddenly he comes up with mike and camera and pins me down to have me televised universally naked, I hang there like a helpless child till I hear Julien's faint voice in back trees saying (twangily St. Louis) "Don't let him do it!" so after a helpless moment I up and throw him a feeble punch.[5]

Most interviewers seemed to be hostile. To emphasize the earnestness of his writing, at a Viking publicity event Kerouac rolled out the original scroll across the carpet before "thousands of screaming interviewers."[6] Maurice Dolbier of the *New York Herald Tribune* appeared just as Kerouac was rolling it up again. "It took a long time," Dolbier recalled. When it was Dolbier's turn to conduct his interview, Kerouac explained once again his definition of "beat." It was Spengler's Second Religiousness "prophesied for the west":

> And when one's mind began to boggle at the vision of Presley's sideburns and Jean-Paul Sartre and bop-talk and rock-'n'-roll and Brando on a motorcycle as units in a religious revival, you are reminded of the posthumous revival of James Dean and the trance-visions induced by drugs and young wonder. Mr. Kerouac hammers out the case with anonymous instances of strange manifestations, foreshadowings of the end of the world and the Second Coming, hipsters who have seen angels and devils, and reports quite casually that he too has heard the heavenly music while speeding along a California highway.[7]

When Mike Wallace asked, "What is the Beat Generation?" Kerouac quipped that it was just an "old phrase" that he "knocked off one day and they made a big fuss about it." Throughout the interview he assured Wallace that the beat generation was simply a mystical revival, invoking

Spengler, celebrated against a jazz soundtrack, a dose of dope-fueled mysticism, and the vast empty space of the American West:

MW: What is the basis of your mysticism?

JK: What I believe is that nothing is happening.

MW: What do you mean?

JK: Well, you're not sitting here. That's what you think. Actually, we are great empty space. I could walk right through you . . . you know what I mean, we're made of atoms, electrons. We're actually empty. We're an empty vision . . . in one mind.[8]

When Wallace told him that he didn't sound "happy," Kerouac replied that he was "tremendously sad." "It's a great burden to be alive. A heavy burden, a great big heavy burden. I wish I were safe in Heaven, dead," Kerouac said.[9]

Such self-pity elicited less empathy than ridicule. The only ones who took any pity on him at all, it seems, were two nuns, who offered up a mass to be celebrated by the priests of St. Francis of Assisi. Kerouac, touched, responded to them via letter, "Reverend Mothers, Pray for all living creatures."[10]

Many wrongly assumed that Kerouac was Dean Moriarty. Men wanted to fight him, and women wanted to go to bed with him. But Kerouac didn't rise to the bait. Perhaps as penance for once having smashed a violin over the head of a gay violinist in his days at Columbia—an incident that haunted him—Kerouac absorbed the blows. The women who came on to him were deflected by Joyce, who resorted to physical displays of affection to establish her territory. At congratulatory parties, people shook his hand, passed him a bottle of Old Granddad, got him high on goofballs and weed, and watched Kerouac unravel.

His health started declining as a result of his accelerated drug use, alcoholism, and disrupted eating habits. To friends he complained of his "nervous breakdowns."[11] As always, his solace from the turmoil of the outside world lay in his writing and reading. From the pages of Dostoevsky's *The Idiot,* Kerouac fixed his current identity with Prince Myshkin (as Ginsberg had done when he was committed for psychiatric evaluation in 1949). Joyce tried to maintain a semblance of stability by ironing his clothes and cooking him dinners. Her support brought him solace among the throng of users and hangers-on. However, Jack and Joyce's relationship had changed. Alcohol killed their lovemaking, while constant intrusions diminished their quiet time together. Finally, Kerouac's preference for brunettes over blondes brought him back into Helen Weaver's life—much to Joyce's chagrin. At a party Kerouac saw Weaver dressed beautifully in a "lost generation" red flapper dress and wanted to approach her. Sensitive to Joyce's feelings, he forbore, but he wrote to Weaver when he returned to Florida in October 1957. He admitted that she hurt him when she took her psychoanalyst's advice to leave him and told her she should have gone to a Catholic confessional instead of paying such "fakes." Weaver responded by sending him a box of cigars.[12]

Kerouac participated in jazz/poetry readings with composer David Amram, with whom he felt comfortable under most any circumstances. Kerouac first met Amram at one of the many parties around the Village. Gifted with a musician's ear, Kerouac read to Amram's improvisatory playing. Amram also saw Kerouac at the Five Spot and sensed the writer's brooding presence: "Even though he often sat alone, like a wayward meditative Canadian lumberjack in his plaid red-checkered work shirt, he always exuded a special energy. He was that one special person Mingus alluded to, the one we always knew we could play for."[13] Accompanied by poets Howard Hart and Philip Lamantia, Amram and Kerouac performed at the Brata Art Gallery on East Tenth Street. Typewritten and mimeographed handbills appeared all over the Village advertising the performance, resulting in a standing-room-only crowd.[14]

Joyce tried to salvage her relationship with Kerouac. To escape the frantic New York City scene, she and Kerouac traveled upstate to visit Lucien and Cessa Carr. Shortly after arriving there, Kerouac became drunk. When the family doctor made a house call to give the Carr children seasonal flu shots, Kerouac's constant drunken bantering caused Cessa Carr to shout at him, "Shut your big mouth!" At that point Kerouac experienced *satori*: an instant awakening of the senses, an "eye-kick." (He would relate a similar experience in his 1965 novel *Satori in Paris*.) Kerouac had a true flash of enlightenment in which he realized his obnoxious behavior was intrusive and unsettling to his hosts. Despite this, he hammered the keys of the Carr's pump organ for hours while the rest of them slept.

Kerouac left New York in mid-October to be with his mother in Orlando. He slept in the little bedroom, while Gabrielle took to the couch. She was relieved to have Jack back and safe from the temptations of New

York. Kerouac made preliminary notes for a new novel, "Memory Babe," and wrote a three-act play (his second since adapting *Doctor Sax* to a screenplay), originally solicited by Leo Garen, stage manager for an off-Broadway production of *The Threepenny Opera*. Instead of giving the play to Garen, Kerouac wrote to Patricia MacManus that the play would be available within two weeks for her perusal at Sterling Lord's office. Kerouac realized that publishers wanted another *On the Road*. Malcolm Cowley had no use for *Doctor Sax,* even with the chapters Kerouac had added to meet the editor's request for more childhood scenes. On Viking Press stationery Cowley called *Doctor Sax* an "exercise in self-abuse" and *Tristessa,* he determined, was an even more self-indulgent foray into the excesses of automatic writing. He later told Lawrence Lee and Barry Gifford that the projects did not "arouse my enthusiasm." Cowley asked Kerouac (via Lord) for a novel with simply a plot and some characters.[15]

Kerouac worried that *On the Road* was already slipping from the bestseller list and wondered if he ruined his chances by getting drunk instead of making more television appearances. One of the chief reasons that sales had waned was that Viking could not keep up with the demand. He turned his attention toward other moneymaking enterprises, including possible public readings of his work and writing for the theater.

After contacting Helen Weaver, Kerouac wrote to Stella Sampas in Lowell. She had sent him a letter congratulating him on the success of his new novel. "That boy whom Sammy loved so—believed in—could live, love, and write with such intensity. Time has improved you. The boy is a man now and it takes so long to grow up. The whole family takes pride in congratulating you."[16]

His response was friendly, almost brotherly:

Everynight I thank God that it's only a show in His mind. Since thought is unthinkable, and the world a thought in God's mind, what world is there? Think of your dead ancestors, now did they really truly appear and then disappear? T'would seem to me that the nature of appearance and disappearance is in conformity with the nature of non-appearance and non-disappearance. . . . Go to the sources of your spiritual comfort. The world is a primordial mystery and never even happened. Five falling stars every minute on a dark night mountaintop I saw. The name of the mountain was Desolation Peak. I was in bliss. My only friends were deer.

He closed the letter with a poem ("God, be kind! / Free all your dedicate / angels, for me") and promised that he would visit her the next time he returned to Lowell. [17]

He also wrote a testimonial to Lawrence Ferlinghetti endorsing Gregory Corso's work. Recently acquitted on obscenity charges for publishing, distributing, and selling Ginsberg's *Howl and Other Poems,* Ferlinghetti was seeking fresh, original work. Although stylistically Corso and Ginsberg were leagues apart, Kerouac praised his contemporaries as some of the best poets of the country. Corso, he continued, "rose like an angel over the rooftops and sang Italian songs as sweet as Caruso and Sinatra, but in *words."* Ferlinghetti accepted Corso's poems and compiled them under the title *Gasoline,* using Kerouac's comments as a blurb on the book cover. However, when Jack submitted his own *Book of Blues,* Ferlinghetti was hesitant to publish the work, thinking it more prose than poetry.

Kerouac's Orlando exile did little to alert him to how much *On the Road* was affecting the country at large. The best that he could surmise was that the book would reach the top of the bestseller list. Although *On the Road* did make the list, it never reached number one. By day Kerouac spent hours sitting in the yard eating oranges and reading *Don Quixote.* At night he slept outside in his sleeping bag. One evening he glanced at the sky and saw *Sputnik II's* rockets gleaming. Excited, he called his mother out to watch with him. The timing of the Soviet space launch inspired the press to make a mockery of the word "beat." They melded the term with the suffix from the new Russian satellite to create "beatnik." The image of the beatnik—a parody on the be-bop style of Thelonious Monk's goatee and beret—totally derailed any serious allusions to being beat. Now, turtlenecked, bongo-banging beat wannabes plagued the Village. This corruption reached right into Kerouac's living room: on the television screen Louis Nye, portraying a crude caricature of Kerouac (Jack Crackerjack), would hysterically scream, "I saw the best minds of my generation destroyed by naked hysteria . . . kill for the sake of killing!"[18]

Kerouac stayed productive, finishing his play *Beat Generation,* in which he incorporated real-life people like Neal and Carolyn Cassady, Al Sublette, Allen Ginsberg, and Peter Orlovsky. The play's contents highly amused Jack, but he wasn't sure that it had any theatrical merit. Perhaps part of the problem was that he wrote the play over a twenty-four-hour period, determined to ward off sleep until it was completed. He rented a typewriter for $7.73 per month and typed the play, which totaled 103 pages. He sent a copy to Sterling Lord, who sent a telegram requesting additional copies and telling Kerouac that Brando wanted to see it. Even Lillian Hellman expressed interest.[19]

Although he had suggested to Joyce that she come to Florida in October to be with him, the prospect of a new novel caused him to change his mind. He now asked her not to come. Once Kerouac arrived in New York for his contractual nightclub appearances, he did not plan to stay with Joyce but with Henri Cru, who enforced a strict rule that none of Kerouac's "friends" could call him there. Kerouac offered Joyce's apartment to Peter Orlovsky and told him that he intended to meet with Helen Weaver when he arrived.[20]

On another scroll, Kerouac typed twelve feet of "Memory Babe," although he did not have enough material to complete it. Disgusted with the results, he put it aside and worked further on *The Dharma Bums*. As usual, Kerouac took Benzedrine to sustain himself through the long bouts of writing that ultimately produced the novel. To Kerouac, it seemed better than *On the Road*. In December 1957 he boasted of his newest accomplishment to Ginsberg, Orlovsky, and Corso:

> Wanta tell you, I just finished writing my shining new novel The Dharma Bums all about Gary, the real woodsy version of Gary, not surrealistic romantic vision, my own puremind trueself Ti Jean Lowell woods vision of Gary, not what you guys will like particularly, actually, tho, there's a lot of Zen Lunacy throughout and what's best: all the tremendous details and poems and outcries of the Dharma Bums at last gathered together in a rushing narrative on a 100 foot scroll.[21]

He also corrected the galleys for *The Subterraneans* over five nights and restored passages altered by Grove Press. Kerouac was so adamant about having the book published as originally intended that he told Donald Allen he would pay to change the galleys if necessary. With the novel completed, he wrote to friends of his coming to visit New York City for his December 19–25 run doing readings at the Village Vanguard.

Kerouac stood on the edge of the Village Vanguard's stage with a small audience before him and some jazz musicians backing him up. The idea for the readings had originated with Gilbert Millstein, who contacted Max

Gordon, owner of the Village Vanguard. (Presumably, Millstein was unaware that Kerouac had already read with jazz backing with David Amram a few months earlier.) Gordon agreed and scheduled the writer for a week in December.

The Village Vanguard audience was a tough crowd, and Kerouac was not ready to take the stage as boldly as he may have envisioned while safe in his mother's Orlando home. He arrived with Alene Lee, who watched from the audience as Kerouac made a spectacle (or debacle) of himself. She later recalled that it was "all out of kilter and awful." Lucien Carr remembered that the audiences would start with as few as twenty people and eventually would diminish to fewer than ten.[22] Most nights Kerouac felt excluded by the musicians backing him (except for television personality Steve Allen, who agreed to sit in on piano for the second performance) and resorted to the bottle. In the Vanguard's tiny backstage dressing room, J. J. Johnson and his band (the other act the night of the second performance) saw the unpolished writer trudge into the small room unannounced and thought he was someone who had come in from off the street. Johnson remarked to Kerouac that he thought his writings "deep."[23] The remainder of the week at the Vanguard went no better, and Kerouac's contract was terminated. On January 4, 1958, the *Nation* published an article on Kerouac's reading by Dan Wakefield: "Out of each era in our national history there come a few poets and a few poor boys who wander with words."[24] Contrary to most of Kerouac's critics who were hell-bent on destroying his reputation as a writer, the hip youth of the Village seemed to *get* it. Howard Smith, a staff writer for the *Village Voice*, was one such critic:

> Out front the J. J. Johnson Quartet heats up the buzzing, jammed-in, packed house to a supercharged, pregnant pitch. In a back alcove, near the men's room, sits Jack Kerouac, who has come off his road into the spotlight of the literary world and his sometime home, Greenwich Village, for a stay at the Village Vanguard that was supposed to be indefinite—and was. It lasted seven nights.
>
> His receding hairline touseled, sweating enough to fill a wine cask, Kerouac looks like a member in good standing of the generation he called "beat." Anxious drags on cigarette after cigarette, walking around in tight little circles, fast quick talk to anyone nearby, swigs from an always handy drink, gulps of an always handy coffee, tighten Paisley tie, loosen tie, tighten tie.

"What am I going to read?" . . . and he leafs through a suitcaseful and suddenly realizes no one remembered to bring a copy of his own *On the Road.* His combination manager–literary agent talks slowly and carefully in the assuring way they get paid to talk in, but the girl jazz singer is lilting a flip version of "Look to the Rainbow," and Jack knows he's on next.

He leafs through lots of little pads filled with the tiniest handlettered notes. "When I write I print everything in pencil. My father was a printer. He lost his shop on the horses. If he didn't, I'd be a printer today. I'd probably be publishing the fresh, young poets." . . .

He's getting more nervous, but his speech comes easy in answer to certain questions. "You don't know what a square is? Well, old Rexroth says I'm a square. If he means because I was born a French Canadian Catholic . . . sometimes devout . . . then I guess that makes me a square. But a square is someone who ain't hip. Hipness? Him" (pointing to me) "and I, we're hip."

Trying to keep up with the questions, he goes on at an even faster rate. "I was sitting with Steve Allen out front for a while; he said he wished he had his old 'Tonight' show, so he could put me on. I told him he should wire Jack Paar. . . . Jazzmen and poets are both like babies. . . . No, I decided not to read to music because I feel they don't mix. . . . Well, maybe Allen will sit in on the piano for a while, though. . . . Yair, whatever I write about is all true. . . . I think Emily Dickinson is better than Whitman, as a wordman, that is."

The drink, the sweat, the smoke, the nerves are taking effect. It's time for him to go on. He grabs some of those pads and begins making his way through the maze of tiny night-club tables. They all came to see him, and a few tieless buddies from the old days, a little proud and a little jealous, the fourth estate, the agents, the handshakers, the Steve Allens, the Madison Avenue bunch trying to keep ultra-current; all treating him like a Carmine DeSapio or Floyd Patterson.

He's shorter than they expected, this writer who has been likened to Sandburg but looks like a frightened MC on his first job. They applaud wildly for this 35-year-old who was drunk for the first three weeks that his book made the bestseller list, and now stands before them wearing an outfit of fair middle-class taste, but with a thick, hand-tooled, large-buckled leather belt.

"I'm going to read like I read to my friends." A too-easy murmur of laughter, the crowd is with him. He reads fast, with his eyes untheatrically glued to the little pad, rapidly, on and on as if he wants to get it over with. "I'll read a junky poem." He slurs over the beautiful passages as if not expecting the crowd to dig them even if he went a little slower. "It's like kissing my kitten's belly. . . ." He begins to loosen up and ad lib, and the audience is with him. A fast 15 minutes and he's done.

The applause is like a thunderstorm on a hot July night. He smiles and goes to sit among the wheels and the agents, and pulls a relaxed drag on his cigarette.

He is prince of the hips, being accepted in the court of the rich kings who, six months ago, would have nudged him closer to the bar, if he wandered in to watch the show. He must have hated himself in the morning—not for the drinks he had, but because he ate it all up the way he never really wanted to.

As I was leaving I heard some guy in an old Army shirt, standing close to the bar, remark: "Well, Kerouac came off the road in high gear . . . I hope he has a good set of snow tires."[25]

Relieved of his performance obligations, Kerouac's itinerary opened up so that he could participate with David Amram at a reading before a more receptive audience at Circle in the Square. At a moment's notice, flyers were printed announcing the event, which was packed to the rafters. Once again, poets Philip Lamantia and Howard Hart were willing to participate, as was Amram, who took time off from his post office job to play improvisatory backup. On Friday midnight, two days after Christmas, Kerouac once again took the stage. The Village Vanguard had dampened expectations of any stellar performances by Kerouac, so that the press did not appear this time. Among friends and a less hostile crowd, Kerouac was in rare form. Amram remembers: "Jack made up a whole rap about driving down a dark two-lane highway in the Black Hills of South Dakota and being blinded by a speeding trucker who was bearing down relentlessly in the wrong lane, trying to get home early to make love to his new bride on their farm in North Carolina."[26] Jack also read some of Ginsberg's, Corso's, and Steve Allen's "sensitive lil poems."[27] During the intermission the three sodden poets, drunk on Thunderbird wine, stood in

Sheridan Square Park reading their poetry to anybody who would stop and listen. When they missed the cue to go back onstage, Amram improvised with scat-singing and piano-playing till they returned.[28]

Kerouac's love life was still up in the air, as he vacillated between "big sexy brunettes"[29] and Joyce Glassman. She had not seen him during the first week of December when he was in the city, which hurt her tremendously. She missed all of his readings at the Vanguard when he failed to invite her (except for the second-to-last performance). She realized that Kerouac was not performing as poetic sage but was being forced to play the role of "King of the Beats." This, she knew, would result in his getting drunk each night. Sitting in the back of the club, where the shadows concealed her, Joyce watched Kerouac, head sunk down to his chest, appear to a drumroll. A Thunderbird-infused reading of *On the Road* ruined any chance for Jack to be taken seriously as an artist, though a few people, like Elvin Jones, appreciated the beauty and stark honesty of Kerouac's reading. Backstage, Joyce met Kerouac and left with him after he asked her to get him out of there.[30]

They returned to the Marlton Hotel on Eighth Street, where he was staying after falling out with Henri Cru (in part owing to Kerouac's drunkenness and his portrait of Cru in *On the Road,* an accusation that Jack later felt to be "twaddle and foolishness").[31] In the dingy hotel room she lay on the double bed with him passed out beside her. She felt angry, half sorry for him, half in love, but nonetheless aware that she was more mother figure than lover to him. The following week, they stayed alone in her apartment (Orlovsky did not take Kerouac's suggestion to move in with Joyce), away from the "evil" of the "world." He tried to fend off his desire for drink by sleeping. They did go out on what Joyce and Kerouac termed a "real date." He took her to the Hong Fat Noodle Shop in Chinatown and afterward they went to see *The Sweet Smell of Success* at the Variety Theatre in the Bowery. After a weekend together, Kerouac prepared to return to Orlando, this time accompanied by Robert Frank, who had been hired to photograph Kerouac on the road for *Life* magazine. That morning, Joyce left for her temporary job as a typist while Jack slept. Upon returning, she saw a note left on the pillow. Frank had awakened him with a phone call, and Kerouac was "gone on the road," assuring her that she was "my Angel in a pink slip." Although the note seemed promising enough, she reflected later in her memoir that it was in fact the "beginning of the end."[32]

As Kerouac endured the storm of publicity, those who had been by his side from the mid-1940s through the most depressing, indigent hours of his life were still in self-imposed exile. If Ginsberg, Corso, and Burroughs were perceptive at all about Kerouac, they would have picked up the distress signals in his letters. They were safe from the media bombardment and cared only about "*Howl*'s obscenity trial. Kerouac wrote to Ginsberg on December 28:

> Mad pad in Puerto Rico 13th Street near Ave A . . . where I'm hiding out, this afternoon I finally told everybody I was thru with publicity for the rest of my life. I see where Rexroth says I am an "insignificant Tom Wolfe" (can he really say that about Sax?) Everybody attacking us like mad, Herbert Gold, etc. etc. you and me now equally being attacked. My mother says every knock is a boost. I saw your sweet sweet cousin Joel the other night, he gave me bottle vitamin pills, your father wrote, wants me to come out Paterson "talk." O talk talk, I've talking to 1,500 people in past week. I read fine. Lucien said Yes, I read fine. Lucien said, admires my sticking it out, dear Lucien slept on my bathroom floor on 2 day binge. Wish you were here. Broke up with Joyce because I wanted to try big sexy brunettes then suddenly saw evil of world and realized Joyce was my angel sister and came back to her. Xmas Eve read my prayer to drunken nightclub, everybody listen.[33]

Ginsberg recognized the reality of the situation: Kerouac was left holding "the bag in New York for the whole beat generation and the San Francisco Renaissance all by himself." By the midsummer of 1958, Ginsberg was en route to America to face the country's new fascination with the beats, to stem the opposition to Kerouac's aesthetics, and to rejoin Peter Orlovsky. Unlike Kerouac, Ginsberg thrived on the attention.

To help bridge the broadening rift between Kerouac and his critics, Ginsberg suggested that Kerouac stop selling his wares to please the "market-driven appetites of his agent" and release each novel of his developing Duluoz legend in chronological order. Instead, *Maggie Cassidy* and *Tristessa* were doomed to appear as cheap paperbacks with lurid covers sold largely in five-and-dime book racks. Despite Ginsberg's well-intended advice, he was persona non grata in the Kerouac house, now in Northport, Long Island. Gabrielle had intercepted Ginsberg's letters from Paris to Kerouac and informed her son that Ginsberg and Burroughs were no longer allowed in "her" home, an ultimatum that he thought odd since he was thirty-six years old and the owner of the house in question. Dutifully, and sadly, Kerouac obeyed this command well into the next decade.

Despite the negative reception of Kerouac's public readings in New York, Steve Allen, Norman Granz, and Bill Randall offered him three contracts to read his works on long-playing records. Upon returning to Orlando from New York, he considered the offers. To realize such opportunities, Kerouac knew that he needed to be closer to New York. Via letter, he asked Joyce Glassman to send the real estate section of the *New York Times,* so that he could find a rental until a house became available. However, the claustrophobic pressures of living with his sister and her husband prompted him to purchase a house hastily so he could move in by the spring of 1958. Even his nephew Paul Jr. got on his nerves. Kerouac thought that the ten-year-old boy was "arrogant," "indocile," and "perverse."[34] Kerouac expected the move to New York state to put an end to his nomadic life. There he could "finish my own life be an old graybeard Jack poet writing haiku & praying for deliverance of all living things to heaven, which, if prayer is earnest and desire is true, is not only possible, but done."[35]

Kerouac sent his typewriter out for reconditioning before retyping *The Dharma Bums* from the scroll version onto separate sheets of paper. Meanwhile, his agent fielded offers from numerous magazines wanting to publish Kerouac's smaller pieces: "Alone on a Mountaintop," his description of his fire-lookout job, was placed in the October 1958 edition of *Holiday*; "Lamb, No Lion" in *Pageant*'s February 1958 issue; "Beatific: On the Origin of the Beat Generation" in *Playboy*'s June 1959 issue; and "The Last Word" in *Escapade*'s October 1959 issue. Most notable, at least for Kerouac, was the publication of an excerpt from *Mexico City Blues* in the academic periodiocal *Chicago Review.* Excerpted was the 211th Chorus:

> The wheel of the quivering meat
> conception
> Turns in the void expelling human beings,
> Pigs, turtles, frogs, insects, nits,

Mice, lice, lizards, rats, roan
Racinghorses, poxy bucolic pigtics,
Horrible unnameable lice of vultures,
Murderous attacking dog-armies
Of Africa, Rhinos roaming in the
                    jungle,
Vast boars and huge gigantic bull
Elephants, rams, eagles, condors,
Pones and Porcupines and Pills—
All the endless conception of living
                    beings
Gnashing everywhere in Consciousness
Throughout the ten directions of space
Occupying all the quarters in & out,
From supermicroscopic no-bug
To huge Galaxy Lightyear Bowell
Illuminating the sky of one Mind—
    Poor! I wish I was free
    of that slaving meat wheel
    and safe in heaven dead[36]

Lonely in Orlando, where he thought the locals were "dead," Kerouac craved, for the moment, the companionship of those in New York, the "Nation of People."[37] With Gabrielle, Kerouac whiled away the hours finishing the series of blues poems first started in July 1957, "Orlando Blues." The Forty-fourth Chorus warns readers, "Don't ever come to Florida."[38]

Kerouac returned to New York in March 1958 and met Robert Frank and Joyce Glassman to look for a home. He found one fifty miles from Manhattan in Northport, Long Island. Later, when he ill advisedly went to New York City, accompanied by Gregory Corso, Kerouac suffered a beating at the Kettle of Fish on Macdougal Street. When they left the stuffy confines of the bar, two men stepped from the shadows and attacked the intoxicated Kerouac. They thrashed him, pounding his head against the pavement and breaking his arm. As Corso looked on horrified, he noted that Kerouac did not defend himself.

Corso took the bloodied Kerouac to Joyce, who took him to the New York Infirmary. Emergency room doctors assured Jack that he did not have a concussion. For years afterward, however, Kerouac was convinced that he had suffered brain damage from the assault. The beating further estranged Kerouac from the city and all that it contained, including Joyce. According to Ginsberg, Kerouac was repeatedly involved in drunken altercations:

> That's something that did happen to him when he came in [to New York City], drank, and got into arguments and fights in the San Remo Bar. And he was incapable of fighting back. Not that he was weak but he simply wouldn't strike another person; he believed in the Lamb and so lived that through. There were situations where people attacked him, out of inquisitiveness or jealousy or natural alcoholic anger or irritability—jealousy primarily. Then there was one incident where he actually was down on the sidewalk with a big huge man literally banging his head on the sidewalk. Kerouac said it "did something to his brain," scrambled his brains permanently. So, he was afraid to come into the metropolis after that.[39]

No sooner had he arrived in New York than he was gone. Joyce did not hear from him again for a month. On a men's room wall in the Village, someone had scrawled "Kerouac Go Home."[40]

In February, Grove Press published *The Subterraneans* with an admiring introduction by Henry Miller, who declared that Kerouac took pleasure in "defying the laws and conventions of literary expression which cripple genuine, trammeled communication between reader and writer."[41] Miller wrote:

> When someone asks, "Where does he get that stuff?" say: "From you!" Man, he lay awake all night listening with eyes and ears. A night of a thousand years. Heard it in the womb, heard it in the cradle, heard it in school, heard it on the floor of life's stock exchange where dreams are traded for gold. And *man*, he's sick of hearing it. He wants to move on. He wants to *blow*. But will you let him?[42]

Joyce read *The Subterraneans*. Kerouac's thorough knowledge of himself and everything around him impressed her. The confessional rush of the spontaneous prose was immediate, intense, and irrefutably sad:

Cried in the railyard sitting on an old piece of iron under the new moon and on the side of the old Southern Pacific tracks, cried because not only I had cast off Mardou whom now I was not too sure I wanted to cast off but the die'd been thrown, feeling too her emphathetic tears across the night and the final horror both of us round-eyed realizing we part—but seeing suddenly not in the face of the moon but some-where in the sky as I looked up and hoped to figure, the face of my mother—remembering it in fact from a haunted nap just after supper that same restless unable-to-stay-in-a-chair or on-earth day—just as I woke to some Arthur Godfrey program on TV, I saw bending over me the visage of my mother, with impenetrable eyes and moveless lips and round cheekbones and glasses that glinted and hid the major part of her expression which at first I thought was a vision of horror that I might shudder at, but it didn't make me shudder—wondering about it on the walk and suddenly now in the railyards weeping for my lost Mardou and so stupidly because I'd decided to throw her away myself, it had been a vision of my mother's love for me.[43]

His adamant refusal to submit to Donald Allen's editorial cuts and emendations resulted in a superb work rich with peculiar intellectual en-ergy. Released in softcover, *The Subterraneans* was not light reading, though it was meant to be consumed at one sitting. Kerouac's characteris-tic honesty impressed readers. *The Subterraneans* put Kerouac on the line not only with his family ("not only my mother but my sister whom I may have to live with some day and her husband a Southerner and everybody concerned, would be mortified to hell and have nothing to do with us"), but also with critics.[44] In the novel he documented faithfully a biracial re-lationship—as taboo in 1950s America as Mark Twain's respectful friend-ship between Huckleberry Finn and the slave Jim in the previous century. Predictably, critics were less than impressed. To *Time* magazine, Kerouac was the "Latrine laureate of Hobohemia," and nemesis Kenneth Rexroth ridiculed him in print and declared that "Negroes and Jazz" were two things which Kerouac knew nothing about. David Dempsey (book critic for the *New York Times* and short story writer) seemed to be pursuing a vendetta against Kerouac and his book: "It's a 'boy meets girl' story of the lowest depths, more difficult to read than its predecessor. It is written less for laughs ('kicks') and more as an attempt to put down every recollected fact about an affair between two psychologically 'sick' people." About Jack's spontaneous writing, Dempsey informs readers that "the most notable feature of 'The Subterraneans' is the complete, almost schizophrenic disintegration of syntax—the effort to reproduce, by a sort of reflex action, the uninterrupted continuum of experience enjoyed by subterranean Percepied in his brief affair with a Negro girl." The influential *Times*, once the harbinger of Kerouac's success as a writer, was now dismantling his reputation as a serious postmodern novelist and poet. Such negative reviews, in so large a forum, could reduce his expected income from the novel. At a time when his bank account was in the red (he owed a mortgage of $10,000 for purchasing his home), Jack needed money.[45]

In late April Kerouac, Gabrielle, and an armful of cats moved to 34 Gilbert Street in Northport. He wrote John Clellon Holmes that month: "I have my cats, my mother, my typewriter, my work, and have finally reached that enviable position you have in Saybrook Old [Holmes's Connecticut home], of being in a nice home & officially committed to the tender art of writing artistic literature."[46] It was an idealistic enough assessment. In Northport he was close enough to New York yet far enough away to shield himself from much of the criticism of his novels and poetry, particularly from New York critic Norman Podhoretz and the relentless Rexroth. His mother gave him a roll of nickels to take with him whenever he ventured into town. He became a regular fixture on the barstool and at the pool table: "We all saw him drinking beer and playing coin-operated pool tables at the bars along Main Street. We saw him there late at night, night after night, as dapper as an unmade bed, the sweat rolling from his uncombed hair, and still, no matter the hour, never missing the intent of what you were saying, never ignoring a shade of your meaning."[47]

Norman Podhoretz, editor of the *Partisan Review*, attacked the beats in general and Kerouac in particular in the spring 1958 issue under the misleading title "The Know-Nothing Bohemians." The essay was a scathing critique of the beat aesthetics of Kerouac, Ginsberg, and Burroughs (of whom Podhoretz remarks, "So far, everybody's sanity has been spared by the inability of *Naked Lunch* to find a publisher"). Podhoretz was all too aware of the waves that these writers were creating in American culture, of the undercurrents of sex, drugs, and "criminality" that pervaded the works of Kerouac and company. Podhoretz's observations were sometimes astute, as when he said that Ginsberg's poetry tended to speak "for the darker side of the new Bohemianism. Kerouac is milder." But he rebuked Kerouac for his naïveté over race relations, in particular the love affair between Mardou Fox and Leo Percepied, and Jack's observations of African Americans in *On the Road*: "It will be news to the Negroes to learn that they are so happy and ecstatic; I doubt if a more idyllic picture of Negro life has been painted since certain Southern ideologues tried to convince the world that things were just as fine as fine could be for the slaves on the old plantation."

Podhoretz's evaluation of *The Subterraneans* was more damning than his take on *On the Road*. He called *The Subterraneans* an "inept parody" of Faulkner's "worst" writing, noting that Kerouac's spontaneous prose was the most problematic element of the work. Kerouac's impulse to explore the emotional impact of a thought or event contrasted with the cerebral-based processes that Podhoretz favored. The critic characterized Kerouac's style as infected by solipsism. The line dividing autobiography from fiction, he said, becomes so blurred that the books are "impossible to discuss as novels." Podhoretz indicted the beat ideal as being indirectly responsible for the "spread of juvenile crime in the 1950's." He reasoned that "even the relatively mild ethos of Kerouac's books could accelerate easily into brutality: 'Kill the intellectuals who can talk coherently.'" This allegation—a far cry from the "beatitude" of Kerouac's beat philosophy—displayed a shallow understanding of his work and intentions. Writing to Philip Whalen, Jack summed up his reaction to Podhoretz's *Partisan Review* article simply: "Gad."[48]

25

Northport

May 1958-January 1959

I am watching them churn the last milk
they'll ever get from me.
They are waiting for me to die.
  GREGORY CORSO, "The Mad Yak"

Kerouac retreated to his Northport house. In the yard, he tended a garden seeded with watermelon and corn and pruned the American Beauty roses growing in a rock garden. A makeshift vineyard promised grapes. Kerouac kept his mother company. However, because she had forbidden Ginsberg and Burroughs (among others) to visit, Kerouac lacked stimulating companionship. The Kerouac home did not have a telephone, so Jack had to walk a half mile to a pay phone. Gabrielle, a devout Catholic who festooned the Long Island home with religious artifacts, would not permit women to spend the night. In truth, it was hardly Kerouac's home at all. He was merely a guest abiding by his mother's bigotry.

One Saturday morning in May, Joyce Glassman decided to board the Long Island Railroad to visit Kerouac. She left Manhattan with a loaf of pumpernickel bread that he had asked her to bring. She dressed conservatively and pulled her hair into a French twist in an effort to create a favorable impression on Gabrielle. When she got off the train, she knew better than to expect Kerouac to be waiting for her. She boarded a bus with the explicit directions to his house that he had given her. At the door Gabrielle greeted her by immediately asking what train she would be "going back on." Joyce, who had never met Gabrielle before, remembers her as a "grandmotherly" type: apron wrapped around a simple housedress, tightly wrapped hair, and thick glasses magnifying eyes that Kerouac described as "hard to find" in the accumulation of swelling flesh.[1] Gabrielle had cooked a roast, an unusual gesture, Joyce thought, since it was a seasonably warm May day.[2]

Joyce noted the simplicity of the décor—a throwback to the depression-era homes that Gabrielle kept in Lowell. In the family parlor, the furniture was an ugly "orangey" maple. On the wall hung crucifixes and a portrait of the Virgin Mary that reflected the abiding faith that still gripped mother and son. "You would not think the writer who was the avatar of the Beat Generation lived there," she wrote years later in her memoir. She saw that Kerouac was already drunk. Glumly, he took Joyce upstairs to see his study and to show her the manuscript of *The Dharma Bums*. When she attempted to kiss him, he backed away from her. Meanwhile, Gabrielle started shouting from the bottom of the stairs. It was—as others had recalled—as if Gabrielle and Jack were husband and wife.[3]

Later, Gabrielle greeted a group of teenagers at the door and allowed them to enter. The teens convinced Kerouac to accompany them to a party, where one girl told him that he was the "saddest man" she had ever known. Later, Joyce joined Jack for an immense dinner, which Gabrielle had prepared. At the table Kerouac drank wine and ignored the food. After a while, he rested his head on the table and closed his eyes. Gabrielle said to Joyce, "You see—he doesn't eat." She then asked Joyce if it was time to catch her train and shooed her out of the kitchen. Kerouac was still passed out. Momentarily rousing him, Joyce asked him to take her to the station; he resisted. Greatly saddened, she went alone.[4]

According to Ginsberg, the relationship between mother and son was a "weird companionship" that he likened to "down-home peasants" uninhibitedly exchanging insults, "not restrained at all in their family squabbles fired by alcohol." According to Ginsberg, one such exchange took place during one of the rare instances he was allowed inside their Long Island home:

> We sat by the television set and there was a retrospective news broadcast about Hitler and the concentration camps. Kerouac and his mother were both drinking. She was also a great tippler, both were drunk, and they began arguing among themselves. And then some

German refugee came on the screen and talked about the Holocaust and Kerouac's mother said in front of me: "They're still complaining about Hitler, it's too bad he didn't finish them off." Kerouac agreed with her. I sat there and nodded. Then he said to her, "You dirty cunt, why did you say that?" And she said, "You fucking prick, you heard me say that before." And then began an argument of violence and filth such as I had never heard in any household in my life. I was actually shocked.[5]

Though Gabrielle and Jack's relationship was certainly questionable, one must doubt Ginsberg's veracity for two reasons: the timing of his accounts and his rejection by Gabrielle and Stella Kerouac. After Jack's death, Stella's refusal to allow Ginsberg access to Kerouac's archives (per Jack's strict orders) undermined the poet's plans to publish their correspondence. Frequently, Kerouac made it clear that he did not want to have much to do with Ginsberg. In early 1964, Kerouac made plain his stance on Ginsberg:

> I've just turned down $3,000 because I didn't want to be in the same film with Ginsberg, please do not identify my biography with his, or with Corso's. They've both become political fanatics, but have begun to revile me because I don't join them in their political opinions (in person, that is), and I am sick of them and their beatnik friends.[6]

Others of Jewish extraction, such as Joyce Johnson and David Amram, did not see any evidence of full-blown anti-Semitism on the part of Jack or his mother. Amram was an occasional visitor to the Northport home and frequently spoke to Gabrielle in French. One time she inquired about Jewish editor Lenny Gross, whom Jack had met at Brooklyn College in 1958, when he appeared there to do a reading with Amram, Howard Hart, and Philip Lamantia. Amram remembers: "Like everyone else who ever met him, Gabrielle was crazy about him. 'Le petit Lenny. Il est adorable. When are *you* getting married?' she asked, suddenly breaking into English. 'When will you find yourself a nice Jewish girl and have a family? You're not getting any younger.'"[7]

Amram's account, to say the least, is in stark contrast to Ginsberg's. It is easier to believe that Gabrielle disliked Ginsberg's homosexuality and drug-taking rather than his Judaism. Ginsberg's campaign to subtly smear Kerouac's legacy only began to take place after Kerouac's death. It is reasonable to infer that Kerouac, who once wrote in *Mexico City Blues,* "I keep fallin in love with my mother," would never stoop so low as to call her a "dirty cunt." According to Amram, "Kerouac would never have dreamed of using any vulgarities in front of his mother. In the twelve years I knew him, no matter how much he drank, or how much we smoked, I never heard him use *that* word in relation with Gabrielle."[8]

In June, Kerouac freed himself from lethargy and gloominess long enough to address a variation of the same old editorial problem. A Viking Press copy editor had received his manuscript for *The Dharma Bums* and had taken the liberty of altering the text. He complained to Gary Snyder:

> Well old shitface I had the same problem with Viking Press and the ms. of The Dharma Bums, that I had with Grove Press and the ms. of Subterraneans. I had to have a showdown and take the galley and re-store it 3,500 places to its original freshness and purity of dharma bum way of talking. Now its in perfect shape again. The only technical error in it, I think, is in my estimate of the height of the Matterhorn camp, that is, our big concave rock: I said 9000 feet, and the height of the little alpine lake at the foot of Matterhorn itself, I said 12,000 I'm afraid, and the height of Matterhorn Peak itself. Can you send me that and I'll rectify.[9]

He offered (as he did with *The Subterraneans*) to pay the publisher to rein-state the text to its original form. Kerouac's editor at Viking, Helen Taylor, told Kerouac to amend the original typescript, a difficult process, as there was no room to write in the already crowded margins: "You see, it's obvi-ous that you've restored to the original certain things you agreed to change on your first visit here. Also you have accepted other changes without comment. The things that have been corrected, like 'further' to 'farther' and numerous other small details, must stand corrected, and starting from a new manuscript would mean doing all those things again."[10] In June 1958 Kerouac responded to Taylor with his changes. He demanded that he compare the final copy with the original scroll: "Since I'm paying for this and my reputation depends on it, I want to make sure we put out a book we can be really proud of. Just leave the secrets of syntax and narra-tive to me."[11]

Kerouac's agent fielded an offer from MGM to buy the film rights to *The Subterraneans* for $15,000. Sterling Lord had declined a $100,000 offer for film rights to *On the Road,* thinking he could get a better price. A second offer from Tri-Way Productions promised Kerouac $25,000. Instead, Kerouac received only $2,500 before the company closed its doors for good.[12]

Kerouac continued writing a new novel, a process he found difficult. He would pace his yard at night thinking about the plot and mechanics of the new novel. To help him write, a physician prescribed Dexamyls, an artificial stimulant. As he wrote (listening to a new phonograph that he had purchased), the drugs took their toll on his health and did nothing to cure his writer's block. In June 1958, Kerouac completed a 35-foot scroll and titled it on the outside "Memory Babe."

Gradually, Kerouac began to refuse the local college students who constantly rang his doorbell wanting to party with the King of the Beats. He wrote to local editors asking that his Long Island home not be disturbed. It was, he explained to Whalen, a "refuge of an aged quiet lady and a quiet writer Buddhist."[13] It was, in fact, a dreary exile; Kerouac spent days and weeks in front of the television. The summer heat was stultifying. Even his love life ("lots of mad young girls after me these days," he told Gary Snyder) was put on hold until the weather cooled.[14]

In the heat Kerouac labored over *The Dharma Bums* galleys. Because local (as well as Manhattan) newspapers continued to attach his street address to articles written about him, Jack still received uninvited visitors at his Long Island home. Fan mail regularly filled his mailbox. Kerouac intended *The Dharma Bums* to succeed both commercially and critically. He wrote to Viking Press editor Tom Guinzburg and enclosed some text written expressly for the novel's dust jackets. He headed the proposed dust jacket text by defining the Sanskrit word for *dharma* (Truth) and a synopsis of the work. Most telling was Kerouac's effort to distance himself from the stigma of the beat credo: "In this new novel, Jack Kerouac departs from the 'hipster' movement of the Beat Generation and leads his readers towards a conception of 'continual conscious compassion' and a peaceful understanding truce with the paradox of existence."[15] Assuring readers that the novel was filled with 'original descriptions' of the American Northwest and people from all walks of life, Viking chose not to use Kerouac's own words but instead used a dust jacket design similar to that used for *On the Road.*

Kerouac told Gary Snyder that he would be receiving a libel release form from Viking since the main character was largely based on Snyder. There was nothing libelous in the book, Kerouac assured him. He changed basic facts of Snyder's personal life such as girlfriends, family, and locations.[16]

The Dharma Bums was published on October 2, 1958. The book release party, attended by Ginsberg, became one long drunken binge. The novel's reception was predictable, with most critics ridiculing Kerouac's heartfelt tribute to the Buddhist religion that underpinned the outdoorsy novel. To help support the novel, Ginsberg wrote a favorable review for the *Village Voice* (published on November 12, 1958). In it, he emphasized the importance of Kerouac's prose and noted that *The Subterraneans*, which could be considered Kerouac's stylistic breakthrough, was published without editorial changes. To support this assertion, he included a lengthy excerpt from *The Subterraneans* as well as Kerouac's "Essentials of Spontaneous Prose." The review was a much needed corrective to the plethora of critics who chose to lampoon the writer rather than critically assess the work. Ginsberg, always willing to risk ridicule, assured the *Village Voice* readers that Kerouac was America's "new visionary poet": "There has not been criticism that has examined his prose purpose—nor his hip-beat insight and style—nor, finally, his holy content. It takes one to find one. Don't expect much understanding from academic journalists who, for all their pretense at civilization, have learned little but wicked opinion."[17] Novelist Henry Miller wrote to Kerouac saying the review was "quite wonderful."

Despite defending Kerouac's prose in print, Ginsberg found it startling that Jack would publish as his fourth novel a vastly more simplistic text and would disregard his spontaneous prose dictum. He feared that Kerouac would now seek to appease critics and Madison Avenue publishers. To defend his decision, Kerouac wrote to Ginsberg in December about his work in progress, *Old Angel Midnight,* which promised to burst current writing conventions.

Despite Ginsberg's *Village Voice* endorsement, looked upon as a sort of Valentine from one beat to another, the novel's climb on the charts was less than expected. The novel's protagonist Gary Snyder (Japhy Ryder), wrote to Kerouac approving of his friend's portrait: "*The Dharma Bums* is a beautiful book & I am amazed & touched that you should say so many nice things about me because that period was for me a really great process of learning from you, not just your vision of America and of people but your immediate all-embracing faith & thank you for sending me a copy."[18] Snyder would later reveal in interviews that he felt that Kerouac embellished his character portrait to suit his narrative. Kerouac could see right through the praise, and in February 1959 he wrote to Snyder, concerned that he had disappointed his friend. He was also frustrated with criticism that he lacked competent insight into Buddhism. His diatribe against all organized religions echoed his father's anticlerical stance:

> I don't think the book was as bad as you think; when you look at it again in future years, when the world will've gotten worster, you'll look back and appreciate the job I did on "you" and on Dharma Bumism. For Mrs. Sasaki to say that "it was a good portrait of Gary but he doesn't know anything about Buddhism" is just so fuckin typical of what's wrong with official Buddhism and all official religions today— woe, clashings, divisions, sects, jealousies, formalities, materialism, do-goodism, actionism, no repose, no universal love-try, no abandoning of arbitrary conceptions for a moment. Even Suzuki [Buddhist scholar D. T. Suzuki, who had met Kerouac in 1958] was looking at me through slitted eyes as tho I was a monstrous impostor of some kind (at least I feel that way I dunno).[19]

Viking Press bound a copy of *The Dharma Bums* in black leather and marbled endpapers (as the company had done earlier with *On the Road).* Kerouac inscribed the book to his mother, telling her that his fourth novel would help pay for the home, cat food, and brandy.

Almost one week before Ginsberg's review appeared, Kerouac summoned the courage to participate in a Hunter College symposium sponsored by Brandeis University. Needing money to move, he accepted the invitation for a $100 honorarium. Other participants included British author Kingsley Amis, anthropologist Ashley Montagu, and *New York Post* editor James Weschler. Weschler was amazed by the turnout and realized that most, like himself, were there simply to see Jack Kerouac. The beats, it seemed, had greatly raised the reading public's reception of them despite the New York critics who consistently panned their writings. In the audience were Arthur Schlesinger Jr. and Elbert Lenrow (Kerouac's New School professor who taught the course on the twentieth-century novel in America in

1948–1949), who doubted that Kerouac could hold his own in a serious debate. In fact, in Lenrow's opinion, Kerouac destroyed the proceedings by turning the symposium into a one-man reading: "Kerouac determined that this would be a hostile encounter, pitting the three panelists against himself. They were ready to prove once and for all that the thought of the beat generation was no more a philosophy than rock and roll was music." A lumberjack-shirted Kerouac took the podium first. Drinking from a brandy-filled flask, he gave a seemingly free-form "speech." He told the audience that, rather than wondering if there was a beat generation, they should wonder if there was a "world."

> I want to speak *for* things, for the crucifix I speak out, for the Star of Israel I speak out, for the divinest man who ever lived who was a German [Bach] I speak out, for Lao-tse and Chuang-tse I speak out, for D. T. Suzuki I speak out . . . why should I attack what I love out of life. This is Beat. Live your lives out? Naw, *love* your lives out. When they come and stone you at least you won't have a glass house, just your glassy flesh.[20]

After only five minutes, moderator Dean Kaufmann signaled for Kerouac to step down. Ginsberg, who was in the audience, witnessed what he construed to be a setup intended to mock the blissfully stoned writer. Intent on belittling Kerouac's importance as a writer, Weschler began his assault. He accused Kerouac of speaking like a "jaded traveling salesman" who told "obscene bedtime stories to the young." Kerouac tried to bait Weschler by taking his hat, pushing it onto his own head, and slouching down in his seat, mimicking the way that Weschler sat. Jack asked him if he believed in the "destruction of America."

"No," Weschler replied.

Kerouac: "What do you believe in, come here, come here and tell me what you believe in. . . . You told me what you don't believe in. I want to know what you *do* believe in. This is a university, we've got to learn. I believe in love, I vote for love."

Weschler: "I believe in the capacity of the human intelligence to create a world in which there is love, compassion, justice, and freedom. I believe in fighting for that kind of world. I think what you are doing is to try to destroy anybody's instinct to care about this world."

Kerouac: "I believe, I believe in the dove of peace."

Weschler: "So do I."

Kerouac: "No, you don't. You're fighting with me for the dove of peace."

Weschler found it difficult to converse with Kerouac, thinking that he talked as if he were from "outer-space." Kerouac continued, "Well, Mr. Weschler, I was sitting under a tangerine tree in Florida one afternoon and I was trying to translate the *Diamond Sutra* from Sanskrit to English and I said, shall I call it a personal god or an impersonal god, and at that moment a little tangerine dropped out of the tree, and they only drop out of a tree about once every six weeks, and landed right square in the middle of my head. Right, boing; I said, okay, personal god."

Weschler interjected, "I just want to say, Mr. Kerouac, that as an editor I have to write about Dwight D. Eisenhower's press conference every week—"

"He's very witty," Kerouac interrupted.

"—and it's possible to reduce life to an area of so little sense that there would hardly be any reason for all these people to have come here tonight, or for us to be here. I don't think we render any service by doing that—" Weschler attempted to continue.

"Education is education," Kerouac interrupted once more.

"Well, as Eisenhower would say, government is government," Weschler responded testily.

"And as Dulles would say, statesmanship is statesmanship," Kerouac concluded.

Professor Montagu then took the podium: "What I am trying to say is that it is not condemnation or contempt that is called for but compassion and understanding, that the Beat Generation is not something either to bemoan or disown but a suffering confusion of human beings crying out for sympathetic understanding. The Beat Generation represents the ultimate expression of a civilization whose moral values have broken down and in many ways, what is even worse, a civilization with little faith or conviction in the values it professes to believe." It was, he summed up, the "cult of unthink" that the beat generation fostered.

Amis's views were dismissive of Kerouac's assertion that the beats were a literary movement rooted in spiritualism and love for humanity. Instead, the panelists treated the beats as little more than a perverse social phenomenon. Amis stated, "There was no genuine union between the so-called angry young men of Great Britain, who had at least voiced a certain definable—and not monolithic—protest against the grayness of life, and the rambling wrecks from American Tech—who had ostentatiously proclaimed themselves the beat generation."

After the event, Elbert Lenrow left the building and glimpsed Kerouac and Ginsberg fleeing a throng of pursuers wanting their autographs.

As the year came to a close, Kerouac unconsciously began to dissolve relationships with several people. Joyce Glassman barely saw or heard from him anymore. Neither did Burroughs. Ginsberg and Orlovsky only saw Kerouac for a brief period when Gabrielle spent a month babysitting for Caroline in Florida. Cassady was imprisoned (and could not have cared less about Kerouac or his book), while Carolyn heard less from him as well. Most of Kerouac's correspondence was directed at his family, John Clellon Holmes, and editors at various publishing houses. Alcohol fostered his emotional distance, as did the isolation of his Long Island home (with shades drawn and Gabrielle guarding the doorway). Occasional writing, the childhood baseball game that he still played avidly, and editorial matters absorbed his time. College students rang his doorbell, and sometimes he found them at his dinner table devouring Gabrielle's roast. One Northport friend remembers that "there were constant interruptions. The kids tracked him down, of course. College girls would knock on his door and seeing Jack, older than his sleek book-jacket pictures, they would ask if they might talk to Mr. Kerouac. This happened often and never failed to disappoint him."[21] As he told John Montgomery, he was "sick," afflicted with the weight of a "sad heart."[22]

Despite his reclusiveness, Kerouac was drawn back to Manhattan in October and stayed the whole week during Gabrielle's absence. He stayed with Joyce Glassman, and when he departed, he left her hungover, high on "conversation," and sleep deprived. Writing to her girlfriend Elise Cowen, Joyce said that Jack was sick and always falling asleep on the floor—any floor. The weekend after writing Elise, Joyce ended her relationship with Kerouac in front of an Italian restaurant in the Village. In the company of some artists, Jack started flirting with artist Dody Muller in full view of Joyce, who called him a "big bag of wind." Kerouac responded with a line borrowed from Cole Porter: "Unrequited love's a bore." She stormed away and when she turned to see if he was still standing in the neon-lit Village street, he was gone. Dody had his heart. For the moment.

Despite the thematic undercurrents of Buddhism in his latest novel, Kerouac's preoccupation with Catholicism took over his religious sensibilities. Gone were the Buddhist references in his notebooks, replaced by frequent prayers and drawings of Christ. He even considered replacing the Buddhist references in *Visions of Gerard* with Catholic allusions.

Kerouac decided to move himself and his mother once more to Orlando, figuring that Florida would help reinvigorate his writing. There, he could concentrate on his writing and rework the novels that he had hoped would ultimately be published. Also, it cost less to live in Florida, and Jack was ever mindful of his limited income. To afford this sudden move, Kerouac hoped *The Dharma Bums* would sell well. It didn't. He was short the $7,500 needed to pay off the mortgage. He was still waiting for his advance for *Doctor Sax,* scheduled by Grove Press for publication in paperback in 1959. He didn't care whether it was published in hardcover or not, so long as it was published. This attitude, endorsed by his agent, belittled the importance of his spontaneous prose works, if only by their shoddy appearance on the bookshelf.

Kerouac continued seeing Dody Muller, a Manhattan artist and widow of painter Jan Muller. She was exactly Kerouac's type: dark-haired, artistic, and intellectually adept. She was also a private person and understood his reclusive nature perfectly. When they walked the Village streets or drank at the Cedar Tavern, she kept the hordes of women at bay. Composer David Amram remembers Dody in his memoir of those years: "She told me that Jack was so emotional and operated on such an intense level of feelings, that she found she could relate to him as she would with a woman friend. She could talk or listen to him without being buffeted by aggression or smothered by a wall of insensitivity."[23]

Kerouac learned from Dody the basics of oil painting. The circle of artists whom she knew socially (Kline, de Kooning, Hartigan, and others) all appreciated him as an artist and not as a celebrity. With Gabrielle gone throughout November, Kerouac invited Dody to his house, where she went to work freeing him from the squalor into which his home had fallen. Kerouac also visited Buddhist scholar D. T. Suzuki. Kerouac had received word that Suzuki wanted to see him and called from a phone booth while Orlovsky and Ginsberg waited outside. A woman answered and told him that Suzuki would be available within a half hour. They ran to First Avenue, hailed a cab, and arrived together at Suzuki's home. They stood on the stoop. Kerouac rang the bell and, not getting a response, rang it again three times slowly. Suzuki opened the door. He was an old man with long eyelashes and bushy eyebrows. He brought the trio upstairs and prepared green tea for them. In Suzuki's presence, Kerouac and Ginsberg wrote some haiku. Kerouac felt a paternal presence in Suzuki and wished to stay with him, but Jack had an appointment with Viking Press that afternoon and had to leave. (Suzuki, exhausted, was already trying to usher the men from his home.)

Kerouac was still being asked to write freelance articles for magazines. *Escapade* hired him to write a bimonthly column on baseball. Kerouac was determined not to write another novel until *Visions of Cody* and *Doctor Sax* were published. Ginsberg continued to solicit material from him for the beat anthology. Kerouac was also asked to supply a blurb for Vladimir Nabokov's recent novel, *Lolita. Holiday* magazine was willing to pay Kerouac $1,200 to travel to Canada to write an article; he declined the offer, having neither the time nor the inclination to travel. It seemed that the world around Kerouac was cashing in on his idea. His lawyer informed him that in Vermont a play was being adapted from *On the Road.*[24]

By the end of 1958, Kerouac began to feel the familiar pinch for money. He needed a new typewriter ribbon, a new battery for his transistor radio, a new desk, oil paint and canvas, and a tape recorder to record Henri Cru monologues. His savings were needed to pay off his Long Island mortgage, which he did in early December. Despite his need for cash, he refused to read his work in tandem with Ginsberg at Yale University. As he lamented in a letter to Gary Snyder: "I wanted to give you an idea of what a crock of shit it is to have to satisfy every tom dick and harry stranger in the world. No wonder Hemingway went to Cuba and Joyce to France. I was in love with the world thru blue purple curtains when I knew you and now I have to look at it thru hard iron eyes."[25] Writing to editor Tom Guinzburg to thank him, Kerouac also tried to interest Viking in another novel. Sterling Lord tried once more to place *Tristessa* and *Maggie Cassidy,* among others. Both novels were fated to paperback oblivion. Viking had already rejected *Visions of Gerard* and *Doctor Sax,* thanks to the remarks of a reader protected by the initials "C.C." The reader's report stated, "Actually, when you've had one of Jack's Lowell memoirs you've had them all." Although the reader thought that *Maggie Cassidy* was the best of the lot, *Tristessa* was "awful." The experimental prose was lost on the reader. Despite the critical acclaim for *On the Road,* the editors no longer regarded Kerouac as a serious writer.

Robert Lax visited Kerouac in Northport. Lax had agreed to publish an excerpt from *Visions of Gerard* in *Jubilee* magazine the next September. On New Year's Eve, Kerouac ventured into Manhattan to celebrate with Dody Muller, Lucien Carr, and Robert Frank. Jack's inebriated crawl through the Village included sitting in on drums at the Artists' Club, emerging wild haired and sweating. It was such a drunken debacle that guilt hovered over Kerouac for the next several weeks.

His meeting Robert Frank was meant to lead to collaboration; together, they planned to film Kerouac's recent rewrite of *The Beat Generation*. A three-act play based on the collaborative poem "Pull My Daisy" was another opportunity to earn some much-needed money. Kerouac had already written a generous introduction for Frank's book of road photography, *The Americans*. In it, Kerouac inserted a long paragraph from "Visions of Neal" as well as writing original descriptive prose to accompany the stark, gritty black-and-white photographs:

> Car shrouded in fancy expensive designed tarpolian to keep soots of no-soot Malibu from falling on new simonize job as owner who is a two-dollar-an-hour carpenter snoozes in house with wife and TV, all under palm trees for nothing, in the cemeterial California night, ag, ack—In Idaho three crosses where the cars crashed, where that long thin cowboy just barely made it to Madison Square Garden as he was about a mile down the road—*"I told you to wait in the car"* say people in America so Robert sneaks around and photographs little kids waiting in the car, whether three little boys in a motorama limousine, ompious & opiful, or poor little kids can't keep their eyes open on Route 90 Texas at 4 A.M. as dad goes to the bushes and stretches.[26]

In January, Kerouac mailed his signed contracts for the Italian translations of *On the Road* and *The Subterraneans*. The novels were eventually translated into several languages.

When Gabrielle returned from one of her numerous visits to Caroline, right away Kerouac sensed her loneliness and unhappiness. Gabrielle's cat Timmy was missing, Tyke refused to eat, and the gray, cold winter held fast. Depressed, Kerouac wrote a haiku:

> Lost cat Timmy—
> he wont be back
> In a blue moon[27]

Traditionally, a haiku, a form that dates from the sixteenth century, is a Japanese verse form consisting of seventeen syllables in three lines of five, seven, and five syllables. This form of poetry is meant to express a single idea, feeling, or image. Kerouac's adaptation of the form bears mention since he compiled a collection of the poems for publication, *Book of Haikus* (2003). He altered the spelling, adding an "s" to haiku, signaling his radical though respectful nod to the ancient art. He also dispensed with the syllabic form. His reworking of haiku is in the tradition of several poets, including Ezra Pound, Robert Frost, Amy Lowell, Conrad Aiken, William Carlos Williams, and W. B. Yeats. Kerouac scholar Regina Weinreich, in her introduction to *Book of Haikus,* states:

> Strict critics doubt whether these are haiku at all. Because Kerouac makes distinctions among the various short poems in his canon, one might well question these departures from the strict Japanese models he so admired. While Kerouac was well versed in the haiku books of his time, and a diligent, disciplined practitioner of the genre, he also felt free, exercising a kind of poetic license in their experimental use.[28]

Kerouac dropped haiku into novels such as *Maggie Cassady* and *Desolation Angels.* They also constantly dotted the pages of his notebooks, sometimes nakedly revealing his state of mind:

> Waiting with me for
> the end of this ephemeral
> Existence—the moon[29]

To ward off his mother's boredom, Jack bought her a new twenty-one-inch television so she could watch *The Lawrence Welk Show* on Saturday nights and game shows in the afternoons. But her misery stemmed not only from boredom but also from heartbreak. It saddened Gabrielle to watch her son's decline. Jack's alcoholism and pronounced indifference to his welfare and health troubled her. His weight increased, reaching 180 pounds by February. She felt that New York City was too close to Northport; her home was still besieged by interlopers intent on meeting Kerouac. In contrast, Caroline's household was wholesome, and Gabrielle wanted to be closer to the Blakes, although they were having marital problems. Yet she felt she was a burden to them. She pressed Kerouac to move to Florida as soon as possible. However, the Blakes were planning to move away from Florida. Paul had found a job as a radar technician and they planned on moving before the end of January. Perhaps dreading financial and personal duty, Kerouac tried to persuade them to return to Florida. He wrote to Caroline, arguing that it would benefit himself, Gabrielle, and her family. He mentioned the outrageous Long Island taxes, living costs, and Gabrielle's loneliness. Kerouac offered to contribute the down payment on several wooded lots on which to build a duplex that would allow them all to live together while preserving the Blakes' privacy. Paramount for Kerouac was the freedom to come and go without fear of neglecting his mother.[30]

Al Aronowitz of the *New York Post* came to interview Kerouac and right away noted his slovenly appearance. Wearing an untucked heavy flannel shirt, worn shoes, and gas station pants, Kerouac greeted Aronowitz at the door, ushered him in, and handed him a beer. Gabrielle was there and chimed in every so often to defend Jack and assure Aronowitz that her son was a "good boy." She had just come back from shopping and unloaded from a paper bag six-packs of beer. Later, she popped into Kerouac's bedroom, where he was showing Aronowitz his scrapbook of newspaper clippings, and consented to a small interview of her own. Afterwards, she pointed out a silver crucifix over Kerouac's bed and rosary beads on his night table, and asked, "If he was so bad, would he have that?" Next to the crucifix hung a clipboard with sheets of paper on which Jack scribbled dream notes. They were, he told Aronowitz, his "bedside sheets." Confused, Gabrielle thought that he meant the sheets the next-door neighbor was airing outside.

"No," he corrected, "bedside sheets, pieces of paper hanging by the bedside!"

"Oh," she said, "explain yourself."

"I did," he chuckled. "You don't listen. You're airing sheets."

When Aronowitz's interview was published in the *New York Post*, Kerouac thought it a "hatchet job." Writing to Aronowitz on January 12, 1959, Kerouac declared that he was a man of "stature" who would ultimately be "recognized when the dust settles." To say the least, the taped two-hour interview did little to bolster Kerouac's confidence in the American press.[31]

26

Pull My Daisy

January–September 1959

Why not make them
higher, and higher, and
higher—until they fall down?

ROBERT CREELEY, "Buildings"

January and February 1959 were hectic months for Kerouac. He mailed signed contracts to Sterling Lord, including one for a Swedish translation of *The Dharma Bums*. Grove Press, preparing *Doctor Sax* for publication, sent Kerouac the proofs to correct. He was also trying to ensure that *Old Angel Midnight* would be printed in unexpurgated form in the literary journal *Big Table* (along with selections from Burroughs's *Naked Lunch*). Grove Press accepted *Mexico City Blues,* and selections from *Visions of Cody* would finally appear in *New Directions*. It was a victory of a sort for Kerouac, who wanted to silence naysayers like Ginsberg who thought he had sold out in writing the novel *The Dharma Bums*.

Kerouac had also recently done a voice-over for the film *Pull My Daisy,* filmed in artist Alfred Leslie's loft in January. The black-and-white short, filmed without sound, starred French actress Delphine Seyrig. Assorted beats, like Ginsberg and Orlovsky, played themselves with the exception of Gregory Corso, who played Jack. Other contributors included Dody Muller, Richard Bellamy, Larry Rivers, Mary Frank, Alice Neal, and David Amram. The majority of the actors had little or no experience. Director Robert Frank adapted the filming to the work schedules of each person. For Frank, it was a chance to capture a unique group of people free from the worst portraits of them invented by the press. A cast party on the day of filming created chaos in Alfred Leslie's loft. This Frank recorded with a slow camera crawl around the room before settling on a conversation between Corso (puffing on a joint) and Ginsberg, who dropped his pants just as the camera reached him. Corso then doused Ginsberg with ketchup, french fries, cold grease from a skillet, and red wine. Similar episodes were intended to test the patience of Leslie and Frank, who remained calm.

Kerouac visited the studio later and saw the squalor of the set. "Good God, Alfred, my shoes are stuck to the floor," said Jack, laughing. "Neal's house never looked this bad. Carolyn wouldn't have allowed it." He hoped that Corso, Orlovsky, and Ginsberg would stop their spontaneous disruptions and stick to the story. Filming ended one week later, and Kerouac's narration and Amram's score were to be added later. From this work, Frank created a patchwork of grainy impressionistic images of tenement squalor. Amram's score required a jazz ensemble and chamber musicians, all paid union scale from the meager production budget.[1]

In Jerry Newman's studio, Kerouac recorded his narration for *Pull My Daisy.* Hoisting a bottle of Chateauneuf-du-Pape, Kerouac quaffed half before delivering his first line as silent images flickered on the screen: "Early morning in the universe . . ." The narration was based loosely on the treatment that Jack had originally written. After much prodding, Kerouac agreed to record another take of the narration, although he believed that the first take was the best ("touched by the hand of God"). A composite narration was created from the two takes to create a twenty-eight-minute monologue. (The rest of the audiotape, as well as approximately fifty hours of film outtakes, was destroyed in a fire at Alfred Leslie's studio several years later.)

Kerouac next turned his efforts to *Doctor Sax.* He praised Grove Press for its sensitive proofreading, marvelous typesetting, and attention to detail. For the title page, he submitted a penciled sketch of Doctor Sax and assured editor Jeanne Unger that if there were no further mistakes to be found, the book was ready for publication in April. The novel, with its mix of realism and mysticism, was, he told Stella Sampas, an "honor of art." Most important for its author, *Doctor Sax* was a departure from the type of work associated with "bearded beatniks." Its focus was Lowell, his refuge from the present world: "The Lowell of my mind satisfies my need for Lowell as I get older. The Lowell of my mind is my only Lowell. Lowell was a kingdom."[2]

In February 1959, Dody Muller went the same route as Joyce Glassman and Helen Weaver. Jack was too erratic to settle down at that point in his life, even though he thought of marriage. Kerouac reacted, according to Dody, emotionally rather than intellectually. "His plans never seemed to come through despite his best intentions. Jack was too unsettled."[3] Dody loved him, but she was tired of his drunkenness, mood swings, and obnoxious intrusions (often accompanied by rowdy sycophants) into her art studio. Also, the ever protective Gabrielle disliked Dody's dark complexion and bohemian lifestyle. Dody wanted to focus only on her painting and not be embroiled in a turbulent, emotional love affair. Drunk on Old Crow highballs, Kerouac wrote to John Clellon Holmes—one of the few who could tolerate Jack's behavior of late—and lamented losing once more a woman whom he loved. He wanted true love, but felt too "old" and "fat" to be desirable to anyone at all. His view of himself stemmed more from self-loathing than from his actual looks. Kerouac's appearance on the *Steve Allen Show* that year shows a man with the same charm and rugged good looks as the photograph on *The Town and the City* dust jacket.

Furthermore, he was unhappy that he had alienated some friends and sensed a distancing from Gary Snyder ever since the publication of *The Dharma Bums*. But his sense of betrayal did not alter his behavior for the better. Using as an excuse his deadline for two *Holiday* articles, he backed out of a March reading engagement with Ginsberg, Corso, and Orlovsky scheduled at Harvard University. Kerouac appeared instead at the Artist's Club on February 15. He stood dramatically on a stepladder with arms outstretched and recited portions of *On the Road* to an enraptured audience, including Ginsberg, Corso, and LeRoi Jones. At a reading several weeks later by Frank O'Hara, Kerouac was in the audience. He began drunkenly criticizing O'Hara: "You're ruining American poetry, O'Hara!" In response to Kerouac's jeering, O'Hara countered, "That's more than you ever did for it."[4] Later, when O'Hara saw Kerouac at the Cedar Bar, Kerouac asked, "What's the matter, don't you like me?" O'Hara responded, "It's your writing I like—it's not you."[5]

Kerouac was wary of appearing in public, on or off the stage. Gabrielle had warned him not to get "plastered so often," as he did whenever he was in New York. Her concern pushed her to the extreme of allowing Ginsberg, Orlovsky, and Corso into her house so as to stop Jack from making ill-fated visits to the city. Besides affecting his health, drinking contributed to his slovenly appearance and lowered his productivity. "I just noticed today it all began last April right after that bum pounded my brain head with his big fingered fist ring . . . maybe I got brain damage, maybe once I was kind of drunk, but now am brain-clogged drunk with the kindness valve clogged by injury."[6]

Tapped dry, Kerouac took out his notebooks ("Book of Sketches," "Tics & Daydreams," earlier called "Tics") from May and June 1953 and considered publishing them. He also assumed editorial responsibilities for an anthology commissioned by Avon Books. The twenty-five-cent *Beat Generation Anthology* was to be published three times a year. Kerouac would have the final say over its contents. He began to solicit material from Ginsberg, Michael McClure, Chris MacClaine, Philip Whalen, William Everson, Samuel Greenberg, and Lawrence Ferlinghetti. He intended to include material collected over the years from various contingents of the New York scene as well as excerpts of letters from Cassady and Ginsberg and the August 1958 letter from Corso, who would not consent to publication unless he got paid a lot of "loot, a good sum too."[7] Kerouac worked through the spring, but soon began to fear that his efforts would be in vain. Avon, he felt, was dragging its feet. Kerouac suspected that Avon's new owner, William Randolph Hearst, would break the deal, and indeed the project was canceled.[8]

The publication of *Doctor Sax* did even less to further his literary reputation or to earn him much-needed money. On the day of its publication, a book party was held in his honor, but Kerouac failed to appear. Writing to Barney Rossett, he apologized, explaining that he got drunk with a "colored girl" instead.[9] Kerouac was dismayed that *Doctor Sax* did not receive major reviews beyond David Dempsey's critique in the *New York Times:* "'Dr. Sax' is not only bad Kerouac; it is a bad book. Much of it is in bad taste, and much more is meaningless. It runs the gamut from the incoherent to the incredible, a mishmash of avant-gardism (unreadable), autobiography (seemingly Kerouac's) and fantasy (largely psychopathic)."[10]

Barnaby Conrad of *Saturday Review* was even less appreciative:

> The result, unhappily, seems to me to be "stupefying in its unreadability." "Doctor Sax" is a series of mystical, unorganized reminiscences of an autobiographical nature, the formula of which seems to have been: take one part of the murkiest of Kafka, two parts of Wolfe's streamingest thoughts, three parts of the most scatological of Joyce, and then mix them all together with neither taste nor selectivity.[11]

Time magazine did respond favorably ("Kerouac's best book"), but it did not help sales. *Doctor Sax,* issued as a trade paperback, vanished from store shelves and was remaindered. Kerouac corresponded with Lawrence Fer-linghetti about issuing *Old Angel Midnight,* to which he had added new chapters.

By the end of June, the house on Gilbert Street had been sold. The buyers did not assume occupancy until August, so Kerouac, having sent his mother to Florida, stayed in the empty house and slept on the floor. He was still intent on building a duplex. Kerouac wrote to Caroline fran-tically trying to solidify his plans. His joint checking account with Gabrielle would make it easier for Caroline to pay the builders. He even offered to pay the first month's rent for the temporary housing that they would need. With Caroline overlooking construction and keeping Gabrielle company, Jack would be free to travel to Mexico City.

Mexico City Blues was in production at Grove Press, as was *Maggie Cas-sidy* (due out in July 1959).[12] *Maggie Cassidy,* for which Kerouac was paid $7,500, would be marketed as a novel by the "Bard of the Beat Genera-tion," despite Cowley's belief that it was "too thin" to stand on its own. The ad copy assured prospective readers that *Maggie Cassidy* revealed a "startling new dimension" in Kerouac's "personality" by creating a "bril-liant and profoundly moving novel of adolescence and first love." Again, the critics attacked. Like *Doctor Sax, Maggie Cassidy* was soon remain-dered. To repeat the scenario a third time, *Mexico City Blues* was published mere months after *Maggie Cassidy.* It was a more difficult read for Ameri-cans spoon-fed on anthologized canonical poetry. The free-form poems bordered on gibberish to those unaccustomed to spontaneous prose.

James Laughlin asked Kerouac to write a preface for the December limited-edition publication of *Visions of Cody,* to be published in selected excerpts—by Kerouac's estimate, it was a fourth of the manuscript in full. Kerouac also completed the typing of *Old Angel Midnight* and drew a de-sign that he hoped to have on its cover. He also typed 250 pages of *Book of Sketches.* His adamant desire to build in Florida spurred him on. In Au-gust, the plans collapsed, and Kerouac found himself temporarily home-less. In Northport he scoured the newspaper for another home. By Octo-ber 1959, he found an unassuming house on Earl Avenue. He moved into it just as *Mexico City Blues* was presented to readers who, for the most part, concluded that Kerouac would not be writing another *On the Road* anytime soon.

27

"I Am the Flames"

October 1959–October 1960

Constantly risking absurdity
and death
whenever he performs
above the heads
of his audience

LAWRENCE FERLINGHETTI, "Constantly Risking Absurdity"

Despite Kerouac's conviction that his brain had been damaged by his Village beating, he continued experimenting with narcotics. In October 1959, he ingested mescaline and composed a "report" of its effects. Huddled in the blankets on his bed, he found that the effects of the drug were similar to his experiences with peyote, minus the nausea and vomiting. The mescaline hallucinations severed his birth-and-death preoccupations and left him floating in a blissful high. He realized that he was absolutely right about his spontaneous prose method, and he told Ginsberg that he contemplated this revelation in the light of a "haunted October moon." He planned to use mescaline monthly and to experiment further with LSD, which Ginsberg had offered him. In the short run, the high created a false sense of security in Kerouac, and he regarded the next few weeks with unflagging optimism.[1]

The new house in Northport was equipped with a telephone; Kerouac found its endless ringing bothersome. Herbert Huncke, released from Rikers Island, called Kerouac, needing a $25 loan. Kerouac told Ginsberg that though he relented and sent a check, he was not "Frank Sinatra." Telegrams and fan mail also intruded: "When I got home there were 30 letters and telegrams each one insanely demanding something. I see now clearly that I have to quit the whole scene for good. I don't want to see anyone or talk to anyone, I want to go back into my own mind. Its murder pure and simple."[2]

MGM wanted Kerouac to write a publicity piece for its film version of *The Subterraneans.* To escape this onerous obligation, he retreated to the West Coast. The trip west would last from early to mid-November 1959. He was scheduled to read on Steve Allen's November 16 television show and to speak at a film festival where *Pull My Daisy* was to be honored as the "Best American Experimental Film of 1959." Also on Jack's itinerary was a visit to Cassady, who was doing time in San Quentin.[3]

The first of Kerouac's eleven bimonthly columns appeared in the June 1959 issue of *Escapade.* It was a forum in which he could reveal his views without fear of ridicule or confrontation. In his first column Kerouac defended his literary technique:

> My position in the current American literary scene is simply that I got sick and tired of the conventional English sentence which seemed to me so ironbound in its rules, so inadmissible with reference to the actual format of my mind as I had learned to probe it in the modern spirit of Freud and Jung, that I couldn't express myself through that form any more. How many sentences do you see in current novels that say, "The snow was on the ground, and it was difficult for the car to climb the hill"? By the childish device of taking what was originally two short sentences, and sticking in a comma with an "and," these great contemporary "craftsmen" think they have labored out a sentence. As far as I can see it is two short sets of imagery belonging to a much longer sentence the total imagery of which would finally say something we never heard before if the writer dared to utter it out.[4]

He also assured *Escapade's* readers that the best literature that America had to offer was yet to come. There was Burroughs's *Naked Lunch,* Corso's and Ginsberg's poetry, and finally his own *Book of Dreams, Some of the Dharma,* and *Visions of Cody* (an excerpt of which he would submit as his last column in April 1960).

The October column dipped into Buddhism, a topic he had not touched in the last year:

I see that I *have* reached the other shore because it no longer matters to me about "happiness" in this or any other world, "crossing the shore" has simply been the recognition that there's nothing to yearn after, nothing to think, my Essence of Mind, the universal One Sea of mysterious mentality, so that I raise a private toast to my mother and all beings (silently) wishing them the Sweet Dharma Truth instead of a Happy "New Year"—the sweet Dharma Truth, the unrecognizable recognition that which blots out (as snow blots out the blottable pitiful shapeliness of ogroid earth—[5]

On November 12, a train left Grand Central terminal heading for California with Kerouac in one of its boxcars. He was still reeling from the sting of a television parody that he had seen the previous night. He did feel, though, some sense of accomplishment: he had completed typing "Book of Sketches" and was ready to take on his notebooks containing "Tics & Daydreams."

In Hollywood, Kerouac appeared, somewhat nervously, on Steve Allen's show. Before the taping, the show's producers and Allen urged Kerouac to rehearse, but he refused. During the taping, though, Kerouac performed splendidly. Looking gaunt and distant, holding *On the Road* before him, Jack read a passage from *Visions of Cody* that he had taped into the book. He was more determined than ever to show that his real writing had yet to appear in print. (After he left Allen's piano and went to the side of the soundstage, Kerouac vomited.) In Seattle, Caroline watched her brother's performance with friends gathered in her living room.

The rest of the California trip was a shambles. Kerouac had been scheduled to be a guest speaker at a comparative religion class taught at San Quentin by Gavin Arthur, who had read *On the Road*. Gary Snyder promised to introduce Arthur to Cassady and predicted that he would be the first person to enroll in the course. Right away, Arthur sensed who Cassady was when he noticed his face beaming with enthusiasm. After the class, Cassady introduced himself by saying that Arthur might know him better as Dean Moriarty. In future classes Arthur brought in guest speakers, including Snyder and Ginsberg. The next scheduled speaker was Kerouac, but he failed to show up. Three consecutive parties weakened his commitment. Arthur attempted unsuccessfully to reschedule Kerouac's appearance for the following day, but Kerouac was still hungover. To fill in for Kerouac, Arthur solicited Alan Watts, who dutifully made it.[6]

A visit to the Metro-Goldwyn-Mayer studio spent watching film rushes of *The Subterraneans* was fruitless, as Kerouac declined to provide any publicity for the bastardized version of his novel. In the film, Mardou Fox was now a white woman played by Leslie Caron. The ending of the film would sell out the novel. Mardou would get pregnant and Leo would promise to get a job and marry her. Presumably, director Ranald MacDougall, following the screenplay by Robert Thom, preferred to see the lovestruck heroine steered onto the path of respectability. Kerouac's stay was dotted with occasional meals with Hollywood executives and a party held in his honor at the Matador.

Negative publicity continued to dog Kerouac. This time, it was *Life* magazine, which launched an attack on Kerouac's public image. The November 30, 1959, feature was written by staff journalist Paul O'Neil. The title of the article, "Beats: Sad But Noisy Rebels," was emblazoned on *Life*'s glossy cover. O'Neil aimed to highlight the beats' dislike of all things materialistic. He disparaged Kerouac's athletic experience at Columbia and compared his writing to "goulash." The journalist's bitterness was evident. O'Neil also didn't do any favors for Carolyn Cassady, who had kept her husband's incarceration a secret from her family. O'Neil mentioned not only his stay in San Quentin but also the crime that put him there, calling Cassady the "Johnny Appleseed of the Marijuana Racket." After being told that her sister and father had read the article, Carolyn approached her mother, who responded that it would have been "better" if Neal had killed his children rather than disgrace their name.[7]

When attending the film festival in San Francisco, an intoxicated Kerouac fell from the stage. This incident did not help the reception of *Pull My Daisy*, which was either greeted with hostility and suspicion or dismissed outright. Albert Saijo, a student of Zen Buddhism, and poet Lew Welch offered to drive Kerouac from California to Northport. Saijo recalls:

Shortly after we moved into Hyphen-House [a communal house in San Francisco] we heard that Jack was coming to San Francisco from Hollywood where he had appeared on the Steve Allen Show. Then he was there, in the kitchen, seated at the table, with red plaid hunting cap sat back on his head, and red check flannel shirt worn with tails out, and dress slacks with creases gone, knockabouts on his feet, looking downhome and French-Canadian. He was then at the height of his fame after *On the Road, The Subterraneans,* and *The Dharma Bums.* He looked tired and he was drinking heavily, but he appeared to be on a binge and determined to party on. He never lacked company. His celebrity drew company.[8]

Welch's Willys Jeepster (nicknamed "Willy"), with its mattress in the back, an extra two-gallon gas can, a new tire, and a cracked windshield, was primed for a trip east. However, they feared bad weather in the Rockies and wanted to drive further south before turning the car east. In Chinatown Jack shopped for souvenirs for his mother. In the Mojave Desert, he initiated a morning jog. The car ride across country was, to Kerouac, an "enlightening trip." With a St. Christopher medal affixed to the dashboard, they drove to Las Vegas, where Lew Welch lost $22. As they traversed the United States, the trio composed collaborative poetry. Saijo was in the backseat, and Kerouac was in the front with Welch, who recorded their on-the-spot haiku in his yellow notebook. In Arizona, they pulled the car to the side of the road, and Kerouac yanked a wooden cross left there to mark an automobile fatality. He later gave the cross to Ginsberg.[9]

By the first week of December, they were in New York. They stopped by Ginsberg and Orlovsky's Second Street apartment to visit before going on to Long Island. On Earl Avenue in Northport, Gabrielle was there to greet them and cook dinner. Jack showed Welch and Saijo his attic study with its straight-back chair, desk, and electric typewriter. Welch and Saijo slept the night in comfortable beds before heading back west. Kerouac bade his friends farewell and settled into his new home.

Before long, he was again immersed in the self-destructive behavior that would dominate the final nine years of his life.[10] Philip Whalen came to visit Kerouac in Northport, but failed to rouse either him or Gabrielle from their drunken slumber. In his "Handelian" attic Kerouac wrote in his journals and typed old material from his notebooks, as the *Messiah* boomed from his phonograph. That December, Barney Rossett held a reception for *Mexico City Blues.* Kerouac appealed once more to Rossett to publish the complete *Visions of Cody.* Rossett refused, since *New Directions* had recently published its limited edition of excerpts. Jack wanted to publish *Old Angel Midnight* with Ferlinghetti's City Lights, but the literary journal *Big Table,* under the impression that it retained exclusive publishing rights, was uncooperative. He offered Ferlinghetti a number of different manuscripts, including the complete text of "October in the Railroad Earth"; his play, *The Beat Generation; Book of Dreams;* "Book of Sketches"; and *Some of the Dharma.* Since Ferlinghetti's specialty was his Pocket Poets series, such voluminous submissions could have been published only in excerpted form. For now, Ferlinghetti paid Kerouac for the publishing rights to a poem, "Rimbaud," which City Lights printed as a broadside.

> Screaming in the barn
>   Rimbaud writes Season in Hell,
> his mother trembles—
> Verlaine sends money & bullets
>   into Rimbaud—
>   Rimbaud goes to the police
>   & presents his innocence
>   like the pale innocence
>   of his divine, feminine Jesus
> —Poor Verlaine, 2 years
> in the can, but could have
> got a knife in his heart[11]

Jack met with Alfred Leslie about publishing his narration for *Pull My Daisy* (published by Grove Press in July 1961). Offers of publication from small presses and periodicals continued to stream in as Kerouac became gradually preoccupied with his health, both physical and mental. His hopes of reviving his literary reputation hinged on the success of *Mexico City Blues.* Kenneth Rexroth crushed those hopes in the pages of the *New York Times*: "It's all there, the terrifyingly skillful use of verse, the broad knowledge of life, the profound judgements, the almost unbearable sense of reality. I've always wondered what ever happened to those wax work figures in the old rubber-neck dives in Chinatown. Now we know; one of them at least writes books."[12]

It was, Kerouac felt, not objective criticism but was based on Rexroth's less-than-favorable estimate of him as a person. Kerouac told Gary Snyder that Rexroth lied on television when he stated that Kerouac was shooting heroin in front of his children. Despite Rexroth's harsh criticism, Jack liked his poetry and praised its qualities to Snyder. Rexroth, however, was not alone in his views, as others ran with his criticism. The backlash caused a despondent Kerouac to feel that he could no longer express himself without critics dissecting his every word. But the vicious and unrelenting criticism did not extend beyond the United States. Increasingly, his work was being translated and read by audiences in other countries more attuned to its spiritual sensibilities: Sweden, Germany, France, Spain, Japan, and Holland. Most of his income came from these translations.

The sad cycle of Kerouac's life continued. Kerouac brooded over his weight as a blizzard covered Long Island. Another Christmas with lonely Mémère, who missed her daughter and grandson, and Kerouac filled the Earl Avenue home with the sounds of *St. Matthew's Passion* drifting from the attic. At his desk he typed a letter to Ginsberg, whom Ferlinghetti had invited to a poetry reading in Santiago, Chile. He promised to send Ginsberg a copy of his Hanover LP released in October 1959, *Blues and Haikus*. The record featured pianist Al Cohn and saxophonist Zoot Sims backing Jack as he read "American Haikus" and other poems.

By year's end, *Tristessa* had been sold to Avon Books for $7,500. Despite the sale, he continued with a new work, "Beat Traveler," to boost his lagging income. However, he needed a kick start to begin writing. He asked a local doctor for a prescription for Benzedrine. To "offset" the negative effects of the amphetamine, Kerouac also asked for a phenobarbital. Thinking that Kerouac had suicidal tendencies, the physician refused. Instead, he agreed to prescribe Dexamyls. Kerouac wrote to his editor Donald Allen asking for a connection to acquire some Benzedrine. Kerouac promised in return to sell "Beat Traveler" to Grove Press and even to reduce his writing to the "simple prose" found in *On the Road* and *The Dharma Bums*.[13] Before long, Donald Allen came through with the drugs. Fortified with speed, Kerouac rolled a sheet of paper into his typewriter on January 17 and tried to begin writing. However, despite the Benzedrine coursing through his system, he could not get started. Kerouac continued to write his *Escapade* column but did not complete much else. To buttress his writing efforts, he read the second volume of Proust's *Remembrance of Things Past*, Erich Fromm (he thought the psychoanalyst's findings were "phoney shit"), and a new book by D. T. Suzuki.[14]

Kerouac wrote to a woman he had been seeing, Lois Sorrels, announcing his plans finally to get a driver's license in the spring.[15] The next day, he again attempted to write "Beat Traveler"—to no avail. By mid-February, the novel had hardly progressed at all: four false starts were all he had to show for his efforts. It was evident that he was wrong about the creative efficacy of Benzedrine. Amphetamines didn't fuel his novels of the early 1950s; pure, burning ambition motivated him. After completing forty thousand words, Kerouac put the manuscript away. The work would eventually emerge as *Lonesome Traveler,* a collection of travelogue pieces assembled piecemeal along with such high-caliber prose as "October in the Railroad Earth," retitled "The Railroad Earth."

All of his poet acquaintances were publishing new work. The answer to his writing problems, Kerouac felt, was to leave Northport. He blamed some of his writer's block on the constant stream of visitors, and he planned to buy a cabin with acreage in upstate New York, much to Gabrielle's chagrin. She told Caroline that she was "working overtime" to dislodge these plans from her son's mind. Whatever she did to thwart his plans eventually succeeded. To Kerouac's detriment, Gabrielle continued to interfere with his life. He needed to get away, to feel like the Ti Jean of old, to reorganize his splintered identity. He felt that the "monster they've built up in the papers is beginning to take shape inside my body like Burroughs' 'Stranger.'"[16] Kerouac also felt that the beat philosophy, which he held to be sacred, had been co-opted by "political types" like Norman Mailer and "West Venice Communists," and he feared that the beat movement would become a leftist political movement undermined by "brutality" and "racism."[17]

> The original idea of Beatific Joy such as was experienced by Sal Paradise in *On the Road* and by the narrator of *Howl* to some extent and by Neal in his letters and by the Hart Kennedy in Holmes' *Go* . . . all that will be lost in social get-togetherness (since Beatitude is and has always been an individualistic phenomena, as is pointed out in William James' chapter on *The Value of Saintliness*). . . . In short, as I am still Beatific in my personal reverence for God's show in its Essence, and still pray occasionally in solitude, and am going to end my life more or less of a religiously minded hermit, I have no more to do with Beatnikness as it is coming to be now.[18]

Kerouac prepared a newly typed version of *Book of Dreams.* This latest version included dreams not in the original manuscript. In June, Ferlinghetti returned the manuscript, and Kerouac penciled in further name changes. Ferlinghetti suggested that he delete passages that mentioned his former wives. As with his other novels, Kerouac had ideas for its cover. Although he mentioned using a photo by Fred McDarrah, Ferlinghetti chose a photo by Robert Frank showing Kerouac sleeping on a bed during their trip to Florida. Not wishing to retype the *Book of Dreams* manuscript, Kerouac penciled in his changes and mailed it back to City Lights. Philip Whalen agreed to retype the work once it reached San Francisco.[19]

Jack's romance with Lois Sorrels continued. According to a letter to Ginsberg, she made it through Gabrielle's doorway and had sex with Kerouac in his attic.[20] When he wasn't with Lois, he taped jazz from the local radio station WFAM and, so inspired, wrote an *Escapade* column about his friend Seymour Wyse, who once claimed that jazz was "dead." In a provocative essay published in *Escapade* in December 1960, Kerouac proved differently, listing a who's who of jazz's greatest trumpeters, saxophonists, pianists, scat singers, and bass players, among others.

Ferlinghetti offered Jack the use of his cabin in Big Sur. Kerouac accepted the invitation and planned to leave Long Island in the summer of 1961. He had good reasons for wanting to leave. That June saw the film premiere of *The Subterraneans*. The film tanked and received dismal reviews, with an exceptionally brutal one from *Time:*

> The bushy-bearded Beat Generation is a collective hair farm that the average solid citizen does not dig. Nevertheless, in this picture, which bears about as much relationship to Jack Kerouac's novel as Hollywood does to Endsville, producer Arthur Freed attempts to sell the beatniks back to the mass culture they are desperately and often comically trying to escape. He shaves them down, scrubs them up and presents them, in deadly earnest, as pioneers in the great American tradition, as "the Young Bohemians . . . the makers of the future." Unhappily, the notion is so translucently ludicrous and the picture so poorly put together that in box-office terms all this cold water flattery will probably get the movie-makers nowhere.[21]

Despite the film's poor reception, the movie distracted Kerouac from his work. More urgently than ever, he sought escape from New York, if only to continue reworking *Book of Dreams*. In July, Kerouac boarded a train for Chicago, where he transferred to the Zephyr to Oakland. For the first time in a long time, he was happy watching his beloved America flying past the roomette's window seat—much better than hopping a flatcar and enduring inclement weather. He found it "all so easy and dreamlike compared to my harsh hitch hikings before I made enough money to take transcontinental trains." En route, he brewed instant coffee and ate the sandwiches that he had prepared at home.[22]

In Oakland he found a room in a motel and woke with the same sickness and self-loathing that had greeted his Long Island mornings. He could hear the moans in nearby rooms, vomiting drunks, and the creaking of ancient steps. It was, he knew, the creepings of delirium tremens, every bit as vicious and unrelenting as those associated with kicking heroin. That same night, Kerouac hoisted his rucksack—with a St. Christopher medal sewn into a flap by Gabrielle—and boarded a bus to Monterey. It arrived just after midnight. Kerouac hired a cab to take him the rest of the way, fourteen more miles, to Big Sur. Kerouac knew that finding Ferlinghetti's cabin in this unfamiliar terrain was next to impossible, so he laid his rucksack in the sand and slept by a murmuring creek.

In the morning, Kerouac crossed the bridge. He was silenced and a bit intimidated by the vastness of the canyon. He shuddered when he looked over the railings and saw the remnants of a car that had plunged over the side of the bridge. Once he crossed, he saw a lone mule, which he named Alf. Before long, he found the cabin. He rested on a cot on the porch and wondered whether he could last alone out there for three weeks.

At night, the only things that kept Kerouac company were Big Sur's nocturnal offerings: a bat fluttering in his cabin, a rat skittering over his head while he was lying down, outside a raccoon scraping near the cabin, in the hollows of the canyon an owl hooting. In the corner of his cabin he laid out a meal of cheese and chocolate for a resident mouse. When his sleeping bag ripped and the down feathers began poking out, Jack repaired it by hand with his sewing kit. By the light of a kerosene lantern, he read Ferlinghetti's copy of *Dr. Jekyll and Mr. Hyde,* and during the days took his notebook to the beach to write. Despite the breathtaking view, Kerouac found the experience saddening; even the flies were as "sad as the fog on the peaks."[23]

The Big Sur trip began to unfold miserably for him. The thirst for alcohol got the better of him, but he still managed to complete some new work. Sitting by the sea and watching waves crash against the cliffs, Kerouac composed in mid-August a poem, "Sea," in which he re-created the sounds of the ocean in words (imitating Joyce):

> Breathe our iodine, filthy yr drink,
> faint at feet wet, drop
>   yr profile move it in the sea,
> float weeded watery Adonais
>   longs for thee—& Shelley three,
>   that's three—burn in salt
> with slow most change—
>   We've had no crack at eternity
> in a billion years of trying—
>   one grain of sand possesses
> 3 thousand worlds of glee—
> not to mention me—
> Ah sea[24]

Looking up, he saw the headlights of cars crossing the bridge high above. Kerouac wondered if the drivers, tucked safely behind their steering wheels, knew that he was in the remote depths of the canyon "in all that windy fury sitting in the dark writing in the dark." One day Kerouac hiked from the beach, up the canyon trail, and back onto the highway to mail some letters. Soon afterward, he left the cabin to return to San Francisco. He cut a lonely figure hitchhiking along the highway, traveling seven miles without one car stopping to offer him a ride. The soles of his boots wore thin, and his feet blistered in the late August heat that melted the tar of the road. He sat at the side of the road, took off his boots, and soothed his feet as best he could with his first-aid kit. A small truck pulled over, and the driver offered him a ride to the next gas station. When the driver saw the condition of Kerouac's feet, he took Jack straight to the bus station in Monterey.

In San Francisco, in a reasonably comfortable skid-row motel room, Kerouac slept soundly that night. The next morning, he went to City Lights and found Ferlinghetti, who told Kerouac that his cat, Tyke, was dead. Kerouac was devastated. The cat had died the day after he left New York, and Gabrielle buried it in the backyard under the house's honeysuckle vines amid—as she noted in a letter to her son—a chorus of noisy starlings. It was, for the sensitive Kerouac, as upsetting as the news of Gerard's death had been. Jack was concerned for his mother, who was alone in the house and who had taken to barring the front door after some unwanted visitors broke a pane of glass in search of the absent writer.

Kerouac predictably began an exhausting drunken bar crawl through North Beach, chugging down double bourbons and ginger ale. Accompanying him was Philip Whalen, who watched with helpless alarm the cycle of Kerouac's self-abuse. Whalen left Kerouac to pursue quiet study of his own and only saw him sporadically for the rest of Jack's West Coast stay.

Kerouac also met Cassady, newly freed from San Quentin. His release, on June 3, 1960, into mainstream society saw for the moment a rehabilitated Neal. In prison, he had been taking courses in the school of religion, even earning an award of recognition for the successful completion of a course called "Meaning of Life in Buddhism."[25] The shift was not a hard one because of his incarceration. Cassady had attained the bliss Kerouac only wished for. To support his family, Cassady had a job waiting for him recapping tires—the only job available for a convicted felon. Neal promised Carolyn that he would do right by her and even bought matching gold rings to seal their marriage vows. However, he had a woman on the side, Jacqueline Gibson, with whom he had been corresponding regularly and who wanted him to divorce Carolyn as soon as he was released.

One night a banging on the patio door announced Kerouac, accompanied by a few drinking friends (including Lew Welch and Paul Smith, a musician). The visit arose from Kerouac's spur-of-the-moment desire to introduce Welch to the real-life Dean Moriarty. However, Neal was working late and was not at home. When Carolyn greeted him with a kiss, the sodden Kerouac pushed her away and barked gruffly a "crude remark." Shocked, Carolyn phoned Neal, who told her to have them come by the shop after midnight when his boss had left. Although Carolyn offered to make dinner for them, Kerouac decided to buy dinner elsewhere and bring it back. Over the course of the visit, his demeanor changed and he warmed to Carolyn. After midnight they left to see Neal, and before long, they were back with both cars careening into the driveway, breaking the stillness of the Los Gatos suburb. Kerouac, Welch, and Smith slept over that night. The next morning, a somewhat sober Kerouac awoke to find Carolyn making coffee. It relieved Carolyn that he had forgotten their initial encounter. They sat and talked. She noted that one thing had changed about Kerouac: he did not make any more promises to quit drinking. "He knew he was being slowly pulled down into the quagmire, and his will was too weak to resist. His tormented eyes foretold the future, his face like that of a character from Poe."[26]

Kerouac made plain to her the ruinous effect fame had on his mental and physical health. Buddhism, he told her, was useless, as were the last three weeks in Big Sur, which only added boredom to his bleak life. Soon, the other two men woke, eager to get back to the city. Before they left, Carolyn drove Kerouac to a liquor store to get some wine. They returned and said good-bye to Neal, who was still sleeping off his late night. A few days afterward, Neal was laid off precisely when his mortgage was due. In desperation he asked Kerouac for a loan. Kerouac agreed, eager to contribute after all the times the Cassadys had put him up in their home. Soon thereafter, Kerouac appeared at their Los Gatos house en route to Big Sur. With him were Lawrence Ferlinghetti, local artist Victor Wong, and Philip Whalen. Since Neal was unemployed, he went to Big Sur with them, violating his probation.

It was a great get-together of artists and poets. Michael McClure drove down to Big Sur with his wife. At night they read their poems aloud, with Kerouac holding court and reading "Sea." During the visit to the cabin Kerouac took an interest in Wong's art. Wong had brought along his colored pencils and paper and set to work impressing and inspiring Kerouac. The next day, they all went skinny-dipping in the hot springs, except for Neal and Jack.

Kerouac noted of Cassady in *Big Sur*: "ever since he's come out of San Quentin there's been something hauntedly boyish about him as tho prison walls had taken all the adult dark tenseness out of him."[27] Neal returned home and found work with the Los Gatos Tire Company. Soon after he started his latest job, a maroon jeep replaced the run-down Rambler. The Cassadys decided to test their new vehicle by driving to Big Sur after Neal finished work on Friday. It would be, they thought, a surprise for Jack. After a terrifying taste of Cassady's driving along Big Sur's sinuous cliff highways, they arrived at the cabin. Neal knocked on the door before opening it wide. A wave of California sunshine swept the darkened interior, save for the last flickering embers in the hearth. Kerouac had been talking to Michael McClure about his poem, "Fuck Ode," when they saw Cassady's arm reaching toward them from the doorway. It was, to Kerouac, the arm of an "archangel." Seventeen-year-old Paul Smith had been sitting hearthside, McClure's wife Joanna and their child at a table. Neal and Carolyn approached them laughing. Kerouac yelled out, "My God! It's a band of angels."

That day they left Big Sur for Old Town. Carolyn had become involved in a theatrical production. She was enthusiastic about sharing this interest with Jack. When they arrived at a roadside café, Kerouac, who was drinking beer and wine intermittently, refused to eat anything. The Cassadys left him and went into the café. Before long, the wail of sirens sounded. The interior of the Cassadys' new Jeep was in flames, which were promptly extinguished. Kerouac, present when it happened, was assumed to be at fault, although he was never confronted. A cigarette was found smoldering between two mattresses.

During the ride to the theater, Carolyn noted that as Jack became more inebriated, Neal became increasingly aloof. Arriving late in Old Town, Neal dropped Carolyn off and then took Jack away from the dressing room, where he was embarrassing himself by imitating the western drawl of the owner, Frank Dean. In a nearby saloon, Kerouac banged on the player piano, bawling western songs till he was thrown out. Angry, frustrated, and tearful, Carolyn was furious at Neal and Jack for taking no interest in her work. Neal suggested that she find a ride back on her own. He took Kerouac to meet Jacqueline, a single mother of one boy, in the hopes that she and Jack would become romantically involved and save Cassady's marriage.[28]

Neal's matchmaking was a dubious proposition at best. Carolyn felt that Neal intended to prove that he was through with his mistress. One week later, Kerouac appeared at the Cassady home to retrieve the knapsack that he had left there and to have Carolyn sew a tear in his flannel shirt. Soon, Carolyn discovered that Kerouac had left Jacqueline sitting in the car with her son. Carolyn insisted that he bring the two inside. Once Jackie was in the house, she carried on a civil conversation about motherhood with Carolyn. Meanwhile, Neal paced the floor in a mix of jealousy and regret. This did not escape Kerouac's notice; he became sick with worry that he had angered his friend. At the urging of Lew Welch, they all left. It was the last time Carolyn would ever see Kerouac.[29]

Kerouac paid an extra $69 for red wine, champagne, pastries, and a steak dinner on the plane back to New York. As he flew over the country that he had crisscrossed so many times via foot, train, and car, Kerouac wrote in his journal. He was giddy with the prospect of using the past few weeks, bleak as they were, to create a future novel. He knew that he needed to write new material, since his stockpile of completed but unpublished "novels" had dwindled to a handful of oddball experimental works. *Tristessa,* published while Kerouac was at Big Sur, had received a warm, appreciative review from the *New York Times.* The critic, Daniel Talbot, sensed Kerouac's empathic nature and sincerity, remarking that despite being "embarrassing, even sloppy," inevitably he was "more truthful, entertaining and honest than most writers on the American scene."[30] Despite the praise, the cheesy pulp paperback would not generate significant revenue for Kerouac.

Once in Northport, Kerouac realized that he was at a crossroads. He had to choose whether to write easy-to-swallow works like *The Dharma Bums* or to pursue experimental works like "The Railroad Earth." He created in his notebook a revised listing of his Duluoz legend, this time adding five new installments. "Memory Babe" would span the years 1927 to 1936; *Vanity of Duluoz,* from 1939 to 1943; "Visions of Julien," from 1944 to 1946; "Beat Traveler," from 1957 to 1960; and an unnamed novel would document Kerouac's trip to Hollywood to read for Steve Allen.[31] The beat writing anthology that Kerouac had so arduously labored upon was returned to Sterling Lord with Kerouac's suggestion that his agent submit it to Dial Press. There was still work to be done on *Book of Dreams.*

Kerouac had ordered the eleventh edition of the *Encylopaedia Britannica,* for which he paid $35. He had first seen the set when he was sixteen years old in Lowell High School's library. When it arrived, he placed the set, all twenty-nine volumes, on his shelf to read whenever he wanted. Kerouac would avidly peruse the set for the remaining years of his life.[32] He also read Ferlinghetti's novel *Her* on the toilet for so long that he boasted a red ring around his ass: "*Her* is very good, will surprise lotta people, is strange long thinlegged shadow Paris sidewalk dream of birds."[33]

Hoping to re-create the flawed idealism of the Big Sur experience, despite his bad memories of the delirium tremens nightmare he had experienced there, Jack only assumed that it could be improved upon closer to his home turf. He once more broached the idea of buying a cabin somewhere in New England to Gabrielle. In September, Kerouac went north to Laconia, New Hampshire, a town nestled in the White Mountains, to look at some land for sale. Fearing that the purchase would signal a move back to Lowell, Gabrielle resisted until her son gave up. So he stayed in Northport, in the drab living room where his mother served him Christian Brothers port, and in his attic room playing his solitary baseball game and writing futile entries in his notebooks. At other times, he sat in the yard, bored and waiting for something to happen. When nothing did, he drank even more. To escape Gabrielle, he went into the city with increasing frequency. That fall, like so many Americans, Kerouac watched the presidential debates between John F. Kennedy and Richard M. Nixon. On election night, he stayed up till 5 A.M. watching Kennedy's victory, "fascinated" by "gatecrashing beatniks" who swarmed the headquarters of the Washington GOP. The next day, he went downtown to buy some books, the Frank Sinatra album *No One Cares*, a new winter coat and hat, and a pint of whiskey. He would play the Sinatra album when he made a tape of himself reading passages from *Dr. Sax* and *Old Angel Midnight* for Lois Sorrels.[34]

The following month, *Lonesome Traveler* was released. The motley collection of travel-themed pieces gave readers the opportunity to experience Kerouac's style in brief encounters. There was Kerouac's winter 1951 visit to San Pedro, California ("Piers of the Homeless Night"); his spring 1952 Mexican sojourn ("Mexico Fellaheen"); his 1952 railroad brakeman job ("The Railroad Earth"); his stint as a steward on the SS *William Carruthers* ("Slobs of the Kitchen Sea"); New York City jazz encounters sketched with his inquisitive eye ("New York Scenes"); fire watching in the High Cascades ("Alone on a Mountaintop"); an ill-fated winter 1957 jaunt through Europe ("Big Trip to Europe"); and a fine retrospective on changing America and its less-than-tolerant treatment of Kerouac's beloved vagrants ("The Vanishing American Hobo"). In the *New York Times*, freelance critic Daniel Talbot declared: "There really is not too much to say about this book, except that it is vintage Kerouac; it is not quite a travel book, nor is it quite fiction; it is again a collection of Kerouac's nerve-ends vs. the universe; it has flashes of poetry, truth, daffiness, lapses of embarrassing writing, and in the end is much more readable than most 183-page books I could think of."[35]

If the book was not a financial triumph for Kerouac, it was at least an artistic one. The truth and honesty of his writing style—only suggested in *On the Road*—was recognized, at last, by a major periodical.

PART 5

Ghostly Friend in God

28

The Sad Light of the Old Decade

October 1960–October 1962

When the universe fails to see Jack, then Jack will die.
GREGORY CORSO to ALLEN GINSBERG, fall 1958

It was time; it was the beginning of America's psychedelic revolution in which the country's youth questioned (sometimes violently) the Establishment's decision to send even more young men and women to be decimated by war. America's involvement in Vietnam was most noticeable when they began sending troops into the country from April 1965 until March 1968. The country's elders would be as beleaguered as Kerouac when the social revolt of their children was exemplified by growing their hair long, embracing mystical religions, experimenting with drugs, and, eventually, plugging their acoustic guitars into amplifiers. It was also the start of President Kennedy's New Frontier. After the sluggish Republican moderation of the 1950s, Kennedy's objective was to respark America's engine by calling for health care and increased expenditure on aid for education. However, the ultra-conservative majority in Congress would block such ideas from 1961 through 1963. Instead, the economy of the 1960s would be reinvigorated through foreign policy and the effort to exceed the Soviet Union's quest to reach space. The notion to "ban the bomb" would also come to symbolize the era. Worldwide demonstrations in France, Germany, and Britain would follow suit in America. Marches, demonstrations, rallies, and clashes with police would be seen with increasing regularity on the six o'clock news on televisions throughout America. However, Kerouac's concern for this was marginal, and he chose to spend the remainder of his short life writing, reading, and keeping up with his unquenchable thirst for alcohol, which was becoming more and more hopelessly an addiction.

In 1960, Kerouac was thoroughly disenchanted with America's perception of him as a "beatnik." He voiced his protest in the static pages of his notebook: "Realized last night how truly sick and tired I am of being a 'writer' and 'beat'—it's not me at all—yet everybody keeps hammering it into me—that's why I wanta be alone with the dumb beasts of the country so I begin to feel like Ti Jean again instead of their goddam *Jack Karrawack*." What Kerouac resented was the emphasis the public was placing on his celebrity instead of the books he was publishing with regularity. "They're going to INSIST that I fit their preconceived notion of the 'Beatnik Captain,' as tho I was some degenerate Bearded insurrectionist."[1] On a broader palette, Kerouac foresaw that his "vision of America" was being annihilated by the "beatnik movement"and that it was nothing more than "a big move-in from intellectual dissident wrecks of all kinds and now even anti-American, America-haters of all kinds with placards who call themselves *beatniks*." Kerouac recognized that his individualism made him fear the worst; he accurately predicted a split between two camps, "America-lovers" and "America-haters." But he was insistent that he would go on "scribbling" and, ultimately, get a cabin from which he could just "admire" and not "get involved in discussions about *society problems*."[2]

But the rumblings of America that Kerouac detested Allen Ginsberg thrived on. In the fall of 1960 Ginsberg had returned from Peru, where he consumed yage after an extensive search for the plant and drank it as a potion. The hallucinogenic experience opened a door: "I felt my body, like an independent serpent with a material universe life of its own, crawl over bend & curl on snakelike spasms of vomiting, assaulted by the Presence of the Knower which I identified with (rather than the serpent body) as an alien & superior permanent Ghost. Constantly interrupting into Matter at moments of radiant instability."[3]

Ginsberg composed some of his poetry in drug-induced bliss: yage, nitrous oxide, cocaine, and, eventually, LSD-25. Enthusiastic about the creative possibilities, he encouraged Kerouac to partake. On the evening of October 7, high on the ayahuasca potion that Allen had brought back from South America, Kerouac spontaneously composed a poem, with Ginsberg at his side transcribing.

Also he says he said, "God (for I was God to him
for a moment) why did you create the world?"—
　　　　　but then sighed back, to himself, "Oh-aghoh"—
Accepting! "Because to ask a personal god why he Created the
Being is tantamount to telling him to go kill himself—which
is not polite, nice"
　　　　　Also said—looking at me—"This is one of the most
sublime or tender or lovely moments of all our lives together . . ."
　　　　　I sat there feeling like a secret wizard.[4]

For three days in mid-October, Kerouac stayed with Allen at his East Second Street apartment. In a small way it echoed the first years of their
friendship during the mid-1940s. It also offered him a reprieve from his
mother's oppressive domination. In November, Ginsberg took his experimentation one step further by eating psilocybin mushrooms under the
guidance of Timothy Leary. Naked, Ginsberg wandered to a phone and
told the operator that he was God. After phoning William Carlos
Williams and Norman Mailer, and trying unsuccessfully to reach Nikita
Krushchev, Ginsberg called Kerouac in Northport to declare, "I am high
and naked and I am the King of the Universe. Get on the plane. It is
time!" Kerouac replied, "I can't. My mother won't let me go."[5]

In October Kerouac wrote a second preface for *Book of Dreams* after
discarding the first. He sent it to Ferlinghetti to use as "blurb notes" after
refusing to write a new one. To do so would cause him, he told Ferlinghetti, "weeks of anguish." What he did submit was effective for it gave
the confused reader a keyhole to peep through and witness Kerouac's *Book
of Dreams* creative process: "I wrote nonstop so that the subconscious
could speak for itself in its own form, that is, uninterruptedly flowing &
rippling—Being half awake I hardly knew what I was doing let alone writing."[6] However, his aesthetics were hardly ever a concern to his reading
public, for much of his work was reduced to fodder meant to capitalize on
the name of "Kerouac"; under that name, most of his readers sought to
fall again under the spell of *On the Road* and *not* the subconscious mean-
derings of his dream states. Kerouac, though, looked beyond the current
perception of him. In a letter written to a college instructor at Carnegie
Tech in Pennsylvania, Granville Jones, Kerouac asserted that "Academic
recognition" would bring importance to his art and not the "temporary
admiration for the wrong reasons coming from the wrong thinkers."[7]

On January 12, 1961, Kerouac went into the city to bring his tape recorder in for repairs and buy a new sleeping bag and rucksack. Afterward, he visited Lucien Carr and got drunk before dropping by Ginsberg's place to meet Timothy Leary. Kerouac took some LSD and concluded that attaining instant enlightenment was impossible: "Walking on water wasn't built in a day." In his journal, Kerouac expounded on the effects of LSD: "The psychic clairvoyance lasted till early this morning—I've been sleeping it off—(too much to live with, in fact too much for Samahdi peace)."[8]

Twenty years later Leary's interpretation was that Kerouac "opened the neural doors to the future, looked ahead, and didn't see his place in it." Kerouac was convinced that LSD was not the key to enlightenment. One of his more extravagant theories was that the drug was a communist strategy to brainwash America's youth. Nevertheless, he would drop acid every so often out of boredom or with friends.

During the month of January 1961, Kerouac experienced a number of setbacks, both professional and personal. *Book of Dreams,* published by City Lights, was not reviewed at all and subsequently sold poorly. This was exceptionally troubling to Kerouac, since he had chosen, for one of the few times in his life, to intentionally revise his writing. He deliberately changed some words like "fucking" to "boffing" in order to avoid having the book banned.[9] Also, *Lonesome Traveler* was remaindered. And one afternoon his doorbell rang and Jack was served a summons by Lewis B. Stackell, the attorney for his former wife Joan (Haverty) Aly, who was demanding $17,500 for back payment of child support.

Desperately, Kerouac retained Eugene Brooks as his attorney and prepared to foil Joan's efforts by demanding a paternity test. Joan assumed, like many, that Jack was living in luxury from the royalties of his numerous books, and she was convinced of his wealth. Joan told reporters that Kerouac's bank account held at least $50,000. Reading the papers and seeing them slam his name in print infuriated Kerouac and upset his family. Gabrielle was afraid to show her face in the Northport shops; she complained to Caroline that her nerves were shot from the constant negative publicity and the reporters who appeared constantly at the door. At one point, a stranger forced his way into the house. Kerouac told Philip Whalen: "An absolute stranger came in the house t'other night wanting to borrow $150! It's sinister. Everybody wants money; they're all doing ANYTHING for money. It wouldn't be so sinister if it hadn't been for the fact that I did *not* write my books in expectation of ever even publishing them let alone making money."[10]

Gabrielle was alarmed not only by the surge of negative publicity but also by how it frayed Jack's nerves. The publicity caused him to drink even more Christian Brothers port on the rocks every day. "He keeps himself 'stewed' to forget his troubles," she wrote Caroline.[11] Kerouac saw this flaw in himself and revealed that alcoholism was turning him into an "ugly ghoul."[12]

In an attempt to clear his name outside of court, Jack conceded to give his side of the story to the press. Alfred Arbelli, a reporter for the *New York Daily News*, was allowed into the Kerouac parlor. During the course of a few hours, Kerouac told him about the troubling months of 1951 in which Kerouac was certain Joan Haverty had committed adultery:

> I was compelled to leave the apartment in which we were living at my wife's insistence. Some weeks after our separation, I visited her at our apartment and attempted to make a reconciliation, but she met me at the outer door and told me I could not come in because another man was in bed. I did not even learn through her that she was pregnant, but only through a mutual friend. She later remarried and moved to Missouri and had twins by her second husband. Then, at the end of 1960, she separated from her second husband and returned to New York.[13]

Joan countered that she was burdened with all of the medical bills when Jan was born. Under the impression that Kerouac had sold a novel to Hollywood (possibly *The Subterraneans*), she figured that the time was ripe to collect much-needed income for Jan's upbringing. Desperate to slant the press in her favor, Joan conveniently revised history, declaring that Kerouac had abandoned *her* in June 1951.

The negative press and lawsuit soured Kerouac's immediate outlook. Joan's reappearance only intensified the misogyny that lurked within him. He told Philip Whalen that the solution to his problems was to have nothing more to do with women—not Lois Sorrels or Jacqueline Gibson, who he concluded was a "predator." However, his venting was short-lived, and Lois continued to visit him. The one woman from whom he should have distanced himself, the one whom he praised and pilloried during his drunken tirades, stoically remained Gabrielle.[14]

In February, Kerouac and Gabrielle assessed Kerouac's finances with Eugene Brooks after a court hearing before Justice Samuel Gold. Kerouac feared that any jury would be prejudiced against him and that the judge would lecture him "on my evil influence on American youth."[15] Kerouac had a doctor's note prepared stating his abnormally low sperm count. During this time, Jack's royalty statements revealed that he was earning only an average of $90 per week. Desperately, Joan sold her story to the magazine *Confidential,* which printed it under the blazing headline "My Ex-Husband Jack Kerouac Is an Ingrate."

Jack and Gabrielle endured Northport's hostile public opinion, but by the spring of 1961 they decided to sell their house and move back to Orlando. Caroline's family had also returned to Orlando with her husband and son. The Blakes and the Kerouacs each purchased a house on Alfred Drive, united in the belief that their familial bonding would improve their financial resources. Also, it was a relief for Jack to be able to share the responsibility for his mother's welfare.

Intellectually, Kerouac was in top form. He immersed himself in a vast array of reading materials, most of which dealt with Western philosophy: Schopenhauer, Kant, and Spinoza. They were, he concluded, "all great minds" who "agreed" with Buddha's precepts of enlightenment. Kerouac also read Ginsberg's newest work, "Kaddish," a mammoth and emotional poetic memorial to his mother, Naomi: "The whole package, with later visionary poems, makes one explosive book." To Kerouac, Ginsberg's impassioned writing took on the dimensions of a Dostoyevsky novel.

In subtle ways, Kerouac was gaining notoriety as a fresh and influential prose stylist—despite the all-too-common media baiting and the public focus on his personality rather than his work. He was impressed to hear that actor Charles Laughton had read from his books at Boston Symphony Hall, along with excerpts from Thomas Wolfe and Walt Whitman. Kerouac was also receiving numerous letters from college students writing theses on his work. He helped Boston College graduate student Bernice Lemire, also from Lowell, with her thesis, centered around the early influences of his formative years, Giving her permission to access his high school records, Kerouac explained the biographical parallels of his Lowell fiction, as well as aspects of his maternal and paternal genealogy. He also supplied her with boyhood contacts, like G. J. Apostolos and Henry Beaulieu.[16]

As Kerouac began asserting his political views, they increasingly revealed a conservative stamp. When Lawrence Ferlinghetti solicited Kerouac's support for the Fair Play for Cuba Committee (brought to infamy by New Orleans attorney general Jim Garrison's evidence of a link between Kennedy assassin Lee Harvey Oswald and his distribution of Fair Play for Cuba leaflets on New Orleans's Dumaine Street Wharf in June 1963), he responded that he had his own "revolution" in America. (Kerouac was never one to participate in any political demonstration, Burroughs recalled.)[17] Instead, Kerouac told Ferlinghetti that he and his fellow writers and poets should "join hands" in the spirit of poetry not politics.[18] Jack also questioned Ferlinghetti's choice of politics, asking him if Cuba's choice of the death penalty (the firing squad) was not "evil." Ferlinghetti replied to Kerouac that he was being "brainwashed by yer one-eyed cyclopses," the television set where Jack and Gabrielle spent so much of their time nursing their port and ice.[19]

Although Kerouac never voted, he preferred Eisenhower's vice president, Richard M. Nixon (but welcomed the new tenant in the White House, Democrat John F. Kennedy).[20] Later, Gabrielle became a staunch supporter of Kennedy, but for reasons of her own. In a January 21, 1961, *Time* article, First Lady Jacqueline Kennedy revealed that each week she read everything from "Colette to Kerouac."[21] This remark, Gabrielle gleefully hoped, would not only turn public opinion toward Kerouac but would also boost his lagging book sales.

Life in Orlando had not changed; the bleakness, boredom, and stifling heat predominated. A coma patient lived across the street, and behind their one-story terrazzo-floored ranchito, a new development of over a dozen houses was being built, "piling up more horror in what was my huge empty back field wastes of piney barrens."[22] However, he did have his privacy; his temporary anonymity allowed him to no longer have to hide behind the drapes when people knocked on his door. Nin lived two doors down and, with her 1960 Pontiac, could take Gabrielle shopping. Paul also had his own car, and Kerouac would join him on trips to area bars. Soon, the drinking escalated. In a bar where he and Paul drank, men laughed behind Jack's back. Even his nephew was embarrassed by his uncle's "silly behavior" when Jack appeared at his school. At home, his alcoholism intensified. He once remarked to Philip Whalen that he had finished off a fifth of Martell cognac but failed to see the damage alcohol in general was slowly doing to him: "But that cognac, after years of horrible hopeless nightmares, I see that Cognac as being at least the only drink in the world, with soda and ice, that won't actually kill you."[23] He confessed his "inadequacy" in the pages of his journal: "I'll be in an insane asylum soon (asylum)—Paralysis, melancholia, alcoholic manic depression, guilt horror, self inadequacy, maniacal appearance." At the bottom of the page he made his plea, "O God help me," and added a penciled sign of Christ's cross.[24]

To ward off the prison of reality, Kerouac took to writing. He gleaned some poems from his 1954 notebook and created a typescript he titled "San Francisco Blues." He sent the poem to Donald Allen, who promptly rejected it. Although Kerouac was eager to submit manuscripts such as *Desolation Angels,* Sterling Lord suggested that he slow the pace of submissions to avoid flooding the market with novels, something he should have advised after *The Dharma Bums* was published. Even an offer by Grove Press, which dangled a $1,000 advance for *Desolation Angels,* did not dissuade Lord from his belated commonsense strategy.

In June 1961, Kerouac went to Mexico City to revive his creative process. It was one of several last-ditch efforts. In May 1961, he had written to Timothy Leary requesting some "SM," or Siberian mushrooms (*Amanita muscaria*), after Ginsberg told him they would enable Jack to complete a chapter each day.[25] In Mexico City he rented 13-A Cerrada de Medellín, a "dismal dusty streetdoor apartment" where Burroughs had previously lived with his late wife. Kerouac scribbled by candlelight approximately fifty thousand words depicting the time spent in Berkeley with his mother. He also composed a poem, "Cerrada Medellin Blues," made up of two extended "solos" that, for once, took up longer than a page length. The first solo was separated into twelve choruses, the second into ten. In July 1961 he completed the work and set it aside to be later inserted into his *Book of Blues*:

> My hand is moved
> by holy angels
> The life we are in
> is invisible
> Holy Ghost[26]

Despite his burst of productivity, his stay was soured when thieves jimmied open his window while he was at a movie theater. Having left the theater (he was offended by a scene where Catholic nuns were about to be "laid") he returned to his room to find that his bathrobe, raincoat, sleeping bag, sweater, and prayer beads had been stolen.[27] Most importantly, for him, the thieves also made off with his notebook documenting his forty-first fantasy-baseball game (where his Cincinnati Blacks were in first place and the Detroit Reds in second).[28]

His addictions and deteriorating mental condition followed him north across the border. "Disgusted" from the trip, he returned home after a month, satisfied that he at least had something that he could use for a later work, which he tentatively titled "An American Passed Here." Despite his dislike for Florida, he was glad to be in his own bed. Contentedly, he recorded in his notebook on September 4 that he had dreamed of the Virgin Mary, the "Universal Mother," who had comforted him in his "half-sleep" state. Increasingly, it wasn't the solid stream of writing that he took solace in, but religion. In his journals and in his paintings, the crucified Christ and the comforting Universal Mother populated most of his artistic output.[29]

Two months after his return from Mexico, on September 18, in the air-conditioned confines of his Orlando home, Kerouac sat at his desk determined to write something of substance. He typed twenty-four thousand words of his stay in Big Sur but rejected the results. Part of his problem, he realized, was his excessive intake of amphetamines. On September 24 he wrote in his notebook: "Strange few days wherein I didn't know what I was doing (?)—Wrote more but insanely disorganized—Took too many bennies yet kept exercising—Will have to start BIG SUR all over again even—Something's wrong—What I need is a kick in the ass—Wasting all this genius for stories—Tho it ain't all bad."[30]

On September 30, he began to write what would eventually become sixty thousand words depicting his nervous collapse at Big Sur. The preparation for the novel, Kerouac wrote Holmes on December 29, included "putting together all of the musings of the past year, together with allied musings of past 4 years since I wrote Bums" and underpinning the story with the "dominant figure of the sea itself, on the shore where the Sur cabin was in tangled woods." It exhilarated him to complete this much original work, even though the effort was facilitated by the Mexican Benzedrine surging through his bloodstream as he typed relentlessly on a scroll rolled into his typewriter. Excited, he wrote to his agent three hours after its completion (which took ten days of focused writing). Kerouac described his work as "a narrative drama which was written with more excitement than *Dharma Bums,* is probably a better "novel," doesn't preach, sometimes runs breathless like *On The Road,* surpasses *Tristessa* for sad misery, has flashes of greatest prose of *Visions of Cody* and *Sax*."[31]

Although he could not regard the merits of *Big Sur* objectively, he assured Sterling Lord that the next book would be a "Comedy and nothing else."[32] Several days later, he wrote to Philip Whalen and Carolyn Cassady to tell them about his newest work depicting the "night of the end of Nirvana" when "masses of devils" chased after him. To Whalen, he also described life in Orlando:

> Mémêre [sic] is very happy here tho as usual she complains. Well, there are some complaints, like all summer you gotta have the aircon-ditioner on or die (I wouldnta moved here without it) which makes you cough—But next summer if she'll only just sweat in the yard a half hour a day, at flowers, lawn, etc., cough will just go away—also, tho, most horrible, one of these modern tracts with endless rows of perfect new houses but all of them without exception full of flat housewives looking out the window when someone dares to try to walk to the stores which are too far away anyway under broiling sun in flat treeless waste, ugh. But my sister is next door and there's family fun for old Mémêre, which is bettern waiting for me under cracking old boughs of New England's November, really (with all its witches and graveyards).[33]

Carolyn was touched that Kerouac wrote to her and she promptly replied. That fall, he was impressed by Ken Kesey's novel *One Flew over the Cuckoo's Nest,* of which Viking sent advanced bound galleys, hoping to receive a blurb. The prose he found "unusually good" and he generously called Kesey "a great man and a great new american novelist!" to Viking editor Tom Guinzburg.[34]

In the late fall of 1961, buoyed by the creative burst of early October, Kerouac planned other works. He once more offered Ferlinghetti *Old Angel Midnight* as well as *Book of Haikus,* which he planned to compose by extracting various haiku inserted throughout his journals and letters. However, it would not be a slapdash effort meant to earn money. Kerouac took pains to abide by and be appreciated for his informed mastery of the poetic form. According to Kerouac scholar Regina Weinreich (who collected and edited the posthumous edition of *Book of Haikus* in 2003), Kerouac had a working knowledge of the haiku form, though he tended to be more "playful than rigorous" in his poetry. His selection and revisions for *Book of Haikus* was deliberate and conscientious. When choosing a haiku, Kerouac "revised his poems in order to achieve greater concision" in structure, oftentimes taking a poem and revising it by deleting extraneous description. Hence, a last line in one haiku that reads "At noon in May" was eventually stripped of the last two words in its final published form. This, as theorized by Weinreich, minimized the syllabic count as well as an unnecessary seasonal reference. However, Ferlinghetti did not want Kerouac's collection of haiku, for he was discouraged by the sales of *Book of Dreams* that past year.

In November 1961, Kerouac went to New England where his original objective was to look for land to build a cabin; first he traveled to Old Orchard Beach, Maine, where he "walked among the Canucks." In Cape Cod, Massachusetts, a "Negro bouncer knocked me out in a roadhouse." He then went to New York.

In New York, many of his old friends and acquaintances saw that the alcohol not only affected Jack physically (his face was red and starting to bloat) but also distorted his personality blackly. Such was the appalling change in Kerouac that Burroughs did not even look him up when he came to New York to meet Grove publisher Barney Rossett. Lucien Carr also got a dose of the bilious Kerouac early that fall: they wrestled in Jerry Newman's studio until their clothes were torn and they were both smeared with blood. Later, when Lucien, Jacques Beckwith, and Kerouac went to Vermont to look for land (where Jack could put his cabin), they all sat in a kitchen drinking. Kerouac toppled Lucien's chair as he leaned back on the rear legs—not once, but three times. Clearly, the gentle, introverted writer Lucien had known at Columbia had turned into a mean drunk. Upon returning to New York, Kerouac spent thirty days sodden with whiskey, in what he deemed to be the "biggest drunk of all."

> Also, ate 12 S[iberian] mushrooms in one afternoon and wanted to telegram Winston Churchill something about an old Baron crying for his hounds in his "weird wield wier," thinking, on psilocybin, one baron to another he'd understand—Gad, how self—aggrandized you get on SM's—Last time, remember, I was Genghiz Khan—I incidentally wrote Timothy Leary and Pearl that I think this is the Siberian sacred mushroom used by Brainwash-inventor Airapatianz to empty American soldier prisoners in Korean brainwash program—Because if

you become so emptied you don't even care if you're Kerouac or Ginsberg or Orlovsky, and what that meant to you before, then you're ready to become anything at all, for any reason, even perhaps an assassin?[35]

He took temporary respite at the lofts of two painters, Hugo Weber and Yseult Snepvangers, where Kerouac practiced the art he was growing increasingly fond of, painting. One time the three pinned up an enormous canvas on which Kerouac painted a pietà ornamented with a white dove floating against a murky black sky. However, the effect was ruined when more and more paint was splashed onto the canvas with less-than-desirable results. With his inhibitions gone, he picked up a sixty-five-year-old "ex–movie star" and attempted to make love to her.[36] Attending the Village Gate to see a performance by tenor saxophonist Stan Getz, a "dirty and ragged" Kerouac was thrown out (according to Kerouac) by the club's founder, Art D'Lugoff (to this day D'Lugoff does not remember meeting or ejecting Kerouac). Unfazed by his ejection, Jack went across the street to a "hobo bar" only to be retrieved by Getz and seated in front of the bandstand.[37] At the White Horse Tavern, which catered to drinking regulars like Norman Mailer and Dylan Thomas, Kerouac was barred from entering ever again.[38] Despite his own drunken fiascos, Kerouac feared most his drinking sprees with Lucien Carr. After a plate-glass window was broken (and paid for by Willem de Kooning) in the city, they almost got "killed" and then arrested. Decidedly, he told Lois Sorrels, "I'm laying off Lucien . . . I've got to change now or never—No more N.Y. trips even for 'business' goddamit." Determinedly he decided to abstain from alcohol when he became aware of the alarming state of his declining health. He felt like he was having a heart attack and experienced "breathless sweating & trembling" after his New York City debacle. Only when he returned home and prayed, he told Lois, did he get better.[39] Sometime in 1961 he spit up blood.

Back in Florida, the pressures of the approaching court date for Joan Haverty's child support hearing began to weigh heavily on him. After typing thirty-five pages of *Big Sur* from the scroll, he wrote Lois at four in the morning griping that he would "show that bitch up for what she is. . . . I only hope her Puerto Rican fuckass aint got the same blood type I have." Paranoid of marriage, he explained to Lois that the only reason he hadn't married her was that he knew "what legal marriages end up with." He made no qualms about telling her that even she could "turn against me in legal marriage."[40]

In January 1962, Sterling Lord sold two of Kerouac's novels to Farrar, Straus and Cudahy, much to the chagrin of Viking. Since Farrar, Straus and Cudahy had accepted *Visions of Gerard*, rejected by Malcolm Cowley years earlier, the company exercised its option on *Big Sur*.[41] For this two-book deal Lord obtained $10,000 for Kerouac, his largest advance yet. He was thankful to Robert Giroux not only for endorsing the advance but also for refusing to edit his works. *Visions of Gerard* was scheduled for publication in September 1963. However, though Kerouac was fond of *Big Sur*, he was not sure it would sell at all since the public's fascination with all things *beat* had diminished.

To Stella Sampas, Jack attempted to paint a rosy picture of life in Orlando. His reaction to Stella, who described for Jack her "domestic happiness" in caring for her mother, was that she was "innocent of the fact that you are happier than most people in the world." His bland portrait of domesticity revealed his daily routine of late: "I just get up, read in the sun, eat, watch TV, walk and write till 6 A.M.—Florida peace has been good to me because I finally wrote a new novel . . ."[42]

Kerouac and Eugene Brooks were back before the judge in February 1962 to contest Joan Haverty's child support suit. This time Kerouac met Jan, who bore, he later admitted, a startling resemblance to him. He and Jan gave blood samples, which ultimately proved inconclusive. Despite the results, in March the court ordered Kerouac to pay $52 a month for child support. Jan's meeting with Jack would be only one of two visits in her lifetime. Her 1962 meeting was highlighted, historically, by a trip to a corner bar in Brooklyn, where she, her mother, and her stepsisters watched John Glenn orbit Earth for the third time. On Tenth Street, Kerouac and Jan went to a liquor store, where, Jan claimed, Jack purchased a bottle of Harvey's Bristol Cream sherry. Louis Ginsberg wrote to Allen, then traveling in India: "Kerouak [*sic*] admitted his paternity in his case, defended by Eugene, and has to pay twelve dollars a week for support. Eugene had him sleep over his house a few nights so he could get Kerouak sober in the courtroom for the trial."[43] Jack, though, was still convinced that he was not Jan's father: "No law'll make me recognize that poor kid as anybody's daughter but Joan; lovers of June 1951 (Rosario)—I know my own blood when I see it."[44] Corso, who had witnessed Kerouac's diatribes against his alleged paternity, wrote to Ginsberg:

Saw your brother, he's fine, and Jack too, but he not so fine, drunk, and can't talk straight with him. Wanted to, he just cares about his self and demands I respect that self, but I can't if he just sits about bubbling drunkenly how great he is and how bad who else is, so unreal, unrelated, that he truly bored me—and your brother did try to make sense to him about trial, his wife had him get blood test, and test shows that kid is Jack's, and Jack no want that baby. He said she said: "Jack, I don't care if you're my father or not, (double negative girl) I'll still love you." Poor Jack, to hear something like that can break your heart. Anyway I was in no mood after three years of separation to hear his boring diatribes.[45]

The rest of his New York stay was predictable. Ousted from the Hotel Ashley, which did not tolerate the frequent visits to his room by "Negro visitors" and a "girl," he found (eventually) the couch of a friend on which he could crash. He vented on an eleven-page typescript all of his worldly concerns, titling the work "Telling the World Off." When he returned south from the northeast in the train, Kerouac wept for the first time in many years thinking of his father's death in 1946.

In Orlando, he sent out a flurry of drunken letters (one of which he did not mail) to Robert Giroux excusing his behavior. In one of them Jack extolled the virtues of Yeats, whom he felt to be the most "important" writer of the century, followed by James Joyce and Marcel Proust. Kerouac emphasized the "holy" writers of the literary canon: Balzac, Dostoyevsky, Henry Vaughan, George Herbert, Keats, James Boswell, Alexander Pope, Thomas Traherne (the author of the mystical treatise *The Cloud of Unknowing*), St. John, and St. Matthew. Tacked onto the end of the list was "Jean Kerouac."[46] In a demonstration of his compassion and empathy, he wrote a letter to hospitalized Hugo Weber asking if there was anything "special" he could do for him. He told Weber that the "turning point of his narrative art" was when Jack was hospitalized in 1951 for phlebitis: "It was there, day after day in bed thinking, that I formulated all these volumes (16) I've written since (most of them save six so far published). But I mean I was *so happy* in the hospital."[47]

Convinced that his literary reputation as a serious artist would only grow over time, he began to arrange his impressive and expansive archives. Since 1939, he had acquired hundreds of letters, which he placed in order by correspondent and stored in a recently purchased four-drawer file cabinet. Besides the literary importance that his archive had, it served as a reference tool when memory failed him during his writing.

Kerouac wrote to Ferlinghetti with ambitious plans to write novels centered around Ginsberg, Peter Orlovsky, Corso, Burroughs, and G. J. Apostolos of Lowell. He also detailed the novel he had written with its setting around Ferlinghetti's Big Sur cabin: "Everybody in it (of course I won't call it Bixby Canyon and won't make it 18 miles south of Monterey, etc.) even Victor Wong is in it, fact quite a lot . . . You in it, of course, tho I was going to have lots more at the 'end' when I come to your house 706 but suddenly saw the novel should end at the cabin with Lew Welch and Jacky etc."[48]

Concerning his sister and her husband, Jack was growing increasingly at odds. He had begrudgingly loaned the Blakes money to build an addition to their home. A dispute arose over repayment. But he could not truly vent his feelings for in some ways he was more dependent than ever on them. He needed his sister to drive him to replenish his liquor cabinet or to mail the many letters that he wrote from sheer boredom. It was an awkward dependency that made it hard to collect what was owed from the Blakes.

On his return he opened a letter from Lois Sorrels in which she told him that her mother had died. In consideration of her grief, and remembering his own father dying in his arms in 1946, Kerouac invited Lois to stay with him in Orlando and even offered to pay her round-trip fare. Her presence in Orlando, however, incited a weeklong drinking binge. He could not even take advantage of having sex with Lois in his guest bedroom because alcohol had rendered him impotent. His drinking habits were changing; he was forced to drink primarily whiskey and rum after he found that the excessive intake of wine had turned his tongue white. A few months earlier, Kerouac had painted a false picture of contentment to Stella Sampas: "As I grow older I more and more come to the life of a kind of literary monk—No friends, no girlfriends either down here, on purpose—I'm just happy to be alone and studying—I'm reading everything, history, poetry, philosophy, the works—I don't get drunk anymore except on special occasions—I'm actually entering a happy phase of my life at 40."[49] Bored one day in his home, he ingested some psilocybin mushrooms and wrote in his notebook some "holy notes," intending to show them to Timothy Leary. His conclusion about the experience was blunt: "Awakening is a lot of shit."[50]

A letter from Ginsberg did "awaken" him to the fact that "young hepcats" in Bombay had translated *Old Angel Midnight* and *Scripture of the Golden Eternity* into Parmathi, a dialect of Bombay, India. Overseas, numerous titles of Kerouac's were being published; among them was an Italian translation of *Book of Dreams* as well as excerpts of the same published behind the Iron Curtain in Czechoslovakia.[51]

On September 11, 1962, *Big Sur* was published. The *New York Times* reviewed the hardcover edition, giving an appreciative nod toward its literary merits. *New York Times* book critic William Wiegand, an English professor from San Francisco State College, wrote:

> What Kerouac has achieved, most importantly, in "Big Sur" is a sense of structure and pacing which the early books lack. The scenes absolutely click for a change. They "signify." An orgy is no mere orgy; it has motive and consequence. Things are, in short, not as Zen as they used to be, and this is all to the good. Prose narrative can be "spontaneous" without being nonsensical.[52]

Herbert Gold, in the *Saturday Review*, found the novel both "troubling and touching" and said Kerouac was a "writer in addition to being a phenomenon."[53] However, the number of tepid reviews caused Kerouac to lash out at New York City critics. He contended that they favored Jewish writers like Saul Bellow, J. D. Salinger, and Philip Roth. He concluded that the only fans of his books of late were those who stole them from bookshelves. On September 14, *Time* magazine chose to ridicule the personality rather than offer objective criticism and to deprecate Kerouac's nervous collapse as a "howling emotional crisis":

> Alas, a cruel thought has intruded upon Kerouac's world. Though he has managed to write a book about this fell experience, it is clear that things will never be the same again—"like those pathetic five high-school kids," he explains, "who came to my door one night wearing jackets that said 'Dharma Bums' on them, all expecting me to be 25 years old . . . and here I am old enough to be their father." What can a beat do when he is too old to go on the road? He can go on the sauce. In *Big Sur* he does.[54]

The scathing attack on his character flaws shook Kerouac, though he remained skeptical of *Time* when they had given James Jones's novel *The Thin Red Line* a negative review, dismissing their criticism as "fairy talk."

Kerouac, perhaps realizing that his point of view would never be taken seriously by such a huge corporate magazine, suggested to Ferlinghetti that he pen a "hairy letter" to *Time* that would be so "pungent" that it couldn't be excerpted "without thorns." In defense of Kerouac, Ferlinghetti wrote "[y]our snide, sneering, condescending, semi-literate, semi-dishonest, spiteful attack on Jack Kerouac and his latest book, *Big Sur,* is disgusting. The fact that you've concentrated on Kerouac himself more than on his book makes your review particularly despicable."[55] *Time* did not publish Ferlinghetti's letter.

Gregory Corso's reaction to reading *Big Sur* was one of alarm. In 1963 he penned a letter to Ginsberg:

> Jack needs a lesson, I don't care what you say, his *Big Sur* at first I thought it all right but rereading it I see that he is lost, blind. He sees only his worthless skin, his woe his beatnik plight. . . . I tell you he needs help, a real good awakening or he is forever lost. Just don't say "aw good old Jack" because you won't be helping him much that way. I love Jack as much as you and know what Jack is and man is human and no one can be perfect as we poets but they can be made to wake up by God. Read *Big Sur* and see what I mean. He is in Florida, I last saw him a year ago. He was obnoxious, drunk and yet his eyes betrayed him for indeed he is hurt and a good soul.[56]

Jack's crisis intensified until Gabrielle became alarmed and feared not just for his health but also for his life. To disguise her concern, she told Jack, "I want to go home, back to New England." It wasn't hard convincing him. Jack was disgusted with his and his mother's dependency on Caroline and Paul for rides to the market. A jaunt by foot meant either walking along a busy highway with no sidewalks or trudging through a thorny briar-patched field populated by deadly copperheads. The noise of neighborhood children playing in front of his house echoed throughout the rooms, their voices resounding up and down the street (a situation that Kerouac blamed on the lack of trees, which had been cut down by the builders). The surrounding neighborhood, in Jack's estimation, was a "glorified slum" that filled him with "nightmares." He considered buying a car and having Lois Sorrels drive him to New England, look for a house, and then marry him. However, Gabrielle intervened: "Never mind that Lois, go see John Holmes and he'll help you, you've got plenty of time to find a wife and you don't have to get married just for that." Holmes, to Gabrielle, was a "good clean New England boy" and the "only one I liked who came to the house." Jack realized, after she told him, "how right she was." Writing to John and Shirley Holmes in Connecticut, Gabrielle implored them to help Jack find a house there. John replied that he would do anything to help his friend. Three days after the Kerouacs received his letter, Jack was on a train.

In the northeast Kerouac felt liberated, partially because the weather revived him and his fondness for October, but also because he was away from his mother, who absorbed so much of his energy and thoughts. He was also safer among friends who understood him. John Clellon Holmes at least empathized with his friend's self-destructive mind-set. He realized that since 1960 Kerouac had cared "less and less about things like 'career' and 'reputation.'" What puzzled Holmes was what motivated Kerouac to continue at all. Intuitively, Holmes felt that Kerouac would not "live much beyond forty." Because Holmes and Shirley were going on a two-week trip to New Hampshire in late August (after Holmes had finished a nonfiction book he was writing called *Nothing More to Declare*), Jack planned his trip for September.[57]

The idealism behind a move to New England was not meant merely to placate Gabrielle; it was an idyllic retreat for Jack as well: "I could live again in the trees and grasses and could walk in the fields when tired of books (like you do) and at the same time be close enough to receive your visits any time you felt like coming to shoot the bull." As idealistic as it was for Kerouac, it ultimately would bring more harm than good. His desperate attempts to flee his alcoholism and personal misery were in vain; the addictions within him dogged his heels as relentlessly as *On the Road*'s Shrouded Stranger pursued Sal Paradise.

In Old Saybrook, Connecticut, Kerouac was content just to talk, not about anything in particular, but to release the demons rattling his tormented mind. At first, Holmes drove Kerouac around to look at a few homes. But, quite predictably, it became a drunk fest that Holmes himself could not sustain. It began with casual tippling and reminiscing about all the years they had known each other. A week later, Jack had abandoned the objective of his journey altogether. Unshaven and hair unkempt, he did not leave his chair. He was content to spend days in an undershirt rank with body odor, torn pajama bottoms, and Japanese slippers. He ate next to nothing and chain-smoked unfiltered Camels; a cigarette hung habitually from his mouth. He consumed wine, scotch, and (by Holmes's estimate) a fifth of Courvoisier each day. Jack was, as he inscribed in Lucien Carr's copy of *Big Sur*, caught in the throes of "alcoholic sorrow."[58] Despite this, Holmes renewed his effort to motivate Kerouac. Showered and shaved, Kerouac sat in the backseat of Holmes's car sweating out the need to drink. Sensing the futility of the search for a home, Holmes gave up and brought Kerouac to a bar in Essex, Connecticut. After many beers, Kerouac started arguing with the bartender. Jack's behavior turned erratic. Back at Holmes's house, Shirley cooked them dinner, and Kerouac switched to hard liquor. He turned to Holmes abruptly and announced, "I've got to get out of here." He asked Holmes to take him to Lowell, where he wanted to visit G. J. Apostolos. Holmes refused to make a trip so suddenly at that late hour. Kerouac decided that he would take a taxi. Shirley called New London and found a company willing to let its car venture out of state. Holmes prepared a mason-jar cocktail of brandy and soda that would last the drive. When the driver came to the door and saw Jack, he was understandably concerned. Holmes assured him that Kerouac was harmless but warned the cabbie that the passenger would talk his ear off. Sixty-two dollars in cab fare later, Kerouac was back in Lowell.

Lowell had become run-down over the last decade; the scars of economic collapse were evident in the abandoned mills and numerous boarded-up tenements that once composed Little Canada. Friends of Jack's were now middle-aged, most too busy to keep steady company with their famous friend. Unimpressed with his literary fame, many chose to read about him in the *Lowell Sun* instead of seeking him out among Lowell's many bars and taverns. Kerouac found a small room to rent by the Boston and Maine train depot. From there, at four o'clock in the morning, he called and woke G. J. Apostolos, declaring "I'm here!" That Sunday, September 16, after making an intoxicated visit to Mary Carney in South Lowell, Kerouac continued his drinking, one beer after another, and bombarded fellow Lowellians with strung-out imagery that linked *Maggie Cassidy* with guardian angels and *Hamlet* soliloquies. Apostolos remembers, "It would be morning to night, drinking, drinking, drinking."[59]

In vain, Jack tried to get his bar-stool companions to accompany him to return to his old school, the Bartlett, to toss one down by the light of the autumn moon. According to the *Lowell Sun*, he stopped traffic to perform a spontaneous poetry reading while holding in one hand the ever-present jug of booze. Another time, he demonstrated a Cossack dance at a rock club. Debauched and often demented, Kerouac was still jubilant to be among old friends. Mary Sampas noted that he seemed only mildly bothered by *Time's* putdown; he was more anxious to read the other reviews of *Big Sur* appearing in most papers that week. He was hardly himself now among the barkeepers and patrons who piled into downtown bars when the *Lowell Sun* announced his visit. However, when he was away from the gawking public, he was genial and gentlemanly. When Mary Sampas's teenaged daughter and her friend met Kerouac, they encountered a "tanned, clean-shaven, good-looking, handkissing courtier" who proffered advice to them and signed an autograph complete with a spontaneous haiku.

In Nicky Sampas's bar, Kerouac sat at a table absently drawing pietàs on bar napkins and dispensing autographs to jaded barflies who wanted to share their brush with fame with family and friends. Thrilled with the notion of being back in his hometown, Kerouac courted his fame with the same degree of exuberance as he had his winning touchdown at the Lowell High School Thanksgiving football game victory over Lawrence in 1939. However, his reception by many who had once known him in his youth was shame, pity, and alarm. The transformation from dark, handsome brooder to an unkempt Falstaff was too sudden and unwarranted. Lowell Tech professor Charles Giarvais, who knew Kerouac from high school, remembered seeing him in a Market Street bar:

> The once dark-maned, clear-eyed Endymion youth had become a soggy, booze-bloated hulk. He was bombed and he was noisy. He wore a pair of fatigue pants, a plaid shirt, three quarter shoes, and a hunter's cap which reminded me of the kind Admiral "Bull" Halsey wore on the bridge of his ship. What I didn't know then was that all but four or five of my remaining contacts with Kerouac would be under these conditions: he in a state of alcoholic euphoria and I, sharply sober, gathering in every syllable that streamed from his brain. The booze never diminished his giant mind though, and his physical senses rivaled those of Roderick Usher.[60]

Giarvais solicited Kerouac to do a radio interview, to which he agreed. Hosted by Giarvais and local attorney James Curtis, the program *Dia-*

logues in Great Books' endeavor was to discuss the merits of classical and modern literature. Kerouac appeared that October morning at the WCAP radio station in downtown Lowell accompanied by Stella Sampas. Before him he placed a pint of booze and, for the next half hour, gave Lowell a dose of concentrated *Kerouacisms*:

> JIM CURTIS: I heard thunder last night and as I walked down Market Street I looked to the right and there he was . . .
>
> JACK KEROUAC: You heard what?
>
> JC: Thunder.
>
> JK: Thunder?
>
> JC: Thunder. Now Jack, tell me about this thunder? What are you doing in Lowell?
>
> JK: Louis Thunder is my name.
>
> CHARLES GIARVAIS: Louis Thunder? I thought it was "Milestone"?
>
> JK: Louis Milestone . . . gallstone . . . death.
>
> JC: Alright fine.
>
> CG: Jack how did you happen to all of a sudden come to Lowell after an absence of about eight or nine years as I recall you were telling us?
>
> JK: Let's see, why did I come to Lowell? I came here to see George Apostolos.

Kerouac's comments ranged from debating Shakespeare's authorship, to his own revision techniques ("Once God moves the hand . . . to go back and revise is a sin!"), to Gerard. When Curtis asked who Gerard was, a "twilight haze veiled Kerouac's face, but through the veil we now could see a bewildered little boy striving to find his way out of the sudden darkness." Kerouac said softly, "Gerard is my brother. He died when he was nine. I was four at the time. When he was on his deathbed, nine nuns filed into his room and said 'Gerard, repeat what you told us about Heaven.'"[61]

After spending a week in Lowell, Kerouac left with $280 borrowed from Stella Sampas's brother Tony. Two Lowell acquaintances offered to drive him to New York to see Lucien Carr. He bounced around "Auld Manhattoes" for ten days before returning to Orlando, where he promptly repaid Sampas.

Jack and Gabrielle decided to move back to Northport. In November, he bought a house, intending to move by year's end. When he went to the home to buy it, the "witch" (as Kerouac labeled her in an interview) who lived there was "burning dolls in a bonfire out in the yard in the driveway in front of the barn." Nevertheless, Jack got drunk with her "because she was lonely." Kerouac remained suspicious of the area; in the home at 34 Gilbert Street, which he had sold to David Roberts in 1959, he told interviewers that there was a "poltergeist in the dining room cupboard which was left there by a previous witch. You see Northport is full of witches. On Halloween night, when I get high I go out in the yard with my cat. His tail goes up and a big arch . . . the back goes up. I look around, I see ghosts everywhere. I have to do the sign of the cross." Standing in the yard, holding his frightened cat in his arms, Kerouac yelled to the sky, "go back to your graaaaves!" Regardless of Kerouac's past experiences with the paranormal, he signed the papers to purchase the home to live there with his mother.[62]

On Christmas Eve, he and Gabrielle stepped off the train to greet the familiar freezing cold. They were back, for the last time, in Northport. To Philip Whalen, Jack assessed the many moves his mother had made (with and without him):

> Since I was born on Lupine road in 1922 Memere has moved & changed household furniture 26 times . . . Lupine, Burnaby, Beaulieu, Hildreth, Lilley, West, Sarah, Phebe, Aiken, Moody, Gersham, West Haven Conn., Crawford, then Brooklyn, Ozone Park, Denver Colo., Richmond Hill upstairs, Kinston N.C., Richmond Hill downstairs, Rocky Mount N. C., Orlando Fla. (2 addresses), 1943 Berkeley Way Berkeley Calif., Clouser St. Orlando Fla., Gilbert St. Northport, Orlando again, then Earl Avenue Northport, then Orlando again (here) and now we go to Northport again in best house Memere ever had with 2 baths, fireplace, 24 trees in yard, completely finished basement all of it a rumpus room with wood paneling and kentyle floors, big workbench shots where I can paint, easy walk to A & P store and paper store and all fine . . . and the air divine . . . my good old winter air.[63]

Only after Jack had died did Gabrielle finally maintain a stable residence.

29

Days of Autumn

Spring 1963–Summer 1964

Man is not made for defeat.

ERNEST HEMINGWAY, *The Old Man and the Sea*

In his journal Kerouac hopelessly pondered the "autumn" of his life. He wrote that the "springtime" of his life had nurtured the experiences that had become the fodder for his fiction; the "summer," the realization of actual composition; the "autumn," his postfame years and subsequent collapse depicted so candidly in *Big Sur.* He assured himself that "winter" would see him a "silent hermit" writing haiku and spiritual prose freed from the destruction of youthful ambitions. He vowed, once more, to stop drinking and prayed to the Virgin Mary to help him quit. Until then, he sat in the new Northport house, sometimes in a "more or less drunk stupor."[1]

Kerouac's first goal was to write another volume in his legend of Duluoz. His father's life in Lowell unreeled before Jack as he unpacked his archive and read through old correspondence and copies of *Spotlight Print.* He planned to release other works over the next several years: *Vanity of Duluoz,* his reworking of an early manuscript from his youth; *Desolation Angels* (at one point he revised the title to "Generation Angels" before changing it back to its original); and "Passing Through," the 1961 material written in Mexico City. During the winter Jack wrote sporadically and read Spengler and Tolstoy while listening to Mozart's *Requiem.* He also made regular payments to Joan for child support. To mislead her as to his whereabouts, he mailed the check to his sister in Orlando for forwarding.

When Joan asked for more money, he ignored the request. Despite his financial obligations, Kerouac paid for a cedarwood fence to surround his property so that he could sit in the yard in privacy.

Spring 1963 brought restlessness. He paced his yard at four in the morning trying to conjure the ideas needed to jump-start his work. Gabrielle watched television and fed the starlings that constantly flocked into the yard. Ever mindful of his mother's peace of mind, Kerouac kept friends like Lois Sorrels and Jacques Beckwith away from the house. He also did not want anything that would distract him from his writing. His personal contacts in Northport, of late, were limited to people with whom he had business.[2] He did help out Lois by writing an introduction for her volume of poems, describing her as a "fairy trapped in a buttercup," a "somber poet" who "is likely to reach an extremely mysterious middle age and write mysterious shroudy verse about moors and miles of moor in her mind. Anyway, she happened."[3] Despite Kerouac's praise, the book was not published during his lifetime.

That spring, Kerouac also dealt with issues in Italy over the translation of *The Subterraneans,* which incited pornography charges after being banned in 1960. On May 23, Kerouac defended his work in a letter that addressed the novel's "significance," "artistic background," and "style." Interracial sex was very much taboo not only in America but also in Italy and probably was the cause of the pornography charge. Regarding the novel's artistry, Kerouac drew a parallel to Dostoyevsky's "confessional form" in *Notes from the Underground,* which he tried to achieve in the retelling of a complex relationship without offending "certain basic sensibilities in polite society." As for the novel's style:

> This is the style I've discovered for narrative art, whereby the author stumbles over himself to tell his tale, just as breathlessly as some raconteur rushing in to tell a whole roomful of listeners what has just happened, and once he has told his tale he has no right to go back and delete what the hand hath written, just as the hand that writes upon the wall cannot go back.

It was a confessional form of storytelling that had its origins in his Catholic upbringing; of the confessional booths of Saint Louis de France where "to withhold any reasonably and decently explainable detail from the Father was a sin."[4] He addressed the missive to the judge hearing the case and sent it to Barney Rossett at Grove Press to forward on his behalf. Kerouac insisted that the letter serve as a preface to the Italian edition. The letter was published in the October–November 1963 issue of *Evergreen Review.*

Though Kerouac was formal in his defense of his literature, he was tactless when Gary Snyder sent him a thesis written by a Japanese student in his college class. Through a haze of alcohol, responding to the bigotry seeded in his psyche, Kerouac accused Snyder of not taking him or his work seriously. He derided the student's ethnicity and heritage, calling her a "dopey Jap cunt." He asked Snyder how he could "sit there and be spanked on the ass by the soft flat boards of brow beaten crewcutted Jap idiots and not roar at them with a Sword of what you used to call Wisdom?" Despite Kerouac's tirade, Snyder remained cordial. Few others remonstrated; it was easier to stay silent.[5]

Neal Cassady, in New York with yet another mistress, came to Northport with a few friends whom he had picked up en route. Although happy to see Neal, Jack was suffering a fit of delirium tremens after another attempt to stop drinking. He also did not appreciate Neal's companions, who parked a stolen car in front of his house, raided his refrigerator, and put their feet on his coffee table. Despite the fracas, the few minutes that Jack spent alone with Neal revealed Cassady, according to Kerouac, to be as "sweet & gentle & polite & intelligent & interesting as he ever was."[6]

Visions of Gerard, released as scheduled in September 1963, received little to no attention except as a literary curiosity. Illustrated with ink drawings by James Spanfeller, the thin novel was published as a quality hardcover. It failed, as usual, to impress the *New York Times*, which viewed the book as an aching personal memoir skewed by the writer's "relentless voice," which drowned out the characterization of Gerard with "jaunty, garrulous hipster yawping": "It is not enough to say that the style does not evoke or intensify the emotion. It betrays and debases it. The dead boy deserved better of its eulogist." The reviewer, a professor of literature at Bennington College, also slammed Kerouac's language as "slack, unending sentences which pile clause on clause on clause, faulty syntax, gross inaccuracy of language" that "do not make a style—not even an anti-style. They simply violate the language and corrupt feeling. Thus deadened by Kerouac's prose, we cannot respond to the boy's agony." The *New York*

Herald Tribune was especially hostile, calling the novel "slapdash" and "grossly sentimental." Like his other books, *Visions of Gerard* eventually slipped out of print.[7]

The middle part of the decade was approaching. America's involvement in Vietnam was accelerating; by September 1963, sixteen thousand U.S. troops were stationed in Southeast Asia. On November 22, John F. Kennedy was assassinated as his motorcade passed through downtown Dallas, Texas. Vice President Lyndon B. Johnson, sworn in two hours after Kennedy's death, would intensify U.S. involvement in Vietnam. Civil rights clashes were also escalating, with racial tensions rising in the South and riots in the Watts section of Los Angeles. Martin Luther King Jr.'s pacifistic civil disobedience continued amid threats from southern racists. Malcolm X promoted violent self-defense—the very antithesis of King's Christian principles. The United States was slowly becoming a nation gone awry. In response, Kerouac retreated into the solace of Catholicism. The image of the cross frequently came to him when he closed his eyes and he was certain that he could never understand "its mysterious penetration into all this brutality." Over and over again, he expressed faith in his journals that salvation through suffering "will turn out true."[8]

At this time, Ginsberg tried to persuade Kerouac to sign a petition in defense of comedian Lenny Bruce, who was being tried for obscenity. Bruce's exposure of the hypocritical underpinnings of organized religion—a regular mainstay of his nightclub act—clashed with Kerouac's conservative Catholic beliefs. Kerouac refused to sign. Ginsberg's increasing public protests began to override his poetic output, a point of contention for Kerouac, who remarked to John Clellon Holmes that he didn't want to be connected with Ginsberg anymore, "with his Pro-Castro bullshit and his long white robe Messiah shot." He was convinced that Ginsberg, along with all of the other "beatniks," had nothing "new" to tell him.[9] Such was his disenchantment with Ginsberg's politics that Kerouac refused a $3,000 offer to appear in a film with him, although he did permit Andy Warhol to film him sitting on a couch with Ginsberg and Corso in the pop-art silent film *Couch*. Kerouac also resisted an attempt by Italian translator Fernanda Pivano to include him in a beat anthology. Kerouac reasoned to Pivano that she would be doing him "a disservice as an individual voice in America, and I do mean individual, i.e., *alone*."

Despite his plea, she ignored his wishes and forged ahead, editing a bilingual anthology, *Poesia degli ultimi Americani* (published in 1964).[10]

Kerouac's drinking continued to escalate; he was visibly wearied of life. He was disgusted with Corso, who wanted to move his wife into Kerouac's home and adopt one of the ideas of Jack's adolescent novels as his own. Corso blasted Kerouac for not wanting to involve himself "politically" with him or Ginsberg.[11] One embarrassing foray into the public lecture circuit occurred during a March 1964 reading at Harvard University's Lowell House Junior Common Room. During the proceedings Kerouac told the students, "I'm not afraid of Mao Tse-Tung or Arthur Schlesinger, 'cause I'm straight Catholic!" Harvard's tutorial staff paced worriedly as they watched America's beat warrior pontificate untethered on their podium. He opined that Emily Dickinson, James Joyce, and T. S. Eliot were "the greatest poets of the twentieth century" and that "Marcel Proust, Jean Genet and William Faulkner" were the "greatest prose writers." But "Hemingway was nowhere. He wrote childish sentences, like Beckett does." Reading from *Mexico City Blues,* Kerouac insisted on a glass of cognac as he traded jibes with Irish poet Desmond O'Grady (who was in the process of obtaining his doctorate). "When his host, Albert J. Gelpi Jr., instructor in English, suggested that they just forget the whole thing and go out for a drink, Kerouac gestured at the packed crowd and said, 'But these people are here; they can't all go to the bar.' Finally, the drunk but coherent writer was handed a glass through the window, eliciting sympathies from the amused audience."[12]

On April 14, 1964, under local painter and drinking pal Stanley Twardowicz's persuasion, Kerouac consented to sit down with librarians from the Northport Public Library for a recorded interview.[13] Seated in Twardowicz's art studio with the library's assistant director (among others), Jack lucidly conversed (despite profusely imbibing) about Marcel Proust, Thomas Wolfe, John F. Kennedy, the Kerouac family, and his 1957 travels to Morocco, Paris, London, and Marseilles. During the interview, Kerouac offered to paint a pietà of Christ "being taken down from the cross by Mary and Saint Peter and Saint John and Martha with Judas hanging in the background." Ill-advisedly, the loud recorded jazz playing and frequent interjections and interruptions on behalf of those present muddled what could have been a very revealing and interesting audio document.

Of notable interest are Kerouac's comments on Ginsberg, religion, a run-in with an FBI agent, race relations in the South, and anti-Semitism.

Discussing an appearance by Allen Ginsberg, who was scheduled to discuss the "fall of America" on television that month, Kerouac explained, "That's where *we* differ." Asked why he wouldn't "argue" with Ginsberg on television, Kerouac responded, "There is no end to the quibbling that goes on in this world. The best thing for a guy like me to do is not to quibble, but to keep quiet and have fun." When the interviewer pressed Kerouac further by expressing that Ginsberg was a "talented man," Kerouac replied: "He does not like America! He is my college friend, we use to walk over the Brooklyn Bridge together singing to Hart Crane. He's become political. He mailed his beard to the district attorney of New York. He shaved off his beard, put it in an envelope and mailed it to the district attorney protesting censorship." Kerouac goes on to describe a film scenario that Ginsberg had written. Most offensive to Kerouac, besides a lingering shot of Ginsberg's mother's "asshole," was a "collection of broken dolls all glued together into the form of a cross":

> So I told him, I said "go down the delicatessen, buy a link of pork sausage, drive four nails into the wall and put up your Star of David." He insulted the cross man, Christ is not a broken doll! Ever since then I can't sell a book! These beatnik poets have been insulting Jesus and the Virgin Mary right and left for the last six years in poems, including Ferlinghetti and all those guys! They insult Jesus and the Virgin Mary but they never have insulted the Star of David!

Kerouac's anger and sensitivity toward those who mocked Catholicism extended even to filmmaker and photographer Robert Frank, who wanted to film Russian author Isaac Babel's short story "The Sin of Jesus." Kerouac adamantly explained: "I told him, 'Don't make a movie called *The Sin of Jesus*, Jesus never sinned!' He says, 'Who do you think you are? You know everything?' Kerouac spat to the ground and continued, 'I haven't talked to him since. Do I write a book called *The Sin of Moses*? I don't insult other people's religions. Why do the Jews insult the Catholics all the time?'" When Kerouac's interviewers objected personally, he continued, "No, in print and in public they insult!"

Of Kerouac's Catholic church experience as a child, he told of an incident in a confessional booth when he confessed that he looked at the "dong" of the boy standing next to him at the basement urinal of Saint Louis de France School: "Know what the priest said?" Kerouac asked the interviewer, "How big was it?" A female guest present at the interview asked Kerouac if his story was true: "Yes, he was an old sex fiend or something. I thought it was a sin. I'm telling you it's true." Kerouac continued with his perception of the origin of the Catholic church: "I haven't been to communion since I was fourteen years old. If Saint Paul . . . ya see Saint Paul is a latecomer. He is the one that developed the entire Catholic church. In the beginning he was against Jesus. You know that don't you? Then he came over to his side after Jesus died and he himself became a martyr didn't he? But he, according to Oswald Spengler, was a great administrative thinker who built up the executive framework of the Catholic church. Jesus himself was just a barefooted cat who didn't think about executive frameworks. Just a barefooted man who went around and told everybody the same thing: 'Be kind.' Little kids would come up to him and grab his lap and the old fathers would say 'GET AWAY! GET AWAY! GET AWAY! Jesus is talking!' He'd say, 'Uh uh, suffer the little ones to come unto me for they are innocent of heart.'"

The interviewer, perhaps objecting to Kerouac's claims that Ginsberg was a Russian communist, brought up a Supreme Court ruling making it illegal to make such an unfounded accusation. This elicited Kerouac's indifference:

> I don't give a flinging fuck! I'll tell you elsewhere . . . the FBI picked me up one night because I had the highest IQ at Newport Naval Base in the navy. They said, "Are you a Communist officer in the Communist Party?" I said, "No! I just have a high IQ!" Then I went around and came back five, six years later this guy picked me up in a jazz joint. Turned on his tape recorder and made me talk. You know how the end of the tape was? I was fucking him in the mouth. [Kerouac laughs.] That's the FBI for ya. Take that back to J. Edgar Hoover.

If Kerouac sought to shock his interviewers, he continued to do so by blaming Lyndon B. Johnson for John F. Kennedy's assassination: "They're going to get [Barry] Goldwater now." Concerning race relations in the country, Kerouac's anger summoned forth the subject of First Lady Jacqueline Kennedy and civil rights: "Jackie Kennedy, the wife of Jack Kennedy, is all for civil rights of the Negroes and integrating schools.

How come she don't send her children to integrated schools? She sends them to private schools. If I had a kid I'd send him to an integrated public school! What's wrong with public schools?" When Kerouac's interviewers reminded him that he went to Horace Mann, Kerouac replied, "I was integrated with Jews!" Of Abraham Lincoln, Kerouac opined that the late president was a "hypocrite": "Usually the people that are most vociferous for civil rights have Negro help who wash their toilets, do their cooking . . . as my mother says, 'wipe their asses.' My mother and I would never have Negro servants or any other kind of servants. But the people that are most vociferous for civil rights are people who hire Negroes to wash their toilet bowls! Hypocrites!"

Twardowicz responded that at least they were being hired for jobs, to which Kerouac objected, "Yeah but not washing toilet bowls! Wash your own toilet bowl! You ever see me wash a toilet bowl? When I mess up a toilet bowl, I take big pieces of paper and I put my hand right in there and I wash it all off and I flush it away. Then I wash my hands with soap and water. You don't hire no Negroes to do that!"

Another radical foray was Kerouac's theory that the strife over civil rights for African Americans was initiated by an "invasion" of Russian Jews into America. Insisting that he was not anti-Semitic, Kerouac explained:

> Half of my boyhood buddies were killed fighting against Hitler in Europe. Now half my team is gone. They're dead. In order to save the Jews from the concentration camps, the Jews came here: medicine, dentists, lawyers . . . they're very smart, I don't have anything against them. After they had established themselves here, they then took the Negro out and flung him at America and hide behind his skirts so that we will forget about anti-Semitism because we're worried about Negroes now. You see I know there is no *plan* for that, no *paranoic* plan, no planning committee, but that's what's happening! However the Negroes, they don't take no shit from nobody, so they'll work it out themselves. I mean in other words, the Negroes don't like the Jews.

Stunning his interviewers, Kerouac laughed and continued in jest by stating "I don't like them either!" Realizing that there were people of Jewish extraction present at the interview, Kerouac quickly followed with "I don't dislike them as a group." He insisted that there was a radical "movement" at hand in America's disrupted social strata. When the 1964 interview was transcribed for *Athanor* magazine, it was altered heavily by the editor's pen.[14]

In time for Easter morning, Kerouac went to Lowell and, afterwards, to Nashua to visit the graves of his father and brother. Returning to Northport, he played his baseball game in his bedroom, continued his introspective jottings in his notebooks, organized his archive, and listened to a tape of Mozart's *Requiem* recorded from a radio broadcast, an opportunity he had been waiting for for "years."[15] His finances reached a new low and he had to borrow almost $300 from Tony Sampas and $20 from Stella. Again, he bemoaned his living expenses in Northport and before long prepared to move once again to Florida. The move required money, and he met with his agent to attempt to generate some much-needed cash. For consideration there were two novels: *Desolation Angels* and *Visions of Cody*. The strife and quarreling in his immediate family continued to disrupt his thoughts. Upset with his brother-in-law and nephew, Jack jotted down his thoughts about his sister's current domestic situation:

He's [Paul Blake Sr.] completely abandoned her and his son after 17 years living and hoping together, much of it spent mulcting money first from Ma then me—Borrowed 5 thou from me, paid back only 1 thou—Meanwhile Lil Paul is now staying away from home 3 days at a time, hits his mother, and acts like a hood—Says "I don't have to work, my father doesn't work"—Big Paul hiding in Wash. probably living with an older woman—hoping to become a Washington Wheeler Dealer but cant even spell! and still my sister hopes he'll come home (where the law wants him for debts!)[16]

To appease Gabrielle and bring her closer to Caroline, Jack sold the Northport home at a loss as well as the reprint rights for his books to foreign publishers. Satisfied that the costs could be covered, he prepared to move south again.

30

The Ghost Hells of My Heart

Fall 1964–January 1967

When a true genius appears in this world you may know him by the
sign that the dunces are all in confederacy against him.
  JONATHAN SWIFT, *Thoughts on Various Subjects*

By 1963, Neal Cassady was a strung-out convicted felon constantly high
on marijuana and crashing on barbiturates. Neal, it seemed to many, was
living out the role of Dean Moriarty. One year earlier, Cassady met Ken
Kesey, author of *One Flew over the Cuckoo's Nest*, at a party, and joined his
band of acid-headed disciples, the Merry Pranksters. In a garish bus, with
a speed-crazed Cassady at the wheel, they set out from California on June
14, 1964. Two months later, the bus reached New York so that Cassady
could see Kerouac once more.

They met, for the last time, in a Madison Avenue apartment. Kerouac
smoked some pot and allowed himself to be draped with a scarf fashioned
from an American flag. Despite the high hopes of the Pranksters, who anticipated a historical literary reunion of sorts, Jack and Neal had little to
say to each other. When Kesey approached Kerouac, telling him that his
place in history was assured, Kerouac responded simply, "I know."

In September, the Kerouacs moved to muggy St. Petersburg. They
chose a respectable, quiet, middle-income house on 5155 Tenth Avenue
North. Invigorated by the new surroundings, Kerouac prowled the town,
attended baseball games, and searched for new bars in which to drink and
play pool. He became a pool table regular, an eerie shadow of Leo in the
1930s when he managed the Pawtucketville Social Club. Often he walked
down the street at midnight with his mother.

Caroline still lived in Florida with her son, Paul Jr., but was on hard times. She had arteriosclerosis, and her weight had dropped to ninety pounds. Her marriage had deteriorated. Paul moved out of their home and stopped sending her money for support. Her finances in ruin, she had to sell some furniture and, later, her home. She moved into an Orlando apartment with Paul Jr., now a teenager. He did not contribute to their finances. Desperately, Caroline weeded and cut her landlady's lawn to reduce her rent.[1]

On September 19, 1964, after Jack returned from a day of drinking at a bar, he saw his mother shaken with grief. His sister was dead. Caroline Kerouac Blake was only forty-five when she died. On the day of her death Caroline made a long-distance phone call to her husband in Washington, D.C. Their conversation did not go well. She abruptly hung up on Paul after telling him, "All right, if that's the way you want it!" Shortly afterward, she suffered cardiac arrest and was rushed to Orlando's Florida Sanitarium and Hospital, where she died in the middle of the afternoon. Gabrielle wrote to Jack's friends, Stanley and Anne Twardowicz, in Northport, relaying the news: "Just when everything was going to be fine and good for us all. My heart is broke. My only little girl gone."[2] Kerouac, crushed by grief, locked himself in his bathroom during Nin's funeral. On October 19 he wrote John Clellon Holmes:

Yes, Nin died and as time goes on I think about it more and more, in my own way. Up at night at 2 A.M. I sit and remember up a storm as tho I were still writing *Sax* and *Maggie*. There was a reason, tho, and I have nothing to do with it. Get older and you get more mystified. Youth has a way of sluffing off death and graves and even makes purple armpit poetry about it, as I did. But when in real life there's a red-neoned funeral parlor on the end of your street, and gloom hits you, yet, ah, I'll still not die in a stain coffin in Lowell. Oh, but maybe fall off Mount Sumeru (Everest). The trouble here is, Nin woulda had a lot of fun with me and my Maw here, picnics etc. a very stimulating city is St. Petersburg, you'd be surprised.[3]

On September 22, Caroline was buried at the Greenwood Cemetery in an unmarked grave. Kerouac could not afford to buy a gravestone. Paul Blake vowed to buy one but had not done so by the time he died eight years later.[4] Jack blamed Caroline's death in part on her harried life: doing homework for her son and his friends, entertaining a constant stream of "gossiping" friends, struggling to subsist. Jack took his mother's copy of *Visions of Gerard* and pressed into the pages a flower from Nin's funeral.

The women in Florida didn't talk to Kerouac, because (he felt) they were "afraid" of him. In Gunther's he played pool, while outside white men played tackle sandlot football with "niggers"; someone ended up in the hospital after most games. Kerouac let the South's intolerance seep into his mind. Yet, all the while, he decorated the margins of his pages and the bottoms of his letters to friends with angels fluttering over a haloed Christ. Death continued to haunt him. In 1961 he had experienced an eerie foreboding: "When I threw up blood the other day, I thought I might be hemorrhaging to death, quietly there in bed, I realized I loved only Heaven anyway."[5]

The memories triggered a renewed effort to rewrite his old manuscript of *Vanity of Duluoz*. In his "Reading Notes" notebook, he outlined the work. The book, he knew, would span the years from 1938 to 1942. Locales would include Pawtucketville; Manhattan and the Columbia University campus; Washington, D.C.; Paterson, New Jersey; Denver, Colorado; San Francisco; and Rocky Mount, North Carolina. He planned to take all of his 1939–1948 letters and his 1949 correspondence with Robert Giroux about *The Town and the City* to serve as guideposts for composition. He also had a clear vision of the characters. His personal pseudonym, Jack Duluoz, would be used in this novel; as for the rest of his family, Leo would appear as Emil, Gabrielle as Ma and Ange. Charley Bissonette (Caroline's first husband, Charles Morissette) and several of Kerouac's Pawtucketville friends would round out the last written installment of the Duluoz legend. It would be a sober, no-frills, first-person departure from his spontaneous prose-writing style. He had also laid out a rough chapter treatment, estimating it would take ten sittings to complete the book. He would begin with his Nashua game, which would "hearken back" to his Lowell sandlot games before returning to his Lowell-Lawrence clash on Thanksgiving 1938. The high school and college games would end on the third sitting. There was his time in Hartford and West Haven; the stint aboard the SS *Dorchester*; the composition of "The Sea Is My Brother" and his navy conflicts. In the eighth sitting he planned to cover his incarceration at the Bronx jail and the degradation of his Self-Ultimacy period. Finally, Jack would write of the death of his father, Ozone Park, and the preparations for the composition of *The Town and the City*. Though he stuck to this chapter outline, it would ultimately take him longer than ten sittings to complete the novel.[6]

Meanwhile, Sterling Lord sold two of Kerouac's manuscripts, from 1956 and 1961, to Coward-McCann after lunching with its publisher,

John J. Geoghan: *Desolation Angels* and "An American Passed Here." Ellis Amburn, editor for the company, took the two manuscripts home and read them, resorting to getting high on weed when he couldn't untangle Kerouac's message from his writing style. Amburn found *Desolation Angels* an engaging, stellar example of Kerouac's mature writing style. "An American Passed Here" wasn't as well written, in his opinion, but nevertheless was historically important, highlighting Kerouac's postfame years: "They did for the Beat Generation what Hemingway's *A Moveable Feast* had done for the Lost Generation; they showed us how literary and cultural movements are born." This was the "publishing theme" that Amburn suggested. However, Geoghan felt that the two short novels would not sell separately. The solution was to merge the two manuscripts and to sell them under one title: *Desolation Angels.* Lord told Kerouac that Coward-McCann wanted to market the novel for its historical importance (much as Viking did with *On the Road*) and to promote it with enough energy and imagination to renew the reading public's interest in Kerouac. This dedication to the work was the best the company could offer beyond a modest advance.[7]

At first, Kerouac resisted, hoping for two advances. He was also ambivalent when Amburn told him that an influential writer would write a foreword, and responded, "Why should I give another writer a free ride?" Coward-McCann stood firm. Sterling Lord was persuasive, and Kerouac finally accepted. On November 19, 1964, Amburn wrote to Kerouac suggesting that *Village Voice* editor Seymour Krim write the foreword. A little over a week later, the copyediting on the novel was completed, including Kerouac's corrections. His philosophy hadn't changed: there were to be no editorial changes save those he submitted after inspecting the copyedited manuscript.[8]

Rebounding somewhat from his sister's death, Kerouac refocused his attention on the Buddhist precepts of suffering and the Catholic fascination with sin and redemption. These themes would underpin the evolving notebook ponderances of *Vanity of Duluoz*. Life, to Kerouac, was now a "brute creation beautiful and cruel." He questioned how a bud could be considered "beautiful" when the life force only "encouraged the bud to flower out" and ultimately die. It was, in a sense, Kerouac's awareness of the mortification of his body as alcohol physically took its toll on him. Kerouac also said that a young person experimenting with LSD only sought to seek the "beautiful cruelty and the cruel beauty of the brute creation." Even Jack's dying father, who "gave you hopeful birth," "cops out," leaving "you flat with the burden (your self) of his own folly." In Kerouac's view, man merely inhabited a "bag" of skin, much as an astronaut dons a spacesuit to survive the harsh environment in which he floats. A soul can only be freed when the bag is broken, releasing the "ashes" back into the "Universal sea." The only "perfect bag," Jack mused, was a bottle of booze.[9]

Kerouac's final resurgence of active writing was sparked, in part, by reading Richard Ellmann's 1959 biography of James Joyce. Reinvigorated by linking his own circumstances with Joyce's, he was convinced that writing more novels could assure him a lasting audience. There was his Duluoz saga to complete. He needed to fill in the empty years from the high school period of *Maggie Cassidy* to that of *On the Road*. Creating such "installments" was, he felt, no less an effort than Joyce composing *Ulysses* and *Finnegans Wake*. Kerouac's works were "narratives in time" and not the "universal and linguistic mellings" of Joyce—if only Jack could lift himself from the lethargy that Scotch with beer chasers induced. He reached a new low when, drunk, he spent Thanksgiving night in jail for urinating in public.[10]

By the end of 1964, *Desolation Angels* was being prepared for galleys. Kerouac was still uneasy about merging what he had originally conceived as two novels. Examining the galleys, he struggled with the transition between the first half, "Desolation Angels" and the second half, "Passing Through" (the title chosen instead of "An American Passed Here," which Jack assumed he could save for a future work). Resigned, he told John Clellon Holmes, "Whatever people say about my work is of no consequence to my work, and of no consequence to my reasons for working." In the end, he wrote to "keep from dying of boredom and diffuseness of heart."[10]

In January 1965 he corrected the galleys and was pleased with the results. More than ever, he felt on the "right track" with the grand design of the Duluoz legend. However, he still had not seen Seymour Krim's foreword. When he saw it the next month, he objected to Krim's references to homosexuality. He insisted that he was not "queer" and that his associations with Ginsberg and Burroughs since the early 1940s were solely for artistic reasons. His stance was that of the naïve provincial absorbing the "big evil city scene": "[Y]ou must know me, you met me, you know I'm not queer, and at that time when I met Burroughs and Ginsberg I was just off the football team and in those days (1943) it was no easy trick to find a non-queer football player who didn't look down his nose at a queer. But these guys were such great writers and thinkers, and over the objections of my father, I hung out with them to learn new ideas and techniques."[11]

To drive his point home, Kerouac told Krim that he had sex, by his count, with approximately 250 women in New York during the World War II years between his two merchant marine voyages.[12] Kerouac advised Krim to avoid using expletives, as he had done, lest they harm the book's distribution. Overall, though, Krim's contribution to *Desolation Angels* satisfied him. Writing to Krim, Jack alerted him to the degrading financial status his fame had led him to: "Would you believe that I'm not coming to N.Y. for the publication of this book because I cant afford it, really? By 'really' I mean, it would eat into my next rent money. Can you explain to me why a guy with a name as 'famous' as mine and fourteen books and translated into fifteen languages around the world has to worry about the rent?"[13]

As was his wont, and despite his tenuous finances, Kerouac planned a European trip for the spring. This time he wanted to go to France to research his genealogy. Kerouac planned to pay for the trip from the money from *Desolation Angels*. He also knew that he had to get away from St. Petersburg, where his regular intake of Scotch with beer chasers and the beatings that he regularly absorbed were ruining his health. When he prowled the streets, mostly by himself, he tended to gravitate toward the roughest barrooms, full of sullen drunks and whiskey-fueled rowdies unimpressed by his celebrity. In March one man (a northern drifter, Kerouac concluded) attacked him. Jack told his agent on March 23, 1965:

> Now I have punctured lung and two broken ribs from a meaningless barroom attack (sneak) on my person. Luckily I got out alive by wrestling the maniac over on his back and then walking out. I broke my own ribs with the off-balance twisting effort. Lung is okay, says the doctor, and ribs are joining and mending. I was alone in a strange bar. I'm through with going out alone and through with hard liquor forever. That's enough of the rough stuff. There was no provocation for these sudden punches into my face. I was just telling my name.[14]

The injuries compelled him to postpone his Paris trip. Determined to alter his destructive pattern of living, he abstained from hard liquor for a few weeks. To help him stop drinking, he took prescribed tranquilizers. When he was sober, Jack stayed in, watching television. When he was bored and there were no shows to watch, he read *The Last Tycoon*, completing the book sometime during April 1965.[15]

Royalties became so meager that for the first time Kerouac considered taking Sterling Lord's advice to sell part of his archive. When he reviewed his archive, he noticed that a pencil-written 1948 diary was missing. He first made an inquiry to Northport neighbor Stanley Twardowicz: "I'm hoping I drunkenly gave it to Northport Library instead of having it stolen by those teenage bums the last weeks in N'Port."[16] However, it wasn't a "teenage bum" who pilfered the valuable document depicting part of his "on the road" journey. In a brochure he received from the University of Texas at Austin, Jack saw a photostat of a page from the missing journal. He traced the sale back to Gregory Corso, who had stolen the notebook from Northport in the early 1960s and sold it to the House of Books in New York for $1,000 to support his heroin habit. The store had sold the journal to the university.

A $1,000 check arrived from Coward-McCann, which had arranged for him to receive immediate payment for a paperback sale to Bantam Books.

Desolation Angels was published and received what Kerouac expected: some hostile reviews that criticized his free style, and others that recognized the writer's stature in American literature. As usual, the *New York Times*, in a review on May 2, 1965, observed that Kerouac's celebration of life (as conveyed in his past published efforts) was nothing more than a "vast, inconsequential epic of himself and his friends, no longer even attempting to disguise memoir with the trappings of fiction, and offering this as the sacred book of the Movement, the canonical work." Almost as an afterthought, reviewer Saul Maloff concluded, "If only he were putting us on; but no, he is beyond compare the most sincere writer we have."[17]

Kerouac took the $1,000 check from Coward-McCann and converted it into traveler's checks, leaving enough behind for his mother for emergencies. He bought a ticket for Paris. He did not plan to spend all the money in Paris, since he expected Sterling Lord to wire him some of the money due him from foreign royalties. He expected to visit the Bibliothèque Nationale in Paris and to finish "Sea" by describing the cold crash of the Atlantic against the coast of Brittany. He would conclude his trip by renting a room in Amsterdam and spending a quiet week reading, drinking coffee, strolling through the streets, and watching films.

He boarded an Air France jet in Florida and arrived the next morning in Paris. Kerouac noted the contrast to humid and hot St. Petersburg. The streets remained wet and skies overcast, for it had been raining in Paris for almost a month. Kerouac took a bus to Les Invalides and rented a cheap room. He visited the Hotel des Invalides, to visit the namesake of his boyhood church, Saint Louis de France. In the classically built church with its baroque interior, Jack sat in his rumpled raincoat, enraptured by the mournful strains of the organ, perhaps staring at the sarcophagus that held the body of Napoleon I. Jack's hat was upturned in his lap. A family passing by took pity, thinking him homeless, and dropped 20 centimes into his hat. Later in his hotel room, he had sex with a forty-three-year-old prostitute whom he met at Montparnasse, paying her $120. Much of the rest of the journey was seen through a haze of cognac.

Kerouac had little luck investigating his genealogy. His plan to research the Kerouac name began with a visit to the Bibliothèque Nationale, where he learned that the Nazis had burned the crucial documents in 1944. The librarians were also less than helpful when they smelled the alcohol exuding from him.[18] Back on the streets, he took a "luscious" Arab girl to a performance of Mozart's *Requiem* at St. Germain des Près. Afterward he looked for the graves of Balzac and Pascal and went to a Beckett film. At the National Archives, Jack's research was again thwarted; he was told that records were not stored there, only manuscripts. A trip to the Bibliothèque Mazarine was equally fruitless. At the offices of Gallimard, his French publisher, they did not believe that he was Jack Kerouac and told him that neither the publisher nor his editor was available. Frustrated, he was ready to leave Paris after five days and bought a one-way plane ticket to the Breton city of Brest. When he arrived at the boarding gate, he suddenly had to go to the bathroom, which meant a brisk quarter-mile walk back up the terminal. When he returned to the gate, the plane was already taxiing down the runway. In it was the suitcase he had already checked. After a fifteen-mile taxi ride to Gare Montparnasse, he boarded a train to complete the journey. Predictably, the rest of the voyage came to nil, though he felt that he had the makings of another novel.[19]

July 1965 saw him working feverishly to recapture the cognac blur of his European trip. His writing filled over three notebooks, totaled thirty thousand words, and was completed in seven consecutive nights. In this work he abandoned his experimental prose style to increase the book's salability. Because of the trip, he now lacked enough money to support himself and his mother. Royalties for *Desolation Angels* weren't expected until

1966, and those due from Viking; Farrar, Straus; Grove Press; and a host of overseas publishers were still outstanding. For the present Jack and his mother remained solely dependent on Gabrielle's monthly Social Security check.

In August he typed his new novel, *Satori in Paris,* determined that it be published as is. Although he recognized the sparseness of the material, he reasoned that the novel was no less substantial than *The Subterraneans* or *Tristessa.* Writing to Lord in August he said:

> There seems to be a general new distaste in the culture since 1960 for works of realistic sentimentality (add Tennessee Williams' new position of disfavor to mine here), a trend towards the Ian Fleming type of sadistic facetiousness and "sickjoke" grisliness about human affairs, a grotesque hatred for the humble and the suffering heart, an admiration for the mechanistic smoothy *killer of sincerity,* a new infernal mockery sniggering down the alleys of the earth (not to mention down the corn-rows outside the Drive-In movies.) I just felt that nobody is going to care any more about my vow to write the truth only as I see it, and with sympathetic intention, "thru the keyhole of my eye."[20]

Nostalgically, he "remembered my father's tearful blue eyes and honest Breton face, and I am mindful of what my mother just said: that my way and my philosophy will come back, some great catastrophe is going to make people wake up again, my works and my fellow ham human beings who work in the same spirit, will outlast the sneerers, the uncooperative and unmannerly divisionists, the bloody Godless forever."[21]

Despite his substandard income, Kerouac resisted Ginsberg's suggestion that they compile their letters with Neal Cassady's for publication. In the fall of 1965, after a five-day drinking spree, Kerouac's conspicuous presence increasingly alerted residents that a "celebrity" was among them. The less-than-appreciative portion of St. Petersburg threw stones at his door and treated him like a court jester when he frequented bars. College kids sneered at his beer belly; others harassed Gabrielle for being the mother of the town "buffoon." He was arrested for vagrancy while sleeping in a parked car. The solution to all this hostility was to move.[22]

Having no family in St. Petersburg besides her son, Gabrielle grew lonelier. Also, her nerves became frayed every time someone lobbed rocks at her door. Jack's physical decline only exacerbated her depression and agitation. The arrival of a royalty check for $2,229 in October made relocating once again possible. As Sterling Lord circulated *Satori in Paris* around Manhattan, Kerouac left for New England to find a new house. Although he aborted the househunt soon after arriving, he did connect with some old friends. The three-week jaunt included a drunken side trip to Lowell, where he visited Stella Sampas and drank with Tony and Nicky Sampas at Nicky's bar on Gorham Street. One Sunday morning Jack returned to the house on Beaulieu Street where his brother had died and saw a statue of the Virgin Mary on the small strip of grass that constituted the lawn. On the next street over was Saint Louis de France, the church where he was baptized. He attended Sunday mass. At the Parkway Lounge in downtown Lowell, Kerouac ate with Tony Sampas. On the way home, he visited John Clellon Holmes and his wife in Old Saybrook. Kerouac's appearance was so shocking that Holmes wondered whether he would ever see his old friend again. He wouldn't.

By December, Kerouac was back in Florida, having been driven there by some new companions: Clifford and Patricia Mitchell and Paul Bourgeois. Bourgeois, according to Kerouac, overstayed his welcome, and Jack begrudged him the hospitality. Bourgeois, a self-described "Indian chief" whom Kerouac dubbed "cousin," was more Jack's drinking companion than anything else. Bourgeois later found work at an ice cream stand, thus ending his brief, sodden connection to Kerouac.[23]

Fans of Kerouac—some of them hippie college students—continued to knock on his door hoping for a night out with a famous (and notorious) author. Sometimes he went, but most times he hid in his mother's bedroom while Gabrielle shooed them away. One of her techniques was to tell unwanted guests that Jack was drinking miles away; they'd vanish in the Florida night in a frantic quest to catch up with him. He did make regular appearances at the Wild Boar, a college bar, where he reigned as celebrity "writer-in-residence," entertaining patrons with wild impressions and free-form, bar-stool spontaneous rap. Professors would come to the bar to taunt Jack, but he rarely took their bait: "I create what you profess."

Sterling Lord finally sold *Satori in Paris* to Grove Press (after Coward-McCann declined). The sale garnered Kerouac a $2,000 advance. With these funds and $2,000 more from his English publisher, Kerouac was able to shop for a house in Massachusetts. He returned to Cape Cod to find a new place, this time by getting a motel and walking around for a few days until he found a house. The move was intended not only to satisfy his restless mother but also to connect with his Lowell youth so he could complete *Vanity of Duluoz*. He planned to use his correspondence from 1938 to 1949 as a guide. He wanted to "individualize & isolate characters away from 'Duluoz' & weave him in & out." The other option was to write in the first person as briefly as possible. To underpin the thematic continuity of his new book, he listed a "collection of statements that are absolutely true to Be Used as an Answer to All the Shitty Questions and Arguments of This Shit World":

> 1. All Creatures Tremble From Fear of Punishment
> 2. If Any Of You Be Free of Sin, Throw the First Stone
> 3. Who am I to throw Stones?
> 4. All Life Is Suffering
> 5. The Cause of Death Is Birth
> 6. Tears follow laughter, defeat follows victory[24]

One other way Kerouac revisited his Lowell youth was to write a "film drama" based on his novel *Doctor Sax;* he titled it "Dr. Sax & The Great World Snake" in his 1965 "G" journal. The idea eventually became a typescript in 1967 (as Jack's handwriting reveals on the manuscript). The mind's eye of the writer, writing with a pencil by the flickering light of a railroad lantern, in turn focuses on an eleven-year-old boy, Jacky Duluoz, sitting on the steps of a tenement doorway with his friends Lousy and G. J. The screenplay relies heavily on the novel, but is embellished at times with descriptive scenes of 1930s Lowell. Most striking is Jacky Duluoz's stroll through the grotto with his mother and Blanche. As they ascend the stairs to the looming crucifix (Kerouac likens its appearance to that of Salvador Dalí's oil painting *Saint John of the Cross*), the shot turns to Dr. Sax hanging from the orphanage walls with suction cups watching Jacky. Death, floods, gnomes, and snakes abound in Kerouac's bizarre film treatment. Like the novel, the screenplay culminates in an apocalyptic clash between a "Great Bird" and the "Great World Snake," which battle to hold sway over Duluoz's Lowell. Afterwards, Jacky bounces along the grotto by daylight with a rose in his hair and asks two praying women ascending the steps to the cross on their knees: "Boy did you see that giant bird catch that snake? Whoo!" The women turn to each other; one spins a finger in circles to her ear. It is plausible to believe that that was what most people were doing behind Kerouac's back in real life.[25]

By the early spring of 1966, Kerouac and Gabrielle were living in a modest house in Hyannis, Massachusetts, sold to them by John and James K. Atsalis, who first met Jack in their grocery store. They were driven north by a St. Petersburg friend, Betty Watley. On the trip, Gabrielle and Jack drank and talked as Betty drove. Predictably, funds remained tight. Kerouac sweated out the arrival of the next installment of royalties from Coward-McCann. He had used most of his savings to buy the house and was barely surviving with checks (ranging from $7 to $22 a week) from Sterling Lord's office.

The summer on Cape Cod—a sweltering haze of humidity and salty sea air—brought in tourists by the thousands. Now in her early seventies, Gabrielle was no longer the strong, faithful mother laboring at the shoe factory to support her son's artistic whims. Without her daughter, she was now dependent solely on a son who was still dependent on her. The darker side of their relationship was revealing itself in drunken insults and rash actions. Mother and son relied on the bottle to facilitate conversation between them. Attempting to conquer his alcoholism, Kerouac turned to a friend of Tony Sampas, Dr. Dan DeSole, who had visited Kerouac earlier that August and had prescribed Benadryl and Valium (under the mutually agreed code word "Wild Turkey"). After ten days on the medications Jack found alcohol "distasteful" and was able to write more productively. Kerouac hoped that he could write something of value, as long as he could avoid being "blind drunk."[26] To ward off the craving, Kerouac built a fence around his yard so he could sun himself all day in his "all-together," as Gabrielle expressed it.[27]

She was still perversely protective of her son. One summer afternoon she closed the door on Ginsberg and Orlovsky, who, with Jack's consent, had driven from New York City to visit him. Kerouac hid in the house to avoid them. Misery pervaded the home when Pitou, their cat, which had a gangrenous tail, died in Gabrielle's arms.[28] Cats were a constant fixation for the Kerouacs, as observed by John Atsalis when he came into their home. When the company of cats and his mother was not enough, Jack took to the phone. Those who were on the receiving end of his long-distance calls were old girlfriends like Helen Weaver, Lois Sorrels, Edie Parker, Carolyn Cassady, and Helen Elliott. The caliber of his calls ranged from sexual taunts to romantic reveries. But most times those he called could not fathom the dark, whiskey-blurred depths of his scattershot, brooding intelligence. Other recipients of calls were Ed White, Al Gelpi, Stanley Twardowicz, Tony Sampas, Lucien Carr, and Allen Ginsberg. Kerouac often baited Ginsberg with anti-Semitic crudities or ridiculed his "Messiah shot" of antiwar rhetoric and college campus protests. The phone bills, in conjunction with the liquor bill, were catastrophic to his budget.

In September 1966, Jack walked downtown with his mother to purchase a hundred capsules of vitamin C, as advised by Dan DeSole. The next day, intoxicated from a pint of sherry, Jack found Gabrielle slumped over in her chair with her head between her legs and foam bubbling from her lips. He dragged his mother to her bed and, after an hour, tried to sit her up so she could vomit, but she kept slumping over to her right and staring with glazed eyes. Kerouac called a doctor he knew, who came over and diagnosed a massive stroke. The doctor called an ambulance, which took her to Cape Cod Hospital in Hyannisport. There she underwent comprehensive testing and physical therapy. Nine days later, she began to feel the left side of her face and she moved her left leg. After a while, she also felt some sensation in her left arm. Kerouac was at her bedside every day. The nurses called Gabrielle "Zsa Zsa Gabor the Movie Star." She was allowed to come home but remained bedridden. Bitterly, she blamed the appearance of Ginsberg on her doorstep for her stroke. To help ease her suffering, Jack got her two new kittens they named Timmy and Tuffy.

Several weeks earlier, when Gabrielle first exhibited signs that something was amiss, Kerouac had contacted Stella Sampas. Stella was living in her mother's Stevens Street home with her brother John and caring for her mother, Maria. Kerouac had casually suggested marriage in 1964. Having loved Jack all her life, she normally would have accepted. She had followed his artistic growth and read each of the complimentary novels his publishers mailed her. There was, however, the hard fact that she was a middle-aged woman, almost five years older than Kerouac. She wrote Jack and Gabrielle in July 1966:

Dear Mrs. Kerouac & Jack—

I am relieved to know that you are perfectly well and I'm sure that you can handle all problems as they arise. As you know, Jack did come to Lowell and again brought up the subject of he and I getting married.

I don't know how to pursue the subject. You are his mother and know him much better than I could.

This much I can write, I love Jack—have loved him very much for a very long time and have never given the thought of marrying anyone but him.

I look in the mirror, and this is what holds me back. I'm no beauty. Probably too old to bear children. Jack deserves much more than I can offer.

This much I can offer—love—devotion and each and every effort to make him happy.

As for his previous marriages, all I can say is that whatever was lacking in these attempts I will try to avoid.

Look to your heart, and give me your blessing to share your son's future life.

Love—

Stella[29]

Gabrielle was initially against the proposal, as she was when Jack suggested marrying Lois Sorrels. In 1964, after Jack had proposed, Stella had visited the Kerouacs in Northport. When she arrived, Jack was out drinking and Gabrielle sent her away promptly. Disappointed, she stayed overnight with her uncle, Michael Sampas, a retired colonel living nearby in the city of Huntington. The next day she returned to Lowell. By July 1966, Gabrielle had softened and replied favorably to Stella.[30]

The lone survivor of his family (apart from his mother), all Jack had to do was glance at his mother's sewing basket before he began weeping. He wrote to John Clellon Holmes that he was "annoyed" by people's "arrogant assumption" that "to support" one's parents "in their old age is some kind of feebleminded mistake instead of what it really is: love on the only unselfish level."[31] On September 27, Stella left Lowell, by arrangement with Jack that month, to stay with Gabrielle. Kerouac wrote in his notebook: "Stella slaves and I do nothing but drink and think."[32] With Stella nursing Gabrielle and overseeing her rehabilitation, Jack could now go to Italy to help publicize the Italian edition of *Big Sur*, which was about to be published by Mondadori. Although he was reluctant to leave Cape Cod, the trip meant earning a sorely needed $1,000 honorarium.

In Italy, Kerouac's books were widely read. Many young readers kept copies of his and Ginsberg's books in their sleeping bags when they took to the road themselves, thereby kick-starting a rucksack revolution. Mondadori saw that Kerouac, the young, intense writer who peered so powerfully from his book jackets, was now rumpled, bloated, and insolent. In a televised interview with Fernanda Pivano, he drank from a glass of whiskey and spoke incoherently, asking questions like where Leonardo's

Last Supper was and imitating Mussolini. At Cavour Bookshop, for a celebration of the publication of *Big Sur* as the five-hundredth book in Mondadori's Medusa series, Kerouac slept in a chair during the proceedings.
Back in the States, Kerouac wrote to Sterling Lord complaining that, during the television interview and a seminar that he attended, he hardly got
a word in "edgewise." "Everybody had long prepared statements explaining me even to myself."[33] Apart from visiting the Vatican, singing poorly
in a Rome nightclub, and painting a pietà with Italian artist Franco Angeli
in his studio, he did not see the sense in having gone to Italy at all. Un-
dermining the whole trip was Jack's serious worry for his mother, which
understandably drained his spirits.

Permanently paralyzed, Gabrielle was released from rehabilitation at
the hospital and Stella returned to Lowell. Realizing he was Gabrielle's
sole support, Jack was determined not to place her in a nursing home.[34]
He purchased rubber sheets and a portable commode with the intention
of caring for her with the aid of a visiting nurse. Again Stella offered to
visit the Kerouacs once a week by bus to help care for Gabrielle, who was
now gaining mobility with the help of a wheelchair. Over the ensuing
weeks, Jack continued to care for her. Whenever she rang the bell that
dangled over her bed, Jack would lift and carry her to the portable commode. He also did the cooking: chicken pot pies, soft-boiled eggs, and
oyster soup. When she slept, he hurried to the local store and was back
within a half hour. A local friend of Gabrielle's came to the house to bathe
her. The family physician, however, did not visit, and Jack assumed that
he didn't "care." Kerouac was finally comfortable with the combination of
his income (he received his check from Italy in October) and his mother's
Social Security check. In mid-October, Kerouac wrote to Stella: "Okay,
sister . . . You heard what I said, S I S T E R. . . . come on over if you want
but remember it's not an emergency situation any more as far as care
goes—As for her progress, I don't understand it—Maybe the death of my
sister Caroline has taken the gumption out of her, I don't know."[35] He
contemplated moving to Lowell, where family friend Laurette Sullivan ran
a private nursing home on Andover Street. If she agreed to help, Kerouac
would be free to work on *Vanity of Duluoz*. However, the plan did not
materialize because he was still staunchly resistant (as was Gabrielle) to
placing her in an assisted-living home.[36]

Previous biographers have assumed that Kerouac only married Stella
because he could not care for himself, much less meet the demands im-
posed by Gabrielle's illness. However, the selfless, nurturing Stella was

willing to take on the arduous task. Jack and Stella's relationship ranged across thirty years of visits, correspondence, and phone calls. She and her family fostered important aspects of Kerouac's growth. There was a sign of Jack's true intentions when he wrote in a letter, "my mother is paralyzed, I had to get a wife to help."[37] Regardless of his intentions expressed under duress, Jack harbored true affection for his old friend.

They married in the backyard of his Hyannis home on November 19, 1966, with a justice of the peace officiating. In her unassuming home-made dress Stella was radiantly happy, as was Kerouac, jubilant to finally be a formal part of his late friend Sebastian Sampas's family. Sipping his Scotch, he called John Clellon Holmes to report the good news. Although he was happy for them, Holmes knew intuitively that Stella had "dealt herself a tough hand when she got into that."[38] Kerouac intended to have the ceremony performed twice more in Lowell: at Stella's Greek Orthodox church in February 1967 and, later, at his boyhood church in Centralville. Neither ceremony took place.

The Kerouacs' move to Lowell in January 1967 was a practical one, bringing Stella closer to her ailing mother as well as reintroducing Kerouac to his hometown. He had also worn out his welcome in Hyannis, a town used to the calm and noble reserve of the Kennedy compound. Shortly after his marriage, he was arrested twice for public drunkenness. Somehow he got Coward-McCann to lend him $4,000 to help pay for the new house in Lowell.

Sterling Lord had sold *Vanity of Duluoz* as a hardcover original to Coward-McCann for an advance of $1,500. As early as 1964, Kerouac had discussed the planned novel with Ellis Amburn. He told Amburn that he wanted to make as much money as popular spy novelist John le Carré. Kerouac would use material relating to Lucien Carr and his murder of David Kammerer, despite Carr's objections. With a new wife, a new novel, and a return to Lowell, Kerouac greeted his remaining years with an uncharacteristic optimism. In October 1967, he reflected in his notebook: "I still mourn for my Pitou [his cat that had died]—Stella I love now—Mémère has a constant friend, and I a great wife."[39]

31

The Golden Baby of Heaven

January 1967–October 1969

Shove yr. apples
and shove yr. eyes,
I wanta leave Clean
   JACK KEROUAC, notebook entry, 1965

The Highland section of Lowell was just far enough away from the city's downtown area that it retained its quiet and order, much like neighboring Chelmsford. The green split-level house at 271 Sanders Avenue was only a couple of miles from Stella's family home, where her mother, Maria, also required care. It wasn't Kerouac's first choice; he had tried to buy his old childhood home on Beaulieu Street. So it was in the Highlands that the Kerouacs settled in December 1966, paying the asking price of $31,000 for the house. One Lowell resident, Kerouac's paper boy, remembered that from "the doorway the house was usually in darkness with an eerie blue television light flickering. His mother occupied the dining room in an enormous hospital bed, invalid."[1] Kerouac hadn't sold the house in Hyannis, on which he was still paying the mortgage. He was also responsible for outstanding taxes, Gabrielle's medical costs not covered by Medicare, and Jan's child support payments. (Thinking of his ex-wife and her giving birth to Jan contributed to the morbid broodings he scribbled into his notebook: "Women and their predilection for giving birth so as not to bear the stigma of barrenness are skeletons inventing skeletons.")[2] By June 1967, these obligations (and the mortgage) prevented Jack from buying a much-needed new typewriter. His bill for his late-night phone calls averaged $150 a month.

Despite her husband's moodiness, preoccupations, and eccentricity, Stella was giddy with joy about her first marriage. She was grateful to have Gabrielle around to advise her on Jack's likes and dislikes. For his part, Kerouac purchased and kept by his chair a Greek dictionary, partially for his research and to look up some of Stella's occasional Greek (though English was her native language). However, beneath the honeymoon façade, Kerouac's restive desire to move yet again was stirring within him. Although Gabrielle was admitted to Holy Ghost Hospital in Cambridge, one of Massachusetts's best rehabilitative centers for stroke victims, soon after they moved to Lowell, the Massachusetts winters made her doubt the wisdom of staying in New England any longer. After three weeks of rehabilitation, Gabrielle expressed her dislike of the hospital and wanted to return home. Kerouac was equally miserable. In his notebook, he jotted: "She's on her deathbed, 73, and she doesn't want you, 45, to get off of it. Consider Unreasonableness."[3] The main cause of his misery was his inability to begin meaningful work on his contracted novel. He procrastinated during the winter of 1967 and planned to start in earnest in March. His creative frustration and alcoholism added to his considerable financial pressure. At times, he had to borrow money from Stella's brothers, which he paid back diligently.

There was interest in him and his work that winter, when friends and fans asked him about the absence of his books (notably *Satori in Paris*) from area shops like Prince's Book Store and Pollard's in downtown Lowell. Also, some filmmakers from Canada invited him to participate in their documentary on the Franco-American experience in New England. Although at first he refused unless paid "star wages" for his troubles, he relented and made the trip to Montreal, where he was filmed and interviewed in French.

When he returned to Lowell in mid-March, Kerouac sat down at his electric typewriter, rolled in a scroll of paper, and started to write. He altered the original 1942 version of *Vanity of Duluoz*. Unlike the composition of his previous novels, Kerouac's writing this time came in sporadic, brief bursts. His alcoholism made focusing extremely difficult. What drive he did have was fueled by financial duress and the "pep" pills that he regularly took. As he wrote, Kerouac read passages into his tape recorder or to his patient brother-in-law Tony Sampas, who acted as a sort of confidant. The Sampas brothers treated Kerouac like family: they drove him where he needed to go; hosted him at Nicky's bar; and, as they did throughout his life, supported his work. But the allegiance came at a cost to them—watching a loved one dive headlong into ruin. The alcoholism that had ravaged Kerouac for over a decade was now plainly evident. Neighbors were accustomed to seeing him walking at dusk along Walker Avenue. Wearing a short jacket, baseball cap, with head lowered and hands in pockets, he was "an overwhelmingly lonely figure."[4] "The only thing that people try to avoid, loneliness, is the only thing that makes their life precious," he had written in 1966.[5] His Lowell physicians called him, among themselves, the "walking dead man."[6]

At the end of March 1967, Kerouac wrote to Sterling Lord apologizing for a drunken phone call that he made from Nicky's after he had spent the night "writing 18,000 words on *Vanity of Duluoz*."[7] The call was one of dozens that ran up his phone bill.

The proximity of Lowell taverns and bars made it easy for Kerouac to find another drinking hole when ejected from the last. He continued his slovenly habit of public urination and was often arrested for it. When he wasn't delivering sexually overt crudities from his bar stool, he was drawing napkin sketches of pietàs, angels, cardinals, and crosses. In such moments Kerouac found temporary solace in religion. He remained devout in his Catholicism. On his bedroom wall hung a sheet of paper with two prayers written in French from St. Augustine ("Charité") and St. Teresa of Avila ("L'amour du Prochain").

As usual, the bulk of his income trickled in from foreign publishers like Gallimard, which had recently accepted *Satori in Paris* (Kerouac signed the contract that March). He had earned enough money to purchase a reconditioned Smith-Corona typewriter that made it possible to retype the *Vanity of Duluoz* scroll onto separate sheets of paper. By the spring of 1967, he was in dire straits once again and had to borrow money from Sterling Lord to pay for groceries and bills. In June he sent Lord two copies of *Vanity of Duluoz*, one of which his brother-in-law John Sampas duplicated at his Boston office. Kerouac had made his deadline, a heroic achievement.

Coward-McCann was pleased with Kerouac's "generous" effort and proceeded to copyedit the manuscript (scheduled for release the following year). Meanwhile, Kerouac was left to his own devices, trying to string together enough money to meet all of his financial demands. At Nicky's bar he ran up a tab and borrowed money in $10 increments. Not only did he lack money, he was also running out of fresh material. In his archive he searched for earlier work that would be relevant in the revolutionary 1960s. He reread much of Wolfe's work "in search of the secret of writing at great length about one short episode." The *Viking Portable Kerouac Reader,* initiated by John Clellon Holmes, had been abandoned, largely owing to the complexity of obtaining permissions from the many publishers that had bought Kerouac's work over the years.

In November 1967, a fifteen-year-old, pregnant Jan Kerouac located her father's house and knocked on the door. She was accompanied by her long-haired boyfriend, John Lash, and was planning on going to Mexico after her visit. It wasn't the first time she had tried to make contact with Jack; Jan had made inquiries through Sterling Lord's office, but at Jack's insistence, they refused to reveal his whereabouts. Stella answered the door (as was her custom when neither Jack nor Gabrielle wanted to, thus unintentionally making Jack's wife appear to be the "villain" when she turned away their visitors).⁸ Jack's welcome to Jan was distant. Acknowledging his paternity faintly, he assured her that she could use the Kerouac name to write books once she reached Mexico. The reunion was brief; Gabrielle was disturbed by the girl's presence in the house.

Jan left and headed south, where she gave birth to a stillborn baby and buried it beneath the hot sands of the desert. Jack clearly looked upon his paternity as a hapless mistake that fell in line with the flaws of the human condition: "Women are hooked on the habit of birth and death, which are synonymous, but men, ignorance itself personified, suspecting it, nevertheless follow along like goats."⁹ He never saw his daughter again.

That year, poet Ted Berrigan, approached Kerouac for an interview for the *Paris Review.* Berrigan was accompanied by William Saroyan's son Aram and fellow poet Duncan McNaughton. During the interview, Kerouac explained his spontaneous prose-writing technique: "I got the idea for the spontaneous style of *On the Road* from seeing how good old Neal Cassady wrote his letters to me, all first person, fast, mad, confessional, completely serious, all detailed, with real names in his case however (being letters)." He also talked about *Visions of Cody's* dictating techniques, haiku writing, Lou Little and his years at Columbia, Burroughs and *Naked Lunch,* Buddhism, his family's genealogy; and the background of the novels *Tristessa* and *The Subterraneans.* Finally, he asserted his conservative outlook on American society: "I'm pro-American and the radical political involvements seem to tend elsewhere. . . . The country gave my Canadian family a good break, more or less, and we see no reason to demean said country."[10]

The winter of 1967 assailed Lowell with snowstorms, and Kerouac got his exercise shoveling snow from his driveway. Stella snapped a photo of a beaming Jack, ruddy from cold and exertion. But alcoholism was eroding Jack's resilience. His hometown did not give Kerouac the respect he so greatly desired. "Stinktown on the Merrimack" chose to ignore or deride its native son. His depression deepened; before long, he agreed with Gabrielle to look for a house in Florida the following spring. In the house the alcoholism continued; Kerouac was now a two-fisted drinker, holding malt liquor in one hand and Scotch in the other. Stella had few visitors. Even some of her family, like her sister-in-law Betty Sampas, were hesitant to visit after Gabrielle made it plain that she did not like her young children in the house. The Sampas family felt that it would be the wrong time for Kerouac to move; in Lowell he was protected. In Florida, the uncertainty of familiar strangers in bars added a potent caliber of dread to Stella who, for all intents and purposes, would be treading unfamiliar ground. But the plan surfaced again and again as Gabrielle made plain her desire to move away from the cold winters of Lowell.

In February 1968, the month of *Vanity of Duluoz*'s publication, Mexican Indians in San Miguel walking along the train tracks found a body lying beside the tracks. It was Neal Cassady, comatose from a drug overdose. He had traveled to Mexico to meet a new girlfriend, Janice Brown, in Celaya. She was confident that she could help him with his savage drug addiction, but they soon squabbled. Determined to walk from Celaya to San Miguel along the train tracks, Cassady left Janice. At the train station he met some revelers celebrating a wedding. They offered him pulque, a potent Mexican drink derived from the sap of the maguey plant, which he rejected because hard liquor made him deathly ill. Instead he took a handful of speed and Seconal. Shortly afterward, he began walking, but exhaustion and the heat overtook him only a few yards down the track. Somewhere along the way his steps faltered and he collapsed. The Indians who found him brought him to a hospital, where doctors failed to revive him. No one claimed his corpse. Ken Kesey sent funds, via his lawyer, to pay for Neal's cremation. His ashes were sent to Carolyn.

Carolyn's phone call on February 4 at first left a sobered Kerouac in a vehement state of denial that "old Neal" was dead; he believed instead that Cassady was in Africa incognito. More than ever, he sensed his own fragility and mortality. He told Carolyn that he would be joining Neal "soon."

Kerouac traveled to Europe (Germany, Spain, and Portugal) with his brothers-in-law Tony and Nick Sampas in March 1968. They returned to Lowell after Jack became disenchanted with Germany. He felt Germans were harsh and cold. In Portugal he solicited a prostitute, paying her to stare into his eyes.

In March 1968, an autobiographical sports article by Kerouac for the *Atlantic Monthly* called "In the Ring" appeared. It carried the reader from 1968 back to the "grimly drab lamps" of 1930s Lowell when his father managed a boxing gymnasium with family friend Roland Bouthelier (Armand Gauthier).

> So I remember the time in about 1931 when I heard Roland being given sincere instructions in a dressing room smelling of big men sweat and liniment and all the damp smells that come from the showers and the open windows. "Go out there etc.," and out comes me and my Pa and we sit right at ringside, he lights up his usual 7-20-4 or Dexter cigar, the first match is on, his own promoted match, it's Roland Bouthelier against wild Mad Turk McGoo of the Lower Highlands and they come out and face each other; they lean over and clap big arms and hands over each other's necks and start mauling around and pretty soon one of them makes a big move and knocks the other guy down on the soft hollowly bouncing canvas.[11]

Though the writing paled in comparison with that of a decade earlier, it was nonetheless sincere.

To raise money for his move to Florida, Kerouac asked Sterling Lord to send Coward-McCann three manuscripts to option at $5,000 each: the complete version of *Visions of Cody;* a new novel titled "Beat Spotlight"; and another called "The Second Coming," the latter two still existing only as outlines. "The Second Coming" would echo the fantastical element of *Doctor Sax;* in the new novel the second coming of Christ materializes in the sky as a dark cloud. The imminent apocalypse causes the earth to rumble and people to rush from homes into the streets crying out to be saved. However, the earth stops shaking and the people's fear subsides. It was a thin story, to say the least, but Kerouac hoped that he could make it significant enough to sell. It was never written, let alone optioned.[12]

Vanity of Duluoz: An Adventurous Education, 1935–1946 was released in February 1968 to lackluster reviews. The *New York Review of Books* reviewed the novel in the same column as Jeremy Larner's book *The Answer* and William H. Gass's *In the Heart of the Heart of the Country*:

> If Jack Kerouac's *Vanity of Duluoz* and Jeremy Larner's *The Answer* were put together between one cover they would make a saga on the regenerative powers of each generation to consider itself unique and to write about this with an ineptness and banality indistinguishable from its predecessor. Kerouac, in his forties, Larner, in his twenties, both take up the search for identity, and grimly turn it into exercises so similar that one wonders whether America is not producing a literary Snopes family which we are doomed to see advertising itself with steamy prose every twenty years or so. It is uncanny how these two books, one an autobiography, the other written in the first-person singular, blend together to chronicle an inbred sensibility whose only purpose seems to be to publish vague musings about itself.[13]

The *New York Times*, especially, demolished any interest a publisher would have in a Kerouac novel. His name was dead in industry circles, for he was viewed as being unpublishable, not for his experimental prose but because he was seen as written out and incapable of quality. To Allen Ginsberg, Kerouac wondered earnestly why there was a "conspiracy" against him.[14] His notebooks made bigoted references to the "Jewish mafia," which he felt put his books out of print. He was even offended by those Jews who spoke French: "Every time I hear a 'cultured Jew' speak 'French' it cuts into my heart to hear such Corruption."[15]

In desperation, Jack turned to his archive to raise money for household expenses and his mother's medical needs. In July 1968, Kerouac defended the negotiation of the sale of his correspondence with Ginsberg to Andreas Brown of Gotham Book Mart:

> In case you think I'm being "commercial," I want you to know that this is the worst financial moment of my life: my mother is paralyzed, I had to get a wife to help, my books are being turned down by publishers ("*Visions of Cody*") (the complete one), so I have no money but small savings left, no prospects, magazines only ask me for Letters-to-the-Editor free prose, or "my own obituary," my health worsened by

ten years in the last single year. . . . I'm in debt to a local bank for $1,300, the right is accusing me of "corrupting youth" and the left is accusing me of "do-nothingism."[16]

Kerouac's drinking landed him in the tank for walking downtown with an open can of beer in his hand. In the jail cell of Lowell's police department, Kerouac caught a cold and consequently suffered from strep throat. However, he was glad that the incident did not reach the papers. On another occasion, Jack was imbibing in downtown's SAC club and passed out between the booths. The management locked the doors and left. When they opened up early the next day, they found him sitting at the bar drinking. They threatened to call the police, but Jack persuaded them to call either Stella or Tony. Tony retrieved Jack and paid Jack's hefty tab.[17] Not aware of, or concerned about, the hazard that he posed to himself and the community when he was drunk, Kerouac blamed the "civil rights movement" for making police paranoid and "jittery" of "everybody they see on the sidewalk."[18]

Kerouac brought Stella to the hospital in Lowell after they had intercourse; she was a virgin and had bled profusely the first time they had sex. His average income of $60 a week compelled Stella to borrow constantly from her brothers just to make ends meet. When the offer came to appear on William F. Buckley's *Firing Line* television show, Kerouac accepted eagerly, despite his apprehension about making a spectacle of himself on television. He wanted to publicize his "need to reprint" *Vanity of Duluoz* and to promote *Visions of Cody* and the yet-to-be-written "Beat Spotlight," which was to address the years after the publication of *On the Road*. "The Second Coming" had fallen by the wayside. Impatient and worried about their finances, Stella wrote a letter to Sterling Lord. She reminded Lord that Jack was planning to take Gabrielle to Florida and to write a "future book" (presumably "Beat Spotlight"). Also, Jack had received notice from Viking Press that the expected royalty rate from any "special editions" of *On the Road* would drop from 15 percent to 10 percent. *On the Road*, Stella asserted, was Jack's "most valuable property." Besides Viking, other American publishers, including City Lights and Grove Press, had yet to send him any royalty statements. She found it unbelievable that Kerouac the writer had slipped beneath the radar of American culture, that he was perceived to be no longer relevant: "Apparently, the American people seem to ignore Jack's works and we are wondering if this is really so."[19] Writing to his agent later that month, Kerouac said that Stella "oughta mind her own business and wash her dishes."[20]

He arrived in New York City for his appearance on *Firing Line* on September 3, 1968, escorted by Lowell friends Billy Koumentzelis, Nicky, and Tony Sampas. Kerouac was drunk on Scotch and beer imbibed on his three-hour drive from Lowell. In Manhattan, Kerouac took them to his old haunt, the West End Bar, before going to the Delmonico Hotel, where *Firing Line* put him up. Also staying there were Jean Genet and William S. Burroughs, who was writing an *Esquire* article on the 1968 Democratic convention. When Kerouac suggested that Burroughs come with him to the television studio, he refused, not wishing to witness this "outrage." Kerouac also saw his old friend Ginsberg. His obvious disdain for Ginsberg extended, to some degree, to his opinion of the hippie movement. In his notebook he compared a 1901 photo of a Jewish refugee woman from Russia and her child waving a little American flag to a photograph of Ginsberg and his "gang" using the American flag as a "shroud coat" and waving a "Viet Cong flag 60 years later."[21] This, to Kerouac, was the two polarities that defined what was happening to America. Before Kerouac left to tape the show, Ginsberg bade adieu to Kerouac for the last time in person, telling him "Goodbye drunken ghost."

During the taping, Kerouac slouched on his swivel chair and looked every bit the rumpled belligerent drunk at the end of the bar at Nicky's. Despite his appearance, Kerouac's wit and intellect were every bit as sharp, and at times sharper, than those of his two co-guests, poet Ed Sanders and sociologist Lewis Yablonsky. When a frustrated Yablonsky was nonplussed by Kerouac's interjections, he asked, "why couldn't you keep quiet while I was talking? I'll keep quiet when you talk?" Attempting to make plain his sentiments about the beat movement, Kerouac sent his "thumbs-down to Ginsberg over there in the back." Crudely he stated that he would throw Ginsberg "to the lions." When Buckley asked Kerouac his first question, he stammered for a moment, leading the impatient Kerouac to rudely reply, "get your question over with."

> WB: What distinguishes the hippie movement from simply an ortho-
>   dox, radical Adamite movement?
> JK: A*d*omite? *Adam*? Adam and Eve or A*t*om?

WB: Adam.

JK: It's Adam and Eve? What's Adamite? When they wear their hair long, layers, in caves?

WB: Back to nature [. . .]

JK: We might have to in due time due to the Atom . . . ite bomb. (laughs loudly)

WB: Hey that was good wasn't it?

JK: I'm good all the time boy. [22]

When Buckley asked Kerouac what the "evolution" was from the beats to the hippies, Kerouac explained:

I'm 46 years old and these kids are 18, but it's the same movement. It's apparently some kind of Dionysian movement in late civilization in which I did not intend any more than I suppose Dionysius did. [. . .] It's just a movement which is supposed to be licentious but it isn't really. The hippies are good kids, they're better than the beats. See Ginsberg and I . . . well Ginsberg . . . boring, we're all in our forties and we started this and the kids took it up. A lot of hoods, hoodlums and communists jumped on our backs, well on my back not *his* [Ginsberg]. Ferlinghetti jumped on my back and turned the idea that I had that the beat generation was a generation of beatitude and pleasure in life, and tenderness into what they call in the papers "beat mutiny," "beat insurrection," words I never used. Being a Catholic I believe in order, tenderness, and piety.

Buckley responded: "Well then your point was that a movement which you conceived as relatively pure has become idealogized and misanthropic and generally . . ."

JK: A movement that was considered what?

WB: Pure.

JK: Yes it was pure in my heart.

Though Kerouac was intoxicated, his perception of his work and legacy to Buckley was sober, oftentimes cutting through the academic navel-gazing of Yablonsky and Sanders with his savage wit and intelligence. He conjured forth aphorisms as well as occasional forays into literary anecdote (such as about Tolstoy) to prove his points. Though to the television-viewing adults of America, Jack came off as out of touch with his times, he was in fact years ahead of them.

In Lowell, Jack's drinking continued unabated. On one occasion he took Joe Chaput to a Boston bar frequented by a black clientele. Kerouac's unrestrained racial taunts and imitation of southern black speech forced Chaput and Kerouac to leave before they were violently ejected.

In September 1968, Jack, Gabrielle, and Stella left for St. Petersburg. Joe Chaput, Jim Dumphy, and Red Doherty helped load the Kerouacs' belongings into a station wagon. Their cats accompanied them in pet carriers. The trip was punctuated by Jack's frequent blasts on the harmonica and by slugs from a bottle of Johnny Walker Red and cans of malt liquor that accumulated around his feet.

They moved into a house at 5169 Tenth Avenue North, next door to the one that they had lived in earlier. One of the first things Kerouac did was to go to the home of his friend Betty Watley so he could introduce her to Stella. Watley's children alerted her that a man had passed out on her lawn; when Betty saw who it was, she was happy to see Jack once again.[23]

In the new house Jack unpacked and arranged his belongings as he had at all previous residences. In his bedroom was his office: his desk and a carefully organized file cabinet. With money from Italian royalties, Kerouac planned to build a five-foot fence around the property and pay the first month's mortgage. Before long, he had to think of new ways to generate income. Keith Jennison at Viking had the original scroll for *On the Road*. Kerouac instructed Lord to retrieve the scroll from Jennison in the hope that it could be sold: "It's my personal property, also my concrete physical property in that it's my paper and my ink and no one else's. I'll be needing this to tide me over middle age in a very surprisingly unlucky literary career."[24] Another scroll Kerouac created were notes for *Beat Spotlight*. The length of his typing grew to ten feet before it faltered to a stop. This he planned to have his agent sell.

Beat Spotlight failed to find a publisher, so Kerouac retrieved a 1951 story, "Pic," to rewrite for possible publication.[25] Pic (the nickname of Pictorial Review Jackson) was an African American boy from North Carolina. At the end of the third draft of *On the Road*, Sal and Dean meet Pic. Kerouac scrapped the end and saved the characters for a story. Kerouac mailed the manuscript to his agent, who kept it in his office and was only able to sell it after Kerouac's death. Meanwhile, Stella found some work at a department store, Webb City, as a seamstress for approximately one month. She earned $1.70 per hour; occasionally she had to borrow from her brothers.[26]

Sterling Lord secured a $1,500 assignment for Kerouac from the *Chicago Tribune*; even more money was possible after it was syndicated in other newspapers. "After Me the Deluge" (variously titled "What Am I Thinking About?," "Man, Am I the Grandaddy-O of the Hippies," and "The Bippie in the Middle") discussed his disassociation from the radical political climate.

> I've got to figure out first how I could possibly spawn Jerry Rubin, Mitchell Goodman, Abbie Hoffman, Allen Ginsberg and other warm human beings from the ghettoes who say they suffered no less than the Puerto Ricans in their Barrios and the blacks in their Big and Little Harlems, and all because I wrote a matter-of-fact account of a true adventure on the road (hardly an agitational propaganda account) featuring an ex-cowhand and an ex-footballer driving across the continent north, northwest, Midwest and southland looking for lost fathers, odd jobs, good times, and girls and winding up on the railroad. Yup, I'd better convince myself that these thinkers were not on an entirely different road.[27]

In the current political climate, Kerouac wrote, he had nowhere to turn, as he liked neither the hippies eating peanut butter sandwiches in the park nor the upper-echelon paper shufflers and political fund-raisers. His solution was simply to "drop out" in the "Great American Tradition," to "go to sleep and suddenly in my deepest inadequacy nightmares wake up haunted and see everyone in the world as unconsolable orphans yelling and screaming on every side to make arrangements for making a living yet all bespattered and gloomed-up in the nightsoil of poor body and soul." It was a potent, sobering essay from a lonely, despondent, and unsober mind.

Other than staying in his air-conditioned home, there was no escape from Florida's scorching heat except slugging down boilermakers. Dan De-Sole offered Kerouac a paying gig: a trip to Michigan to give a lecture. Knowing he was unable to undertake such an endeavor, Kerouac replied that he conducted a "seminar" regularly in his rocking chair. On September 20, wanting company, he invited Edie Parker to visit, with Gabrielle's consent, wiring, "Have money available for air fare . . . So forget that job and come quick as you can. Jack Kerouac."[28] Once she was there, she would have to pay her own expenses; there would be no "moochy-moochy." However, soon after sending the telegram, he wrote to her that he, Gabrielle, and Stella had all decided that she should not come.[29]

Inadvertently, Kerouac slipped into his character Pic's African American dialect at the Cactus Bar. Unfortunately, the bar was frequented by "Negro soul-brothers" who thought that he was mocking them. He told Edie in a letter: "I was stupid enough to take a 100% disabled retired Air Force Lieutenant to a Negro bar in St. Pete here, where he put his arm affectionately around the Negro band manager while the band was rehearsing. The manager, 22, slugged him. I jumped up and said, 'He's not a queer.' 'So, you want it too!?' said the ex-boxer." Kerouac was tossed from the bar into the parking lot, where several black men took turns beating him, breaking his ribs. As usual, Kerouac did not fight back. He was stitched up in the hospital and given a tetanus shot. Afterward, he spent four hours in jail with black eyes, a twisted knee, and bruised arms. Stella paid the $25 bail at eight o'clock that evening.[30]

Stella quit her job to stay home with the two invalids, one crippled by a stroke, the other by alcohol and a savage assault. Jack had taken to treating himself; he feared hospitals and lacked money for follow-up medical treatment. Stella had to maintain his correspondence for a while, while he sat in the yard alone and adrift. The swampy humidity soaked his T-shirts. October arrived and Jack wanted desperately to return to Lowell. He called John Clellon Holmes; they spoke for an hour. Or, rather, Holmes listened as Kerouac winded his boozy monologues until well past midnight, when an exhausted Holmes hung up at last. Before he did, Jack dared Holmes to call him back. It was the last time that Holmes ever spoke to him.

Leo Kerouac's last surviving brother, Jack's godfather Jean-Baptiste, died on October 8. He had accomplished what most in the Kerouac bloodline had failed to do: live a full life. He died at age eighty-two, leaving behind no children and a second wife, whom he had married in 1956 when he was sixty-nine.

Jack sent Sterling Lord the conclusion of *Pic,* dedicating the novel to Dan DeSole. He was also anxious to hear about any royalties from Europe.

On the evening of October 19, Kerouac was lying in his yard on a cot

Stella had purchased for him with S&H green stamps. A lifelong insomniac, he wrote in his notebook. When he could not write any more, he took out his father's letters and read them, the haunted voice almost audible. By his side, his wife listened patiently as he talked about Leo. After a while, they sat up with Gabrielle, eager to talk about those Lowell days when they were all together. Jack called Tony Sampas Sr. (who was in bed with his girlfriend). Tony did not want to talk to Jack, who was complaining about Stella, and hung up the phone. This angered Kerouac, and he hastily wrote a vitriolic letter to his nephew, Paul Blake Jr.:

> This is Uncle Jack. I've turned over my entire estate, real, personal, and mixed, to Mémère, and if she dies before me, it is then turned to you, and if I die thereafter, it all goes to you. The will is locked in a bank vault of the Citizens National bank of St. Petersburg. I have a copy of the new will in the house just for reference. My St. Pete attorney who did this for me is Fred Bryson. I just wanted to leave my "estate" (which is what it really is) to someone directly connected with the last remaining drop of my direct blood line, which is, me sister Carolyn [sic], your Mom, and not to leave a dingblasted fucking goddamn thing to my wife's one hundred Greek relatives. I also plan to divorce, or have her marriage to me, annulled.[31]

The next morning, Jack drank his breakfast—whiskey—despite Stella's offer to cook for him. Instead he ate from a can of tuna as he watched television. On his lap was an open notebook. He got up and went to the bathroom; Stella heard him cry out for her. Startled, she rushed in and found him bowed over the toilet bowl vomiting blood. The vicious beating at the Cactus Bar had been the final blow. Over his objections, Stella called an ambulance and rushed him to St. Anthony's Hospital in St. Petersburg. Jack sat in the receiving room for a few minutes waiting for a doctor to become available. He was then strapped to a stretcher and had to be held down while the doctor performed a blood transfusion. Kerouac's weakened body rejected the donated blood; he continued to spew gory vomit. Stella, despondent and helpless, could only watch her husband shouting that he did not want to die. From the waiting room, Betty Watley could hear Jack screaming in pain. Thirty pints of blood were transfused into his body before Kerouac lapsed into unconsciousness.

He lay in a bed, his body stained with blood, IVs stuck into his hands.

32

The Deluge

Success is counted sweetest
By those who ne'er succeed.
To comprehend a nectar
Requires sorest need.
EMILY DICKINSON

John Clellon Holmes was reading about Jack in some journals when his wife, Shirley, called to him that she had heard on the radio that Jack had died. Holmes said, "There were the bad moments waiting for a repeat of the newscast; there were the waves of awareness coming up and receding." Dread mixed with the dull ache of a long-awaited expectation of the inevitable. Ginsberg called him. "He didn't live much beyond Neal, only a year and a half."[1]

Allen was at his home in Cherry Valley, New York, preparing for a poetry reading at Yale University when he heard of Jack's death. At the reading, Ginsberg answered the students' questions about Kerouac. They wanted to know where he fit in "today." Holmes remembered:

> Allen sighed and leaned on the lectern towards the microphone on his elbows, and didn't say anything for fifty seconds. I knew what he was thinking: How could you sum it up in a few glib words? How could you bring back the eager Jack, Jack of the tender eyes, the raucous Jack of midnights, Jack's earnest sweat, maddening Jack of the end of the

nights, maudlin Jack of all the songs, the Jack who knew for sure, canny Jack who trusted to his whims, Jack simple as a cornflower, fist-proud Jack, the bongo-Jack of saucepans, Jack of the Chinese restaurants, Jack mooning under streetlamps about guilt, the Jack of Jacks?—when all they probably knew anything about was drunken, contentious Jack, bigoted, mind-stormed Jack, the Jack of sneers, the boozy bum of Buckley, the imitator of Stepin Fetchits who wrote all those unreadable books, and somehow now appeared to have drunk a hole in his Balzac-belly. How could you? No way.

Ginsberg's answer was concise and insightful: "Well he was the first one to make a new crack in the consciousness."[2]

Before they left, they carved Kerouac's name into a Cherry Valley tree in the name of "American poetry." Together they drove to Lowell, Massachusetts, for Kerouac's second wake. The first wake was held, with an open casket, at the Rhodes Funeral Home. Kerouac's soft, slightly thinning black hair was combed back like it was when he was a young man. His hairy hands clutched rosary beads. He wore the same jacket he had first worn at the *Firing Line* taping less than a year earlier. His mother had picked out his clothes. Distraught, Gabrielle was wheeled into the funeral parlor in her wheelchair, wailing, half in Québecois French and half in English, how "pretty" her youngest child looked. She was despondent that she was now alone, having outlived her husband and all of her children. After a daylong wake, the body was prepared for a flight to Boston.

At Logan Airport, the casket was put into a hearse and transported to Archambeault's Funeral Home, next door to the Franco-American Catholic school grotto that haunted Jack so much that he had featured it in *Doctor Sax*. On Thursday, October 23, over one hundred mourners—hippies, beats, blue-collar workers, professors and students, the Sampas family, and a coterie of Kerouac's fellow bar crawlers—attended the wake. One floral wreath held a copy of *Maggie Cassidy*. It stated simply, "Thank you."

Linking arms, Ginsberg, Corso, and Orlovsky approached the casket. Corso filmed some shaky, grainy footage of the corpse—much to the shock of those around him. Ginsberg told Kerouac to "get up, you son of a bitch." He reached out and caressed the cold, unfurrowed brow, which so many times before had been sweaty with excitement, contemplation, or brooding. Ginsberg later said that there was "really nothing inside"—echoing Kerouac's own poetic sensibility. Near the casket Stella, dressed in black, greeted mourners.

The pallbearers carried the casket down the long canopied walkway to the waiting hearse. It drove less than a half mile to Saint Jean de Baptiste Church, where nearly thirty-five years earlier Kerouac had served as an altar boy. Father "Spike" Morissette said the mass. Afterward, the cars of the mourners followed the hearse through a veritable tour of Jack's Lowell novels: through downtown Lowell of his teenaged years, where he was both sports hero and brooding loner; past the Commodore Ballroom, where he had enjoyed the latest swing bands with the keen ear that helped shape his prose; and into South Lowell, where he had courted Mary Carney. He was buried in Edson Cemetery in the Sampas family plot, next to Sebastian.

Ginsberg threw a handful of dirt and a rose onto the casket, as fall leaves blew in the grass. Crows cawed from the twisted branches of the elm and oak trees. Later, a tombstone was erected. Stella's brother John was with her when she selected the stone. Around John's neck hung a religious medallion of a dove, symbolizing the Holy Spirit, descending from Heaven toward the earth. She chose to have that imagery etched onto the stone. She composed the epitaph: "He Honored Life." Under her husband's name she had her own inscribed.

Stella managed the estate mostly by keeping Jack's archives safe and largely unseen by most people. Shrewdly and stubbornly, she resisted the many who wanted to write biographies of her husband. She turned away the first to ask, Ann Charters. Kerouac had allowed her to write a bibliography of his published works under his supervision in 1966 while he was living in Hyannis. During the course of her work, Kerouac awoke one morning and accused her of going through his papers and snapping a "Bowery bum" photo of him (he was hungover at the time). Stella's refusal did not stop Charters, who wrote a biography using interviews with the many friends and associates who had their own versions of Kerouac. She also used Kerouac's books in lieu of the many detailed notebooks, letters, and journals that were denied to her. As flawed as the biography was, she created the first published chronology.

Stella had expressly forbidden the publication of Jack's letters in her lifetime, a request that was honored. Besides, Stella hardly had time to manage the estate, as she was caring for Gabrielle in their St. Petersburg home. In March 1971, she considered returning to Lowell. Writing to her brother John and her mother, Stella explained, "All I have is a paralyzed Memere & the kittens & surely we can make a comfortable life in such a large house." However, she decided to remain in St. Petersburg where Gabrielle was being treated by a physical therapist. Gabrielle remained in her bedroom, and all visiting was done there; the only television perpetually stayed on next to her bed. Stella cooked Greek food and scrimped along on their limited income. Most of the time she wore Jack's T-shirts. Before long, she grew "very leery of people" who tried to gain access to Jack's archive. Among those who were turned away were the Blakes, both father and son: "They never came over until Jack died. In the house they started going through things until Stella asked them to leave."[3] Ginsberg was similarly shut out, even though Gabrielle eventually tolerated his presence in her house. In 1972, Ginsberg was asked to write an essay memorializing Kerouac as a foreword to *Visions of Cody*, which had been accepted by McGraw-Hill. Ginsberg's comments were respectful, a eulogy of sorts not only for Kerouac but also for a piece of a bygone America:

> I don't think it is possible to proceed further in America without first understanding Kerouac's tender brooding compassion for bygone scene & personal Individuality oddity'd therein. Bypassing Kerouac one bypasses the mortal heart, sung in prose vowels; the book is a giant mantra of appreciation and adoration of an American man, one striving heroic soul.[4]

Ginsberg was also one of the earliest advocates of Kerouac as a poet:

> Kerouac's poetry looks like the most "uncrafted stuff" in the world. He's got a different idea of craft from most people who use the word craft. I would say Kerouac's poetry is the craftiest of all. And as far as having the most craft of anyone, though those who talk about craft have not yet discovered it, his craft is spontaneity; his craft is having the instantaneous recall of the consciousness; his craft is the perfect executive conjunction of archetypal memorial images articulating present observation of detail and childhood epiphany fact.[5]

Gabrielle had another stroke in 1973 and, at age seventy-eight, died in her bed in her St. Petersburg home. Stella brought her body back to Nashua, New Hampshire, where she was buried alongside her husband, Leo, and son Gerard. Eventually, Kerouac's daughter, Jan, was buried there also. She died on June 7, 1996, in Albuquerque, New Mexico.

Aside from *Visions of Cody*, Kerouac's books were mostly out of print.

Not until the 1990s, after the death of Stella Kerouac, would Kerouac begin to earn his rightful place in the literary pantheon.

Stella Sampas Kerouac died on February 10, 1990. Having inherited the estate from Gabrielle in 1973, she in turn willed it to her surviving brothers. In the estimate of her youngest brother, John, the estate was "moribund."[6] The first priority of the Sampas family was to bring capital into an estate valued at less than $50,000 at the time of Kerouac's death (presumably including his real estate). John Sampas, in conversations with his family, figured that it was time to publish the archive. Michael Sampas had died after Stella, in September 1990. Tony Sr. had suffered a heart attack. John, being the youngest, felt the most capable. He had the family draw up a legal document appointing him as literary executor. To generate income, some archival material was sold to pay property taxes for the St. Petersburg home as well as those back taxes owed on his publishing royalties. Some items in the archive were sold to book dealers, but most were later bought back. The estate hired Lowell poet and editor Paul Marion to help catalog the vast archive.[7]

The first part of the archive to be published was a book of poetry that Kerouac had submitted to Lawrence Ferlinghetti during the 1960s, *Pomes All Sizes*. John Sampas next wanted to publish *Some of the Dharma* and submitted Jack's typescript to Viking. After *The Portable Jack Kerouac Reader* (1995) and the first volume of selected letters in 1995, Ann Charters was hired by the estate to transcribe and edit a second volume from hundreds of Kerouac's letters. After the publication of the letters, Charters told an interviewer:

> I really was tremendously impressed by the effort he [Kerouac] had to go through to find his own voice. I wanted to document this. It, to me, was a sign of his commitment, because if it had been easy I would feel differently about it. I mean it looks easy only because he worked so hard at finding it. And to me what documented this in a way that no one had ever shown were those letters to Neal Cassady in the end of 1950 and the beginning of 1951, before he sits down to write the scroll manuscript of *On the Road*. And his letters, his response to Neal's "Joan Anderson" letter—I'd known about that of course, but I didn't know that he sat down to do it to Neal, to begin to mine his own memories. It's about a hundred pages of manuscript, and they were just an eye-opener to me. So I think they're the core of unknown Kerouac in the Letters.[8]

In the same year as the first volume of selected letters came *Book of Blues; Some of the Dharma* followed in 1997. The work was published exactly as Kerouac had meticulously typed and annotated it, on the fortieth anniversary of the publication of *On the Road*. In 1999 a collection of Kerouac's juvenilia, edited by Paul Marion, was published. The estate also took the novel step of publishing one of Kerouac's shorter works, the 1945 novella *Orpheus Emerged*, in e-book form. Said *Publishers Weekly:* "Rebellion, self-destructive behavior, alcoholism—all the Kerouac hallmarks are in evidence in this newly recovered novella by the Beat Movement legend, the first to be published since his death in 1969. Written in 1945 (six years before his first novel, *The Town and the City*, and 12 years before *On the Road*), it remains fresh and vital, though it lacks the 'spontaneous prose' style that made Kerouac famous."[9] More satisfying and vital to the Kerouac oeuvre was the unexpurgated *Book of Dreams*, published once more by City Lights. Though it received little critical attention, its unique vitality to the whole of Kerouac's art was felt by most informed readers:

> [M]any facets of Kerouac's oeuvre appear here much less polished, and more naked and powerful: "—My mother and I are arm in arm on the floor, I'm crying afraid to die, she's blissful and has one leg in pink sexually out between me, and I'm thinking 'Even on the verge of death women think of love & snaky affection'—Women? who's dreaming this?" Lost love, madness, castration, cats that speak, cats in danger of their lives, people giving birth to cats, grade school classrooms, Mel Torme, Zsa Zsa Gabor, Tolstoy and Genet all make repeated appearances, lending the collection a repetitive, nonprogrammatic logic and exposing an unfamiliar sort of vulnerable beauty in Kerouac's iconic persona.[10]

In spring 2003 came *Book of Haikus*, another splendid representation of Kerouac's poetic output. Regina Weinreich's choices (out of an estimated one thousand haiku) were gleaned from notebooks, journals, novels, and various other items in his vast archive. Asia Africa Intelligence Wire astutely observed in a favorable review:

> The book provides a self-portrait of a flawed but still-brilliant and beautiful mind. The book is a minefield of potent Kerouac imagery set in Buddhist/Catholic observations of nature in places like Desolation

Peak, Northport and "road haikus" [. . .] [T]he collection is big enough that the reader can make his or her own judgment. And the book provides an opportunity to observe Kerouac's process, his using the same images and tropes in different contexts. Apparently rethinking and revision, at least in haiku, were more a part of his work habits than the tales of one-draft novels let on."[11]

Book of Haikus also revealed to the world that the work did not represent bottom-of-the-barrel material, but that there were still works of merit forthcoming from the Kerouac archive. Works still to be published include "Book of Sketches"; the early novel "The Sea Is My Brother," and the novella "The Night Is My Woman"; Kerouac's road journals, edited by Douglas Brinkley; the original scroll of *On the Road*; and several volumes of correspondence with Holmes, Ginsberg, and Cassady.

In Boulder, Colorado, poets Anne Waldman and Ginsberg founded the Jack Kerouac School for Disembodied Poetics as part of the Naropa Institute, the first accredited Buddhist college in America. Some citizens concerned to honor their hometown son formed Lowell Celebrates Kerouac!, which holds an annual festival in his honor. The city also broke ground in 1988 for a memorial park dedicated to Kerouac, which elicited a negative reaction from such staunch critics of Kerouac as Norman Podhoretz. Stella Sampas attended the opening ceremony with sculptor Ben Woitena, who had created some marble tablatures for the park, each engraved with passages from Kerouac's published works.

Kerouac's original April 1951 *On the Road* scroll set a world record for the highest paid bid for a literary manuscript at auction. Owner of the NFL's Indianapolis Colts, Jim Irsay, bought it for a staggering $2.43 million. Carolyn Cassady blasted the auction as a "blasphemy" to the London *Guardian*.[12] However, it was auctioned to pay off estate taxes owed after the death of the scroll's last owner, Anthony Sampas, who inherited it from his sister Stella. Reporter Noan Schoenberg for the *Chicago Tribune* writes:

> Not everyone would share Irsay's elation. Some scholars and curators say that such an important literary holding should, ideally, be in the hands of a public institution, such as a major library. Among their concerns: the scroll, which was typed on cheap pieces of paper attached to each other by means of paste and tape, is fragile. It is also of immense value to scholars, who have not yet performed comprehen-

sive studies of the hand-written corrections that dot the manuscript. Another potentially fruitful area of study is the difference between the scroll and the finished book, over which Kerouac had little editorial control.[13]

Soon after Irsay's successful bid, he had the document undergo an extensive preservation treatment in the Lilly Library at Indiana University. Irsay claims he has made the document available to scholars and will continue to do so in the future. In 2007, the fiftieth anniversary of *On the Road*'s publication, the scroll will finish a three-year tour across the country in various institutions. Plans to publish the manuscript as is are a certainty.

In August 2001, John Sampas placed the entire archive under his control in the Berg Collection of Jack's beloved New York Public Library. The collection, according to a publicist for the New York Public Library, will reevaluate Kerouac as the driving force behind the beat generation and as a major American postmodernist author. The archive, added to those items that were placed there throughout the 1990s, is quite extensive. Containing over 1,050 manuscripts and typescripts (including novels, short stories, prose pieces, poems, and fragments), the archive documents works in progress; completed works; 130 notebooks for almost all of his works (published and unpublished); 52 journals dating from 1934 to 1960 (which include material used in *The Town and the City* [1950], *On the Road* [1957], *Big Sur* [1962], and other works); 72 publishing contracts; 55 diaries dating from 1956 to 1969; about 1,800 pieces of correspondence; such archival curiosities as two sets of more than 100 hand-written cards for his fantasy-baseball game and hundreds of pages meticulously documenting and reporting all the games played between 1936 and 1965; and Kerouac's harmonicas. All of these were saved by Kerouac, who was certain of the value of his legacy.

Acknowledgments

It is gratifying to acknowledge the assistance of the numerous individuals and institutions in the making of this biography. One person in particular deserves special mention: my sincere thanks to John Sampas for sharing his wealth of knowledge of Jack Kerouac and for his adept management of this important American writer's legacy. John was always available to discuss matters of Kerouac biography. Thanks also to Sterling Lord Literistic for permission to quote from Kerouac's published works.

For their help, in more ways than one, thanks to David Amram, for his infectious enthusiasm toward my ideas and for his thoughtful foreword; Adira Amram, who assisted me graciously with research in New York City; Cindy Adler and Michael Barton, for their extremely helpful comments and corrections on portions of the first draft; and Brenda LaFlemme, for proofreading vital parts of the second draft. Also invaluable was input from Judy and Kerry Machado, the late John Pendergast, Ed Metz, Victor Bockris, Lucien Carr, Stan Isaacs, Cliff Lewis, Claire Ignacio, John Cohen, "Duke" Chiungos, Jeannette Brown, Joseph Salvano, James Dowling, James Atsalis, Joseph Sullivan, Betty Watley, Betty Sampas, Matthew Velasquez, Aaron Latham, Howard Smith, Jim Sampas, and several Lowell citizens who preferred to stay anonymous lest they be "implicated." Thanks to Steve Edington for his crucial study of Kerouac's Canadian roots; offshoot sources led to other secrets of Kerouac's Canadian/Breton ancestors. My indebtedness to other Kerouac scholars living and dead is indicated in the source notes to this volume. No list, however, can do ample justice to the vast number of individuals, institutions, and collections that made this biography possible. To those especially I remain indebted.

For their enormously informative staff and scholarly resources I thank Isaac Gerwitz and his assistants at the Berg Collection at the New York Public Library: Diana Burnham, Philip Milito, and Stephen Crook. Thanks to the University of Massachusetts and its Center for Lowell History, especially to Martha Mayo, Shirley Rathbun, Francis Endyke, and James McNamara. Sincere appreciation to Jo August Hills of the Lowell National Park Service, for sharing with me the many precious documents archiving Lowell's rich history; the Allen Ginsberg Trust and the Wylie Agency, for permissions to quote from unpublished works of Allen Ginsberg; the Newberry Library, for various items pertaining to Viking's publishing relationship with Kerouac; and the Malcolm Cowley Archive. Others who have helped over the years to enrich my knowledge of Kerouac and the beats include Hilary Holladay, Douglas Brinkley, Michael Schumacher, Paul Marion, Matt Theado, and Ben Giamo. The late Allen Ginsberg cleared up many inconsistencies in prior biographies about the literary influences of the beat generation when I briefly interviewed him in 1994. I am grateful to photographer Elliott Erwitt for his wonderful images (one of which graces the book's cover), to Antonio Rubino for his 1962 Northport pictures of Kerouac, and again to John Sampas for photographs from the Kerouac and Sampas family albums.

To Grove Press, I express my gratitude for permission to include brief excerpts from the copyrighted works of Jack Kerouac, published by Grove Press: *Dr. Sax* ©1959, *Satori in Paris* ©1985, *Mexico City Blues* ©1959, *Pic* ©1971, *Lonesome Traveler* ©1960, and *The Subterraneans* ©1958. Grove Press also kindly granted permission to use excerpts from a copyrighted work of Allen Ginsberg: *Journals: Early Fifties, Early Sixties,* edited by Gordon Ball ©1977.

I thank City Lights Books for granting permission to quote brief excerpts from the copyrighted works of Jack Kerouac: *Book of Dreams* ©2001, *Scattered Poems* ©1971, *The Scripture of the Golden Eternity* ©1994, and *Pomes All Sizes* ©1992.

I also express my thanks to HarperPerennial for permission to use brief excerpts from the copyrighted works of Allen Ginsberg: *Spontaneous Mind: Selected Interviews 1958–1996,* edited by David Carter ©2001; *Family Business: Selected Letters between a Father and Son,* edited by

Michael Schumacher ©2001; *Journals Mid-Fifties 1954–1958,* edited by Gordon Ball ©1996; and *Collected Poems 1947–1980,* ©1988.

I thank Riverhead Books for permission to quote brief excerpts from a copyrighted work of Jack Kerouac: *Desolation Angels* ©1993.

Thanks to Grey Fox Press for permission to use brief excerpts from the copyrighted works of Jack Kerouac: *Trip Trap: Haiku on the Road* (with Albert Saijo and Lew Welch) ©1998; *Good Blonde and Others* ©1993; *Heaven and Other Poems,* edited by Donald Allen ©1977; and *Old Angel Midnight* ©1993.

To I Books, thanks for permission to use brief excerpts from a copyrighted work of Jack Kerouac: *Orpheus Emerged* ©2000, by the Estate of Stella Kerouac.

Special thanks are in order for the staff of Taylor Trade Publishing: former associate publisher Michael Dorr for acquiring this project and contributing his beautiful poem; former marketing director Michael Messina for his assistance in developing marketing strategies early in the publishing process; Hector DeJean and Elizabeth Weiss; Chris Joaquim for her early copyediting of the manuscript and Cheryl Hoffman for further editing; production editor Lynn Weber for her excellence and grace under pressure; and Gisele Henry of the graphic design department for creating such a wonderful cover design.

Thanks also to those many unnamed individuals who gave small but very important details and insights into this complex man's life. I hope, in some small way, that I have contributed to the growing field of Kerouac studies.

Thank you to Carolyn Cassady for her help in the revised edition.

Above all, thanks to my wife Tina for her tolerance, strength of mind, love, and support during the researching and writing of this book, which, to say the least, strengthened the bonds of our marriage by testing every facet of its union.

Fictional Names in the Novels of Jack Kerouac

Jack Kerouac used different names to refer to his friends in his books, varying the aliases from book to book. Here's a list of some of the people and their fictional counterparts.

Alan Ansen
Book of Dreams—Irwin Swenson
On the Road—Rollo Greb
The Subterraneans—Austin Bromberg

William Burroughs
Book of Dreams—Bull Hubbard
Desolation Angels—Bull Hubbard
On the Road—Old Bull Lee
The Subterraneans—Frank Carmody
The Town and the City—Will Dennison
Vanity of Duluoz—Will Hubbard

Bill Cannastra
Visions of Cody—Finistra

Lucien Carr
The Town and the City—Kenneth Wood

Carolyn Cassady
On the Road—Camille
Visions of Cody—Evelyn

Cathy Cassady
On the Road—Amy Moriarty
Visions of Cody—Emily Pomeray

Jamie Cassady
On the Road—Joanie Moriarty
Visions of Cody—Gaby Pomeray

John Allen Cassady
Big Sur—Timmy John Pomeray
Visions of Cody—Timmy Pomeray

Neal Cassady
Big Sur—Cody Pomeray
Book of Dreams—Cody Pomeray
Desolation Angels—Cody Pomeray
The Dharma Bums—Cody Pomeray
On the Road—Dean Moriarty
Visions of Cody—Cody Pomeray

Hal Chase
On the Road—Chad King
Visions of Cody—Val Hayes

Gregory Corso
Book of Dreams—Raphael Urso
Desolation Angels—Raphael Urso
The Subterraneans—Yuri Gligoric

Elise Cowen
Desolation Angels—Barbara Lipp

Henri Cru
Desolation Angels—Deni Bleu
Lonesome Traveler—Deni Bleu
On the Road—Remi Boncoeur
Visions of Cody—Deni Bleu
Vanity of Duluoz—Deni Bleu

Robert Duncan
Desolation Angels—Geoffrey Donald

Lawrence Ferlinghetti
Big Sur—Lorenzo Monsanto

William Gaddis
The Subterraneans—Harold Sand

Bill Garver
Desolation Angels—Old Bull Gaines
Tristessa—Old Bull Gaines
Visions of Cody—Harper

Allen Ginsberg
Big Sur—Irwin Garden
Book of Dreams—Irwin Garden
Desolation Angels—Irwin Garden
The Dharma Bums—Alvah Goldbrook
On the Road—Carlo Marx
The Subterraneans—Adam Moorad
The Town and the City—Leon Levinsky
Vanity of Duluoz—Irwin Garden
Visions of Cody—Irwin Garden

Louis Ginsberg
Desolation Angels—Harry Garden

Joyce Glassman
Desolation Angels—Alyce Newman

Diana Hansen
On the Road—Inez
Visions of Cody—Diane

Joan Haverty
On the Road—Laura

Luanne Henderson
On the Road—Mary Lou
The Subterraneans—Annie
Visions of Cody—Joanna Dawson

Al Hinkle
Book of Dreams—Ed Buckle
On the Road—Ed Dunkel
Visions of Cody—Slim Buckle

Helen Hinkle
On the Road—Galatea Dunkel
Visions of Cody—Helen Buckle

John Clellon Holmes
Book of Dreams—James Watson
On the Road—Tom Saybrook
The Subterraneans—Balliol MacJones
Visions of Cody—Wilson

Herbert Huncke
Book of Dreams—Huck
On the Road—Elmer Hassel
The Town and the City—Junky

Natalie Jackson
Book of Dreams—Rosemarie
The Dharma Bums—Rosie Buchanan

Randall Jarrell
Desolation Angels—Varnum Random

Frank Jeffries
On the Road—Stan Shepard
Visions of Cody—Dave Sherman

David Kammerer
The Town and the City—Waldo Meister

Lenore Kandel
Big Sur—Romana Swartz

Caroline Kerouac
The Dharma Bums—Nin
Doctor Sax—Catherine "Nin" Duluoz
Maggie Cassidy—Nin

Gabrielle Kerouac
Doctor Sax—Ange
On the Road—Sal's Aunt
The Town and the City—Marguerite Martin
Vanity of Duluoz—Ange

Gerard Kerouac
Doctor Sax—Gerard Duluoz
The Town and the City—Julian Martin
Visions of Gerard—Gerard Duluoz

Jack Kerouac
Big Sur—Jack Duluoz
Book of Dreams—Jack Duluoz
Desolation Angels—Jack Duluoz
The Dharma Bums—Ray Smith
Maggie Cassidy—Jack Duluoz
On the Road—Sal Paradise
Satori in Paris—Jack Duluoz
The Subterraneans—Leo Percepied
The Town and the City—Peter Martin
Tristessa—Jack Duluoz
Vanity of Duluoz—Jack Duluoz
Visions of Cody—Jack Duluoz
Visions of Gerard—Jack Duluoz

Leo Kerouac
Doctor Sax—Emil "Pop" Duluoz
Maggie Cassidy—Emil "Pop" Duluoz
The Town and the City—George Martin
Vanity of Duluoz—Emil "Pop" Duluoz
Visions of Gerard—Emil "Pop" Duluoz

Philip Lamantia
Desolation Angels—David D'Angeli
The Dharma Bums—Francis DaPavia
Tristessa—Francis DaPavia

Robert LaVigne
Big Sur—Robert Browning
Desolation Angels—Levesque

Norman Mailer
Desolation Angels—Harvey Marker

Michael McClure
Big Sur—Pat McLear
Desolation Angels—Patrick McLear
The Dharma Bums—Ike O'Shay

Locke McCorkle
Desolation Angels—Kevin McLoch
The Dharma Bums—Sean Monahan

James Merrill
Desolation Angels—Merrill Randall

John Montgomery
Desolation Angels—Alex Fairbrother
The Dharma Bums—Henry Morley

Jerry Newman
Book of Dreams—Danny Richman
The Subterraneans—Larry O'Hara
Visions of Cody—Danny Richman

Peter Orlovsky
Book of Dreams—Simon Darlovsky
Desolation Angels—Simon Darlovsky
The Dharma Bums—George

Edie Parker
The Town and the City—Judie Smith
Vanity of Duluoz—Edna "Johnnie" Palmer
Visions of Cody—Elly

Kenneth Rexroth
The Dharma Bums—Rheinhold Cacoethes

Gary Snyder
Big Sur—Jarry Wagner
The Dharma Bums—Japhy Ryder

Allen Temko
Book of Dreams—Irving Minko
On the Road—Roland Major
Visions of Cody—Allen Minko

Gore Vidal
The Subterraneans—Arial Lavalina

Esperanza Villanueva
Tristessa— *Tristessa*

Joan Vollmer
On the Road—Jane
The Subterraneans—Jane
The Town and the City—Mary Dennison
Vanity of Duluoz—June

Ed Uhl
On the Road—Ed Wall
Visions of Cody—Ed Wehle

Alan Watts
Big Sur—Arthur Wayne
Desolation Angels—Alex Aums

Lew Welch
Big Sur—David Wain

Philip Whalen
Big Sur—Ben Fagan
The Dharma Bums—Warren Coughlin

William Carlos Williams
Desolation Angels—Dr. Williams

Reprinted with permission
http://www.emptymirrorbooks.com/alias.htm,
February 13, 2004.

Appendix B

Books That Comprise the Duluoz Legend

Book	Published	Written	Time Covered
Atop an Underwood	1999	1936–1943	Various
Visions of Gerard	1963	January 1956	1922–1926, Lowell, MA
Doctor Sax	1959	July 1952	1930–1936, Lowell, MA
The Town and the City	1950	1946–1949	1935–1946, Lowell, MA, & NY
Maggie Cassidy	1959	early 1953	1938–1939, Lowell, MA
Vanity of Duluoz	1968	1968	1939–1946, Lowell, MA, & NY
On the Road	1957	1948–1956	1946–1950, Various Road Trips
Visions of Cody	1960	1951–1952	1946–1952, Various Road Trips
The Subterraneans	1958	Oct. 1953	Summer 1953, NY
Tristessa	1960	1955–1956	1955–1956, Mexico City
The Dharma Bums	1958	November 1957	1955–1956, West Coast, NC
Desolation Angels	1965	1956 and 1961	1956–1957 West Coast, Mexico, Tangier, NY
Big Sur	1962	Oct. 1961	Summer 1960, Big Sur
Satori in Paris	1966	1965	June 1965, Paris and Brittany

Reprinted with permission from http://www.emptymirrorbooks.com/duluoz.html, February 13, 2004.

Notes

All letters by Jack Kerouac have been quoted from their original source in the University of Massachusetts, Lowell, or the New York Public Library. However, for the reader's ease, the citations are from the two volumes of Selected Letters, *which will be more accessible to readers than the original sources.*

Chapter 1: The Kerouacs of Nashua

1. Patricia Dagier and Hervé Quéméner, *Jack Kerouac, au bout de la route . . . la Bretagne.* Éditions An Here, 177. February 11, 2000.

2. Patricia Dagier, "The Enigma of the Kerouac Ancestor Is Finally Resolved." Lecture to the French-Canadian Genealogical Society, January 10, 2001.

3. Quebec National Archives. Fonds Gouverneur, French Regime, cote (R1), R1/1.

4. Quebec National Archives. Fonds Intendant, E1, Series E1, S1/11, ordinance.

5. Jack Kerouac, *Satori in Paris* (New York: Grove Press, 1966), 72.

6. Dagier, "Enigma."

7. Jack Kerouac, *Visions of Gerard* (New York: Viking, 1987), 79. The most popular dime-novel hero of his day, Frank Merriwell, the hero of Street and Smith's *Tip Top Weekly*, was first introduced to readers on April 18, 1889. He typically relied as much upon mental as physical prowess. The books created a genre of humor/romance stories.

8. Steve Edington, *Kerouac's Nashua Connection* (Nashua, N.H.: Transition, 1999).

9. Jack Kerouac to R. Dion Levesque, December 28, 1950, University of Massachusetts, Lowell.

10. Edington, *Kerouac's Nashua Connection,* 22.

11. *Lowell City Documents,* 1916 (Courier Citizen, Lowell).

12. Jack Kerouac, " . . . Legends and Legends . . .," in *Atop an Underwood: Early Stories and Other Writings,* ed. by Paul Marion (New York: Viking Penguin, 1999), 147.

13. Jack Kerouac, *The Town and the City* (New York: Barnes & Noble Books, 2001), 18.

14. Jack Kerouac, *Desolation Angels* (New York: Riverhead Books, 1995), 381.

15. *Lowell City Documents,* 1916 (Courier Citizen, Lowell).

16. Marriage certificate of Leo and Gabrielle Kerouac, October 15, 1915, Saint Louis de Gonzague Church record.

17. Mary Blewett, ed., *Surviving Hard Times* (Lowell, Mass.: Lowell Museum, 1982).

18. Jack Kerouac, *Visions of Gerard*, 74.

19. *L'Etoile*, March 27, 1922. Lowell, Mass.

20. *Lowell Sun*, March 25, 1922.

21. *Lowell Sunday Telegram*, March 19, 1922.

22. *Lowell City Documents*, 1922 and 1923.

23. *Lowell Sun*, March 12, 1922.

24. *Lowell Telegram*, March 12, 1922. Weather conditions are consistent with Kerouac's description in *Doctor Sax*.

25. Jack Kerouac, *Doctor Sax* (New York: Grove Press, 1959), 16–17.

26. Baptismal record of Jack Kerouac in Saint Louis de France archive, Lowell.

27. *Lowell City Documents*, 1924.

28. According to a list Jack Kerouac had made of his childhood addresses, Kerouac Estate, Lowell, Mass.

29. Jack Kerouac to Yvonne Le Maitre, September 8, 1950, in *Selected Letters: 1940–1956*, ed. Ann Charters (New York: Viking Penguin, 1995), 228–229.

30. Kerouac to Yvonne Le Maitre, September 8, 1950, in *Selected Letters: 1940–1956*, 229.

31. *Lowell City Documents*, 1926.

32. Jack Kerouac, *Book of Dreams* (galley) (San Francisco: City Lights, 2001), 98.

33. Kerouac to Neal Cassady, December 28, 1950, in *Selected Letters: 1940–1956*, 259.

34. Kerouac to Caroline Kerouac Blake, March 14, 1945, in *Selected Letters: 1940–1956*, 87.

35. *History of St. Louis de France* (Lowell, Mass.: St. Louis Rectory, n.d.), www.stlouisschool.org.

36. Kerouac, *Visions of Gerard*, 24.

37. Kerouac, *Book of Dreams*, (San Francisco: City Lights Books, 2001), 288.

38. Kerouac, *Doctor Sax*.

Chapter 2: The Ethereal Flower

1. Donald Motier, *Gerard: The Influence of Jack Kerouac's Brother on His Life and Writing* (Harrisburg, Pa.: Beaulieu Street Press, 1991).

2. Motier, *Gerard*, 4–5.

3. Jack Kerouac, 1963 radio interview with Charles Jarvis and James Curtis on program *Dialogues in Great Books* on WCAP, Lowell, M

4. *New World Medical Dictionary* (Paris: Black & Foster, 1998), 248.

5. Kerouac, *Visions of Gerard*, 68–69.

6. Kerouac, *Visions of Gerard*, 103.

7. Kerouac, *Visions of Gerard*, 110.

8. Kerouac, *Book of Dreams*, 117.

9. Kerouac to Neal Cassady, January 3, 1951, in *Selected Letters: 1940–1956*, 268. Kerouac categorized Sigmund Freud and his dream theories as part of the "Four Horsemen of the Apocalypse," which also included Ivan Pavlov, Karl Marx, and Ignorance (Kerouac to Gary Snyder, May 23, 1964, in *Selected Letters: 1940–1956*, 415). Kerouac's resentment toward Freud may have begun when he was blasted with criticism by friends and critics for his devoted and unselfish attachment to his mother.

10. Kerouac to Neal Cassady, January 3, 1951, in *Selected Letters: 1940–1956*, 272.

11. Kerouac to Caroline Kerouac Blake, March 14, 1945, in *Selected Letters: 1940–1956*, 87.

12. Kerouac, *Book of Dreams*, 153.

13. Kerouac, *Visions of Gerard*, 6.

14. *Lowell City Documents*, 1928.

15. Kerouac, *Book of Dreams*, 289.

16. Kerouac to Neal Cassady, January 9, 1951, in *Selected Letters: 1940–1956,* 283–284.

17. Kerouac to Neal Cassady, January 9, 1951, in *Selected Letters: 1940–1956,* 284.

18. *Biographies of the Saints* (New York: Lourdes Press, 1984), 46.

19. Kerouac, *Doctor Sax*, 4.

20. Kerouac, *Desolation Angels*, 373.

21. *Lowell City Documents*, 1929.

22. Jack Kerouac, journal entry 1944, in *A Jack Kerouac CD-ROMnibus* (New York: Viking Penguin, 1995).

23. *Lowell City Documents*, 1931.

24. Jack Kerouac, *Visions of Cody* (New York: Viking Penguin, 1993).

25. Jack Kerouac to R. Dion Levesque, December 28, 1950, University of Massachusetts, Lowell.

26. Thomas Dublin, *Lowell: The Story of an Industrial City* (Washington, D.C.: National Park Service, 1992), 89.

27. Kerouac, *Town and the City*, 30–31.

28. *Lowell City Documents*, 1932.

29. Gertrude Maher, interview with the author, May 5, 1997, Dracut, Mass.

30. Kerouac, *Town and the City*, 18.

31. Kerouac, *Desolation Angels*, 374.

32. Gabrielle Courbet, interview with the author, June 21, 2001, Lowell, Mass.

33. Kerouac, *Visions of Cody*, 27.

34. *The Lowell Sun*, October 1962. "Conversation with Kerouac," September 20, 1962.

Chapter 3: "Wits Abound in Lowell Too"

1. Lowell National Park archives, photo of Massachusetts Mills sign with existing tenants of Massachusetts Mills.

2. Gertrude Maher, interview with the author, May 5, 1997, Dracut, Mass.

3. *Lowell City Documents,* 1934.

4. Kerouac, *Visions of Cody,* 27.

5. Jack Kerouac, "The Turf Journal," *Kerouac CD-ROMnibus.*

6. Jack Kerouac, "Stake Special," *Kerouac CD-ROMnibus.*

7. Kerouac, *Book of Dreams*, 100.

8. Stan Isaacs, *The 1969 Chronicles: A Sportswriter's Notes.*

9. Kerouac to R. Dion Levesque, December 28, 1950, University of Massachusetts, Lowell.

10. Kerouac, January 1934 journal entries, *Kerouac CD-ROMnibus.*

11. Kerouac, "The Whole World Is on Fire," *Kerouac CD-ROMnibus.*

12. Jack Kerouac, "Home at Christmas," *Glamour,* December 1961.

13. Charles Jarvis, *Visions of Kerouac* (Lowell, Mass.: Ithaca Press, 1974), 41.

14. Kerouac, *Doctor Sax*, 125.

15. Edington, *Kerouac's Nashua Connection*, 42.

16. "Weed of Crime," *The Shadow,* radio broadcast (starring Orson Welles), circa 1938.

17. Kerouac, *Doctor Sax*, 155.

Chapter 4: Now a Flood Will Bring the Rest

1. John Sampas, interview with the author, August 18, 2000, Lowell, Mass.

2. Kerouac, *Doctor Sax*, 176.

3. "Locals Seek Relief," *Lowell Sun*, March 15, 1936, p. 2.

4. John Clellon Holmes, "Rocks in Our Beds," in *Gone in October* (Hailey, Idaho: Limberlost Press, 1985), 12.

5. Jeanette Brown, interview with the author, May 22, 2000, Lowell, Mass.

6. Kerouac, *Visions of Cody,* 317.

7. Kerouac, *Doctor Sax,* 81.

8. G. J. Apostolos, Oral History Project, University of Massachusetts, Lowell, Center for Lowell History.

Chapter 5: Order, Tenderness, and Piety

1. Jack Kerouac, "I Remember the Days of My Youth," in *Atop an Underwood: Early Stories and Other Writings,* ed. Paul Marion (New York: Viking Penguin, 1999), 50–51.

2. Joe Sarota, Oral History Project, University of Massachusetts, Lowell, Center for Lowell History.

3. Jack Kerouac, "Sports News," circa 1936, New York Public Library, Berg Collection.

4. Mike D'Orso, "Saturday's Hero: A Beat," *Sports Illustrated,* October 23, 1989.

5. David Pevear, "Jack Kerouac's Legend as a Football Player Tough to Read," *Lowell Sun,* January 2, 2000, p. 1

6. *Lowell Sun,* September 3, 1938, p. 12.

7. According to Jack Kerouac from a variety of sources, most notably Jack Kerouac, *Vanity of Duluoz* (New York: Viking, 1998), 20.

8. Odysseus Chiungos, interview with the author, May 6, 1999, Chelmsford, Mass.

9. Chiungos, interview.

10. James Dowling, interview with the author, May 10, 1999, Lowell, Mass.

11. Jack Kerouac, *Maggie Cassidy* (New York: McGraw-Hill, 1978), 20.

12. Kerouac, *Maggie Cassidy,* 133.

13. Gertrude Maher, interview with the author, May 5, 1997, Dracut, Mass.

14. Joseph Sullivan, interview with the author, April 7, 1999, Lowell, Mass.

15. Kerouac, *Vanity of Duluoz.*

16. Kerouac, *Visions of Cody,* 270.

17. *Lowell Sun,* November 23, 1938.

18. Pevear, "Jack Kerouac's Legend."

19. Kerouac, *Visions of Cody,* 270.

20. Kerouac, *Visions of Cody,* 76.

21. John Sampas, interview with the author, December 2002, Lowell, Mass.

22. "Editor Still Nurses $1200 He Made from Amateur Boxing," *Lowell Free Press,* April 8, 1939, p. 13.

23. Joseph Sullivan, interview with the author, April 7, 1999, Lowell, Mass.

24. Kerouac, "Background," in *Atop an Underwood,* 4.

25. Kerouac, "Background," in *Atop an Underwood,* 4.

26. Kerouac, *Vanity of Duluoz,* 29.

27. "Tower Theatre Plays Host to Rats—Rodents Slink Away Patrons," *Lowell Free Press,* March 25, 1935.

28. Advertisement, *Lowell Evening Leader,* March 15, 1939.

29. Kerouac, "Background," in *Atop an Underwood,* 4.

30. Jack Kerouac, notebook, fall 1939, New York Public Library, Berg Collection.

31. Frank Leahy to Jack Kerouac, July 13, 1939, *Kerouac CD-ROMnibus.*

32. Kerouac, *Vanity of Duluoz,* 28–29.

33. Jack Kerouac, notebook, fall 1939, New York Public Library, Berg Collection.

Chapter 6: Aloof from Teeming Humanity

1. Kerouac, journal entry, fall 1939, New York Public Library, Berg Collection.

2. Horace Mann Yearbook, 1941.

3. Kerouac, "One Long Strange Dream," in *Atop an Underwood*, 20.

4. Kerouac, "Count Basie's Band Best in Land: Group Famous for 'Solid Swing,'" in *Atop an Underwood*, 21–22.

5. Kerouac, *Maggie Cassidy*, 176.

6. Kerouac, "If I Were Wealthy," in *Atop an Underwood*, 79.

7. Kerouac to Mrs. A. B. Chandler, April 12, 1950, Heritage Book Shop and Bindery catalog.

8. Kerouac, "A Play I Want to Write," in *Atop an Underwood*, 28.

9. Kerouac, "Background," in *Atop an Underwood*, 5.

10. Kerouac, "Radio Script: The Spirit of '14," in *Atop an Underwood*, 44.

11. Kerouac, "Go Back," in *Atop an Underwood*, 25.

12. Kerouac, "Go Back," in *Atop an Underwood*, 26.

13. Kerouac, *Vanity of Duluoz*, 65.

14. Kerouac, *Vanity of Duluoz*, 64.

15. Kerouac, "Where the Road Begins," in *Atop an Underwood*, 59–60.

16. Scotty Beaulieu in *Jack's Book: An Oral Biography of Jack Kerouac*, ed. Barry Gifford and Lawrence Lee (New York: Viking, 1979), 25. Kerouac writes of "Kid Faro" with a "green suit and ring" and gold tooth in an early piece of juvenilia called "From Radio City to the Crown" (*Atop an Underwood*, 138).

17. Kerouac, "No Connection: A Novel That I Don't Intend to Finish," in *Atop an Underwood*, 93–95.

18. Kerouac, "I Know That I Am August," in *Atop an Underwood*, 41–42.

19. Thomas Wolfe, *Look Homeward, Angel* (New York: Charles Scribner's Sons, 1929), dustjacket.

20. Thomas Wolfe, *Of Time and the River* (New York: Charles Scribner's Sons, 1935), 550.

21. Jack Kerouac, journal entry, fall 1939, New York Public Library, Berg Collection.

Chapter 7: A Kernel of Eternity

1. Kerouac to Sebastian Sampas, February 26, 1941, in *Selected Letters: 1940–1956*, 7.

2. Thomas Wolfe, *The Complete Short Stories of Thomas Wolfe*, ed. Francis E. Skipp (New York: Collier, 1989), 107.

3. Kerouac, "There's Something about a Cigar," in *Atop an Underwood*, 66.

4. Kerouac, "The Birth of a Socialist," in *Atop an Underwood*, 87.

5. Kerouac to Sebastian Sampas, April 15, 1941, in *Selected Letters: 1940–1956*, 10–11.

6. Sebastian Sampas to Jack Kerouac, May 22, 1941, Kerouac Estate.

7. Doris Miller to Jack Kerouac, October 17, 1941, Kerouac Estate.

8. Kerouac, "Definition of a Poet," in *Atop an Underwood*, 122.

9. Kerouac, "Definition of a Poet," in *Atop an Underwood*, 121.

10. Kerouac, "Odyssey," in *Atop an Underwood*, 115–116.

11. Kerouac, *Vanity of Duluoz*, 85.

12. *Lowell City Documents*, 1939, 1940, and 1941.

13. Kerouac, "Farewell Song, Sweet from My Trees," in *Atop an Underwood*, 112.

Chapter 8: The Furious Poet

1. Kerouac to Caroline Kerouac, late summer 1941, in *Selected Letters: 1940–1956*, 12.

2. Kerouac to Caroline Kerouac, late summer 1941, in *Selected Letters: 1940–1956*, 15.

3. Jack Kerouac, "At 18, I Suddenly Discovered the Delight of Rebellion," in *Atop an Underwood*, 118.

4. Sebastian Sampas to William Saroyan, circa 1942, New York Public Library, Berg Collection.

5. Kerouac to Sebastian Sampas, mid-September 1941, in *Selected Letters: 1940–1956*, 16.

6. Kerouac, "Here I Am at Last with a Typewriter," in *Atop an Underwood*, 131.

7. Kerouac to Sebastian Sampas, New York Public Library, Berg Collection.

8. Ralph Waldo Emerson, *Self-Reliance* (New York: Library of America, 1983), 259.

9. Kerouac to Sebastian Sampas, mid-September 1941, in *Selected Letters: 1940–1956*, 16.

10. Kerouac to Sebastian Sampas, undated 1941, New York Public Library, Berg Collection.

11. Sebastian Sampas to Jack Kerouac, late 1941, New York Public Library, Berg Collection.

12. Kerouac, "The Birth of a Socialist," in *Atop an Underwood*, 92.

13. Kerouac to Sebastian Sampas, October 1941, in *Selected Letters: 1940–1956*, 17.

14. Kerouac, "Old Love-Light," in *Atop an Underwood*, 126–127.

15. Kerouac, "I Tell You It Is October!" in *Atop an Underwood*, 128.

16. Kerouac, "Background," in *Atop an Underwood*, 65.

17. Kerouac, "Hartford after Work," in *Atop an Underwood*, 143.

18. Kerouac, "Credo," in *Atop an Underwood*, 153–154.

19. Kerouac, "Hungry Young Writer's Notebook," in *Atop an Underwood*, 156.

20. Kerouac, "Today," in *Atop an Underwood*, 167.

21. Kerouac, "Today," in *Atop an Underwood*, 168.

22. Kerouac, *Visions of Cody*, 12.

23. Kerouac, *Visions of Cody*, 12.

Chapter 9: The Wound of Living

1. Kerouac, "Background," in *Atop an Underwood*, 179.

2. "U.S.-JAP War On! Bomb Pearl Harbor!" *Lowell Sun,* December 8, 1941, p. 1.

3. Kerouac, "Search by Night," in *Atop an Underwood*, 172.

4. Kerouac, "Background," in *Atop an Underwood*, 179.

5. Jack Kerouac, "Richmond Hill Blues," in *Book of Blues* (New York: Viking, 1995), 82.

6. "Pay envelopes of Lowell Workers Much Fatter during Last Month," *Lowell Sun,* December 17, 1941, p. 27.

7. Kerouac, "The Joy of Duluoz," in *Atop an Underwood*, 184.

8. Kerouac, "Today," in *Atop an Underwood*, 168.

9. Jack Kerouac, *Vanity of Duluoz* (New York: Viking Penguin, 1994), 111.

10. Kerouac to Norma Blickfelt, July 15, 1942, in *Selected Letters: 1940–1956*, 23.

11. Kerouac to Norma Blickfelt, July 15, 1942, in *Selected Letters: 1940–1956*, 21–23.

12. Joseph Salzano, phone interview with the author, January 5, 2003.

13. Joseph Salzano, phone interview with the author, January 5, 2003.

14. Joseph Salzano, phone interview with the author, January 5, 2003.

15. Joseph Salzano, phone interview with the author, January 5, 2003.

16. Kerouac to Norma Blickfelt, August 25, 1942, in *Selected Letters: 1940–1956*, 28.

17. Kerouac to Norma Blickfelt, August 25, 1942, in *Selected Letters: 1940–1956*, 26–28.

18. Joseph Salzano, phone interview with the author, January 5, 2003.

19. Gabrielle Kerouac to Jack Kerouac, fall 1942, New York Public Library, Berg Collection. Gabrielle's spelling and grammar have been retained in all of her quoted material.

20. Gabrielle Kerouac to Jack Kerouac, fall 1942.

21. Gabrielle Kerouac to Jack Kerouac, fall 1942.

22. Jack Kerouac, *Vanity of Duluoz*

23. Kerouac to Sebastian Sampas, November 19, 1942, New York Public Library, Berg Collection.

24. Kerouac, "Background," in *Atop an Underwood*, 180.

25. Thorstein Veblen, *The Theory of the Leisure Class* (New York: Viking, 1931).

26. Kerouac to Sebastian Sampas, February 1943, in *Selected Letters: 1940–1956*, 39–40.

Chapter 10: Among the Philistines

1. Kerouac to Sebastian Sampas, March 21, 1943, New York Public Library, Berg Collection.

2. Sebastian Sampas to Jack Kerouac, March 15, 1943, New York Public Library, Berg Collection.

3. Kerouac to Sebastian Sampas, March 24, 1943, New York Public Library, Berg Collection.

4. Gabrielle Kerouac to Jack Kerouac, March 24, 1943, in *Selected Letters: 1940–1956*, 49.

5. Kerouac to Sebastian Sampas, March 25, 1943, in *Selected Letters: 1940–1956*, 54.

6. Kerouac to Cornelius Murphy, circa spring 1943, New York Public Library, Berg Collection.

7. Kerouac to Cornelius Murphy, circa spring 1943, New York Public Library, Berg Collection.

8. Kerouac to Gabrielle Kerouac, March 30, 1943, New York Public Library, Berg Collection.

9. Gabrielle Kerouac to Jack Kerouac, May 3, 1943, New York Public Library, Berg Collection.

10. Sebastian Sampas to Jack Kerouac, May 26, 1943, New York Public Library, Berg Collection.

11. Kerouac to John Macdonald, April 1943, in *Selected Letters: 1940–1956*, 56.

12. Kerouac to Cornelius Murphy, circa mid-1943, New York Public Library, Berg Collection.

13. Sebastian Sampas to Jack Kerouac, May 26, 1943, New York Public Library, Berg Collection.

14. Oswald Spengler, *The Decline of the West*, vol. 2 (New York: Knopf, 1945), 169. It seems that both Kerouac and Sebastian Sampas read from the second volume of the 1928 translation by Charles F. Atkinson.

15. Spengler, *Decline of the West* (vol. 2), 3.

16. Kerouac, "The Wound of Living," in *Atop an Underwood*, 230.

17. Kerouac, "Beauty as a Lasting Truth," in *Atop an Underwood*, 227.

18. Kerouac to Cornelius Murphy, circa mid-1943, New York Public Library, Berg Collection.

19. Kerouac, journal entry, January 1944, in *Orpheus Emerged* (New York: Live-Reads, 2000), 355.

20. Sebastian Sampas, "Taste the Nightbane" and "Puptent Poets of the Mediterranean," *Stars and Stripes* (Italy), 1945.

21. Kerouac to Sebastian Sampas, March 1944, New York Public Library, Berg Collection.

22. Kerouac to Stella Sampas, October 17, 1950, New York Public Library, Berg Collection.

23. Kerouac, "My Generation, My World," in *Atop an Underwood*, 229.

24. Kerouac to Edie Parker, September 18, 1943, in *Selected Letters: 1940–1956*, 71.

25. Kerouac, "The Romanticist," in *Atop an Underwood*, 236.

26. Seymour Wyse, "My Really Best Friend: An Interview with Seymour Wyse," in *Kerouac at the "Wild Boa," and Other Skirmishes*, ed. John Montgomery (San Anselmo, Calif.: Fels & Firn Press, 1986), 79–81.

27. Kerouac to Ian MacDonald, March 21, 1944, New York Public Library, Berg Collection.

28. Edington, *Kerouac's Nashua Connections*, 44.

29. Kerouac to Ian MacDonald, March 21, 1944, New York Public Library, Berg Collection.

30. Allen Ginsberg, "The Art of Poetry, No. VIII," *Paris Review*, Spring 1966, included in *Spontaneous Mind—Selected Interviews, 1958–1996* (New York: Harper Perennial, 2001), 35.

31. Michael Schumacher, *Dharma Lion: A Biography of Allen Ginsberg* (New York: St. Martin's Griffin, 1992), 35.

32. Allen Ginsberg, *Spontaneous Mind: Selected Interviews, 1958–1996* (New York: Harper-Collins, 2001), 543.

33. Allen Ginsberg, "Gay Sunshine Interview," September 25, 1972, in *Spontaneous Mind*, 305–306.

34. Caroline Kerouac to Jack Kerouac, July 12, 1944, University of Massachusetts, Lowell.

35. Kerouac, *Visions of Cody*, 185.

36. *Visions of Cody*.

37. Kerouac, *Vanity of Duluoz*, 232–234.

38. Kerouac, "The Prisoner's Song," *Kerouac CD-ROMnibus*.

39. Kerouac, "Jail Notes '44," *Kerouac CD-ROMnibus*.

40. Edie Kerouac to Lucien Carr, August 26, 1944, Kerouac Estate, Lowell, Mass.

41. Kerouac to Mrs. Parker [Edie's mother], September 1, 1944, in *Selected Letters: 1940–1956*, 76–77.

42. Edie Parker, interview in film *What Happened to Kerouac?* Directed by Richard Lerner & Lewis MacAdams (New York: Winstar Home Entertainment, 2001).

43. Edie Parker, interview in film *Kerouac* by John Antonelli. (New York: Goldhil Home Media I, 2003).

44. *New York World-Telegram*, September 15, 1944, New York Public Library, Berg Collection.

45. Kerouac, *Vanity of Duluoz*, 248.

46. Kerouac to Mrs. Parker, September 1, 1944, in *Selected Letters: 1940–1956*, 77.

47. Gabrielle Kerouac to Edie Kerouac, November 26, 1944, University of Massachusetts, Lowell, Center for Lowell History.

48. Gabrielle Kerouac to Jack Kerouac, September 15, 1944, in *Selected Letters: 1940–1956*, 79.

49. Kerouac to Allen Ginsberg, October 1944, in *Selected Letters: 1940–1956*, 81.

50. Gabrielle Kerouac to Edie Kerouac, November 26, 1944, University of Massachusetts, Lowell, Center for Lowell History.

51. Gabrielle Kerouac to Edie Kerouac, November 26, 1944, University of Massachusetts, Lowell, Center for Lowell History.

52. Kerouac, *Vanity of Duluoz*, 255.

53. Kerouac, "Waiting for Céline," October 26, 1944, New York Public Library, Berg Collection.

54. Kerouac, *Vanity of Duluoz*, 255.

55. Kerouac, "Definition of Art for the Layman," *Kerouac CD-ROMnibus*.

56. Kerouac, *Vanity of Duluoz*, 256.

57. Kerouac, "Au Revoir a l'Art," New York Public Library, Berg Collection.

Chapter 11: True Thoughts Abound

1. Jack Kerouac and William S. Burroughs, "And the Hippos Were Boiled in Their Tanks," title page, New York Public Library, Berg Collection.

2. Kerouac, *Vanity of Duluoz*, 260.

3. Edie Parker, interview in film *Kerouac*.

4. Kerouac to Caroline Kerouac Blake, March 14, 1945, in *Selected Letters: 1940–1956*, 89.

5. Kerouac, *Vanity of Duluoz*, 260–261.

6. Kerouac to Caroline Blake, March 14, 1945, New York Public Library, Berg Collection.

7. Kerouac to Caroline Blake, March 14, 1945, New York Public Library, Berg Collection.

8. Kerouac, journal entry, *Kerouac CD-ROMnibus*.

9. Kerouac, *Orpheus Emerged*, 251.

10. Kerouac, *Orpheus Emerged*, 85–86.

11. Kerouac, *Orpheus Emerged*, 248.

12. Kerouac, *Orpheus Emerged*, 250.

13. Kerouac, *Orpheus Emerged*, 250.

14. Kerouac, *Visions of Cody*, 190.

15. Kerouac, *Visions of Cody*, 187–188.

16. John Sampas, phone interview with the author, July 14, 2003.

17. Kerouac, *Visions of Cody*, 188.

18. Kerouac to Allen Ginsberg, August 1945, Columbia University, Allen Ginsberg archive.

19. Schumacher, *Dharma Lion*, 57–58.

20. Kerouac, "Notes, September 5, 1945," *Kerouac CD-ROMnibus.*

21. Kerouac, *Vanity of Duluoz*, 262.

22. Kerouac, *Vanity of Duluoz*, 262–263.

23. Kerouac, *Town and the City*, 401.

24. Kerouac, "Reading Notes—1965," New York Public Library, Berg Collection.

25. Neal Cassady, *The First Third and Other Writings* (San Francisco: City Lights, 1971).

26. Marriage annulment for John and Edie Kerouac, Kerouac Estate.

27. Edie Parker to Stella Kerouac, undated letter, Kerouac Estate.

28. Jack Kerouac, "Prayer," circa 1947, *Atlantic Monthly*, November 1998, 52.

29. Douglas Brinkley, introduction to Kerouac, *Town and the City*, x.

30. Neal Cassady, *The First Third*, 39–40.

31. "Application for Admission to the J. K. Mullen Home for Boys for Neal Cassady," in *The Beats: A Literary Reference*, ed. Matt Theado (New York: Carroll & Graf, 2003), 338–339.

32. Cassady, *The First Third*, 184–185.

33. Kerouac to Hal Chase [unmailed], April 19, 1947, in *Selected Letters: 1940–1956*, 107.

34. Kerouac to Gabrielle Kerouac, July 24, 1947, in *Selected Letters: 1940–1956*, 110.

35. Kerouac to Gabrielle Kerouac, July 28, 1947, in *Selected Letters: 1940–1956*, 110.

36. Kerouac to Gabrielle Kerouac, July 29, 1947, in *Selected Letters: 1940–1956*.

37. Gifford and Lee, *Jack's Book*, 153.

38. Carolyn Cassady, *Off the Road: My Years with Cassady, Kerouac, and Ginsberg* (New York: Viking, 1990), 12.

39. Neal Cassady to Allen Ginsberg, March 14, 1947, in *As Ever: The Collected Correspondence of Allen Ginsberg and Neal Cassady* (Berkeley, Calif.: Creative Arts Book Company, 1977), 6.

40. Steven Watson, *The Birth of the Beat Generation* (New York: Pantheon, 1995), 87.

41. Kerouac to Neal Cassady, September 13, 1947, in *Selected Letters: 1940–1956*, 125.

42. Kerouac to Neal Cassady, September 13, 1947, in *Selected Letters: 1940–1956*, 127.

43. Kerouac to Neal Cassady, September 13, 1947, in *Selected Letters: 1940–1956*, 128.

44. Neal Cassady to Jack Kerouac, December 1947, in *Selected Letters: 1940– 1956*, 136.

45. Neal Cassady to Jack Kerouac, December 1947, in *Selected Letters: 1940– 1956*, 136.

46. Kerouac, journal entry, January 1, 1948, *New Yorker*, June 22 and 29, 1998, edited by Douglas Brinkley.

47. Kerouac, journal entry, April 17, 1948, *New Yorker*, June 22 and 29, 1998.

Chapter 12: Toward a New Vision

1. Neal Cassady to Jack Kerouac, n.d., in *Selected Letters: 1940–1956*, 154.

2. William S. Burroughs to Jack Kerouac and Allen Ginsberg, June 5, 1948, in *The Letters of William Burroughs: 1945–1959* (New York: Viking, 1993), 21.

3. Kerouac to Neal Cassady, June 27, 1948, in *Selected Letters 1940–1956*, 155.

4. Neal Cassady to Allen Ginsberg, May 1948, in *As Ever*, 36.

5. Neal Cassady to Allen Ginsberg, May 1948, in *As Ever*, 36.

6. Ginsberg, *Spontaneous Mind*, 473.

7. Ginsberg, *Spontaneous Mind*, 36.

8. Kerouac, journal entry, June 2, 1948, *New Yorker*, June 22 and 29, 1998.

9. Kerouac, journal entry, July 22, 1948, *Kerouac CD-ROMnibus*.

10. Kerouac, journal entry, July 3, 1948, *New Yorker*, June 22 and 29, 1998.

11. Kerouac, journal entry, July 24, 1948, *Kerouac CD-ROMnibus*.

12. Kerouac, journal entry, July 25, 1948, *Kerouac CD-ROMnibus*.

13. Kerouac, journal entry, July 25, 1948, *Kerouac CD-ROMnibus*.

14. Kerouac, journal entry, July 28, 1948, *Kerouac CD-ROMnibus*.

15. Arthur Knight and Kit Knight, eds., *Kerouac and the Beats: A Primary Sourcebook* (New York: Paragon House, 1988), 173. (Also recorded in Jack Kerouac's journal.)

16. Kerouac, journal entry, August 17, 1948, *New Yorker*, June 22 and 29, 1998.

17. Kerouac, journal entry, August 23, 1948, *New Yorker*, June 22 and 29, 1998.

18. Kerouac, journal entry, August 23, 1948, *New Yorker*, June 22 and 29, 1998.

19. Kerouac, journal entry, September 9, 1948, *New Yorker*, June 22 and 29, 1998.

20. Gifford and Lee, *Jack's Book*, 129.

21. Gifford and Lee, *Jack's Book*, 129.

22. Kerouac to Neal and Carolyn Cassady, July 10, 1948, in *Selected Letters 1940–1956*, 158–161.

23. Jack Kerouac, journal entry, July 10, 1948, *Kerouac CD-ROMnibus*.

24. Kerouac to Ed White, October 29, 1948, *Missouri Review* 17, no. 3 (1994): 116–117.

25. Kerouac to Neal Cassady, October 2, 1948, in *Selected Letters 1940–1956*, 165.

26. Kerouac to Neal Cassady, October 2, 1948, in *Selected Letters 1940–1956*, 165.

27. Kerouac to Neal Cassady, October 3, 1948, in *Selected Letters 1940–1956*, 169.

28. Kerouac to Ed White, October 29, 1948, *Missouri Review* 17, no. 3 (1994).

29. Kerouac to Neal Cassady, October 18, 1948 (photocopy obtained from anonymous source).

30. Kerouac to Ed White, October 29, 1948, *Missouri Review* 17, no. 3 (1994): 118.

31. Elbert Lenrow, "Memoir: The Young Kerouac." *Narrative*, January 1994: 65–66.

32. Jack Kerouac, "The Minimalism of Thomas Wolfe in His Own Time," *Narrative*, January 1994: 72.

33. Lenrow, "Young Kerouac," 77.

34. Lenrow, "Young Kerouac," 77.

35. Lenrow, "Young Kerouac," 77.

36. Kerouac to Ed White, October 29, 1948, *Missouri Review* 17, no. 3 (1994).

37. Kerouac to Ed White, November 30, 1948, *Missouri Review* 17, no. 3 (1994).

38. John Clellon Holmes to Jack Kerouac, November 30, 1948, in *The Beats*, 390.

39. John Clellon Holmes, interview, in Gifford and Lee, *Jack's Book*.

40. William Burroughs to Jack Kerouac, November 30, 1948, in *Letters of William S. Burroughs: 1945–1959*, 27.

41. Kerouac to Neal Cassady, December 8, 1948, in *Selected Letters: 1940–1956*, 175.

42. Kerouac to Allen Ginsberg, December 15, 1948, in *Selected Letters: 1940–1956*, 176.

43. Jack Kerouac to Ed White, November 30, 1948, *Missouri Review* 17, no. 3 (1994): 119.

44. Kerouac, notebook draft of "Whitman: A Prophet of the Sexual Revolution," *Kerouac CD-ROMnibus*.

45. Kerouac, *Visions of Cody*, 346.

46. Cassady, *Off the Road*, 101.

47. William S. Burroughs to Allen Ginsberg, January 16, 1949, in *Letters of William S. Burroughs*, 35.

48. Cassady, *Off the Road*, 75.

49. William S. Burroughs to Allen Ginsberg, January 30, 1949, in *Letters of William S. Burroughs, 1945–1959*, 38.

Chapter 13: What Kicks

1. Gifford and Lee, *Jack's Book*, 137.
2. Gifford and Lee, *Jack's Book*, 128.
3. Kerouac, journal entry, January 3, 1949, *New Yorker*, June 22 and 29, 1998.
4. Kerouac, journal entry, January 3, 1949, *New Yorker*, June 22 and 29, 1998.
5. Gifford and Lee, *Jack's Book*, 130.
6. Kerouac, journal entry, January 3, 1949, *New Yorker*, June 22 and 29, 1998.
7. William S. Burroughs to Allen Ginsberg, January 30, 1949, in *Letters of William S. Burroughs: 1945–1959*, 37.
8. Gifford and Lee, *Jack's Book*, 131.
9. Gifford and Lee, *Jack's Book*, 132.
10. Gifford and Lee, *Jack's Book*, 137.
11. Gifford and Lee, *Jack's Book*, 137.
12. Gifford and Lee, *Jack's Book*, 137.
13. Jack Kerouac, journal entry, February 1, 1949, *New Yorker*, June 22 and 29, 1998.
14. William S. Burroughs to Allen Ginsberg, January 30, 1949, in *Letters of William S. Burroughs: 1945–1959*, 38.
15. Kerouac to Neal Cassady, January 8, 1951, in *Selected Letters 1957–1969*, 275–277.

Chapter 14: Back East

1. Kerouac, journal entry, February 6, 1949, *New Yorker*, June 22 and 29, 1998.
2. Douglas Brinkley, "The American Journey of Jack Kerouac," in *The Rolling Stone Book of the Beats* (New York: Hyperion, 1999), 112.
3. Kerouac, journal entry, February 7, 1949, *New Yorker*, June 22 and 29, 1998.
4. Kerouac, journal entry, February 7, 1949, *New Yorker*, June 22 and 29, 1998.
5. Kerouac, journal entry, February 9, 1949, *New Yorker*, June 22 and 29, 1998.
6. Kerouac, journal entry, February 9, 1949, *New Yorker*, June 22 and 29, 1998.
7. Kerouac, journal entry, February 25, 1949, *New Yorker*, June 22 and 29, 1998.
8. Tim Hunt, *Kerouac's Crooked Road: Development of a Fiction* (University of California Press, November 1996), 95.
9. Kerouac, journal entry, March 25, 1949, *Atlantic Monthly*, November 1998.
10. Kerouac to Tom Guinzburg, January 17, 1962, in *Selected Letters 1957–1969*, 326.
11. Kerouac, journal entry, April 23, 1949, *New Yorker*, June 22 and 29, 1998.
12. Kerouac, journal entry, April 23, 1949, *New Yorker*, June 22 and 29, 1998.
13. Kerouac to Alan Harrington, April 23, 1949, in *Selected Letters 1940–1956*, 188.
14. Kerouac, untitled essay, circa 1949, *Atlantic Monthly*, November 1998.
15. Kerouac to Ed White, May 9, 1949, *Missouri Review* 17, no. 3 (1994): 123.
16. Kerouac to Ed White, May 9, 1949, *Missouri Review* 17, no. 3 (1994): 123–131.
17. Ted Morgan, *Literary Outlaw: The Life and Times of William S. Burroughs* (New York: Avon, 1988), 168.
18. Schumacher, *Dharma Lion*, 107.
19. Watson, *Birth of the Beat Generation*, 111–112.
20. Neal Cassady to Jack Kerouac, in Cassady, *Off the Road*, 95.
21. Neal Cassady to Jack Kerouac, in Cassady, *Off the Road*, 97.
22. Kerouac to Alan Harrington, April 23, 1949, in *Selected Letters: 1940–1956*, 187.
23. Kerouac, journal entry, April 17, 1949, *New Yorker*, June 22 and 29, 1998.

24. Kerouac, journal entry, April 23, 1949, *New Yorker*, June 22 and 29, 1998.

Chapter 15: Denver Doldrums

1. Kerouac, journal entry, April 17, 1949, *New Yorker*, June 22 and 29, 1998.

2. Kerouac to Hal Chase, May 15, 1949, in *Selected Letters: 1940–1956*, 189–190.

3. Kerouac, journal entry from "Ten-Day Writing Log," May 22, 1949, *Kerouac CD-ROMnibus*.

4. Kerouac to Allen Ginsberg, June 10, 1949, in *Selected Letters: 1940–1956*, 191.

5. Kerouac to Allen Ginsberg, June 10, 1949, in *Selected Letters: 1940–1956*, 193.

6. Kerouac, journal entry from "Ten-Day Writing Log," May 23, 1949, *Kerouac CD-ROMnibus*.

7. Kerouac to Elbert Lenrow, June 28, 1949, in *Selected Letters: 1940–1956*, 202–203.

8. Kerouac to Neal Cassady, July 28, 1949, in *Selected Letters: 1940–1956*, 211.

9. Kerouac to Neal Cassady, July 28, 1949, in *Selected Letters: 1940–1956*, 212.

10. Kerouac, *Visions of Cody*, 293.

11. Kerouac to John Clellon Holmes, June 24, 1949, in *Selected Letters: 1940–1956*, 200.

12. Allen Ginsberg, "The Literary History of the Beat Generation" (unpublished lecture transcribed from private audiotape), October 1992, Lowell, Mass.

Chapter 16: Go Moan for Man

1. Ginsberg, *Spontaneous Mind*, 473.

2. Kerouac to Allen Ginsberg, July 26, 1949, in *Selected Letters: 1940–1956*, 210.

3. Neal Cassady to Jack Kerouac, July 3, 1949, in *The Portable Beat Reader*, ed. Ann Charters (New York: Viking, 1992), 193.

4. Kerouac, journal entry, August 1949, *New Yorker*, June 22 and 29, 1998.

5. Kerouac to Neal Cassady, July 28, 1949, in *Selected Letters: 1940–1956*, 214.

6. Kerouac, journal entry, *New Yorker*, June 22 and 29, 1998.

7. Jack Kerouac to Neal Cassady, July 28, 1949, in *Selected Letters: 1940–1956*, 211.

8. Kerouac, *Visions of Cody*, 293.

9. Cassady, *Off the Road*, 100.

10. Kerouac to Neal Cassady, July 28, 1949, in *Selected Letters: 1940–1956*, 213.

11. Kerouac, *Visions of Cody*, 295.

12. Cassady, *Off the Road*, 100.

13. William Burroughs to Jack Kerouac, September 26, 1949, in *Letters of William S. Burroughs: 1945–1959*, 53.

14. Cassady, *Off the Road*, 195.

15. Kerouac, journal entry, September 21, 1949, *New Yorker*, June 22 and 29, 1998.

16. William S. Burroughs to Jack Kerouac, September 26, 1949, in *Letters of William S. Burroughs: 1945–1959*, 53.

17. Kerouac, *Town and the City*, 317.

18. Kerouac, *Selected Letters: 1940–1956*, 221.

19. Kerouac, journal entry, February 18, 1950, *New Yorker*, June 22 and 29, 1998.

20. John Brooks, review of *The Town and the City* by Jack Kerouac, *New York Times*, March 5, 1950.

21. Howard Mumford Jones, "Back to Merrimac," *Saturday Review of Literature*, March 11, 1950.

22. Charles Sampas, editorial, *Lowell Sun*, March 12, 1950.

23. Kerouac to Stella Sampas, October 17, 1950, in *Selected Letters: 1940–1956*, 235.

24. Kerouac to Frank Morley, July 27, 1951, cited in Douglas Brinkley's introduction to *The Town and the City* (London: Viking Penguin U.K., 2000), xi.

25. William Burroughs to Jack Kerouac, September 26, 1949, in *Letters of William S. Burroughs: 1945–1959*, 53.

26. Gifford and Lee, *Jack's Book*, 153.

27. Jack Kerouac to John Clellon Holmes, July 10, 1950, University of Massachusetts, Lowell, Center for Lowell History.

28. Jack Kerouac to John Clellon Holmes, July 10, 1950.

29. Kerouac to John Clellon Holmes, July 1950, University of Massachusetts, Lowell, Center for Lowell History.

30. Jack Kerouac to Yvonne Le Maitre, September 8, 1950, in *Selected Letters: 1940–1956*, 229.

31. Kerouac, journal entry, February 18, 1950, *New Yorker*, June 22 and 29, 1998.

32. Allen Ginsberg to Jack Kerouac, undated March 1950 (photocopy from anonymous source).

33. Gifford and Lee, *Jack's Book*, 77.

Chapter 17: Shadow Changes into Bone

1. Gifford and Lee, *Jack's Book*, 232–233.

2. Douglas Brinkley, ed., "The Kerouac Papers," *Atlantic Monthly.*

3. Jack Kerouac, *Pic* (New York: Grove Press, 1988), 125.

4. Kerouac to Neal Cassady, October 6, 1950, in *Selected Letters: 1940–1956*, 230.

5. Al Aronowitz, "Jack Kerouac: Beyond the Road," *New York Post*, October 22, 1969.

6. Allen Ginsberg to Neal Cassady, October 31, 1950, in *As Ever*, 72.

7. Allen Ginsberg to Neal Cassady, October 31, 1950.

8. Allen Ginsberg to Neal Cassady, November 18, 1950, in *As Ever*, 81.

9. Cassady, *Off the Road*, 126.

10. Neal Cassady to Allen Ginsberg, November 15, 1950 in *As Ever*, 80.

11. Neal Cassady to Allen Ginsberg, November 25, 1950 in *As Ever*, 88.

12. Joan Haverty Kerouac, *Nobody's Wife: The Smart Aleck and the King of the Beats* (Berkeley, Calif.: Creative Arts Book Company, 2000), 128.

13. Joan Kerouac, *Nobody's Wife*, 129.

14. Joan Kerouac, *Nobody's Wife*, 132.

15. Joan Kerouac, *Nobody's Wife*, 134.

16. Ginsberg and Cassady, in *As Ever*, 88–89.

17. Kerouac, *Visions of Cody*, 24–25.

18. Cassady, *Off the Road*, 132.

19. Cassady, *Off the Road*, 133.

20. Kerouac to Carolyn Cassady, December 14, 1950, University of Massachusetts, Lowell, Center for Lowell History.

21. Joan Kerouac, *Nobody's Wife*, 156–157.

22. Kerouac to Neal Cassady, December 3, 1950, in *Selected Letters: 1940–1956*, 240.

23. Neal Cassady to Jack Kerouac, December 17 (?), 1950, in *Portable Beat Reader*, 197.

24. Kerouac to Neal Cassady, December 27, 1950, in *Selected Letters: 1940–1956*, 243.

25. Kerouac to Neal Cassady, December 28, 1950, in *Selected Letters: 1940–1956*, 247.

26. Kerouac to Neal Cassady, December 28, 1950, in *Selected Letters: 1940–1956*, 248.

27. Kerouac to Neal Cassady, January 9, 1951, in *Selected Letters: 1940–1956*, 287–289.

28. Kerouac to Neal Cassady, January 9, 1951, in *Selected Letters: 1940–1956*, 290.

29. Joan Kerouac, *Nobody's Wife*, 168–169.

30. Joan Kerouac, *Nobody's Wife*, 160–161.

31. Ann Charters, commentary in *Selected Letters: 1940–1956*, 321.

32. John Clellon Holmes to Ann Charters, June 23, 1987, in *The Beats*, 393.

33. Joan Kerouac, *Nobody's Wife*, 176–177.

34. Kerouac to Alfred Kazin, February 20, 1951, in *Selected Letters: 1940–1956*, 312.

35. Joan Kerouac, *Nobody's Wife*, 192.

36. Kerouac to Stella Sampas, January 25, 1951, New York Public Library, Berg Collection.

37. Kerouac to John Clellon Holmes, June 3, 1952, in *Selected Letters: 1940–1956*, 367.

38. Kerouac to Ed White, April 1951, *Missouri Review* 17, no. 3 (1994): 141.

39. Allen Ginsberg to Neal Cassady, May 7, 1951, in *As Ever*, 106.

40. Neal Cassady to Allen Ginsberg, May 7, 1951, in *As Ever*, 109.

41. Neal Cassady to Allen Ginsberg, May 10, 1951, in *As Ever*, 108.

42. Kerouac to Neal Cassady, May 22, 1951, in *Selected Letters: 1940–1956*, 316.

43. John Clellon Holmes, journal entry, April 27, 1951, *Moody Street Irregulars* Summer/Fall 1979.

44. Kerouac, *On the Road*, 84.

45. Joan Kerouac, *Nobody's Wife*, 202.

46. Charters, in *Selected Letters: 1940–1956*, 320 fn.

47. Kerouac to Neal Cassady, June 24, 1951, in *Selected Letters: 1940–1956*, 320.

48. Kerouac to Neal Cassady, June 10, 1951, in *Selected Letters: 1940–1956*, 318.

49. Knight and Knight, *Kerouac and the Beats*, 152–153.

50. Jack Kerouac, "Editorial Explanation of Various Techniques of the Duluoz Legend," in *Some of the Dharma* (New York: Viking Penguin, 1999), endpapers.

51. Kerouac, *Visions of Cody*, 8–9.

52. Kerouac, foreword, in *Visions of Cody*.

53. Neal Cassady to Jack Kerouac, in Cassady, *Off the Road*, 146.

54. Kerouac to Neal Cassady, June 24, 1951, in *Selected Letters: 1940–1956*, 321.

55. Kerouac to Neal Cassady, August 31, 1951, in *Selected Letters: 1940–1956*, 324.

Chapter 18: Beat Fellaheen

1. Kerouac to Neal Cassady, August 31, 1951, in *Selected Letters: 1940–1956*, 324.

2. Kerouac to Neal Cassady, October 1, 1951, in *Selected Letters: 1940–1956*, 326.

3. Kerouac to Stella Sampas, August 30, 1951, in *Selected Letters: 1940–1956*, 323.

4. Kerouac to Allen Ginsberg, May 18, 1952, in *Selected Letters: 1940–1956*, 356–357.

5. Kerouac, *Visions of Cody*, 48.

6. Kerouac to Neal Cassady, October 9, 1951, in *Selected Letters: 1940–1956*, 327.

7. Neal Cassady to Allen Ginsberg, May 15, 1951, in *As Ever*, 110.

8. Kerouac, *Visions of Cody*, 131.

9. Kerouac, *Kerouac CD-ROMnibus*.

10. Kerouac, *Kerouac CD-ROMnibus*.

11. Kerouac to John Clellon Holmes, March 12, 1952, in *Selected Letters: 1940–1956*, 335.

12. Knight and Knight, *Kerouac and the Beats*, 114–120.

13. Jack Kerouac, "Mexico Fellaheen," in *Lonesome Traveler* (New York: Grove Press, 1989), 33.

14. Allen Ginsberg to Neal Cassady, July 3, 1952, in *As Ever*, 131.

15. Kerouac to Neal and Carolyn Cassady, May 27, 1952, in *Selected Letters: 1940–1956*, 359.

16. William Burroughs to Allen Ginsberg, June 4, 1952, in *Letters of William S. Burroughs: 1945–1959*, 124.

17. Kerouac, *Doctor Sax*, 19.

18. Kerouac to John Clellon Holmes, June 17, 1952, University of Massachusetts, Lowell.

19. Kerouac to John Clellon Holmes, editor's note, in *Selected Letters: 1940–1956*, 375.

20. Carolyn Cassady, *Off the Road*, 186–187.

21. Kerouac, "Mexico Fellaheen," in *Lonesome Traveler*, 34.

22. Kerouac to Allen Ginsberg, October 8, 1952, in *Selected Letters: 1940–1956*, 379.

23. Kerouac to Stella Sampas, December 10, 1952, in *Selected Letters: 1940–1956*, 391.

24. Kerouac to Allen Ginsberg, October 8, 1952, in *Selected Letters: 1940–1956*, 378–379.

25. Neal Cassady, "Letter of Recommendation for Jack Kerouac," in *The Beats*, 155.

Chapter 19: The Shrouded Traveler

1. Cassady, *Off the Road*, 197.

2. Neal Cassady to Allen Ginsberg, October 4, 1952, in *As Ever*, 133.

3. Kerouac to John Clellon Holmes, October 12, 1952, in *Selected Letters: 1940–1956*, 381–382.

4. Jack Kerouac, poem, October 1952 notebook, New York Public Library, Berg Collection.

5. Kerouac, *Lonesome Traveler*, 80.

6. Ben Giamo, *Kerouac, the Word and the Way* (Carbondale: Southern Illinois University Press, 2000), 99–100.

7. Kerouac, "The Happy Truth," New York Public Library, Berg Collection.

8. Kerouac to Neal and Carolyn Cassady, December 9, 1952, in *Selected Letters: 1940–1956*, 385–386.

9. Kerouac to John Clellon Holmes, December 9, 1952, in *Selected Letters: 1940–1956*, 389.

10. Kerouac to Stella Sampas, December 10, 1952, in *Selected Letters: 1940–1956*, 391.

11. Kerouac to Stella Sampas, December 10, 1952, in *Selected Letters: 1940–1956*, 391.

12. Allen Ginsberg to Neal Cassady, January 1953, in *As Ever*, 137.

13. Kerouac, *Maggie Cassidy*, 20.

14. Kerouac, *Maggie Cassidy*, 73.

15. Kerouac to Allen Ginsberg, February 21, 1953, in *Selected Letters: 1940–1956*, 397.

16. Kerouac to John Clellon Holmes, March 9, 1953, University of Massachusetts, Lowell.

17. Kerouac to Neal Cassady, April 1953, in *Selected Letters: 1940–1956*, 400.

18. Allen Ginsberg to Neal Cassady, May 14, 1943, in *As Ever*, 144.

19. Allen Ginsberg to Neal Cassady, June 22, 1953 in *As Ever*, 149.

20. Kerouac, "Editorial Explanation."

21. Jack Kerouac, "*Book of Daydreams*," New York Public Library, Berg Collection.

22. Kerouac, "Book of Daydreams."

23. Kerouac, "Editorial Explanation."

24. Jack Kerouac, *Book of Tics*, New York Public Library, Berg Collection.

25. Jack Kerouac, "Slobs of the Kitchen Sea," in *Lonesome Traveler*, 94–95.

26. Gregory Corso to Jack Kerouac, August 25–28, 1958, in *An Accidental Autobiography: The Selected Letters of Gregory Corso*, ed. Bill Morgan (New York: New Directions, 2003), 126.

27. Gifford and Lee, *Jack's Book*.

28. Gifford and Lee, *Jack's Book*.

29. Jack Kerouac, *The Subterraneans* (New York: Grove Press, 1981), 67.

30. Kerouac, *Subterraneans*, 66.

31. Kerouac, *Book of Dreams*, 165.

32. Kerouac, *Book of Dreams*, 6.

33. Allen Ginsberg to Neal Cassady, June 22, 1953, in *As Ever*, 147.

34. Allen Ginsberg to Neal Cassady, November 14, 1953, in *As Ever*, 156–157.

35. Phyllis Jackson to Malcolm Cowley, May 12, 1953, Newberry Library, Malcolm Cowley Archive.

36. Helen K. Taylor to Malcolm Cowley, October 22, 1953, Newberry Library, Malcolm Cowley Archive.

37. Kerouac to Malcolm Cowley, November 21, 1953, in *Selected Letters: 1940–1956*, 402.

38. Cassady, *Off the Road*, 224–225.

39. Cassady, *Off the Road*, 227.

40. Jack Kerouac, *Book of Blues*, 1.

41. Kerouac, "San Francisco Blues–80th Chorus," in *Book of Blues*, 81.

42. Kerouac to Carolyn Cassady, April 22, 1954, in *Selected Letters: 1940–1956*, 408–409.

Chapter 20: Lake of Light

1. Kerouac, *Book of Dreams*, xv.

2. Allen Ginsberg to Louis and Edith Ginsberg and Eugene Brooks, July 10, 1954, in *Family Business: Selected Letters between a Father and Son* (New York: Bloomsbury, 2002), 30.

3. Kerouac to Carolyn Cassady, May 17, 1954, in *Selected Letters: 1940–1956*, 420.

4. Dwight Goddard, ed., "The Surangama Sutra," in *The Buddhist Bible* (Boston: Beacon Press, 1970), 112.

5. Goddard, "Surangama Sutra," 112.

6. Goddard, "Surangama Sutra," 113.

7. Kerouac to Carolyn Cassady, July 2, 1954, in *Selected Letters: 1940–1956*, 427.

8. Kerouac to Carolyn Cassady, July 2, 1954, in *Selected Letters: 1940–1956*, 426–427.

9. Kerouac, *Some of the Dharma*, 140.

10. Mary Carney to Jack Kerouac, October 1954, New York Public Library, Berg Collection.

11. Kerouac, *Some of the Dharma*, 140.

12. Kerouac to Stella Sampas, October 12, 1955, in *Selected Letters: 1940–1956*, 527.

13. Kerouac, *Some of the Dharma*, 141.

14. Mary Carney to Jack Kerouac, circa 1954, Berg Collection, New York Public Library.

15. Kerouac, "Easter Eve 1954," in *Some of the Dharma*, 47.

16. Kerouac, *The Portable Kerouac* (New York: Viking Penguin, 1995), 222–223.

17. Kerouac to Malcolm Cowley, June 1, 1955, University of Massachusetts, Lowell.

18. Kerouac to Carolyn Cassady, in *Selected Letters: 1940–1956*, 442.

19. Kerouac, "Book of Samadhi," in *Some of the Dharma*, 90.

20. Kerouac, "From July 29, 1954," in *Some of the Dharma*, 93.

21. Kerouac, "Yet Today Aug. 24 '54," in *Some of the Dharma*, 103.

22. Kerouac to Alfred Kazin, in *Selected Letters: 1940–1956*, 450.

23. Kerouac, *Some of the Dharma*, 61.

24. Kerouac, *Some of the Dharma*, 185.

25. Kerouac to Allen Ginsberg, January 18, 1955, in *Selected Letters: 1940–1956*, 457–458.

26. Kerouac to Allen Ginsberg, January 18, 1955, in *Selected Letters: 1940–1956*, 458.

27. Kerouac, *Some of the Dharma*, 268.

28. Jack Kerouac, "Wake Up," *Tricycle: The Buddhist Review* (Summer 1993), 13.

29. Jack Kerouac, "Wake Up," *Tricycle: The Buddhist Review* (Fall 1993), 13.

30. Jack Kerouac, "Wake Up," *Tricycle: The Buddhist Review* (Spring 1995), 23.

31. Kerouac, *Some of the Dharma*, 112.

32. Kerouac to Carolyn Cassady, after April 15, 1955, in *Selected Letters: 1940–1956*, 476.

33. Jack Kerouac, "Canto Tres" from "Macdougal Street Blues," in *Il Libro dei Blues* (Poesia Del, Italy 1999), 160.

34. Kerouac, *Some of the Dharma*, 166.

35. Kerouac, *Some of the Dharma*, 124.

36. Kerouac, *Some of the Dharma*, 305.

37. Kerouac to Allen Ginsberg, September 1–6, 1955, in *Selected Letters: 1940–1956*, 510.

38. Kerouac, *Some of the Dharma*, 335.

39. William S. Burroughs to Jack Kerouac, June 9, 1955, in *Letters of William S. Burroughs: 1945–1959*, 275.

40. Kerouac, *Some of the Dharma*, 305.

41. Kerouac to Allen Ginsberg, June 1, 1955, *Kerouac CD-ROMnibus.*

42. Kerouac to Allen Ginsberg, June 1, 1955, *Kerouac CD-ROMnibus.*

43. Kerouac to Arabelle Porter, May 28, 1955, in *Selected Letters: 1940–1956,* 487.

44. Kerouac to Allen Ginsberg, early April 1955, in Knight and Knight, *Kerouac and the Beats,* 130.

45. Kerouac to Carolyn Cassady, after April 15, 1955, in *Selected Letters: 1940–1956,* 478.

Chapter 21: The Sage of Rocky Mount

1. Kerouac, *Some of the Dharma,* 336.

2. Jack Kerouac, *Tristessa* (New York: Viking Penguin, 1992), 8.

3. Kerouac, *Tristessa,* 8.

4. Kerouac, *Tristessa,* 10-11.

5. Kerouac, *Tristessa,* 57.

6. Kerouac to Allen Ginsberg, August 7, 1955, in *Selected Letters: 1940–1956,* 505.

7. Evelyn Levine, interoffice Viking memo, Newberry Library, Malcolm Cowley Archive.

8. Allen Ginsberg, "Dream Record: June 8, 1955," in *Collected Poems: 1947–1980* (New York: Harper & Row, 1988), 124.

9. Watson, *Birth of the Beat Generation,* 180.

10. Jane Kramer, *Allen Ginsberg in America* (New York: Random House, 1969), 140.

11. Kerouac to Sterling Lord, August 19, 1955, in *Selected Letters: 1940–1956,* 510.

12. Kerouac, *The Portable Kerouac,* 173.

13. Jack Kerouac, *Mexico City Blues* (New York: Grove Press, 1959), i.

14. Kerouac to Malcolm Cowley, September 11, 1955, in *Selected Letters: 1940–1956,* 516.

15. Kerouac, *Some of the Dharma,* 339.

16. Charters, in *Selected Letters: 1940–1956,* 539 fn.

17. Kerouac to Gary Snyder, January 16, 1956, in *Selected Letters: 1940–1956,* 540.

18. Kerouac to Neal Cassady, April 1955, in Kinght and Knight, *Kerouac and the Beats,* 129.

19. Kerouac to Malcolm Cowley, September 11, 1955, in *Selected Letters: 1940–1956,* 515.

20. Kerouac, *Book of Dreams.*

21. Kerouac, *Some of the Dharma,* 358.

22. Kerouac, *Some of the Dharma,* 354.

23. Malcolm Cowley to Jack Kerouac, October 12, 1955, Newberry Library, Malcolm Cowley Archive.

24. Malcolm Cowley to Jack Kerouac, November 8, 1955, Newberry Library, Malcolm Cowley Archive.

25. Contract between Zoetrope Studios and Stella Kerouac, courtesy of John Sampas, literary executor of the Estate of Jack and Stella Kerouac.

26. Kerouac to John Clellon Holmes, October 12, 1955, in *Selected Letters: 1940–1956,* 522.

27. Kerouac, *Some of the Dharma,* 346.

28. Kerouac, "Little Main Street Blues," in *Some of the Dharma,* 359–360.

29. Kerouac, "Little Pureland Blues," in *Some of the Dharma.*

30. Kerouac, *Some of the Dharma,* 364–365.

31. Kerouac, *Some of the Dharma,* 365.

32. Kerouac, *Some of the Dharma,* 366.

33. Kerouac, *The Dharma Bums,* 134.

34. Kerouac, *Some of the Dharma,* 367.

35. Kerouac, *Some of the Dharma,* 367.

Chapter 22: Passing Through

1. Jack Kerouac, foreword to *Scattered Poems* (San Francisco: City Lights, 1971).
2. Kerouac, *Some of the Dharma*, 380.
3. Kerouac to Gary Snyder, January 15, 1956, in *Selected Letters: 1940–1956*, 539.
4. Kerouac to Philip Whalen, February 7, 1956, in *Selected Letters: 1940–1956*, 549.
5. Kerouac to Philip Whalen, January 16, 1956, in *Selected Letters: 1940–1956*, 543.
6. Kerouac, *Some of the Dharma*, 406.
7. Kerouac, "Desolation Blues," in *Il Libro dei Blues*, 168.
8. Kerouac to Malcolm Cowley, May 9, 1956, in *Selected Letters: 1940–1956*, 575–577.
9. Ann Charters, in *Selected Letters: 1940–1956*, 577 fn.
10. Jack Kerouac, *Old Angel Midnight* (San Francisco: Grey Fox Press, 1993), 9.
11. Michael McClure, "Jack's Old Angel Midnight," preface to Kerouac, *Old Angel Midnight*, xvii.
12. Kerouac to Gary Snyder, May 1956, in *Selected Letters: 1940–1956*, 581.
13. Kerouac to Gary Snyder, May 1956, in *Selected Letters: 1940–1956*, 581–583.
14. Kerouac. *Book of Haikus*, ed. Regina Weinreich (New York: Viking Penguin, 2003), 85.
15. Kerouac, *Kerouac CD-ROMnibus*.
16. Kerouac, *Desolation Angels*, 5.
17. Kerouac, *Desolation Angels*, 24–25.
18. Kerouac, *Desolation Angels*, 32–33.
19. Kerouac to Sterling Lord, October 7, 1956, in *Selected Letters: 1940–1956*, 589.
20. Kerouac, *Desolation Angels*, 255.
21. Kerouac, *Il Libro dei Blues*, 184–289.
22. Helen Weaver, *Woodstock Times* 1983. www.ulsterpublishing.com.
23. Weaver, *Woodstock Times*.
24. Kerouac to Helen Weaver (circa late December/early January 1956/57).
25. Allen Ginsberg, interview with the author, October 4, 1992, Lowell, Mass.

Chapter 23: Before the Fall

1. Kerouac, *Desolation Angels*, 313.
2. Jack Kerouac, "Washington DC Blues," recording from *Jack Kerouac Reads On the Road* (2000). Rykodisc.
3. Kerouac, *Desolation Angels*, 314.
4. Kerouac to Allen Ginsberg, December 26, 1956, in *Selected Letters: 1940–1956*, 594.
5. Viking memo, March 22, 1957, Newberry Library, Malcolm Cowley Archive.
6. Viking Manuscript Acceptance Report, April 8, 1957, Newberry Library, Malcolm Cowley Archive.
7. Kerouac to Keith Jennison, December 26, 1956, in *Selected Letters: 1940–1956*, 596–597.
8. Kerouac to Edith Dietz, January 20, 1957, University of Massachusetts, Lowell.
9. Kerouac to Edith Dietz, January 20, 1957, University of Massachusetts, Lowell.
10. Jack Kerouac, unpublished letter and drawing to Helen Weaver, undated, circa November 1956. Book dealer's catalog, www.alibris.com.
11. Helen Weaver, phone interview with the author, July 23, 2002.
12. Joyce Johnson, *Door Wide Open: A Beat Love Affair in Letters, 1957–1958* (New York: Viking Penguin, 2000).
13. Johnson, *Door Wide Open*, 3–6.
14. William S. Burroughs to Jack Kerouac, April 22, 1954, in *Letters of William S. Burroughs: 1945–1959*, 203–207.
15. Johnson, *Door Wide Open*, 7.

16. Kerouac to Sterling Lord, March 25, 1957, University of Massachusetts, Lowell.

17. Kerouac, *Desolation Angels*, 347.

18. Kerouac to Joyce Glassman, March 1957, in Johnson, *Door Wide Open*, 11–12.

19. Kerouac, *Desolation Angels*, 358.

20. Kerouac to Gary Snyder, April 3, 1957, University of Massachusetts, Lowell.

21. Kerouac to Sterling Lord, April 20, 1957, University of Massachusetts, Lowell.

22. Kerouac to Gary Snyder, April 3, 1957, University of Massachusetts, Lowell.

23. Kerouac to Ed White, in *Selected Letters: 1957–1969*, ed. Ann Charters (New York: Viking, 2000), 31.

24. Kerouac to Allen Ginsberg and William S. Burroughs, May 1967, in *Selected Letters: 1957–1969*, 36–37.

25. Kerouac to Sterling Lord, April 20, 1957, University of Massachusetts, Lowell.

26. Johnson, *Door Wide Open*, 22.

27. Kerouac to Neal Cassady, March 25, 1957, in *Selected Letters: 1957–1969*, 23.

28. Kerouac to William S. Burroughs and Allen Ginsberg, early May 1957, in *Selected Letters: 1957–1969*, 35.

29. Kerouac, *Desolation Angels*.

30. Kerouac to Sterling Lord, June 26, 1957, University of Massachusetts, Lowell.

31. Kerouac to Gary Snyder, June 24, 1957, University of Massachusetts, Lowell.

32. Kerouac to Joyce Glassman, late May 1957, in Johnson, *Door Wide Open*, 23.

33. Kerouac, "Sketch for Book of Sketches," in *Some of the Dharma*, 344.

34. Kerouac to Malcolm Cowley, July 4, 1957, University of Massachusetts, Lowell.

35. Kerouac to Malcolm Cowley, July 4, 1957, University of Massachusetts, Lowell.

36. Kerouac to Joyce Glassman, mid-June 1957, in Johnson, *Door Wide Open*, 31.

37. Kerouac to Joyce Johnson, June 27, 1957, in Johnson, *Door Wide Open*, 30–33.

38. Johnson, *Door Wide Open*, 35.

39. Kerouac to Malcolm Cowley, July 21, 1957, University of Massachusetts, Lowell.

40. Kerouac to Patricia MacManus, July 19, 1957, in *Selected Letters: 1957–1969*, 58–59.

41. Spengler, *Decline of the West*, 310.

42. Spengler, *Decline of the West*, 310.

43. Jack Kerouac, "Aftermath: The Philosophy of the Beat Generation," in *Good Blonde and Others* (San Francisco: Grey Fox Press, 1993), 49.

44. Kerouac, "Aftermath."

45. Kerouac to Allen Ginsberg, August 9, 1957, in *Selected Letters: 1957–1969*, 66.

46. Kerouac to Joyce Glassman, July 28, 1957, in Johnson, *Door Wide Open*, 44–45.

47. Kerouac to Philip Whalen, mid-August 1957, University of Massachusetts at Lowell.

48. Kerouac to Joyce Glassman, August 23, 1957, in *Selected Letters: 1957–1969*, 71.

49. Kerouac to Joyce Glassman, August 23, 1957, in *Selected Letters: 1957–1969*, 71.

50. Gilbert Millstein, review of *On the Road*, by Jack Kerouac, *New York Times*.

51. Joyce Johnson, *Minor Characters* (New York: Penguin USA, 1999).

Chapter 24: Everything Exploded

1. Kerouac, *Book of Dreams*, 303.

2. Gifford and Lee, *Jack's Book*, 240–241.

3. Phoebe Lou Adams, "Ladder to Nirvana," *Village Voice*, October 1957.

4. Jerry Tallmer, "Jack Kerouac: Back to the Village—But Still on the Road," *Village Voice*, September 18, 1957.

5. Kerouac, *Book of Dreams*, 312.

6. Kerouac to Allen Ginsberg, October 1, 1957, in *Selected Letters: 1957–1969*, 76.

7. Maurice Dolbier, "Beat Generation Roadster," review of *On the Road*, by Jack Kerouac, *New York Herald Tribune*, September 22, 1957.

8. Mike Wallace, interview with Jack Kerouac, *New York Post*, January 28, 1958.

9. Mike Wallace, interview with Jack Kerouac, *New York Post*, January 28, 1958.

10. Kerouac to Stella Sampas, October 25, 1957, University of Massachusetts, Lowell.

11. Kerouac to Allen Ginsberg, October 1, 1957, in *Selected Letters: 1957–1969*, 76.

12. Kerouac to Helen Weaver, October 22, 1957, in *Selected Letters: 1957–1969*, 85.

13. David Amram, *Offbeat: Collaborating with Kerouac* (New York: Thunder's Mouth Press, 2002), 6.

14. Amram, *Offbeat*, 17.

15. Gifford and Lee, *Jack's Book*, 242.

16. Stella Sampas to Jack Kerouac, September 15, 1957, New York Public Library, Berg Collection.

17. Kerouac to Stella Sampas, October 1957, New York Public Library, Berg Collection.

18. Kerouac to Allen Ginsberg, October 6, 1959, in *Selected Letters: 1957–1969*, 251.

19. Kerouac to John Clellon Holmes, November 8, 1957, University of Massachusetts, Lowell.

20. Kerouac to Allen Ginsberg, Peter Orlovsky, and Gregory Corso, December 10, 1957, New York Public Library, Berg Collection.

21. Kerouac to Allen Ginsberg, Peter Orlovsky, and Gregory Corso, December 10, 1957, New York Public Library, Berg Collection.

22. Gifford and Lee, *Jack's Book*, 251–252.

23. Dan Wakefield, *The Nation*, January 4, 1958.

24. Wakefield, *The Nation*, January 4, 1958.

25. Howard Smith, "Jack Kerouac: Off the Road, into the Vanguard, and Out," in *The Village Voice Reader: A Mixed Bag from the Greenwich Village Newspaper* (New York: Grove Press, 1962).

26. Amram, *Offbeat*, 19.

27. Kerouac to Allen Ginsberg, January 8, 1958, in *Selected Letters: 1957–1969*, 114.

28. Amram, *Offbeat*.

29. Kerouac to Allen Ginsberg, December 28, 1957, in *Selected Letters: 1957–1969*, 107.

30. Johnson, *Door Wide Open*, 114.

31. Kerouac to Joyce Glassman, February 4, 1958, in *Selected Letters: 1957–1969*, 127.

32. Johnson, *Door Wide Open*, 115–116.

33. Kerouac to Allen Ginsberg, December 28, 1957, in *Selected Letters: 1957–1969*, 107.

34. Kerouac to Joyce Glassman, January 13, 1958, in *Selected Letters: 1957–1969*, 121.

35. Kerouac to Philip Whalen, January 7, 1958, New York Public Library, Berg Collection.

36. Jack Kerouac, "211th Chorus," in *Mexico City Blues*, 211.

37. Kerouac to Joyce Glassman, January 13, 1958, in Johnson, *Door Wide Open*, 119.

38. Jack Kerouac, "Orlando Blues," in *Book of Blues*, 241.

39. Allen Ginsberg, "Kerouac's Ethic," in *Deliberate Prose: Selected Essays 1952–1995* (New York: HarperPerennial, 2000), 359.

40. Kerouac to Gary Snyder, July 14, 1958, University of Massachusetts, Lowell.

41. Henry Miller, preface to *The Subterraneans* by Jack Kerouac (New York: Grove Press, 1958).

42. Miller, preface to *Subterraneans*.

43. Kerouac, *Subterraneans*, 103.

44. Kerouac, *Subterraneans*, 45.

45. Kerouac to Philip Whalen, undated, University of Massachusetts, Lowell.

46. Kerouac to John Clellon Holmes, April 13, 1958, University of Massachusetts, Lowell.

47. Michael McGrady, "Jack Kerouac: Beat Even in Northport," in *The Kerouac We Knew* (San Anselmo, Calif.: Fels & Firn Press, 1987), 11.

48. Kerouac to Philip Whalen, June 12, 1958, University of Massachusetts, Lowell.

Chapter 25: Northport

1. Jack Kerouac, "Brooklyn Bridge Blues," in Jack Kerouac, *Kicks Joy Darkness* (audio recording, Rykodisc, 1997).

2. Johnson, *Door Wide Open*, 141.

3. Johnson, *Door Wide Open*, 142.

4. Johnson, *Door Wide Open*, 140–144.

5. Ginsberg, "Kerouac's Ethic," 359.

6. Kerouac to Fernanda Pivano, early 1964, in *Selected Letters: 1957–1969*, 429.

7. Amram, *Offbeat*, 125.

8. David Amram, interview with the author, June 20, 2003. Putnam Valley, N.Y.

9. Kerouac to Gary Snyder, June 19, 1958, University of Massachusetts, Lowell.

10. Helen K. Taylor to Jack Kerouac, June 12, 1958, Newberry Library, Malcolm Cowley Archive.

11. Kerouac to Helen Taylor, June 18, 1958, in *Selected Letters: 1957–1969*, 149.

12. Kerouac to Allen Ginsberg, August 28, 1958, in *Selected Letters: 1957–1969*, 169.

13. Kerouac to Philip Whalen, June 1958, University of Massachusetts, Lowell.

14. Kerouac to Gary Snyder, July 21, 1958, University of Massachusetts, Lowell.

15. Kerouac to Tom Guinzburg, July 1958, in *Selected Letters: 1957–1969*, 157.

16. Kerouac to Gary Snyder, July 14, 1958, University of Massachusetts, Lowell.

17. Allen Ginsberg, review of *The Dharma Bums* by Jack Kerouac, *Village Voice*, November 12, 1958.

18. Gary Snyder to Jack Kerouac, December 1958, in *Selected Letters: 1957–1969*, 177.

19. Kerouac to Gary Snyder, February 23, 1959, in *Selected Letters: 1957–1969*, 214.

20. Jack Kerouac, "On the Origins of a Generation," in *Good Blonde*, 56–57.

21. McGrady, "Jack Kerouac," 11.

22. Kerouac to John Montgomery, after November 6, 1959, in *Selected Letters: 1957–1969*, 186–187.

23. Amram, *Offbeat*, 88.

24. Kerouac to Sterling Lord, January 8, 1959, University of Massachusetts, Lowell.

25. Kerouac to Gary Snyder, December 1, 1958, University of Massachusetts, Lowell.

26. Jack Kerouac, "Introduction to *The Americans: Photographs by Robert Frank*," in *Good Blonde*, 22.

27. Jack Kerouac, "Beat Generation Haikus," in *Book of Haikus*, ed. Regina Weinreich (New York: Viking Penguin, 2003), 151.

28. Regina Weinreich, introduction to Kerouac, *Book of Haikus*, xxvii.

29. Kerouac, "Beat Generation Haikus," 148.

30. Kerouac to Caroline Kerouac, January 29, 1959, University of Massachusetts, Lowell.

31. Al Aronowitz, "The Beat Papers of Al Aronowitz," Column 22, June 1, 1997.

Chapter 26: Pull My Daisy

1. Amram, *Offbeat*, 59.

2. Kerouac to Stella Sampas, February 13, 1959, New York Public Library, Berg Collection.

3. As told to David Amram by Dody Muller, author interview with David Amram, March 28, 2002.

4. Ann Charters, commentary, in *Selected Letters: 1957–1969*, 219.

5. Ellis Amburn, *Subterranean Kerouac: The Hidden Life of Jack Kerouac* (New York: St. Martin's Press, 1998), 337.

6. Jack Kerouac to Allen Ginsberg, Gregory Corso, and Peter Orlovsky, March 24, 1959, in *Selected Letters: 1957–1969*, 220.

7. Gregory Corso to Allen Ginsberg, September 4, 1959, in Corso, *Accidental Biography*, 208.

8. Kerouac to Philip Whalen, June 10, 1959, University of Massachusetts, Lowell.

9. Kerouac to Barney Rossett, May 8, 1950, in *Selected Letters: 1957–1969*, 228.

10. David Dempsey, "Beatnik Boogeyman on the Prowl," *New York Times*, May 3, 1959.

11. Barnaby Conrad, "Barefoot Boy with Dreams of Zen," *Saturday Review*, May 22, 1959, 23.

12. Kerouac to Caroline Kerouac Blake, late May 1959, in *Selected Letters: 1957–1969*, 234.

Chapter 27: "I Am the Flames"

The phrase "I Am the Flames" is part of a handwritten response by Kerouac to a poem Ginsberg had written in his September 1959 journal.

1. Kerouac to Allen Ginsberg, October 19, 1959, in *Selected Letters: 1957–1969*, 252–253.

2. Kerouac to Allen Ginsberg, November 2, 1959, in *Selected Letters: 1957–1969*, 254.

3. Kerouac to John Clellon Holmes, November 8, 1959, University of Massachusetts, Lowell.

4. Jack Kerouac, "The Last Word—One," *Escapade*, June 1959; reprinted in Kerouac, *Good Blonde*, 159.

5. Jack Kerouac, "The Last Word—Three," *Escapade*, October 1959; reprinted in Kerouac, *Good Blonde*, 167–168.

6. Cassady, *Off the Road*, 335–336.

7. Ann Charters quoting Carolyn Cassady from November 2, 1996, panel for the San Francisco Book Fair, in *Selected Letters: 1957–1969*, 263.

8. Saijo, "Recollection," in Jack Kerouac, Albert Saijo, and Lew Welch, *Trip Trap: Haiku on the Road* (San Francisco: Grey Fox Press, 1998), 5.

9. Kerouac, Saijo, and Welch, *Trip Trap*, 18.

10. Saijo, "Recollection," 10.

11. Jack Kerouac, excerpt from "Rimbaud," in *Scattered Poems* (San Francisco: City Lights, 1971), 34.

12. Kenneth Rexroth, "Discordant and Cool," book review, *New York Times*, November 29, 1959.

13. Kerouac to Donald Allen, December 1959, in *Selected Letters: 1957–1969*, 273.

14. Kerouac to Philip Whalen, January 18, 1960, in *Selected Letters: 1957–1969*, 278.

15. Kerouac to Lois Sorrels, January 19, 1960, University of Massachusetts, Lowell.

16. Kerouac, journal entry, April 18, 1960, *Kerouac CD-ROMnibus*.

17. Kerouac, journal entry, January 11, 1960, *Kerouac CD-ROMnibus*.

18. Kerouac, journal entry, January 11, 1960, *Kerouac CD-ROMnibus*.

19. Kerouac to Lawrence Ferlinghetti, February 1960, in *Selected Letters: 1957–1969*, 283.

20. Kerouac to Allen Ginsberg, June 20, 1960, in *Selected Letters: 1957–1969*, 294.

21. Film review, *Time*, June 20, 1960.

22. Jack Kerouac, *Big Sur* (New York: Viking Penguin, 1992), 5.

23. Kerouac, *Big Sur*, 16–21.

24. Kerouac, *Big Sur*, 237–238.

25. Certificate of Recognition, June 22, 1959, collection of Carolyn Cassady.

26. Cassady, *Off the Road*, 347.

27. Kerouac, *Big Sur*, 91.

28. Kerouac, *Big Sur*, 138.

29. Cassady, *Off the Road*, 358.

30. Daniel Talbot, book review of *Tristessa* by Jack Kerouac, *New York Times*, June 19, 1959.

31. Kerouac to Sterling Lord, May 5, 1961, University of Massachusetts, Lowell.

32. Kerouac to Allen Ginsberg, September 22, 1960, in *Selected Letters: 1957–1969*, 304.

33. Kerouac to Lawrence Ferlinghetti, October 18, 1960, in *Selected Letters: 1957–1969*, 312.

34. Kerouac, November 9, 1960, journal entry, *Kerouac CD-ROMnibus*.

35. Daniel Talbot, "On the Road Again," *New York Times*, November 27, 1960.

Chapter 28: The Sad Light of the Old Decade

The title of this chapter is taken from a line in the poem "Sunrise" by Allen Ginsberg, dated January 1, 1960.

1. Kerouac, journal entry, April 18, 1960, *Kerouac CD-ROMnibus*.

2. Kerouac to Granville Jones, November 22, 1960, in *Selected Letters: 1957–1969*, 313–314.

3. Allen Ginsberg, *Journals: Early Fifties Early Sixties* (New York: Grove Press, 1977), 129.

4. Ginsberg, *Journals*, 144.

5. Ginsberg, *Journals*, xxii.

6. Jack Kerouac to Lawrence Ferlinghetti, October 1960, New York Public Library, Berg Collection.

7. Kerouac to Granville Jones, November 22, 1960, in *Selected Letters: 1957–1969*, 313.

8. Kerouac, journal entry, January 19, 1961, *Kerouac CD-ROMnibus*.

9. Kerouac to Lawrence Ferlinghetti, fall 1960, University of Massachusetts, Lowell, Center for Lowell History.

10. Jack Kerouac to Philip Whalen, February 2, 1961, University of Massachusetts, Lowell.

11. Gabrielle Kerouac to Caroline Blake, January 25, 1961, in *Selected Letters: 1957–1969*, 319.

12. Kerouac to Philip Whalen, February 2, 1961, in *Selected Letters: 1957–1969*, 321.

13. Alfred Arbelli, "Beat Bard Denies He's the Daddy-O," *New York Daily News*, December 14, 1961.

14. Jack Kerouac to Philip Whalen, February 2, 1961, University of Massachusetts, Lowell.

15. Jack Kerouac to Ed White, August 7, 1961, *Missouri Review* 17, no. 3 (1994).

16. Kerouac to Bernice Lemire, June 15, 1961, New York Public Library, Berg Collection.

17. William S. Burroughs, interview in film *Kerouac*.

18. Kerouac to Lawrence Ferlinghetti, May 25, 1961, in *Selected Letters: 1957–1969*, 333.

19. Kerouac to Ferlinghetti, February 1, 1961, University of Massachusetts, Lowell, Center for Lowell History.

20. Kerouac, November 9, 1960 journal entry, *Kerouac CD-ROMnibus*.

21. *Time*, January 21, 1961.

22. Kerouac to Philip Whalen, October 17, 1961, University of Massachusetts, Lowell.

23. Kerouac to Philip Whalen, October 17, 1961, University of Massachusetts, Lowell.

24. Kerouac, journal entry, March 8, 1961, *Kerouac CD-ROMnibus*.

25. Kerouac to Timothy Leary, May 1961, Leary Archives.

26. Kerouac, excerpt from 8th Chorus, 1st Solo, "Cerrada Medellin Blues," *Book of Blues*, 256.

27. Kerouac to John Clellon Holmes, August 9, 1961, University of Massachusetts, Lowell, Center for Lowell History.

28. Jack Kerouac, notebook, Berg Exhibit, Victorians, Moderns, and Beats, May 2002, New York Public Library, Berg Collection.

29. Kerouac, 1961 Working Notebook A, New York Public Library,. Berg Collection.

30. Kerouac, notebook entry, September 24, 1961, *Kerouac CD-ROMnibus.*

31. Kerouac to Sterling Lord, October 9, 1961, University of Massachusetts, Lowell.

32. Kerouac to Sterling Lord, October 9, 1961, University of Massachusetts, Lowell.

33. Kerouac to Philip Whalen, October 17, 1961, in *Selected Letters: 1957–1969,* 347.

34. Kerouac to Tom Guinzburg, October 19, 1961, in *Selected Letters: 1957–1969,* 353.

35. Kerouac to Allen Ginsberg and Peter Orlovsky, December 28, 1961, in *Selected Letters: 1957–1969,* 363.

36. Kerouac to Carolyn Cassady, January 7, 1962, in *Selected Letters: 1957–1969,* 369.

37. Kerouac to John Clellon Holmes, December 29, 1961, University of Massachusetts, Lowell, Center for Lowell History.

38. Kerouac to John Clellon Holmes, August 8, 1962, University of Massachusetts, Lowell, Center for Lowell History.

39. Kerouac to Lois Sorrels, circa April 1961, University of Massachusetts, Lowell, Center for Lowell History.

40. Kerouac to Lois Sorrels, December 18, 1961, University of Massachusetts, Lowell, Center for Lowell History.

41. Kerouac to Tom Guinzburg, January 17, 1962, in *Selected Letters: 1957–1969,* 372–374.

42. Jack Kerouac, journal entry, January 11, 1961, New York Public Library, Berg Collection.

43. Louis Ginsberg to Allen Ginsberg, March 20, 1962, in *Family Business,* 178.

44. Kerouac, journal entry, March 1962, Estate of Jack and Stella Kerouac, Lowell, Mass.

45. Gregory Corso to Allen Ginsberg, March 9, 1962, in *Accidental Autobiography,* 307.

46. Kerouac to Robert Giroux, unmailed letter dated 1962, New York Public Library, Berg Collection.

47. Kerouac to Hugo Weber, 1961, *Kerouac CD-ROMnibus.*

48. Kerouac to Lawrence Ferlinghetti, October 23, 1961, *Selected Letters: 1957–1969,* 314.

49. Jack Kerouac to Stella Sampas, February 9, 1962, *Selected Letters: 1957–1969,* 374–375.

50. Kerouac, Working Notebook B, 1962, New York Public Library, Berg Collection.

51. Kerouac to Lawrence Ferlinghetti, October 6, 1962, University of Massachusetts, Lowell.

52. William Wiegand, "A Turn in the Road for the King of the Beats," *New York Times,* September 16, 1962.

53. Herbert Gold, "Squaring Off the Corners," book review of *Big Sur* by Jack Kerouac, *Saturday Review,* September 22, 1962.

54. "Lion and Cubs," book review of *Big Sur, Time,* September 14, 1962.

55. Lawrence Ferlinghetti, letter to the editor of *Time* (unpublished), September 15, 1962, in *Selected Letters: 1957–1969,* 395.

56. Gregory Corso to Allen Ginsberg, March 7, 1963, in *Accidental Autobiography,* 352.

57. Kerouac to John Clellon Holmes, August 8, 1962, University of Massachusetts, Lowell.

58. Jack Kerouac inscription in *Big Sur,* formerly owned by Lucien Carr, New York Public Library, Berg Collection. The full inscription reads "To Lucien my dear friend & compatriot in alcoholic sorrow & Sorrow otherwise, & Cessa, his Wife, Sweet Lady Forever—from Jack (Kerouac) Forever XXX."

59. Gifford and Lee, *Jack's Book,* 298.

60. Jarvis, *Visions of Kerouac,* 176.

61. Kerouac, 1963 radio interview, *Dialogues in Great Books.*

62. Kerouac, interview by the librarians of Northport Public Library, April 14, 1964, Northport Public Library.

63. Kerouac to Philip Whalen, December 13, 1962, in *Selected Letters: 1957–1969,* 403.

Chapter 29: Days of Autumn

1. Kerouac to Philip Whalen, January 14, 1963, in *Selected Letters: 1957–1969*, 405.

2. Kerouac to Lois Sorrels and Jacques Beckwith, undated, University of Massachusetts, Lowell.

3. Jack Kerouac, foreword to unpublished poetry collection, *Some Collected Poems of Lois Sorrels* (written May 7, 1963).

4. Jack Kerouac, "Written Address to the Italian Judge," in *Good Blonde*, 80–81.

5. Kerouac to Gary Snyder, May 23, 1963, in *Selected Letters: 1957–1969*, 413–414.

6. Kerouac to Carolyn Cassady, August 16, 1963, in *Selected Letters: 1957–1969*, 422.

7. Saul Maloff, "A Yawping at the Grave," *New York Times*, September 8, 1963.

8. Jack Kerouac, entry 1965, Reading Notes, New York Public Library, Berg Collection.

9. Kerouac to John Clellon Holmes, December 11, 1963, in *Selected Letters: 1957–1969*, 427.

10. Kerouac to Fernanda Pivano, early 1964, in *Selected Letters: 1957–1969*, 30.

11. Kerouac to Fernanda Pivano, early 1964, in *Selected Letters: 1957–1969*, 378.

12. "Jack Kerouac Reads, Etc., at Lowell," *Harvard Crimson*, March 25, 1964.

13. Jack Kerouac, interview by the librarians of Northport Public Library, April 14, 1964, Northport Public Library.

14. Kerouac to Andreas Brown, July 14, 1968, in *Selected Letters: 1957–1969*, 514.

15. Kerouac to Stella Sampas, April 22, 1964, in *Selected Letters: 1957–1969*, 380.

16. Jack Kerouac, journal entry, spring 1964, Estate of Jack and Stella Kerouac, Lowell, Mass.

Chapter 30: The Ghost Hells of My Heart

1. Kerouac to John Clellon Holmes, October 16, 1964, University of Massachusetts, Lowell.

2. Gabrielle Kerouac to Stanley and Anne Twardowicz, September 19, 1964, in *Selected Letters: 1957–1969*, 436.

3. Kerouac to John Clellon Holmes, October 16, 1964, University of Massachusetts, Lowell.

4. John Sampas, interview with the author, March 28, 2003, Lowell, Mass.

5. Jack Kerouac, Working Notebook A, 1961, New York Public Library, Berg Collection.

6. Jack Kerouac, Working Notebook C, 1963–1964, New York Public Library, Berg Collection.

7. Ellis Amburn, *Subterranean Kerouac: The Hidden Life of Jack Kerouac* (New York: St. Martin's Press, 1998), 335.

8. Amburn, *Subterranean Kerouac*, 335.

9. Jack Kerouac, Reading Notes, 1965, New York Public Library, Berg Collection.

10. Kerouac to John Clellon Holmes, December 8, 1964, University of Massachusetts, Lowell.

11. Kerouac to Seymour Krim, February 13, 1965, University of Massachusetts, Lowell, Center for Lowell History.

12. Kerouac to Seymour Krim, February 13, 1965, University of Massachusetts, Lowell, Center for Lowell History.

13. Kerouac to Seymour Krim, April 20, 1965, University of Massachusetts, Lowell.

14. Kerouac to Sterling Lord, March 23, 1965, in *Selected Letters: 1957–1969*, 449.

15. Kerouac to Seymour Krim, April 20, 1965, University of Massachusetts, Lowell, Center for Lowell History.

16. Kerouac to Stanley and Anne Twardowicz, March 22, 1965, University of Massachusetts, Lowell.

17. Saul Maloff, "A Line Must Be Drawn," *New York Times*, May 2, 1965.

18. Kerouac, *Satori in Paris*, 33.

19. Kerouac to Sterling Lord, June 11, 1965, in *Selected Letters: 1957–1969*, 455–457.

20. Kerouac to Sterling Lord, August 10, 1965, in *Selected Letters: 1957–1969*, 462.

21. Kerouac to Sterling Lord, August 10, 1965, in *Selected Letters: 1957–1969*, 462.

22. Kerouac to John Clellon Holmes, September 18, 1965, University of Massachusetts, Lowell.

23. Kerouac to Tony Sampas, November 29, 1965, in *Selected Letters: 1957–1969*, 467.

24. Jack Kerouac, Working Notebook F, New York Public Library, Berg Collection.

25. Kerouac, *Dr. Sax and the Great World Snake*, audio recording (New York: Gallery Six Press, 2003).

26. Kerouac to Dan DeSole, August 11, 1966, New York Public Library, Berg Collection.

27. Gabrielle Kerouac to Stanley and Anne Twardowicz, January 20, 1965, University of Massachusetts, Lowell.

28 Kerouac, notebook entry, 1966, *Kerouac CD-ROMnibus.*

29. Stella Kerouac to Gabrielle and Jack Kerouac, July 21, 1966, Estate of Stella Kerouac.

30. John Sampas, interview with the author, March 28, 2003, Lowell, Mass.

31. Kerouac to John Clellon Holmes, September 22, 1966, in *Selected Letters: 1957–1969*, 482.

32. Kerouac, notebook entry, 1966, *Kerouac CD-ROMnibus.*

33. Kerouac to Sterling Lord, October 8, 1966, in *Selected Letters: 1957–1969*, 484.

34. Kerouac to Sterling Lord, October 8, 1966, in *Selected Letters: 1957–1969*, 483–484.

35. Kerouac to Stella Sampas, in *Selected Letters: 1957–1969*, 486.

36. Kerouac to Stella Sampas, *Selected Letters: 1957–1969*, 485–486.

37. Kerouac to Andreas Brown, *Selected Letters: 1957–1969*, 514.

38. Gifford and Lee, *Jack's Book*, 304.

39. Kerouac, notebook entry, October 1967, *Kerouac CD-ROMnibus.*

Chapter 31: The Golden Baby of Heaven

1. "By a Lowellite—Footnotes from Lowell" in *The Kerouac We Knew* (San Anselmo, Calif.: Fels & Firn Press, 1987), 26.

2. Jack Kerouac, Working Notebook G, New York Public Library, Berg Collection.

3. Kerouac, Working Notebook G, New York Public Library, Berg Collection.

4. "By a Lowellite," 26.

5. Jack Kerouac, notebook entry, 1966, *Jack Kerouac ROMnibus.*

6. John Sampas, interview with the author, March 30, 1997, Lowell, Mass.

7. Kerouac to Sterling Lord, March 30, 1967, in *Selected Letters: 1957–1969*, 494.

8. Betty Sampas, interview with the author, September 6, 2003, Lowell, Mass.

9. Kerouac, Working Notebook G, New York Public Library, Berg Collection.

10. Ted Berrigan interviewing Jack Kerouac, unedited audiotape, 1968.

11. Kerouac, "In the Ring," in *Good Blonde*, 152–153.

12. Kerouac to Sterling Lord, April 20, 1968, in *Selected Letters: 1957–1969*, 511–512.

13. "Prop Art," *New York Review of Books*, April 7, 1968.

14. Kerouac to Allen Ginsberg, June 4, 1968, in *Selected Letters: 1957–1969*, 512.

15. Kerouac, Working Notebook G, New York Public Library, Berg Collection.

16. Kerouac to Andreas Brown, July 14, 1968, in *Selected Letters: 1957–1969*, 514.

17. John Sampas, interview with the author, March 28, 2003, Lowell, Mass.

18. Kerouac to Allen Ginsberg, June 4, 1968, in *Selected Letters: 1957–1969*, 513.

19. Stella Kerouac to Sterling Lord, August 27, 1968, in *Selected Letters: 1957–1969*, 516.

20. Kerouac to Sterling Lord, September 28, 1967, in *Selected Letters: 1957–1969*, 520.

21. Kerouac, Working Notebook G, New York Public Library, Berg Collection.

22. Jack Kerouac, *Firing Line* transcript, September 3, 1968.

23. Betty Watley, phone interview with the author, March 15, 2003.

24. Kerouac to Keith Jennison, December 3, 1968, in *Selected Letters: 1957–1969*, 523.

25. Jack Kerouac, journal entry, October 4, 1951, *Kerouac CD-ROMnibus*.

26. Betty Watley, phone interview with the author, March 15, 2003.

27. Kerouac, "What Am I Thinking About?" in *Good Blonde*, 192.

28. Western Union Telegram photocopy, September 20, 1969, University of Massachusetts, Lowell.

29. Kerouac to Edie Parker, September 21, 1969, University of Massachusetts, Lowell.

30. Kerouac to Edie Parker, September 8, 1969, University of Massachusetts, Lowell.

31. Kerouac to Paul Blake Jr., October 20, 1969, in *Selected Letters: 1957–1969*, 544.

32. Death certificate of Jack Kerouac, October 21, 1969.

33. Kerouac, "211th Chorus."

Chapter 32: The Deluge

1. John Clellon Holmes, "Gone in October," in *Gone in October: Last Reflections on Jack Kerouac* (Hailey, Idaho: Limberlost Press, 1985), 38.

2. Holmes, "Gone in October," 41.

3. Betty Watley, phone interview with the author, March 15, 2003.

4. Allen Ginsberg, "The Great Rememberer," in *Visions of Cody*, vii.

5. Mary Jane Fortunato, Lucille Medwick, and Susan Rowe, "Craft Interview with Allen Ginsberg," in *Spontaneous Mind*, 247–248.

6. John Sampas, interview with the author, March 28, 2003.

7. John Sampas, interview with the author, March 28, 2003.

8. Interview with Ann Charters, Dan Barth, March 28, 1995.

9. *Publishers Weekly*, December 4, 2000, 38.

10. *Publishers Weekly*, May 14, 2001, 64.

11. "Kerouac's Haiku a Revelation," Asia Africa Intelligence Wire, May 11, 2003.

12. "Kerouac Scroll Nets Record," *Writer*, September 2001, 13.

13. Nara Schoenberg, "Uninhibited NFL Owner Keeps Kerouac Manuscript on His Coffee Table," *Chicago Tribune*, August 12, 2002.

Selected Bibliography of Jack Kerouac's Work

Note: Years in bold indicate the year of publication. Years within brackets indicate the original date of writing.

The Duluoz Legend

1957
[1951] *On the Road.* Viking Penguin.

1958
[1953] *The Subterraneans.* Grove Press.
[1957] *The Dharma Bums.* Viking Penguin.

1959
[1952] *Doctor Sax.* Grove Press.
[1953] *Maggie Cassidy.* Viking Penguin.

1960
[1955–56] *Tristessa.* Viking Penguin.
[1958–60] *Lonesome Traveler.* Grove Press.

1961
[mid-1950s] *Book of Dreams.* City Lights.

1962
[1961] *Big Sur.* Viking Penguin.

1963
[1956] *Visions of Gerard.* Viking Penguin.

1965
[1956, 1961] *Desolation Angels.* Riverhead Books.

1966
[1965] *Satori in Paris.* Grove Press.

1968
[1967] *Vanity of Duluoz.* Viking Penguin.

1972
[1951–52] *Visions of Cody.* Viking Penguin.

Oher Works

1950
[1946–48] *The Town and the City.* Harcourt, Brace.

1960
[1956] *The Scripture of the Golden Eternity.* City Lights.

1971
[1951] *Pic.* Grove Press.

1993

[1956–59] *Old Angel Midnight.* Grey Fox Press.

[various dates] *Good Blonde and Others.* Grey Fox Press.

1995

Selected Letters: 1940–1956. Viking Penguin.

1997

[1953–56] *Some of the Dharma.* Viking Penguin.

1999

[various dates] *Atop an Underwood: Early Stories and Other Writing.* Viking Penguin.

Selected Letters: 1957–1969. Viking Penguin.

2002

[1945] *Orpheus Emerged.* I Books.

Forthcoming

Windblown World: The Journals of Jack Kerouac, 1945–1954. Viking Penguin.

Poetry

1959

[1955] *Mexico City Blues.* Grove Press.

1971

[various dates] *Scattered Poems.* City Lights.

1973

[1959] *Trip Trap: Haiku along the Road from San Francisco to New York, 1959.* With Albert Saijo and Lew Welch. Grey Fox Press.

1977

[various dates] *Heaven and Other Poems.* Berkeley, Calif.: Grey Fox Press.

1992

[various dates] *Pomes All Sizes.* City Lights.

1995

[various dates] *Book of Blues.* Penguin.

2003

[various dates] *Book of Haikus.* Penguin Poets.

Index

175–76, 185–86, 192, 207–8, 219,
226, 405
music and, 156, 174
On the Road and, 234–35, 316, 349, 463
Parker, Frankie Edith, and, 208
persona of, 154, 180, 182
poetry and, 313
prose style of, 225
reading of, 220, 282–83, 287–88
religion and, 286–88, 318, 405
sexuality and, 143, 149, 152, 232, 262, 309
sketch and, 241–42
Solomon, Carl, and, 243
on soul, 227
The Town and the City and, 220
travels of, 174–76, 179–86, 212–13, 231
work of, 172, 192, 219, 242, 405–6
writing and, 147, 150, 152, 156, 164, 196,
206–7, 220, 225–27, 242–43
Cassady, Neal, Sr., 142–43, 145–46
Cassady, Shirley Jean, 145
Catholicism
beatniks and, 440
Book of Haikus and, 481
Buddhism and, 288
Doctor Sax and, 35, 476
Ferlinghetti, Lawrence, and, 440
Frank, Robert, and, 440
Ginsberg, Allen, and, 440
Haverty, Joan, and, 294
intolerance of, 16
Kerouac, Gabrielle, and, 35, 41, 292,
374–75
Kerouac, Jack, and, 22–24, 34–36, 53, 71,
144–45, 229, 253–54, 272, 286, 288,
321–23, 341, 375, 384, 388, 420–21,
436, 438–41, 447, 462, 469
Kerouac, Leo, and, 288
Kirouac, Jean-Baptiste, and, 6–7
sin and, 12–13
suffering and, 253–54, 438
Visions of Gerard and, 322–23, 384
See also Jesus; Virgin Mary
Cayce, Edgar, 282–83, 287–88
Céline, Louis-Ferdinand, 118, 221, 245, 343
Centralville
annexation of, 10
culture of, 16
Kerouac, Jack, and, 28, 240, 278
society in, 10–11, 17
See also Lowell
"Cerrada Medellin Blues," 420
Cézanne, Paul, 161, 215, 345
Chandler, Billy, 67, 115, 257
Chaput, Joe, 470

character
America and, 161
in *Beat Generation*, 361
in *Big Sur*, 427
in *On the Road*, 88, 161, 171, 189–91, 207,
233–35, 313, 315–16, 332
in *Orpheus Emerged*, 134–35, 144
in *The Town and the City*, 134, 143–44,
154, 209, 211
in *Vanity of Duluoz*, 93–94, 446
in *Visions of Gerard*, 207
voice and, 217–18
Charters, Ann, xiii, 477, 479–80
Chase, Haldon "Hal"
Cassady, Neal, Jr. and, 142–43, 146
Kerouac, Jack, and, 136, 142–43, 146, 148,
154, 166, 172–73
Night of the Wolfeans and, 136
sexuality and, 136
Chicago Review, 368–69
Chicago Tribune, 471, 481–82
Chiungos, Odysseus "Duke," 47
Chuang-tse, 381
Churchill, Winston, 81
Cicero, 202
Citizen Kane, 87, 92
"cityCityCITY," 300–303
City Lights, 399, 416, 480
Clements, J. C., 259
Clift, Montgomery, 316
Coffey, Margaret, 52, 54, 108
Coffey, Pauline, 19
Cohn, Al, 400
Cold War, 301
Cole, Pat, 194–95
Columbia Jester Review, 117
Columbia Spectator, 70
Columbia University
education at, 70
Kammerer, David, murder and, 137
matriculation at, 68–74, 102
recruitment by, 51, 55–57
reinstatement at, 97, 101–2
social life at, 78, 115–16
sports at, 69, 72–74, 83, 102–4
withdrawal from, 83, 85, 91, 104–5
communism, 109, 401, 416, 441, 469. *See also*
Marxism; socialism
"Confidence Man," 189
Confidential, 418
Connecticut, 80, 82, 87–88
Conrad, Barnaby, 392
Conrad, Joseph, 159–60
Coppola, Francis Ford, 316–17
Corso, Gregory

210, 245, 302, 324, 426, 436
  inspiration of, 54, 144–45, 148, 358
  The Town and the City and, 210
  on worship, 187
Dowling, James, 47
"Dr. Sax & The Great World Snake," 454
drawing. *See* art
dreams
  "Book of Daydreams—San Luis Obispo"
    and, 273
  Book of Dreams and, 14, 415
  Buddhism and, 287, 337–38
  Duluoz Legend and, 273
  fear and, 357
  Kerouac, Jack, and, 20–21, 63, 68, 105,
    193–94, 273, 276–77, 278–79, 285,
    287, 289–90, 328, 337, 355, 357, 388
  Lowell and, 289–90, 315
  Visions of Gerard and, 314–15
Dreiser, Theodore, 153, 166, 168–69, 172, 257
"Dreiser and Lewis: Two Visions of American
  Life," 168
Dreyer, Carl, 198
"Drinking Pomes," 321
drugs
  Allen, Donald, and, 400
  beat generation and, 358
  in "Benzedrine Vision—Mexico Thieves
    Market—Memoirs of a Bebopper,"
    264–65
  Burroughs, Joan Vollmer, and, 138, 139,
    182–83
  Burroughs, William S., and, 138, 139, 172,
    194–95, 209, 252, 254, 301, 340, 341
  Cassady, Neal, Jr. and, 147, 207–8, 242,
    243–44, 262, 264, 282, 444, 464
  Cole, Pat, and, 194–95
  Corso, Gregory, and, 308, 450
  Ginsberg, Allen, and, 331, 376, 414–15
  Kerouac, Gabrielle, and, 376
  Kerouac, Jack, and, 130, 132, 140, 144,
    147, 184, 201, 213, 218, 222, 225,
    241, 243–44, 246, 248–49, 252, 254,
    255, 258, 262, 264–65, 266, 269–70,
    270–71, 272, 274, 282, 293, 301, 308,
    309, 313, 315, 317, 320, 321, 323,
    331, 341, 343, 344, 348, 358, 362,
    378, 394, 400–401, 414–15, 416, 420,
    421, 423–24, 427, 447, 461, 471
  Leary, Timothy, and, 415, 416, 420
  Orlovsky, Lafcadio, and, 331
  Orlovsky, Peter, and, 331
  in *Vanity of Duluoz*, 140
  Villanueva, Esperanza, and, 308–9
  writing and, 140, 264–65, 378, 400–401,
    421

Dube, Amanda, 9, 321
Duluoz Legend
  Cowley, Malcolm, and, 314
  dreams and, 273
  gaps in, 348–49, 408, 448
  influences on, 68
  writing, 95, 314
  See also *specific works*
Dumphy, Jim, 470

"The Ecstasy of Life and Death," 265
"Editorial Explanation of Various Techniques of
  the Duluoz Legend," 273
education of Jack Kerouac
  childhood, 15–16, 21–22, 23, 29–30, 34,
    38, 44, 45, 56, 94
  college, 70, 78, 83, 85, 91, 97, 102, 104–5,
    164, 166, 166–70, 174, 193
  college preparatory, 61–63
  self, 92, 100
The Egyptian Book of the Dead, 129
Eliot, T. S., 18, 439
Ellington, Duke, 232
Elliott, Helen, 331, 455
Ellmann, Richard, 448
Emerson, Ralph Waldo, 85, 117, 129, 202, 307
empathy, 77, 89, 97, 120, 324–25
emptiness
  beat generation and, 358
  Buddhism and, 273, 283, 292
  Kerouac, Jack, and, 205, 273, 283, 292,
    294, 304, 358, 360
Encyclopedia Britannica, 408
enlightenment. *See* awakening
Enrique, 248–50, 274
Escapade, 368, 385, 395–96, 400, 402
Esquire, 356, 468
Essays, 85
"Essentials of Spontaneous Prose," 379
L'Etoile, 8, 10, 27
Europe, 344–46, 450–51, 457–58, 465
Evergreen Review, 437
Everitt, Rae, 216, 236, 242
Everson, William, 392
evil, 214
existentialism, 68, 71–72
"Explaining the Beat Generation," 351–52, 353
Eyre and Spottiswoode, 211

Fair Play for Cuba Committee, 418–19
Fantasia, 78
"Farewell Song, Sweet from My Trees," 80, 86,
  87, 89
Farewell to Arms, 112
Farrar, Straus, 216, 425
"The Father of My Father," 6–7

Mann, Thomas, 100, 118, 129, 199
Mao Tse-Tung, 439
Marion, Paul, xvi, 479, 480
Marius the Epicurean, 52–53
marriages of Jack Kerouac
    to Haverty, Joan, 218, 220–24, 228–29,
        230–31, 232–33, 235–36, 238, 240,
        254, 267, 424–25
    to Parker, Frankie Edith, 124–25, 126,
        127–28, 130, 132, 138, 143
    to Sampas, Stella, 267, 456–57, 458–59,
        461, 473
    See also love; romances of Jack Kerouac
"The Martin Family," 325
Marton, Howie, 77–78
Marx, Karl, 494n9
Marx Brothers, 25
Marxism, 167, 169. *See also* communism; social-
    ism
Mary, 14
"Mary Carney." See *Maggie Cassidy*
Massachusetts, 453–54, 455
materialism
    beat generation and, 352, 397
    Kerouac, Jack, and, 205, 257
    On the Road and, 160, 191
    war and, 257
Matthew, Saint, 426
Maugham, W. Somerset, 124
Mazur, Hank, 46
McCallister, Lon, 121
McClure, Joanna, 406
McClure, Michael
    Beat Generation Anthology and, 392
    Kerouac, Jack, and, 325, 406
    Mexico City Blues and, 326
    "Old Angel Midnight" and, 326
    poetry and, 313, 322
McCoy, Tim, 26
McCullough, Ian, 105
McDarrah, Fred, 402
McKnight, Nicholas, 137
McNaughton, Duncan, 463–64
meditation
    Haverty, Joan, and, 229, 230
    Kerouac, Jack, and, 63, 73, 87, 229,
        264–65, 286, 287, 290, 292–93, 295,
        299, 314, 321, 337–38
    See also awakening; Buddhism
Melody, "Little Jack," 195–96
Melville, Herman, 118, 129, 189, 245
memories, 20–21, 299, 329
"Memory Babe," 360, 362, 378, 408
Merchant Marines, 97–102, 104, 105, 117–18,
    240

Merrimack Mills, 25–26
Merrimack News Company, 29
Merrimack River
    in *Doctor Sax*, xi
    flooding of, 37, 39–41
    Kerouac, Jack, and, 12, 32, 39–40, 44–45
Merriwell, Frank, 7
Merry Pranksters, 444
"The Mexican Girl," 312, 323, 342
Mexico, 248, 250
Mexico City
    earthquake in, 352
    homes in, 266, 330–31
    Lowell compared with, 213, 252–53
    travels in, 213–15, 248–56, 264–67, 307–9,
        330–31, 350–52, 420–21
Mexico City Blues
    foreshadowing, 292
    Grove Press and, 389
    Lord, Sterling, and, 311–12
    McClure, Michael, and, 326
    mother-son relationship in, 377
    promotion of, 439
    publication of, 368–69, 389, 393, 398–99
    review of, 399–400
    Rossett, Barney, and, 398
    writing, 309
"Mexico Fellaheen," 250, 409
MGM, 378, 395, 397
Michaud, Louise Kirouac, 8
Miller, Doris, 78
Miller, Glenn, 64
Miller, Henry, 324, 370, 379
Miller, Lou, 62
Millstein, Gilbert, 353–54, 355, 362–63
"The Minimization of Thomas Wolfe in His
    Own Time," 169
Minor Characters, xvi
Mitchell, Clifford, 453
Mitchell, Patricia, 453
Mix, Tom, 26
Modern Utopia, 67
Mondadori, 457
Monk, Thelonious, 361
Montagu, Ashley, 380, 382
Montgomery, John, 314, 348
The Moon is Down, 112
Moorehead, Agnes, 36
Morissette, Caroline. *See* Kerouac, Caroline
Morissette, Charles, 48, 80, 121
Morissette, "Spike," 477
Morley, Frank, 212
"Morning Dhyana," 294
Mother Tongue, 29
movies

317–18, 321, 326, 328–29, 348, 384, 392, 408, 414, 421, 427, 443, 446, 447–48, 451, 460, 472–73
  as young adult, 108, 128, 142, 189
  See also journals of Jack Kerouac
Notes from the Underground, 92, 148, 159, 436
"Nothing," 68
Nothing More to Declare, 430
"A Novella of Children and Evil," 254
La nuit et ma femme, 14
Nye, Louis, 361

O'Dea, Jim, 67, 257
O'Dwyer, William, 325–26
O'Grady, Desmond, 439
O'Hara, Frank, 391
O'Neil, Paul, 397
October, 87, 151, 265, 430
"October in the Poolhall." *See* "October in the Railroad Earth"
"October in the Railroad Earth"
  Ferlinghetti, Lawrence, and, 399
  foreshadowing, 66
  in *Lonesome Traveler*, 409
  Lord, Sterling, and, 295
  prose style of, 263–64, 408
  publication of, 401
  selling, 295, 399
  writing, 263–64
Odessa, 150–51
"Ode to the Setting Sun," 260
Offbeat: Collaborating with Kerouac, xvi
Offices, 202
Off the Road: My Years with Cassady, Kerouac, and Ginsberg, xvi, 246–47
Of Time and the River, 73, 170, 220
"Old Angel Midnight"
  Big Table and, 399
  City Lights and, 399
  Ferlinghetti, Lawrence, and, 393, 399, 422
  Ginsberg, Allen, and, 379
  McClure, Michael, and, 326
  prose style of, 326
  publication of, 389, 427–28
  revision of, 389
  selling, 399, 422
  writing, 326, 348, 379, 393
"Old Bull Balloon," 265–66
"Old Love-Light," 87
"Old Lucien Midnight." *See* "Old Angel Midnight"
One Flew over the Cuckoo's Nest, 422
On the Road
  A. A. Wyn and, 243, 251
  America and, 160, 166, 188–89, 191

beat generation and, 352, 356, 357–58
Big Sur and, 421
Burroughs, William S., and, 252
Carr, Lucien, and, 236, 238
Cassady, Carolyn, and, 481
Cassady, Neal, Jr. and, 234–35, 316, 349, 463
character in, 88, 161, 171, 189–91, 207, 233, 234, 234–35, 313, 315–16, 332
Cowley, Malcolm, and, 241, 280, 291, 293, 303, 312–13, 315–16, 325, 326, 329–30, 335, 344, 349
Cru, Henri, and, 366
death in, 214
Denver and, 142
Doctor Sax and, 234
Dreiser, Theodore, and, 172
Everitt, Rae, and, 242
Farrar, Straus and, 216
father-son relationship in, 190, 191
fear in, 184
Ginsberg, Allen, and, 234, 238, 251–52, 256, 258, 280, 316
Giroux, Robert, and, 200, 212, 216, 236, 238
Harcourt, Brace and, 236, 238
Holmes, John Clellon, and, 171, 216, 233, 235, 236, 238
imprisonment in, 204
individualism in, 183
inspiration for, 150, 160, 232, 279
Jackson, Phyllis, and, 280
Jennison, Keith, and, 335, 470
Knopf and, 293, 295
Levine, Evelyn, and, 309
libel and, 313, 315–16, 332, 335
Lord, Sterling, and, 312, 324, 332, 345–46, 349, 378, 470
MacManus, Patricia, and, 351
manuscript acceptance report on, 335–36
materialism and, 160, 191
Morley, Frank, and, 212
movies and, 316–17, 356, 378
Plimpton, George, and, 303
politics and, 471
promotion of, 351, 355–56, 356–58, 360, 362–65, 366, 391, 396
prose style of, 171–72, 251–52, 400, 409, 463
publication of, 242, 243, 257–58, 316–17, 332, 335–36, 337, 342, 344, 349–50, 351, 353–54, 355–58, 386, 482
race relations and, 373
rejection of, 236, 237–38, 251–52, 257–58, 280, 293, 295